The Editor

STEPHEN A. BARNEY is Professor Emeritus of English at the University of California, Irvine. He is the author of *Studies in "Troilus": Chaucer's Text, Meter, and Diction; Allegories of History, Allegories of Love;* and *Word-Hoard: An Introduction to the Old English Vocabulary.* He is the editor of *Chaucer's "Troilus": Essays in Criticism* and *Annotation and Its Texts.* His edited text of *Troilus and Criseyde* appears in *The Riverside Chaucer,* edited by Larry D. Benson et al.

A NORTON CRITICAL EDITION

Geoffrey Chaucer

TROILUS AND CRISEYDE
with facing-page IL FILOSTRATO

AUTHORITATIVE TEXTS

THE TESTAMENT OF CRESSEID
by Robert Henryson

CRITICISM

Edited by

STEPHEN A. BARNEY
UNIVERSITY OF CALIFORNIA, IRVINE

W • W • NORTON & COMPANY • *New York* • *London*

W. W. Norton & Company has been independent since its founding in 1923, when William Warder Norton and Mary D. Herter Norton first published lectures delivered at the People's Institute, the adult education division of New York City's Cooper Union. The Nortons soon expanded their program beyond the Institute, publishing books by celebrated academics from America and abroad. By midcentury, the two major pillars of Norton's publishing program—trade books and college texts—were firmly established. In the 1950s, the Norton family transferred control of the company to its employees, and today—with a staff of four hundred and a comparable number of trade, college, and professional titles published each year—W. W. Norton & Company stands as the largest and oldest publishing house owned wholly by its employees.

The text of this book is composed in Fairfield Medium
with the display set in Bernhard Modern.
Composition by Binghamton Valley Composition.
Manufacturing by the Courier Companies—Westford Division.
Production manager: Benjamin Reynolds.

Library of Congress Cataloging-in-Publication Data
Chaucer, Geoffrey, d. 1400.
Troilus and Criseyde, facing page Filostrato : context, criticism / Geoffrey Chaucer ;
edited by Stephen A. Barney.
p. cm.
Chaucer's Troilus and Criseyde compared on facing pages to Boccaccio's Filostrato.
Includes bibliographical references

ISBN 0-393-92755-5 (pbk.)

1. Troilus (Legendary character)—Poetry. 2. Chaucer, Geoffrey, d. 1400. Troilus and Criseyde. 3. Troilus (Legendary character) in literature. 4. Cressida (Fictitious character)—Poetry. 5. Trojan War—Literature and the war. 6. Cressida (Fictitious character) 7. Troy (Extinct city)—Poetry. 8. Trojan War—Poetry. I. Barney, Stephen A. II. Boccaccio, Giovanni, 1313–1375. Filostrato. English. III. Title.

PR1895.B37 2005
821'.1—dc22   2005053928

W. W. Norton & Company, Inc., 500 Fifth Avenue, New York, N.Y. 10110 0017
www.wwnorton.com
W. W. Norton & Company Ltd., Castle House, 75/76 Wells Street, London WIT 3QT

4 5 6 7 8 9 0

amatissimae
Cerisae
dedicavi
librum
libra
non sat est

Contents

Introduction

Troilus and Criseyde is the most important English writing between the eras of *Beowulf*, perhaps of the tenth century, and Spenser's *Faerie Queene*, begun in the 1580s. Before *Paradise Lost* (1667) it is the most accomplished English narrative in design, ambition, and poetic craft.

The Background of Troilus and Criseyde

Chaucer finished writing *Troilus and Criseyde* in the early-to-middle 1380s, when he was about forty years old.[1] It is a good guess that by then he had written a number of other works, among them his poetic translation of the immensely popular French allegory about courtship, the *Romance of the Rose*, his prose translation of Boethius's Latin *Consolation of Philosophy*, and his adaptation, which became the Knight's Tale of the *Canterbury Tales*, of Boccaccio's Italian poem, *Il Teseida delle nozze d'Emelia* (*The Story of Theseus concerning the Nuptials of Emily*). Along with these he had probably composed at least two, perhaps all three, of his longer "minor poems": *The Book of the Duchess*, *The House of Fame*, and *The Parliament of Fowls*. He had completed his apprenticeship as a poet.

Troilus and Criseyde itself is a very free adaptation of Boccaccio's *Filostrato* (literally, "The One Made Prostrate by Love," i.e., "The Love-Stricken"). The *Filostrato* was written around 1335, and the *Teseida* around 1340. Comparison of Chaucer's poem with the *Filostrato*, its main source, is the first and essential step toward a criticism of Chaucer's art. Hence in this Norton Critical Edition of *Troilus and Criseyde* a translation of Boccaccio's poem is provided on facing pages.[2] It is

---

1. For the date of *Troilus and Criseyde*, and for most matters of fact about the poem, see Windeatt 1992 and Barney 1987. The only solid evidence for dating *Troilus and Criseyde* is the date of the death of Thomas Usk, executed on March 4, 1388. Usk refers to *Troilus and Criseyde* in his *Testament of Love*. It is generally thought that Usk composed the *Testament* while a political prisoner between December 1384 and June 1385. See Ramona Bressie, "The Date of Thomas Usk's *Testament of Love*," *Modern Philology* 26 (1928): 17–29; Virginia B. Jellech, *Dissertation Abstracts International* 31 (1971): 6060–61A; and John F. Leyerle's conclusions as reported in Gary W. Shawver, ed., *The Testament of Love* (Toronto: U of Toronto P, 2002). Some think that Usk's narrator's stance as a prisoner is conventional and prefer the dates 1385–86 for the composition of the *Testament*. See Lucy Lewis, "The Identity of Margaret in Usk's *Testament of Love*," *Medium Aevum* 68 (1999): 63–72 and Joanna Summers, "Gower's *Vox Clamantis* and Usk's *Testament of Love*," *Medium Aevum* 68 (1999): 55–62. See also *Troilus and Criseyde* 3.624–25.
2. A fine edition of *Troilus and Criseyde* that includes the Italian text of the *Filostrato* along with a running commentary about Chaucer's adaptation of it is Windeatt 1984. C. S. Lewis's famous study of Chaucer's adaptation is included below. For editions and translations of the *Filostrato* see the Selected Bibliography.

   Although Boccaccio's poem is clearly Chaucer's main source, he may have used a French translation of it as an aid—as he used a French translation of Boethius's Latin. Like all members of his class, Chaucer was absolutely bilingual in English and French. See Robert A. Pratt, "Chaucer and the *Roman de Troyle et de Criseida*," *Studies in Philology* 53 (1956): 509–39, and Hanly 1990.

obvious that Chaucer deeply transformed the story as he recast Boccac-
cio's work—in fact, more than 5500 of the 8239 lines of *Troilus and
Criseyde* are Chaucer's independent work.

The first three of these earlier works give a good idea of the direction
Chaucer's work was taking. Along with the amatory works of his poetic
soulmate, Ovid, the thirteenth-century *Romance of the Rose* lent him
the materials for a refined and elegant way of talking about love, for the
making of a comedy of manners. Like Chaucer, his immediate French
precursors and models—the poets Deschamps, Froissart, and especially
Machaut—were deeply influenced by the *Romance*. The distinctive lan-
guage and style of *Troilus and Criseyde* owes much to this French tra-
dition.[3] Second, Boethius's *Consolation* provided a philosophical
framework for *Troilus and Criseyde*, especially with regard to the themes
of human happiness, fortune, and predestination[4]—and possibly pro-
vided the idea of arranging his poem into five books. And third, Boccac-
cio's *Teseida* opened for Chaucer the possibility of combining classical,
epic matter and machinery with a medieval romance plot of chivalric
love. Hence the heroic (and satiric) tones of the great Roman poets could
be welded to the intricate analyses of lovers' interiors and their courtly
worlds characteristic of medieval romance. When to these we add the
pervasive influence on *Troilus and Criseyde* of Dante's *Divine Comedy*,
we find the makings of a poetic ambition as richly varied and grand as
that of the Renaissance masters from Spenser to Milton, worthy to

> kis the steppes where as thow seest pace
> Virgile, Ovide, Omer, Lucan, and Stace.   (V.1791–92)

The story of Troilus and Criseyde is older than Boccaccio's account,
and Chaucer seems to have set about in scholarly fashion to examine a
number of earlier sources with care: a number of details from them
appear in *Troilus and Criseyde*. He takes for granted, in *Troilus and
Criseyde* and earlier poems, that his audience knew the story of the Tro-
jan War. The ultimate source is Homer's *Iliad*, the epic that looms trag-
ically behind Chaucer's love story, and contains the names of most of
the characters in *Troilus and Criseyde*: Troilus, Pandarus (a Lydian
archer, killed by Diomedes), Calchas (a Greek seer), Diomedes, Priam,
Hector, Paris, Helen, Deiphebus, Cassandra, Achilles, and others. Miss-
ing is the character of Criseyde. A captive woman, Chryseis (accusative:
Chryseida), whose name means "daughter of Chryses," appears in the
Iliad, and is in fact the initiating cause of the "wrath of Achilles," but
she has nothing to do with Chaucer's Criseyde.

Of course Chaucer did not read Greek, but many versions of the story
of Troy were available to him in French and Latin, languages he read
easily. Any medieval student who learned Latin would read Vergil and
Ovid, who everywhere allude to the Trojan matter. Two works, probably
originally in Greek of the first century C.E., were received by the Middle

---

3. The classic study here is Muscatine 1957. See also James I. Wimsatt, "The French Lyric Element
   in *Troilus and Criseyde*," *Yearbook of English Studies* 15 (1985):18–32 and the Green 1979 essay
   printed in this Norton Critical Edition.
4. See especially *Troilus and Criseyde* III.813–33, Criseyde on the fragility of happiness, and IV.953–
   1085, Troilus on free will and predestination. For a list of parallels between *Troilus and Criseyde*
   and the *Consolation of Philosophy* see Windeatt 1992:99–100.

Ages as what they claimed to be, eyewitness accounts of the Trojan War. These were translated into Latin, the *Journal of the Trojan War* by Dictys of Crete (fourth century C.E.), and the *History of the Destruction of Troy* by Dares the Phrygian (sixth century C.E.). Chaucer refers to Dares in the *Book of the Duchess*, the *House of Fame*, and *Troilus and Criseyde* (I.146, 1771), and to Dictys in *Troilus and Criseyde* (I.146). He probably had read neither work, but he did read a Latin poem of about 1190 by Joseph of Exeter, the *Iliad of Dares Phrygius*, which was commonly known as "Dares," and which Chaucer may well have thought was Dares's actual work.[5] He translates directly from Joseph's poem in *Troilus and Criseyde* V.799–840. Yet Dares and Dictys write nothing of the love affair between Troilus and Criseyde.

The basic story of Chaucer's poem, the love of Troilus for a woman (named Briseida) and her infidelity with Diomedes, was first told by the French poet Benoît de Sainte-Maure, in interwoven episodes in his *Roman de Troie* (late 1150s).[6] Benoît uses the name Briseida for the woman whom Boccaccio would call Criseida; like the name Criseyde, "Briseida" is the accusative form of Briseis, "daughter of Brises." In the *Iliad* she is the slave girl whom Agamemnon seized from Achilles, and her Homeric story has nothing to do with Benoît's invention of her affair with Troilus. Chaucer adopts a number of details directly from Benoît, but he tellingly omits the many generalized antifeminist comments that Benoît makes as he tells of Briseida's infidelity.

The *Roman de Troie* was adapted into Latin prose by the Sicilian Guido de Colonne's *History of the Destruction of Troy*, which was completed in 1287. Like Benoît, Guido claims to follow Dares and Dictys as his sources. Because the *History* is in Latin, it, like Dares and Dictys, was taken as a more authoritative source than the French of Benoît. Thus Chaucer names Guido in the *House of Fame*, but never names Benoît—or Boccaccio! Chaucer uses only a few details from Guido, and suppresses Guido's general view of the love of Troilus and Briseida as emblematic of overheated passion and mutability.

The author whom Chaucer's narrator does claim as his major source, whom he merely translates and sets into rhyme (II.8–18), is a Latin writer whom he names Lollius. We have good evidence that medieval writers, misunderstanding a passage in Horace, actually thought that there was a classical authority on the Trojan War named Lollius.[7] But no such author existed, and Chaucer is simply being sly. He both claims for himself an authentic ancient source, and, while characterizing his narrator as a plodding and hapless intermediary, manages to defer the question of his actual source, the altogether too modern and vernacular *Filostrato*.

Boccaccio undertook the same reading program that Chaucer did, and

5. Dares and Dictys are translated in Frazer 1966, and Joseph of Exeter in Roberts 1970. Two other Latin histories of the Trojan War were known in the medieval West, but there is no evidence that Chaucer used them: the *Latin Iliad*, perhaps of the first century C.E., and the *Destruction of Troy*, before the ninth century.
6. Relevant passages from Benoît are translated in Havely 1980 and Gordon 1934, with important omissions as signaled by Mieszkowski, "R. K. Gordon and the *Troilus and Criseyde* Story," *Chaucer Review* 15 (1980): 127–37. A good account of Chaucer's use of Benoît (and of all the sources) is in Windeatt 1992:37–137.
7. See Robert A. Pratt, "A Note on Chaucer's Lollius," *Modern Language Notes* 65 (1950): 183–87.

based his Filostrato mainly on Benoît (and a prose redaction of it), along with a number of earlier Italian accounts of the history of Troy.[8] His changing of the name of Briseida to Criseida is but a small part of his vast elaboration of the lovers' story. As compared with its predecessors, *Filostrato* has much more complicated investigations of his characters' interior lives. Whereas the earlier accounts focused almost entirely on Briseida's departure from Troy and her shifting of affections, Boccaccio invented the whole first part of the story, from the lovers' first sight of one another to the consummation scene. Chaucer augmented still further the earlier part of the action, and hence emphasized the rising comic action. He likewise redistributed the rather disorderly nine Parts of the *Filostrato* into his more studied, and carefully marked, five Books. Boccaccio's introduction of the go-between Pandaro (whose character likewise reflects a tradition of prior go-betweens in love affairs, from Ovid to Dante) enormously enriches the comic possibilities of the story. And though both lovers are more experienced, more overtly sensual, and may seem somewhat cynical as compared with Chaucer's pair, Boccaccio largely suppresses the blatant antifeminism of the sources.[9] The narrative was ready for Chaucer to work on.

Toward a Criticism of Troilus and Criseyde

The beginnings of a critical approach to the poem might adopt the old-fashioned categories of genre, characterization, style, setting, and theme.

GENRE

Chaucer refers to the five segments of *Troilus and Criseyde* as books (II.10, III.1818, IV.26) and he calls the whole poem *a sorwful tale* (I.14), a *storie* (II.31), several times a *boke*, and most pregnantly *litel myn tragedye* (V.1786). By tragedy Chaucer probably means loosely a story that tells of one *that stood in greet prosperitee*, fell, and *endeth wrecchedly* (Prologue to the Monk's Tale 1975–77), rather than an Aristotelian drama of character or fate.[1]

Regardless of Chaucer's own genre terms, critics a century ago liked to speak of *Troilus and Criseyde* as a drama, and analyzed the poem's structure into "scenes." Some found precedent for Chaucer's division of the poem into five parts in Seneca's five-act tragedies, though Chaucer may not have known Senecan drama.[2] Indeed, we find a progression of different scenes of action in narrative as well as drama (and our most famous ancient play, *Oedipus Rex*, has after all only one scene.) Still, we may justly label as dramatic Chaucer's use of dialogue in the poem,

---

8. On Boccaccio's sources see Maria Gozzi, "Sulle fonti del *Filostrato*: Le narrazioni di argomento troiano," *Studi sul Boccaccio* 5 (1969): 123–209.

9. Especially on the development of the character of Briseida/Criseyde in the tradition see Mieszkowski 1971 and Donaldson 1979.

1. In his usual contrary way, Ovid says, "Tragedy surpasses every kind of writing in gravity; also it always has as its subject love" (*Tristia* 2.381–82). On medieval conceptions of tragedy see Kelly 1997.

2. Others think Boethius's five books in the *Consolation of Philosophy* may have given Chaucer the idea.

surely the richest dialogue in English before Shakespeare, and his adroit exposition of character and the play of "dramatic irony" made possible by dialogue.[3] Reminiscent of Greek tragedy is the sharpest and largest irony of all, the fact that the rather narrow domestic action is set in doomed Troy.

Troilus and Criseyde may have acquired the label "drama" because it is good, and drama is good. In like manner, recent criticism suspects that to speak of it as a "novel"—Kittredge called it "the first novel, in the modern sense, that was ever written in the world, and one of the best"[4]—blends what should be kept distinct, out of a desire to equate a good poem with a favored genre. At least it can be said that, like a novel, the poem resists classification.

If the poems of Chrétien de Troyes and the books to which Don Quixote was addicted define the genre "romance," then Chaucer's and Boccaccio's poems are not romances: their plots are too simple; their settings too classical and, in the medieval view, too historical; their adventures insufficiently marvelous; their main characters too limited in their powers; their milieux too urban, too caught up in intricate social forces; their tones too skeptical, too profoundly critical of aristocratic mores. Yet like a novel *Troilus and Criseyde* seems to contain a romance within it, one constructed by Pandarus and lived by Troilus, and to reflect on the romance conventions of intense private morality: loyalty, honor, truth, the knightly code. Both Troilus and Criseyde are more conscious of, and more troubled by, the chivalric codes of decency in love affairs than their counterparts in the *Filostrato*: they are, in a rich sense, chaste. *Troilus and Criseyde* can usefully be compared with the genre "historical romance," debased in popular fiction since the eighteenth century, but still the vehicle of some of the best fiction from Homer's *Odyssey* to Faulkner's *Absalom, Absalom!*

Finally, epic. The story has its origins in Homeric epic, and in many ways it resembles the trio of French romanticized epics produced in the middle of the twelfth century, the "romans" of Thebes, of Aeneas, and (by Benoît) of Troy, ultimately derived from Statius, Vergil, and Homer. The division of *Troilus and Criseyde* into books, its occasional flights into the "high style" of ornate poetry appropriate, the medieval rhetoricians taught, to epic matters, and its elaborate invocations of various figures standing for the Muses remind us of these epic forebears. Here Chaucer seems to outdo even the classicizing Boccaccio, introducing more epic devices in his formal prologues, and even inserting a brief retelling of Statius's *Thebaid*, complete with a Latin summary (V.1485–1510).

Chaucer calls the Theban story *gestes olde* (V.1511), just as he calls the matter of the Trojan War *the Troian gestes* of Homer and the later "authorities" on Troy, Dares and Dictys (I.145–46). But a gest in this sense or an epic in the tradition of the *Iliad* focuses on military action, whereas Chaucer insistently avoids the scene of the battlefield as *a long digression / Fro my matere* (I.143–44; see also V.1765–71). His arena is the bedroom. At the end of the poem he alludes to the opening lines of

---

3. Chaucer in smaller scope matches this brilliant dialogue with later work like the Prologue to the Canon's Yeoman's Tale, the Friar's Tale, and the Pardoner's Tale.
4. George Lyman Kittredge, *Chaucer and His Poetry* (Cambridge: Harvard UP, 1915, 1970), p. 109.

the *Aeneid* and the *Iliad* (V.1766, 1800–801) as if to remind us of what he has *not* written. In embracing some of the conventions but eschewing the matter of epic, he makes us think of great epic themes—the destruction of cities, heroic enterprise, divine and fatal destiny, the subordination of private happiness to public demands—while at the same time presenting a world of social comedy and intimate and scrupulous moral probing. Chaucer's poem is funnier and brighter than Boccaccio's, but its allusions to poems of national doom make it also more poignant and grave.

CHARACTERIZATION

Chaucer invites us to respond to the principal characters of the poem as if they were not fictional, and if we avoid asking the wrong questions we may indeed judge them—and we may be wrong. The poet seems to tease us to ask such questions as whether Criseyde had children (I.132–33; Boccaccio says she had none), or whether she knew Troilus was at Pandarus's house (III.575–79), or how old she is (V.826). More important, indeed crucial, are such questions as whether Criseyde succumbs to love too willingly, or shifts her affections too culpably; whether Pandarus is a true friend or a slimy, opportunistic pimp; whether Troilus is a moony boy or a paragon of integrity. More demandingly than the *Filostrato*, the poem requires us to raise such questions.

Chaucer focuses our attention on the question of how people decide what to do, the essential moral question. The agent of that focus is Chaucer's most notable addition to Boccaccio's poem, the narrator. *Troilus and Criseyde*'s narrator intrudes everywhere, openly manages and comments on the story, and speaks more or less consistently "in character." Like the pilgrim narrator of the *Canterbury Tales* or the narrators of the dream visions, he tempts us to imagine him as a freestanding persona, a character in the poem as subject to our judgment as the others. Broadly, he presents himself, especially at first, as a comic figure, the embodiment of the rhetorical topic of "affected modesty" writ large, helplessly inept at love, something of a pedantic historian doing his best to render his source (the fictitious Lollius) to an audience of adepts in the arts of Cupid; later, as the reluctant purveyor of offensive story matter; and finally, if we take the conclusion of the poem as a continuation of the narrator's voice, as a serious Christian poet who urges the rejection of worldly vanity and the higher love of *that sothfast Crist* (V.1860).

This narrator guides our moral criticism. He protests (too much?) that Criseyde's loving of Troilus was no *sodeyn love* (II.666–86). He excuses Criseyde for pity, and observes that *swich is this world* (V.1099, 1748). He constantly praises Troilus for virtue and honor, *trewe as stiel in ech condicioun* (V.831), and claims that his martial prowess is a product of his love (III.1776–77). He admires the energy, at least, of Pandarus in his machinations (III.484–90, 512–13). Yet this same narrator provides us, willy-nilly, with the materials for a harsh criticism of the principals: Criseyde may be thought *slydynge of corage* (V.825); Troilus and Pandarus are caught up in more than one lie (Troilus's feigned sickness and his feigned jealousy of Horaste); Pandarus worries about his status as a procurer (III.253–56)—his name after all later became our word "pander."

In comparison with Boccaccio's characters, Chaucer's extend the range of what we find in the *Filostrato*. By pushing out the extremes, he contrives more pronounced oppositions, clearer dilemmas. Troilus is more idealistic, more driven to universalize his feelings, than Troilo, and yet (or, and hence?) he is a more comic figure, farcically abashed especially when it comes to the rude business of the bedchamber. Chaucer's Criseyde is a much more complicated figure than the Criseida of the *Filostrato*. She is dominated, as C. S. Lewis argued, by fear, and yet she is often confident and assertive (for the ambivalence see, e.g., I.176–82). Boccaccio's Pandaro suggests that, as a widow, Criseyde will be amorous. Likewise Chaucer's Criseyde is erotically motivated, but her passions are rendered more delicately and indirectly. Pandarus is altogether livelier and funnier than Boccaccio's Pandaro. Perhaps because he is the precursor of Shakespeare's officious and ineffectual Polonius, we may well guess that he is a generation older than his niece (in Boccaccio, his cousin), although he is himself an unrequited lover (II.57–63). Yet Pandarus is also a darker figure than his Italian counterpart: he himself raises the moral problem of procuring for friendship (III.239–80), and his suggestion to Troilus, grieving over the decision to send Criseyde to the Greeks, that he simply take another mistress (IV.400–27) seems worse than crude.

STYLE

Using the common classical and medieval division of styles into high, middle, and low, we might describe the style of *Troilus and Criseyde* as rarely reaching higher, but often reaching lower, than that of the *Filostrato*. A stylistic maneuver typical of the poem is the utterance of a lofty sentiment, full of such rhetorical adornments as apostrophe, anaphora, extended simile, antithesis, mythological allusion, metaphor, and other figures, only to be deflated by some ridiculous gesture or common-sensical riposte. Chaucer repeats in the poem the old joke about over-wrought ornamentation: *The dayes honour, and the hevenes yë, / The nyghtes foo—al this clepe I the sonne . . .* (II.904–905).

To Troilus is given much of the high style of the poem, especially in several lyric set-pieces that Chaucer adds to the *Filostrato*, beginning with his song in the first book, translated from a sonnet by Petrarch (I.400–20). His speech often conforms to the style of medieval lyrics in the tradition of "courtly love": he is given to superlatives, to absolutes, to self-searching soliloquies, to talk of heaven and hell and death (see Davis Taylor 1976).

Pandarus is something of a shrewd and earthy Mercutio to Troilus's Romeo. We might imagine him with Rosalind saying "men have died from time to time, and worms have eaten them, but not for love" (*As You Like It* IV.i.101). Boccaccio used a few proverbs, but Chaucer adds so many as to make proverbial speech, with its folksy tone of common wisdom, an especially prominent feature of his style, and most of the proverbs are spoken by Pandarus. Naturally Troilus is exasperated by

Pandarus's persistent homely lore: *For thy proverbes may me naught availle* (I.756). The styles of the two men differ as analytical and spiritual intellect differs from unsifted public opinion.

A fascinating quality of the style of *Troilus and Criseyde* is its potential for ambiguity: it is hard to pin down the tone. Early in the poem we read in a description of Criseyde that

> *the pure wise of hire mevynge*
> *Shewed wel that men myght in hire gesse*
> *Honour, estat, and wommanly noblesse.* (I.285–87)

How far may we allow *gesse*—which in Middle English can mean "guess, discern, suppose, conclude, imagine, believe"—with its possible intimation of doubt about her character, to color our response, even this early in the poem? Troilus falls in love, and our narrator is moved to apostrophe: *O blynde world, O blynde entencioun!* (I.211). Who reads correctly, those who hear in this passage a moral critique of the vanity of earthly affections that culminates in the final stanzas of the poem, or those who hear a playful parody of pretentious poetizing about a condition—amorous bedazzlement—entirely commonplace and scarcely culpable?

SETTING

Boccaccio certainly saw the implications of setting an essentially private love story amidst the great events of Troy and its public love story, the rape of Helen (see McCall 1962). Troilus's name, "little Troy," reinforces the point. We hear the words "Troy" and "destroy" echoing through the poem. Early commentators on the Trojan War, both pagans and Christians, tended to ascribe Troy's fall not simply to blind destiny or to the interventions of pagan gods, but rather to the pride and lust of the Trojans. This moral view of the justice of Troy's fall scarcely colors the mood of the poem until the public intrusion into the lovers' affair in the fourth book. Then Pandarus advises Troilus simply to abduct Criseyde, appealing to his manliness, his kinship with Paris. Troilus declines, seeing that the town is at war *For ravysshyng of wommen* (IV.548)—his counterpart in the *Filostrato* does not advance this argument. In spite of Troilus's effort to avoid *so gret unright* (IV.550), his end finally coincides with that of Troy.

The Greek Diomede finds it in his interest, while wooing Criseyde, to emphasize the impending destruction of Troy (V.883–910), and the narrator, about to report the death of Hector, says that Fortune *Gan pulle awey the fetheres brighte of Troie*, and alludes to the old motif of the translation of empire from nation to nation (V.1541–47). Neither Boccaccio nor Chaucer mentions the final doom of Troy at the end of their poems, but that doom and the question of its meaning looms in the background of the story.

Chaucer's most extended addition to the *Filostrato* is the episode at Deiphebus's house, which brings together for the first time the smaller world of the love affair—perhaps symbolized by Troilus's cramped chamber—and the great world of Trojan public affairs. There we see Helen of Troy, and we hear of a letter from Hector, but the scene revolves around a business of litigation involving Criseyde and one Poliphete, and of course the focus of the scene is on Troilus' feigning illness and his private meeting with Criseyde. The episode presents court politics, aristocratic graciousness, and amorous scheming, where we in the shadow of Chapman's Homer might have looked for the brilliant glow of the great characters of the *Iliad*. The matter of Troy handed down to Chaucer constrained him to recount the death of Troilus in war, as a piece of epic history. Chaucer in various ways seems to resist this limitation on his narrative freedom, and to do what he can, by concentrating on the bedroom rather than the battlefield, to leave his principal characters free and therefore able to choose and liable to judgment. He strains to make Troy a theater not of war but of love.

THEME

Among the issues presented in *Troilus and Criseyde* are the conflict of public and private good; the differing value systems of courtly chivalry, paganism, and Christianity (in short, the nature of happiness and the meaning of *trouthe*); the interplay of fiction and history, literary allusion and immediate experience; the consequences of gender; the role of time; the significance of the literary structure. Chaucer particularly emphasizes, even in his first stanza, two other themes here briefly considered: fortune and love.

Much more insistently than Boccaccio, and conspicuously under the influence of Boethius's *Consolation of Philosophy*, our narrator reverts to the bundle of themes associated with fortune: the reversals of worldly affairs (*aventures . . . Fro wo to wele*, I.4), the destiny of the stars, the fate of vain wishes, the ineluctable fixity of past history, and the limitations of human aspirations in the arena of the mutable goddess Fortune and her fickle wheel. Chaucer adds to Boccaccio the remarkable scene in which Troilus argues in Boethian terms about the classic problem of free will and divine predestination, concluding (as Boethius had not) that *al that comth, comth by necessitee* (IV.958).

But to these grim conclusions we hear Pandarus respond, *Who say (saw) evere a wis man faren so?* (IV.1087). So much of the poem turns on decisions—will Criseyde love Troilus? how will the lovers respond to the exchange of prisoners?—that we would deny much to deny the power of human choice, however fatalist we may be. Chaucer does not solve the problem of fate and free will, but in *Troilus and Criseyde* he explores it in all gravity, as he would later explore it comically in the Nun's Priest's Tale. Boccaccio's poem ends by making it an exemplum of bad female behavior; Chaucer ends appropriately with a request that young lovers direct their love to God.

The topic of love is introduced in the third line of *Troilus and Criseyde*, and recurs in the last line. The poem raises the question, what should a person desire, and poses the terms of the question in various ways. Of Troilus we ask whether his loving is celestial or natural (the terms in I.977–79), a matter of noble ideals or of Bayard the horse, driven from within and without (I.218–20). The bustling of Pandarus raises the questions of whether love is a matter of relieving an itch, the efficient cause of farce, and whether *frendes love* (III.1591) springs from purity of heart or from a complex combination of voyeurism, careerism, lust for power, and displaced or vicarious desire. Criseyde's conduct must make us ask how love and fidelity are linked, whether a love that can change can be true.

The very center of *Troilus and Criseyde* (the 4120th of its 8239 lines) falls at III.1271, within the three stanzas of a speech by Troilus in worship of love and at the climax of the poem in the consummation scene (III.1254–74). This hymn to love is furthermore bracketed by two other universalizing love-paeans, the Proem to book Three, and the song of Troilus near the same book's end (III.1744–71). The central stanzas repay study; from their first line, O Love, O Charite, they collect in compressed form many of the terms designating types of love. Troilus first, surprisingly, evokes charity—religious selflessness, grace, love of God and neighbor: "charity" has never meant "erotic love" in English. Then Venus, as planet (astrological cause of love) and goddess; and the wedding god, Hymen (in a context where a wedding might well be, but is not, in question). Troilus then apostrophizes love as the *holy bond of thynges*, the opposite of Strife in Empedocles's physics, a cosmic force that holds atoms together. Then, love as the enabler of grace (either a lady's favor or God's grace), in a passage significantly drawn from that other great love-poet, Dante. The allusion is to the last canto of the *Divine Comedy* (*Paradise* 33.13–18), St. Bernard's prayer to the Virgin Mary. Troilus's speech refers to a number of features of noble loving: worship and praise itself, benevolence, fidelity, sorrow and joy, honor, succor, diligent service, grace, the devotions of the "religion of love."

This little anatomy of love is further bracketed by the addresses to lovers at the beginning and end of the poem. In the former our narrator strikingly first presents himself as inept at loving *for myn unliklynesse*. He seems, like Pandarus (with whom he is often compared as the architect of the affair), to seek his reward in love's religion by merely helping other lovers to recognize their suffering in Troilus's:

> For so hope I my sowle best avaunce,
> To prey for hem that Loves servauntz be,
> And write hire wo, and lyve in charite.   (I.47–49)

This is surely playful, but just as surely plays with very serious matters: charity and the salvation of the soul.

Equally playful and serious is the ending of the poem. Where the narrative proper actually ends, and whether the final stanzas are in our usual narrator's proper voice, and whether the poem's close (a palinode?) contravenes the relatively worldly view of love that the story has presented, are matters of vigorous dispute. But there is no question that Chaucer here, after (playfully?) asserting that his purpose is to warn women against treacherous men (V.1779–85), shows Troilus finally in contempt of the *blynde lust* of this world (1824), and recommends that we love him who for love of us died on the cross (1842–44), and concludes praying that Jesus make us worthy of his mercy *For love of mayde and moder thyn benigne. Troilus and Criseyde* displays the many forms of loving, noble and divine and fleshly, farcical and elegant and violent, comic and tragic.

Life of Chaucer

Like Spenser and Milton, Chaucer was a civil servant, and his public offices ensured that many documents mentioning him, nearly five hundred, have been preserved—though none of the life records refers to his career as a poet.[5] He served three kings of England: Edward III, Richard II (1377–99), and Henry IV. The Chaucer family were wealthy vintners—wholesale wine dealers—who settled in London in the late thirteenth century. Geoffrey Chaucer was born to Agnes and John Chaucer in the early 1340s. Where he received his early education is not known, but it is obvious that he acquired a good grounding in Latin to accompany the English and French he grew up speaking. Some evidence suggests that he studied law at the Inns of Court.

The first document naming Chaucer records grants to him in 1357 from the Countess of Ulster, daughter-in-law of Edward III. He was probably a page in the noble household, and it seems he was being prepared for government service, not for the family business. He learned young of the courtly manners we find reflected in *Troilus and Criseyde*, and also how to wield arms. Chaucer's whole life was spent during the Hundred Years' War with France, and he was in fact captured on the battlefield near Reims and briefly held for ransom, but set free in early 1360. At some point he assumed the title of esquire (one of his sons, Thomas, was knighted).

We know nothing of his activities until we next hear of him in 1366, when he received a safe-conduct to travel through Navarre in modern Spain. This is the first of many documents recording Chaucer's travels to the continent, on the king's business. His principal occupation for several years seems to have been as envoy. He also traveled abroad in 1368, in 1369 (with the powerful Duke of Lancaster, John of Gaunt, son and father of kings), and in 1370. In 1372–73 he made an extended visit to Italy—Genoa and Florence at least—negotiating trade and perhaps military matters. Conceivably he met both Petrarch and Boccaccio at that time. Possibly Chaucer already knew some of the language from Italian merchants in London before this mission, and was chosen for it partly for that reason. He traveled several times again on the king's business in 1376–77, and again to Italy (Lombardy) in 1378. Here he dealt with the Visconti family, powerful rulers of Milan and patrons of the arts. His last recorded journey abroad was to Calais, in 1387.

Chaucer held a number of other important positions in the government, and the records show that he was amply remunerated by John of Gaunt and the three kings. In 1374 he moved to a rent-free apartment over Aldgate in London, and in the same year he was appointed controller of the customs on wool, leather, and sheepskins in the port of London, a job he held for twelve years. Wool was England's prin-

5. See Crow and Olson 1966 and the section on Chaucer's life in the introduction to Benson 1987 by Crow and Virginia E. Leland. For biographies of Chaucer see the Selected Bibliography.

cipal export, and Chaucer's job was in effect to serve as auditor of the immense customs proceeds.

From 1385 to 1389 he served with a number of influential men on a commission of peace for the county of Kent. By then he may have already changed his residence to Kent, perhaps to Greenwich. In 1386 he was elected as one of the two members of the House of Commons from Kent. He was obviously recognized as a substantial citizen. In 1389 he was named clerk of the king's works, responsible for the fabric of royal residences and other buildings, including the Tower of London. He left this work in 1391, and took up the post of deputy forester of a royal forest in Somerset, another job with large responsibilities. In 1399 Chaucer changed residence for the last time, leasing a house in the precincts of Westminster Abbey. He died late in the year 1400.

By 1366 Chaucer had married Philippa, probably the daughter of a knight of Hainault, Gilles de Roet. Philippa's sister Katherine Swynford was John of Gaunt's mistress, whom he finally married in 1396. Philippa died some time in or soon after 1387. In 1380 Chaucer was released by Cecilia Chaumpaigne *de raptu meo*. Whether the *raptus* was a physical rape, or an abduction of some sort, is not clear, nor is it clear that Chaucer was guilty.

Three fellow writers set down comment on Chaucer during his lifetime. In the mid-1380s the French poet Eustache Deschamps, whose work Chaucer sometimes drew from, spoke of him as a "great translator," particularly with reference to his translation of the *Romance of the Rose*. He was also praised by his fellow Londoner Thomas Usk in the *Testament of Love*, and by the Kentish poet John Gower in his *Confessio Amantis*. Whether Chaucer was ever patronized specifically as a poet we don't know, but the 1374 grant to him by John of Gaunt may have been a reward for the *Book of the Duchess*, which in a barely disguised allegory laments the death of the duke's first wife, Blanche, in 1368.

Chaucer's Language

PRONUNCIATION[6]

Words are usually, as in Modern English, stressed on the first syllable unless they have a prefix (*defénce, afféccìoun*), but borrowings from French often stress the last syllable apart from final *-e* (*benígne, honóur, servýse*). Endings like *-nésse, -énce, -áunce, -ýnge* in rhyme position take stress. The common ending *-cióun* has two syllables, with the stress on the last. A number of words are variable (like the modern word "diverse"): in *Troilus and Criseyde* I.843 *Fórtune* has stress on the first syllable; in I.849 it is *Fortúne*. Proper names vary, especially two-syllabled *Tróilus, Pándar(e), Críseyd(e)*, three-syllabled *Troílus, Pándarùs, Criséyde*, and even four-syllabled *Criséÿdè* (II.1424). (Here and in the text the dieresis mark over a vowel (*ë*) means that it is to be pronounced as a separate syllable.) The best guide is the meter.

The consonants are pronounced as in Modern English (including the

6. See Kökeritz 1978. For inflectional forms see the "Notes on Inflections" in Davis et al. 1979.

ch sound of *chaunce* and the *g* sound of *age*—not the French sounds), with some exceptions. The *g*, *k*, and *w* in combinations like *gnaw*, *knee*, and *wrecche* were fully pronounced, as was the *l* in *folk*, *half*, but the *gn* combination in French words like *signe*, *benigne* was pronounced simply as *n*. Initial *h* in words borrowed from French (*honour*, *habit*) is silent—so the scribes usually spelled Helen and Hector as *Eleyne*, *Ector*—and in short common words like *he*, *him*, *hem*, *hire*, *hit*, *han*, initial *h* is either silent or weakly pronounced. In words like *is* and *was* the *s* was usually unvoiced, so that the words rhymed with *this* and *glas*. Exactly how *r* was pronounced is not known, but especially between vowels it should be trilled or rolled as in the continental European languages or Scots. The sound of *gh* in words like *knight*, *broght* is that of the *ch* in German *ich* and *ach*. The former sound (after *i*, *e*, *y*) is that of a strongly pronounced *h* of the word "hue"; the latter sound (after *a*, *o*, *u*) is the more guttural sound of Scottish *loch*.

Chaucer's vowel sounds differed substantially from ours, and had roughly the values of Latin and modern continental languages like French and German. As in Scots or Irish English, long vowels were truly long, drawn out so as to produce the sounds we hear as lilting. The accompanying table will give an idea of the pronunciation, but listening to a teacher or a good recording of Chaucer will help the most. Unstressed vowels like those in the final syllables *-o*, *os*, *ed* have the "uh" (schwa) sound of the last syllable of *sofa* and the first syllable of *control*. Chaucer has no vowel like that of modern "but"; his word *but* rhymes with "put" (with rounded *u*). The spellings *y* and *i* are interchangeable; they have the same value.

Hardest to pronounce at speed are the long vowels of short words: Chaucer's *he* is pronounced like "hay" (but as a pure vowel, not a diphthong), and his *to* sounds like a pure-vowel version of modern "toe." Also tricky are the long *u* vowels that Chaucer texts spell *ou* or *ow*: Chaucer's *flour* (flower) rhymes with modern "tour," and *fowl* (bird) with "drool." The spelling *o* in common words like *love*, *monk*, *sonne* never had an *o* sound, but the rounded *u* sound of "put": the *o* spelling merely avoided a confusing series of "minim" strokes in writing, such that *munk* would look, in medieval script, like iiiiiiik (without the dots on the *i*'s). Variant spellings of words generally reflect actual variants of pronunciation, so that we should pronounce *hye* and *heigh*, both meaning "high," or *nat* and *noght*, both meaning "not," in two different ways.

Final *-es* and *-ed* normally had full pronunciation as syllables. The pronunciation of final *-e* depends on complex inflectional rules, but on the whole the spelling in this Norton Critical Edition (which is slightly normalized) in conjunction with the meter will be a reliable guide. Very frequently a final *-e* (or often another final vowel like the *-o* of *to* or *unto*) will precede a word beginning with a vowel or an *h* that is not pronounced or weakly pronounced; in these cases the *-e* is elided or slurred, at least for metrical purposes. Hence, near the beginning of *Troilus and Criseyde*, *parte fro* and *sothe for* are each pronounced as having three syllables, while *sone of* and *clepe I* and *have he* have two syllables; *unto any* has three, *the advérsité* has four (and scribes would often spell such a combination as *thadversite*). Exceptions to these rules include *thise*,

CHAUCER'S SPELLING

VOWELS

CHAUCER'S SPELLING	ME PRONUNCIATION	EXAMPLES	EVOLUTION IN NE
a	[a], as in NE *top*	*after, at*	usually becomes [æ], as in NE *after, at*
a, aa	[a:], as in NE *father*	*take, caas*	becomes [e], as in NE *take, case*
e	[ɛ], as in NE *best*	*best, hem*	no change
e, ee	[ɛ:], as in NE *bed*	*heeth, ese, see*	becomes [i], spelled *ea*, as in NE *heath, ease, sea*
e, ee	[e:], as in NE *take*	*swete, be, see*	becomes [i], spelled *e* or *ee*, as in NE *sweet, be, see*
i, y	[I], as in NE *hit, in*	*hit, in*	no change
i, y	[i:], as in NE *seed*	*I, ride*	becomes [ai], as in NE *I, ride*
o	[ɔ], as in NE *long*	*of, oxe*	usually becomes [ə] or [a], as in NE *of, ox*
o, oo	[ɔ:], as in NE *law*	*go, hope, so*	becomes [o], as in NE, *go, hope, so*
o, oo	[o:], as in NE *note*	*roote, to, good*	becomes [u] or [U], as in NE, *root, to, good*
u, o¹	[U], as in NE *put*	*up, but, come*	usually becomes [ə], as in NE *up, but, come*
ou, ow	[u:], as in NE *to*	*hous, town*	becomes [aU], as in NE *house, town*
u, eu, ew	[y], as in Fr. *tu*²	*vertu, salewe*	no NE equivalent

DIPHTHONGS

CHAUCER'S SPELLING	ME PRONUNCIATION	EXAMPLES	EVOLUTION IN NE
ai, ay, ei, ey	[æI], somewhere between NE *hay* and *high*	*day, sayn, they*	becomes [ei], as in NE *day, say, they*
au, aw	[aU], as in NE *out*	*cause, draw*	becomes [ɔ], as in NE *cause, draw*
eu, ew³	[Iu], close to NE *few*	*newe, reule*	becomes [Iu] or [u], as in NE *few, rule*
oi, oy	[ɔI], as in NE *joy*	*joye, point*	no change
ou, ow	[ɔU], a glide between the vowels of NE *law* and *to*	*thought, bowe*	becomes [ɔ] or [o], as in NE *thought, bow*

1. A few words with the short [U] sound in ME are spelled with *o* instead of *u*: *sone* (NE *son*), *sonne* (NE *sun*), *come, love, some*. These words were originally spelled with *u* in Old English; the *o* spelling is an orthographic change only.

2. This sound occurs only in a few words recently borrowed from French.

3. A few words—the most familiar are *feve*, *lewed, shew, shrewe*—should be pronounced [eu] instead of [Iu].

The table is reproduced by permission from the companion Norton Critical Edition of the *Canterbury Tales*, ed. V. A. Kolve and Glending Olson (New York and London: W. W. Norton & Company, 1989), p. xv.

oure, hire (pronoun), *here* (adverb), *youre*, regularly one syllable, as well as such words as *wel, frend, blynd, desir, out*, all of which the scribes sometimes spelled with an *-e* that should not be pronounced. Further, the unstressed vowels in words like *ever(e)* and *over(e)* were regularly elided (cf. later poets' *e'er, o'er*), so that *evere in* and *over al* each have two syllables.[7]

Most of Chaucer's grammatical forms and syntactic usages are the same as in Modern English, and difficult instances are handled in the marginal glosses and footnotes in the text. A few differences should be noted. More nouns have plurals in *-en* than in Modern English ("oxen," "children"): the word for "eyes" is *yën*. *Hors* and *thing* and *cas* are plural as well as singular forms. A few nouns have no final *-s* in the possessive: *lady, herte*, and kinship nouns like *fader, brother*—so *my lady grace* is "my lady's grace."

I and *ich* freely vary as the first person pronoun. The word *its* had not yet come into English, and the possessive of *hit* ("it") was *his*. Chaucer uses the singular *thou* and (objective) *thee* for the familiar second person pronoun (compare French *tu*, German *du*), the plural *ye* and (objective) *yow* for plural and formal singular address. (Surprisingly, Troilus and Criseyde use the *ye* forms with one another, even in bed.) The words for "them" and "their" are *hem* (to be distinguished from singular *him*) and *hire*—and "her" is also *hire*. The word *men* is sometimes a singular pronoun meaning "one." The word *who* is used as an interrogative but never as a relative pronoun; Chaucer uses *that* or *which that* instead. *That* sometimes means "that which."

Gan, "began," very frequently is merely an auxiliary verb marking the past tense, meaning "did": *gan to take*, "did take, took"; *gan hir bet biholde*, "beheld her better." The verb *do(n)* often means "do," but often means "cause": *don us bothe dyen*, "cause us both to die." See the Glossary.

The infinitives of verbs end in *-e* or *-en*, except for those whose stems end in a vowel, like *go/gon*. The infinitive of the verb meaning "slay," then, can be *slee* or *slen* or *sleen*. In the present tense the verbs have these endings, familiar from the King James Bible and Shakespeare:

ich ride	*we ride(n)*
thou ridest	*ye ride(n)*
he/she/hit rideth	*they ride(n)*

Parentheses enclose optional endings, *ride* or *riden*. Thus the plural forms are all the same, as they are in the past tense as well. For metrical reasons Chaucer will sometimes contract the *-eth* ending, and assimilate the final consonant of the stem to the dental sound of the final *-th*, so that *cometh* becomes *comth*, *rideth* becomes *rit*, *listeth* becomes *list*, *wortheth* becomes *worth*, *bideth* ("abides") and *biddeth* ("asks") become *bit*. *Halt* and *stant* are contractions of *holdeth* and *stondeth*.

In the subjunctive (very frequently used in *Troilus and Criseyde*), the present tense singular ends in *-e*, and the past tense in *-(n)*.

---

7. For the handling of final *-e* see Barney 1993.

Two classes of verbs, strong and weak, correspond to the Modern English strong verb "ride, rode, ridden," with stem vowel change indicating the change of tense, and the weak verb "walk, walked, walked," with the past and past participle indicated by *-ed* (sometimes pronounced and sometimes spelled *-t*). Strong verbs in the past tense have no ending for the first and third person singular, *-e* for the second person singular, and *-e(n)* for the plural:

I sang	we songe(n)
thou songe	ye songe(n)
he/she/hit sang	they songe(n)

The past participle of strong verbs ends in *-e(n)*. Both strong and weak past participles may freely receive the prefix *y-* or *i-*: *ycomen, iseyd* "having come, having said."

Weak verbs have different past tense inflections that follow on the *-(e)d* or *-t* that marks the past tense (*demen* means "deem, judge, think"):

ich herde, demede, kepte	we herde(n), demede(n), kepte(n)
thou herdest, demedest, keptest	ye herde(n), demede(n), kepte(n)
he/she/it herde, demede, kepte	they herde(n), demede(n), kepte(n)

The past participle of weak verbs is like the past plural but without the *-e(n)*: *herd, demed, kept.*

The pronoun *thou* is sometimes contracted and suffixed to its verb: *slepestow*, "are you sleeping"; *dorstestow*, "did you dare." The very common verb *list* or *lest*, "pleases," a contraction of *listeth*, is usually impersonal in use, with a pronoun as indirect object: *hire lyst*, "it pleases her, she is pleased." Its past tense is *liste*: *hem liste*, "it pleased them, they were pleased."

The negative particle *ne*, "not," is often attached to following verbs that are highly frequent: *nam*, "am not"; *not* (= *ne wot*), "knows not"; *nadde* (= *ne hadde*), "did not have"; *nil, nolde* (= *ne wil, ne wolde*), "don't wish, didn't wish." In Middle English double (or triple) negatives do not make a positive, but merely add emphasis: *she nis nat*, "she isn't."

The Versification of Troilus and Criseyde

Like several of Chaucer's other poems, *Troilus and Criseyde* is written in "rime royal," a seven-line stanza in iambic pentameter rhyming *ababbcc*. Chaucer was not the first to use the stanza in English, but he was among the first, as he practically introduced the iambic pentameter line (and the couplet in the same meter) into the poetic tradition.[8] His use of the form both for narration and in representing speech demonstrates absolute mastery.

The line regularly contains ten syllables, or eleven when it concludes with a final *-e(n)*. The syllables are arranged with alternating stress; hence each line has five sequences ("feet") of lesser stress followed by greater stress: iambic pentameter. The five stresses need not all be strong; it only matters that a syllable in the stressed position receives more stress than the adjacent syllables. Exceptions to these norms are

8. See Martin Stevens, "The Royal Stanza in Early English Literature," *PMLA* 94 (1979): 62–76.

not very numerous. Stress may be inverted so that the first of a pair receives greater stress, especially in the first foot, rarely if ever in the last two feet. Some lines omit the first unstressed syllable, and are called "headless." Very rarely a line will omit an unstressed syllable in mid-line, with the line thus containing nine syllables (or ten with a final *-e(n)*). Also rare is the addition of an extra unstressed syllable somewhere within the line.

The following pair of stanzas will represent how the meter works. Fully stressed syllables receive an acute accent (á); syllables only relatively stressed receive a grave accent (à). Any final *-e* that is not pronounced, usually because of its elision before another vowel or initial *h-*, is here italicized. Often a sequence of little words will not have an obvious pattern of stress. In these cases the metrical benefit of the doubt may be given to the normal alternating pattern, and the even-numbered syllables be marked with the grave accent. Obviously a skilled, dramatic reading of the poem will not thump out the meter mechanically.

> The dóuble sórwe of Tróïlùs to téllen,
> That wàs the kýng Priámus sóne of Tróye,
> In lóvynge, hòw his áventùres féllen
> Fro wó to wéle, and àfter òut of jóie,
> My púrpos ìs, er thàt I párte frò ye.⁹
> Theзíphonè, thow hélp me fòr t'endíte
> Thise wóful vérs, that wépen às I wríte.   (I.1–7)

> Thow bíddest mè I shùlde lóve anóther
> Al frésshly néwe, and lát Criséyde gó!
> It líth nat ìn my pówer, léeve bróther;
> And thóugh I mýght, I wólde nàt do só.
> But kánstow pláyen ráket, tó and fró,
> Nettle ín, dok óut, now thís, now thát, Pandáre?
> Now fóule fálle hire fòr thi wó that cáre!   (IV.456)

This second stanza exhibits the lively variation of excited speech, yet still maintains the basic meter. The sixth line may be read as scanned, or the first two feet may be inverted or read with emphatic level stress. Broadly speaking, Chaucer does not press against the self-imposed constraints of iambic pentameter as much as Shakespeare ("When to the sessions of sweet silent thought"), but he presses more than Pope ("Belinda smiled, and all the world was gay").

The Text

No copy of *Troilus and Criseyde* in Chaucer's own handwriting survives.¹ The earliest manuscripts are from near the beginning of the fifteenth century. No scribe copies exactly what he sees; hence we cannot know with absolute certainty what Chaucer wrote. The texts of Chaucer

---

9. As object of the preposition *fro*, the pronoun *ye* should regularly be in the objective case, *yow*. The rhyme and the scribes' (and probably Chaucer's own) spelling show that the word was so unstressed that its vowel was here reduced to schwa; nowhere else in *Troilus and Criseyde* does this lapse of grammar occur.
1. Some of the documents in the *Chaucer Life Records* may be in Chaucer's own hand.

that we read have to be taken with faith in the scribes who copied them and the editors who adjudicate and emend the scribes' work. Let the reader beware.

It is important to note that all the punctuation and capitalization of this Norton Critical Edition are supplied by the editor. The punctuation involves many decisions about the meaning of the text that are arguable. Even the capitalization amounts to substantial editorial intervention: when is *Love* or *Fortune* a personification, a pagan god, or simply a common noun? Medieval scribes punctuated and capitalized their texts according to their own whim, without authorial sanction, and much less fully than we now take for granted; their marks are of little help to the modern editor.

Luckily *Troilus and Criseyde* is preserved in a number of excellent manuscripts, and there is less doubt about the text than about such works as *Piers Plowman* or the plays of Shakespeare. There are sixteen complete or nearly complete handwritten copies of the poem from the fifteenth and sixteenth centuries, along with three early printed editions that have some textual authority, and sixteen small fragments. Among the best of the manuscripts are those held at Corpus Christi College, Cambridge, at the Pierpont Morgan Library, and at St. John's College, Cambridge. The first of these is the main basis of the present text; it has been published in a facsimile edition.[2]

Very few lines of *Troilus and Criseyde* have no variant readings, at least in spelling, which was obviously not fixed in the Middle Ages. There are in fact thousands of variant readings in the manuscripts that are "substantive," that is, that present different words or inflections. The modern editor must winnow this mass of variation by means of sophisticated techniques of textual criticism. Among the criteria for selecting the most likely authentic reading are the general trustworthiness of the particular manuscript, how that manuscript is related to other copies, how the reading accords with the scribe's usual habits or with what we can determine about Chaucer's normal usage, and how the text reflects the main source, the *Filostrato*. Often the best method is to determine which variant most likely gave rise to the others.

Windeatt's edition of *Troilus and Criseyde* prints all of the substantive variant readings, and *The Riverside Chaucer* from which the present Norton Critical Edition is drawn presents practically all of the variants that would make a difference in our understanding of the poem.[3] A couple of examples can indicate the kinds of questions about the text that an editor must resolve. The real problems with the text are in fact few, and the texts of *Troilus and Criseyde* presented by modern editors differ little from one another and are largely, though not absolutely, reliable.

A typical rather trivial instance: III.302–303 reads:

> O tonge, allas, so often here-byforn
> Hath mad ful many a lady bright of hewe. . . .

2. M. B. Parkes and Elizabeth Salter, ed. *Troilus and Criseyde: A Facsimile of Corpus Christi College MS 61* (Cambridge, Eng.: D. S. Brewer, 1978). Studies of the textual problems of *Troilus and Criseyde* are treated in Barney 1993.
3. Windeatt 1984; Barney 1987.

For *Hath mad ful* the great majority of the early copies, including a couple of the most reliable, and three of the nine modern editors who consulted the manuscripts read *Hastow mad(e)*, "hast thou made, i.e., have you made." This variant assumes what a first glance would suggest, that *O tonge* means "O thou tongue" in a direct address (an apostrophe) to the tongue. But it is hard to explain why six early copies would change this straightforward reading to the apparently ungrammatical *Hath mad ful*. The solution is easy: *O* here is not the marker of direct address, but is rather the adjective "one" in a common spelling. The correct reading is a little tricky, and caused most scribes and some editors to stumble.

More interesting: in IV.596 Pandarus is urging Troilus to refuse to let Criseyde leave:

> It is no rape, in my dom, ne no vice,
> Hire to withholden that ye love moost. . . .

Only three of the early manuscripts and one other modern editor (McCormick) accept this reading. For *rape in my dom* two manuscripts have *jape in my(n) dom(e)*, which is very unlikely (joking is not in question) but on the whole supports the *rape in my dom* reading. All the other early copies, and the other seven modern editors, read *shame unto yow* with minor variants. It is easy to see why early scribes would remove the strong and indelicate wording about rape, but hard to see why they would avoid writing *shame unto yow*. It is, however, conceivable that Chaucer himself wrote both versions, which are somehow preserved in some of the copies. Hence the present Norton Critical Edition retains *rape in my dom*, but its editor lacks absolute confidence in the decision.

The Text of
Troilus and Criseyde,
with facing-page
Il Filostrato

Il Filostrato of
Giovanni Boccaccio[†]

"Filostrato" is the title of this book and the reason is that it agrees excellently with the theme of the book. "Filostrato" is as much as to say "a man vanquished and laid prostrate by love"; as one can see, Troilo was vanquished by love both by fervently loving Criseida and then again by her departure.

Proem

Filostrato salutes his Filomena who is more pleasing than any other woman.

Many times already, most noble lady, it has happened that I, who almost from childhood to the present time have been in the service of Love, finding myself in his court among noble men and beautiful ladies who were dwelling in it together with me, heard proposed and discussed this question, namely: a young man fervently loves a lady, of whom no other thing is granted him by Fortune except that he can sometimes see her, or sometimes speak of her with someone, or think sweetly to himself. Which then of these three things is the greatest delight to him? It never happened that any of these three things—one by one person and one by another—was not defended by many zealously and with acute arguments. And since this question appeared to be excellently suited to my feelings which were more ardent than fortunate, I recall that, overcome by false opinions, I, mingling often with the disputants, held and defended the view that the delight of being able to think sometimes of the beloved object was far greater than that which either of the other two could afford. Among the other arguments offered by me to that end, I affirmed that it was not the least part of the lover's bliss to be able to make the beloved object kindly disposed according to the desire of him who was thinking about her and to render her kind and responsive in accordance with that desire—even though that might last only as long as the thought—which certainly could not happen when seeing her or talking to her. O foolish judgment, O ridiculous opinion, O vain argu-

† This translation was made by Robert P. apRoberts and Anna Bruni Benson from the Pernicone 1937 Italian text, and published as *Giovanni Boccaccio: Il Filostrato* (New York and London: Garland, 1986). Reprinted by permission.

ment, how far from the truth you were! Bitter experience now demonstrates it to me, wretched me. O sweetest hope of an afflicted mind, and sole comfort of a transfixed heart, I shall not be ashamed to disclose to you with what force into my darkened intellect entered the truth against which I, childishly erring, had taken arms. And to whom could I tell this, who could provide alleviation for the punishment given to me—I know not if I should say by Love or by Fortune—for the false opinion I had, if not you?

Therefore, most beautiful lady, after you had suddenly disappeared from my eyes, which are more delighted by your angelic face than by any other thing, by taking yourself from Naples in the most gracious season of the year and going to Sannio, I affirm it to be true that what I ought to have known much better through your presence, but did not recognize, was immediately made known to me through its contrary, that is, through deprivation of it. That deprivation has saddened my soul so far beyond any proper limit that I can understand clearly enough how much was the happiness, then little recognized by me, which came to me from the gracious and beautiful sight of you. But so that this truth may appear somewhat more manifest, it shall not be painful to me to tell what happened to me after your departure in elucidating my great error, nor do I wish to forgo telling it, although it is explained elsewhere more fully than here.

I say, therefore—may God soon through the sight of your beautiful face restore my eyes to their lost peace—that, after I knew that you had left here and had gone to a place where no proper reason for seeing you could ever lead me, these eyes, through which Love drew the very sweetest light of yours into my mind, have, beyond any assurance which my words can offer, bathed my face and filled my sorrowing breast so many times with so many and such bitter tears that not only has it been a miraculous thing where so much moisture might have come from, but also this moisture by its power would have brought pity not only to you, who, I believe, are as pitiful as you are gentle-born, but to one who might be my enemy, even if he had a breast of iron. This has not happened only as often as I have remembered having lost your charming presence with sad consequences, but whatever has appeared before my eyes has been a cause of their greater misery. O me, how many times in order to feel less suffering they have spontaneously turned away from looking at the temples and the loggias and the squares and the other places in which formerly, longing and desirous, they sought to see, and sometimes joyfully saw, your countenance, and sorrowfully they forced my heart to recite to itself that unhappy verse of Jeremiah: "Oh how solitary abides the city which before was full of people and a mistress of nations!" [Lamentations; I, 1] Certainly, I will not say that everything saddens them equally, but I will affirm that there is only one thing which somewhat lessens their sadness as they look about and that is to look at that country, those mountains, that part of the sky, among which and under which I firmly believe you to be. Every breeze, every soft wind that comes from there, my face welcomes, as if, without doubt, it had touched yours. Nor does this mitigation, however, last long, but just as we sometimes see flames darting over oily things, so above the afflicted heart this sweetness dances, fleeing suddenly because of the supervening thought which shows me that I cannot see you, and my desire for this is already kindled beyond all measure.

What shall I say of the sighs which in the past pleasing love and sweet hope used to draw inflamed from my breast? Certainly I have nothing other to say of them except that, multiplied in many duplications of the gravest anguish, a thousand times each hour they are violently forced out through my mouth. And likewise my words, which formerly were sometimes stirred by I know not what hidden joy proceeding from your serene aspect into amorous songs and into discourses full of ardent love, are heard now calling upon your name, which is full of grace, and upon love for mercy, or upon death for an end of my sorrows; now they can be heard by anyone near me changed into the greatest lamentations.

In such a life, therefore, I live far away from you, and without any profit I understand how much was the good, the pleasure, and the delight which, badly understood by me, came to me in the past from your eyes. And although both tears and sighs have indeed given me enough time to be able to speak of your worth and also to think of your elegance, your well-bred manners, your ladylike hauteur, and your appearance, which is more beautiful than any other (all of which I still regard with my mind's eye) and, moreover, although I do not say that my soul does not feel any pleasure from such speech or reflection; nevertheless this pleasure comes mixed with a very fervent desire which kindles all my other desires into such a flame to see you that I can scarcely control them, after they have overthrown every suitable propriety and reasonable consideration, from pulling me to where you are staying. But, still overcome by the desire to respect your honor more than my health, I restrain them; and having no other recourse, and feeling the way to seeing you again closed to me for the reason shown, I return to my interrupted tears. Alas, how much has Fortune, cruel and hostile to my pleasures, always been to me a strict teacher and corrector of my errors! Now, poor me! I know; now I feel; now I understand very clearly how much more good, how much more pleasure, how much more gentleness dwelt in the true light of your eyes, seeing it with my own, than in the false flattery of my thoughts.

So, therefore, O splendid light of my mind, by depriving me of your love-inspiring sight, Fortune has brought to an end the cloudiness of error that was sustained by me in the past. But in truth such bitter medicine was not needed to purge my ignorance; a lighter punishment would have brought me back to the right way. Now it happens this way: my powers, though my reason may be great, cannot resist those of Fortune. And however it goes, I have indeed come through your departure to such a point, as my letters have previously declared to you. And with my very deep suffering, I have become certain of something of which, because I was not certain of it at first, I supported the contrary.

But now I must come to that end toward which, in writing up to here, I have been aiming, and I say that, seeing myself in such bitter adversity through the act of your departure, I first proposed to keep my anguish completely within my sad breast in order that it might not, through being revealed, by chance be in the future the cause of a more dire adversity.

And because I continued this way uncontrolled by force, there was a time when I came very near to death by despair, which indeed if it had come then would have been, without any doubt, dear to me. But afterward, through I know not what hidden hope of being destined to see you again and to turn my eyes again to their first felicity, there was born in me not only a fear of death but a desire for long life—even though, not seeing you I should have to lead it miserably. And I knew very clearly that if, as I had proposed, I held the sorrow engendered in me completely hidden in my bosom, it was impossible that, among the many times that it would become abundant and overstep every bound, it would not vanquish my powers, already become very weak, so much that death would follow without fail from it, and then in consequence I should not see you. Moved by more useful advice, I changed my proposal and wished to let it be disclosed and to give it an outlet from my sad breast with some suitable lamentation in order that I might live and be able to see you again and might by living remain yours a longer time. No sooner did such an idea come into my mind before the way to implement it occurred to me; this occurrence, which seemed inspired by a secret divinity, I took as the most sure sign of future well-being. And the way was this: I wanted to be able, in the person of someone emotionally overcome as I was and am, to relate my sufferings in song.

I began therefore to turn over in my mind, with solicitous care, old stories in order to find one which I could make into a likely shield for my secret and amorous suffering. Nor did any one more suitable for such a need come into my mind than that of the valorous young Troilo, son of Priam, the most noble king of Troy, to whose life mine has been very similar after your departure insofar as it was sorrowful—if any credence can be given to ancient stories—because of love and because of the distance away of his lady, after Criseida, who was greatly loved by him, was returned to her father Calchas. Therefore, from his person and from his fortunes, I took a form excellently suited to my intention, and subsequently in light rhyme and in my Florentine idiom, with a style which would excite pity, I composed his sorrows equally with my own; these, as I sang from time to time, I found very useful according to my expectation in the beginning.

It is true that, before his very bitter tears, part of his happy life is found in a similar style, which I set down not because I wish anyone to believe that I can glory in a similar happiness, since fortune never was so favorable to me, nor even forcing myself to hope for it, can I in any way believe that it may happen to me, but I have written it for this reason: because when someone's happiness is seen, the quantity and the quality of the misery which comes after may be much better understood. That happiness is, nevertheless, in conformity with the facts of my case, inasmuch as I drew from your eyes no less pleasure than Troilo took from the amorous fruit which fortune granted him with Criseida.

Therefore, worthy lady, I composed these rhymes into the form of a little book, in perpetual testimony, to those who see it in the future, both of your worth, with which in the person of another these rhymes are in large part adorned, and of my sorrow; and having set them down, I thought it unfitting that they should first come into the hands of any other person before yours, who have been their true and only inspiration. Therefore, although this may be a very small gift to send to such a great lady as you are, nevertheless, because the affection of myself, the sender, is very great and full of pure loyalty, I dare, however, to send them to you, somewhat confident that, not because of my merit but because of your benignity and courtesy, they will be received by you. If it comes to pass that you read them, as many times as you find Troilo weeping and grieving for the departure of Criseida, that many times you may clearly recognize and know my own cries, tears, sighs, and distresses; and as many times as you find the beauty, the good manners, or any other thing praiseworthy in a lady written of Criseida, that often you can understand them to be spoken of you. Of other matters of which there are many in them beside these, none, as I have already said, pertains to me or is set down there concerning me, but because the story of the noble young lover requires it. And if you are as perceptive as I believe you to be, you will be able to understand the greatness and the nature of my desires, what their limit is and what thing more than any other they ask for, and if they merit any pity. Now I know not if they might be so effective that they can touch your chaste mind with any compassion as you read them to yourself, but I pray Love that he may lend them this power. If that happens, as humbly as I can, I pray you that you give consideration to your return, so that my life, which, hanging on the slenderest thread, is with effort sustained by hope in uncertainty, can, when I see you, joyfully return to its former certainty. And if this cannot happen as soon as I would desire, at least with some sigh or piteous prayer to Love for me, bring it about that he may give some peace to my suffering, and may comfort again my distracted life. My long discourse asks by itself for an end, and therefore, in giving one, I pray to him who has placed my life and my death in your hands that he will kindle in your heart that desire which alone can be the cause of my salvation.

Part One

Here begins the first part of the book called "Filostrato," of the amorous labors of Troilo, in which is recounted how Troilo fell in love with Criseida, and the amorous sighs and the tears he had for her before he disclosed his hidden love to anyone; and first the invocation of the author.

1

Some are accustomed in their beginnings to piously invoke the favor of Jove, while others call on the power of Apollo; I used to pray in my need to the Muses of Parnassus, but Love has recently made me change my old and customary habit since I fell in love with you, my lady.

2

You, lady, are the clear and beautiful light through which I live, guided in this world of darkness; you are the North Star which I follow in order to come to port; anchor of safety, you are she who is all my welfare and my comfort; you are Jove to me, you are Apollo to me; you are my Muse! I have experienced this and know it.

3

Therefore, because your departure, which is more grievous to me than death and more distressing, makes me wish to write about the sorrowful life of Troilo after the amorous Criseida had departed from Troy and how before that his life was full of joy, it is fitting for me to come to you for grace if I hope to be able to finish my enterprise.

4

And so, O beautiful lady, to whom I have been, and always shall be, faithful and subject; O lovely light of those beautiful eyes in which Love has placed all my delight; O sole hope of him who loves you more than himself—with a perfect love, guide my hand, direct my creative power, in the work which I am about to write.

Troilus and Criseyde†

Book One

The double sorwe of Troilus to tellen,
That was the kyng Priamus sone of Troye,°   *the son of King Priam of Troy*
In lovynge, how his aventures fellen
Fro wo to wele,° and after out of joie,   *well-being*
5   My purpos is, er that I parte fro ye.[1]
Thesiphone,² thow help me for t'endite°   *to compose*
Thise woful vers,° that wepen as I write.   *verses*

To the clepe° I, thow goddesse of torment,   *call*
Thow cruwel Furie, sorwynge evere in peyne,
10   Help me, that am the sorwful instrument,
That helpeth loveres, as I kan,° to pleyne;°   *insofar as I can / complain*
For wel sit it,° the sothe° for to seyne,°   *it is fitting / truth / say*
A woful wight° to han° a drery feere,°   *creature / have / companion*
And to a sorwful tale, a sory chere.°   *expression*

15   For I, that God of Loves servantz serve,
Ne dar to Love, for myn unliklynesse,
Preyen for speed, al sholde I therfore sterve,³
So fer am I from his help in derknesse.
But natheles,° if this may don gladnesse   *nevertheless*
20   Unto any lovere, and his cause availle,°   *further, advance*
Have he my thonk, and myn be this travaille!°   *labor*

---

† The text of *Troilus and Criseyde* is reprinted, with a few small corrections, from *The Riverside Chaucer*, Third Edition, gen. ed. Larry D. Benson (Boston: Houghton Mifflin, 1987). Copyright © 1987 by Houghton Mifflin Company. Reprinted by permission. The editor of *Troilus and Criseyde* for the Riverside edition is Stephen A. Barney.

1. Before I part from you. Here "ye" is a reduced form of the regular objective form "yow," and the rhymes "Troye : joie : fro ye" are evidence of Chaucer's pronunciation of final *e* at line end. Likewise in the General Prologue to the *Canterbury Tales* (line 523) he rhymes "to me" with "Rome."

2. Following epic precedent, Chaucer invokes divine aid for his poetry, but because of his sorrowful subject matter he invokes not a Muse but the terrible Tisiphone, one of the three classical Furies who punish the perpetrators of unavenged crimes.

3. For I, who serve the servants of the God of Love, dare not, because of my unsuitableness, pray to Love for success, even though I should therefore die. As part of his stance as an outsider in matters of love, Chaucer's narrator alludes to an equally humble title of the pope, "Servant of the Servants of God." The allusion introduces a favorite medieval analogy that Chaucer exploits to the full, the "religion of love," with its god, its worship and services, its saints and sins and confessions.

5

You are pictured in my sad heart with such force that you can do more there than I can; impel my disconsolate voice in such a way that it may express my sorrow in another's pain, and make it so pleasing that whoever hears it may become compassionate. If these words acquire any praise, let the honor be yours and the labor mine.

6

And you lovers, I pray that you listen to what my tearful verse will say, and if it happens that you feel any sense of pity awakening in your hearts, I beg you that you pray for me to Love because of whom I, like Troilo, live sorrowfully, far from the sweetest pleasure that was ever of concern to any creature.

But ye loveres, that bathen° in gladnesse,   *who bask*
If any drope of pyte in yow be,
Remembreth yow on passed hevynesse
25 That ye han felt, and on the adversite
Of othere folk, and thynketh how that ye
Han° felt that Love dorste° yow displese,   *Have / dared*
Or° ye han wonne hym with to° gret an ese.   *Or else / too*

And preieth[4] for hem that ben° in the cas°   *those who are / plight*
30 Of Troilus, as ye may after here,°   *hear*
That Love hem brynge° in hevene to solas;°   *may bring them / comfort*
And ek° for me preieth to God so dere   *also*
That I have myght to shewe, in som manere,
Swich peyne and wo as Loves folk endure,
35 In Troilus unsely° aventure.   *unhappy, unfortunate*

And biddeth ek° for hem that ben despeired° *pray also / are in despair*
In love, that nevere nyl° recovered be,   *will not*
And ek for hem that° falsly ben apeired°   *those who / injured*
Thorugh wikked tonges, be it he or she;
40 Thus biddeth God,° for his benignite,   *pray to God*
So graunte hem° soone owt of this world to pace,° *So to grant them / pass*
That ben despeired out of Loves grace.

And biddeth ek for hem that ben at ese,
That God hem graunte ay good perseveraunce,
45 And sende hem myght hire° ladies so to plese *their*
That it to Love be worship° and plesaunce.   *honor*
For so hope I my sowle best avaunce,°   *to advance, to benefit*
To prey for hem° that Loves servauntz be,   *By praying for those who*
And write hire wo, and lyve in charite,

50 And for to have of hem compassioun,
As though I were hire owne brother dere.
Now herkneth° with a good entencioun,°   *listen / will*
For now wil I gon streght to my matere,°   *subject matter*
In which ye may the double sorwes here
55 Of Troilus in lovynge of Criseyde,
And how that she forsook hym er° she deyde. *ere, before*

---

4. The requests for prayers in this and the following stanzas imitate the form of the "bidding prayer" of the Mass, when the priest requests prayers for various people.

How Calchas fled from Troy and the occasion and the reason why.

7

The Greek kings were round about Troy, strong in arms, and each one according to his power showed himself daring, proud, valiant, and meritorious, and with their troops they ever pressed the city more from day to day, all agreeing to a mutual desire, to avenge the outrage and the rape done by Paris to Queen Helen.

8

At this time Calchas, whose high knowledge had already mastered every will of the great Apollo, wishing to hear the truth about the future, as to which would prevail—the long endurance of the Trojans or the great valor of the Greeks—know and saw that, after a long war, the Trojans would be dead and their land destroyed.

9

Therefore, the prophetic sage planned to depart secretly; and having chosen the time and place to flee, he made his way toward the Greek forces, where he saw many come to meet him who received him with joyful faces, hoping from him the highest good counsel in each and every event and peril.

How Criseida goes to Hector to excuse herself from the fault of Calchas her father.

10

A great clamor arose when it was generally known throughout the city that Calchas had fled from it, and people spoke about it diversely but all condemned it and said that he had done wrong and was guilty of acting like a traitor; and many people could scarcely be restrained from rushing out to burn his house.

Yt is wel wist° how that the Grekes stronge   *known*
In armes with a thousand shippes wente
To Troiewardes, and the cite longe
60   Assegeden, neigh ten yer er they stente,[5]
And in diverse wise° and oon entente,°   *manners / purpose*
The ravysshyng to wreken° of Eleyne,°   *avenge / Helen of Troy*
By Paris don, they wroughten° al hir peyne.°   *employed / efforts*

Now fel it° so that in the town ther was   *it happened*
65   Dwellynge a lord of gret auctorite,
A gret devyn,° that clepid° was Calkas,[6]   *divine, soothsayer / named*
That in science so expert was that he
Knew wel that Troie sholde destroied be,
By answere of his god, that highte° thus: *was called*
70   Daun° Phebus or Appollo Delphicus.[7]   *Lord*

So whan this Calkas knew by calkulynge,
And ek° by answer of this Appollo,   *also*
That Grekes sholden swich° a peple brynge,   *such*
Thorough which that Troie moste ben fordo,°   *fordone, destroyed*
75   He caste anon° out of the town to go;   *plotted forthwith*
For wel wiste° he by sort° that Troye sholde   *knew / casting lots*
Destroyed ben, ye,° wolde whoso nolde.°   *yea / whether anyone wished it or not*

For which for to departen softely
Took purpos° ful this forknowynge wise,°   *Intended / prescient sage*
80   And to the Grekes oost° ful pryvely°   *host, army / secretly*
He stal anon;° and they, in curteys wise,   *stole (away) forthwith*
Hym diden bothe worship° and servyce,   *honor*
In trust that he hath konnynge hem to rede°   *ability to counsel them*
In every peril which that is to drede.

85   Gret rumour gan,° whan it was first aspied   *uproar began (to go)*
Thorough al the town, and generaly was spoken,°   *it was rumored everywhere*
That Calkas traitour fled was and allied
With hem° of Grece, and casten to be   *them*
    wroken°   *they planned to be avenged*
On hym that falsly hadde his feith so broken,
90   And seyden° he and al his kyn at-ones   *(they) said*
Ben worthi for to brennen,° fel° and bones.   *burn / skin*

---

5. Besieged, nearly ten years before they ceased.
6. In the *Iliad*, Calchas is not the Trojan Criseyde's father but a Greek. In Chaucer's poem he is a "lord" in Troy, but events indicate that his daughter would not be of high enough status to consider marrying a prince. As a "divine" he receives oracles and is skilled at what his name echoes, "calkulynge," i.e., astrological reckonings or such other means of foretelling the future as casting or drawing lots ("sort"; line 76).
7. Among the large numbers of "touches of antiquity," as Kittredge called them, that Chaucer derived from the *Filostrato* or inserted on his own. Here, somewhat pedantically, he augments Boccaccio's "Apollo" with the god's other name, Phoebus, and his epithet "Delphicus," from his oracle at Delphi.

11

Calchas had left in this bad situation a daughter, without making known to her any of his plans, a widow, who was so beautiful and so angelic to see that she did not seem a mortal: Criseida she was named, and in my judgment she was as prudent, noble, wise, and well-mannered as any other lady who had ever been born in Troy.

12

Hearing the threatening outcry caused by her father's flight and very dismayed at being in the midst of such a fearful rage, in mourning habit and with tears she flung herself on her knees at the feet of Hector, and with a very pitiful voice and look, excused herself and accused her father, ending up her speech by requesting mercy.

13

Hector was merciful by nature; and so, seeing the weeping of her who was fairer than any other creature, with kind words he comforted her greatly, saying: "Let your father who has offended me deeply go with bad luck and you yourself remain with us in Troy, safe and happy without harm, as long as it pleases you.

14

"Be assured that you shall always have from all of us the favor and the honor you would have if Calchas were here; may the gods give him his right reward!" She thanked him for this greatly and would have thanked him more but he would not permit it; with that she arose and returned to her house, and there lived quietly.

15

There she dwelt as long as she was in Troy with the household that it was suitable for her dignity to maintain, wonderfully noble in her habits and her deeds. And since she had never been able to have any children, she did not need to care for any son or daughter; and by everyone who knew her she was loved and honored.

Now hadde Calkas left in this meschaunce,°   *unfortunate situation*
Al unwist° of this false and wikked dede,   *unaware*
His doughter, which that was in gret penaunce,°   *misery*
95 For of hire lif she was ful sore in drede,
As she that nyste° what was best to   *As a woman who knew not*
     rede;°   *the best counsel*
For bothe a widewe was she and allone
Of any frend to whom she dorste hir mone.°   *dared to complain*

Criseyde was this lady° name al right.   *lady's*
100 As to my doom,° in al Troies cite   *judgment*
Nas° non so fair, forpassynge° every wight,°   *There was / surpassing / creature*
So aungelik was hir natif beaute,
That lik a thing inmortal semed she,
As doth an hevenyssh perfit creature
105 That down were sent in scornynge° of nature.   *contempt*

This lady, which that alday° herd at ere°   *constantly / by ear*
Hire fadres shame, his falsnesse and tresoun,
Wel neigh° out of hir wit for sorwe and fere,   *nigh*
In widewes habit large° of samyt° broun,   *ample / samite, rich silk*
110 On knees she fil biforn Ector° adown   *Hector, Troilus's eldest brother*
With pitous vois, and tendrely wepynge,
His mercy bad,° hirselven excusynge.   *prayed for*

Now was this Ector pitous of nature,
And saugh that she was sorwfully bigon,°   *in a sorry plight*
115 And that she was so fair a creature;
Of his goodnesse he gladede hire anon,
And seyde, "Lat youre fadres treson gon
Forth with meschaunce,° and ye yourself in joie   *with bad luck*
Dwelleth with us, whil yow good list,° in Troie.   *as long as you please*

120 "And al th'onour° that men may don yow   *the honor*
     have,°   *may cause you to have*
As ferforth as° youre fader dwelled here,   *As much as when*
Ye shul have, and youre body shal men save,
As fer as I may ought° enquere or here."   *at all*
And she hym thonked with ful humble chere,
125 And ofter wolde,° and° it hadde ben his wille,   *And would have more often / if*
And took hire leve,° and hom,° and held hir stille.   *said goodbye / (went) home*

And in hire hous she abood° with swich meyne°   *stayed / household, retinue*
As til° hire honour nede was to holde;°   *to / it was necessary to maintain*
And whil she was dwellynge in that cite,°   *city*
130 Kepte hir estat,° and both of yonge and olde   *She maintained her status*
Ful wel biloved, and wel men of hir tolde.
But wheither that she children hadde or noon,
I rede° it naught, therfore I late° it goon.[8]   *read / let*

8. But Boccaccio expressly says that she was unable to have children (*Filost.* I.15).

At the sacrifices made to Pallas in the temple, Troilo mocks at lovers; at which time he himself becomes enamored.

16

Things went on between the Trojans and the Greeks as they very often do in war; sometimes the Trojans rushed out of their city vigorously at the Greeks, and oftentimes the Greeks, if the story does not err, advanced very fiercely even up to the moats, plundering round about, burning and destroying castles and estates.

17

And although the Trojans were tightly pressed by their Greek enemies, it did not happen that the divine sacrifices were for that reason ever neglected, for everyone always maintained the usual customs; and they honored Pallas in every respect more than any other god with greater and more solemn honor, and regarded her more than any other.

18*

Therefore when the beautiful season came which dresses the fields again with herbs and flowers, and during which every animal becomes gay and shows its love in diverse acts, the Trojan fathers had the accustomed honors prepared for the fateful Palladium; to that festival both ladies and knights came alike and all very willingly.

*[The following is an example of Boccaccio's *ottova rima* stanza, rhyming *ababacc*, translated as stanza 18 above and adapted by Chaucer in *Troilus and Criseyde* I.155–68:

18

Per che, venuto il vago tempo il quale
riveste i prati d'erbette e di fiori,
e che gaio diviene ogni animale
e 'n diversi atti mostra suoi amori,
il Troian padri al Palladio fatale
fêr preparare li consueti onori;
alla qual festa donne e cavalieri
fûr parimente, e tutti volentieri.]

The thynges fellen,° as they don of werre,°　　　　　*happened / in war*
135　Bitwixen hem of Troie and Grekes ofte;
For som day boughten they of Troie it derre,[9]　　*fortune*
And eft° the Grekes founden nothing° softe　　　*back*　*in turn / in no way*
The folk of Troie; and thus Fortune on lofte°　　*and forth*　*on high, aloft*
And under eft gan hem to whielen° bothe　　　　　　*wheeled them*
140　Aftir hir course,[1] ay whil that° thei were wrothe.　　　*as long as*

But how this town com° to destruccion　　　　　　　　　*came*
Ne falleth naught to purpos me to telle,[2]
For it were a long digression
Fro my matere, and yow to long to dwelle.°　　*too long for you to dwell upon*
145　But the Troian gestes,° as they felle,　　　　　　　*stories*
In Omer, or in Dares, or in Dite,[3]
Whoso that kan° may rede hem as they write.　　　*Whoever is able*

But though that Grekes hem of Troie shetten,°　　　　*shut in*
And hir cite biseged al aboute,
150　Hire olde usage nolde they nat letten,°　　*they did not wish to leave off*
As for to honoure hir° goddes ful devoute;°　　　　*their / devoutly*
But aldirmost° in honour, out of doute,　　　　　　*most of all*
Thei hadde a relik,° heet° Palladion,[4]　　*relic, devotional image / called*
That was hire trist° aboven everichon °　　*trusted object / everything*

155　And so bifel,° whan comen was the tyme　　　　　　*it happened*
Of Aperil, whan clothed is the mede°　　*Spring*　　*mead, meadow*
With newe grene, of lusty Veer the pryme,°　　*the outset of delightful springtime*
And swote° smellen floures white and rede,　　　　　*sweet*
In sondry wises° shewed, as I rede,　　　　　　　　　　*manners*
160　The folk of Troie hire observaunces° olde,　　　*religious observances*
Palladiones feste° for to holde.°　　　　*religious festival / observe*

And to the temple, in al hir beste wise,°　　　　*manner, finery*
In general° ther wente many a wight,°　　*As one company / person*
To herknen of° Palladions servyce;　　　　　　*To listen to*
165　And namely,° so many a lusty° knyght,　　*especially / vigorous*
So many a lady fressh and mayden bright,
Ful wel arayed, both meeste, mene, and leste,[5]　　*all all dressed up*
Ye, bothe for the seson and the feste.

9. For on some days the Trojans bought it more dearly (at a higher price), i.e., had the worse of it.
1. The goddess Fortune rolled them up and down on her wheel, the common emblem of the fickle revolutions of fortune.
2. To relate does not accord with my purpose.
3. Chaucer cites what were understood to be the ancient and authoritative accounts of the Trojan War, even though he knew none of them directly: Homer, Dares the Phrygian, and Dictys of Crete. On them, see the Introduction.
4. The Palladium was an image of Pallas Athena, sacred to the Trojans. In some accounts, Troy fell when it was lost—so Vergil's *Aeneid*, a poem Chaucer knew thoroughly, 2.162–70. Having first sight of one's beloved in a church (or temple) was a literary convention; compare Aeneas's meeting with Dido, Dante's meeting with Beatrice, and Petrarch's meeting with Laura.
5. Very well clothed, the greatest, middling, and least of them, i.e., everyone.

19

Among those was the daughter of Calchas, Criseida, who was wearing black garments, and who was as much fairer than any other lady as the rose overcomes the violet in beauty; and she alone more than any other made the great festival gay, standing in the temple very close to the door, proud, pleasing, and discerning in her movements.

20

Troilo went about, as young men are accustomed to, looking now here, now there through the great temple, and with his companions he strolled about placing himself now here, now there; and he began to praise now this woman, now that, and to disparage some, like one to whom none of them was more pleasing than another, and he rejoiced in being free.

21

Walking about in such a manner, when he saw some man who, sighing to himself, gazed at some woman intently, he sometimes laughingly pointed him out to his companions saying: "That poor man has said goodbye to his liberty; it weighed so on him that he has placed it into the hands of that lady: see indeed how vain his thoughts are.

22

"What's the use in loving? The way a leaf turns itself with the wind, so a thousand times a day their hearts change, and they don't care for the sorrow any lover of theirs feels for them, nor does any woman know what she wants. O happy's that man who is not taken by their charm, and knows how to abstain from love!

23

"I have already experienced through my great folly what this accursed fire is. And if I were to say that love was not courteous to me, and did not give me delight and joy, certainly I'd be lying; but all the good together that I gathered in my desire for love was little or nothing compared to the torments and to the sad sighs.

Among thise othere folk was Criseyda,
170 In widewes habit° blak; but natheles,°   *garb / nevertheless*
Right as oure firste lettre is now an A,[6]
In beaute first so stood she, makeles.°   *peerless*
Hire goodly lokyng° gladed° al the prees.°   *appearance / gladdened / crowd*
Nas nevere yet seyn thyng to ben preysed derre,[7]
175 Nor under cloude blak so bright a sterre

As was Criseyde, as folk seyde everichone°   *everyone*
That° hir behelden in hir blake wede.°   *Who / weeds, clothing*
And yet she stood ful lowe° and stille allone,   *humble*
Byhynden other folk, in litel brede,°   *in a cramped space*
180 And neigh° the dore, ay undre shames drede,°   *near / ever in fear of shame*
Simple of atir and debonaire of chere,[8]
With ful assured° lokyng and manere.   *confident*

poised, afraid to be shamed

This Troilus, as he was wont to gide°   *accustomed to guide*
His yonge knyghtes, lad hem° up and down   *them*
185 In thilke° large temple on every side,   *that same*
Byholding ay° the ladies of the town,   *ever, constantly*
Now here, now there; for no devocioun
Hadde he to non, to reven hym his reste,°   *to rob him of his sleep*
But gan to preise and lakken whom hym leste.°   *disparage whom he pleased*

seen many women but never in love

190 And in his walk ful faste° he gan to wayten°   *closely / watch*
If knyght or squyer° of his compaignie   *squire*
Gan for to syke,° or lete his eighen baiten°   *began to sigh / eyes feed*
On any womman that he koude espye.°   *see*
He wolde smyle and holden° it folye,   *consider*
195 And seye hym° thus, "God woot,° she slepeth softe   *say to him / knows*
For love of the,° whan° thow turnest ful ofte!   *you / while*

to be in love is foolish

"I have herd told,° pardieux,° of youre lyvynge,°   *heard tell / by god / behavior*
Ye loveres, and youre lewed observaunces,°   *ignorant devotions*
And which a° labour folk han° in wynnynge   *what sort of a / have*
200 Of love, and in the kepyng which doutaunces;°   *perplexities*
And whan youre prey is lost, woo and penaunces.°   *suffering*
O veray° fooles, nyce° and blynde be ye!   *veritable / foolish*
Ther nys nat oon kan war by other be."°   *one who can be cautioned by another*

And with that word he gan caste up the° browe,   *to raise his*
205 Ascaunces,° "Loo! is this naught wisely spoken?"   *As if to say*
At which the God of Love gan loken rowe°   *roughly, angrily*
Right for despit, and shop for to ben wroken.[9]
He kidde° anon his bowe nas naught broken;   *made known*

Apollo

wanted to avenge Troilus

6. Possibly Chaucer here makes a flattering allusion to Queen Anne, who married King Richard II, Chaucer's benefactor, in January 1382.
7. There has never yet been seen a thing more dearly to be praised.
8. Simple in clothing and meek (or, gracious) of countenance.
9. With insulted defiance (or, resentment, scorn) indeed, and he plotted to be avenged.

24

"Now I am out of it, thanks for that be to him who had more pity for me than I myself—I mean Jove, the true god, from whom comes every grace—and I live in peace; and although it may be useful to me to watch others, I guard myself from the wayward path and I gladly laugh at those who are snared; I don't know whether I should call them lovers or morons."

25

O blindness of human minds, how often the effects follow all contrary to our intentions! Troilo goes about now, snapping at the weaknesses and the anxious loves of other people, without thinking of what heaven hastens to lead him into, whom Love transfixed more than any other before he left the temple.

For sodeynly he hitte hym atte fulle—°   *at the full, hard*
210 And yet° as proud a pekok kan he pulle.°   *even now / pluck*

O blynde world, O blynde entencioun!°   *intention, human aspiration*
How often falleth al the effect contraire°   *opposite result*
Of surquidrie° and foul presumpcioun;   *pride*
For kaught is proud, and kaught is debonaire.°   *the meek one*
215 This Troilus is clomben° on the staire,[1]   *has climbed*
And litel weneth° that he moot° descenden;   *thinks / must*
But alday° faileth thing that fooles wenden.°   *always / supposed*

As proude Bayard[2] gynneth° for to skippe   *begins*
Out of the weye,° so pryketh° hym his   *path, road / pricks, prods*
  corn,°   *grain, feed*
220 Til he a lasshe have of the longe whippe—   *prideful horse*
Than thynketh he, "Though I praunce al byforn°   *in front*
First in the trays,[3] ful fat and newe shorn,°   *recently trimmed*
Yet am I but an hors, and horses lawe
I moot° endure, and with my feres° drawe"—   *must / companions*

225 So ferde it by° this fierse and proude knyght: *So it happened with* (Troilus)
Though he a worthy kynges sone were,
And wende° nothing hadde had swich myght   *supposed*
Ayeyns° his wille that shuld his herte stere,°   *against will / Against / steer or stir*
Yet with a look his herte wex a-fere,°   *caught fire*
230 That° he that now was moost in pride above,°   *So that / superior*
Wax° sodeynly moost subgit unto love.   *Grew*

Forthy ensample° taketh of this man,   *warning / Therefore an example*
Ye wise, proude, and worthi folkes alle,
To scornen° Love, which that so soone kan   *love / With regard to scorning*
235 The fredom of youre hertes to hym thralle;°   *enslave*
For evere it was, and evere it shal byfalle,
That Love is he that alle thing may bynde,   *love binds*
For may no man fordon° the lawe of kynde.°   *annihilate / nature*

That this be soth,° hath preved° and doth yit.°   *true / proven (true) / still*
240 For this trowe° I ye knowen alle or some,°   *believe / one and all*
Men reden° nat that folk han gretter wit°   *read / intelligence*

---

1. The image of the wheel of Fortune is here altered to that of a staircase.
2. The overbold blind Bayard—a common name for a horse, from its bay color—was a proverbial figure. The extended simile here (and elsewhere in *Troilus*) imitates, in homely fashion, a technique of classical epics and such works as Dante's *Divine Comedy*, well known to Chaucer.
3. First in the traces or harness, as lead horse in a tandem team.

26

While Troilo was thus going about mocking now one, now another, and often on this lady or that gazing intently, it happened by chance that, through the crowd, his wandering eyes lighted on the place where the charming Criseida, under a white veil in a black habit, was standing among the other ladies at this solemn festival.

27

She was tall and every single one of her limbs was well proportioned to her height, and her face was adorned with celestial beauty, and in her appearance there showed a womanly dignity; and with her arm she held her mantle before her face, making room in front of her by pushing back the crowd.

Than they that han be° most with love ynome;°   *those who have been / taken*
And strengest folk ben therwith overcome,
The worthiest and grettest of degree: *all fall*
245 This was, and is, and yet men shall it see.[4]   *in love*

And trewelich it sit° wel to be so,   *it is fitting*
For alderwisest° han therwith ben plesed;   *the wisest of all*
And they that han ben aldermost° in wo,   *who have been most of all*
With love han ben comforted moost and esed;
250 And ofte it hath the cruel herte apesed,°   *appeased*
And worthi folk maad worthier of name,
And causeth moost to dreden vice and shame.

Now sith it may nat goodly ben withstonde,°   *well be withstood, endured*
And is a thing so vertuous in kynde,°   *nature*
255 Refuseth nat to Love for to ben bonde,°   *to be bound to (the god of) Love*
Syn, as hymselven liste,° he may yow bynde;   *as he pleases*
The yerde° is bet° that bowen wole and wynde°   *rod / better / twist*
Than that that brest,° and therfore I yow rede°   *bursts / counsel*
To folowen hym that° so wel kan yow lede.   *who*

260 But for to tellen forth in special°   *in particular*
Of this kynges sone of which I tolde,
And leten° other thing collateral,   *leave aside*
Of hym thenke I my tale forth to holde,
Both of his joie and of his cares colde;
265 And al his werk,° as touching° this matere,   *conduct / with regard to*
For I it gan,° I wol therto refere.°   *Because I began it / return*

Withinne the temple he wente hym forth pleyinge,
This Troilus, of every wight aboute,°   *(playing) around with everyone*
On this lady, and now on that, lokynge,
270 Wher so° she were of town or of withoute;   *Whether*
And upon cas bifel° that thorugh a route°   *by chance it happened / crowd*
His eye percede, and so depe it wente,   *saw her!*
Til on Criseyde it smot,° and ther it stente.°   *struck / stopped*

And sodeynly he wax° therwith astoned,°   *grew / astounded*
275 And gan hir bet° biholde in thrifty wise.°   *better / prudently*
"O mercy, God," thoughte he, "wher hastow woned,°   *dwelt*
That art so feyr and goodly to devise?"°   *look upon*
Therwith his herte gan to sprede° and rise,   *swell*
And softe sighed,° lest men myghte hym here,   *he sighed softly*
280 And caught ayeyn his firste pleyinge chere.°   *playful manner*

She nas nat° with the leste of hire stature,°   *was not / in her height*
But alle hire lymes° so wel answerynge   *limbs, body parts*
Weren to wommanhod, that creature
Was nevere lasse° mannyssh in semynge;   *less / appearance*

---

4. And one shall see it still. Echoing the *Gloria Patri:* "That was in the beginning, is now, and ever shall be."

28

And as she turned to herself again, that act—somewhat disdainful as if to say, "No one may stand here"—was pleasing to Troilo. And he continued to stare longer at her face, which seemed in itself more worthy of great praise than any other, and he took the highest delight in gazing fixedly among those other persons at her bright eyes and her angelic face.

29

Nor did he, who was so wise a little before in rebuking others, perceive that Love with his darts dwelt inside the rays of those beautiful eyes, nor yet did he recall the outrageous things he had said before to his servants, nor did he notice the arrow which ran to his heart until it stung him thoroughly.

30

Because this lady with the black mantle was pleasing to Troilo beyond any other, without saying what reason kept him there so long, he gazed secretly at the object of his high desire from afar, and looked as long as the honors to Pallas lasted without disclosing anything to anyone; then with his companions he went out from the temple.

31

Nor did he leave it as he had entered it, free and joyful, but he left it thoughtful and in love beyond his belief, keeping his desire well hidden so that the outrageous things which he had said earlier about others might not be turned against him if by chance the passion into which he had fallen should become known.

285 And ek the pure wise of hire mevynge⁵
    Shewed wel that men myght in hire gesse°   *infer, perceive*
    Honour, estat,° and wommanly noblesse.   *(high) social standing*

    To Troilus right wonder wel with alle°   *withal*
    Gan for to like° hire mevynge and hire chere,° *began to please / mien*
290 Which somdel deignous° was, for she let falle   *disdainful*
    Hire look a lite aside in swich manere,
    Ascaunces,° "What, may I nat stonden here?"   *As if to say*
    And after that hir lokynge gan she lighte,°   *brighten*
    That nevere thoughte hym seen° so good a *it seemed to him to have seen*
       syghte.

295 And of hire look in him ther gan to quyken
    So gret desir and such affeccioun
    That in his herte botme° gan to stiken   *heart's bottom*
    Of hir his fixe° and depe impressioun.⁶   *fixed*
    And though he erst° hadde poured° up and down, *formerly / gazed*
300 He was tho° glad his hornes in to shrinke:⁷   *then*
    Unnethes wiste he how to loke or wynke.⁸

    Lo, he that leet° hymselven so konnynge,°   *considered / clever*
    And scorned hem that Loves peynes dryen,°   *suffer*
    Was ful unwar° that Love hadde his dwellynge   *unaware*
305 Withinne the subtile stremes° of hire yën;°   *beams / eyes*
    That sodeynly hym thoughte° he felte dyen,   *it seemed to him*
    Right with hire look, the spirit° in his herte: *vital spirit*
    Blissed be Love, that kan thus folk converte!

    She, this in blak, likynge° to Troilus   *pleasing*
310 Over alle thing, he stood for to biholde;
    Ne his desir, ne wherfore° he stood thus,   *for what reason*
    He neither chere made,° ne word tolde;   *revealed by his expression*
    But from afer,° his manere for to holde,°   *afar / to keep up appearances*
    On other thing his look som tyme he caste,
315 And eft° on hire, whil that servyse laste.°   *again / lasted*

    And after this, nat fullich al awhaped,°   *stunned*
    Out of the temple al esilich° he wente,   *slowly*
    Repentynge hym that he hadde evere ijaped° *made fun*
    Of Loves folk, lest fully the descente
320 Of scorn fille° on hymself; but what he mente,° *should fall / meant*
    Lest it were wist° on any manere syde,°   *known / anywhere, by anyone*
    His woo he gan dissimilen° and hide.   *dissimulate, disguise*

5. And also the very manner of her movements.
6. The idea that the lady's figure is imprinted in the lover's heart is commonplace. In the *Consolation of Philosophy* Boethius attributes to the Stoics the notion that sensory images are imprinted on the soul like letters on a wax tablet (5.m4.6–20).
7. In chagrin, Troilus draws the horns (of his pride) into his shell, like a snail. The figure was proverbial.
8. He scarcely knew how to keep watching or close his eyes.

Troilo, pleased with Criseida, decides, thinking of her, to follow his new love, giving thanks for being enamored.

32

When Criseida had left the noble temple, Troilo returned to his palace with his companions, and there joyfully he remained with them for a long time; in order to hide his amorous wound better, he mocked those who loved for a good while, and then pretending that other matters constrained him, he told each one to go where he pleased.

33

And after everyone had left, he went all alone into his room, where he sat down sighing at the foot of his bed, and he began to recall the pleasure he had had that morning from the sight of Criseida, enumerating one by one the true beauties of her face and praising them all.

Whan he was fro the temple thus departed,
He streght anon° unto his paleys torneth.　　　　　　*immediately*
325　Right with hire look thorugh-shoten and thorugh-
　　　　darted,°　　　　　　　　　　　*shot and pierced through*
Al feyneth he in lust that he sojorneth,[9]
And al his chere and speche also he borneth,°　　　　*polishes*
And ay° of Loves servantz every while,　　　　　*continually*
Hymself to wrye,° at hem he gan to smyle,　　　　　*conceal*

330　And seyde, "Lord, so ye lyve al in lest,°　　　*in what delight you live*
Ye loveres! For the konnyngeste of yow,
That serveth most ententiflich° and best,　　　*attentively, eagerly*
Hym tit° as often harm therof as prow.°　　*There befalls him / profit*
Youre hire is quyt ayeyn°—ye, God woot°　*You are repaid in return / knows*
　　how!—
335　Nought wel for wel, but scorn for good servyse.
In feith, youre ordre is ruled in good wise![1]

"In nouncerteyn° ben alle youre observaunces,　　　　*uncertainty*
But° it a sely° fewe pointes be;　　　　　*Unless / trifling*
Ne no thing asketh so gret attendaunces°　　*attentions, diligence*
340　As doth youre lay,° and that knowe alle ye;　*religion, religious law*
But that is nat the worste, as mote I the!°　　*so may I prosper*
But, tolde I yow° the worste point, I leve,°　　*if I told you / believe*
Al seyde I soth, ye wolden at me greve.[2]

"But take this: that° ye loveres ofte eschuwe,°　　*that which / avoid*
345　Or elles doon, of good entencioun,
Ful ofte thi lady wol it mysconstruwe,
And deme° it harm in hire oppynyoun;　　　　　　*judge*
And yet if she, for other enchesoun,°　　　　　　*reason*
Be wroth,° than shaltow have a groyn° anon.　　*angry / scolding*
350　Lord, wel is hym that° may ben of yow oon!"　　*he fares well who*

But for al this, whan that he say° his tyme,　　　　　*saw*
He held his pees°—non other boote hym　　　　　*peace*
　　gayned—°　　　　　　　　　　　*remedy helped him*
For love bigan his fetheres so to lyme[3]
That wel unnethe until° his folk he fayned°　*with great difficulty to / pretended*
355　That other besy nedes° hym destrayned;°　*pressing business / constrained*
For wo was hym, that what to doon he nyste,°　　　*didn't know*
But bad° his folk to gon wher that hem liste.°　　*asked / it pleased them*

And whan that he in chambre was allone,
He doun upon his beddes feet° hym sette,　　　*the foot of his bed*
360　And first he gan to sike,° and eft° to grone,　　*sigh / in turn*
And thought ay° on hire so, withouten lette,°　　*ever / ceasing*
That,° as he sat and wook,° his spirit mette°　*So that / stayed awake / dreamed*

9. Although he pretended to pass the time pleasantly.
1. Truly, your (religious) order is well ruled, i.e., has a good set of regulations, as if of a monastic
　　order.
2. Even if I spoke truly, you would complain to me.
3. (The god) of Love began to lime (i.e., spread sticky birdlime on) his feathers in such a way.

34

He praised her actions and her bearing, and by her manners and carriage he judged her to be of a very noble heart, and he thought it a great fortune to love such a lady, and a much greater if through long diligence he might be able to bring it about that he might be loved by her as much as he loved her, or nearly as much, or at least not to be refused as a suitor.

35

In his imagination the light-hearted youth, with no forethought of his future weeping, argued that neither exertion nor sighing could be lost for such a lady and that his desire, if it were ever known by any, ought to be much praised, and hence his suffering less blamed if discovered.

36

Therefore, deciding to follow such a love, he thought that he would work discreetly, first proposing to hide the flame already conceived in his amorous mind from every friend and servant, unless it were necessary to reveal it, finally judging that a love revealed to many gets as its reward not joy but harm.

37

And beyond these he proposed to himself many other things, some about disclosing his love to his lady and some about attracting her to him, and here he joyfully gave himself to singing, with high hopes and completely disposed to love Criseida alone, feeling no appreciation for any other lady he might ever see or who had ever pleased him before.

That he hire saugh a-temple,° and al the wise   *in the temple*
Right of hire look, and gan it newe avise.°   *consider, review*

365 Thus gan° he make a mirour of his mynde   *did*
In which he saugh° al holly° hire figure,   *saw / wholly*
And that° he wel koude° in his herte fynde.   *that (figure) / could*
It was to hym a right good aventure°   *happenstance, piece of luck*
To love swich oon,° and if he dede his cure°   *such a one / took pains*
370 To serven hir, yet myghte he falle in° grace,   *enter into, obtain*
Or ellis for oon of hire servantz pace.[4]

Imagenynge that travaille nor grame
Ne myghte for so goodly oon be lorn
As she, ne hym for his desir no shame,   ←*swift turnabout*
375 Al were it wist, but in pris and up-born
Of alle lovers wel more than biforn,[5]
Thus argumented he in his gynnynge,°   *beginning*
Ful unavysed° of his woo comynge.   *unaware*

Thus took he purpos *choice* loves craft to suwe,[6]
380 And thoughte° he wolde werken pryvely,°   *he planned that / secretly*
First to hiden his desir in muwe°   *if reveal*   *in secret (in a pen for birds)*
From every wight yborn,° al outrely,°   *harm*   *born person / utterly*
But° he myghte ought recovered° be therby,   *Unless / at all benefited*
Remembryng hym that love to wide yblowe°   *too widely rumored (blown)*
385 Yelt° bittre fruyt, though swete seed be sowe.   *Yields*

And over al this, yet muchel° more he thoughte   *much*
What for to speke, and what to holden inne;
And what° to arten° hire to love he soughte,   *how / urge*
And on a song anon-right° to bygynne,   *forthwith*
390 And gan loude° on his sorwe for to wynne;°   *aloud / overcome or complain*
For with good hope he gan fully assente   *religious*
Criseyde for to love, and nought repente.   *undertones*

And of his song naught only the sentence,°   *meaning, gist*
As writ myn auctour° called Lollius,[7]   *authority, source*

---

4. Or else pass for one of her servants.
5. Supposing that no labor or suffering could be wasted on behalf of such a goodly person as she was, nor could there be any shame because of his desire, even if it were known, but (that he would be) esteemed and elevated much more than before by all lovers.
6. Thus he formed his intention to follow the art of love.
7. Here and in V.1653 below, Chaucer names his source "Lollius"; see the Introduction. He has in fact, as usual, been following Boccaccio's *Filostrato*, and the *Canticus Troili*, lines 400–420 below, fairly closely translates Petrarch's Sonnet 132 (also numbered Sonnet 88). Chaucer nowhere names Boccaccio, and he names Petrarch only in the *Canterbury Tales*.

Petrarch's "*S'amor non è*"

"If this is not love, what then is it that I am feeling? But if it is love, by God, what is it, and what kind of thing? If it is good, whence is this bitter, mortal effect? If it is wicked, wherefore is its every torment so sweet? If by my own desire I am burning, whence is the weeping and complaint? If against my will, what is the good of complaining? O living death, O delightful evil, how do you have such power over me if I don't wish to consent? And if I consent, I grieve with great wrong. Among such contrary winds, in a frail boat, I find myself in the deep sea without a helm, so light in understanding, so laden with error that I myself don't know what I want, and I shiver in the middle of summer, burning in winter." [Editor's translation.]

38

And to Love he sometimes said with devoted speech: "Lord, now this soul is yours which used to be mine; this pleases me because you have given to me to serve—I don't know if I should say a lady or a goddess, for there was never under a white veil in black clothes so beautiful a lady as this one appears to me.

39

"You stand in her eyes, my true lord, a place that is worthy of your power; therefore if my service pleases you at all, I pray you obtain from them the salvation of my soul, which lies prostrate beneath your feet, for the sharp arrows which you shot so wounded it when you showed me the beautiful face of this lady."

395 But pleinly,° save° oure tonges° difference,   *fully / except for / language's*
I dar wel seyn, in al, that Troilus[8]
Seyde in his song, loo, every word right thus
As I shal seyn; and whoso list it here,°   *whoever wishes to hear it*
Loo, next° this vers he may it fynden here.   *next to*

Canticus Troili°   *Troilus's Song*

400 "If no love is, O God, what fele I so? *a*   *stop time of the narrative*
And if love is,[9] what thing and which is he? *b*
If love be good, from whennes° cometh my woo? *a*   *whence*
If it be wikke, a wonder thynketh me,° *b*   *it seems to me*
When every torment and adversite *b*
405 That cometh of hym may to me savory thinke,° *c*   *seem pleasant*
For ay° thurst I, the more that ich° it drynke. *c*   *always / I*

"And if that at myn owen lust° I brenne,°   *desire / burn*
From whennes° cometh my waillynge and my pleynte?°   *whence / lament*
If harm agree° me, wherto pleyne° I thenne?   *is agreeable to / why lament*
410 I noot, ne whi unwery that I feynte.[1]
O quike° deth, O swete harm so queynte,°   *living / curious, strange*
How may of the in me swich quantite,[2]
But if that° I consente that it be?   *Unless*

"And if that I consente, I wrongfully
415 Compleyne, iwis.° Thus possed° to and fro,   *certainly / tossed*
Al stereles° withinne a boot am I *quatrain &*   *rudderless*
Amydde the see, bitwixen wyndes two *couplet*   *sea*
That in contrarie stonden° evere mo.   *blow in opposite directions*
Allas, what is this wondre° maladie?   *wondrous*
420 For hote of° cold, for cold of hote,° I dye."   *from / heat*

And to the God of Love thus seyde he
With pitous° vois, "O lord, now youres is   *piteous*
My spirit, which that oughte youres be.
Yow thanke I, lord, that han° me brought to this. *knight's tale*   *have*
425 But wheither goddesse or womman, iwis,°   *certainly*
She be, I not, which that ye do me serve;[3]
But as hire man I wol ay° lyve and sterve.°   *ever / die*

"Ye stonden in hir eighen myghtily,[4]
As in a place unto youre vertu digne;°   *worthy of your strength*
430 Wherfore, lord, if my service or I
May liken° yow, so beth to me benigne;   *please*
For myn estat roial° I here resigne   *royal estate, rank*

8. I make bold to say, in its entirety, that which Troilus.
9. Chaucer translates Petrarch's *S'amor non è*, "If this be not love," and *Ma s'egli è amor*, "But if it be love," as "And if love exists"—perhaps deliberately generalizing. The paradoxes and oxymorons in the song—thirst from drinking, pleasing harm, living death, and the like—are typical of late medieval lyric, and especially a signature of "Petrarchan" poetry.
1. I don't know—nor why, though not weary, I languish.
2. How may there be such a quantity of you in me.
3. She whom you cause me to serve may be, I don't know.
4. You have a mighty presence in her eyes.

How Troilo was overcome by love beyond his foreseeing and what his life was.

40

The fierce flames of love did not spare his royal blood nor the power or greatness of his soul, nor did they care for the bodily strength that was in Troilo or for his prowess, but as in suitable material, dry or half-dry, fire kindles itself, so, put into the lover, they kindled each and every part of him.

41

So often from day to day with thinking and with the pleasure from it he prepared more dry tinder within his proud heart, and imagined that he would draw sweet water from her beautiful eyes for his intense ardor; therefore he cunningly sought to see them often, not perceiving that by them the fire was kindled more.

42

When he went here or there, walking or sitting, alone or accompanied, as he might wish, eating or drinking, night or day and in whatever place, he was constantly thinking about Criseida; and he said that her worth and her delicate features surpassed Polyxena in every beauty, and likewise Helen.

43

Nor did an hour of the day pass that he did not say to himself a thousand times: "O clear light which fills my heart with love, O beautiful Criseida, may God will it that your worth, which deprives my face of color, may be moved to a little pity for me; no one except you can make me joyful; you alone are the woman who can help me."

44

Every other thought, both of the great war and of his well-being, had fled and in his breast was heard only what spoke of the high virtue of his lady, and, thus encumbered, he was eager only to cure his amorous wounds, and toward this end he placed every thought, and all his suffering and his delight.

Into hire hond, and with ful humble chere°   *demeanor*
Bicome hir man, as to my lady dere."

435 In hym ne deyned spare blood roial
The fyr of love—wherfro God me blesse—
Ne him forbar in no degree,[5] for al
His vertu° or his excellent prowesse,   *strength, excellence*
But held hym as his thral° lowe in destresse,   *thrall, slave*
440 And brende° hym so in soundry wise ay newe,° *burned / ever anew in sundry ways*
That sexti tyme° a day he loste his hewe.°   *So that sixty times / color*

So muche, day by day, his owene thought,
For lust to° hire, gan quiken° and encresse,   *desire for / grow lively*
That every other charge he sette at nought.° *responsibility he discounted*
445 Forthi° ful ofte, his hote fir to cesse,°   *Therefore / stop*
To sen hire goodly lok he gan to presse;°   *he pushed forward*
For therby to ben esed° wel he wende,°   *comforted / supposed*
And ay the ner° he was, the more he brende.° *nearer / burned*

For ay the ner the fir, the hotter is—
450 This, trowe° I, knoweth al this compaignye;   *believe*
But were he° fer or ner, I dar sey this: *whether he was*
By nyght or day, for wisdom or folye,
His herte, which that is his brestez yë,°   *breast's eye*
Was ay on hire, that fairer was to sene
455 Than evere were Eleyne or Polixene.[6]

Ek° of the day ther passed nought an houre   *Also*
That to hymself a thousand tyme he seyde,
"Good goodly,° to whom serve I and laboure   *excellent one*
As I best kan,° now wolde God,° Criseyde, *As best I can / may God will*
460 Ye wolden on me rewe, er that° I deyde!°   *before / I die*
My dere herte, allas, myn hele and hewe°   *health and color*
And lif is lost, but° ye wol on me rewe!"°   *unless / take pity*

Alle other dredes weren from him fledde,
Both of th'assege° and his savacioun;°   *siege / safety*
465 N'yn him desir noon other fownes bredde[7]
But argumentes to his conclusioun:
That she of him wolde han compassioun,

---

5. The fire of love (from which may God spare me) did not deign to spare the royal blood in him, nor held off from him at all.
6. Helen of Troy, famous for her beauty, or Polyxena, Troilus's sister.
7. Nor did desire breed any other offspring (i.e., other arguments) in him. *Fownes* (cf. "fawns") are the young of any animal.

45

The sharp battles and the bitter clashes which Hector and his other brothers made, followed by the Trojans, did not, however, turn him from his thoughts of love; although often in the most perilous assaults those who happened to be watching saw him, more than any other, work marvels in arms.

46

Nor did hatred of the Greeks move him to this, nor the longing which he had for victory to liberate Troy, which he saw still gripped by siege, but his desire for glory to be more pleasing caused all this; and through love, if the story speaks the truth, he became so fierce and strong in arms that the Greeks feared him as they did death.

Troilo, inflamed more than ever, first believes that Criseida has another lover; afterwards he reasons with himself concerning her and complains to Love.

47

Already love had taken his sleep from him and diminished his food and so multiplied his anxiety, that by now pallor truly showed his state in his countenance, although he concealed it carefully with a feigned smile and with ingenuous speech, and whoever saw it thought that it happened because of the distress he felt from the war.

48

And how things happened is not quite certain: whether Criseida did not perceive all this because of the way he had concealed his state or whether she pretended not to notice it. But this is very clear and obvious, that it certainly seemed that she cared nothing for Troilo and for the love he bore her, but remained unmoved, as if she were not loved at all.

49

As a result Troilo felt such grief as could not be told, sometimes fearing that Criseida might be taken by love for another and, despising him because of that, would not want to receive him as a suitor; nor, pondering repeatedly a thousand ways, could he see how to make her aware in an honorable way of his burning desire.

And he to ben° hire man while he may dure.°   *that he would be / endure, live*
Lo, here his lif, and from the deth his cure!

470 The sharpe shoures felle of armes preve[8]
That Ector or his othere brethren diden
Ne made hym only therfore ones meve;[9]
And yet was he, where so men wente or riden,°   *walked or rode*
Founde oon the beste, and longest tyme abiden[1]
475 Ther° peril was, and dide ek swich travaille°   *Where / labor*
In armes, that to thenke it was merveille.

But for° non hate he to the Grekes hadde,   *because of*
Ne also for the rescous° of the town,   *rescue*
Ne made hym thus in armes for to madde,°   *rage*
480 But only, lo, for this conclusioun:°   *end, purpose*
To liken° hire the bet° for his renoun. *Clover*   *please / better*
Fro day to day in armes so he spedde°   *prospered*
That the Grekes as the deth° him dredde.°   *plague / dreaded*

And fro this forth tho refte hym love his slep,[2]
485 And made his mete° his foo, and ek° his sorwe   *food / also*
Gan multiplie, that, whoso tok kep,°   *whoever heeded it*
It shewed in his hewe° both eve and morwe.   *color, countenance*
Therfor a title° he gan him for to borwe°   *(false) name, diagnosis / assume*
Of other siknesse, lest men of hym wende°   *were to think*
490 That the hote fir of love hym brende,°   *burned*

its cuz the war

And seyde° he hadde a fevere and ferde amys.°   *he said / fared badly*
But how it was, certeyn, kan I nat seye,
If that his lady understood nat this,
Or feynede hire she nyste,° oon of the tweye;°   *pretended not to know / two*
495 But wel I rede° that, by no manere weye,°   *read / by no kind of conduct*
Ne semed it that she of hym roughte,°   *reckoned, cared about him*
Or° of his peyne, or whatsoevere he thoughte.   *Either*

But thanne felte this Troilus swich wo
That he was wel neigh wood;° for ay° his drede   *mad, insane / always*
500 Was this, that she som wight° hadde loved so,   *(other) person*
That nevere of hym she wolde han taken hede,°   *have paid attention (to him)*
For which hym thoughte° he felte his herte blede;   *it seemed to him*
Ne of his wo ne dorste° he nat bygynne   *dared*
To tellen hir, for al this world to wynne.°   *even to win the whole world*

8. The sharp, cruel assaults of the proof (deeds) of combat.
9. Didn't make him move even once for that reason.
1. Found (to be) the very best, and the one who stayed the longest.
2. And from this time forth, then, love robbed him of his sleep.

50

Therefore, when he had a moment's leisure, he began to complain of Love, saying to himself: "Troilo, now you, who used to mock at others, are caught! No one was ever consumed by love as much as you, from poorly knowing how to guard yourself from it; now you are caught in the snare which you blamed others so much for being caught in, and you were not watching out for yourself.

51

"What will those other lovers say about you if this love of yours is known? They will all ridicule you; they will say about you: 'Look—the wise one who once used to ridicule our sighs and our longing complaints has now arrived where we are; praised be Love, who has brought him to such a pass!'

52

"What will be said of you among the excellent kings and lords if this is known? Indeed, they who are very displeased by this can say: 'See how this man has taken leave of his senses who, in these distressing and sorrowful times, has been newly snared by love! Where he ought to be fierce in war, his thoughts are consumed in loving.'

53

"And now, sorrowing Troilo, since it has been fated for you to love, if you were taken by one who might feel love just a little, you might find consolation! But she for whom you weep feels nothing more than a stone, and so remains as cold as ice which hardens in the open air, while you melt away like snow before the fire.

54

"And if I now even come to the port to which my misfortune leads me, this would be a grace and great comfort to me, for by dying I would leave every pain, because if my suffering, which no one yet suspects, were to be discovered, my life would be full of a thousand insults each day, and more than any other I would be called a poor dog.

55

"Ah, help me, Love! And you for whom I weep, who has taken me more than any other ever was; ah, be a little pitiful to him who loves you much more than his own life; moved by him who holds me in these woes for you, lady, turn now your beautiful face toward him; I pray you for it! Ah, do not deny me this grace.

56

"If you do this, lady, I shall revive like a flower in the fresh meadow in spring, and no waiting afterwards will be grievous to me, or seeing you

505　But whan he hadde a space from his care,
　　　Thus to hymself ful ofte he gan to pleyne;
　　　He seyde, "O fool, now artow° in the snare,　　　　　　　*you are*
　　　That whilom japedest° at loves peyne.　　　　　　　*Who formerly mocked*
　　　Now artow hent,° now gnaw thin owen cheyne!　　　*caught*
510　Thow were ay wont° ech lovere reprehende　　　*ever wont, accustomed*
　　　Of thing fro which thou kanst the° nat defende.　　*yourself*

　　　"What wol° now every lovere seyn of the,　　　　　*will*
　　　If this be wist,° but evere in thin absence　　　　*known*
　　　Laughen in scorn, and seyn, 'Loo, ther goth he
515　That is the man of so gret sapience,
　　　That held us loveres leest in reverence.
　　　Now, thanked God,° he may gon° in the daunce　　*thank God / take part*
　　　Of hem that Love list febly for to avaunce.'³

　　　"But, O thow woful Troilus, God wolde,°　　　　　*may God will*
520　Sith° thow most° loven thorugh° thi destine,　　*Since / must / because of*
　　　That thow beset were on swich oon° that　　　*might be bestowed on such a one*
　　　　　sholde
　　　Know al thi wo, al lakked hir° pitee!　　　　　*though she lack*
　　　But also° cold in love towardes the　　　　　　*as*
　　　Thi lady is as frost in wynter moone,
525　And thow fordon° as snow in fire is soone.　　*destroyed*

　　　"God wold I were aryved in the port
　　　Of deth, to which my sorwe wol me lede!
　　　A, Lord, to me it were a gret comfort;
　　　Than were I quyt° of languisshyng in drede;　　　*free*
530　For, be myn hidde sorwe iblowe on brede,⁴
　　　I shal byjaped° ben a thousand tyme　　　　　　*mocked*
　　　More than that fol of whos folie men ryme.⁵

　　　"But now help, God, and ye, swete,° for whom　　*sweetheart*
　　　I pleyne, ikaught, ye, nevere wight° so faste!　　*creature, person*
535　O mercy, dere herte, and help me from
　　　The deth, for I, whil that my lyf may laste,
　　　More than myself wol love yow to my laste;

---

3. Of those whom it pleases Love to promote but feebly.
4. For if my hidden sorrow were blown (i.e. by loose tongues) abroad.
5. Troilus may think of any foolish lover whom poets write about (*ryme*), or may have in mind a specific fool such as Till Eulenspiegel, the legendary German peasant-clown.

disdainful and haughty; if this is grievous to you, at least, proud one, cry out to me, who am ready to please you in everything, 'Kill yourself,' and I shall surely do this, thinking to please you by that act."

57

Then he said many other words, weeping and sighing, and like one who is used to loving too much and finds no mercy for his cries, he called her name, but they were all vain words and lost themselves in the wind, because none of them came to her; and so his torments multiplied a hundred times each day.

Part Two

Here begins the second part of the "Filostrato," in which Troilo makes his love known to Pandaro, cousin of Criseida, who comforts him and discloses his secret love to Criseida, and with prayers and blandishments induces her to love Troilo; and first, after talking of other things, Troilo discloses his love completely to Pandaro, a noble Trojan youth.

1

One day while Troilo was brooding in such a way alone in his room, a Trojan youth of noble lineage and of great spirit entered unexpectedly, who, seeing him lying stretched out and all tearful on his bed, cried out, "What is this, dear friend? Has the bitter time thus already overcome you?"

2

"Pandaro," said Troilo, "what fortune has led you here to see me waste away? If our friendship has any power, may it oblige you to please go from here because I know that to see me die will be more grievous to you than any other thing; and I am not going to stay alive any longer, so much is my strength vanquished and lost.

3

"Do not believe that the siege of Troy, or the suffering of arms, or any fear is the cause of my present distress; this is among other things my least concern. Something else constrains me to really wish that I might die, and because of it I sorrow at my calamity; do not, my friend, feel concern that this is so, for it is best that I conceal it and do not tell it to you."

And with som frendly lok gladeth° me, swete,   *gladden*
Though nevere more thing ye me byheete."°   *promise*

540 Thise wordes, and ful many an other to,°   *to the same effect*
He spak, and called evere in his compleynte
Hire name, for to tellen hire his wo,
Til neigh that he° in salte teres dreynte.°   *Until he almost / drowned*
Al was for nought: she herde nat his pleynte;
545 And whan that he bythought on° that folie,   *considered*
A thousand fold his wo gan multiplie.

Bywayling° in his chambre thus allone,   *As he lamented*
A frend of his that called was Pandare⁶
Com oones in unwar,° and herde hym groone,   *Came in once unexpectedly*
550 And say° his frend in swich destresse and care: *saw*
"Allas," quod he, "who causeth al this fare?°   *to-do*
O mercy, God! What unhap° may this meene?   *misfortune*
Han now thus soone Grekes maad yow leene?°   *lean, enfeebled*

"Or hastow° som remors of conscience,   *do you have*
555 And art now falle in som devocioun,
And wailest for thi synne and thin offence,
And hast for ferde caught attricioun?⁷
God save hem that biseged han oure town,
That so kan leye oure jolite on presse,⁸
560 And bringe oure lusty° folk to holynesse!"°   *cheerful, lusty / a holy state.*

Thise wordes seyde he for the nones° alle,   *nonce*
That with swich thing he myght hym angry maken,
And with angre don° his wo to falle,   *cause*
As for the tyme,° and his corage° awaken.   *Temporarily / spirit*
565 But wel he wist,° as fer as tonges spaken,   *knew*
Ther nas° a man of gretter hardinesse°   *was not / toughness, courage*
Thanne he, ne more desired worthinesse.

"What cas,"° quod Troilus, "or what aventure°   *chance event / happenstance*
Hath gided the° to sen me langwisshinge,   *led you*
570 That am refus of° every creature?   *rejected by*
But for the love of God, at my preyinge,°   *beseeching*
Go hennes° awey; for certes° my deyinge   *hence / surely*
Wol the disese, and I mot nedes deye;⁹
Therfore go wey, ther is na more to seye.

575 "But if thow wene° I be thus sik for drede,   *suppose*
It is naught° so, and therfore° scorne nought.   *not / on that account*

---

6. On Pandare, or Pandarus (depending on the meter), see the Introduction.
7. And have out of fear succumbed to "attrition" (an imperfect kind of penitence for sin, motivated not by love of God but by fear of damnation).
8. Who in this way can shut up our happiness in a cupboard.
9. Will distress you—and I must needs die.

4

Pandaro's pity then increased and his desire to know it. And so he replied, "If your friendship is now, as it used to be, a pleasure to you, disclose to me what cruelty it is that makes you care so much to die; it is not the act of a friend to keep anything hidden from his friend.

5

"I wish to share this pain with you even if I can not comfort your distress, since it is proper for a friend to share everything, pain and pleasure; and I believe you know well how I have loved you in right and in wrong and how I would do for you any great service, whatever it might be or whatever action it might involve."

6

Troilo then drew a great sigh and said, "Pandaro, since it still pleases you to wish to hear about my suffering, I shall tell you briefly what undoes me, not because I hope that an end or peace can be brought to my desire through you, but only in order to satisfy your great plea, which I do not know how to bring myself to deny.

7

"Love, against whom whoever defends himself is sooner taken and works in vain, so much inflames my heart with a fond delight that I have put every other thing far from me, and this so distresses me, as you can see, that I have scarcely restrained my hand a thousand times from taking my life.

8

"Let it suffice, my dear friend, to hear of my sorrows, which I have never disclosed this much; and I pray you by God, if you are faithful to our love, that you do not disclose this desire to another because much harm could follow to me from this. You know what you have wished to know; go away and leave me here to fight with my distress."

Ther is another thing I take of hede°   *am concerned about*
Wel more than aught° the Grekes han yet wrought,   *anything*
Which cause is of my deth, for sorowe and thought;°   *anxiety*
580   But though that I now telle it the ne leste,°   *don't want to tell you of it*
Be thow naught wroth; I hide it for the beste."

This Pandare, that neigh malt° for wo and routhe,°   *melted / ruth, pity*
Ful ofte seyde, "Allas, what may this be?
Now frend," quod he, "if evere love or trouthe°   *allegiance*
585   Hath ben, or is, bitwixen the and me,
Ne do thow nevere swich a crueltee
To° hiden fro thi frend so gret a care!   *As to*
Wostow naught° wel that it am I, Pandare?   *Know you not*

"I wol parten° with the al thi peyne,   *will share*
590   If it be so I do the° no comfort,   *cause you*
As it is frendes right, soth for to seyne,°   *to tell the truth*
To entreparten wo as glad desport.[1]
I have, and shal, for trewe or fals report,
In wrong and right iloved the al my lyve:°   *life*
595   Hid nat thi wo fro me, but telle it blyve."°   *quickly*

Than gan this sorwful Troylus to syke,°   *sigh*
And seide hym thus: "God leve° it be my beste°   *grant / best for me*
To telle it the; for sith° it may the like,°   *since / please you*
Yet wol I telle it, though myn herte breste.°   *should burst*
600   And wel woot° I thow mayst do me no reste;°   *know / bring me no peace*
But lest thow deme° I truste nat to the,   *suppose*
Now herke,° frend, for thus it stant° with me.   *listen / stands*

"Love, ayeins the which whoso defendeth
Hymselven most, hym alderlest avaylleth,[2]
605   With disespeyr° so sorwfulli me offendeth,°   *despair / attacks*
That streight unto the deth myn herte sailleth.
Therto desir so brennyngly° me assailleth,   *ardently*
That to ben slayn it were a gretter joie
To me than kyng of Grece ben° and Troye.   *to be*

610   "Suffiseth this, my fulle frend Pandare,
That° I have seyd, for now wostow° my wo;   *That which / you know*
And for the love of God, my colde care,
So hide it wel—I tolde it nevere to mo,°   *more (people), others*
For harmes myghten folwen mo than two
615   If it were wist°—but be thow in gladnesse,   *known*
And lat me sterve,° unknowe,° of my destresse."   *die / (with my grief) unknown*

---

1. To share sorrow as well as pleasant amusements.
2. Love, against which it profits him least who defends himself most—i.e., struggling against love makes it stronger.

9

"O," said Pandaro, "how have you been able to keep such a great fire hidden from me, because I would have given you counsel or aid, and have found some way to your peace?" To him Troilo said, "How should I have had it from you, whom I have seen always sorrowful for love, and you do not know how to help yourself in this matter? How then do you think to satisfy me?"

10

Pandaro said, "Troilo, I know that you speak the truth, but many times it happens that he who does not know how to guard himself from poison may keep another healthy through good counsel, and of old the one-eyed man has been seen to walk where the man with full sight does not walk well; and although a man does not take good counsel, he can give it in another's peril.

"How hastow° thus unkyndely° and longe   *have you / unnaturally, unkindly*
Hid this fro me, thow fol?" quod Pandarus.
"Paraunter thow myghte after swich oon longe,[3]
620 That myn avys anoon° may helpen us."   *immediately*
"This were a wonder thing," quod Troilus;
"Thow koudest nevere in love thiselven wisse.°   *inform, manage yourself*
How devel maistow° brynge me to blisse?"   *How the devil can you*

"Ye, Troilus, now herke,"° quod Pandare;   *listen*
625 "Though I be nyce,° it happeth° often so,   *foolish / happens*
That oon that excesse doth ful yvele fare[4]
By good counseil kan kepe his frend therfro.°   *from it*
I have myself ek° seyn a blynd man goo°   *also / walk*
Ther as° he fel that couthe loken wide;°   *Where / could see clearly*
630 A fool may ek a wis-man ofte gide.°   *guide*

"A wheston is no kervyng instrument,[5]
But yet it maketh sharppe kervyng tolis;°   *carving tools sharp*
And there thow woost that I have aught myswent,[6]
Eschuw thow that, for swich thing to the scole is.°   *is a lesson for you*
635 Thus often wise men ben war° by foolys.   *are warned*
If thow do so, thi wit is wel bewared;°   *employed*
By his° contrarie is every thyng declared.°   *its / revealed, defined*

"For how myghte evere swetnesse han ben knowe
To him that nevere tasted bitternesse?
640 Ne no man may ben inly° glad, I trowe,°   *wholly / believe*
That nevere was in sorwe or som destresse.
Eke° whit by blak, by shame ek worthinesse,   *Also*
Ech set by other, more for other semeth,[7]
As men may se, and so the wyse it demeth.°   *the wise man judges it*

645 "Sith° thus of two contraries is o lore,°   *Since / one thing taught*
I, that° have in love so ofte assayed°   *who / experienced*
Grevances, oughte konne, and wel the more,°   *should know how all the better*
Counseillen the of that thow art amayed.
Ek the ne aughte nat ben yvel appayed,[8]
650 Though° I desyre with the for to bere   *Even though*
Thyn hevy charge;° it shal the lasse dere.°   *burden / harm you less*

"I woot wel that it fareth thus be me°   *it goes thus with me*
As to thi brother, Paris, an herdesse°   *shepherdess*

---

3. Perhaps you might be longing for such a person.
4. That a person whom excess causes to fare very badly. *Excesse* can mean intemperance in general, or here immoderate passion in love.
5. The whetstone comparison and the idea that things are made known by their contraries form part of Pandarus's string of proverbs and bits of traditional wisdom. This stanza was copied as an independent poem in the fifteenth century.
6. And at the point where you are aware that I have gone wrong in any way.
7. When each is set by the other, one seems more (distinct) because of the other.
8. To advise you about that about which you are dismayed. Also you should not be displeased.

11

"I have loved unfortunately, and I still love to my misfortune; and this happens because I have not, as you, loved another secretly. What God wills shall be at last. The love which I have always borne you, I bear you and shall bear you, nor shall anyone ever know what may be told me by you.

12

"Therefore, my friend, rest secure in me, and tell me who may be the cause of this grievous and hard life, and do not ever fear my reproof for loving, for the sages have declared in their wise discourses that love could not be taken away from the heart unless it was set free by itself after a long time.

Which that icleped° was Oenone — *named*
655 Wrot in a compleynte of hir hevynesse.⁹
Yee say° the lettre that she wrot, I gesse?"° — *saw / suppose*
"Nay, nevere yet, ywys,"° quod° Troilus. — *certainly / said*
"Now," quod Pandare, "herkne, it was thus:

" 'Phebus,¹ that first fond° art of medicyne,' — *invented*
660 Quod she, 'and couthe° in every wightes° care — *knew (about) / person's*
Remedye and reed,° by herbes he knew fyne,° — *(medical) advice / fully*
Yet to hymself his konnyng° was ful bare,° — *knowledge / barren, useless*
For love hadde hym so bounden in a snare,
Al for the doughter of the kyng Amete,
665 That al his craft ne koude his sorwes bete.'° — *remedy, assuage*

"Right so fare I, unhappyly for me. — [handwritten: *Pandarus is also in unrequited love*]
I love oon best, and that me smerteth sore;° — *hurts me badly*
And yet, peraunter,° kan I reden° the — *perhaps / counsel*
And nat myself; repreve° me na more. — *rebuke*
670 I have no cause, I woot° wel, for to sore° — *know / soar*
As doth an hauk that listeth° for to pleye; — *is pleased*
But to thin help yet somwhat kan I seye.

"And of o° thing right siker° maistow be, — *one / assured*
That certein, for to dyen in the peyne,²
675 That I shal nevere mo discoveren the;° — *betray you (reveal your love)*
Ne, by my trouthe,° I kepe° nat restreyne — *troth / care, am concerned*
The fro thi love, theigh that it were Eleyne° — *Helen (of Troy)*
That is thi brother° wif, if ich it wiste:° — *brother's (Paris's) / knew*
Be what she be, and love hire as the liste!³

680 "Therfore, as frend, fullich in me assure,° — *place your trust*
And tel me plat° what is th'enchesoun° — *flatly, frankly / occasion, reason*
And final cause⁴ of wo that ye endure;
For douteth nothyng,° myn entencioun — *have no doubt*
Nis nat to yow of reprehencioun,° — *reproach*
685 To speke as now, for no wight may byreve
A man to love,⁵ tyl that hym list to leve.° — *it pleases him to leave off*

"And witteth° wel that bothe two ben° vices: — *know / are*
Mistrusten alle, or elles alle leve.° — *believe*
But wel I woot,° the mene° of it no vice is, — *know / mean (middle way)*

9. The syntax is elliptical: Pandarus fares as Oenone wrote to Paris (that she fared), i.e., both suffered in love. Paris deserted the nymph Oenone for Helen of Troy; Ovid records her complaint in his *Heroides* 5, to which Pandarus seems (anachronistically, as often) to allude.
1. The god Phoebus Apollo was commonly recognized as the inventor the art of medicine. For a time he served as a shepherd for Admetus, king of Thessaly, and fell in love with Admetus's daughter. In Luke 4:23, Jesus explicitly cites the notion of the physician unable to heal himself as already a proverb.
2. That certainly, even though I should die under torture.
3. Let her be whoever she may be, and love her as you please.
4. Pandarus alludes to the system of four "causes" that Aristotle devised (e.g., in the *Physics*), here referring to the efficient cause (the immediate occasion) and the final cause (the end to which a thing tends). The other two causes are the material and the formal. Just below (line 689) he touches on another Aristotelian doctrine, the superiority of the mean over the extremes in human behavior.
5. In speaking of the present circumstances, for no one can stop a man from loving.

13

"Leave your anguish, leave your sighs, and mitigate your sorrow by talking, because doing this makes sufferings pass, and ardor lessens much more when he who is a lover sees companions in similar desires; and I, as you know, love against my will and no increase of pain can draw me from it.

14

"Perhaps she who torments you will be such that I shall be able to do a lot for your pleasure, and I would satisfy your wish, if I could, more than I would ever my own if only I may hear who she is for whom you have this pain. Rise up; do not lie down; think that you can talk with me as with your own self!"

15

Troilo stood somewhat doubtful, and after drawing a bitter sigh and flaming all red in his face with shame, he replied: "Dear friend, a very proper reason has prevented me from making my love manifest and clear to you because she who has brought me to this state is a relative of yours." And he said not a word more.

690 For to trusten som wight° is a preve°   *person / proof*
Of trouth;° and forthi wolde I fayn remeve°   *loyalty, integrity / gladly remove*
Thi wrong conseyte, and do the som wyght triste[6]
Thi wo to telle; and tel me, if the liste.°   *it pleases you*

"The wise seith, 'Wo hym that is allone,
695 For, and° he falle, he hath non helpe to ryse';[7]   *if*
And sith° thow hast a felawe, tel thi mone;°   *since / moan, complaint*
For this nys naught, certein, the nexte wyse°   *nearest (i.e., best) way*
To wynnen love—as techen us the wyse—
To walwe° and wepe as Nyobe the queene,[8]   *wallow*
700 Whos teres yet in marble ben yseene.

"Lat be° thy wepyng and thi drerynesse,°   *Leave off / sadness*
And lat us lissen° wo with oother speche;   *alleviate*
So may thy woful tyme seme lesse.
Delyte nat in wo thi wo to seche,[9]
705 As don thise foles that hire° sorwes eche°   *their / augment*
With sorwe, whan thei han mysaventure,°   *bad luck*
And listen naught to seche hem° other cure.   *don't wish to seek for themselves*

"Men seyn, 'to wrecche is° consolacioun   *to a wretched person it is*
To have another felawe° in hys peyne.'   *fellow, companion*
710 That owghte wel ben oure opynyoun,
For bothe thow and I of love we pleyne.
So ful of sorwe am I, soth for to seyne,°   *to tell the truth*
That certeinly namore harde grace°   *no more bad fortune*
May sitte on me, for-why ther is no space.[1]

715 "If God wol, thow art nat agast° of me,   *frightened*
Lest I wolde of thi lady the bygyle!°   *defraud you*
Thow woost° thyself whom that I love, parde,°   *know / by God (pardieu)*
As I best kan, gon sithen longe while.°   *since a long time ago*
And sith thow woost I do it for no wyle,°   *guile*
720 And sith I am he that thow trustest moost,
Tel me somwhat, syn° al my wo thow woost."   *since*

Yet Troilus for al this no word seyde,
But longe he ley as stylle as° he ded were;   *as if*
And after this with sikynge° he abreyde,°   *sighing / started up*
725 And to Pandarus vois° he lente his ere,°   *voice / ear*
And up his eighen° caste he, that in feere°   *eyes / fear*
Was Pandarus, lest that in frenesie°   *frenzy, madness*
He sholde falle, or elles soone dye;

---

6. Your incorrect notion, and cause you to trust in some person.
7. "The wise one" often means Solomon, who was thought to have composed most of the "wisdom books" of the Bible, including Proverbs, the Song of Songs, and Ecclesiastes (and the Book of Wisdom in the Vulgate Bible known to Chaucer). Here Pandarus quotes Ecclesiastes 4:10.
8. In the *Metamorphoses* Ovid tells the story of Niobe of Thebes, who was turned to stone while weeping over the slaughter of her fourteen children by Apollo. The stone still weeps.
9. Take no delight, in your grief, in (obsessively) seeking out your grief.
1. May befall me, because there is no space. Alternative punctuation would be translated, "Why? There is no space." Pandarus has no room for more trouble.

And cryde "Awake!" ful wonderlich° and sharpe; — *amazingly (loud)*
730 "What! Slombrestow° as in a litargie?° — *Are you asleep / lethargy, oblivion*
Or artow° lik an asse to° the harpe, — *are you / confronting*
That hereth sown° whan men the strynges plye,° — *sound / ply, pluck*
But in his mynde of that no melodie
May sinken hym to gladen, for that° he — *because*
735 So dul ys of his bestialite?" — *Pandarus is hilarious*

And with that, Pandare of his wordes stente;° — *ceased*
And Troilus yet° hym nothyng answerde, — *still*
For-why° to tellen nas nat his entente° — *Because / intention*
To nevere no man, for whom that he so ferde;[2]
740 For it is seyd, "Men maketh ofte a yerde° — *rod*
With which the maker is hymself ybeten° — *beaten*
In sondry manere," as thise wyse treten,° — *dissertate, say*

And namelich° in his counseil° tellynge — *especially / in confidence*
That toucheth° love that oughte ben secree;° — *That which concerns / secret*
745 For of himself° it wol ynough out sprynge, — *of its own accord*
But if that it the bet governed be.[3]
Ek som tyme it is a craft to seme fle° — *expedient to seem to flee*
Fro thyng whych in effect° men hunte faste; — *in fact*
Al this gan Troilus in his herte caste.° — *ponder*

750 But natheles,° whan he hadde herd hym crye — *nevertheless*
"Awake!" he gan to syken° wonder soore, — *sigh*
And seyde, "Frend, though that I stylle° lye, — *quietly*
I am nat deef. Now pees,° and crye namore, — *peace, be quiet*
For I have herd thi wordes and thi lore;° — *learning, instruction*
755 But suffre° me my meschief° to bywaille, — *allow / misfortune*
For thy proverbes may me naught availle.° — *help*

"Nor other cure kanstow° non for me; — *fuck you too Troilus / do you know*
Ek I nyl nat° ben cured; I wol deye. — *Also I don't wish to*
What knowe I of the queene Nyobe?
760 Lat be thyne olde ensaumples,° I the preye." — *examples, illustrative stories*
"No," quod Pandarus, "therfore I seye,
Swych is delit of foles to bywepe° — *weep over*
Hire wo, but seken bote they ne kepe.[4]

"Now knowe I that ther° reson in the failleth. — *in this matter*
765 But tel me, if I wiste what° she were — *knew who*
For whom that the al this mysaunter ailleth,° — *misfortune afflicts*
Dorstestow° that I tolde in hire ere° — *Do you dare / ear*
Thi wo, sith° thow darst naught thiself for feere, — *since*
And hire bysoughte on the to han som routhe?"[5]
770 "Why, nay," quod he, "by God and by my trouthe!"

---

2. To any person ever, on whose account (i.e., for which lady) he behaved so.
3. Unless it is controlled the better. Unless one restrains blabbing about affairs of the heart, the news will freely emerge.
4. But they don't care to seek out a remedy.
5. And (do you dare that I) should beseech her to have some pity on you?

"What, nat as bisyly,"° quod° Pandarus, *diligently / said*
"As though myn owene lyf lay on this nede?"° *depended on this crisis*
"No, certes,° brother," quod this Troilus, *certainly*
"And whi? For that thow scholdest nevere spede."° *prosper, succeed*
775 "Wostow° that wel?"—"Ye, that is out of drede,"° *Do you know / beyond doubt*
Quod Troilus. "For al that evere ye konne,° *know, can do*
She nyl° to noon swich wrecche as I ben wonne."° *won't / be won over*

Quod Pandarus, "Allas! What may this be,
That thow dispeired° art thus causeles? *in despair*
780 What! lyveth nat thi lady, bendiste?° *bless us*
How wostow so that thow art graceles?° *out of favor*
Swich yvel° is nat alwey booteles.° *evil / remediless*
Why, put nat° impossible thus thi cure, *suppose it is not*
Syn thyng to come is oft in aventure.° *in doubt, a matter of chance*

785 "I graunte wel that thow endurest wo
As sharp as doth he Ticius in helle,⁶
Whos stomak foughles tiren° evere moo *fowls tear*
That hightyn volturis,° as bokes telle; *are called vultures*
But I may nat endure that thow dwelle
790 In so unskilful° an oppynyoun *unreasonable*
That of thi wo is no curacioun.° *there is no cure*

"But oones nyltow,° for thy coward herte, *will you not*
And for thyn ire and folissh wilfulnesse,
For wantrust,° tellen of thy sorwes smerte,° *lack of trust / painful*
795 Ne to thyn owen help don bysynesse° *make an effort*
As muche as speke a resoun° moore or lesse? *argument, word*
But list as he that lest of nothyng recche—⁷
What womman koude° loven swich a wrecche? *could*

"What may she demen oother° of thy deeth, *otherwise*
800 If thow thus deye, and she not° why it is, *know not*
But that for feere is yolden° up thy breth, *has yielded*
For° Grekes han biseged° us, iwys?° *Because / besieged / indeed*
Lord, which a thonk than shaltow han° of this! *what thanks then shall you have*
Thus wol she seyn, and al the town attones,° *as one, together*
805 'The wrecche is ded, the devel have his bones!'

"Thow mayst allone here wepe and crye and knele—
But love a womman that she woot° it nought, *so that she knows*
And she wol quyte° it that thow shalt nat fele; *requite, return*
Unknowe, unkist,° and lost that is unsought. *unknown, unkissed*
810 What, many a man hath love ful deere ybought° *paid for very dearly*
Twenty wynter that his lady wiste,⁸
That° nevere yet his lady° mouth he kiste. *Who / lady's*

---

6. As does that one, Ticius. Boethius and others describe the giant Tityus's eternal punishment in Hades: *Consolation of Philosophy* 3.m12.41–43.
7. But rather you lie there like a person who is pleased to care about nothing.
8. Who knew his lady for twenty years.

"What° sholde he therfore° fallen in dispayr,   *Why / for that reason*
Or be recreant° for his owne tene,°   *act the coward / vexation*
815 Or slen° hymself, al be his lady° fair?   *slay / though his lady be*
Nay, nay, but evere in oon° be fressh and grene°   *forever / green, vigorous*
To serve and love his deere hertes queene,
And thynk it is a guerdon° hire to serve,   *reward*
A thousand fold moore than he kan deserve."

820 Of that word took hede° Troilus, ~~bout damn time~~ *paid attention*
And thoughte anon° what folie he was inne,   *forthwith*
And how that soth° hym seyde Pandarus,   *the truth*
That for to slen° hymself myght he nat wynne,°   *by slaying / gain (anything)*
But bothe don unmanhod° and a synne,   *an unmanly deed*
825 And of his deth his lady naught to wite;°   *(would be) not to blame*
For of his wo, God woot, she knew ful lite.°   *little*

And with that thought he gan ful sore syke,°   *sigh*
And seyde, "Allas! What is me best to do?"
To whom Pandare answered, "If the like,°   *it please you*
830 The beste is that thow telle me al thi wo;
And have my trouthe,° but° thow it fynde so   *pledge / unless*
I be thi boote,° er° that it be ful longe,   *That I am your remedy / before*
To pieces do me drawe and sithen honge!"[9]

"Ye, so thow seyst," quod Troilus tho,°   *then*
835 But, God woot, it is naught the rather° so.   *any the sooner*
Ful hard were it to helpen in this cas,°   *plight*
For wel fynde I that Fortune is my fo;
Ne al the men that riden konne or go°   *can ride or walk*
May of hire cruel whiel[1] the harm withstonde;
840 For as hire list she pleyeth with free and bonde."[2]

Quod Pandarus, "Than° blamestow Fortune   *Then*
For thow art wroth; ye, now at erst° I see.   *for the first time*
Woost thow nat wel that Fortune is comune°   *common*
To everi manere wight° in som degree?   *person*
845 And yet thow hast this comfort, lo, parde,°   *by God, pardieu*
That, as hire° joies moten overgon,°   *their / must pass away*
So mote° hire sorwes passen everechon.°   *must / every one*

"For if hire whiel stynte any thyng° to torne,   *cease at all*
Than cessed she° Fortune anon° to be.   *she would cease / forthwith*
850 Now, sith° hire whiel by no way may sojourne,°   *since / stop*
What woostow if° hire mutabilite   *How do you know whether*
Right as thyselven list wol don by the,[3]
Or that she be naught fer° fro thyn helpynge?°   *far / aid*
Paraunter° thow hast cause for to synge.   *Perhaps*

9. Have me drawn (by horses) to pieces and afterwards hanged. These were (in reverse order!) common sentences for capital crimes.
1. Again referring to the "cruel wheel" of Fortune.
2. For as she pleases she (i.e., Fortune) plays with both free people and slaves.
3. Will behave for you just as it pleases you.

16

Then he fell back flat on his bed weeping bitterly and hiding his face. Pandaro said to him: "My good friend, little faith has put this distrust in your breast; come, stop this miserable complaint which you are making because, as I hope not to be killed, if she whom you love is my sister, you will have your pleasure with her if it is in my power.

17

"Get up, tell me, say who she is, tell it to me at once, so that I, who would wish nothing else, may see a way to your comfort. Is she a lady who is in my household? Ah, tell me quickly, because if she is the one who I am thinking that she may be, I do not believe the sixth day will pass before I shall draw you from such a painful state."

18

Troilo answered nothing to this but each moment he covered up his face more; and yet, hearing what Pandaro was promising, he hoped to himself somewhat more, and wished to speak, and then restrained himself, he was so much ashamed to disclose it to him; but with Pandaro pressing him, he turned toward him weeping and let loose these words:

19

"My Pandaro, I wish I were dead when I think what love has compelled me to, and if I could have concealed it without doing you wrong, I would still be dissembling; but I can do so no more, and if you are as perceptive as you usually are, you can see that Love has not decreed by rule whom a man shall love and disregarded who it is that his desire elects.

20

"Others, as you know, love their sisters, and sisters their brothers, and daughters sometimes their fathers, and fathers-in-law their daughters-in-law; it even comes about sometimes that mothers love their stepsons; but love has taken me for your cousin, which strongly distresses me—I say for Criseida." And this said, he fell back weeping on his bed, face downwards.

21

When Pandaro heard her named, laughingly he spoke thus: "My friend, I pray you by God not to be discouraged. Love has put your desire in a place such that he could not place it better because she is truly worthy of it, if I have any understanding of manners, or of greatness of soul, or of worth, or of beauty.

855 "And therfore wostow what I the biseche?°   *do you know what I ask of you*
Lat° be thy wo and tornyng to the grounde;   *Let*
For whoso list° have helyng of his leche,°   *is pleased / physician*
To hym byhoveth first unwre his wownde.[4]
To Cerberus[5] yn helle ay° be I bounde,   *forever*
860 Were it for my suster, al thy sorwe,
By my wil° she sholde° al be thyn to-morwe.   *According to my wish / ought to*

"Look up, I seye, and telle me what° she is   *who*
Anon,° that I may gon about thy nede.°   *Immediately / needful task*
Knowe ich hire aught?° For my love, telle me this.   *at all*
865 Thanne wolde I hopen rather for to spede."°   *expect to succeed the better*
Tho° gan the veyne° of Troilus to blede,   *Then / blood vessel*
For he was hit, and wax° al reed° for shame.   *he grew / red*
"A ha!" quod Pandare; "Here bygynneth game."°   *Now the hunt begins*

And with that word he gan hym for to shake,
870 And seyde, "Thef, thow shalt° hyre name telle."   *must*
But tho° gan sely° Troilus for to quake   *then / hapless*
As though men sholde han led hym into helle,
And seyde, "Allas, of al my wo the welle,°   *fount, source*
Thanne is my swete fo called Criseyde!"
875 And wel neigh° with the word for feere he deide.°   *nearly / died*

And whan that Pandare herde hire name nevene,°   *named*
Lord, he was glad, and seyde, "Frend so deere,
Now far aright,° for Joves name in hevene.   *fare well, prosper*
Love hath byset the° wel; be of good cheere!   *set you up*
880 For of good name and wisdom and manere°   *conduct*

4. It behooves him first to reveal his wound.
5. Cerberus, the three-headed watchdog of Hades.

22

"No lady was ever more worthy, none was ever more joyous and more eloquent, none more agreeable or more gracious, none among any of them ever had a greater soul; nor is there anything so noble that she would not undertake it as ably as any king would and that her heart would not allow her to carry to its conclusion, if only she had the power to.

23

"My cousin has only one quality, somewhat troublesome to you, aside from those mentioned: she is more chaste than other ladies and has scorned the things of love more; but if nothing else vexes us, believe me I will find a way with my pleasing words to deal with this according to your need; be patient, restraining carefully your burning desire.

She hath ynough, and ek of gentilesse.°   *good breeding, gentility*
If she be fayr,° thow woost thyself, I gesse,°   *fair, lovely / suppose*

"Ne nevere saugh a more bountevous°   *benevolent, generous*
Of hire estat,° n'a° gladder, ne of speche   *In her social condition / nor a*
885 A frendlyer, n'a more gracious
For to do wel, ne lasse hadde nede° to seche   *nor one who had less need*
What for to don; and al this bet to eche,
In honour, to as fer as she may strecche,
A kynges herte semeth by hyrs a wrecche.[6]

890 "And forthi loke° of good comfort thow be;   *And therefore see to it that*
For certeinly, the ferste poynt is this
Of noble corage° and wel ordeyne,°   *spirit, heart / regulated*
A man to have pees° with hymself, ywis.°   *peace / certainly*
So oghtist thow, for noht but good it is
895 To love wel, and in a worthy place;
The oghte not to clepe° it hap,° but grace.   *call / chance*

"And also thynk, and therwith glade the,°   *make yourself glad*
That sith° thy lady vertuous is al,°   *since / entirely*
So foloweth it that there is some pitee
900 Amonges alle thise other° in general;   *these other virtues*
And forthi° se that thow, in special,°   *therefore / in particular*
Requere naught that is ayeyns hyre name;[7]
For vertu streccheth naught hymself° to shame.   *does not extend itself*

"But wel is me° that evere that I was born,   *it is a good thing for me*
905 That thow biset° art in so good a place;   *situated*
For by my trouthe, in love I dorste have sworn
The sholde nevere han tid thus fayr a grace.[8]
And wostow why? For thow were wont to chace°   *harass*
At Love in scorn, and for despit him calle
910 'Seynt Idiot, lord of thise foles alle.'

"How often hastow maad thi nyce° japes,   *foolish*
And seyd that Loves servantz everichone°   *every one*
Of nycete ben verray Goddes apes;[9]
And some wolde mucche hire mete° allone,   *munch their food*
915 Liggyng° abedde, and make hem° for to grone;   *lying / themselves*
And som,° thow seydest, hadde a blaunche fevere,[1]   *one*
And preydest God he sholde nevere kevere.°   *recover*

"And som of hem took on hym,° for the cold,   *put on (clothing)*
More than ynough, so seydestow° ful ofte.   *you said*
920 And som han feyned° ofte tyme, and told   *feigned, made a pretense*

---

6. And to enlarge on this even more, with regard to honor, to the extent that she can reach, compared with hers a king's heart seems a wretch's.
7. Ask for nothing that goes against her good reputation.
8. That so lovely a good fortune was destined (*sholde*) never to have befallen (*tid*) you.
9. In their folly are true "God's apes" (natural-born fools). Cf. II.370.
1. "Blanch (white) fever," an illness that makes one pale, is one of the conventional maladies of "love-sickness," along with loss of appetite, sleeplessness, swooning, etc. Troilus exhibits these symptoms.

How that they waken,° whan thei slepen softe;   stayed awake
And thus they wolde han brought hemself alofte,[2]
And natheles° were under at the laste.   nevertheless
Thus seydestow, and japedest ful faste.°   quite persistently, strongly

925 "Yet seydestow that for the moore part°   for the most part, more often
Thise loveres wolden speke in general,°   (not of a particular lady)
And thoughten that it was a siker art,°   safe course
For faylyng, for t'assaien overal.[3]
Now may I jape of the, if that I shal;°   would
930 But natheles,° though that I sholde deye,   nevertheless
That thow art non of tho,° I dorste° saye.   those / dare

except the cry baby option. he is that one.

"Now bet° thi brest, and sey to God of Love,   beat (as a penitent)
'Thy grace, lord, for now I me repente,
If I mysspak,° for now myself I° love.'   spoke amiss / I myself
935 Thus sey with al thyn herte in good entente."°   intention, conscience
Quod Troilus, "A, lord! I me consente,°   consent for myself
And preye to the my japes° thow foryive,°   mocking / forgive
And I shal nevere more whyle I live."

"Thow seist wel," quod Pandare, "and now I hope
940 That thow the goddes° wrathe hast al apesed;°   god's (god of Love's) / appeased
And sithen° thow hast wopen° many a drope,   since / wept
And seyd swych thyng° wherwith thi god is plesed,   such things
Now wolde nevere god but thow were esed![4]
And thynk wel, she of whom rist° al thi wo   arises
945 Hereafter may thy comfort be also.

"For thilke° grownd that bereth the wedes wikke°   that same / noxious
Bereth ek thise holsom° herbes, as ful ofte   wholesome
Next° the foule netle, rough and thikke,   Next to
The rose waxeth swoote° and smothe and softe;   grows sweet
950 And next the valeye is the hil o-lofte;°   aloft, on high
And next the derke nyght the glade morwe;°   morning
And also joie is next the fyn° of sorwe.   end

"Now loke° that atempre° be thi bridel,   see to it / reined in
And for the beste ay suffre to the tyde,[5]
955 Or elles al oure labour is on ydel:°   in vain
He hasteth° wel that wisely kan abyde.°   hastens / bide time, endure
Be diligent and trewe, and ay wel hide;°   always hide (your affair) well
Be lusty,° fre;° persevere in thy servyse,   cheerful, vigorous / generous
And al is wel, if thow werke in this wyse.°   work this way

2. And in this way they wished to have brought themselves on top (in the lady's favor, as it were on top of the wheel of Fortune).
3. To avoid failure, to try (wooing) everywhere.
4. Now may God (or, the god of Love) desire nothing except that you may be comforted. Medieval manuscript spelling did not regularly distinguish by capital letters between the Judeo-Christian God, a pagan god, or a special figure like the god of Love. Capitalization in modern printed texts has no authority beyond the editors' best guesses.
5. And as the best course ever be patient in accordance with the times. The phrase *suffre to the tyde* (time) is of uncertain meaning: an alternative, "suffer until the time (of success)."

24

"You can see well then that Love has put you in a place worthy of your virtue; therefore stand firm in your high proposal, and hope well for your salvation, which I believe will follow soon, if you do not forfeit it with your lamenting. You are worthy of her and she of you, and I shall use all my cunning here.

25

"And do not believe, Troilo, that I do not see well that such loves are not proper for a worthy lady and what, furthermore, may come from it both to her and to hers if such a thing should ever come to the mouth of the people; because, through our folly, she in whom honor ought to be has become shameful after she has been made so through love.

26

"But if desire is restrained in its working and all things are not made known, it seems to me possible to hold the opinion that each lover, as long as he is discreet in deed and in appearance, can follow his high desire without any shame to those to whom shame and their honor hold importance.

27

"I believe certainly that in desire every woman lives amorously, and nothing else restrains her but fear of shame; and if to such discomfort a full remedy can properly be given, foolish is he who does not ravish her, and little it seems to me does the pain smart her. My cousin is a widow and has desires, and if she should deny it, I would not believe her.

960 "But he that departed° is in everi place   *divided*
    Is nowher hol,° as writen clerkes wyse.   *whole*
    What wonder is, though swich oon° have no grace?   *is it if such a person*
    Ek wostow° how it fareth of som servise,   *also you know*
    As° plaunte a tree or herbe, in sondry wyse,   *As (for example) to*
965 And on the morwe° pulle it up as blyve!°   *morning / just as quickly*
    No wonder is, though it may nevere thryve.

    "And sith° that God of Love hath the bistowed   *since*
    In place digne unto° thi worthinesse,   *appropriate to*
    Stond faste, for to good port hastow° rowed;   *you have*
970 And of thiself, for any hevynesse,°   *despite any sorrow*
    Hope alwey wel; for, but if drerinesse°   *unless dejection*
    Or over-haste oure bothe labour shende,[6]
    I hope of this to maken a good ende.

[handwritten note: ✳ metaphor throughout of life being a man in a boat, tossed by fate wheresoever she deems]

    "And wostow why I am the lasse afered°   *afraid*
975 Of this matere with my nece trete?°   *to treat of, discuss*
    For this have I herd seyd of wyse lered,[7]
    Was nevere man or womman yet bigete°   *begotten*
    That was unapt° to suffren loves hete,°   *not disposed / heat*
    Celestial,° or elles love of kynde;°   *heavenly / natural*
980 Forthy° som grace[8] I hope in hire to fynde.   *Therefore*

    "And for to speke of hire in specyal,°   *particular*
    Hire beaute to bithynken° and hire youthe,   *consider*
    It sit° hire naught to ben celestial   *suits*
    As yet, though that hire liste bothe and kowthe;[9]

6. Or overhasty action should ruin the labor of the two of us.
7. Heard tell from wise, learned men (or, a man). The following assertion probably derives from Dante, *Purgatory* 17.91–93: "Never was Creator or creature . . . without love, either natural or of the spirit."
8. Pandarus's persistent use of metaphors of the "religion of love," where he acts as father confessor to Troilus as penitent sinner, lends force here to the term *grace*, commonly meaning (somewhat euphemistically) the lady's favor in a love affair, but here with further allusion (if now only playfully) to the grace associated with love *celestial*. Pandarus represents himself as a priest of love, a physician of love, and a *wis-man*, a sage of love full of proverbs and traditional lore.
9. Even though she might both be pleased to and know how to (engage in heavenly love).

28

"Therefore, knowing you to be wise and discreet, I can please her and both of you, and give equal comfort to each, on the condition that you keep it hidden, and it will be as if it were not; and I would do wrong, if in this matter I did not do everything in my power in your service; but you must be discreet then in keeping such deeds concealed from others."

29

Troilo listened to Pandaro so satisfied in mind that he seemed to himself to be already beyond all his torment, and love rekindled itself more in him; but after he had been silent for a time, he turned to Pandaro and said to him, "I believe what you have said of her, but the difficulty seems in my eyes the greater because of this.

30

"But how, however, will the ardor that I carry within diminish, since I have never seen that she perceives my love? She will not believe it if you tell it to her; then for fear of you she will blame this passion, and you will achieve nothing. And even if she felt it in her heart, to show you that she is chaste, she would not be willing to listen to you.

985 But trewely, it sate° hire wel right nowthe°   would suit / now
A worthi knyght to loven and cherice,°   cherish
And but she do,° I holde it for a vice.   unless she does so

"Wherfore I am, and wol ben, ay redy°   will be ever ready
To peyne me° to do yow[1] this servyse;   To take pains
990 For bothe yow° to plese thus hope I   you both
Herafterward; for ye ben bothe wyse,
And konne it counseil kepe° in swych a wyse   know how to keep it secret
That no man shal the wiser of it be;
And so we may ben gladed° alle thre.   gladdened

995 "And, by my trouthe, I have right now of the
A good conceyte°_in my wit, as I gesse,   conceit, idea
And what it is, I wol now that thow se.
I thenke, sith° that Love, of his goodnesse,   since
Hath the converted out of wikkednesse,
1000 That thow shalt ben the beste post,° I leve,°   pillar (of the church) / believe
Of al his lay,° and moost° his foos to greve.°   religion / the most / afflict

"Ensample why,° se now thise wise clerkes,   To exemplify why
That erren aldermost ayeyn a lawe,²
And ben converted from hire° wikked werkes   their
1005 Thorugh grace of God that list hem to hym drawe,³
Thanne arn° thise folk that han moost God in awe,   are
And strengest feythed° ben, I undirstonde,   And are strongest in faith
And konne° an errowr° alderbest° withstonde."   know how / heresy / best of all

Whan Troilus hadde herd Pandare assented°   to have consented
1010 To ben his help in lovyng of Cryseyde,
Weex° of his wo, as who seith,° untormented,   He became / so to speak
But hotter weex his love, and thus he seyde,
With sobre chere,° although his herte pleyde:°   sober countenance / delighted
"Now blisful Venus helpe, er that I sterve,°   die
1015 Of the, Pandare, I mowe som thank deserve.⁴

"But, deere frend, how shal my wo be lesse
Til this be doon? And good,° ek telle me this: good friend
How wiltow seyn° of me and my destresse,   How will you speak
Lest she be wroth—this drede I moost, ywys—°   indeed
1020 Or nyl nat here or trowen how it is.⁵

1. The shift from the singular pronouns *thow* and *the* to *ye* and *yow* here merely marks Pandarus's plural reference to both Troilus and Criseyde—he consistently addresses his close friend Troilus as *thow*. Elsewhere less intimate friends address each other with the formal plural *ye*; observation of the use of these pronouns reveals subtle social distinctions that could be made by earlier English writers.
2. Who err (fall into heresy) most of all against a religious faith. A *lay* or *lawe* is literally a law, but the word commonly means a religious law (like Torah) and hence simply a religion or faith.
3. Through the grace of God, which (*or*, Who) is pleased to draw them to Him. Examples of the special zeal of converts would be Paul and Augustine.
4. That I might (in the future) deserve some thanks from you, Pandarus. Troilus asks the goddess of Love to allow him in turn some day to assist in Pandarus's own unrequited love affair.
5. Or will not hear or believe how it stands.

31

"And furthermore, Pandaro, I do not wish you to believe that I would desire anything unbecoming to such a lady. I would wish only that it be agreeable to her that I love her: this would be to me a sovereign grace if I should obtain it. Seek for this and I do not ask more of you." Then he lowered his face, somewhat ashamed.

32

Laughing, Pandaro replied to him, "There is no harm in what you say. Let me act, because I have at hand amorous flames and speeches of similar kind, and I have known before how to bring more difficult things to their conclusion under unusual conditions. This labor will be all mine, and I wish that the sweet result may be yours."

33

Troilo leapt quickly to the ground from his bed, embracing and kissing him, then swearing that to win the Greek war triumphantly would be nothing to him compared to this passion which gripped him so tightly. "My Pandaro, I put myself in your hands; you sage, you friend, you know all that is needed to put an end to my grief."

Al this drede I, and ek for the manere
Of the, hire em,° she nyl no swich thyng here."⁶   *uncle*

Quod Pandarus, "Thow hast a ful gret care
Lest that the cherl may falle out of the moone!⁷
1025 Whi, Lord! I hate of the thi nyce fare!°   *foolish (or, too scrupulous) to-do*
Whi, entremete of that thow hast to doone!°   *meddle in your own business*
For Goddes love, I bidde° the a boone:°   *beg / favor*
So lat m'alone, and it shal be thi beste."⁸
"Whi, frend," quod he, "now do right as the leste.°   *it pleases you.*

1030 "But herke, Pandare, o° word, for I nolde°   *one / would not wish*
That thow in me wendest° so gret folie,   *would suppose*
That to my lady I desiren sholde°   *might desire anything*
That toucheth° harm or any vilenye;°   *has to do with / base conduct*
For dredeles° me were levere° dye   *beyond doubt / I had rather*
1035 Than she of me aught elles understode
But that that myghte sownen into° goode."   *be conducive to, tend toward*

Tho lough° this Pandare, and anon answerde,   *laughed*
"And I thi borugh? Fy! No wight doth but so.⁹
I roughte naught° though that she stood and herde°   *wouldn't care / heard*
1040 How that thow seist! but farewel, I wol go.
Adieu! Be glad! God spede° us bothe two!   *grant success to*
Yef° me this labour and this bisynesse,°   *Give / busy task*
And of my spede° be thyn al that swetnesse."   *success*

Tho° Troilus gan doun on knees to falle,   *Then*
1045 And Pandare in his armes hente° faste,   *seized*
And seyde, "Now, fy on the Grekes alle!
Yet, parde,° God shal helpe us atte° laste.   *by god, pardieu / at the*
And dredelees, if that my lyf may laste,
And God toforn,° lo, som of hem shal smerte;°   *before God (I swear) / feel pain*
1050 And yet m'athenketh that this avant m'asterte!¹

"Now, Pandare, I kan na more seye,
But, thow wis, thow woost, thow maist, thow art al!²
My lif, my deth, hol° in thyn hond I leye.°   *wholly / lay*
Help now!" Quod he, "Yis,° by mi trowthe, I shal."   *Indeed*
1055 "God yelde° the, frend, and this in special,"°   *grant / particular*
Quod Troilus, "that thow me recomande°   *you commend me*
To hire that to the deth me may comande."

---

6. All this I fear, and also that, for the sake of propriety, she will hear of no such affair from you, her uncle. The sense of *for the manere* is ambiguous: "for the sake of appearances" or "in accordance with the custom" or "considering the circumstances" are all possible, or the phrase could be construed with the following line—"because of the behavior (or, situation) of you, (as) her uncle. . . ."

7. You're worried "lest the churl (i.e., the man) fall out of the moon!"—that is, worried about an unlikely event. That one may see the figure of a man in the moon and that he might fall are common medieval as well as current notions.

8. Just leave me alone, and that will be best for you.

9. And I your guarantor (of honorable behavior)? Fie! No one does otherwise. Precisely what no one does is left ambiguous: act as a guarantor? behave honorably? claim to intend to behave honorably?

1. And yet I regret that this boast escaped my lips.

2. But you wise one, you know, you can do, you are all!

Pandaro discloses to Criseida the love which Troilo bears her and despite her opposition urges her to love him.

34

Pandaro, eager to serve the youth whom he loved so much, having left him to go where he pleased, took himself to where Criseida lived. As she saw him come toward her, she rose to her feet and greeted him from afar, and Pandaro her, and taking her by the hand, he led her with him into a gallery.

This Pandarus, tho° desirous to serve   *then*
His fulle° frend, than seyde in this manere: *fast*
1060 "Farwell, and thenk° I wol thi thank deserve!   *believe*
Have here my trowthe, and that thow shalt wel here."³
And went his wey, thenkyng on this matere,°   *matter*
And how he best myghte hire biseche of grace,°   *entreat her for her favor*
And fynde a tyme therto,° and a place.   *for it*

1065 For everi wight° that hath an hous to founde°   *person / build*
Ne renneth naught° the werk for to bygynne   *doesn't run*
With rakel° hond, but he wol bide a stounde,°   *rash / wait a while*
And sende his hertes line out fro withinne⁴
Aldirfirst° his purpos for to wynne.°   *First of all / attain*
1070 Al this Pandare in his herte thoughte,
And caste° his werk ful wisely or° he wroughte.°   *plotted / before / set to work*

But Troilus lay tho° no lenger down,   *then*
But up anon upon his stede bay,°   *bay (colored) steed*
And in the feld he pleyde tho leoun;⁵
1075 Wo was that Grek that with hym mette a-day!°   *met with him by day*
And in the town his manere tho forth ay°   *manner thenceforth always*
So goodly was, and gat hym so in grace,°   *so advanced him in favor*
That ecch° hym loved that° loked on his face.   *each person / who*

For he bicom° the frendlieste wight,   *became*
1080 The gentilest,° and ek the mooste fre,°   *noblest / generous*
The thriftiest,° and oon the beste⁶ knyght   *most successful, admirable*
That in his tyme was or myghte be;
Dede were his japes and his cruelte,
His heighe port° and his manere estraunge,°   *haughty bearing / aloof*
1085 And ecch of tho° gan for a vertu chaunge.   *those (vices)*

Now lat us stynte° of Troilus a stounde,°   *stop (talking) / while*
That fareth lik a man that hurt is soore,
And is somdeel of akyngge of his wownde
Ylissed wel, but heeled no deel moore,⁷
1090 And, as an esy pacyent,° the loore°   *compliant patient / advice*
Abit° of hym that gooth aboute his cure;   *abides, heeds*
And thus he dryeth forth his aventure.°   *endures his situation*

*Explicit liber primus.*⁸   religious love + courtly love both make you a better person, apparently

---

3. Have here my pledge of loyalty, and you shall indeed hear about that (i.e., my deserving your thanks).
4. And send out the (plumb-)line of his heart from within. The analogy is drawn from the *New Poetry* of Geoffrey of Vinsauf (ca. 1200), preserved in some two hundred manuscripts. The passage is also excerpted in other works possibly known to Chaucer.
5. And in the battlefield he played then the lion, i.e., he fought fiercely. A tenet of medieval lore about love is that loving stimulates courageous behavior.
6. The idiom *oon the beste* regularly means not "one of the best" but "the very best."
7. And is in part well comforted from the aching of his wound, but in no way healed the more.
8. Here ends the first book.

Book Two

Incipit prohemium secundi libri.[1]

Owt of thise blake wawes° for to saylle, — waves
O wynd, o wynd, the weder gynneth clere;° — the weather begins to clear
For in this see the boot hath swych travaylle,
Of my connyng, that unneth I it steere.[2]
5 This see clepe I° the tempestous matere — I call
Of disespeir° that Troilus was inne; — despair
But now of hope the kalendes° bygynne. — first day

O lady myn, that called art Cleo,[3]
Thow be my speed° fro this forth,° and my Muse, — cause of success / henceforth
10 To ryme wel this book til I have do;° — have finished
Me nedeth° here noon other art to use. — I need
Forwhi° to every lovere I me excuse, — For which reason
That of no sentement° I this endite,° — personal feeling / compose
But out of Latyn in my tonge it write.[4]

15 Wherfore I nyl° have neither thank ne blame — will not
Of al this werk, but prey yow mekely,
Disblameth° me if any word be lame, — Don't blame
For as myn auctour° seyde, so sey I. — authoritative source
Ek° though I speeke of love unfelyngly, — Also
20 No wondre is, for it nothyng of newe is.[5]
A blynd man kan nat juggen° wel in hewis.° — judge, discriminate / hues

Ye knowe ek that in forme of speche° is chaunge[6] — linguistic usage
Withinne a thousand yeer, and wordes tho° — then
That hadden pris,° now wonder nyce° and — value / wondrously foolish
straunge
25 Us thinketh hem,° and yet thei spake hem° so, — They seem to us / them
And spedde° as wel in love as men now do; — prospered
Ek for to wynnen love in sondry ages,
In sondry londes, sondry ben usages.° — various are the customs

And forthi° if it happe° in any wyse, — therefore / should happen
30 That here be any lovere in this place
That herkneth, as the storie wol devise,° — relate
How Troilus com to his lady grace,° — passed into his lady's favor

---

1. Here begins the Proem (Prologue) to the Second Book.
2. For in this sea the boat of my wit (poetic craft) has such heavy going that I may steer it only with difficulty. Chaucer carefully explains the analogy in the following lines; it is borrowed from the opening lines of Dante's *Purgatory*, and hence suggests a gradual movement up from the depths of misery.
3. As Tisiphone was the "Muse" of Book One, the narrator here invokes an actual Muse, Clio, traditionally the Muse of history, likewise invoked by Statius at the beginning of the *Thebaid* (see line 84 below).
4. The narrator still makes as if faithfully to follow his Latin (thus classical and authoritative) source, Lollius; see I.394 above. Thus, he says, his task is merely to put the story into adequate English rhyme—he has no experience in love matters of this kind.
5. It is no wonder, for it (the story I tell, or my incapacity to speak of love) is no new thing.
6. The idea expressed in this stanza derives ultimately from Horace, *Art of Poetry* 70–71, probably by way of the quotation of Horace's passage in Dante, *Convivio* 1.5.55–66.

And thenketh, "So nold I nat° love purchace,"°   *I wouldn't / obtain*
Or wondreth on his speche or his doynge,°   *behavior*
35 I noot;° but it is me no wonderynge.°   *don't know / cause for wonder*

For every wight° which that to Rome went°   *person / goes*
Halt nat o path,° or alwey o manere;   *Holds not to one path*
Ek in som lond were al the game shent,°   *ruined*
If that they ferde° in love as men don here,   *behaved*
40 As thus, in opyn doyng or in chere,
In visityng in forme, or seyde hire sawes;[7]
Forthi° men seyn, "Ecch contree hath his° lawes."   *Whence / its*

Ek scarsly ben ther in this place thre
That have in love seid lik, and don, in al;[8]
45 For to thi purpos° this may liken the,°   *for your purposes / please you*
And the right nought; yet al is seid or schal;[9]
Ek som men grave° in tree,° some in ston wal,   *carve / wood*
As it bitit.° But syn° I have bigonne,   *happens / since*
Myn auctour shal I folwen,° if I konne.   *follow*

Explicit prohemium secundi libri.

Incipit liber secundus.[1]

50 In May, that moder° is of monthes glade,   *mother*
That° fresshe floures, blew and white and rede,   *So that*
Ben quike° agayn, that wynter dede made,   *Are alive*
And ful of bawme is fletyng every mede,[2]
Whan Phebus doth his bryghte bemes sprede
55 Right in the white Bole,[3] it so bitidde,°   *came to pass*
As I shal synge, on Mayes day the thrydde,[4]

That Pandarus, for al his wise speche,
Felt ek his part° of loves shotes keene,°   *share / sharp arrowshots*
That, koude he nevere so wel° of lovyng preche,   *though he could ever so well*
60 It made his hewe a-day° ful ofte greene.   *hue by day*
So shop it that hym fil that day a teene[5]
In love, for which in wo to bedde he wente,
And made, er° it was day, ful many a wente.°   *before / turn*

The swalowe Proigne, with a sorowful lay,°   *song*
65 Whan morwen com,° gan make hire   *morning came*
    waymentynge°   *lamenting*

7. As in this way, in public conduct or in bearing, in formal visiting, or if they uttered their expressions (i.e., the talk people here utter in their wooing).
8. Who have spoken and performed everything in the same way in matters of love.
9. And you, not at all; yet all (this love-talk) is said, or will be.
1. Here ends the Proem of the Second Book. Here begins the Second Book.
2. And every mead is overflowing with balmy fragrance.
3. When Phebus (Apollo, the sun) spreads his bright beams in the white Bull (in the zodiacal sign of Taurus). In Chaucer's time May 3 would be over twenty-one degrees (two-thirds) into Taurus.
4. Chaucer twice elsewhere, in the Knight's Tale and the Nun's Priest's Tale, specifies the date May 3. Of various explanations that have been proposed, perhaps the most likely is that the date had personal meaning for him.
5. So it was destined that a malaise came to him that day.

Whi she forshapen was;[6] and evere lay
Pandare abedde, half in a slomberynge,
Til she so neigh° hym made hire cheterynge°   near / chattering
How Tereus gan forth hire suster take,
70   That with the noyse of hire he gan awake,

And gan to calle, and dresse hym up to ryse,[7]
Remembryng hym his erand was to doone°   (still) to be accomplished
From Troilus, and ek his grete emprise;°   enterprise
And caste and knew in good plit was the moone
75   To doon viage,[8] and took his way ful soone
Unto his neces palays° ther biside.°   palace / nearby
Now Janus, god of entree, thow hym gyde![9]

Whan he was come unto his neces place,°   house
"Wher is my lady?" to hire folk° quod° he;   retinue / said
80   And they hym tolde, and he forth in gan pace,°   pass
And fond° two othere ladys sete° and she,   found / seated
Withinne a paved parlour, and they thre
Herden a mayden reden hem the geste°   read to them the story
Of the siege of Thebes,[1] while hem leste.°   it pleased them

85   Quod Pandarus, "Madame, God yow see,°   watch over
With youre book and all the compaignie!"
"Ey,° uncle myn, welcome iwys,"° quod she;   Oh! / indeed
And up she roos, and by the hond in hye°   quickly
She took hym faste, and seyde, "This nyght thrie,°   thrice last night
90   To goode mot° it turne, of yow I mette."°   may / dreamed
And with that word she doun on bench hym sette.

"Ye,° nece, yee shal faren wel the bet,°   Yea / do all the better
If God wol, al this yeer," quod Pandarus;
"But I am sory that I have yow let°   hindered

6. Procne, sister of Philomena and wife of Tereus, was metamorphosed (*forshapen*) into a swallow, and Philomena into a nightingale, after they avenged Tereus's rape of Philomena. A gloss in one of the manuscripts of *Troilus and Criseyde* refers to the source of the story, Ovid's *Metamorphoses* 6.412–674.
7. And began to call (his household servants), and prepare to rise. The principal characters in the poem are all wealthy enough to employ a retinue of servants and live in great houses.
8. And he made a calculation (perhaps by consulting a "moonbook") and knew that the moon was well situated for undertaking some business. Both Calchas's and Pandarus's astrological calculations turn out to be correct. Medieval Christians on the whole assumed that the heavenly bodies indeed influence earthly events, but held it heresy to try to predict an individual's future on the basis of his or her hour and day of birth.
9. Now Janus, god of entry, may you guide him! The narrator himself explains the mythological figure he introduces, Janus, the two-faced Roman god of entryways, eponym of the month of January.
1. The siege of Thebes is narrated in Statius's twelve-book Latin epic, the *Thebaid* (ca. 91 C.E.) and in the French epic-romance, the *Roman de Thèbes* (mid-twelfth century). Chaucer knew both works, or a later abbreviation of the latter. The siege took place before the Trojan War, but of course the poems are much later. Here Chaucer takes various small details from both poems. Criseyde seems to translate the French poem's title in line 100 (though *romaunce* could mean any narrative of adventure), and Pandarus distinctly refers to the *Thebaid*'s twelve books (on the Vergilian model) in line 108. In some manuscripts the *Roman de Thèbes* was bound together with one of the sources of *Troilus and Criseyde*, the *Roman de Troie* (see Introduction). Possibly Chaucer wants us to imagine (all with implicit and playful anachronism) Criseyde as hearing the French poem, as an aristocratic London lady might, and Pandarus as referring to Statius's epic, implying the knowledge of Latin more often reserved to European educated males. In V.1485–510 below, Troilus's (well educated!) sister Cassandra summarizes the *Thebaid*. In any case the violence of the Theban siege forms a dark background to the Trojan siege.

95 To herken of youre book ye preysen° thus.   *that you esteem*
   For Goddes love, what seith it? telle it us!
   Is it of love? O, som good ye me leere!"°   *teach me*
   "Uncle," quod she, "youre maistresse° is nat here."   *mistress, beloved*

   With that thei gonnen° laughe, and tho° she seyde,   *began to / then*
100 "This romaunce is of Thebes that we rede;
   And we han herd how that kyng Layus deyde
   Thorugh Edippus° his sone, and al that dede;°   *Oedipus / action*
   And here we stynten° at thise lettres rede—²   *stopped*
   How the bisshop, as the book kan telle,
105 Amphiorax, fil thorugh the ground to helle."³

   Quod Pandarus, "Al this knowe I myselve,
   And al th'assege° of Thebes and the care;°   *siege / trouble*
   For herof ben ther maked° bookes twelve.   *of this have been written*
   But lat be this, and telle me how ye fare.
110 Do wey youre barbe,⁴ and shew youre face bare;
   Do wey° youre book, rys up, and lat us daunce,   *Put away*
   And lat us don to May som observaunce."°   *appropriate attention*

   "I!° God forbede!" quod she. "Be ye mad?   *Oh!*
   Is that a widewes lif, so God yow save?°   *may God save you*
115 By God, ye maken me ryght soore adrad!°   *very severely frightened*
   Ye ben so wylde, it semeth as ye rave.
   It satte me wel bet ay° in a cave   *would suit me better always*
   To bidde and rede° on holy seyntes lyves;   *pray and read*
   Lat maydens gon to daunce, and yonge wyves."

120 "As evere thrive I,"° quod this Pandarus,   *May I ever prosper*
   "Yet koude I telle a thyng to doon yow pleye."°   *amuse you, please you*
   "Now, uncle deere," quod she, "telle it us
   For Goddes love; is than th'assege aweye?°   *then the siege lifted*
   I am of Grekes so fered° that I deye."   *afraid*
125 "Nay, nay," quod he, "as evere mote° I thryve,   *may*
   It is a thing wel bet than swyche fyve."⁵

   "Ye, holy God," quod she, "what thyng is that?
   What! Bet than swyche fyve? I! Nay, ywys!
   For al this world ne kan I reden° what   *tell*
130 It sholde ben; some jape I trowe° is this;   *believe*
   And but youreselven telle us what it is,

2. Statius alludes to the unwitting killing of Laius by his son Oedipus; the *Roman de Thèbes* tells the story in full. The maiden reading the story stopped at some *lettres rede*, rubrics that indicate the beginning of a section of the narrative.
3. Chaucer uses the French spelling of the prophet named Amphiaraus in Statius. He is called bishop and archbishop in the *Roman de Thèbes*. Apparently anachronistic is the title *bisshop* as are the references to *seyntes lyves* in line 118 below, *religious* (normally, "nun"), line 759 below, and *gospel*, V.1265—but even these can be taken in context as non-Christian terms.
4. The *barbe*, part of Criseyde's *widewes habit* (I.170 above), is "a piece of pleated cloth, forming part of the headdress of widows or nuns, and worn over or under the chin so as to cover the neck and bosom" (*Middle English Dictionary*).
5. It is a better thing than five such things (as the raising of the Greek siege of Troy).

My wit is for t'arede it al to leene.[6]
As help me God, I not nat what ye meene."

"And I youre borugh, ne nevere shal, for me,
135 This thyng be told to yow, as mote I thryve!"[7]
"And whi so, uncle myn? Whi so?" quod she.
"By God," quod he, "that wol I telle as blyve!°   *forthwith*
For proudder womman is ther noon on lyve,°   *alive*
And ye it wiste,° in al the town of Troye.   *If you know about it*
140 I jape nought, as evere have I° joye!"   *may I have*

Tho gan she wondren moore than biforn
A thousand fold, and down hire eyghen° caste;   *eyes*
For nevere, sith the tyme that she was born,
To knowe thyng desired she so faste;°   *eagerly*
145 And with a syk° she seyde hym atte laste,   *sigh*
"Now, uncle myn, I nyl yow nought displese,
Nor axen° more that may do yow disese."°   *ask / discomfort*

So after this, with many wordes glade,
And frendly tales, and with merie chiere,°   *merry demeanor*
150 Of this and that they pleide,° and gonnen wade°   *amused themselves / go, delve*
In many an unkouth, glad, and dep matere,°   *strange, happy, and deep matter*
As frendes doon whan thei ben mette yfere,°   *have met together*
Tyl she gan axen hym how Ector ferde,[8]
That was the townes wal and Grekes yerde.°   *rod, scourge*

155 "Ful wel, I thonk it God," quod Pandarus,
"Save in his arm he hath a litel wownde;
And ek his fresshe brother Troilus,
The wise, worthi Ector the secounde,
In whom that alle vertu list habounde,[9]
160 As alle trouthe and alle gentilesse,
Wisdom, honour, fredom, and worthinesse."

"In good feith, em,"° quod she, "that liketh me°   *uncle / it pleases me (that)*
Thei faren wel; God save hem bothe two!
For trewelich I holde it gret deynte°   *dignity, honor*
165 A kynges sone in armes wel to do,
And ben of goode condiciouns therto;°   *character in addition*
For gret power and moral vertu here
Is selde yseyn in o persone yfeere."[1]

"In good faith, that is soth," quod Pandarus.
170 "But, by my trouthe, the kyng hath sones tweye—°   *two sons*
That is to mene,° Ector and Troilus—   *to be understood*
That certeynly, though that I sholde deye,

6. My understanding is entirely too feeble to grasp it.
7. And I swear, this thing will never be told to you as far as I'm concerned, so may I prosper!
8. Until she asked him how Hector fared. Troilus's eldest brother is regularly portrayed as the chief Trojan hero.
9. In whom all virtue is pleased to be abundant.
1. Are seldom seen conjoined in one person.

Thei ben as voide° of vices, dar I seye,   *devoid*
As any men that lyven under the sonne:
175 Hire myght is wyde yknowe, and what they konne.°   *can do*

"Of Ector nedeth it namore for to telle:°   *there is need to say no more*
In al this world ther nys a bettre knyght
Than he, that is of worthynesse welle;°   *fount, source*
And he wel moore vertu hath than myght;
180 This knoweth many a wis and worthi wight.
The same pris° of Troilus I seye;   *evaluation, praise*
God help me so, I knowe nat swiche tweye."°   *of two such men*

"By God," quod she, "of Ector that is sooth.°   *the truth*
Of Troilus the same thyng trowe° I;   *believe*
185 For, dredeles, men tellen that he doth
In armes day by day so worthily,
And bereth hym here at hom so gentily°   *courteously*
To everi wight, that alle pris hath he
Of hem that me were levest preysed be."²

190 "Ye sey right sooth,° ywys," quod Pandarus;   *quite truly*
"For yesterday, whoso° had with hym ben,   *whoever*
He myghte han wondred upon Troilus;
For nevere yet so thikke a swarm of been°   *bees*
Ne fleigh,° as Grekes for hym gonne fleen,°   *fled / did flee*
195 And thorugh the feld,° in everi wightes eere,°   *battlefield / person's ear*
Ther nas no cry but 'Troilus is there!'

"Now here, now ther, he hunted hem so faste,
Ther nas° but Grekes blood—and Troilus.   *was nothing*
Now hem° he hurte, and hem° al down he caste;   *these / those*
200 Ay wher° he wente, it was arayed° thus: *Everywhere / disposed*
He was hire deth, and sheld° and lif for us,   *shield*
That, as° that day, ther dorste non   *as for*
    withstonde°   *none dared stand up to him*
Whil that he held his blody swerd in honde. *hahahahaha*

"Therto° he is the frendlieste man   *In addition*
205 Of gret estat that evere I saugh my lyve;°   *during my life*
And wher hym lest, best felawshipe kan
To swich as hym thynketh able for to thryve."³
And with that word tho Pandarus, as blyve,°   *forthwith*
He took his leve, and seyde, "I wol gon henne."°   *hence*
210 "Nay, blame have I, myn uncle," quod she thenne.

"What aileth yow to be thus wery° soone,   *weary, bored*
And namelich° of wommen? Wol ye° so?"   *especially / Will you (behave)*

---

2. That he has great esteem among those by whom I would most like to be praised.
3. And wherever it please him, he can (display) the best fellowship to such people as seem to him able to succeed.

Nay, sitteth down; by God, I have to doone°   *I have (business) to do*
With yow, to speke of wisdom° er ye go."   *(my need for) wise counsel*
215 And everi wight that was aboute hem tho,
That herde that, gan fer awey to stonde,
Whil they two hadde al that hem liste in honde.⁴

Whan that hire tale° al brought was to an ende,   *their conversation*
Of hire estat and of hire governaunce,°   *her management (of her affairs)*
220 Quod Pandarus, "Now tyme is that I wende.°   *should depart*
But yet, I say, ariseth, lat us daunce,
And cast youre widewes habit° to mischaunce!°   *garb / to bad luck (to the devil)*
What list yow thus yourself to disfigure,
Sith yow is tid° thus fair an aventure?"   *has befallen*

225 "A, wel bithought!° For love of God," quod she,   *well (i.e., cleverly) conceived*
"Shal I nat witen° what ye meene° of this?"   *know / mean*
"No, this thing axeth leyser," tho quod he,⁵
"And eke me wolde muche greve,° iwis,   *grieve, disturb*
If I it tolde and ye it toke amys.°   *you took it amiss*
230 Yet were it bet my tonge for to stille°   *to keep quiet (or, to silence)*
Than seye a soth° that were ayeyns° youre wille.   *truth / against*

"For, nece, by the goddesse Mynerve,°   *Minerva, Roman goddess of wisdom*
And Jupiter, that maketh the thondre rynge,
And by the blisful Venus that I serve,
235 Ye ben the womman in this world lyvynge—
Withouten paramours, to my wyttynge—⁶
That I best love, and lothest am to greve;°   *am most loath to disturb*
And that ye weten° wel yourself, I leve."°   *know / believe*

"Iwis, myn uncle," quod she, "grant mercy!°   *many thanks (grand merci)*
240 Youre frendshipe have I founden evere yit.°   *always encountered*
I am to no man holden,° trewely,   *beholden*
So muche as yow, and have so litel quyt;°   *requited, repaid*
And with the grace of God, emforth my wit,°   *as far as I can*
As in my gylt° I shal yow nevere offende;   *by my fault*
245 And if I have er this,° I wol amende.°   *before now / make amends*

"But for the love of God I yow biseche,
As ye ben he that° I love moost and triste,°   *are he whom / trust*
Lat be to me youre fremde manere speche,⁷
And sey to me, youre nece, what yow liste."°   *what it pleases you (to say)*
250 And with that word hire uncle anoon hire kiste,
And seyde, "Gladly, leve° nece dere!°   *beloved / dear*
Tak it for good, that° I shal sey° yow here."   *what / tell*

With that she gan hire eighen° down to caste,   *eyes*
And Pandarus to coghe gan a lite,°   *began to cough a little*

4. While the two of them had in hand (i.e., discussed) all they wanted to.
5. "No, this matter takes time," he said then.
6. Apart from amorous relations, in my understanding.
7. Leave off your stranger's manner of speech to me.

35

There he spent time in laughter and sweet words, in merry jests and very affectionate talk, as is customary on such occasions between relatives, like one who wishes to come to his point by ingenious arguments, if he can; and he began to look into her beautiful face very fixedly.

36

Criseida, who noticed this, smilingly said: "Cousin, have you never seen me that you go about memorizing me like this?" To whom Pandaro replied: "You know very well that I have seen you and intend to see you, but you seem to me more beautiful than usual, and, in my opinion, you have more to praise God for than any other beautiful lady."

37

Criseida said, "What does this mean? Why more now than in the past?" To which Pandaro replied gaily and quickly, "Because yours is the most fortunate face that any lady ever had in this world; if I am not deceived, I have heard that it pleases a most excellent man so beyond measure that he is undone by it."

38

When she heard what Pandaro was saying, Criseida, ashamed, reddened somewhat and resembled a morning rose. Then she addressed these words to Pandaro, "Do not laugh at me who would rejoice in every good for you. The man to whom I am pleasing must have little to do, for never before has this happened to me since I was born."

255　And seyde, "Nece, alwey—lo!—to the laste,°　　　　　*in the end*
　　　How so it be that som men hem delite[8]
　　　With subtyl art hire tales° for to endite,°　　　　*stories / compose*
　　　Yet for al that, in hire entencioun°　　　　　　　　*intent*
　　　Hire tale is al for som conclusioun.

260　"And sithe° th'ende is every tales strengthe,　　　　*since*
　　　And this matere is so bihovely,°　　　　　　　　*useful, fitting*
　　　What sholde I peynte or drawen it on lengthe[9]
　　　To yow, that ben my frend so feythfully?"
　　　And with that word he gan right inwardly°　　　　*closely, deeply*
265　Byholden hire and loken on hire face,
　　　And seyde, "On swich a mirour goode grace!"°　　*(may there be) good fortune!*

　　　Than thought he thus: "If I my tale endite°　　　*compose*
　　　Aught harde, or make a proces any whyle,
　　　She shal no savour have therin but lite,[1]
270　And trowe° I wolde hire in my wil bigyle;°　　*believe / deliberately deceive*
　　　For tendre wittes wenen° al be wyle°　　　　*suppose / all is guile*
　　　Theras° thei kan nought pleynly° understonde;　*Where / plainly (or, fully)*
　　　Forthi hire wit to serven wol I fonde"—[2]

　　　And loked° on hire in a bysi wyse,°　　　　*he looked / intently*
275　And she was war° that he byheld hire so,　　　*aware*
　　　And seyde, "Lord! so faste ye m'avise!°　　　*you gaze at me so hard*
　　　Sey° ye me nevere er now? What sey° ye, no?"　*Saw / say*
　　　"Yis, yys," quod he, "and bet wol° er I go!　　*I will all the better*
　　　But be my trouthe, I thoughte now if ye°　*I was just thinking whether you*
280　Be fortunat, for now men shal it se.

　　　"For to every wight som goodly aventure°　　　*good fortune*
　　　Som tyme is shape,° if he it kan receyven;°　*destined / receive*
　　　But if° he wol take of it no cure,°　　　　*Unless / fail to heed it*
　　　Whan that it commeth, but wilfully it weyven,°　*(will) neglect it*
285　Lo, neyther cas° ne fortune hym deceyven,　　*happenstance*
　　　But ryght his verray° slouthe and wrecchednesse;°　*his very own / sorry state*
　　　And swich a wight° is for to blame, I gesse.　　*such a person*

　　　"Good aventure, O beele° nece, have ye　　　*beautiful*
　　　Ful lightly° founden, and° ye konne it take;　*Quite easily / if*
290　And for the love of God, and ek of me,
　　　Cache° it anon, lest aventure slake!°　　　*Seize / slacken, wane*
　　　What° sholde I lenger proces° of it make?　*Why / elaboration*
　　　Yif° me youre hond, for in this world is noon—　*Give*
　　　If that yow list°　a wight so wel bygon.°　*If you please / well-favored*

295　"And sith I speke of° good entencioun,　　　*out of*
　　　As I to yow have told wel herebyforn,°　　*just now*

8. Although it may be that some people take delight.
9. Why should I embellish it or drag it out at length.
1. In any way difficult, or make an elaborate rendition for any time, she shall take but little delight in it.
2. Therefore I will try to accommodate (my rhetoric) to her intelligence.

39

"Let us put aside all jests," said Pandaro then. "Tell me, have you yourself been aware of it?" To which she replied, "No more of one than of another, as surely as I wish not to die. It is true that I see someone pass here from time to time who always gazes fixedly at my door; I do not know if he goes searching to see me or goes musing about something else."

40

Pandaro said then, "Who is this man?" To whom Criseida said, "Truly I do not know him, nor do I know anything further to tell you about him." And Pandaro, who perceived that she was not speaking of Troilo but of someone else, immediately spoke to her thus: "He whom you have wounded is a man who is known by all."

41

"Who then is he who is so pleased to see me?" Criseida said. Then Pandaro said to her, "Lady, since he who circumscribed the world made the first man, I do not believe he ever put a more perfect soul into anyone than that of him who loves you so much that it could never be possible to say how much.

42

"He is noble of soul and of speech, very virtuous, and desirous of honor, in natural judgment wiser than any other man, and no one is greater in knowledge; valiant and spirited, and bright of face, I cannot tell all his worth. Ah, how fortunate is your beauty, since such a man values it more than any other!

43

"Well is the jewel placed in the ring, if you are as wise as you are beautiful. If you become his, as he has become yours, the star will be well joined with the sun; nor was a youth ever so well joined to any maid as you will be to him if you are wise: you will be happy if you will recognize it.

44

"Everyone who lives has fortune in this world only once if he knows how to take it; whoever lets it go, when it comes, weeps for his calamity by himself without blaming another. Your lovely and beautiful face has found it for you; now learn how to use it. Let me weep, who was born in an evil hour, and who was displeasing to God, to the world, and to Fortune."

And love° as wel youre honour and renoun°   *I love / renown, reputation*
As creature° in al this world yborn,   *(any) creature, person*
By alle the othes that I have yow sworn,
300 And° ye be wrooth therfore,° or wene° I lye,   *If / for that reason / suppose*
Ne shal I nevere sen yow eft with yë.°   *eye*

"Beth naught agast,° ne quaketh naught! Wherto?°   *frightened / For what?*
Ne chaungeth naught for fere so youre hewe!°   *hue*
For hardely° the werst of this is do;°   *certainly / done, over with*
305 And though my tale° as now be to yow newe,   *recounting, news*
Yet trist° alwey ye shal me fynde trewe;   *trust, have faith*
And were it thyng that me thoughte unsittynge,[3]
To yow wolde I no swiche tales brynge."

"Now, good em,° for Goddes love, I preye,"   *uncle*
310 Quod she, "come of,° and telle me what it is.   *come on! hurry up!*
For both I am agast what° ye wol seye,   *as to what*
And ek me longeth it to wite, ywis;°   *I long to know it, indeed*
For whethir it be wel or be amys,°   *may be good or bad*
Say on, lat me nat in this feere dwelle."
315 "So wol I doon; now herkeneth! I shall telle:

"Now, nece myn, the kynges deere sone,
The goode, wise, worthi, fresshe, and free,°   *vigorous, and generous*
Which° alwey for to don wel is his wone,°   *For whom / habit*
The noble Troilus, so loveth the,
320 That, but° ye helpe, it wol his bane° be.   *unless / destruction*
Lo, here is al! What° sholde I moore seye?   *Why*
Doth what yow lest° to make hym lyve or deye.[4]   *what pleases you*

"But if ye late° hym deyen, I wol sterve—°   *let / die*
Have here my trouthe, nece, I nyl nat lyen—°   *will not lie*
325 Al sholde I° with this knyf my throte kerve."°   *Even if I were obliged / cut*
With that the teris breste° out of his yën,°   *burst / eyes*
And seide, "If that ye don° us bothe dyen   *you cause*
Thus gilteles, than have ye fisshed fayre!
What mende ye, though that we booth appaire?[5]

330 "Allas, he which that° is my lord so deere,   *who*
That trewe man, that noble gentil knyght,
That naught° desireth but youre frendly cheere,°   *nothing / look, demeanor*
I se hym dyen, ther he goth upryght,°   *where he (seems to) walk erect*
And hasteth hym° with al his fulle myght   *he hastens*
335 For to ben slayn, if his fortune assente.°   *destiny should concur*
Allas, that God yow swich a beaute sente!

"If it be so that ye so cruel be
That of his deth yow liste nought to recche,[6]

---

3. And if it were a matter that seemed improper to me.
4. Pandarus evokes the convention of romance that unrequited love causes death.
5. In this way (since we are) without guilt, then you have made a fine catch! How does it help you, if we both should perish?
6. That you are pleased to care nothing about his death.

45

"Are you tempting me, or do you speak the truth," said Criseida, "or are you out of your senses? Who ought to have full pleasure of me if he should not first become my husband? But who is this man, tell me; is he who is so lost through me a stranger of a citizen? Tell me if you are willing to, and if you ought to tell it to me, and do not cry 'ah me' without reason."

46

Pandaro said, "He is indeed a citizen, not of the lesser kind, and he is very much my friend; I have drawn from his breast, perhaps by the power of destiny, what I have disclosed to you. He lives in weeping, miserable and wretched, because the splendor of your countenance inflames him so, and that you may know who loves you so much, Troilo is he who more than any other desires you."

47

Criseida then halted slightly, looking at Pandaro, and turned such a color as the air does in the morning, and with difficulty held back the tears which came to her eyes ready to fall. Afterwards, as her lost courage returned, she murmured first a little to herself and sighing spoke thus to Pandaro:

That° is so trewe and worthi, as ye se,   *He who*
340 Namoore than of a japer or a wrecche—⁷
    If ye be swich, youre beaute may nat strecche°   *cannot extend (far enough)*
    To make amendes of so cruel a dede;
    Avysement° is good byfore the nede.°   *Deliberation / crisis*

    "Wo worth the faire gemme vertulees!⁸
345 Wo worth that herbe also that dooth no boote!° *provides no remedy*
    Wo worth that beaute that is routheles!°   *ruthless, pitiless*
    Wo worth that wight that tret ech° undir foote! *treads each person*
    And ye, that ben of beaute crop and roote,⁹
    If therwithal° in yow ther be no routhe,°   *together with that / pity*
350 Than is it harm° ye lyven, by my trouthe! *harmful that, too bad that*

    "And also think wel that this is no gaude;°   *trick*
    For me were levere° thow and I and he¹   *I'd rather*
    Were hanged, than I sholde ben his baude,°   *pimp*
    As heigh as° men myghte on us alle ysee!° *(hanged) so high that / see*
355 I am thyn em;° the shame were to° me,   *uncle / would fall on*
    As wel as the, if that I sholde assente°   *concur, participate*
    Thorugh myn abet° that he thyn honour shente.° *abetting, help / injured*

    "Now understond, for I yow nought requere°   *ask*
    To bynde yow to hym thorugh no byheste,°   *promise*
360 But only that ye make hym bettre chiere° *countenance, bearing*
    Than ye han doon er° this, and moore feste,° *before / cheerful attention*
    So that his lif be saved atte leeste;°   *at the least*
    This al and som, and pleynly, oure entente.²
    God help me so, I nevere other mente!°   *meant, intended*

365 "Lo, this requeste is naught but skylle,° ywys, *is only reasonable*
    Ne doute of resoun,° pardee,° is ther noon. *reasonable fear / by God*
    I sette° the worste, that ye dreden° this: *I pose, hypothesize / fear*
    Men wolde wondren sen hym come or goon.³
    Ther-ayeins° answere I thus anoon,° *Against that (fear) / forthwith*
370 That every wight, but he be fool of kynde,° *unless he is a congenital fool*
    Wol deme° it love of frendshipe° in his mynde. *think / (mere) friendly affection*

    "What,° who wol demen, though° he se a man *Why / even though*
    To temple go, that he th'ymages eteth?° *is eating the sacred images*
    Thenk ek° how wel and wisely that he kan *Also consider*
375 Governe hymself, that he no thyng foryeteth,° *forgets, neglects*
    That° where he cometh he pris° and thank hym *So that / praise*
    geteth.°   *receives*

---

7. No more than (you would care) about a trifler or a vile person.
8. Woe betide the fair gem that is without virtue! The "virtue" of a gem is its magical healing property.
9. And you, who are the crown and root of beauty. The *crop* of a plant is its crown of foliage; the idiom *crop and roote* means "the entirety, the be-all and end-all."
1. In the passion of the moment Pandarus shifts to the familiar "thou" form of address for a stanza.
2. This is the whole story, and fully (*or*, candidly), our intention. The word *this* is a common contraction of "this is."
3. That people would be curious about seeing him come or go (to visit you).

And ek therto,° he shal come here so selde,°   *also in addition / seldom*
What fors were it° though al the town byhelde?°   *would it matter / observed it*

"Swych love of frendes regneth al this town;
380 And wre yow in that mantel evere moo,[4]
And God so wys be my savacioun,[5]
As I have seyd, youre beste is° to do soo.   *it is best for you*
But alwey, goode nece, to stynte his woo,°   *bring his distress to a stop*
So lat youre daunger sucred ben a lite,[6]
385 That of his deth ye be naught for to wite."°   *blame*

Criseyde, which that herde hym in this wise,
Thoughte, "I shal felen° what he meneth, ywis."   *feel out*
"Now em,"° quod she, "what wolde ye devise?°   *uncle / advise*
What is youre reed° I sholde don of this?"   *counsel*
390 "That is wel seyd," quod he. "Certein, best is
That ye hym love ayeyn° for his lovynge,   *in turn*
As love for love is skilful guerdonynge.°   *a reasonable recompense*

"Thenk ek how elde wasteth° every houre   *old age consumes*
In ech of yow° a partie° of beautee;   *each of you (i.e., women) / part*
395 And therfore er that age the devoure,
Go love; for old, ther wol no wight of the.[7]
Lat this proverbe a loore° unto yow be: *teaching*
To late ywar,° quod Beaute, whan it paste;°   *Too late aware / has passed*
And Elde daunteth Daunger at the laste.[8]

400 "The kynges fool is wont to crien loude,
Whan that hym thinketh a womman berth hire hye,[9]
'So longe mote° ye lyve, and alle proude,°   *may / all such proud people*
Til crowes feet be growe under youre yë,°   *eye(s)*
And sende yow than a myrour in to prye,[1]
405 In which that ye may se youre face a morwe!'°   *in the morning*
I bidde wisshe yow° namore sorwe."   *I would wish you*

With this he stynte,° and caste adown the heed,°   *stopped / his head*
And she began to breste a-wepe anoon,°   *burst out weeping forthwith*
And seyde, "Allas, for wo! Why nere I° deed?   *were I not*
410 For of this world the feyth is al agoon.°   *has all passed away*
Allas, what sholden straunge° to me doon,   *strangers*
Whan he that for my beste frend I wende°   *whom I took for my best friend*
Ret me to love, and sholde it me defende?[2]

4. Such amity prevails in Troy—and conceal yourself in that cloak (of amity) always.
5. And may God thus surely be my salvation; *or*, And may God so wise be, , , ,
6. Let your haughtiness be sweetened a little, in such a way. *Daunger* in medieval love-talk is the lady's disdain, aloofness, standoffishness. The word derives via French from the root of Latin *dominari*, "to be master, to tyrannize." See II.1376 below.
7. Go love; for (when you are) old, at that point no person will want you.
8. And Old Age intimidates/subdues Haughtiness in the end.
9. The king's jester is wont to cry out aloud when it seems to him that a woman carries herself haughtily. The Fool in *King Lear* exemplifies the *kynges fool*, traditionally an enunciator of sometimes embarrassing truths.
1. And a mirror be sent then for you to peer into.
2. Advises (*redeth*) me to love, but who should prohibit me from it (i.e., from loving).

48

"I used to believe, Pandaro, that, if ever I had fallen into such folly that Troilo might have come into my desire, you would have beaten me, not merely restrained me, as a man who ought to seek my honor. O God help me! What will others do since you now strive to make me follow the rules of love?

49

"I know well that Troilo is great and brave and any great lady ought to be happy with him, but since my husband was taken from me, my desire has been ever far from love, and I have still a sorrowful heart for his grievous death and shall have while I live, calling to memory his departure.

50

"And if anyone ought to have my love, certainly I would give it to him if only I believed that it would please him. But as you should clearly know, the fancies which he now has often occur and last four or five days and then pass away lightly, since love changes as thought changes.

51

"Therefore let me lead such a life as Fortune has prepared for me; he will easily find a lady, both submissive and sweet to love at his pleasure; it is fitting for me to remain chaste. Pandaro, for God's sake, please may this reply not seem grievous to you, and try to comfort him with new pleasures and other amusements."

52

Pandaro felt himself abused when he heard what the lady said, and he almost rose to leave. Then, however, he stopped and turned toward her, saying, "I have praised to you, Criseida, a man whom I would recommend to my own sister or to my daughter or to my wife if I had one; may happiness be granted to me by God.

53

"For I feel that Troilo is worth a much greater thing than your love would be. Yesterday I saw him in such a state from this love that I strongly pitied him. Perhaps you do not believe it and, therefore, do not care about it. I know well that you would necessarily pity him if you were to know what I do of his passion. Ah, have pity on him for love of me.

"Allas! I wolde han trusted, douteles,
415 That if that I, thorugh my dysaventure,°   *misfortune*
Hadde loved outher° hym or Achilles,   *either*
Ector,° or any mannes creature,°   *Hector / human creature*
Ye nolde han had° no mercy ne mesure°   *would have had / moderation*
On me, but alwey had me in repreve.°   *reproach*
420 This false world—allas!—who may it leve?°   *believe in it, trust it*

"What, is this al the joye and al the feste?°   *festivity, pleasure*
Is this youre reed?° Is this my blisful cas?°   *counsel / situation*
Is this the verray mede° of youre byheeste?°   *actual reward, payoff / promise*
Is al this paynted proces° seyd—allas!—   *ornate and specious discourse*
425 Right for this fyn?° O lady myn, Pallas!°   *end / Pallas Athene*
Thow in this dredful cas° for me purveye,°   *frightening situation / provide*
For so astoned° am I that I deye."   *stunned*

Wyth that she gan ful sorwfully to syke.°   *sigh*
"A, may it be no bet?"° quod Pandarus;   *better (than this)*
430 "By God, I shal namore come here this wyke,[3]
And God toforn, that° am mystrusted thus!   *As God is my witness, I who*
I se wel that ye sette lite° of us,   *count for little*
Or of oure deth! Allas, I woful wrecche!
Might he yet lyve, of me is nought to recche.[4]

435 "O cruel god, O dispitouse Marte,°   *spiteful, cruel Mars*
O Furies thre of helle,[5] on yow I crye!
So lat me nevere out of this hous departe,
If I mente harm or vilenye!°   *villainy, impropriety*
But sith° I se my lord mot nedes° dye,   *since / must needs*
440 And I with hym, here I me shryve, and seye[6]
That wikkedly ye don° us bothe deye.[7]   *cause*

"But sith it liketh yow° that I be ded,   *since it pleases you*
By Neptunus, that god is of the see,°   *sea*
Fro this forth° shal I nevere eten° bred   *From this time forth / eat*
445 Til I myn owen herte° blood may see;   *heart's*
For certeyn I wol deye as soone as he."
And up he sterte,° and on his wey he raughte,°   *started / set off*
Tyl she agayn° hym by the lappe° kaughte.   *opposing / garment's fold, hem*

Criseyde, which that wel neigh starf° for feere,   *nearly died*
450 So as° she was the ferfulleste wight°   *Inasmuch as / person*

3. By God, I won't come here any more this week!
4. If only he may yet live, there is nothing to worry about with regard to me.
5. Oh Furies three of hell. See I.6 and accompanying note above.
6. And I (must die) with him, here I make my confession, and say. Pandarus makes as if to confess while at death's door.
7. As the word "die" has two pronunciations in Chaucer's dialect, *dye* and *deye* (lines 439, 441), he admits the two variants, though of single meaning, as separately rhyming. He will also admit homophones as rhymes if they are of different meaning, as the two rhyme words spelled *see* in the next stanza, or the words spelled *longe* in lines 545–46 below. Very rarely will Chaucer rhyme identical words, as *fro* in lines 513, 516 below.

54

"I do not believe that there may be in the world any man more trust-
worthy or more faithful, and no one is as loyal; nor beyond you does he
desire or search; and, though you are dressed in mourning, you are still
young and have the right to love. Do not lose time; remember that old
age or death will take away your beauty."

55

"Alas," said Criseida, "you speak the truth; the years are carrying us away
little by little, and most die before the path given by the celestial fire is
completed. But let us now stop thinking of this, and tell me if I can still
have the solace and joy of love, and in what manner you first became
aware of Troilo.

That myghte be, and herde ek with hire ere°   *ear*
And saugh the sorwful ernest° of the knyght,   *seriousness*
And in his preier ek saugh noon unryght,°   *also saw nothing improper*
And for the harm that myghte ek fallen moore,[8]
455 She gan to rewe° and dredde hire° wonder soore,   *repent, regret / was afraid*

And thoughte thus: "Unhappes fallen thikke°   *Misfortunes happen frequently*
Alday° for love, and in swych manere cas°   *Continually / such a situation*
As° men ben cruel in hemself° and wikke;°   *Where / themselves / wicked*
And if this man sle° here hymself—allas!—   *should slay*
460 In my presence, it wol be no solas.°   *comfort*
What men wolde of hit deme° I kan nat seye;   *judge*
It nedeth me ful sleighly for to pleie."[9]

And with a sorowful sik° she sayde thrie,°   *sigh / thrice*
"A, Lord! What me is tid a sory chaunce!°   *How sad a lot has befallen me!*
465 For myn estat lith in a jupartie,[1]
And ek myn emes° lif is in balaunce;°   *uncle's / at risk*
But natheles, with Goddes governaunce,
I shal so doon,° myn honour shal I kepe,°   *behave so that / preserve*
And ek his lif"—and stynte° for to wepe.   *(she) ceased*

470 "Of harmes two, the lesse is for to chese;°   *one should choose the lesser*
Yet have I levere° maken hym good chere°   *I'd rather / a pleasant demeanor*
In honour, than myn emes lyf to lese.°   *lose my uncle's life*
Ye seyn, ye nothyng elles° me requere?"°   *else / ask of me*
"No, wis,"° quod he, "myn owen nece dere."   *certainly*
475 "Now wel," quod she, "and I wol doon my peyne;°   *take pains (for you)*
I shal myn herte ayeins my lust constreyne.°   *unwillingly constrain*

"But that I nyl nat holden hym in honde,
Ne love a man ne kan I naught ne may
Ayeins my wyl, but elles wol I fonde,
480 Myn honour sauf, plese hym fro day to day.
Therto nolde I nat ones han seyd nay,
But that I drede, as in my fantasye;
But cesse cause, ay cesseth maladie.[2]

"And here I make a protestacioun
485 That in this proces° if ye depper° go,   *business / deeper*
That certeynly, for no salvacioun
Of yow, though that ye sterven bothe two,
Though al the world on o day be my fo,

---

8. And because of the further injury that might also take place.
9. I need to handle the matter very adroitly.
1. For my condition lies in jeopardy.
2. But I will not cajole him with false hopes (*holden hym in honde*, line 477), nor can or may I love a man against my will—but apart from this (*elles*) I will try, as long as my honor is preserved, to please him from day to day. In this connection I would not have denied (your request) once, except that I was afraid in my imaginings—but where the cause may cease, ever the disease will cease. By her last (proverbial) clause Criseyde means that because the cause of her fear—that Pandarus may ask her to perform dishonorably—has ceased, the fear itself ceases.

56

Then Pandaro smiled and replied, "I shall tell it to you since you wish to know it. The day before yesterday, things being quiet because of the truce then made, Troilo wished that I should go strolling with him through the shady woods; there having seated ourselves he began to talk with me of love, and then to sing to himself of it.

57

"I was not near him but, hearing him murmur, I turned my attention toward him, and as far as I can remember, he complained to Love of his torment saying, 'My lord, already what I feel in my heart through the gentle longing which has taken me because of her beauty appears in my face and in my sighs.

58

" 'You dwell there where I bear the image pictured which pleases me more than anything else, and there you behold the soul, which lies prostrated, conquered by your lightning, which holds it bound tightly round, calling ever for that sweet peace which the beautiful and lovely eyes of this lady alone, dear lord, can give to it.

59

" 'Then, for the love of God, if my dying is grievous to you, make it known to this beautiful being, and by imploring her, obtain that joy which cus-

Ne shal I nevere of hym han other routhe."[3]
490 "I graunte wel,"° quod Pandare, "by my trowthe.   *I grant it well, I concur*

"But may I truste wel to yow,"° quod he,   *fully trust in you*
"That of this thyng that ye han hight° me here,   *promised*
Ye wole it holden trewely unto me?"
"Ye, doutelees," quod she, "myn uncle deere."
495 "Ne° that I shal han cause in this matere,"   *Nor*
Quod he, "to pleyne,° or ofter° yow to preche?"   *complain / more often, further*
"Why, no, parde;° what nedeth° moore speche?"[4]   *by God / why is there need*

Tho fellen they in other tales glade,[5]
Tyl at the laste, "O good em," quod she tho,
500 "For his° love, that° us bothe made,   *His, i.e. God's / Who*
Tel me how first ye wisten° of his wo.   *knew, learned*
Woot noon° of it but ye?" He seyde, "No."   *Does anyone know*
"Kan he wel speke of love?" quod she; "I preye
Tel me, for I the bet me shal purveye."°   *will prepare myself the better*

505 Tho Pandarus a litel gan to smyle,
And seyde, "By my trouthe, I shal yow telle.[6]
This other day, naught gon ful longe while,°   *not a very long time ago*
In-with° the palcis° gardyn, by a welle,   *Within / palace*
Gan he and I wel half a day to dwelle,
510 Right for to speken of an ordinaunce,°   *plan*
How we the Grekes myghten disavaunce.°   *repulse*

"Soon after that bigonne we to lepe,°   *leap, exercise*
And casten with oure dartes° to and fro,   *spears*
Tyl at the laste he seyde he wolde slepe,
515 And on the gres adoun° he leyde hym tho;   *down on the grass*
And I afer gan romen° to and fro,   *roamed at a distance*
Til that I herde, as that I welk° alone,   *walked*
How he bigan ful wofully to grone.

"Tho° gan I stalke hym softely byhynde,   *Then*
520 And sikirly,° the soothe° for to seyne,   *certainly / truth*
As I kan clepe ayein° now to my mynde,   *recall*
Right thus to Love he gan hym for to pleyne:
He seyde, 'Lord, have routhe° upon my peyne,   *pity*
Al have I° ben rebell in myn entente;°   *Although I have / intention*
525 Now, mea culpa,[7] lord, I me repente!

---

3. That certainly I shall never take any other form of pity on him (i.e., become his mistress) for any (effort at the) salvation of you, even though you should both die, even if all the world should become my enemy in one day.
4. The words *what nedeth moore speche* may be the narrator's rather than Criseyde's.
5. Then they entered into other pleasant conversation.
6. Possibly the following episode took place, and Pandarus concealed his knowledge when he first spoke with Troilus. This interpretation is made explicit in the *Filostrato* (II.56–62). In other poems, including Chaucer's own *Book of the Duchess*, a narrator seems to conceal what he has overheard from an anguished lover. The convention also occurs elsewhere in the *Filostrato* (VII.77–78 below). But more likely, given Pandarus's wiles and Troilus's less studied grief, Pandarus invents the story to impress Criseyde.
7. A phrase from the formula of contrition, continuing the conceit of the lover's confession: *Mea culpa, mea culpa, mea maxima culpa!*—"My sin, my sin, my most grievous sin!"

tomarily gives peace to your subjects. Ah, do not wish, my lord, that I die. Ah, do this, for the love of God! You see that my anguished soul always cries out day and night since it has such fear that she will slay it.

60

" 'Do you hesitate to kindle your flames under her widow's weeds, my lord? No greater glory will be yours than this; enter into her breast with that desire which dwells in mine and torments me. Ah, bring it about; I pray you for it, compassionate lord, that through you her sweet sighs may bring comfort to my desires.'

61

"And this said, sighing strongly, he bowed his head saying I know not what; then he was silent, almost weeping. Seeing that, there entered into me a suspicion of what the matter was, and I planned, when the time should be more suitable, to ask him one day, smiling, what that song might mean and then the reason for it.

62

"But the time for this did not occur before today when I found him all alone. I went into his room on the chance that he might be there, and he was on his bed, and seeing me he turned away; from this I became somewhat suspicious and drawing nearer found that he was weeping bitterly and was lamenting bitterly.

63

"As I best knew how, I comforted him, and with improvised skill and with varied cunning, I drew from his mouth what troubled him, after I had first pledged my faith to him that I would never tell it to any man. This grief moved me, and because of it I come to you to whom I have in brief conveyed completely in every point what he prays for.

64

"What will you do? Will you remain proud and let him who, through love of you, cares not for himself come to such a cruel death? O horrid destiny, O harsh Fortune, that such a proper man may perish for you!

" 'O god, that° at thi disposicioun°   *God, Who / disposal*
Ledest the fyn by juste purveiaunce[8]
Of every wight, my lowe° confessioun   *humble*
Accepte in gree,° and sende me swich penaunce   *graciously*
530 As liketh the,° but from disesperaunce,°   *As it pleases You / despair*
That may my goost departe° awey fro the,   *Which may separate my soul*
Thow be my sheld, for thi benignite.°   *goodness*

" 'For certes, lord, so soore hath she me wounded,
That° stood in blak, with lokyng of hire eyen,°   *She who / her eyes' glance*
535 That to myn hertes botme it is ysounded,°   *has plummeted*
Thorugh which I woot that I moot nedes deyen.°   *must needs die*
This is the werste, I dar me nat bywreyen;°   *reveal myself*
And wel the hotter ben the gledes rede,
That men hem wrien with asshen pale and dede.'[9]

540 "Wyth that he smot° his hed adown anon,°   *struck, cast / forthwith*
And gan to motre,° I noot° what, trewely.   *mutter / know not*
And I with that gan stille° awey to goon,   *quietly*
And leet° therof as nothing wist° had I,   *let on, pretended / known*
And com ayein anon,° and stood hym by,   *I came back forthwith*
545 And seyde, 'Awake, ye slepen al to° longe!   *too*
It semeth nat that love doth yow longe,[1]

" 'That° slepen so that no man may yow wake.   *You who*
Who sey evere or° this so dul a man?'   *saw ever before*
'Ye, frend,' quod he, 'do ye youre hedes ake[2]
550 For love, and lat me lyven as I kan.'
But though that he for wo was pale and wan,
Yet made° he tho as fresshe a countenaunce   *assumed*
As though he sholde have led the newe daunce.[3]

"This passed forth° til now, this other day,   *So matters stood*
555 It fel° that I com romyng al allone   *happened*
Into his chaumbre, and fond how that he lay
Upon his bed; but man so soore grone°   *for one to groan so grievously*
Ne herde I nevere, and what that was his mone°   *complaint*
Ne wist I nought; for, as I was comynge,
560 Al sodeynly he lefte° his complaynynge.   *left off*

"Of which I took somwat° suspecioun,   *felt in some measure*
And ner I com,° and fond he wepte soore;   *I came nearer*
And God so wys be my savacioun,

---

8. Guides/controls the outcome by just providence/foresight.
9. And the red coals are much the hotter in that people cover them with pale, dead ashes. A proverbial notion derived from Ovid, *Metamorphoses* 4.64.
1. It doesn't seem that love causes you to pine with longing. Pandarus plays off against the convention that lovers are sleepless; see I.921. Troilus has said he knows of lovers' *lyvynge*, behavior, in I.197 above; the tables are turned—see line 550 below, *lat me lyven.* Possibly, with the same import, this line means "It doesn't seem that love pertains to you."
2. May you (lovers) cause your heads to ache.
3. As though he was to be the leader in the new dance. Along with its literal sense (Troilus pretends to be happy and energetic) there is reference to the *daunce* of love, the conduct of courtship.

At least if you were not stingy to him with the sight of your beautiful figure and your eyes, you might perhaps still save him from bitter death."

65

Criseida then said: "From afar you perceived the secret of his breast, although his hand then held it firmly, when you found him weeping on his bed, and so may God make him joyful and sound, and me also, as pity has come to me through your words. I am not cruel, as it seems to you, nor so devoid of pity."

66

She paused awhile, and after a deep sigh, already wounded, she continued: "Ah, I perceive where compassionate desire draws you, and I will do it because I ought to please you by it, and he is worth it, and let it suffice him if I see him; but in order to avoid shame, and perhaps worse, pray him that he be discreet and do what will not be a shame to me, nor to him either.

67

"My sister," said Pandaro then, "you speak well, and I shall pray him to do so. Truly I do not believe that he will fail; I know him to be so well-mannered and discreet—unless it come about through a calamity, may God forbid it—and I shall contrive such recompense in this matter that you shall be pleased. God be with you, and do your duty."

How Criseida, after Pandaro had gone, talked to herself, considering whether she ought to love Troilo or not, and in the end she decides to do so.

68

After Pandaro departed, the beautiful Criseida went alone into her room, revolving in her heart every little word and piece of news from Pandaro in the form in which it had been said, and thinking of Troilo beyond her custom, sighing, joyfully she conversed and talked with herself in this way:

As nevere of thyng hadde I no routhe moore;[4]
565 For neither with engyn,° ne with no loore,°   *ingenuity, stratagem / learning*
Unnethes° myghte I fro the deth hym kepe,   *Hardly*
That yet fele I myn herte for hym wepe.

"And God woot, nevere sith° that I was born   *since*
Was I so besy no man for to preche,
570 Ne nevere was to wight so depe isworn,   *mor An writing thn Boethus*
Or he me told who myghte ben his leche.[5]
But now to yow rehercen al his speche,
Or alle his woful wordes for to sowne,°   *sound, repeat*
Ne bid me naught, but ye wol se me swowne.[6]

575 "But for to save his lif, and elles nought,°   *not for anything else*
And to noon harm of yow, thus am I dryven;
And for the love of God, that us hath wrought,°   *made, created*
Swich cheer hym dooth° that he and I may lyven!   *Behave so to him*
Now have I plat° to yow myn herte shryven,°   *flat out, plainly / confessed*
580 And sith° ye woot that myn entent° is cleene,   *since / intention*
Take heede therof,° for I non yvel meene.   *Pay attention to the matter*

"And right good thrift,° I prey to God, have ye,   *quite good success, luck*
That han swich oon ykaught° withouten net!   *You who have caught such a one*
And be ye wis° as ye be fair to see,   *And if you are as prudent*
585 Wel in the ryng than is the ruby set.
Ther were nevere two so wel ymet,
Whan ye ben his al hool° as he is youre;   *wholly*
Ther myghty God graunte us see that houre!"

"Nay, therof spak I nought, ha, ha!" quod she;
590 "As helpe me God, ye shenden every deel!"°   *spoil everything*
"O, mercy, dere nece," anon quod he,
"What so I spak,° I mente naught but wel,   *Whatever I said*
By Mars, the god that helmed° is of steel!   *helmeted*
Now beth naught wroth,° my blood,° my nece dere."   *angry / kin*
595 "Now wel," quod she, "foryeven be it° here!"   *let it be forgiven*

With this he took his leve, and hom he wente;
And, Lord, he was glad and wel bygon!°   *in a good situation*
Criseyde aros, no lenger she ne stente,°   *stayed, tarried*
But streght into hire closet° wente anon,   *private chamber*
600 And set hire doun as stylle as any ston,
And every word gan up and down to wynde°   *turn over*
That he had seyd, as it com hire to mynde,

4. I never had more pity about anything. The words *As* or *Ther* often stand, untranslatable, at the heads of oaths and strong asseverations; see also lines 588 and 590 below, and compare the modern expression "So help me God!" On *God so wys* see note 5 to 381 above.
5. Was I so busy about haranguing anyone, nor was there ever a person so deeply sworn (i.e., to secrecy), before he told me who his physician might be. Conventionally, as her lover's *leche*, a lady might cure his love-sickness.
6. Don't ask me, unless you wish to see me swoon.

And wex somdel astoned° in hire thought   *grew somewhat astonished*
Right for the newe cas;° but whan that she   *situation*
605 Was ful avysed,° tho fond she right nought°   *Had considered fully / nothing*
Of peril why she ought afered° be.   *frightened*
For man may love, of possibilite,°   *potentially, hypothetically*
A womman so, his herte may tobreste,°   *burst*
And she naught love ayein, but if hire leste.°   *in return, unless it pleased her*

610 But as she sat allone and thoughte thus,
Ascry aros at scarmuch al withoute,[7]
And men criden in the strete, "Se,° Troilus   *See*
Hath right now° put to flighte the Grekes route!"°   *just now / company*
With that gan al hire meyne° for to shoute,   *household*
615 "A, go we se! Cast up the yates wyde!
For thorwgh this strete he moot to paleys ride;[8]

"For other wey is to the yate° noon   *gate*
Of Dardanus, there opyn is the cheyne."[9]
With that com he and al his folk anoon
620 An esy pas° rydyng, in routes tweyne,°   *At a slow gait / two companies*
Right as his happy day was,° sooth to seyne,   *As this was indeed his lucky day*
For which, men seyn, may nought destourbed be
That shal bityden of necessitee.[1]

This Troilus sat on his baye steede
625 Al armed, save his hed, ful richely;
And wownded was his hors, and gan to blede,
On which he rood a pas° ful softely.   *at a walk*
But swich a knyghtly sighte trewely
As was on hym, was nought, withouten faille,
630 To loke on Mars, that god is of bataille.[2]

So lik a man of armes and a knyght
He was to seen, fulfilled of heigh prowesse,
For bothe he hadde a body and a myght
To don that thing,[3] as wel as hardynesse;
635 And ek to seen hym in his gere hym dresse,°   *equip himself in his armor*
So fressh, so yong, so weldy° semed he,   *vigorous*
It was an heven upon hym for to see.°   *to look at him*

His helm tohewen° was in twenty places,   *hewn, hacked*
That by a tyssew heng° his bak byhynde;   *hung by a tissue, band*
640 His sheeld todasshed° was with swerdes and maces,   *broken in pieces*

7. An outcry arose concerning the skirmish outside (the walls of Troy).
8. Ah, let's go see! Throw open the gates wide! He must ride to the palace by way of this street.
9. Where the chain is open. Chains were used to block off streets from horsemen and vehicles. As often, Chaucer draws on sources other than the *Filostrato* for details about the Trojan setting; the gate of Dardanus, one of the six gates of Troy, is named by both Benoît and Guido (see Introduction).
1. Concerning which, people say, that which must happen of necessity may not be prevented. This topic looms large in Book Four.
2. But to look on Mars, who is the god of war, was truly not such a knightly sight, beyond question, as it was to look on him.
3. He was to look at, full of high prowess, for he had both the physique and the power to do that thing (i.e., perform with prowess, possibly with sexual innuendo).

In which men myghte many an arwe fynde
That thirled hadde horn and nerf and rynde;[4]
And ay° the peple cryde, "Here cometh oure joye,   *continually*
And, next° his brother, holder up° of Troye!"   *next to / maintainer, prop*

645 For which he wex° a litel reed for shame   *grew*
When he the peple upon hym herde cryen,
That to byholde it was a noble game
How sobrelich he caste down his yën.°   *eyes*
Criseyda gan al his chere aspien,°   *behold his manner, appearance*
650 And leet it so softe in hire herte synke,
That to hireself she seyde, "Who yaf me drynke?"[5]

For of hire owen thought she wex al reed,
Remembryng hire° right thus, "Lo, this is he   *Recalling to herself*
Which that myn uncle swerith he moot° be deed,   *swears he must*
655 But° I on hym have mercy and pitee."   *Unless*
And with that thought, for pure ashamed,° she   *for very shame*
Gan in hire hed to pulle, and that as faste,°   *very fast (cf. I.300)*
Whil he and alle the peple forby paste,°   *passed by*

And gan to caste° and rollen up and down   *ponder*
660 Withinne hire thought his excellent prowesse,
And his estat,° and also his renown,   *condition, rank*
His wit, his shap,° and ek his gentilesse;   *physique*
But moost hire favour was, for his distresse
Was al for hire, and thoughte it was a routhe
665 To sleen swich oon, if that he mente trouthe.[6]

Now myghte som envious jangle° thus: *some spiteful person chatter*
"This was a sodeyn love; how myght it be
That she so lightly° loved Troilus   *easily, frivolously*
Right for° the firste syghte, ye, parde?"°   *at / by God*
670 Now whoso seith so, mote he nevere ythe!°   *may he never prosper!*
For every thing a gynnyng° hath it nede   *beginning*
Er al be wrought, withowten any drede.°   *Before all is done, doubtless*

For I sey nought that she so sodeynly
Yaf° hym hire love, but that she gan enclyne°   *Gave / began to incline*
675 To like hym first, and I have told yow whi;
And after that, his manhod and his pyne°   *suffering*
Made love withinne hire for to myne,[7]
For which by proces° and by good servyse   *in the course of time*
He gat° hire love, and in no sodeyn wyse.°   *obtained / sudden manner*

680 And also blisful Venus, wel arrayed,
Sat in hire seventhe hous of hevene tho,

---

4. That had pierced horn and sinew and hide—materials of which shields were made.
5. "Who gave me a drink?" That is, any intoxicating beverage, or perhaps a love potion.
6. But what most pleased her was that his distress was all for her, and she thought that it was a pity to slay such a person if he meant well (i.e., had honorable intentions).
7. Made love to mine (i.e., tunnel) within her. Undermining the enemy's fortifications would be part of a siege operation.

Disposed wel, and with aspectes payed,⁸
To helpe sely° Troilus of his woo.   *hapless*
And soth to seyne, she nas not al a foo°   *entirely inimical*
685 To Troilus in his nativitee;°   *at the time of his birth*
God woot that wel the sonner spedde he.⁹

Now lat us stynte° of Troilus a throwe,°   *cease / while*
That rideth forth, and lat us torne faste
Unto Criseyde, that heng° hire hed ful lowe   *hung*
690 Ther as she sat allone, and gan to caste°   *deliberate*
Where on she wolde apoynte hire atte laste,¹
If it so were hire em ne wolde cesse°   *her uncle wouldn't forebear*
For Troilus° upon hire for to presse.   *For Troilus's sake*

And, Lord! So she gan in hire thought argue
695 In this matere of which I have yow told,
And what to doone best were, and what eschue,°   *eschew, avoid*
That plited she ful ofte in many fold.²
Now was hire herte warm, now was it cold;
And what she thoughte somwhat shal I write,
700 As to myn auctour listeth for t'endite.³

She thoughte wel that Troilus persone°   *Troilus's outward appearance*
She knew by syghte, and ek his gentilesse,
And thus she seyde, "Al were it nat to doone°   *Although it would be improper*
To graunte hym love, yet for his worthynesse
705 It were honour with pley and with gladnesse
In honestee° with swich a lord to deele,°   *propriety / deal, converse*
For myn estat,° and also for his heele.°   *social standing / welfare*

"Ek wel woot I my kynges sone is he,
And sith he hath to se me swich delit,
710 If I wolde outreliche° his sighte flee,   *utterly*
Peraunter° he myghte have me in dispit,°   *Perhaps / might scorn me*
Thorugh whicch I myghte stonde in worse plit.°   *plight, condition*
Now were I wis, me hate to purchace,°   *to bring hatred on myself*
Withouten need, ther° I may stonde in grace?°   *where, when / favor*

715 "In every thyng, I woot, ther lith mesure;°   *lies moderation*
For though a man forbede° dronkenesse,   *should forbid*
He naught forbet° that every creature   *doesn't require*

8. And also joyous Venus, well situated, sat then in her seventh house of the sky, favorably inclined,
and propitious in her "aspects" (relations with other planets). The term *hous* refers to one of the
twelve divisions of the sky formed by great circles passing through the north and south points of
the horizon. (Alternatively, it may refer to the house of the zodiacal sign Libra; the omen would
be the same.) The seventh house, just above the western horizon, is Venus's station as the evening
star, and is auspicious. The other planets are also in a favorable relationship with Venus, and
further, as the following lines say, Venus was in a favorable position at Troilus's birth. All the
omens suggest that Troilus will fare well under Venus's influence, that is, in loving.
9. God knows that he prospered all the more speedily.
1. At what place she would settle at the last.
2. Quite often she pleated that (matter) in many a fold (i.e., she turned it over in her mind).
3. According as it pleases my authority/source to compose it. The narrator refers again to his pre-
tended source, Lollius. In fact, in what follows Chaucer diverges persistently from his actual
source, the *Filostrato*.

69

"I am young, beautiful, lovely and gay, a widow, rich, noble, and beloved, without children and leading a quiet life. Why should I not be in love? If perhaps propriety forbids me this, I shall be discreet and keep my desire so hidden that it shall never be known that I have ever had love in my heart.

70

"My youth takes flight each hour; should I lose it so wretchedly? In this land I do not even know any woman without a lover, and, as I know, I see most people fall in love, and I lose my time for nothing. To do as others is not a sin, and no one can be blamed.

Be drynkeles for alwey, as I gesse.°   *suppose*
Ek sith° I woot for me is his destresse,   *Also since*
720 I ne aughte nat° for that thing hym despise,   *I ought not*
Sith it is so he meneth in good wyse.°   *Since it's so that he means well*

"And ek I knowe of longe tyme agon°   *since a long time ago*
His thewes° goode, and that he is nat nyce;°   *moral character / foolish*
N'avantour,° seith men,° certein, he is noon;   *Nor a boaster / it is said*
725 To° wis is he to doon so gret a vice;   *Too*
Ne als I nyl° hym nevere so cherice°   *And because I won't / cherish*
That he may make avaunt, by juste cause,°   *a boast, with just reason*
He shal me nevere bynde in swich a clause.°   *article, legal stipulation*

"Now sette a caas:° the hardest is, ywys,°   *pose a hypothesis / certainly*
730 Men myghten demen° that he loveth me.   *That people might suppose*
What dishonour were it unto me, this?
May ich hym lette of that?° Why, nay, parde!   *prevent him from that?*
I knowe also, and alday° heere and se,   *continually*
Men loven wommen al biside hire leve,°   *quite without their permission*
735 And whan hem leste° namore, lat hem   *it pleases them*
    byleve!°   *leave off, depart*

"I thenke ek how he able is for to have
Of al this noble town the thriftieste°   *worthiest, most admirable*
To ben his love, so° she hire honour save.   *as long as*
For out and out° he is the worthieste,   *out and out, altogether*
740 Save only Ector, which that is the beste;
And yet his lif al lith° now in my cure.°   *lies / keeping, power*
But swich is love, and ek myn aventure.°   *fortune*

"Ne me to love,° a wonder is it nought;   *And (for one) to love me*
For wel woot I myself, so God me spede—°   *may God prosper me*
745 Al wolde I° that noon wiste° of this thought—   *Although I would wish / knew*
I am oon the faireste,° out of drede,°   *the very fairest / doubtless*
And goodlieste, who that taketh hede,°   *whoever takes note (of it)*
And so men seyn,° in al the town of Troie.   *people say*
What wonder is though° he of me have joye?   *is it even though*

750 "I am myn owene womman, wel at ese—
I thank it God—as after myn estat,
Right yong, and stonde unteyd in lusty leese,[4]
Withouten jalousie or swich debat:°   *quarrel, disputing*
Shal noon housbonde seyn to me 'Chek mat!'°   *Checkmate!*
755 For either they ben ful of jalousie,
Or maisterfull, or loven novelrie.[5]

"What shal I doon? To what fyn° lyve I thus?   *For what purpose*
Shal I nat love, in cas if that me leste?

---

4. I am an independent woman, comfortably off—thank God—with regard to my estate (situation in life, or, wealth), quite young, and I stand untethered in a pleasant pasture.
5. Or domineering, or they love novelty (i.e., new loves).

71

"Who will ever want me when I grow old? Certainly no one, and to see one's error then is nothing other than to increase one's woe. It is of no value to repent afterwards or to say sorrowing, 'Why did I not love?' It is good, therefore, to make provision in time: this man who loves you is handsome, well-bred, wise, and well-mannered, and fresher than the lily in the garden.

72

"Of royal blood and of highest worth and your cousin Pandaro praises him so much to you. Then what are you doing? Why not receive him somewhat in your heart as he has you? Why not give your love to him? Do you not hear the pitifulness of his plaint? O, how much happiness will you also have with him if you love him as he loves you!

73

"Now is not the time for a husband and even if it were, to keep one's liberty is much the wiser part. Love which comes from such friendship is always very pleasing between lovers, but, let beauty be as great as one wishes, it will soon grow distasteful to married men, who desire something fresh every day.

74

"Stolen water is a far sweeter thing than wine had in abundance; so the joy of love which is hidden surpasses greatly that of a husband always held in one's arms; then receive with zest the sweet love which is certainly sent to you by God and give satisfaction to his burning desire."

75

Then she stopped awhile; then she turned herself in another direction, saying, "Wretched one, what do you wish to do? Do you not know what a cruel life languishing love draws with it in which it is always necessary that it exists in plaints, in sighs, and in suffering, and then it has, in addition, jealousy, which is much worse than a miserable death?

76

"Besides this, he who now loves you is of much higher rank than you are; this amorous desire will pass from him and he will hold you ever in scorn, and will leave you wretched, full of infamy and shame. Watch what you do, because good sense when it comes too late never was, nor is, nor ever will be of any value.

What, pardieux!° I am naught religious.°   *by God / in a religious order*
760 And though that I myn herte sette at reste
Upon this knyght, that° is the worthieste,   *who*
And kepe° alwey myn honour and my name,   *(though I) preserve*
By alle right,° it may do me no shame."   *By all rights, In fairness*

But right as when the sonne shyneth brighte
765 In March, that chaungeth ofte tyme his° face,   *its*
And that° a cloude is put with wynd to flighte,   *when*
Which oversprat° the sonne as for a space,°   *overspreads, covers / while*
A cloudy thought gan thorugh hire soule pace,°   *pass*
That overspradde hire brighte thoughtes alle,
770 So that for feere almost she gan to falle.

That thought was this: "Allas! Syn° I am free,   *Since*
Sholde I now love, and put in jupartie
My sikernesse,° and thrallen° libertee?   *security / enslave*
Allas, how dorst° I thenken that folie?   *dared*
775 May I naught wel in other folk aspie°   *observe*
Hire dredfull° joye, hire constreinte,° and hire peyne?   *fearful / distress*
Ther loveth noon, that she nath why to pleyne.°   *hasn't cause to complain*

[handwritten:] no one loves who has no reason to complain
[handwritten:] (has loved ?)

77

"But even suppose that this love should endure a long time, how can you know that it is destined to remain concealed? It is very vain to trust to Fortune, and human counsel cannot see well what is advantageous to do; and if it is disclosed openly, you can consider your reputation, which up to now has been so good, lost eternally.

78

"Therefore leave such loves to those to whom they are pleasing." Then after she had said this, she began to sigh strongly, and she could not now thrust from her chaste bosom the handsome face of Troilo; therefore she returned to her first impression, blaming and praising, and in such uncertainty, she made for herself a long delay.

"For love is yet the mooste stormy lyf,
Right of hymself,° that evere was bigonne;   *in itself*
780 For evere som mystrust or nice strif°   *foolish contention*
Ther is in love, som cloude is over that sonne.
Therto° we wrecched wommen nothing konne,°   *Furthermore / know how to do*
Whan us is wo,° but wepe and sitte and thinke;   *When misery befalls us*
Oure wrecche is this, oure owen wo to drynke.⁶

785 "Also thise wikked tonges ben so prest°   *are so ready*
To speke us harm; ek men ben so untrewe,
That right anon as cessed is hire lest,⁷
So cesseth love, and forth° to love a newe.   *(they go) forth*
But harm ydoon is doon, whoso it rewe:°   *no matter who may regret it*
790 For though thise men for love hem first torende,°   *at first tear themselves up*
Ful sharp° bygynnyng breketh° ofte at ende.   *A very eager / breaks off*

"How ofte tyme hath it yknowen be
The tresoun° that to wommen hath ben do!   *treason, treachery*
To what fyn° is swich love I kan nat see,   *To what end, For what purpose*
795 Or wher bycometh it,° whan that it is ago.°   *what becomes of it / gone*
Ther is no wight that woot, I trowe so,⁸
Where it bycometh. Lo, no wight on it sporneth.°   *stumbles (i.e., it vanishes)*
That erst° was nothing, into nought it torneth °   *What at first / turns*

"How bisy, if I love, ek most° I be   *also must*
800 To plesen hem that jangle° of love, and dremen,   *chatter, gossip*
And coye hem, that° they seye noon harm of me!   *cajole them, so that*
For though ther be no cause, yet hem semen
Al be for harm that folk hire frendes quemen;⁹
And who may stoppen every wikked tonge,
805 Or sown° of belles whil that thei ben ronge?"   *the sound*

And after that, hire thought gan for to clere,
And seide, "He which that nothing undertaketh,
Nothyng n'acheveth, be hym looth or deere."°   *whether he likes it or not*
And with an other thought hire herte quaketh.
810 Than slepeth hope, and after drede awaketh.   *— double bind*
Now hoot, now cold; but thus, bitwixen tweye,°   *(torn) between the two things*
She rist hire up, and went hire for to pleye.¹

Adown the steyre° anonright° tho she wente   *stairs / forthwith*
Into the gardyn with hire neces° thre,   *nieces*
815 And up and down ther made many a wente—°   *turn*
Flexippe, she, Tharbe, and Antigone—
To pleyen that it joye was to see;

6. Our misery is this, (that we have) to drink our own woe (i.e., endure trouble of our own making).
   To have to drink one's own woe (or shame) was a proverbial expression similar in force to the
   modern "eat one's hat."
7. That just as soon as their desire has ceased.
8. There is no person who knows, so I believe.
9. For though there be no cause, yet it seems to them that the fact that people please (*quemen*) their
   friends is all for harm (i.e., for some bad purpose).
1. She rises up, and goes (*went* = *wendeth*) out to amuse herself.

And other° of hire wommen, a gret route,°   *others / company*
Hire folowede in the gardyn al aboute.

820 This yerd° was large, and rayled° alle th'aleyes,°   *yard, garden / fenced / pathways*
And shadewed wel with blosmy bowes° grene,   *boughs*
And benched newe, and sonded alle the weyes,²
In which she walketh arm in arm bitwene,
Til at the laste Antigone the shene°   *bright*
825 Gan on a Troian song to singen cleere,
That it an heven was hire vois to here.°   *to hear her voice*

She seyde, "O Love, to whom I have and shal
Ben humble subgit,³ trewe in myn entente,
As I best kan, to yow, lord, yeve ich° al   *I give*
830 For everemo myn hertes lust to rente;°   *my heart's pleasure as tribute*
For nevere yet thi grace no wight sente
So blisful cause as me, my lif to lede
In alle joie and seurte out of drede.⁴ [*free of fear / doubtless*]

"Ye, blisful god, han me so wel byset°   *established*
835 In love, iwys,° that al that bereth lif°   *certainly / all who live*
Ymagynen ne kouth° how to be bet;°   *cannot / better*
For, lord, withouten jalousie or strif,
I love oon which is moost ententif°   *minded, diligent*
To serven wel, unweri or unfeyned,°   *not weary or feigned*
840 That evere was, and leest with harm
    desteyned.°   *stained with harmful intentions*

"As he that is the welle° of worthynesse, [*in my heart, a mirror of Criseyde*]   *the fount, source*
Of trouthe grownd, mirour of goodlihed,°   *excellence*
Of wit Apollo, stoon of sikernesse,°   *security, steadfastness*
Of vertu roote, of lust fynder and hed,°   *of pleasure originator and head*
845 Thorough which° is alle sorwe fro me ded—°   *Through whom / dead, passed*
Iwis, I love hym best, so doth he me;
Now good thrift° have he, wherso° that he be!   *prosperity / wherever*

"Whom shulde I thanken but yow, god of Love,
Of al this blisse, in which to bathe I gynne?°   *I begin to bask*
850 And thanked be ye, lord, for that I love!
This is the righte lif that I am inne,
To flemen° alle manere vice and synne: *banish, put to flight*
This dooth° me so to vertu for t'entende,°   *causes / incline*
That day by day I in my wille amende.°   *grow better*

855 "And whoso seith that for to love is vice,
Or thraldom,° though he feele in it destresse,°   *enslavement / distress*
He outher° is envyous, or right nyce,°   *either / foolish*

---

2. And newly provided with benches, and with all the paths sanded.
3. O Love, to whom I have been and shall be a humble subject.
4. For your favor has never before sent to any person so happy a reason as (you have sent) to me, (a reason) for leading my life in all joy and security free from fear. Alternatively, *thi grace* (line 831) may mean "Your Grace," as a formal address to the god of Love, and *out of drede* (line 833) may mean "doubtless."

Or is unmyghty,° for his shrewednesse,°   *unab[]*
To loven; for swich manere folk, I gesse,
860 Defamen Love, as nothing of hym knowe.
Thei speken, but thei benten nevere his bowe!⁵

"What is the sonne wers, of kynde right,⁶
Though that a man, for fieblesse of his yën,°   *feebleness of his eyes*
May nought endure on it to see for bright?°   *because of its brightness*
865 Or love the wers, though wrecches on it crien?
No wele is worth, that may no sorwe dryen.⁷
And forthi,° who that hath an hed of verre,°   *therefore / glass*
Fro cast° of stones war hym° in the werre!°   *throwing / let him beware / war*

"But I with al myn herte and al my myght,
870 As I have seyd, wol love unto my laste
My deere herte and al myn owen knyght,
In which° myn herte growen is so faste,   *whom*
And his in me, that it° shal evere laste.   *it (our love)*
Al dredde I first° to love hym to bigynne,   *Although I feared at first*
875 Now woot I wel, ther is no peril inne."

And of hir song right with that word she stente,°   *stopped*
And therwithal, "Now nece," quod Cryseyde,
"Who made this song now with so good entente?"
Antygone answerde anoon° and seyde,   *forthwith*
880 "Madame, ywys,° the goodlieste mayde   *indeed*
Of gret estat° in al the town of Troye,   *rank, social condition*
And let° hire lif in moste honour and joye."   *one who leads* (ledeth)

"Forsothe,° so it semeth by hire song,"   *In truth*
Quod tho Criseyde, and gan therwith to sike,⁸
885 And seyde, "Lord, is ther swych blisse among
Thise loveres, as they konne faire endite?"⁹
"Ye, wis,"° quod fresshe Antigone the white,°   *certainly / fair*
"For alle the folk that han or ben on lyve°   *have been or are alive*
Ne konne wel the blisse of love discryve.°   *describe*

890 "But wene ye° that every wrecche woot   *do you suppose*
The parfit blisse of love? Why, nay, iwys!
They wenen all be love, if oon be hoot.¹
Do wey,° do wey, they woot no thyng of this!   *Leave off! Away with you!*
Men moste axe at° seyntes if it is   *must ask of*

---

5. They talk but they never bent his (Love's) bow! As marginal notes in two manuscripts of the poem indicate, Chaucer alludes to a proverb, "Of Robin Hood speak many men who never bent his bow," that is, never attempted dealing do for themselves.
6. How is the sun any the worse, in its own nature.
7. Or (how is) love the worse, though wretches cry out against it? No happiness that cannot endure any sorrow is of value. The following expression about heads of glass is also proverbial, like the modern "People who live in glass houses shouldn't throw stones."
8. Criseyde said then, and began at that to sigh. The word *sike* here is the only clear instance in Chaucer's works of an assonance rather than a full rhyme (though *yeden* in line 936 below is also an imperfect rhyme). A proposed emendation to a word derived from Old Norse, *site*, "be anxious," is unlikely, as it is extremely rare (one recorded use) and found only in the northern dialect area.
9. Such that they can compose (songs) beautifully?
1. They think that all is love, if one (of them) is hot (with passion).

895 Aught° fair in hevene (Why? For they kan telle), *At all*
And axen fendes is it° foul in helle." *whether it is*

Criseyde unto that purpos° naught answerde, *point, argument*
But seyde, "Ywys, it wol be nyght as faste."° *very soon*
But every word which that she of hire herde,° *heard from her (i.e., Antigone)*
900 She gan to prenten° in hire herte faste, *imprint*
And ay gan love hire lasse for t'agaste²
Than it dide erst,° and synken° in hire herte, *at first / (love began) to sink*
That she wex° somwhat able to converte. *So that she grew*

The dayes honour, and the hevenes yë,° *eye*
905 The nyghtes foo—al this clepe° I the sonne— *call*
Gan westren° faste, and downward for to wrye,° *move westward / turn*
As he that° hadde his dayes cours yronne,° *Like one who / run*
And white thynges wexen° dymme and donne° *grew / dun, dark*
For lak of lyght, and sterres for t'apere,
910 That° she and alle hire folk in went yfeere.° *So that / went indoors together*

So whan it liked hire° to go to reste, *it pleased her*
And voided° weren thei that voiden oughte, *withdrawn*
She seyde that to slepen wel hire leste.° *would please her well*
Hire wommen soone til° hire bed hire broughte. *to*
915 Whan al was hust,° than lay she stille and thoughte *hushed*
Of al this thing; the manere and the wise
Reherce° it nedeth nought, for ye ben wise. *Repeat*

A nyghtyngale, upon a cedre grene,
Under° the chambre wal ther as° she ley, *Beside / where*
920 Ful loude song ayein° the moone shene,° *facing toward / bright*
Peraunter in his briddes wise a lay³
Of love, that made hire herte fressh and gay.
That herkned she° so longe in good entente, *She listened to that*
Til at the laste the dede° slep hire hente.° *deadly, deep / seized*

925 And as she slep, anonright tho hire mette⁴
How that an egle, fethered whit as bon,° *bone*
Under hire brest his longe clawes sette,
And out hire herte he rente,° and that anon, *tore*
And dide° his herte into hire brest to gon— *caused*
930 Of which she nought agroos, ne nothyng smerte—⁵
And forth he fleigh,° with herte left for herte. *flew*

Now lat hire slepe, and we oure tales holde° *continue our story*
Of Troilus, that is to paleis riden
Fro the scarmuch° of the which I tolde, *skirmish*
935 And in his chaumbre sit° and hath abiden° *sits / has waited*
Til two or thre of his messages yeden° *messengers went*

2. And love ever began to terrify her less.
3. Perhaps in its bird's manner a song.
4. Immediately then she dreamed. Cf. V.1234–41 below.
5. About which she had no fear, and felt no pain.

Pandaro reports what he has done to Troilo, who, after seeing Criseida, feels strong hope and rejoices greatly.

79

Pandaro, who was content after parting from Criseida, returned directly to Troilo without turning elsewhere, and began from afar to say to him: "Comfort yourself, brother, for I have, I believe, fulfilled a large part of your great desire." And sitting down he told him swiftly without interruption how it had happened.

80

As little flowers drooping and closed by the cold of the night, when the sun whitens them, all open upright on their stems; so in Troilo his tired power recovered itself, and looking to the heavens he began, like a person freed: "Praised be your greatest power, beautiful Venus, and that of your son Love."

81

Then he embraced Pandaro a thousand times and kissed him as much again, so happy that he would not have been more so if a thousand Troys had been given to him; and very softly he went from there, with Pandaro alone, to behold the beauty of Criseida, watching intently if he saw any new behavior in her through what Pandaro had said.

For Pandarus, and soughten hym ful faste,
Til they him founde and broughte him at the laste.

This Pandarus com lepyng in atones,°   *leaping in at once*
940 And seyde thus: "Who hath ben wel ibete°   *beaten*
To-day with swerdes and with slynge-stones,
But Troilus, that hath caught hym an hete?"°   *fever*
And gan to jape,° and seyde, "Lord, so ye swete!°   *joke / how you sweat!*
But ris and lat us soupe° and go to reste."   *sup*
945 And he answerde hym, "Do we as the leste."°   *as you please*

With al the haste goodly that they myghte°   *that they could decently make*
They spedde hem fro the soper unto bedde;
And every wight° out at the dore hym dyghte,°   *person / departed*
And where hym liste upon his wey him spedde.[6]
950 But Troilus, that thoughte his herte bledde
For wo, til that he herde som tydynge,°   *news*
He seyde, "Frend, shal I now wepe or synge?"

Quod Pandarus, "Ly stylle and lat me slepe,
And don thyn hood; thy nedes spedde be![7]
955 And ches° if thow wolt synge or daunce or lepe!   *choose*
At shorte wordes,° thow shal trowen me;°   *In brief / you must trust me*
Sire, my nece wol do° wel by the,   *wishes to do*
And love the° best, by God and by my trouthe,   *you*
But lak of pursuyt make it in thi slouthe.[8]

960 "For thus ferforth° I have thi werk bigonne   *far*
Fro day to day, til this day by the morwe°   *until this morning*
Hire love of frendshipe° have I to the wonne,   *friendly affection*
And therto hath she leyd hire feyth to borwe.
Algate a foot is hameled of thi sorwe!"[9]
965 What° sholde I lenger sermoun° of it holde?   *Why / further palaver*
As ye han herd byfore, al he hym tolde.

But right as floures, thorugh the cold of nyght
Iclosed,° stoupen° on hire stalke lowe,   *Closed up / droop*
Redressen hem ayein° the sonne bright,   *And stand again when facing*
970 And spreden on hire kynde cours by rowe,[1]
Right so gan tho his eighen° up to throwe   *eyes*
This Troilus, and seyde, "O Venus deere,
Thi myght, thi grace, yheried° be it here!"   *praised*

And to Pandare he held up bothe his hondes,
975 And seyde, "Lord, al thyn be that I have!°   *may all I have be yours*
For I am hool,° al brosten° ben my bondes.   *whole, healed / burst*

6. And sped on his way wherever he pleased.
7. And don your hood; your needs have met with success! The phrase *don thyn hood* is of uncertain
sense: keep your shirt on! be at ease! prepare for bed! get ready to go (to sleep)!
8. Unless lack of perseverance, in your sloth, make it (otherwise).
9. And of this she has put down her good word as a pledge. At any rate one foot of your sorrow has
been crippled (hambled). Troilus's anxiety is like a pursuing hound now lamed.
1. And open up (spread) in their natural course in rows.

Looking at Criseida enkindles Troilo more, of which he speaks to Pandaro, who counsels him that he should write to her, and he does so.

82

She was standing at one of her windows, and was perhaps awaiting what happened; neither harsh nor forbidding did she show herself toward Troilo when he looked at her, but at all times over her right shoulder she gazed toward him modestly. Troilo turned away from there delighted at that, giving thanks to Pandaro and to God.

83

And that trepidation which held Criseida between two courses of action fled away as she praised to herself his manners, his pleasing actions, and his courtesy. And so suddenly was she taken that she desired him above every other good, and she strongly grieved at the time lost when she had not known his love.

84

Troilo sings and rejoices wondrously, jousts, gives and spends gladly, and often renews and changes his apparel, loving more fervently each hour; and because of the pleasure involved it is not an irksome thing to him to always follow and see Criseida discreetly who, no less discreet, showed herself to him at prearranged times beautiful and gay.

85

But as we see, through continual experience, the more the wood, the greater the fire, it thus happens that when hope increases very often love also increases; and from then on with greater force than usual Troilo felt the noble desire spur him in his captive heart, from which sighs and torments returned more strongly than at first.

86

Sometimes Troilo lamented strongly to Pandaro about this, saying, "Unhappy me, Criseida with her beautiful eyes has so taken life away from me that I expect to die through the fervent desire that presses so furiously upon my heart that in it I glow and burn. Ah what shall I do, I who should be content with her great courtesy alone?

87

"She gazes at me, and allows me to look at her in a respectable way; this should be enough for my inflamed desires, but my greedy appetite would wish I know not what more, so badly regulated are the ardors that excite it, and he who has not experienced it would not believe how much this flame, which becomes greater each hour, torments me.

A thousand Troyes whoso that me yave,[2]
Ech after other,° God so wys me save,   *one after the other*
Ne myghte me so gladen; lo, myn herte,
980 It spredeth so for joie it wol tosterte!°   *burst*

2. Whoever may have given them to me.

88

"What shall I do then? I don't know what to do except to call on you, beautiful Criseida; you alone are she who can aid me, you worthy lady; you are she who alone can assuage my fire, O sweet light and dear flame of my heart; now if I could be with you a winter's night, then I would remain a hundred and fifty in Hell.

89

"What shall I do, Pandaro? Do you say nothing? You see me glow in such a fire, and do you give the appearance of having no thought for my sighs? Ah, do you see how I burn? Help me, I pray you dearly, tell me what I may do, counsel me a little; if from you or from her I do not have succor, I am caught in the toils of death."

90

Pandaro said then, "I see well and hear what you say, nor have I ever feigned, nor shall I ever pretend to give aid to your sufferings, and always I am ready to do for you not only what is fitting but anything without being urged either by force or by prayer. Let me see openly your noble desire.

91

"In everything I know that you are more perceptive than I, six to one, but nevertheless if I were in your place, I would write to her in my own hand about my entire suffering, and beyond this I would pray her by God, and by love, and by her courtesy that she should care for me, and this letter I shall bear to her without delay.

92

"And besides this, to the limit of my power, I shall again pray her to have mercy on you. We shall be able to see what she will reply, and already my soul believes for a certainty that her response will be sure to please you; and so write, and put all your faith in it, each of your sufferings, and afterwards your desire; leave out nothing that may be expressed there."

"But, Lord, how shal I doon? How shal I lyven?
Whan shal I next my deere herte see?
How shal this longe tyme awey be dryven
Til that° thow be ayein at hire° fro me?   *Until / at her house*
985 Thow maist answer, 'Abid,° abid,' but he   *Abide, Wait, Be patient*
That hangeth by the nekke, soth to seyne
In gret disese abideth for the peyne."

"Al esily,° now, for the love of Marte,"°   *Be easy / Mars*
Quod Pandarus, "for every thing hath tyme.³
990 So longe abid til that the nyght departe,
For also siker° as thow list° here by me,   *as sure / lie down*
And God toforn,° I wol be ther at pryme;°   *as my witness / early morning*
And forthi, werk° somwhat as I shal seye,   *act*
Or on som other wight this charge leye.°   *impose this task*

995 "For, pardee, God woot I have evere yit
Ben redy the to serve, and to° this nyght   *up to*
Have I naught feyned,° but emforth my wit°   *evaded (the task) / as far as I can*
Don al thi lust,° and shal with al my myght.   *performed your every desire*
Do now as I shal seyn, and far aright;°   *fare well*
1000 And if thow nylt, wite al thiself thi care!
On me is nought along thyn yvel fare.⁴

"I woot wel that thow wiser art than I
A thousand fold, but if I were as thow,°   *if I were you*
God help me so, as I wolde outrely°   *by all means*
1005 Of myn owen hond write hire right now
A lettre, in which I wolde hire tellen how
I ferde amys,° and hire biseche of routhe.°   *fared badly / for pity*
Now help thiself, and leve° it nought for slouthe!°   *neglect / sloth*

"And I myself wol therwith° to hire gon;   *with it (i.e., the letter)*
1010 And whan thow woost that I am with hire there,
Worth° thow upon a courser° right anon—   *Mount / swift warhorse*
Ye, hardily,° right in thi beste gere—°   *assuredly / armor*
And ryd forth by the place, as nought ne were,°   *as if no scheme were afoot*
And thow shalt fynde us, if I may, sittynge
1015 At som wyndow, into the strete lokynge.

"And if the list,° than maystow us salue;°   *it pleases you / greet, salute*
And upon me make thow thi countenaunce;°   *And fix your gaze on me*
But by thi lif, be war° and faste eschue°   *wary / strictly avoid*
To tarien ought°—God shilde us fro meschaunce!°   *linger at all / misfortune*
1020 Rid forth thi wey, and hold thi governaunce;°   *keep control of yourself*

---

3. For every thing has its time. From Ecclesiastes 3:1.
4. And if you will not, blame all your trouble on yourself! Your poor progress is not (will not be) owing to me.

93

This advice pleased Troilo greatly, but as a timid lover, he replied, "Ah me, Pandaro, you will see that, as ladies are observed to be bashful, Criseida for shame will reject the letter which you will carry with angry words, and we shall have worsened our state beyond measure."

94

To this Pandaro said: "If it pleases you, do what I say and then let me work, for, as I pray that Love may place me among those with whom he is at peace, I believe that I shall bring you a reply to it made by her own hand. If it displeases you, you can remain timid and saddened by it. You will then lament your torment because it will not remain for you to be made happy through me."

95

Then said Troilo, "Let your pleasure be done; I shall go and write, and I pray Love that through his courtesy he may make fruitful the writing and the letter and the journey." And he went away to his room, and like a wise man at once wrote a letter to his dearest lady, and thus he said:

And we shal speek of the° somwhat, I trowe,°   *you / believe*
Whan thow art gon, to don thyn eris glowe!⁵

"Towchyng° thi lettre, thou art wys ynough.   *With regard to*
I woot thow nylt it dygneliche endite,
1025 As make it with thise argumentes tough;
Ne scryvenyssh or craftyly thow it write;⁶
Biblotte° it with thi teris° ek a lite;°   *Blot / tears / little*
And if thow write a goodly word al softe,°   *tenderly*
Though it be good, reherce° it nought to° ofte.   *repeat / too*

1030 "For though the beste harpour upon lyve°   *harpist alive*
Wolde on the beste sowned° joly harpe   *best sounding*
That evere was, with alle his fyngres fyve
Touche ay o stryng,° or ay o werbul° harpe,   *always (just) one string / tune*
Were his nayles° poynted nevere so sharpe,   *fingernails*
1035 It sholde maken every wight to dulle,°   *be bored*
To here his glee,° and of his strokes fulle.°   *music-making / sated*

"Ne jompre ek no discordant thyng yfeere,⁷
As thus,° to usen termes of phisik°   *For example / medicine*
In loves termes; hold of thi matere
1040 The forme alwey, and do that it be lik;⁸
For if a peyntour wolde peynte a pyk°   *pike*
With asses feet, and hedde it as an ape,°   *give it the head of an ape*
It cordeth naught, so were it but a jape."⁹

This counseil liked wel° to Troilus,   *was well pleasing*
1045 But, as a dredful° lovere, he seyde this: *fearful*
"Allas, my deere brother Pandarus,
I am ashamed for to write, ywys,
Lest of° myn innocence I seyde amys,°   *Lest in / spoke wrongly*
Or that she nolde it for despit° receyve;   *spite, resentment*
1050 Than were I ded: ther myght it nothyng weyve."°   *nothing could avert it*

To that Pandare answered, "If the lest,°   *If you please*
Do that I seye, and lat me therwith gon;°   *go with it (i.e., the letter)*
For by that Lord that formede est° and west,   *east*
I hope of it to brynge answere anon
1055 Of hire hond; and if that thow nylt noon,°   *if you don't wish it*
Lat be, and sory mote he ben his lyve
Ayeins thi lust that helpeth the to thryve."¹

Quod Troilus, "Depardieux,° ich assente!   *By God*
Sith that the list,° I wil arise and write;   *Since it pleases you*

5. When you have gone, (speech that will) make your ears glow! Cf. the modern expression, "make one's ears burn," said of someone being talked about when not present.
6. I know you won't wish to compose it in a haughty style, so as to put on airs with (elaborate) argumentation, or write it in a formal scrivener's manner or artfully.
7. Also don't jumble together discordant things. This stanza recalls Horace's famous advice at the beginning of his *Art of Poetry*.
8. Always keep the (appropriate) form for your subject matter, and make it be in accord.
9. It is not at all fitting, unless it were a joke.
1. Let it go, and may he who helps you to prosper against your will be sorry all his life.

Troilo writes to Criseida that the love he bears her and his sufferings move him to write, and he asks her for her mercy.

96

"How can he who is placed in suffering, in heavy weeping, and in a grievous state, as I am placed for you, lady, wish anyone good health? Certainly it should not be asked of him; and so I depart from what others do, and only because of this you shall not here be wished good health by me because I do not have it unless you give it to me.

97

"I cannot escape what Love wishes, who has before now made bold men more timid than I, and he constrains me to write the words which you will see, and he wishes to be completely obeyed by me as he is used to be; therefore if through me there shall be a mistake in this letter, blame him for it, and I pray you, my sweet hope, to give me pardon.

98

"Your high beauty, and the splendor of your lovely eyes and of your distinguished manners, your dear modesty and your womanly worth, your ways and actions more praised than others have in my mind fixed him for my lord and you for my lady so that no other accident except death will ever be strong enough to draw you away from it.

99

"Whatever I may do, your beautiful image always brings into my heart a thought which hunts out any other which speaks of anyone other than you alone, although of any other my soul has in truth no care, since it has been made a handmaid of your worth in which I alone hope; and your name is always in my mouth, and touches my heart with greater desire every hour.

100

"From these things, lady, is born a fire which tortures my soul day and night without allowing me to find a place to rest. My eyes weep and my breast sighs for this, and I feel myself little by little consumed by this ardor which stirs within me; therefore it is necessary for me to have recourse solely to your power, if I wish to have well-being.

1060 And blisful God prey ich with good entente,
The viage,° and the lettre I shal endite,°   *undertaking / compose*
So spede it;° and thow, Minerva, the white,[2]   *May He (God) prosper it*
Yif° thow me wit my lettre to devyse."°   *Give / compose*
And sette hym° down, and wrot right in this wyse: *And he sat*

1065 First he gan hire his righte° lady calle,   *true*
His hertes lif, his lust,° his sorwes leche,°   *delight / physician*
His blisse, and ek° thise other termes alle   *also*
That in swich cas thise loveres alle seche;°   *seek out*
And in ful humble wise, as in his speche,°   *as to his manner of speaking*
1070 He gan hym recomaunde° unto hire grace;   *commend himself*
To telle al how, it axeth muchel° space.   *asks much*

And after this ful lowely° he hire preyde   *humbly*
To be nought wroth,° thogh he, of his folie,   *angry*
So hardy° was to hire to write, and seyde   *bold*
1075 That love it made,° or elles most he° die,   *caused / otherwise he must*
And pitousli gan mercy for to crye;
And after that he seyde—and leigh ful loude—°   *lied quite palpably*
Hymself was litel worth, and lasse he koude;[3]

2. Minerva the fair. Minerva is the Roman goddess of wisdom, corresponding to the Greek Athena.
3. That he was worth little and knew less.

101

"You alone, when you wish, can bring these vexatious sufferings to sweet peace; you alone, my lady, can bring this painful affliction to true repose; you alone with your works of charity can remove from me the torment which so undoes me; you alone, as my lady, can fulfill that which my heart desires.

102

"Therefore, if anyone ever through pure fidelity, if ever through great love, if through desire to serve well each hour in every case, whether it may result in either good or evil, deserved grace, grant that I may be one of them, my dear lady, grant that I may be that one, I who have recourse to you as to her who is the cause of all my sighs.

103

"I know well that I have never merited by my service that for which I come, but you alone, who have wounded my heart, and no other can make me worthy of a greater thing as you can when you will. O desired happiness of my heart, put down the high disdain of your great soul and be as gracious to me as you are noble in your actions.

104

"Now I am certain that you will be as pitiful as you are beautiful, and will yet turn into sweet joy my grievous pain, discreetly joyous and gracious one, if you do not wish that I should die wretched through loving you so much, delightful lady; and I pray you for it, if my prayer has power, by that love for which you now have greater care.

105

"Although I am a small gift, and of little power, and may be worth much less, I am without fail all yours; now you are wise: if I do not speak fully, you will understand, I know, better what I do not say, and likewise I hope that your deeds will be better and greater than my merits; may Love dispose your heart to this.

106

"I had many more things to say, but in order not to grieve you I shall be silent, and in conclusion I pray the sweet lord Love that, as he has placed you in my delight, so with the same willingness he may put me in your desire, so that, as I am yours, at some time you may become mine, and may never be taken from me."

107

Then after writing all these things on a paper, he folded it in order, and on his cheeks all tearful he bathed his signet, and then sealed it and put it into Pandaro's hand, but first a thousand times and more he kissed it saying, "My letter, you will be blissful when you come into the hands of such a lady."

Pandaro takes the letter from Troilo to Criseida, who before she would take it was disturbed a little.

108

Pandaro, taking the devout letter, went from there to Criseida, who, when she saw him come, left the company with whom she was and went part way to meet him; as an orient pearl looks, so she looked, fearful and desiring; and they greeted one another from afar; then took each other by the hand.

109

Then said Criseida: "What business now brings you here? Have you other news?" Without delay Pandaro said to her, "For you I have good and fair news but not such for another, as these wretched writings will show you of him whom I seem to see dying—so little do you care for him.

And that she sholde han his konnyng° excused,   *understanding, savoir-faire*
1080 That litel was, and ek he dredde° hire soo;   *feared*
And his unworthynesse he ay acused;°   *ever accused, imputed*
And after that than° gan he telle his woo—   *then*
But that was endeles, withouten hoo—°   *cessation*
And seyde he wolde in trouthe° alwey hym holde;   *faithfully*
1085 And radde° it over, and gan the lettre folde.   *(he) read*

And with his salte teris gan he bathe
The ruby in his signet,° and it sette   *signet, seal ring*
Upon the wex deliverliche and rathe,°   *deftly and quickly*
Therwith a thousand tymes er he lette°   *before he left off*
1090 He kiste tho° the lettre that he shette,°   *then / closed up*
And seyde, "Lettre, a blisful destine
The shapyn is:° my lady shal the see!"°   *is destined for you / see you*

This Pandare tok the lettre, and that bytyme°   *early*
A-morwe,° and to his neces paleis sterte,°   *In the morning / hurried*
1095 And faste he swor that it was passed prime,°   *prime, about 9:00 A.M.*
And gan to jape,° and seyde, "Ywys,° myn herte,   *joke / Indeed*
So fressh it is, although it sore smerte,°   *may hurt badly*
I may naught slepe nevere a Mayes morwe;°   *May morning*
I have a joly wo, a lusty° sorwe."   *pleasant*

1100 Criseyde, whan that she hire uncle herde,
With dredful° herte, and desirous to here   *fearful*
The cause of his comynge, thus answerde:
"Now, by youre fey,° myn uncle," quod she, "dere,   *faith*
What manere wyndes gydeth° yow now here?   *kind of wind guides*
1105 Tel us youre joly wo and youre penaunce.°   *suffering*
How ferforth be ye put° in loves daunce?"   *far have you progressed*

"By God," quod he, "I hoppe° alwey byhynde!"   *hop*
And she to laughe,° it thoughte° hire herte brest.°   *laughed / seemed / burst*
Quod Pandarus, "Loke alwey that ye fynde
1110 Game in myn hood;[4] but herkneth, if yow lest!°   *if you please*
Ther is right now come into town a gest,°   *visitor*
A Greek espie,° and telleth newe thinges,   *spy*
For which I come to telle yow tydynges.°   *news*

"Into the gardyn go we, and ye shal here,
1115 Al pryvely,° of this a long sermoun."°   *in privacy / discussion*
With that they wenten arm in arm yfeere°   *together*

---

4. See how you always find game in my hood, i.e., find me amusing.

110

"Take it and look at it diligently, and any reply will make him happy." Criseida stood timorously without taking it, and her gentle aspect changed a little, and then softly she said, "My Pandaro, as I pray Love may place you in a state of peace, have a little respect for me, not merely for the young man.

111

"Consider whether what you now ask for is fitting, and you yourself be a judge of this and look if I do well in taking this, and whether your request is really proper. It is not desirable in order to alleviate the sufferings of another to do an unchaste act. Ah, do not leave it with me, my Pandaro; carry it back, for the love of God."

112

Pandaro, somewhat disturbed at this, said, "This is a strange thing to see—that toward what is most strongly desired by women, each one shows herself, in the presence of others, revolted and angered. I have spoken to you so much about this that you should not now be bashful with me; I pray you that you do not deny me this now."

113

Hearing him Criseida smiled and took it and put it in her bosom. Then she said to him, "When I have leisure, I shall look it over thoroughly, as best I can; if, in doing this, I do less than well, the reason will be that I am not able to do less than your pleasure. May God witness it from heaven and make allowance for my innocence."

Into the gardyn from the chaumbre down;[5]
And whan that he so fer was that the sown
Of that he spak° no man heren myghte,°   *Of what he said / could hear*
1120 He seyde hire thus, and out the lettre plighte:°   *plucked*

"Lo, he that is al holy° youres free°   *wholly / entirely*
Hym recomaundeth lowely° to youre grace,   *Humbly commends himself*
And sente yow this lettre here by me.
Avyseth yow on it,° whan ye han space,°   *Think it over / time*
1125 And of som goodly answere yow purchace,°   *provide yourself*
Or, helpe me God, so pleynly for to seyne,°   *to speak plainly*
He may nat longe lyven for his peyne."

Ful dredfully tho° gan she stonden stylle,   *fearfully then*
And took it naught, but al hire humble chere°   *countenance*
1130 Gan for to chaunge, and seyde, "Scrit ne bille,°   *Writing nor petition*
For love of God, that toucheth swich° matere,   *touches on such a*
Ne bryng me noon; and also, uncle deere,
To myn estat° have more reward,° I preye,   *condition / regard*
Than to his lust!° What sholde I more seye?   *pleasure, desire*

1135 "And loketh° now if this be resonable,   *consider*
And letteth° nought, for favour ne for slouthe,°   *desist / favoritism or sloth*
To seyn a sooth;° now were it covenable°   *true thing / appropriate*
To myn estat, by God and by youre trouthe,
To taken it, or to han of hym routhe,[6]
1140 In harmyng of myself, or in repreve?°   *as a reproach (to me)*
Ber it ayein,° for hym that ye on leve!"°   *Carry it back / believe in*

This Pandarus gan on hire for to stare,
And seyde, "Now is this the grettest wondre
That evere I seigh!° Lat be this nyce fare!°   *saw / foolish behavior*
1145 To dethe mot I smyten be° with thondre,   *may I be struck, smitten*
If for the citee which that stondeth yondre,
Wolde I a lettre unto yow brynge or take
To harm of yow! What list yow thus it make?[7]

"But thus ye faren, wel neigh alle and some,
1150 That he that most desireth yow to serve,
Of hym ye recche leest wher he bycome,[8]
And whethir that he lyve or elles sterve.°   *die*
But for al that that ever° I may deserve,   *for the sake of whatever*
Refuse it naught," quod he, and hente° hire faste,   *seized*
1155 And in hire bosom the lettre down he thraste,°   *thrust*

> LITERALLY
Pandarus is
putting the love
in
movement

---

5. Chaucer here and elsewhere in the poem tells of the subterfuges necessary for obtaining privacy in a medieval/Trojan household, even for the head of the household.
6. To receive it (i.e., the letter), or to have pity on him.
7. Would I wish to bring or convey a letter to you to your harm! Why are you pleased to take it this way?
8. But you (women) behave, nearly all of you, so that you care the least regarding him, as to what may become of him, who most desires to serve you.

Criseida reads Troilo's letter with delight and, being pleased to be kindly toward him, she is strongly disposed to love him.

114

Pandaro left after having given it to her, and she, being very eager to see what it said, having found an occasion, left her company, and went from there to sit in her room, and after unfolding it, read and reread the letter with pleasure, and saw clearly that Troilo was very much more on fire than appeared in his actions.

115

This was pleasing to her because she felt the spirit in her heart transfixed, by which she lived much afflicted, although it did not show outwardly at all. And each written word well noted, she praised and thanked Love for it, saying to herself, "It is fitting that I find both time and place to quench this fire.

116

"For if I let it multiply into too great a flame, it might happen that my hidden desire might be seen in the loss of color of my face, which would be no little calamity to me. And for myself I do not intend to die, or to make another die when with pleasure I can avoid my own and another's distress.

117

"I shall certainly not be so disposed as I have been up to this point. If Pandaro returns for an answer, I shall give it to him amiably and agreeably, even if it should cost me something, as it does not; and Troilo will never be able to call me cruel. I wish that I were now in his sweet arms, pressed face to face!"

And seyde hire, "Now cast it awey anon,
That folk may seen and gauren on us tweye."°   *stare at the two of us*
Quod she, "I kan abyde° til they be gon";   *wait*
And gan to smyle, and seyde hym, "Em,° I preye,   *Uncle*
1160 Swich answere as yow list,° youreself purveye,°   *pleases you / provide*
For trewely I nyl no lettre write."
"No? than wol I," quod he, "so ye endite."[9] *Compose aloud*

Therwith she lough,° and seyde, "Go we dyne."°   *laughed / to dine*
And he gan at hymself to jape° faste,   *poke fun*
1165 And seyde, "Nece, I have so gret a pyne°   *suffering*
For love, that everich other day I faste—"°   *fast, forego eating*
And gan his beste japes forth to caste,°   *throw out, tell*
And made hire so to laughe at his folye,
That she for laughter wende for to dye.°   *thought she would die*

1170 And whan that she was comen into halle,
"Now, em," quod she, "we wol go dyne anon."
And gan some of hire wommen to hire calle,
And streght° into hire chambre gan she gon;   *directly*
But of hire besynesses this was on—[1]
1175 Amonges othere thynges, out of drede—°   *doubtless*
Ful pryvely° this lettre for to rede;   *secretly*

Avysed° word by word in every lyne,   *Having considered*
And fond no lak, she thoughte he koude good,[2]
And up it putte, and wente hire in to dyne.
1180 But Pandarus, that in a studye° stood,   *(brown) study, reverie*
Er he was war,° she took hym by the hood,   *aware (of her presence)*
And seyde, "Ye were caught er that ye wiste."[3]
"I vouche sauf,"° quod he. "Do what you liste."°   *grant it / pleases you.*

Tho wesshen° they, and sette hem down, and ete;   *washed up*
1185 And after noon ful sleighly° Pandarus   *slyly*
Gan drawe hym° to the wyndowe next the strete,   *draw himself, move*
And seyde, "Nece, who hath araied° thus   *decorated*
The yonder hous, that stant aforyeyn° us?"   *stands opposite*
"Which hous?" quod she, and gan for to byholde,
1190 And knew it wel, and whos it was hym tolde;

9. So long as you compose (and dictate) it. Pandarus jokingly suggests that Criseyde cannot write, and there is evidence that many educated medieval women could read but not write. It turns out that she can write, though she claims never to have written a personal letter before (lines 1213– 14 below).
1. But among her occupations this was one.
2. And having found no fault, she thought that he was well skilled (in letter-writing and wooing), that he had savoir-faire.
3. You were caught before you knew (that I was here). Apparently such a surprise granted one a wish.

Pandaro returns for a reply to Criseida, who after some words promises to write one and does so.

118

Pandaro, whom Troilo often urged, returned to Criseida and said smilingly, "Lady, how does my friend's writing impress you?" She turned red instantly without saying anything else but "God knows that." To which Pandaro said, "Have you replied?" Joking, she said to him, "So soon?"

119

"If I am ever to be able to work for you," Pandaro said, "do it now." And she to him: "I do not know how to do it well." "Ah," said Pandaro, "try to satisfy him; Love customarily knows how to teach well. Upon my faith, I have so great a desire to comfort him that you would not believe it. Your reply alone could do this."

120

"I shall do it because it pleases you so much, but may God grant that the matter goes well!" "Ah, yes, it will do so," said Pandaro, "inasmuch as he to whom it gives more pleasure than anything else is worth it." Then he departed, and in a corner of her room where any other was accustomed to come most rarely, she sat down to write in the following manner:

Criseida replies to Troilo in a way which, while neither committing herself nor releasing herself from obligation, cautiously lets him suspect her love.

121

"To you, discreet and powerful friend, whom Love strongly beguiles for me as a man unduly taken by me, Criseida, her honor preserved, sends greeting and then humbly recommends herself to your high worth, desirous of pleasing you as long as my honor and chastity may be safe.

122

"I have had from him who loves you so perfectly that he does not now care for any honor of mine or for my reputation pages full of your writing, in which I read about your wretched life, not without grief, as I hope to have a fortune which may be valuable to me, and although they are decorated with tears, I have gazed at them intently.

And fillen forth in speche° of thynges smale,   *they fell into conversation*
And seten° in the windowe bothe tweye.°   *sat / the two of them*
Whan Pandarus saugh tyme unto his tale,°   *his chance to speak (privately)*
And saugh wel that hire folk were alle aweye,
1195 "Now, nece myn, tel on," quod he; "I seye,
How liketh yow° the lettre that ye woot?°   *pleases you / (now) know*
Kan he theron?° For, by my trouthe, I noot."°   *Has he skill about it? / know not*

Therwith al rosy hewed tho wex she,°   *then she grew*
And gan to homme,° and seyde, "So I trowe."°   *hum / believe*
1200 "Aquite° hym wel, for Goddes love," quod he;   *Repay*
"Myself to medes wol the lettre sowe."[4]
And held his hondes up, and sat on knowe;°   *knelt*
"Now, goode nece, be it nevere so lite,°   *little*
Yif° me the labour it to sowe and plite."°   *Give / fold up*

1205 "Ye, for I kan so writen," quod she tho;
"And ek I noot what I sholde to hym seye."[5]
"Nay, nece," quod Pandare, "sey nat so.
Yet at the leeste thonketh hym, I preye,
Of° his good wille, and doth° hym nat to deye.   *For / cause*
1210 Now, for the love of me, my nece deere,
Refuseth nat at this tid° my prayere!"   *time*

"Depardieux,"° quod she, "God leve° al be wel!   *By God / grant*
God help me so, this is the firste lettre
That evere I wroot, ye, al or any del."°   *as a whole or in any part*
1215 And into a closet,° for t'avise hire° bettre,   *private chamber / take thought*
She wente allone, and gan hire herte unfettre°   *to unfetter*
Out of desdaynes° prisoun but a lite,   *Disdain's, Haughtiness's*
And sette hire down, and gan a lettre write,

Of which to telle in short is myn entente
1220 Th'effect,° as fer as I kan understonde.   *gist, substance*
She thanked hym of al that he wel mente
Towardes hire, but holden hym in honde°   *cajole him with false hopes*
She nolde nought, ne make hireselven bonde°   *bond, unfree*
In love; but as his suster, hym to plese,
1225 She wolde fayn to doon his herte an ese.°   *gladly comfort his heart*
She shette° it, and to Pandare in gan goon,   *closed*
Ther as he sat and loked into the strete,
And down she sette hire by hym on a stoon
Of jaspre, upon a quysshyn gold-ybete,°   *gold-embroidered cushion*
1230 And seyde, "As wisly° help me God the grete,°   *surely / great*
I nevere dide thing with more peyne°   *pain, difficulty*
Than writen this, to which ye me constreyne,"°   *constrain, force*

And took it hym.° He thonked hire and seyde,   *gave it to him*
"God woot, of thyng ful often looth bygonne°   *reluctantly begun*

---

4. I myself in return will sew up the letter. For privacy letters would be folded, sewn, and sealed.
5. "Yea, for I can, indeed, write," she said then; "And also I don't know what I should say to him."

123

"And having considered everything reasonable and having examined your affliction and your demand, your faith, and your hope, I do not see how I can very suitably satisfy your request, wishing well and fully to have regard for what is most received with favor in the world, that is, to live and die with a good reputation.

124

"Although it would be well to please you if the world were such as you would have it be; yet because it is what it is, it is perforce necessary for us to take it as it is; if we do otherwise, desperate punishment might follow from it. Despite myself I still must put aside the pity for you which increased itself in me; you will be little satisfied for it by me.

125

"But so great is the worth which I perceive in you that I know that you will clearly see what is fitting for me and that you will be satisfied with that which I reply to you and will moderate your grave suffering, which greatly displeases and troubles my heart, and in truth, if it were not unbecoming, willingly I should do what would please you.

126

"As you can see, of little value is the writing and the art in this letter, which I would wish might bring you more pleasure, but one cannot do what one now wishes; perhaps the power to do this will sometime take the place of good intentions, and if that possibility does not seem bad to you, give some respite to your sorrow because each word has not been given an answer.

127

"There is no need here for protesting, as you do, that you are unworthy, because I am certain that you would do everything; and in truth, though I am of little value, you could and can have me for yours much more than a thousand times, if the cruel fire does not burn me, which I am certain you would not wish. Nor do I say any more but only that I pray God that your desire and mine be satisfied."

1235 Comth ende good; and nece myn, Criseyde, *with difficulty / won over*
That ye to hym of hard° now ben ywonne°
Oughte he be glad, by God and yonder sonne;° *sun*
For-whi men seith, 'Impressiounes lighte
Ful lightly ben ay redy to the flighte.'[6]

1240 "But ye han played tirant neigh to° longe, *tyrant almost too*
And hard was it youre herte for to grave.° *engrave, make an impression on*
Now stynte, that ye no lenger on it honge,
Al wolde ye the forme of daunger save,[7]
But hasteth you to doon° hym joye have; *cause*
1245 For trusteth wel, to long ydoon hardnesse° *resistance too long maintained*
Causeth despit° ful often for destresse." *resentment*

And right as they declamed° this matere, *discussed*
Lo, Troilus, right at the stretes ende,
Com rydyng with his tenthe som yfere,° *together with his party of ten*
1250 Al softely,° and thiderward° gan bende° *slowly / thither / turn*
Ther as they sete,° as was° his way to wende° *sat / it was / pass*
To paleis-ward;° and Pandare hym aspide,° *toward (his own) palace / spotted*
And seyde, "Nece, ysee who comth here ride!

"O fle° naught in (he seeth us, I suppose), *flee*
1255 Lest he may thynken that ye hym eschuwe."° *avoid*
"Nay, nay," quod she, and wex° as red as rose. *grew*
With that he gan hire humbly to saluwe° *salute*
With dredful chere, and oft his hewes muwe;[8]
And up his look debonairly° he caste, *graciously*
1260 And bekked on° Pandare, and forth he paste.° *nodded to / passed*

God woot if he sat on his hors aright,° *properly*
Or goodly was biseyn,° that ilke° day! *was good to look at / same*
God woot wher° he was lik a manly knyght! *whether*
What° sholde I drecche,° or telle of his aray?° *Why / delay / array, equipment*
1265 Criseyde, which that alle thise thynges say,° *saw*
To telle in short, hire liked al in-fere,° *all together pleased her*
His persoun, his aray, his look, his chere,° *demeanor*

His goodly manere, and his gentilesse,
So wel that nevere, sith that° she was born, *since*
1270 Ne hadde she swych routh of° his destresse; *such pity for*
And how so° she hath hard ben here-byforn, *insofar as*
To God hope I, she hath now kaught a thorn,

6. For which reason people say, "Shallow impressions are ever ready for flight quite lightly/quickly/ easily." Pandarus means that the difficulty of wooing Criseyde suggests that, once she has submitted, her love will endure; she isn't flighty. One manuscript glosses this passage with a Latin proverb, "Levis impressio, levis recessio" (light impression, light recession), i.e., "Soon learned, soon forgotten." This time Pandarus doesn't give her a chance to say that she hasn't been *ywonne* yet (cf. lines 589–90 above).
7. Now cease, so that you no longer remain undecided, even though you wish to preserve the appearance of aloofness.
8. With a fearful demeanor, and often to change his hue.

She° shal nat pulle it out this nexte wyke.°   *That she / week*
God sende mo swich thornes on to pike!⁹

1275 Pandare, which that stood hire faste by,
Felte iren hoot,° and he bygan to smyte,   *That the iron was hot*
And seyde, "Nece, I pray yow hertely,°   *earnestly*
Tel me that I shal axen yow a lite:¹
A womman that were of his deth to wite,°   *blame*
1280 Withouten his gilt, but for hire lakked routhe,°   *because pity was lacking in her*
Were it wel doon?" Quod she, "Nay, by my trouthe!"

"God help me so," quod he, "ye sey me soth.°   *tell me the truth*
Ye felen wel youreself that I nought lye.
Lo, yond he rit!"° Quod she, "Ye, so he doth!"   *yonder he rides*
1285 "Wel," quod Pandare, "as I have told yow thrie,°   *thrice*
Lat be youre nyce° shame and youre folie,   *fastidious*
And spek with hym in esyng° of his herte;   *comforting*
Lat nycete nat do yow bothe smerte."²

But theron was to heven and to doone.³
1290 Considered al thing° it may nat be;   *All things considered*
And whi? For speche;° and it were ek to° soone   *Because of gossip / also too*
To graunten hym so gret a libertee,
For pleynly° hire entente, as seyde she,   *plainly (or, entirely)*
Was for to love hym unwist,° if she myghte,   *without his knowledge*
1295 And guerdoun° hym with nothing but with sighte.   *to reward*

But Pandarus thought, "It shal nought be so,
Yif that I may;° this nyce° opynyoun   *If I am able / foolish*
Shal nought be holden fully yeres° two."⁴   *years*
What° sholde I make of this a long sermoun?   *Why*
1300 He moste assente on that conclusioun,⁵
As for the tyme; and whan that it was eve,
And al was wel, he roos° and tok his leve.   *rose*

And on his wey ful faste homward he spedde,
And right for joye he felte his herte daunce;
1305 And Troilus he fond° allone abedde,°   *found / in bed*
That lay, as do thise lovers, in a traunce
Bitwixen° hope and derk disesperaunce.°   *Between / despair*
But Pandarus, right at his in-comynge,
He song, as who seyth, "Somwhat I brynge,"⁶

9. May God send others such thorns (i.e., pangs of love) to (have to) pluck out! Alternatively *mo* may go with *thornes*, "more of such thorns." Chaucer (or his narrator) may slyly allude to his own difficulties in courting a *hard* (cruel, reluctant) woman (line 1271).
1. Tell me a little concerning what I shall (or, must) ask you about.
2. Don't let scrupulosity cause you both to be in pain.
3. But in this matter there was (required) exertion and activity.
4. Pandarus exaggerates in jest. The usual period of formal mourning by a widow was two years; this may have suggested the number to Pandarus.
5. He had to concur with that conclusion, i.e., with Criseyde's less than complete acquiescence, because of her fear of gossip and fear that things were going too fast.
6. Sang out, as someone who says, "I have brought something for you."

Troilo receives Criseida's reply and examines it with Pandaro, taking joyful hope from it.

128

And when she had spoken in such a way, she folded it and sealed it and gave it to Pandaro, who straightway seeking the youth Troilo, went with it to him and gave it to him with the greatest delight. Having taken it, he read what was written in it sighing with joy, his heart changing according to the words.

129

But in the end, however, carefully repeating to himself everything she had written, he said to himself. "If I understand her, love constrains her, but like a guilty person, she still goes covering herself under a shield; but if love gives me the strength to suffer, she will not be able to last long before she will come to say something entirely different."

130

And the matter also seemed like that to Pandaro, with whom he discussed everything. Therefore more than usual Troilo was cheered, leaving somewhat his sad grief, and he hopes that the hour is destined to come soon which ought to yield up the fruit of his suffering, and this he implores, and day and night beseeches, like one whose heart desires this alone.

Troilo's ardor growing, Pandaro, desirous of serving him, induces Criseida to want to be with him.

131

From day to day his ardor grew more, and although hope helped to sustain him, still he was heavy at heart, and it must be believed that it troubled him greatly; therefore it can be judged that many times out of his great fervor he wrote letters, to which there came to him a reply, now sweet and now bitter, now often and now seldom.

132

Therefore he often complained of Love and of Fortune, which he considered his enemy, and often he said to himself, "Alas, if the nettle of love would prick her even a little, as it pierces and undoes me, my life,

1310 And seyde, "Who is in his bed so soone
Iburied thus?" "It am I, frend," quod he.
"Who, Troilus? Nay, help me so the moone,"°   *moon (a mild oath)*
Quod Pandarus, "thow shalt arise and see
A charme° that was sent right now to the,   *medicinal incantation (the letter)*
1315 The which kan helen the° of thyn accesse,°   *heal you / attack of fever*
If thow do forthwith al thi bisynesse."°   *due diligence*

"Ye, thorough the myght of God," quod Troilus,
And Pandarus gan hym the lettre take,°   *give*
And seyde, "Parde,° God hath holpen° us!   *By God / helped*
1320 Have here a light, and loke on al this blake."°   *black (ink)*
But ofte gan the herte glade° and quake   *gladden*
Of Troilus, whil that he gan it rede,
So as the wordes yave° hym hope or drede.   *According as the words gave*

But finaly, he took al for the beste
1325 That she hym wroot, for somwhat he byheld
On which hym thoughte° he myghte his herte reste,   *it seemed to him*
Al° covered she tho° wordes under sheld.°   *Although / those / a shield*
Thus to the more worthi° part he held,   *favorable*
That what for hope and Pandarus byheste,°   *Pandarus's promise*
1330 His grete wo foryede he at the leste.[7]

But as we may alday° oureselven see,   *every day*
Thorough more wode or col,° the more fir,   *With more wood or coal*
Right so encreese hope,° of what° it be,   *when hope increases / whatever*
Therwith ful ofte encresseth ek desir;
1335 Or as an ook comth of a litil spir,°   *shoot*
So thorugh this lettre which that she hym sente
Encrescen° gan desir, of which he brente.°   *To increase / burned*

Wherfore I seye° alwey, that day and nyght   *say*
This Troilus gan to desiren moore
1340 Thanne he did erst,° thorugh hope, and did his   *at first*
    myght°   *exerted himself*
To preessen° on, as by Pandarus loore,°   *push / instruction*
And writen to hire of his sorwes soore.
Fro day to day he leet° it nought refreyde,°   *allowed / grow cold*
That by Pandare he wroot somwhat or seyde;[8]

1345 And dide also his other observaunces
That til° a lovere longeth° in this cas;°   *to / belong / situation*
And after that thise dees torned on chaunces,[9]

7. At least he set aside the greater part of his suffering.
8. In that (daily) he wrote or said something (conveyed to Criseyde) by Pandarus.
9. And according as these dice turned up one number or another. Dice could indicate one's luck in a love affair.

begging for solace, would soon come to the gracious port which I may die without gaining."

133

Pandaro, who perceived the flames enkindled in the breast of him whom he loved, was often lavish with his prayers to Criseida, and related to her all that he observed of Troilo. Although she heard it gladly, she said, "I can do nothing else; I am doing for him, my dear brother, what you imposed on me."

134

"That is not enough," Pandaro replied. "I wish that you would comfort him and that you would speak to him." To him Criseida said in reply, "This I do not intend ever to do for him, for the crown of my chastity I do not intend on any account to give him; as a brother I shall always love him with firm honorableness for his great goodness."

135

Pandaro replied, "This crown the priests praise in those from whom they cannot take it, and each talks like a saint and then surprises all of you women in sleep. No one will ever know about Troilo; now he suffers much and nevertheless he controls himself well. Very poorly does he act who can do well and does not, and the more a man knows the more loss of time is displeasing to him."

136

Criseida said, "I know that his virtue is sensitive to my honor and that he will not ask from me anything other than what is fitting, so great is his worthiness; and I swear to you by my salvation, that I am, aside from what you ask, a thousand times more his than I am mine, so much does his courtesy please me."

137

"If he pleases you, what are you seeking? Ah, let this thorniness go. Do you intend that he should die of love? You can certainly consider your beauty dear if you kill such a man; ah, tell me, when do you wish him to come to you, when he praises more than he does Heaven, and tell me how and where; do not try to rebuff all his attempts."

138

"Ah me, alas! To what have you led me, my Pandaro, and what do you wish that I should do! You have shattered and broken my virtue; I dare not look you in the face. Ah me, alas, poor me, when shall I recover it? My blood turns to ice around my heart, when I think of what you ask, but you see it clearly and do not care about it.

So was he outher° glad or seyde "Allas!"   either
And held after his gistes ay his pas;[1]
1350 And after swiche answeres as he hadde,[2]
So were his dayes sory outher gladde.

But to Pandare alwey was his recours,°   recourse, resort
And pitously gan ay tyl hym to pleyne,°   always complained to him
And hym bisoughte of reed° and som socours.°   counsel / succor
1355 And Pandarus, that sey his woode peyne,°   saw his wild suffering
Wex wel neigh ded for routhe,° sooth to seyne,   Grew almost dead for pity
And bisily with al his herte caste°   plotted
Som of his wo to slen,° and that as faste;°   slay / quickly

And seyde, "Lord, and frend, and brother dere,
1360 God woot that thi disese doth me wo.°   causes me distress
But wiltow stynten° al this woful cheere,   if you will cease
And, by my trouthe, er it be dayes two,
And God toforn,° yet shal I shape° it so,   as my witness / contrive
That thow shalt come into a certeyn° place,   particular
1365 There as° thow mayst thiself hire preye of   Where
grace.°   pray to her for grace

"And certeynly—I noot if thow woost,°   whether you know it
But tho that° ben expert in love it seye—   those who
It is oon of the thynges forthereth most,°   that most advances (an affair)
A man to han a layser for to preye,[3]
1370 And siker° place his wo for to bywreye;°   a safe / reveal
For in good herte it mot som routhe impresse,°   may imprint some pity
To here° and see the giltlees° in distresse.   hear / a guiltless person

"Peraunter thynkestow:° though it be so,   Perhaps you think
That Kynde° wolde don° hire to bygynne   Nature / cause
1375 To have a manere° routhe upon my woo,   a kind of
Seyth Daunger,° 'Nay, thow shalt me nevere wynne!'[4]   Disdain
So reulith° hire hir hertes gost° withinne,   governs / heart's spirit
That though she bende, yeet she stant on roote;[5]
What in effect° is this unto my boote?°   finally / for my benefit

1380 "Thenk here-ayeins:° whan that the stordy° ook,   on the other hand / sturdy
On which men hakketh° ofte, for the nones,°   one chops / nonce
Receyved hath the happy fallyng strook,°   lucky felling stroke
The greete sweigh doth° it come al at ones,°   momentum causes / once
As don thise rokkes or thise milnestones;°   millstones
1385 For swifter cours comth thyng that is of wighte,[6]
Whan it descendeth, than don thynges lighte.

---

1. And always conformed his pace to his stopovers (gistes), i.e., flowed with the tide.
2. And according to such responses as he received.
3. For a man to have an opportunity to plead (his case to his lady).
4. The personifications of Kynde and Daunger, like that of desdaynes prisoun in line 1217 above, are typical of love-allegories influenced by the thirteenth-century French poem, The Romance of the Rose, which Chaucer translated.
5. That though she may bend, she still stands firmly rooted.
6. For a thing that is weighty takes a swifter course.

139

"I wish that I had been dead the day that I heard you say so much here in this gallery. You put in my heart a desire which I believe will scarcely ever leave it, and which will be the cause of my losing my honor and, alas, of infinite troubles. But now I can do no more; since it is pleasing to you, I am disposed to do your will.

140

"But if any prayer can be effective in your eyes, I pray you, my sweet and dear brother, that everything done and said by us may be hidden from all. You can well see what might follow from it, if such a result should come to light. Ah speak to him about it and make him aware of it, and when the time allows, I will do what his pleasure desires."

141

Pandaro replied: "Guard your lips because neither he on his part, nor I, will ever tell it." "Now do you consider me," said she, "very foolish when you see me all trembling with fear lest it might be known? But since the honor and shame we shall have from it touches you as well as me, I shall pass it over in silence, and act now as it pleases you."

142

Pandaro said: "Do not doubt that we shall indeed use good caution in this matter. When do you want him to come to speak to you? Let me now draw this business to an end because, since it should be done, it is much better that it be done quickly, and love is much better hidden after the deed when you have arranged together what you need to do."

143

"You know," said Criseida, "there are ladies and other people with me in this house, some of whom have to go to the coming festival; then I shall be with him. May this delay not be grievous to him. I shall talk to you then about the manner of coming; only make sure that he is prudent and knows well how to hide his desire."

"And reed that boweth down for every blast,
Ful lightly, cesse wynd,° it wol aryse; *when the wind ceases*
But so nyl nought an ook, whan it is cast;° *toppled, felled*
1390 It nedeth me nought the longe to forbise.[7]
Men shal° rejoissen of a gret empryse° *ought to / undertaking*
Acheved wel, and stant° withouten doute, *(it) stands*
Al han men ben the lenger theraboute.[8]

"But, Troilus, yet telle me, if the lest,° *it please you*
1395 A thing now which that I shal axen the:° *ask you*
Which is thi brother that thow lovest best,
As in thi verray hertes privetee?"° *true privacy of heart*
"Iwis,° my brother Deiphebus,"[9] quod he. *Certainly*
"Now," quod Pandare, "er houres twyes twelve,° *before twice twelve hours*
1400 He shal the ese,° unwist° of it hymselve. *comfort you / unaware*

"Now lat m'alone, and werken° as I may," *and (let me) work*
Quod he; and to Deiphebus wente he tho,
Which hadde his lord and grete frend ben ay;
Save° Troilus, no man he loved so. *Except for*
1405 To telle in short, withouten wordes mo,
Quod Pandarus, "I pray yow that ye be
Freind to a cause which that toucheth° me." *concerns*

"Yis, parde,"° quod Deiphebus, "wel thow woost, *Certainly, by God*
In al that evere I may, and God tofore,° *with God as my witness*
1410 Al nere it but for man I love moost,[1]
My brother Troilus; but sey wherfore
It is; for sith that day that I was bore,° *born*
I nas, ne nevere mo to ben I thynke,
Ayeins a thing that myghte the forthynke."[2]

1415 Pandare gan hym thanke, and to hym seyde,
"Lo, sire, I have a lady in this town,
That is my nece, and called is Criseyde,
Which° some men wolden don oppressioun, *To whom*
And wrongfully han° hire possessioun; *have, seize*
1420 Wherfore I of youre lordship yow biseche
To ben oure frend, withouten more speche."

Deiphebus hym answerde, "O, is nat this,
That thow spekest of to me thus straungely,° *distantly, as if to a stranger*
Criseÿda, my frend?" He seyde, "Yis."
1425 "Than nedeth," quod Deiphebus, "hardyly,° *certainly*
Namore to speke, for trusteth wel that I

7. I need no longer offer you examples.
8. Even though people have been at it for a longer time. The phrase *stant withouten doute* may mean "it stands without doubt," there can be no doubt, or "(an undertaking) that stands beyond doubt."
9. Chaucer's sources Dictys and Benoît (see Introduction) report that Deiphebus was the third of Priam and Hecuba's five sons; Hector was eldest, Troilus youngest.
1. Even if it weren't on behalf of the man I love the most. Deiphebus will give his all for Pandarus, just as he would for his brother Troilus.
2. I have not been, and never more intend to be, opposed to anything so that it might displease you.

Wol be hire champioun with spore and yerde;°   *spur and staff (i.e., weapon)*
I roughte nought though alle hire foos it herde.[3]

"But tel me how—thow woost of this matere—
1430 It myghte best avaylen."° "Now lat se,"   *help*
Quod Pandarus; "if ye, my lord so dere,
Wolden as now do this honour to me,
To preyen° hire to-morwe, lo, that she   *ask, invite*
Come unto yow, hire pleyntes to devise,°   *to set forth her complaint*
1435 Hire adversaries wolde of it agrise.°   *quake with fear*

"And yif I more dorste preye° as now,   *if I may dare request more*
And chargen° yow to han so gret travaille,°   *charge, impose on / trouble*
To han some of youre bretheren here with yow,
That myghten to hire cause bet availle,[4]
1440 Than wot I wel she myghte nevere faille
For to ben holpen,° what at youre instaunce,°   *To be helped / urging*
What with hire other frendes governaunce."°   *oversight, management*

Deiphebus, which that comen° was of kynde°   *given, disposed / by nature*
To alle honour and bounte° to consente,   *goodness*
1445 Answerd, "It shal be don; and I kan fynde
Yet grettere help to this in myn entente.°   *for this in my intention*
What wiltow seyn if I for Eleyne° sente   *Helen (of Troy)*
To speke of this? I trowe° it be the beste,   *believe*
For she may leden° Paris as hire leste.°   *lead / as she pleases*

1450 "Of Ector, which that is my lord, my brother,
It nedeth naught to preye hym frend to be;
For I have herd hym, o tyme and ek oother,°   *at one time or another*
Speke of Cryseyde swich honour that he
May seyn no bet, swich hap to° hym hath she.   *favor with*
1455 It nedeth naught his helpes for to crave;
He shal be swich, right as we wol hym have.°   *such as we would have him be*

"Spek thow thiself also to Troilus
On my byhalve, and prey hym with us dyne."
"Syre, al this shal be don," quod Pandarus,
1460 And took his leve, and nevere gan to fyne,°   *stop*
But to his neces hous, as streyght as lyne,°   *a string*
He com;° and fond hire fro the mete arise,°   *came / rising from dinner*
And sette hym down, and spak right in this wise:

He seide, "O verray God, so have I ronne!°   *run*
1465 Lo, nece myn, se ye nought how I swete?°   *sweat*
I not whether ye the more thank me konne.[5]
Be ye naught war how false Poliphete[6]

---

3. I wouldn't care if all her enemies heard of it.
4. Who might the better be helpful to her cause.
5. I don't know whether you are the more grateful to me (because of my efforts).
6. The figure Poliphete is Chaucer's invention, and Poliphete's renewed oppression of Criseyde may be Pandarus's invention. Chaucer may have drawn the name itself from Vergil's *Aeneid* 6.484, where Polyphœtes/Polybœtes is associated with Antenor (see line 1474 below).

Is now aboute eftsones° for to plete,°   *again / sue at law*
And brynge on yow advocacies° newe?"   *charges, accusations*
1470 "I,° no!" quod she, and chaunged al hire hewe.°   *Oh / hue*

"What is he more aboute, me to drecche[7]
And don me wrong? What shal I doon, allas?
Yet of hymself nothing ne wolde I recche,°   *I wouldn't care at all*
Nere it° for Antenor and Eneas,   *If it weren't*
1475 That ben his frendes in swich manere cas.[8]
But, for the love of God, myn uncle deere,
No fors of that; lat hym han al yfeere,[9]

"Withouten° that I have ynough for us."   *Except, Providing*
"Nay," quod Pandare, "it shal nothing° be so.   *in no way*
1480 For I have ben right now at Deiphebus,
At Ector, and myn oother lordes moo,°   *more*
And shortly maked ech of hem his foo,
That, by my thrift,° he shal it nevere wynne,   *successful work*
For aught he kan,° whan that so he bygynne."   *For all that he can do*

1485 And as thei casten° what was best to doone,   *plotted*
Deiphebus, of his owen curteisie,
Com hire to preye,° in his propre persone,°   *ask / in his own person, himself*
To holde° hym on the morwe° compaignie   *keep / next day*
At dyner, which she nolde nought denye,°   *refuse*
1490 But goodly gan to his preier° obeye.   *entreaty, invitation*
He thonked hire, and went upon his weye.

Whan this was don, this Pandare up° anon,   *(rose) up*
To telle in short, and forth gan for to wende°   *go*
To Troilus, as stille as any ston;
1495 And al this thyng he tolde hym, word° and ende,   *beginning*
And how that he Deiphebus gan to blende,°   *blind, deceive*
And seyde hym, "Now is tyme, if that thow konne,°   *can, know how*
To bere the wel° tomorwe, and al is wonne.   *conduct yourself well*

"Now spek, now prey, now pitously compleyne;
1500 Lat° nought for nyce° shame, or drede, or slouthe!   *Leave off / fastidious*
Somtyme a man mot telle his owen peyne.°   *must reveal his own pain*
Bileve° it, and she shal han on the routhe:°   *Believe / pity*
Thow shalt be saved by thi feyth,[1] in trouthe.
But wel woot I thow art now in drede,
1505 And what it is, I leye,° I kan arede.°   *wager / guess*

"Thow thynkest now, 'How sholde I don al this?
For by my cheres° mosten folk aspie°   *demeanor / see*

---

7. Why is he at it again, to trouble me.
8. Who are his allies in this kind of case. According to Dares (see Introduction), Antenor and Aeneas later were betrayers of Troy; see IV.202–205 below. Here and in his *House of Fame*, where Aeneas is a betraying lover (line 294, etc.), Chaucer emphasizes the unheroic side of Vergil's Trojan hero.
9. It doesn't matter about that; let him (Poliphete) have all (my estate) at once.
1. Chaucer has Pandarus again apply theological language to love matters; see Luke 8:48, 18:42, etc.

That for hire love is that I fare amys;° *badly*
Yet hadde I levere unwist° for sorwe dye.' *unsuspected*
1510 Now thynk nat so, for thow dost gret folie;
For I right now have founden o manere° *one kind*
Of sleyghte,° for to coveren° al thi cheere. *sleight, stratagem / conceal*

"Thow shalt gon over nyght, and that bylyve,° *quickly*
Unto Deiphebus hous as the to pleye,° *as if to amuse yourself*
1515 Thi maladie° awey the bet° to dryve— *sickness / better*
For-whi° thow semest sik, soth for to seye. *Because*
Sone after that, down in thi bed the leye,° *lay yourself*
And sey thow mayst no lenger up endure,° *bear to be up*
And ly right there, and byd thyn aventure.° *await your fortune*

1520 "Sey that thi fevre is wont the for to take° *usually comes on you*
The same tyme, and lasten til a-morwe;²
And lat se now how wel thow kanst it make,° *feign it*
For, parde,° sik is he that is in sorwe. *by God*
Go now, farwel! And Venus here to borwe,° *with Venus present as guarantor*
1525 I hope, and thow this purpos holde ferme,³
Thi grace° she shal fully ther conferme." *Favor to you*

Quod Troilus, "Iwis, thow nedeles° *unnecessarily*
Conseilest me that siklich I me feyne,° *I feign illness*
For I am sik in ernest,° douteles, *in earnest, really*
1530 So that wel neigh I sterve° for the peyne." *die*
Quod Pandarus, "Thow shalt the bettre pleyne,° *complain all the better*
And hast the lasse° need to countrefete, *you have the less*
For hym men demen° hoot that men seen swete.° *judge (to be) / sweat*

"Lo, hold the at thi triste cloos,⁴ and I
1535 Shal wel the deer unto thi bowe dryve."
Therwith he took his leve al softely,° *quietly*
And Troilus to paleis wente blyve.° *quickly*
So glad ne was he nevere in al his lyve,
And to Pandarus reed° gan al° assente, *counsel / wholly*
1540 And to Deiphebus hous at nyght he wente.

What nedeth yow to tellen al the cheere
That Deiphebus unto his brother made,
Or his accesse,° or his sikliche° manere, *onset of fever / ailing*
How men gan hym with clothes for to lade° *to load on bedclothes*
1545 Whan he was leyd,° and how men wolde hym glade?° *put to bed / cheer up*
But al for nought; he held forth ay the wyse° *ever maintained the manner*
That ye han herd Pandare er this devyse.

But certayn is, er Troilus hym leyde,° *lay down*
Deiphebus had hym preied over-nyght° *asked the night before*
1550 To ben a frend and helpyng to Criseyde.

---

2. At the same time (every day), and to last until the next morning.
3. I expect, if you hold firmly to this intention.
4. Hold yourself close at your *triste*, the station toward which deer would be driven in a hunt.

God woot that he it graunted anon-right,°   *immediately*
To ben hire fulle frend with al his myght.
But swich a nede was to preye hym thenne,
As for to bidde a wood man for to renne!°   *ask a mad man to run*

1555 The morwen com, and neighen gan the tyme°   *the time approached*
Of meeltid,° that the faire queene Eleyne   *dinnertime*
Shoop hire to ben, an houre after the prime,[5]
With Deiphebus, to whom she nolde feyne;°   *dissemble*
But as his suster, homly,° soth to seyne,   *familiarly*
1560 She com to dyner in hire pleyne entente.°   *with full purpose, willingly*
But God and Pandare wist al what this mente.

Com ek Criseyde, al innocent of this,
Antigone, hire suster Tarbe also.
But fle we now prolixitee best is,[6]
1565 For love of God, and lat us faste go
Right to th'effect,° withouten tales mo,°   *point / more talk*
Whi al this folk assembled in this place;
And lat us of hire saluynges pace.°   *pass over their greetings*

Gret honour did hem Deiphebus, certeyn,
1570 And fedde hem wel with al that myghte like;°   *be pleasing*
But evere mo "Allas!" was his refreyn,°   *refrain*
"My goode brother Troilus, the syke,
Lith° yet"—and therwithal he gan to sike;°   *Lies (abed) / sigh*
And after that, he peyned hym to glade°   *took pains to gladden*
1575 Hem° as he myghte, and cheere good he made.   *Them*

Compleyned ek Eleyne of his siknesse
So feythfully° that pite was to here,   *sincerely*
And every wight gan waxen for accesse°   *became with regard to fever*
A leche° anon, and seyde, "In this manere   *physician*
1580 Men curen folk."—"This charme° I wol yow   *healing incantation*
    leere."°   *teach*
But ther sat oon, al list hire nought to teche,[7]
That thoughte, "Best koud I yet ben his leche."

After compleynte, hym gonnen they to preyse,
As folk don yet whan som wight° hath bygonne   *person*
1585 To preise a man, and up with pris hym reise°   *exalt him with praise*
A thousand fold yet heigher than the sonne:
"He is, he kan, that° fewe lordes konne."   *he can do what*
And Pandarus, of that they wolde afferme,°   *regarding what they would affirm*
He naught forgat hire preisynge to conferme.

1590 Herde al this thyng Criseyde wel inough,
And every word gan for to notifie;°   *take note of*

---

5. Arranged to be, an hour after prime, i.e., about 10 A.M.—dinnertime.
6. But it is best now to flee prolixity, to be brief. The expression comes from *The Romance of the Rose*, line 18,298.
7. But there sat one person (i.e., Criseyde), although she didn't wish to offer instruction.

For which with sobre cheere° hire herte lough.°   *sober demeanor / laughed*
For who is that ne wolde hire glorifie,°   *who wouldn't glorify herself*
To mowen swich a knyght don lyve or dye?[8]
1595 But al passe° I, lest ye to° longe dwelle;   *pass over / too*
For for o fyn° is al that evere I telle.   *one end, purpose*

The tyme com fro dyner for to ryse,
And as hem aughte, arisen° everichon,   *they ought, they arose*
And gonne° a while of this and that devise.°   *began / converse*
1600 But Pandarus brak° al that speche anon,°   *broke, interrupted / forthwith*
And seide to Deiphebus, "Wol ye gon,
If it youre wille be, as I yow preyde,
To speke here of the nedes of Criseyde?"

Eleyne, which that by the hond hire held,
1605 Took first the tale,° and seyde, "Go we blyve";°   *First began speaking / quickly*
And goodly on Criseyde she biheld,
And seyde, "Joves° lat hym nevere thryve°   *Jupiter / prosper*
That° doth yow harm, and brynge hym soone of lyve,°   *Who / out of life*
And yeve° me sorwe, but he shal it rewe,°   *Give / rue, regret*
1610 If that I may, and alle° folk be trewe!"   *If I'm able, and if all*

"Tel thow thi neces cas," quod Deiphebus
To Pandarus, "for thow kanst best it telle."
"My lordes and my ladys, it stant° thus: *(the situation) stands*
What° sholde I lenger," quod he, "do yow dwelle?"°   *Why / make you wait*
1615 He rong hem out a proces° lik a belle   *rang out the argument for them*
Upon hire foo that highte° Poliphete,   *was named*
So heynous° that men myghten on it spete.°   *hateful / spit*

Answerde of this ech werse of hem than other,[9]
And Poliphete they gonnen thus to warien:°   *curse*
1620 "Anhonged be swich oon,° were he my brother!   *May such a one be hanged*
And so he shal, for it ne may nought varien!"°   *be otherwise*
What shold I lenger in this tale tarien?°   *dwell on this story*
Pleynliche,° alle at ones,° they hire highten°   *Plainly / together / promised*
To ben hire help in al that evere they myghten.°   *could do*

1625 Spak than Eleyne, and seyde, "Pandarus,
Woot ought my lord,° my brother, this   *Does my lord know anything of*
matere—
I meene Ector—or woot it Troilus?"
He seyde, "Ye, but wole ye now me here?
Me thynketh this,° sith that Troilus is here,   *It seems to me*
1630 It were good, if that ye wolde assente,
She tolde hireself hym al this er she wente.[1]

"For he wol have the more hir grief at herte,
By cause,° lo, that she a lady is.   *For the reason*

8. To be able (*mowen*) to cause such a knight to live or die.
9. Each of them responded to this worse (i.e., more vehemently against Poliphete) than the others.
1. That she herself would tell him all this before she left.

And, by youre leve, I wol but in right sterte°   *hurry*
1635 And do yow wyte,° and that anon, iwys,   *let you know*
    If that he slepe, or wol ought here° of this."   *wishes to hear anything*
    And in he lepte, and seyde hym in his ere,°   *told him in his ear*
    "God have thi soule, ibrought have I thi beere!"[2]

    To smylen of° this gan tho Troilus,   *smile about*
1640 And Pandarus, withouten rekenynge,°   *(further) calculation*
    Out wente anon to Eleyne and Deiphebus,
    And seyde hem,° "So° ther be no taryinge,   *said to them / So that*
    Ne moore prees,° he wol wel that ye brynge   *crowding*
    Criseÿda, my lady, that is here;
1645 And as° he may enduren, he wol here.°   *as long as / hear*

    "But wel ye woot, the chaumbre is but lite,°   *little*
    And fewe folk may lightly° make it warm;   *easily*
    Now loketh ye (for I wol have no wite°   *advise (me) / blame*
    To brynge in prees° that myghte don hym harm,   *For bringing in a crowd*
1650 Or hym disesen,° for my bettre° arm)   *discomfort / right*
    Wher it be bet she bide til eft-sonys;[3]
    Now loketh ye that knowen what to doon is.

    "I sey for me, best is, as I kan knowe,°   *as far as I can tell*
    That no wight in ne wente but ye tweye,°   *the two of you*
1655 But° it were I, for I kan in a throwe°   *Unless / short time*
    Reherce hire cas unlik that she kan seye;[4]
    And after this she may hym ones preye°   *once entreat*
    To ben good lord, in short, and take hire leve.
    This may nought muchel° of his ese° hym reve.°   *much / comfort / deprive*

1660 "And ek, for she is straunge, he wol forbere
    His ese, which that hym thar nought for yow;[5]
    Ek oother thing that toucheth nought to here°   *doesn't concern her*
    He wol yow telle—I woot it wel right now—
    That secret is, and for the townes prow."°   *benefit*
1665 And they, that nothyng knewe of his entente,
    Withouten more, to Troilus in they wente.

    Eleyne, in al hire goodly softe wyse,
    Gan hym salue,° and wommanly to pleye,°   *greet / banter*
    And seyde, "Iwys, ye moste alweies arise!"°   *by all means arise, get well*
1670 Now faire brother, beth al hool,° I preye!"   *whole, healed*
    And gan hire arm right over his chulder leye,
    And hym with al hire wit to reconforte;°   *comfort*
    As she best koude, she gan hym to disporte.°   *cheer up*

---

2. May God have your soul; I've brought your (funeral) bier. As a corpse lies on a bier, the joke has sexual meaning: the bier is Criseyde.
3. Whether it may be better for her to wait until afterwards.
4. Go over her case differently from what (i.e., better than) she can say.
5. And also, because she is not a member of his family (as Helen and Deiphebus are), he will forgo his comfort (while Criseyde is present), which he need not do for you.

So after this quod she, "We yow biseke,°   beseech
1675 My deere brother Deiphebus and I,
For love of God—and so doth Pandare eke—°   also
To ben good lord and frend, right hertely,
Unto Criseyde, which that certeynly
Receyveth wrong, as woot° weel here Pandare,   knows
1680 That° kan hire cas wel bet than I declare."   Who

This Pandarus gan newe his tong affile,°   file smooth
And al hire cas reherce, and that anon.
Whan it was seyd, soone after in a while,
Quod Troilus, "As sone as I may gon,°   can walk
1685 I wol right fayn° with al my myght ben oon—°   gladly / one (of those)
Have God my trouthe—hire cause to sustene."°   support
"Good thrift° have ye!" quod Eleyne the queene.   success

Quod Pandarus, "And it youre wille be°   And is it your will
That she may take hire leve,° er that she go?"   leave
1690 "O, elles° God forbede it," tho° quod he,   otherwise / then
"If that she vouche sauf° for to do so."   agree
And with that word quod Troilus, "Ye two,
Deiphebus and my suster lief° and deere,   beloved
To yow have I to speke of o matere,°   a matter

1695 "To ben avysed° by youre reed° the bettre—"   advised / counsel
And fond, as hap was,° at his beddes hed   by chance
The copie of a tretys° and a lettre   treatise
That Ector hadde hym sent to axen red°   ask for advice
If swych a man was worthi° to ben ded,°   deserved / dead, executed
1700 Woot I nought who; but in a grisly wise°   grim manner
He preyede hem anon on it avyse.°   to consider it forthwith

Deiphebus gan this lettre for t'onfolde
In ernest greet;° so did Eleyne the queene;   great seriousness
And romyng outward, faste it gonne byholde,°   examined it carefully
1705 Downward a steire,° into an herber° greene.   Down a staircase / garden
This ilke° thing they redden° hem bitwene,   same / read, took counsel on
And largely,° the mountance° of an houre,   fully / length
Thei gonne on it to reden and to poure.°   pore (over it)

Now lat hem rede, and torne° we anon   turn
1710 To Pandarus, that gan ful faste prye°   surely to espy
That al was wel, and out he gan to gon
Into the grete chaumbre, and that in hye,°   in haste
And seyde, "God save al this compaynye!
Com, nece myn; my lady queene Eleyne
1715 Abideth° yow, and ek my lordes tweyne.°   Is waiting for / two lords

"Rys, take with yow youre nece Antigone,
Or whom yow list; or no fors; hardyly⁶

6. Or whoever pleases you, or—it doesn't matter—indeed.

The lesse prees,° the bet; com forth with me,   *crowding*
And loke° that ye thonken humblely   *take care*
1720   Hem alle thre,° and whan ye may goodly°   *all three of them / properly*
Youre tyme se,° taketh of hem youre leeve,   *see your time (to depart)*
Lest we to longe his restes hym byreeve."°   *deprive him of his rest periods*

Al innocent of Pandarus entente,
Quod tho Criseyde, "Go we, uncle deere";
1725   And arm in arm inward with hym she wente,
Avysed wel° hire wordes and hire cheere;°   *Having well considered / looks*
And Pandarus, in ernestful° manere,   *serious*
Seyde, "Alle folk, for Goddes love, I preye,
Stynteth° right here, and softely yow pleye.°   *Stay / amuse yourselves quietly*

1730   "Avyseth yow° what folk ben hire withinne,   *Consider*
And in what plit oon° is, God hym amende!"°   *plight one person / heal*
And inward thus, "Ful softely bygynne,
Nece, I conjure and heighly yow defende,
On his half which that soule us alle sende,
1735   And in the vertu of corones tweyne,
Sle naught this man, that hath for yow this peyne![7]

"Fy° on the devell! Thynk which oon° he is,   *Fie / what sort of person*
And in what plit he lith;° com of° anon!   *lies / come on, hurry up!*
Thynk al swich taried tyde, but lost it nys.[8]
1740   That wol ye bothe seyn,° whan ye ben oon.°   *say / united*
Secoundely, ther yet devyneth noon°   *no one yet supposes anything*
Upon° yow two; come of now, if ye konne!   *With regard to*
While folk is blent, lo, al the tyme is wonne.[9]

"In titeryng, and pursuyte, and delayes,
1745   The folk devyne at waggyng of a stree;[1]
And though ye wolde han after mirye° dayes,   *desire afterwards to have merry*
Than dar° ye naught. And whi? For she, and she°   *dare / this and that woman*
Spak° swych a word; thus loked° he, and he!   *Spoke / cast a glance*
Las, tyme ilost!° I dar nought with yow dele.   *Alas (for) lost time!*
1750   Com of, therfore, and bryngeth hym to hele!"°   *health*

But now to yow, ye loveres that ben here,
Was Troilus nought in a kankedort,[2]
That° lay, and myghte whisprynge of hem here,°   *Who / hear*
And thoughte, "O Lord, right now renneth my sort°   *my destiny approaches*

---

7. And privately (he spoke) thus, "Begin very quietly, niece; I implore and strictly forbid you, on His behalf Who gave us all a soul, and in the power of two crowns, slay not this man, who has this suffering for you!" The word *inward* (line 1731) may alternatively mean "on the way in." The sense of *the vertu of corones tweyne* has not been determined—the strength of two royal powers?
8. Consider that all such time delaying is but lost.
9. While people are blinded (deceived), lo, all the time is gained; i.e., the iron is hot.
1. In vacillation, in (prolonged) entreaty, and in delays, people make guesses about the waving of a straw, i.e., about trifles.
2. The word *kankedort* seems from context to mean "predicament"; its etymology and exact meaning are unknown.

Part Three

Here begins the third part of the "Filostrato" in which, after the author's invocation, Pandaro and Troilo speak together of the need to keep secret that which later is done with Criseida; to whom Troilo goes secretly, takes his delight and talks with her, departs and returns, lives in rejoicing and in song, but first the author's invocation.

1

O shining light, whose rays have guided me, as I wished, through the halls of love up to this place, now it is fitting that your redoubled light should guide my talent and make it such that the benefit of the sweet reign of Love of which Troilo was made worthy may in each particular appear elucidated through me.

2

To that kingdom comes he who with discretion and with virtue faithfully can suffer entirely the pains of love: by any other way, rarely can he ever come there; therefore be present, O beautiful lady, and my high desire fill with the grace which I ask for while I sing continually your praises.

Troilo lives joyous with Pandaro, who has brought him a glad reply; and, after having talked a long time, he speaks showing his gratitude.

3

Even though Troilo greatly burned, nevertheless things seemed well for him when he thought merely of what might be pleasing to Criseida and when he thought of how she responded unpretentiously to his letters when she wrote, and things seemed even better whenever he saw her: she looked at him with such a sweet look that he seemed to feel the greatest delight.

1755 Fully to deye, or han anon° comfort!"   *immediately*
And was° the firste tyme he shulde hire preye°   *(this) was / beseech*
Of love; O myghty God, what shal he seye?

Explicit secundus liber.[3]

Book Three

Incipit prohemium tercii libri.[1]   *to Venus*

O blisful light of which the bemes clere
Adorneth al the thridde heven faire!
O sonnes lief, O Joves doughter deere,[2]
Plesance° of love, O goodly debonaire,°   *Delight / gracious one*
5 In gentil hertes ay redy to repaire![3]   *health*
O veray° cause of heele° and of gladnesse,   *true / well-being*
Iheryed° be thy myght and thi goodnesse!   *Praised*
    Praise

In hevene and helle, in erthe and salte see
Is felt thi myght, if that I wel descerne,°   *discern, understand (it)*
10 As man, brid, best, fissh, herbe,° and grene tree   *bird, beast, fish, plant*
Thee fele in tymes with vapour eterne.[4]
God loveth, and to love wol nought werne,°   *refuse, deny nothing*
And in this world no lyves° creature   *living*
Withouten love is worth,° or may endure.   *of value*

    You first moved Jove to glad effects
15 Ye Joves first to thilke effectes glade,
Thorugh which that thynges lyven alle and be,
Comeveden,[5] and amorous him made
On mortal thyng, and as yow list, ay ye°   *as it pleased you, always you*
Yeve° hym in love ese or adversitee,   *Gave*
20 And in a thousand formes down hym sente
For love in erthe, and whom yow liste he hente.[6]

3. Here ends the second book.
1. Here begins the proem (prologue) of the third book.
2. Adorn the whole lovely third heaven (i.e., celestial sphere), O beloved of the sun, O dear daughter of Jupiter. Counting out from the earth, Venus (after the moon and Mercury) was the third planetary sphere. The prologue's elaborate invocation to Venus as planet (*blisful light*) and goddess of Love derives from part of a song sung by Boccaccio's Troilo at the height of his happiness in the love affair (*Filostrato* III.74–79). Boccaccio derived the song partly from a poem embedded in Boethius's *Consolation of Philosophy* (2.m8); Chaucer's separate translation of the whole *Consolation* has been preserved, and his translation of this metrum is reproduced at the note to line 1744 below. Chaucer supplied a new song for Troilus (III.1744–71 below), now based directly on the same poem in Boethius. Venus is the *sonnes lief* because the planet accompanies the sun as morning and evening star. She also represents the social love that unites kingdoms and households (line 29), and the cosmic love that binds together the elements of the universe (line 36 and I.237 above), an idea deriving from Empedocles and Lucretius. *Adorneth* is a Southern dialect plural form.
3. Always ready to repair to (enter) noble hearts. Chaucer seems to translate a famous line, quoted by Dante in the *Convivio*, by Guido Guinizelli, "Al cor gentil rempaira sempre Amore."
4. Feel you (i.e., Venus's power) in (their particular) seasons by way of eternal emanation, i.e., the "influence" that planets exert on earthly matters according to medieval astrology.
5. You (Venus) first moved Jupiter to those happy effects (i.e., sexual propagation) through which all things live and have their being.
6. For love you sent him down to earth, and he seized whomever you wished (to have him seize). Among the *thousand formes* Jupiter assumed for his rapes of human women are those of a bull to Europa, a golden shower to Danae, a swan to Leda; see Ovid's *Metamorphoses* for the stories.

Ye fierse Mars apaisen of his ire,[7]
And as yow list, ye maken hertes digne;°   *worthy*
Algates° hem that ye wol sette a-fyre,   *At any rate*
25 They dreden shame, and vices they resygne;°   *resign, give up*
Ye do° hem corteys° be, fresshe and benigne;   *cause / courteous*
And heighe or lowe, after a wight entendeth,°   *as a person is inclined, wishes*
The joies that he hath, youre myght it sendeth.

Ye holden regne° and hous in unitee;   *reign, realm*
30 Ye sothfast° cause of frendship ben also;   *trustworthy*
Ye knowe al thilke covered° qualitee   *that same hidden*
Of thynges, which that folk on wondren° so,   *people wonder at*
Whan they kan nought construe° how it may jo°   *understand / happen (?)*
She loveth hym, or whi he loveth here,°   *her*
35 As whi this fissh, and naught that, comth to were.°   *weir, fish-trap*

Ye folk a lawe han set in universe,[8]
And this knowe I by hem that lovers be,
That whoso stryveth with yow hath the werse.
Now, lady bryght, for thi benignite,°   *goodness*
40 At reverence of hem° that serven the,   *Out of respect for those*
Whos clerc° I am, so techeth me devyse°   *priest, scribe / to narrate*
Som joye of that° is felt in thi servyse.   *that which*

Ye in my naked herte sentement
Inhielde, and do me shewe of thy swetnesse.[9]
45 Caliope,[1] thi vois be now present,
For now is nede: sestow nought° my destresse,   *see you not*
How I mot° telle anonright° the gladnesse   *must / right now*
Of Troilus, to Venus heryinge?°   *Venus's praise*
To which gladnesse, who nede hath,° God hym   *whoever is in need*
    brynge!

Explicit prohemium tercii libri.

Incipit liber tercius.[2]

50 Lay al this mene while Troilus,
Recordyng° his lesson in this manere: *Rehearsing, Memorizing*
"Mafay,"° thoughte he, "thus wol I sey, and thus;   *By my faith*
Thus wol I pleyne° unto my lady dere;   *complain*
That word is good, and this shal be my cheere;°   *look, demeanor*

7. You appease fierce Mars of his wrath. As beneficent planet, Venus counters the influence of the maleficent Mars; as Love, she counters War; as the goddess of myth, she was Mars's lover. Chaucer's short poem "The Complaint of Mars" elaborates these ideas.
8. You have established a law for people in the universe.
9. May you pour feeling (i.e., a sense of what loving is) into my naked (i.e., innocent of experience in loving) heart, and cause me to make a display of your sweetness. Chaucer may allude to the Stoic idea of the mind (*herte*) as a "blank slate" before it experiences sense impressions. Thus Boethius, *Consolation*, 5.m4.18.
1. Chaucer makes a second invocation to Calliope, the muse of epic poetry, called the "best voice" by medieval mythographers.
2. Here ends the prologue of the third book. Here begins the third book.

Troilus trying to want to be his own narrator

forget / way
let him perform / plan

55 This nyl I nought foryeten° in no wise."°
God leve hym werken° as he kan devyse!°

And, Lord, so that° his herte gan to quappe,°   *how / pound*
Heryng hire come, and shorte for to sike!°   *to sigh with quick breaths*
And Pandarus, that ledde hire by the lappe,°   *hem or fold of her garment*
60 Com ner, and gan in at the curtyn pike,[3]
And seyde, "God do boot° on alle syke!°   *give remedy / sick people*
Se who is here yow comen to visite:
Lo, here is she that is youre deth to wite."°   *to blame for*

Therwith it semed as he wepte almost.
65 "Ha, a," quod Troilus so reufully,°   *piteously*
"Wher me be wo,° O myghty God, thow   *Whether I have suffering*
     woost!°   *know*
Who is al° ther? I se nought trewely."   *together*
"Sire," quod Criseyde, "it is Pandare and I."
"Ye, swete herte? Allas, I may nought rise
70 To knele and do yow honour in som wyse."

And dressed hym upward,° and she right tho°   *reared up / then*
Gan bothe hire hondes softe upon hym leye.
"O, for the love of God, do ye nought so
To me," quod she, "I!° What is this to seye?   *Oh!*
75 Sire, comen am I° to yow for causes tweye:°   *I have come / two*
First, yow to thonke, and of youre lordshipe eke°   *patronage also*
Continuance I wolde yow biseke."°   *beseech*

This Troilus, that herde his lady preye
Of lordshipe hym, wax° neither quyk° ne ded,   *became / alive*
80 Ne myghte o° word for shame to it seye,°   *one / respond*
Although men sholde smyten of his hed.°   *smite off his head*
But Lord, so he wex sodeynliche° red,   *suddenly*
And sire, his lessoun, that he wende konne
To preyen hire, is thorugh his wit ironne.[4]

85 Criseyde al this aspied wel ynough,
For she was wis, and loved hym nevere the lasse,
Al nere he malapert, or made it tough,
Or was to bold, to synge a fool a masse.[5]
But whan his shame gan somwhat to passe,
90 His resons,° as° I may my rymes holde,°   *speeches / insofar as / maintain*
I yow wol telle, as techen bokes olde.

In chaunged vois, right for his verray drede,°   *pure, very fear*
Which vois ek quook,° and therto his manere   *quavered*

---

3. Came nearer, and peeked in at the curtain. Beds were surrounded by curtained canopies for privacy and against drafts.
4. And sir (reader or auditor), his lesson, with which he thought he knew how to entreat her, has run out of his mind.
5. Loved him none the less, although he was not presumptuous, or arrogant, or too bold, (as if) to chant a mass to a fool—i.e., to flatter deceptively. The precise sense of the last phrase is uncertain.

Goodly abaist,° and now his hewes° rede,   Becomingly abashed / color
95 Now pale, unto Criseyde, his lady dere,
With look down cast and humble iyolden chere,°   yielding, submissive look
Lo, the alderfirste° word that hym asterte°   very first / escaped
Was, twyes,° "Mercy, mercy, swete herte!"   twice

And stynte° a while, and whan he myghte out   he ceased
    brynge,°   utter (anything)
100 The nexte word was, "God woot, for I have,
As ferforthly° as I have had konnynge,°   Insofar / understanding, wits
Ben youres al, God so my soule save,
And shal° til that I, woful wight, be grave!°   And I shall be / buried
And though I dar, ne kan,° unto yow pleyne,   I neither dare to nor can
105 Iwis,° I suffre nought the lasse° peyne.   Certainly / less

"Thus muche as now, O wommanliche wif,[6]
I may out brynge, and if this yow displese,
That shal I wreke° upon myn owen lif   avenge
Right soone, I trowe,° and do youre herte an ese,°   believe / a comfort
110 If with my deth youre wreththe° may apese.°   wrath / be appeased
But syn that° ye han herd me somwhat° seye,   since / something, a little
Now recche° I nevere how soone that I deye."°   care / die

Therwith his manly sorwe to biholde
It myghte han mad an herte of stoon to rewe;°   feel pity
115 And Pandare wep as° he to water wolde,°   wept as if / would (turn)
And poked evere his nece new and newe,°   again and again
And seyde, "Wo bygon° ben hertes trewe!   Grievously beset
For love of God, make of this thing an ende,
Or sle° us both at ones er ye wende."°   slay / depart

120 "I,° what?" quod she, "by God and by my trouthe,   Oh!
I not nat° what ye wilne° that I seye."   don't know / desire
"I,° what?" quod he, "That ye han on hym routhe,°   Ah! / pity
For Goddes love, and doth° hym nought to deye!"   cause
"Now than thus," quod she, "I wolde hym preye°   request
125 To telle me the fyn of his entente.°   end, goal of his intentions
Yet wist I nevere° wel what that he mente."   I've still never known

"What that I mene, O swete herte deere?"
Quod Troilus, "O goodly, fresshe free,°   noble (lady)
That with the stremes of youre eyen° cleere   beams of your eyes
130 Ye wolde somtyme frendly on me see,°   look on me amiably
And thanne agreen that I may ben he,
Withouten braunche° of vice on any wise,°   branch type (in any way)
In trouthe° alwey to don yow my servise,   loyalty, integrity

"As to my lady right° and chief resort,°   indeed / recourse, sustainer
135 With al my wit and al my diligence;
And I to han, right as yow list, comfort,

6. So much for now, O womanly woman—i.e., O paragon of femininity. In Middle English *wif* means "wife" or generally "woman" depending on the context.

Under yowre yerde, egal to myn offence,[7]
As deth, if that I breke youre defence;°   *violate your prohibition*
And that ye deigne° me so muchel° honoure   *deign to grant / much*
140   Me to comanden aught° in any houre;   *anything*

"And I to ben youre°—verray,° humble, trewe,   *yours / true*
Secret,° and in my paynes° pacient,   *Discreet / suffering*
And evere mo desiren fresshly newe
To serve, and ben ylike° diligent,   *likewise*
145   And with good herte al holly° youre talent°   *wholly / desire*
Receyven wel, how sore that me smerte;°   *however sorely it pains me*
Lo, this mene I, myn owen swete herte."

Quod Pandarus, "Lo, here an hard requeste,
And resonable, a lady for to werne!°   *refuse*
150   Now, nece myn, by natal Joves feste,[8]
Were I a god, ye sholden sterve as yerne,°   *die quickly*
That heren° wel this man wol nothing yerne°   *You who hear / desire*
But youre honour, and sen hym almost sterve,
And ben so loth to suffren° hym yow serve."   *suffer, permit*

155   With that she gan hire eyen on hym caste
Ful esily and ful debonairly,[9]
Avysyng hire,° and hied° nought to faste   *Considering / hastened*
With nevere a word, but seyde hym softely,
"Myn honour sauf,° I wol wel trewely,   *With my honor preserved*
160   And in swich forme as he gan now devyse,°   *propose*
Receyven hym fully to my servyse,

"Bysechyng hym, for Goddes love, that he
Wolde, in honour of trouthe and gentilesse,
As I wel mene, ek menen wel to me,
165   And myn honour with wit and bisynesse°   *intelligence and diligence*
Ay kepe;° and if I may don hym gladnesse,   *Always maintain*
From hennesforth, iwys,° I nyl nought feyne.°   *indeed / hold back*
Now beth al hool;° no lenger ye ne pleyne.   *whole, healed*

"But natheles,° this warne I yow," quod she,   *nevertheless*
170   "A kynges sone although ye be, ywys,
Ye shal namore han sovereignete
Of° me in love, than right in that cas is.°   *Over / is correct in that case*
N'y nyl forbere,° if that ye don amys,°   *Nor will I refrain / wrong*

7. And for me to have, just as pleases you, comfort, under your rod (i.e., subject to your punishing authority), appropriate to my offence. The infinitive *to han* may be absolute, or may depend on *may* in line 131—"and that I may have"; in Middle English if an infinitive is distant from its governing main verb a *to* can go with it.
8. By the feast-day of Jupiter, god of births. Because Jupiter is not especially known as god of nativities, whereas his wife Juno is, the manuscripts may here err in writing *Joves* for the less familiar term *Junos*, which looks very similar in English script around 1400.
9. The adverbs here exemplify the difficulty in glossing Chaucer's subtle vocabulary of manners. *Esily* could mean gently, with the easy manner of a well-brought-up and experienced widow, softly (with affection), comfortingly, leniently, kindly; *debonairly* could mean meekly (as subservient), graciously (as a superior), benignly, kindly, condescendingly, gently, with pleasant disposition, or, in close to the modern sense, suavely, socially gracefully, with savoir-faire. The latter word is from French *de bon aire*, of good disposition/air/demeanor.

To wratthe° yow; and whil that ye me serve,   *be angry with*
175 Chericen yow right after° ye disserve.   *Cherish you just as*

"And shortly, deere herte and al my knyght,
Beth glad, and draweth yow to lustinesse,°   *come to happiness*
And I shal trewely, with al my myght,
Youre bittre tornen° al into swetenesse.   *turn*
180 If I be she that may yow do gladnesse,
For every wo ye shal recovere a blisse"—
And hym in armes took, and gan hym kisse.

Fil° Pandarus on knees, and up his eyen°   *Fell / eyes*
To heven threw, and held his hondes highe:
185 "Immortal god," quod he, "that mayst nought deyen,
Cupide I mene, of this mayst glorifie;°   *you may boast, exult*
And Venus, thow mayst maken melodie!
Withouten hond, me semeth that in the towne,
For this merveille ich here ech belle sowne.¹

190 "But ho! namore° as now of this matere;   *no more*
For-whi° this folk wol comen up anon,   *Because*
That han the lettre red;° lo, I hem here.°   *read / hear*
But I conjure the,° Criseyde, anon,   *implore you*
And to,° thow Troilus, whan thow mayst goon,   *also*
195 That at myn hous ye ben at my warnynge,°   *summons*
For I ful well shal shape° youre comynge;   *arrange*

"And eseth there youre hertes right ynough;
And lat se which of yow shal bere the belle²
To speke of love aright!"°—therwith he lough—°   *correctly / laughed*
200 "For ther have ye a leiser° for to telle."   *an opportunity*
Quod Troilus, "How longe shal I dwelle,°   *abide, wait*
Er this be don?" Quod he, "Whan thow mayst
   ryse,°   *get up (from the sickbed)*
This thyng shal be right as I yow devyse."

With that Eleyne and also Deiphebus
205 Tho° comen upward, right at the steires° ende;   *Then / staircase's*
And Lord, so thanne gan gronen Troilus,
His brother and his suster for to blende.°   *deceive*
Quod Pandarus, "It tyme is that we wende.°   *depart*
Tak, nece myn, youre leve at° alle thre,   *from*
210 And lat hem speke, and cometh forth with me."

She took hire leve at hem ful thriftily,°   *properly, politely*
As she wel koude,° and they hire reverence⁶   *knew how / polite respect*
Unto the fulle diden,° hardyly,   *paid*
And wonder wel speken,° in hire absence,   *spoke*

---

1. It seems to me that, for this miracle, I hear every bell sound without a hand (i.e., spontaneously) in the town. Several medieval stories tell of the miraculous spontaneous ringing of bells, a sign of a joyous occasion.
2. Shall take first place; to "bear the bell" probably meant to win the prize, but possibly meant to lead the flock as a bellwether.

4

Pandaro, as I have said before, had departed from the lady in agreement and, joyful in mind and in countenance, he sought for Troilo whom, when he had gone away, he had left bewildered between joyful hope and sad plaints; and he went looking in this place and in that until he found him brooding in a temple.

5

As soon as he reached him, he drew him aside and began to say to him, "Dear friend, when in the past I saw you languishing so bitterly for love, so much was I attached to you that my heart bore in itself for you a great part of your suffering; I have never rested until I have found a way to give you comfort.

6

"I have for you become a go-between, for you I have cast my honor to the ground, for you I have corrupted the wholesome breast of my sister and have placed your love in her heart; nor will a long time pass before you will see her with more joy than my speech can give you, when you will have the beautiful Criseida in your arms.

215 Of hire in preysing of hire excellence—
Hire governaunce,° hire wit, and hire manere°   *self-control, composure / bearing*
Comendeden,° it joie was to here.°   *They commended / hear*

    Now lat hire wende° unto hire owen place,   *go*
And torne we to Troilus ayein,°   *again*
220 That gan ful lightly of the lettre pace³
That Deiphebus hadde in the gardyn seyn;°   *seen, looked over*
And of Eleyne and hym he wolde feyn°   *fain, gladly*
Delivered ben, and seyde that hym leste°   *it pleased him*
To slepe, and after tales° have reste.   *conversation*

225 Eleyne hym kiste, and took hire leve blyve,°   *quickly*
Deiphebus ek, and hom wente every wight;°   *person*
And Pandarus, as faste as he may dryve,°   *hasten*
To Troilus tho com, as lyne right,°   *then came straight as a string*
And on a paillet° al that glade nyght   *pallet*
230 By Troilus he lay, with mery chere,°   *demeanor*
To tale;° and wel was hem° they were yfeere.°   *talk / it was to them / together*

    Whan every wight was voided° but they two,   *had departed*
And alle the dores weren faste yshette,°   *shut*
To telle In short, withouten wordes mo,
235 This Pandarus, withouten any lette,°   *delay*
Up roos, and on his beddes syde hym sette,
And gan to speken in a sobre wyse
To Troilus, as I shal yow devyse:°   *relate*

    "Myn alderlevest° lord, and brother deere,   *dearest of all*
240 God woot, and thow, that it sat° me so soore,   *affects*
Whan I the saugh° so langwisshyng to-yere°   *saw / this year*
For love, of which thi wo wax° alwey moore,   *grew*
That I, with al my myght and al my loore,°   *instruction, advice*
Have evere sithen° don my bisynesse°   *since / diligence*
245 To brynge the° to joye out of distresse,   *you*

    "And have it brought to swich plit° as thow woost,°   *condition / know*
So that thorugh me thow stondest now in weye°   *on the path*
To faren wel; I sey it for no bost,°   *boast*
And wostow whi? For shame it is to seye:⁴
250 For the have I bigonne a gamen pleye°   *to play a game*
Which that I nevere do shal eft for other,°   *again for another*
Although he were a thousand fold my brother.

    "That is to seye, for the am I bicomen,
Bitwixen game and ernest, swich a meene⁵
255 As maken° wommen unto men to comen;   *[those who] make*
Al sey I nought,° thow wost wel what I meene.   *Though I say nothing*

---

3. Who passed/glanced very quickly over the letter.
4. And do you know why? It is shameful to speak it.
5. Between playfulness and seriousness, such a go-between. The word Pandarus avoids saying is
baude, "pimp." Cf. II.353 above, III.397 below.

7

"But as God, who sees all, knows and as you know, the hope of reward has not led me to this, but only loyalty, which I bear you as a friend, has led me to work so that you may find your reward. Therefore I pray you, if the desired good be not dashed from you by ill fortune, that you act as it is fitting for a wise man to do.

8

"You know that her reputation is one of purity among the people, nor has anything other than good ever been said of her. Now it has happened that you have it in your hands and can take it from her, if you do what you ought not to do; though this can never happen without great shame to me, who am related to her and a go-between likewise.

9

"Therefore I pray you as much as I can that this business be kept secret between us. I have removed from Criseida's heart any sense of shame and every thought that was against you and have so impressed her with talk of your sincere love that she loves you and is disposed to do what it shall please you to command.

For the° have I my nece, of vices cleene,   *For your sake*
So fully maad thi gentilesse triste,°   *trust your noble character*
That al shal ben right as thiselven liste.°   *as pleases you*

260 "But God, that al woot,° take I to witnesse, *I never wrought this for* *knows* *covetous*
That nevere I this for coveitise wroughte,°   *performed for covetousness*
But oonly for t'abregge° that distresse   *to abridge, alleviate*
For which wel neigh thow deidest, as me thoughte.[6]
But, goode brother, do now as the oughte,°   *you ought to*
265 For Goddes love, and kep hire out of blame,
Syn° thow art wys, and save° alwey hire name.°   *Since / protect / reputation*

"For wel thow woost,° the name as yet of here°   *you know / her*
Among the peeple, as who seyth,° halwed° is.   *as one says / hallowed, sainted*
For that man is unbore,° I dar wel swere,   *unborn*
270 That evere wiste° that she dide amys.°   *knew / wrong*
But wo is me, that I, that cause al this,
May thynken that she is my nece deere,
And I hire em, and traitour ek yfeere![7]

"And were it wist° that I, thorough myn engyn,°   *known / machinations*
275 Hadde in my nece yput this fantasie,°   *set this idea, desire*
To doon thi lust° and holly° to ben thyn,   *accede to your pleasure / wholly*
Whi, al the world upon it wolde crie,
And seyn that I the werste trecherie
Dide in this cas, that evere was bigonne,
280 And she forlost, and thow right nought ywonne.[8]

"Wherfore, er I wol ferther gon a pas,°   *step*
The preie ich eft,° althogh thow shuldest deye,°   *I entreat you again / die*
That privete° go with us in this cas;   *secrecy*
That is to seyn, that thow us nevere wreye;°   *reveal*
285 And be nought wroth,° though I the ofte preye   *angry*
To holden secree° swich an heigh matere,°   *secret / high matter*
For skilfull° is, thow woost wel, my praiere.   *reasonable*

"And thynk what wo ther hath bitid er° this,   *happened before*
For makyng of avantes,° as men rede;°   *boasts / read*
290 And what meschaunce° in this world yet ther is,   *misfortune*
Fro day to day, right for that wikked dede;°   *deed (i.e., boasting)*
For which thise wise clerkes that ben dede
Han evere yet proverbed° to us yonge,°   *said in a proverb / young people*
That 'firste vertu is to kepe tonge.'[9]

295 "And nere it that I wilne° as now t'abregge°   *desire / abridge*
Diffusioun° of speche, I koude almoost   *Diffuseness, prolixity*
A thousand olde stories the allegge°   *adduce for you*

6. In which (distress) you almost died, as it seemed to me.
7. And I her uncle, and also her betrayer along with it. Boccaccio's word in the parallel passage is *trattator*, "procurer, go-between"; Chaucer may have thought the word was *traditore*, "traitor."
8. And that she was completely lost, and that you had won nothing at all.
9. That "the first virtue is to hold one's tongue." The widespread proverb originates in the *Distichs* of pseudo-Cato, a popular medieval schoolbook for learning Latin.

10

"Nor to this effect is anything lacking but a time when, as soon as it comes, I shall put you in her arms to take delight there. But, by God, act so that this business may be silent, and in no case may issue from your breast, O my dear friend, and don't be displeased if I pray you for this many times; you see well that my prayer is honorable."

Of wommen lost through fals and foles bost.°   *the boast of false men and fools*
Proverbes kanst thiself ynowe° and woost   *you know yourself enough*
300   Ayeins° that vice, for to ben a labbe,°   *Against / blabbermouth*
Al seyde men soth as often as thei gabbe.[1]

"O° tonge, allas, so often here-byforn°   *One / before this*
Hath mad ful many a lady bright of hewe°   *hue*
Seyd 'Weilaway,° the day that I was born!'   *To have said, "Alas"*
305   And many a maydes sorwe for to newe;°   *renew*
And for the more part, al is untrewe
That men of yelpe,° and° it were brought to   *brag about / if*
    preve.°   *put to the test*
Of kynde non avauntour is to leve.[2]

"Avauntour and a lyere,° al is on;°   *liar / it is all the same thing*
310   As thus: I pose,° a womman grante me   *posit, hypothesize*
Hire love, and seith that other wol she non,°   *she desires none other*
And I am sworn to holden it secree,°   *keep it secret*
And after I go telle it two or thre—
Iwis,° I am avauntour at the leeste,°   *Surely / least*
315   And lyere, for I breke my biheste.°   *promise*

"Now loke thanne,° if they be nought to blame,   *consider then*
Swich manere folk—what shal I clepe° hem, what?—   *call*
That hem avaunte of° wommen, and by name,   *boast of themselves about*
That° nevere yet bihyghte° hem this ne° that,   *(Women) who / promised / or*
320   Ne knewe hem more than myn olde hat!
No wonder is, so God me sende hele,°   *well-being*
Though° wommen dreden with us men to dele.°   *That / have dealings*

"I sey nought this for no° mistrust of yow,   *any*
Ne for no wis-man, but for foles nyce,°   *silly fools*
325   And for the harm that in the werld is now,
As wel for folie ofte as for malice;
For wel woot I, in wise folk that vice
No womman drat,° if she be wel avised;°   *dreads / has considered carefully*
For wyse ben by foles harm° chastised.   *the harm done by fools*

330   "But now to purpos; leve° brother deere,   *beloved*
Have al this thyng that I have seyd in mynde,
And kep the clos,° and be now of good cheere,   *keep (it) to yourself*
For at thi day° thow shalt me trewe fynde.   *at the time destined for you*
I shal thi proces° set in swych a kynde,°   *case / such a condition*
335   And God toforn,° that it shal the suffise,   *with God as my witness*
For it shal be right as thow wolt devyse.°   *arrange (it)*

"For wel I woot, thow menest wel, parde;°   *by God*
Therfore I dar this fully undertake.
Thow woost ek° what thi lady graunted the,   *also*

1. Even if people spoke the truth as often as they chatter idly.
2. By nature no boaster is to be believed.

11

Who could tell fully the joy that the soul of Troilo felt when he heard Pandaro? For the more he spoke, the more his sorrow lessened. The sighs which he had in great plenty left him, and his wretched suffering departed, and his tearful face, now that he felt good hope, became joyful.

12

And just as the new spring reclothes suddenly with leaves and with flowers the shrubs which were bare in the severe season and makes them beautiful and revests the meadows and hills and every riverbank with grass and with the beautiful new flowers, so, at once full of new joy, Troilo assumed again a serene countenance.

13

And after a little sigh, looking Pandaro in the face, he said, "Dear friend, you should remember both how and when you formerly found me weeping in the bitter time that I used to have in loving and also likewise when your words labored hard to know what might be the cause of my sorrow.

14

"And you know how much I restrained myself from disclosing it to you, who are my one and only friend, nor was there at that time any peril in telling it, although, for that matter, it was not a modest act. Think then how I should ever be able to consent to it now, who, while I speak about it with you, tremble with fear that another may hear it. May God take away such a misfortune!

15

"But nevertheless I swear to you by that God who governs equally the heaven and the earth, as I hope not to come into the hands of the cruel Agamemnon, that, if my life were eternal as it is mortal, you can live secure that this secret will, as far as my power is concerned, be retained in me, and in every act will the honor be served of that one who has wounded my heart.

340 And day is set the chartres up to make.[3]
Have now good nyght, I may no lenger wake;
And bid° for me, syn° thow art now in blysse,   *pray / since*
That God me sende deth or soone lisse."°   *comfort*

Who myghte tellen half the joie or feste
345 Which that the soule of Troilus tho° felte,   *then*
Heryng th'effect° of Pandarus byheste?°   *substance / promise*
His olde wo, that made his herte swelte,°   *grow faint*
Gan tho for joie wasten and tomelte,°   *diminish and melt away*
And al the richesse° of his sikes° sore   *abundance / sighs*
350 At ones fledde; he felte of hem namore.°   *no more of them*

But right so as thise holtes and thise hayis,°   *these groves and hedges*
That han in wynter dede ben and dreye,°   *dry*
Revesten hem° in grene whan that May is,   *Reclothe themselves*
Whan every lusty° liketh best to pleye;   *vigorous person*
355 Right in that selve wise,° soth° to seye,   *same manner / truth*
Wax° sodeynliche his herte ful of joie,   *Grew*
That gladder was ther nevere man in Troie.

And gan° his look on Pandarus up caste   *And (he) began*
Ful sobrely, and frendly for to se,°   *to look at*
360 And seyde, "Frend, in Aperil the laste—[4]
As wel thow woost, if it remembre the—°   *if you remember*
How neigh° the deth for wo thow fownde me,   *near*
And how thow dedest° al thi bisynesse   *performed*
To knowe of me the cause of my destresse.

365 "Thow woost how longe ich it forbar to seye°   *I refrained from saying it*
To the, that art the man that I best triste;°   *whom I most trust*
And peril non was it to the bywreye,°   *to reveal it to you*
That wist I wel; but telle me, if the liste,°   *if it please you*
Sith° I so loth was that thiself it wiste,°   *Since / that you might know it*
370 How dorst I mo tellen° of this matere,   *How would I dare tell others*
That quake° now, and no wight may us here?°   *(I) who tremble / hear*

"But natheles,° by that God I the swere,   *nevertheless*
That, as hym list,° may al this world governe—   *as it pleases him*
And, if I lye, Achilles with his spere
375 Myn herte cleve,° al° were my lif eterne,   *cleave, split / even if*
As I am mortal, if I late or yerne°   *early*
Wolde it bewreye,° or dorst, or sholde konne,°   *reveal / should know how to*
For al the good that God made under sonne—

"That rather deye I wolde, and determyne,°   *come to an end*
380 As thynketh° me, now stokked° in prisoun,   *it seems / put in stocks*
In wrecchidnesse, in filthe, and in vermyne,°   *vermin, rodents*

---

3. And the day is established for drawing up the documents, i.e., bringing the affair (as if a legal *proces,* as in line 334 above) to a conclusion.
4. Last April—but whether one (or more), or thirteen (or more) months ago cannot be determined.

16

"How much you have said and done for me I well know and plainly see. Nor should I ever be able to reward you for it in any act, for you have drawn me from Hell and worse to Paradise. But I beg you by our friendship that you do not apply that ugly name to yourself where it is a case of assisting a friend in his need.

17

"Let that name be for wretched, avaricious ones whom gold leads to such service. You have done it to draw me from the bitter anguish which I was in and from the harsh dispute which I had with adverse thoughts, the disturbers of any vestige of sweetness, as should be done for a friend when a friend sees him in tribulation.

18

"And so that you may know how much complete good will I bear for you, I have my sister Polyxena, more praised for beauty than any other, and also there is with her the most beautiful Helen, who is my sister-in-law. Open your heart, if either of them pleases you; then let me work with whichever one it may be.

19

"But since you have done so much—much more than I would have prayed you—fulfill my desire when the opportunity appears to you. To you I appeal and from you alone do I await the high pleasure and my comfort, the joy and the well-being and the solace and the delight. Nor shall I do more than you say; mine shall be the delight and you shall have gratitude for it."

Caytif to° cruel kyng Agamenoun;⁵   *Captive of*
And this in all the temples of this town
Upon the goddes alle, I wol the° swere   *to you*
385 To-morwe day, if that it liketh here.°   *pleases her*

"And that thow hast so muche ido° for me   *done*
That I ne may it nevere more disserve,
This know I wel, al° myghte I now for the   *even if*
A thousand tymes on a morwe sterve.°   *die in one morning*
390 I kan° namore, but that I wol the serve   *can (say)*
Right as thi sclave,° whider so thow wende,°   *slave / wherever you go*
For evere more, unto my lyves ende.

"But here, with al myn herte, I the biseche
That nevere in me thow deme° swich folie   *suppose*
395 As I shal seyn: me thoughte by° thi speche   *it seemed to me from*
That this which thow me dost for compaignie,°   *companionableness*
I sholde wene° it were a bauderye.°   *think / pandering*
I am nought wood,° al° if I lewed° be!   *insane / even / ignorant*
It is nought so, that woot I wel, parde!°   *by God*

400 "But he that gooth for gold or for ricchesse
On swich message,° calle hym what the list;°   *an errand / pleases you*
And this that thow doost, calle it gentilesse,
Compassioun, and felawship, and trist.°   *trust, loyalty*
Departe° it so, for wyde-wher° is wist°   *Distinguish / far and wide / known*
405 How that ther is diversite requered°   *required*
Bytwixen° thynges like, as I have lered.°   *Between / learned*

"And that thow knowe° I thynke nought ne   *so that you may know*
   wene°   *suppose*
That this servise a shame be or jape,°   *trick*
I have my faire suster Polixene,
410 Cassandre, Eleyne, or any of the frape—⁶
Be she nevere so fair or wel yshape,°   *formed*
Tel me which° thow wilt° of everychone,   *which one (of the sisters) / want*
To han for thyn, and lat me thanne allone.⁷

"But, sith thow hast don me this servyse
415 My lif to save and for non hope of mede,°   *reward*
So for the love of God, this grete emprise°   *undertaking*
Perfourme it out,° for now is moste nede;   *See it through*
For heigh and lough, withowten any drede,⁸
I wol alwey thyn hestes° alle kepe.   *commands*
420 Have now good nyght, and lat us bothe slepe."

---

5. Agamemnon, leader of the Greek army at Troy.
6. Helen, or any of the crowd. Polyxena and Cassandra were, according to Benoît, full sisters of
   Troilus; Helen was mistress of his brother Paris.
7. And then let me alone, i.e., leave the business to me.
8. For high and low (i.e., in every circumstance), without any doubt.

20

Pandaro remained pleased with Troilo and each attended to his own needs. But although to Troilo each day seemed to be a hundred with such a woman as the prize, he still suffered patiently and with high argument bore within himself the assaults of love, giving the night to thoughts of love and the day with his men to strenuous Mars.

Troilo is called again to amorous delights, who, taking the supreme sweetnesses with Criseida, solaces himself.

21

In the meantime the opportunity desired by the two lovers came, and so Criseida had Pandaro called to her and explained everything to him. But Pandaro was concerned about Troilo, who the day before had gone with certain men some distance on a particular duty of their war, although he ought to have returned at any moment.

22

He told her this, which it was very grievous to her to hear. But notwithstanding, Pandaro, as a diligent friend, at once sent a speedy servant for him, who, without taking any rest, was in a short time before Troilo who, having heard why he came, joyfully started out to return.

23

And having joined Pandaro, he heard from him fully what he had to do. Therefore he very impatiently awaited the night, which seemed to him to flee; then quietly alone with Pandaro, he took his way toward where Criseida was staying, who, alone and fearful, waited for him.

24

The night was dark and cloudy, as Troilo wished, who went watching each object attentively that nothing might possibly be a disturbance, little or great, to his amorous enjoyment, which he hoped might be the outcome of his severe torment, and through a secret way he entered alone the already quiet house.

25

And in a certain dark and remote place, as was enjoined upon him, he awaited the lady. Nor did he find waiting difficult or hard or not being able to see clearly where he was. But confident and secure he said often to himself, "The courteous lady will soon come, and I shall be more joyful than if I were the sole ruler of the world."

Thus held hym ech of other wel apayed,[9]
That al the world ne myghte it bet amende;°   *improve on it*
And on the morwe, whan they were arayed,°   *dressed*
Ech to his owen nedes gan entende.°   *attend*
425 But Troilus, though as the fir he brende°   *burned*
For sharp desir of hope and of plesaunce,
He nought forgat his goode governaunce,°   *appropriate self-control*

But in hymself with manhod gan restreyne
Ech racle° dede and ech unbridled cheere,°   *rash / unrestrained look*
430 That alle tho that° lyven, soth to seyne,   *those who*
Ne sholde han wist,° by word or by manere,   *known*
What that he mente, as touchyng° this matere.   *with regard to*
From every wight as fer° as is the cloude   *person as distant*
He was, so wel dissimilen he koude.°   *he knew how to dissemble*

435 And al the while which that I yow devyse,°   *recount*
This was his lif: with all his fulle myght,
By day, he was in Martes° heigh servyse—   *Mars's*
This is to seyn, in armes as a knyght;
And for the more part, the longe nyght
440 He lay and thoughte how that he myghte serve
His lady best, hire thonk° for to deserve.   *thanks*

Nil I naught swere,° although he lay ful softe,°   *I will not swear / comfortably*
That in his thought he nas somwhat disesed,°   *distressed*
Ne that he torned on his pilwes° ofte,   *pillows*
445 And wold of that hym missed han ben sesed.[1]
But in swich cas men° is nought alwey plesed,   *a person*
For aught I woot,° namore than was he;   *For all I know*
That kan I deme of possibilitee.[2]

But certeyn is, to purpos for to go,
450 That in this while, as writen is in geeste,[3]
He say° his lady somtyme, and also   *saw*
She with hym spak, whan that she dorst or leste;°   *dared or was pleased to*
And by hire bothe avys,° as was the beste,   *the counsel of the two of them*
Apoynteden° full warly° in this nede,   *they arranged things / prudently*
455 So as they durste,° how they wolde procede.   *dared*

But it was spoken° in so short a wise,   *they held conversation*
In swich await° alwey, and in swich feere,   *watchfulness*
Lest any wight devynen or devyse°   *guess or conjecture*
Wolde of hem two, or to it laye an ere,°   *extend an ear*

9. Thus each considered himself well pleased with the other.
1. And wished to have been put in possession of what he lacked.
2. That I can suppose as a (logical) potentiality.
3. That during this period, as it is written in the story. The narrator again, as in lines 502 and 575 below, alludes to his fictitious source Lollius here where he departs at length from his actual source in the *Filostrato*.

26

Criseida had clearly heard him come; therefore, as had been agreed, she coughed in order that he might hear her; and so that it might not be a displeasure to him to be there, she often speeded her conversation, and she hastened so that everyone might at once take himself to sleep, saying she had such sleepiness that she could no longer stay awake.

27

After everyone had gone to sleep and the house remained all quiet, Criseida thought to go at once where Troilo was in the secret place. When he heard her come, he rose to his feet and with a joyous face went to meet her, waiting silently to be ready at her every command.

28

The lady had in her hand a lighted torch and all alone she descended the stairs and saw Troilo awaiting her in suspense. She greeted him; then said as well as she could: "My lord, if I have offended you by keeping your royal splendor shut up in such a place, I pray you, by God, to pardon me, my sweet desire."

29

Troilo said to her: "Beautiful lady, sole hope and well-being of my mind, the star of your beautiful face, splendid and shining, has been ever before me, and this little place has been dearer to me certainly than my palace and there is no need to ask pardon for this." Then he embraced her, and they kissed each other on the mouth.

460 That al this world so leef to hem ne were[4]
As that Cupide wolde hem grace sende
To maken of hire speche aright° an ende.   *quickly*

But thilke° litel that they spake or wroughte,°   *that same / did*
His wise goost° took ay° of al swych heede,   *spirit / always*
465 It semed hire he wiste° what she thoughte   *knew*
Withouten word, so that it was° no nede   *there was*
To bidde° hym ought to doon, or ought forbeede;°   *ask / forbid anything*
For which she thought that love, al come it° late,   *though it had come*
Of alle joie hadde opned hire the yate.°   *gate*

470 And shortly of this proces for to pace,°   *pass*
So wel his werk and wordes he bisette,°   *employed*
That he so ful stood in his lady grace,°   *lady's favor*
That twenty thousand tymes, er she lette,°   *before she left off*
She thonked God that evere she with hym mette.
475 So koude he hym governe in swich servyse,
That al the world ne myght it bet devyse.°   *arrange*

For whi° she fond hym so discret in al,   *Because*
So secret, and of swich obeïsaunce,°   *such obedience*
That wel she felte he was to hire a wal
480 Of stiel,° and sheld° from every displesaunce;   *steel / shield*
That° to ben in his goode governaunce,   *So that*
So wis he was, she was namore afered—°   *afraid*
I mene, as fer as oughte ben required.[5]

And Pandarus, to quike° alwey the fir,   *quicken, enliven*
485 Was evere ylike prest° and diligent;   *ready, prompt*
To ese° his frend was set al his desir.   *comfort*
He shof ay° on, he to and fro was sent;   *pressed always*
He lettres bar° whan Troilus was absent;   *carried*
That nevere man, as in his frendes nede,
490 Ne bar hym bet than he, withouten drede.°   *doubt*

But now, paraunter,° som man wayten° wolde   *perhaps / expect*
That every word, or soonde,° or look, or cheere   *message*
Of Troilus that I rehercen sholde,
In al this while unto his lady deere—
495 I trowe° it were a long thyng for to here—   *believe*
Or of what wight that stant in swich disjoynte,
His wordes alle, or every look, to poynte.[6]

For sothe, I have naught herd it don er this
In story non, ne no man here,° I wene;°   *nor (has) anyone here / think*
500 And though I wolde, I koude nought, ywys;°   *certainly*

---

4. That all this world was not so dear to them.
5. I mean, to the extent that (Troilus's governance) ought to be required; i.e., within the bounds of propriety, or within Criseyde's tolerance for being governed.
6. Or to describe ("point," set forth in detail) all the words, or every look, of whatever person who stands in such distress.

For ther was som epistel° hem bitwene,   letter
That wolde, as seyth myn autour, wel contene°   fill
Neigh° half this book, of which hym liste   Nearly
   nought° write.   it doesn't please him
How sholde I thanne a lyne of it endite?°   compose

505 But to the grete effect:° than sey I thus,   main point
That stondyng in concord and in quiete,
Thise ilke° two, Criseyde and Troilus,   same
As I have told, and in this tyme swete—°   sweet
Save only often myghte they nought mete,°   meet
510 Ne leiser° have hire speches to fulfelle—°   leisure / fulfill, complete
That it bifel° right as I shal yow telle: befell, occurred

That Pandarus, that evere dide his myght
Right for the fyn° that I shal speke of here,   goal
As for to bryngen to his hows° som nyght   house
515 His faire nece and Troilus yfere,°   together
Wheras at leiser al this heighe matere,
Touchyng here love, were at the fulle upbounde,
Hadde out of doute a tyme to it founde.[7]

For he with gret deliberacioun
520 Hadde every thyng that herto myght availle°   be helpful
Forncast° and put in execucioun,   Planned
And neither left for cost ne for travaille.
Come if hem list, hem sholde no thyng faille;[8]
And for to ben in ought aspied° there,   detected in any way
525 That, wiste he wel, an impossible° were.   impossibility

Dredeles, it cler was in the wynd
Of every pie and every lette-game;[9]
Now al is wel, for al the world is blynd
In this matere, bothe fremde and tame.°   wild and tame, i.e., everyone
530 This tymbur° is al redy up to frame;°   timber / be built (as a house)
Us lakketh nought° but that we witen° wolde   We lack nothing / know
A certeyn houre, in which she comen sholde.

And Troilus, that al this purveiaunce°   these arrangements
Knew at the fulle,° and waited on it ay,°   completely / always
535 Hadde hereupon ek° mad gret ordinaunce,°   also / preparation
And found his cause, and therto his aray,[1]
If that he were missed, nyght or day,
Ther-while° he was aboute this servyse,   While
That he was gon to don his sacrifise,

---

7. At which point all this important subject-matter concerning their love would have been completely wrapped up had a trouble-free opportunity (*out of doute a tyme*) for it been found.
8. And (Pandarus) omitted nothing either for expense or trouble. If it pleased them to come, nothing would be lacking for them.
9. Assuredly, it was clear in the wind from every magpie (i.e., chatterbox) and every spoilsport. Pandarus's plan is downwind, unable to be sniffed out by gossips.
1. And found (as his excuse) his cause, and the arrangements appropriate to it.

540 And moste° at swich a temple allone wake,°   *must / keep watch*
     Answered of Apollo for to be;
     And first to sen the holy laurer quake,[2]
     Er that° Apollo spak out of the tree,   *Before*
     To telle hym next whan Grekes sholde flee—
545 And forthy lette hym no man,° God forbede,   *therefore may no one hinder him*
     But prey Apollo helpen° in this nede.   *to help*

     Now is ther litel more for to doone,
     But Pandare up and, shortly for to seyne,
     Right sone upon the chaungynge of the moone,°   *at the new moon*
550 Whan lightles is the world a nyght or tweyne,°   *two*
     And that the wolken shop hym° for to reyne,°   *sky prepared / rain*
     He streght o morwe° unto his nece wente—   *in the morning*
     Ye han wel herd the fyn of his entente.°   *goal of his intentions*

     Whan he was com, he gan anon to pleye
555 As he was wont, and of hymself to jape;°   *to poke fun at himself*
     And finaly he swor and gan hire seye,
     By this and that, she sholde hym nought escape,
     Ne lenger don° hym after hire to cape;°   *cause / hunt*
     But certeynly she moste, by hire leve,°   *with her permission*
560 Come soupen° in his hous with hym at eve.   *sup*

     At which she lough,° and gan hire faste° excuse,   *laughed / quickly*
     And seyde, "It reyneth;° lo, how sholde I gon?"   *It's about to rain*
     "Lat be," quod he, "ne stant nought° thus to muse.°   *don't stand / ponder*
     This moot° be don! Ye shal be ther anon."°   *must / immediately*
565 So at the laste herof they fille aton,°   *fell at one, into agreement*
     Or elles, softe he swor hire in hire ere,
     He nolde nevere° comen ther° she were.   *would never / where*

     Soone after this, she to hym gan to rowne,°   *whisper*
     And axed° hym if Troilus were there.   *asked*
570 He swor hire nay, for he was out of towne,
     And seyde, "Nece, I pose° that he were;   *posit, set as a hypothesis*
     Yow thurste nevere han the more fere;[3]
     For rather than men myghte hym ther aspie,°   *espy, detect*
     Me were levere° a thousand fold to dye."   *I had rather*

575 Nought list° myn auctour fully to declare   *It does not please*
     What that she thoughte whan he seyde so,
     That Troilus was out of towne yfare,°   *gone*
     As if° he seyde therof soth° or no;   *Regarding whether / the truth*
     But that, withowten await,° with hym to go,   *delay*
580 She graunted hym, sith° he hire that bisoughte,°   *since / beseeched that of her*
     And, as his nece, obeyed as hire oughte.

---

2. And first (Troilus must) see the holy laurel quake. The laurel tree is sacred to Apollo; its quaking
     precedes the god's prophetic speech.
3. You need never have the more fear (even if Troilus were at Pandarus's house).

But natheles,° yet gan she hym biseche, *nevertheless*
Although with hym to gon it was no fere,° *there was nothing to fear*
For to ben war° of goosissh° poeples speche, *wary / gooselike, silly*
585 That dremen° thynges whiche as nevere were, *Who dream up*
And wel avyse hym° whom he broughte there; *to consider well*
And seyde hym, "Em, syn I moste on yow triste,° *must trust in you*
Loke° al be wel, and do now as yow liste."° *See that / as it pleases you*

He swor hire yis,° by stokkes and by stones,[4] *"yes," affirmatively*
590 And by the goddes that in hevene dwelle,
Or elles were hym levere,° soule and bones, *else he would rather*
With Pluto kyng as depe ben in helle
As Tantalus[5]—what sholde I more telle?
Whan al was wel, he roos and took his leve,
595 And she to soper com, whan it was eve,

With a certein° of hire owen men, *certain number*
And with hire faire nece Antigone,
And other of hire wommen nyne or ten.
But who was glad now, who, as trowe ye,° *as you may believe*
600 But Troilus, that stood and myght it se° *see*
Thoroughout° a litel wyndow in a stewe,° *Through / closet, bathroom*
Ther he bishet syn mydnyght was in mewe,[6]

Unwist of every wight° but of Pandare? *Undetected by anyone*
But to the point: now whan that she was come,
605 With alle joie and alle frendes fare° *friendly to-do*
Hire em° anon in armes hath hire nome,° *uncle / taken*
And after to the soper, alle and some,
Whan tyme was, ful softe they hem sette.
God woot, ther was no deynte for to fette![7]

610 And after soper gonnen they to rise,
At ese wel,° with herte fresshe and glade; *well at ease, comfortable*
And wel was hym that koude best devyse° *contrive*
To liken° hire, or that hire laughen made: *please*
He song; she pleyde; he tolde tale of Wade.[8]
615 But at the laste, as every thyng hath ende,
She took hire leve, and nedes wolde wende.° *needs must depart*

But O Fortune, executrice° of wierdes,° *(female) administrator / fates*
O influences° of thise hevenes hye!° *(astrological) influences / high*
Soth is, that under God ye ben oure hierdes,° *shepherds*
620 Though to us bestes ben the causez wrie.° *creatures the causes are hidden*
This mene I now: for she gan homward hye,° *hasten*

4. (Pandarus swore) by tree-trunks and stones, i.e., by the materials of pagan idols.
5. Tantalus was condemned in Hades to stand thirsty in a pool of water that always eluded (tantalized) him.
6. Where he had been shut up, cooped up (*in mewe*) since midnight.
7. God knows, there was no delicacy to be fetched—no dainty food was lacking.
8. This man sang, that woman played an instrument, that man told the tale of Wade. The several references in medieval literature to a legendary hero named Wade do not suffice for us to know his story.

But execut° was al bisyde hire leve°   *done / without her leave*
The goddes wil, for which she moste bleve.°   *remain*

   The bente° moone with hire° hornes pale,   *crescent / its*
625   Saturne, and Jove, in Cancro joyned were,[9]
That swych a reyn from heven gan avale°   *come down*
That every maner° womman that was there   *sort of*
Hadde of that smoky reyn a verray° feere;   *true, intense*
At which Pandare tho lough,° and seyde thenne,   *then laughed*
630   "Now were it tyme a lady to gon henne!°   *for a lady to go hence*

   "But goode nece, if I myghte evere plese
Yow any thyng,° than prey ich yow," quod he,   *in any way*
"To don myn herte as now so gret an ese
As for to dwelle here al this nyght with me,
635   For-whi° this is youre owen hous, parde.°   *Because / by God*
For by my trouthe, I sey it nought a-game,°   *in jest*
To wende° as now, it were to me a shame."   *depart*

   Criseyde, which that koude as muche good°   *who had as much good sense*
As half a world, took hede of his preiere;
640   And syn it ron,° and al was on a flod,°   *since it was raining / in flood*
She thoughte, "As good chep° may I dwellen here,   *profitably*
And graunte it gladly with a frendes chere,°   *friendly demeanor*
And have a thonk,° as grucche° and thanne   *thanks / grumble*
   abide;°   *stay here*
For hom to gon, it may nought wel bitide."°   *go well*

645   "I wol," quod she, "myn uncle lief° and deere;   *beloved*
Syn that yow list, it skile is to be so.[1]
I am right glad with yow to dwellen here;
I seyde but a-game° I wolde go."   *in jest*
"Iwys, graunt mercy,° nece," quod he tho,   *Indeed, great thanks*
650   "Were it a-game or no, soth for to telle,
Now am I glad, syn that yow list° to dwelle."   *it pleases you*

   Thus al is wel; but tho bigan aright
The newe joie and al the feste° agayn.   *merriment*
But Pandarus, if goodly hadde he myght,[2]
655   He wolde han hyed° hire to bedde fayn,°   *hastened / gladly*
And seyde, "Lord, this is an huge rayn!
This were a weder° for to slepen inne—   *weather*
And that I rede° us soone to bygynne.   *advise*

9. The planets Saturn and Jupiter and the crescent moon were conjoined in the zodiacal house of Cancer, causing the rain. The conjunction of the planets with the newly visible moon actually took place on June 9 or 10, 1385. The conjunction (beginning in May 1385) of these largest and most distant known planets in Cancer was thought to be particularly portentous and was noted by contemporary writers; it had not occurred for 600 years. Chaucer may have witnessed the conjunction—perhaps while at work on *Troilus and Criseyde*—or he may have learned of it from an almanac; in either case it suggests that he composed the poem around this time.
1. Since it pleases you, it is reasonable for it to be so.
2. But Pandarus, if he could have done so decently.

"And nece, woot ye wher I wol yow leye,[3]
660 For that° we shul nat liggen° far asonder,°   *So that / lie / apart*
And for ye neither shullen, dar I seye,
Heren noyse of reynes nor of thonder?[4]
By God, right in my litel closet° yonder.   *bedroom*
And I wol in that outer hous allone
665 Be wardein° of youre wommen everichone.°   *guardian / every one*

"And in this myddel chambre that ye se
Shal youre wommen slepen, wel and softe;[5]
And there° I seyde shal youreselven be;   *there where*
And if ye liggen° wel to-nyght, com ofte,°   *lie asleep / come (again) often*
670 And careth nought what weder is alofte.°   *weather is in the sky*
The wyn anon, and whan so that yow leste,[6]
So go we slepe: I trowe° it be the beste."   *believe*

Ther nys no more, but hereafter soone,
The voidë dronke, and travers drawe anon,[7]
675 Gan every wight that hadde nought to done
More in the place out of the chaumbre gon.
And evere mo° so sterneliche it ron,°   *more / fiercely it rained*
And blew therwith so wondirliche° loude,   *amazingly*
That wel neigh no man heren other koude.[8]

680 Tho Pandarus, hire em, right as hym oughte,
With wommen swiche as were hire most aboute,[9]
Ful glad unto hire beddes syde hire broughte,
And took his leve, and gan ful lowe loute,°   *bow*
And seyde, "Here at this closet dore withoute,
685 Right overthwart,° youre wommen liggen° alle,   *Just opposite / lie down*
That whom yow list of hem° ye may here   *Whomever of them it pleases you*
calle."

So whan that she was in the closet leyd,
And alle hire wommen forth by ordinaunce°   *in due order*
Abedde weren, ther as I have seyd,
690 Ther was nomore to skippen nor to traunce,
But boden go to bedde, with meschaunce,
If any wight was steryng anywhere,[1]
And lat hem slepen that abedde were.

3. Do you know where I want you to lie down?
4. And, I dare say, so that you must hear the noise neither of rain nor of thunder.
5. The festivities have taken place in Pandarus's great hall. Apparently he assigns Criseyde a chamber for sleeping off one end of the hall, arranges for her waiting women to sleep in the hall outside her door, draws a curtain across the hall, and assigns himself the far end of the hall beyond the curtain, the *outer hous* (line 664). Chaucer does not describe the arrangements in detail, and we are left ignorant of how Pandarus reaches the little room (*stewe*; line 601, 698) in which Troilus hides.
6. (Bring) the wine forthwith, and when it may please you.
7. The *voidë* (a good-night cup of spiced wine) having been drunk, and the curtain having been drawn forthwith. The French term *voidé* refers to one's withdrawal from a room.
8. That one person almost couldn't hear another.
9. With such women as were most closely attendant on her.
1. There was no more prancing or tramping about, but if any person was stirring anywhere (he was) commanded to go to bed, with a curse.

But Pandarus, that wel koude ech a deel°   *in its entirety*
695 Th'olde daunce,° and every point therinne,   *the old dance, the art of courtship*
Whan that he sey° that alle thyng was wel,   *saw*
He thought he wolde upon his werk bigynne,
And gan the stuwe° doore al softe unpynne;°   *little room's / unlatch*
And stille as stoon, withouten lenger lette,°   *delay*
700 By Troilus adown right he hym sette,

And shortly to the point right for to gon,
Of al this werk he tolde hym word and ende,°   *beginning and end, entirely*
And seyde, "Make the° redy right anon,   *yourself*
For thow shalt into hevene° blisse wende."°   *heaven's / pass*
705 "Now, blisful Venus, thow me grace sende!"
Quod Troilus, "For nevere yet no nede°   *need (of your grace)*
Hadde ich er now, ne halvendel° the drede."   *half*

Quod Pandarus, "Ne drede the nevere a deel,°   *bit*
For it shal be right as thow wolt desire;
710 So thryve I,° this nyght shal I make it weel,°   *may I prosper / well*
Or casten al the gruwel in the fire."²
"Yet, blisful Venus, this nyght thow me enspire,"°   *inspire*
Quod Troilus, "As wys° as I the serve,   *surely*
And evere bet° and bet shal, til I sterve.°   *better / die*

715 "And if ich hadde, O Venus ful of myrthe,
Aspectes badde of Mars or of Saturne,
Or thow combust or let were in my birthe,
Thy fader prey al thilke harm disturne
Of grace, and that I glad ayein may turne,³
720 For love of hym thow lovedest in the shawe—°   *woods, thicket*
I meene Adoun, that with the boor was slawe.⁴

"O Jove ek, for the love of faire Europe,⁵
The which° in forme of bole° awey thow   *Whom / bull*
    fette,°   *fetched, carried off*
Now help! O Mars, thow with thi blody cope,°   *bloody cloak (as god of war)*
725 For love of Cipris,° thow me nought ne lette!°   *Venus (beloved of Mars) / hinder*
O Phebus, thynk whan Dane hireselven shette
Under the bark, and laurer wax for drede;⁶
Yet for hire love, O help now at this nede!°   *in this crisis*

---

2. Or (I shall) throw all the porridge into the fire, i.e., ruin everything—tonight will make or break us.
3. And if I had at my birth, O Venus full of mirth, unfavorable positions of the planets Mars or Saturn, or if you were burnt up (as a planet, too close to the sun) or hindered, pray to your father (Jupiter) for grace to avert all those harmful influences, and pray that I may conversely revert to my happy condition. Troilus here and in the following lines invokes all the planet-gods along with the sun and moon, and refers to several of the myths recounted in Ovid's *Metamorphoses*.
4. I mean Adonis (beloved of Venus), who was slain by the boar.
5. Jupiter assumed the form of a bull when he abducted Europa.
6. O Phebus (Apollo, god of the sun), think about when Daphne shut herself under the bark, and for fear grew into a laurel tree.

"Mercurie, for the love of Hierse eke,°   *also*
730 For which Pallas was with Aglawros wroth,[7]
Now help! And ek Diane,° I the biseke°   *Diana (the moon) / beseech you*
That this viage° be nought to the looth!°   *undertaking / hateful*
O fatal sustren which, er any cloth
Me shapen was, my destine me sponne,[8]
735 So helpeth to this werk that is bygonne!"

Quod Pandarus, "Thow wrecched mouses herte,
Artow agast so° that she wol the bite?   *Are you so frightened*
Wy! Don° this furred cloke upon thy sherte,°   *Why! Put on / over your shirt*
And folwe me, for I wol have the wite.°   *blame*
740 But bid,° and lat me gon biforn a lite."°   *wait / a little before*
And with that word he gan undon a trappe,°   *trapdoor*
And Troilus he brought in by the lappe.°   *hem (of his garment)*

The sterne° wynd so loude gan to route°   *fierce / roar*
That no wight oother noise myghte heere;
745 And they that layen at the dore withoute,
Ful sikerly° they slepten alle yfere;°   *soundly / together*
And Pandarus, with a ful sobre cheere,°   *serious countenance*
Goth to the dore anon, withouten lette,°   *delay*
Ther as they laye, and softely it shette.°   *shut*

750 And as he com ayeynward pryvely,°   *back again stealthily*
His nece awook, and axed,° "Who goth there?"   *asked*
"My dere nece," quod he, "it am I.
Ne wondreth nought,° ne have of it no fere."   *And don't be amazed*
And ner he com° and seyde hire° in hire ere, *he came nearer / said to her*
755 "No word, for love of God, I yow biseche!
Lat no wight° risen and heren of oure speche."   *person*

"What, which wey be ye comen, benedicite?"°   *bless me*
Quod she; "And how, unwist of hem° alle?"°   *undetected by them*
"Here at this secre trappe-dore," quod he.
760 Quod tho Criseyde, "Lat me som wight calle!"
"I!° God forbede that it sholde falle,"°   *Oh! / happen*
Quod Pandarus, "that ye swich folye wroughte!°   *should do such folly*
They myghte demen thyng° they nevere er°   *suspect something / before*
    thoughte.

"It is nought good a slepyng hound to wake,
765 Ne yeve° a wight a cause to devyne:°   *give / conjecture*
Youre wommen slepen alle, I undertake,°   *affirm*
So that, for hem, the hous men myghte myne,°   *undermine*
And slepen wollen° til the sonne shyne.   *they will sleep*
And whan my tale brought is to an ende,
770 Unwist,° right as I com, so wol I wende.°   *Undetected / depart*

7. Pallas Athena was angry with Aglauros and caused her to envy her sister Herse, beloved of Mercury. Hence Mercury turned Aglauros to stone. Chaucer differs from the story in Ovid (*Metamorphoses* 2.708–832) in implying that Mercury's love for Herse made Pallas angry (*wroth*) with Aglauros.
8. O fatal sisters (i.e., the three Fates) who spun my destiny before any cloth was woven for me (i.e., before I was born).

"Now, nece myn, ye shul wel understonde,"
Quod he, "so as ye wommen demen° alle, — *judge, think*
That for to holde in love a man in honde,⁹
And hym hire lief° and deere herte calle, — *beloved*
775 And maken hym an howve above a calle—¹
I meene, as love another in this while—
She doth hireself a shame and hym a gyle.° — *deception*

"Now, wherby that° I telle yow al this: — *the reason why*
Ye woot youreself, as wel as any wight,
780 How that youre love al fully graunted is
To Troilus, the worthieste knyght,
Oon of this world, and therto trouthe yplight,²
That, but it were on hym along,° ye nolde — *unless it were his fault*
Hym nevere falsen° while ye lyven sholde. — *play false*

785 "Now stant it° thus, that sith° I fro yow wente, — *it stands / since*
This Troilus, right platly° for to seyn, — *plainly*
Is thorugh a goter, by a pryve wente,³
Into my chaumbre come in al this reyn,
Unwist of° every manere° wight, certeyn, — *Undetected by / sort of*
790 Save of myself, as wisly have I joye,° — *as surely as I have joy*
And by that feith I shal° Priam of Troie, — *owe to*

"And he is come in swich peyne and distresse
That, but he be al fully wood° by this, — *insane*
He sodeynly mot° falle into wodnesse,° — *must / madness*
795 But if° God helpe; and cause whi° this is. — *Unless / the reason why*
He seith hym told is of° a frend of his, — *that he has been told by*
How that ye sholden love oon hatte Horaste;⁴
For sorwe of which this nyght shal ben his laste."

Criseyde, which that al this wonder herde,
800 Gan sodeynly aboute hire herte colde,° — *grow cold*
And with a sik° she sorwfully answerde, — *sigh*
"Allas! I wende, whoso tales tolde,⁵
My deere herte wolde me nought holde
So lightly fals!° Allas, conceytes° wronge, — *frivolously false / imaginings*
805 What harm they don! For now lyve I to° longe! — *too*

"Horaste! Allas, and falsen Troilus?
I knowe hym nought, God helpe me so!" quod she.
"Allas, what wikked spirit tolde hym thus?
Now certes,° em, tomorwe and° I hym se, — *certainly / if*
810 I shal therof as ful° excusen me, — *fully*

9. To cajole a man with false promises about loving.
1. And make him a hood above a cap, i.e., deceive him, deal doubly with him.
2. The very worthiest (*oon the worthieste*) knight in this world, and have pledged your faith to that.
3. Has through a gutter (perhaps an eavestrough), by a secret passage—or perhaps, by a sewer (privy) passage, if the *stewe* is a bathroom. In any case Troilus's method of entry seems to be Pandarus's invention.
4. One named Horaste. Pandarus invents Troilus's jealousy of Horaste.
5. I would have thought, whoever told (such) tales.

As evere dide womman, if hym like."°   *if it please him*
And with that word she gan ful soore sike.°   *to sigh*

"O God," quod she, "so worldly selynesse,°   *happiness*
Which clerkes° callen fals felicitee,[6]   *learned people, scholars*
815 Imedled° is with many a bitternesse!   *Mingled*
Ful angwissous° than is, God woot," quod she,   *painful*
"Condicioun of veyn° prosperitee: *vain*
For either joies comen nought yfeere,°   *together*
Or elles no wight hath hem alwey here.

820 "O brotel wele° of mannes joie unstable!   *brittle, fragile well-being*
With what wight so° thow be, or how thow pleye,°   *whatever person / you act*
Either he woot° that thow, joie, art muable,°   *knows / mutable*
Or woot it nought; it mot ben oon of tweye.°   *the two*
Now if he woot it nought, how may he seye
825 That he hath verray° joie and selynesse,°   *true / happiness*
That is of ignoraunce ay° in derknesse?   *ever*

"Now if he woot that joie is transitorie,
As every joye of worldly thyng mot flee,[7]
Than every tyme he that° hath in memorie,°   *that (joy) / mind*
830 The drede of lesyng° maketh hym that he   *losing (it)*
May in no perfit° selynesse be;   *perfect*
And if to lese his joie he sette a myte,[8]
Than semeth it that joie is worth ful lite.°   *quite little*

"Wherfore I wol diffyne° in this matere,   *conclude*
835 That trewely, for aught I kan espie,
Ther is no verray weele° in this world heere.   *true well-being*
But O thow wikked serpent, jalousie,
Thow mysbyleved° envyous folie,°   *unbelieving / folly*
Why hastow Troilus mad to me untriste,°   *untrusting*
840 That° nevere yet agylte hym,° that I wiste?"°   *I who / did him wrong / knew of*

Quod Pandarus, "Thus fallen is this cas—"°   *The situation is thus*
"Wy!° Uncle myn," quod she, "who tolde hym this?   *Why!*
Why doth my deere herte thus, allas?"
"Ye woot, ye, nece myn," quod he, "what is.
845 I hope al shal be wel that is amys,
For ye may quenche° al this, if that yow leste—°   *put a stop to / it please you*
And doth right so, for I holde it the beste."

"So shal I do to-morwe, ywys,"° quod she,   *certainly*
"And God toforn,° so that it shal suffise."   *with God as my witness*
850 "To-morwe? Allas, that were a fair!"° quod he;   *a fine thing or a to-do*
"Nay, nay, it may nat stonden in this wise,°   *remain this way*

---

6. Many of Criseyde's thoughts about the limitations of worldly happiness, "false felicity," replicate those of Boethius in *The Consolation of Philosophy*, especially 2.p4, which Chaucer may have translated shortly before writing *Troilus and Criseyde*.
7. Inasmuch as every joy in worldly things must be fleeting.
8. And if he cares a whit about losing his joy. A *myte* is a small coin.

For, nece myn, thus writen clerkes wise,
That peril is with drecchyng in ydrawe;°   *introduced with delay*
Nay, swiche abodes° ben nought worth an   *delays*
    hawe.°   *hawthorn-berry, trifle*

855 "Nece, alle thyng hath tyme, I dar avowe;
For whan a chaumbre afire° is or an halle,   *on fire*
Wel more nede is, it sodeynly rescowe°   *to rescue it immediately*
Than to dispute and axe° amonges alle   *ask*
How this candel in the strawe is falle.°   *has fallen*
860 A, benedicite!° For al among that fare°   *bless me! / to-do*
The harm is don, and fare-wel feldefare!⁹

"And nece myn—ne take it naught agrief—°   *don't take it badly*
If that ye suffre hym° al nyght in this wo,   *let him remain*
God help me so, ye hadde hym nevere lief!°   *never held him dear*
865 That dar I seyn, now° ther is but we two.   *now that*
But wel I woot that ye wol nat do so;
Ye ben to wys to doon so gret folie,
To putte his lif al nyght in jupertie."°   *jeopardy*

"Hadde I hym nevere lief?° by God, I weene°   *dear / believe*
870 Ye hadde nevere thyng so lief!" quod she.
"Now by my thrift,"° quod he, "that shal be seene!   *as I may prosper*
For syn° ye make this ensaumple° of me,   *since / exemplar (of friendship)*
If ich al nyght wolde hym in sorwe se,
For al the tresour in the town of Troie,
875 I bidde° God I nevere mote° have joie.   *pray / may*

"Now loke thanne, if ye that ben° his love   *who are*
Shul putte his lif al night in jupertie
For thyng of nought,° now by that God above,   *For no good reason*
Naught oonly this delay comth of folie,
880 But of malice, if that I shal naught lie.
What! Platly,° and ye suffre hym° in destresse,   *Plainly / if you let him remain*
Ye neyther bounte° don ne gentilesse."   *good deed*

Quod tho Criseyde, "Wol ye don o° thyng   *one*
And° ye therwith shal stynte° al his disese?°   *If / stop / distress*
885 Have heere, and bereth hym this blewe° ryng,   *blue (sign of constancy)*
For ther is nothyng myghte hym bettre plese,
Save I myself, ne more hys herte apese;°   *appease, comfort*
And sey° my deere herte that his sorwe   *tell*
Is causeles; that shal be sene° to-morwe."   *seen, made clear*

890 "A ryng?" quod he, "Ye haselwodes shaken!¹
Ye, nece myn, that ryng moste° han a stoon°   *must / stone (of magical power)*
That myghte dede men alyve maken;

9. And farewell, thrush!—i.e., the bird has flown, it's too late.
1. Either "You shake hazelwoods!" or "Yea, hazelwoods shake!" The tree is also referred to in V.505
and V.1174 below; in each case the meaning is uncertain, but the expressions seem to imply a
mocking skepticism. The sense here may be "You merely go a-nutting" or "Sure, hazelwoods
shake—what else is new?"

And swich a ryng trowe° I that ye have non.   *believe*
Discrecioun° out of youre hed is gon;   *Good sense*
895 That fele I now," quod he, "and that is routhe.°   *a pity*
O tyme ilost, wel maistow corsen slouthe!°   *may you curse sloth (i.e., delay)*

"Woot ye not wel that noble and heigh corage°   *lofty spirit*
Ne sorweth nought, ne stynteth ek, for lite?[2]
But if a fool were in a jalous rage,
900 I nolde setten at his sorwe a myte,[3]
But feffe° hym with a fewe wordes white°   *endow / specious, plausible*
Anothir day, whan that I myghte hym fynde;
But this thyng stant al in° another kynde.   *consists entirely of*

"This° is so gentil and so tendre of herte   *This (man)*
905 That with his deth he wol his sorwes wreke;°   *make up for*
For trusteth wel, how sore that hym smerte,°   *however sorely it pains him*
He wol to yow no jalous wordes speke.
And forthi,° nece, er that his herte breke,   *therefore*
So speke youreself to hym of this matere,
910 For with o° word ye may his herte stere.°   *one / steer, guide*

"Now have I told what peril he is inne,
And his comynge unwist° is to every wight;   *undetected*
Ne, parde,° harm may ther be non, ne synne:°   *by God / sin*
I wol myself be with yow al this nyght.
915 Ye knowe ek how it is youre owen knyght,
And that bi right ye moste upon hym triste,°   *rely*
And I al prest° to fecche hym whan yow liste."   *ready*

This accident° so pitous was to here,   *occurrence*
And ek so like a sooth at prime face,°   *a truth at first sight*
920 And Troilus hire knyght to hir so deere,
His prive° comyng, and the siker° place,   *secret / safe*
That though that she did hym as thanne a grace,°   *favor*
Considered° alle thynges as they stoode,   *Considering*
No wonder is, syn° she did al for goode.   *since*

925 Criseyde answerde, "As wisly God at reste
My soule brynge, as me is for hym wo![4]
And em,° iwis, fayn° wolde I don the beste,   *uncle / gladly*
If that ich hadde grace° to do so;   *power, opportunity*
But whether that ye dwelle° or for hym go,   *remain here*
930 I am, til God me bettre mynde sende,
At dulcarnoun,[5] right at my wittes ende."

2. Doesn't grieve, and also doesn't cease to grieve, for a small matter.
3. I wouldn't care a whit for his sorrow (see line 832 above).
4. As surely as God may bring my soul to rest, how much sorrow I have for him!
5. In Euclid's geometry the 47th proposition is called *dulcarnoun*, from an Arabic phrase meaning "the two-horned," because the geometric diagram resembles a figure with two horns. In line 933 Pandarus says Dulcarnon is called the "putting to flight (*flemyng*) of wretches," but that is the translation of the name given Euclid's 5th proposition, Fuga Miserorum, because at that point in Euclid the weaker students are routed by the difficulty of the proposition.

Quod Pandarus, "Yee, nece, wol ye here?°　　　　　　　*listen*
Dulcarnoun called is 'flemyng of wrecches':
It semeth hard, for wrecches wol nought lere,°　　　　*learn*
935　For verray slouthe° or other wilfull tecches;°　　　*sloth itself / willful faults*
This seyd by hem that ben nought worth two fecches;[6]
But ye ben wis, and that we han on honde°　　　　*what we are concerned with*
Nis neither hard, ne skilful to withstonde."°　　　　*reasonable to avoid*

"Than, em," quod she, "doth herof as yow list.°　　　*it pleases you*
940　But er he com, I wil up first arise,
And for the love of God, syn al my trist°　　　　　　*reliance*
Is on yow two, and ye ben bothe wise,
So werketh now in so discret a wise
That I honour may have, and he plesaunce:
945　For I am here al in youre governaunce."

"That is wel seyd," quod he, "my nece deere.
Ther good thrift on° that wise gentil herte!　　　　*Good luck to*
But liggeth° stille, and taketh hym right here—　　*lie*
It nedeth nought no° ferther for hym sterte.°　　*There is no need / to move*
950　And ech of yow ese otheres sorwes smerte,°　　　*painful*
For love of God! And Venus, I the herye;°　　　　*praise*
For soone hope I we shul ben alle merye."

This Troilus ful soone on knees hym sette
Ful sobrely, right be° hyre beddes hed,　　　　　*by*
955　And in his beste wyse his lady grette.°　　　　*greeted*
But Lord, so she wex° sodeynliche red!　　　　　*grew*
Ne though men sholde smyten of° hire hed,　　*smite off*
She kouthe° nought a word aright° out brynge　*could / indeed*
So sodeynly, for his sodeyn comynge.

960　But Pandarus, that so wel koude feele°　　*who had such good sense*
In every thyng, to pleye anon bigan,
And seyde, "Nece, se° how this lord kan knele!　　*see*
Now for youre trouthe,° se this gentil man!"　　*fidelity*
And with that word he for a quysshen° ran,　　*cushion*
965　And seyde, "Kneleth now, while that yow leste;°　*it pleases you*
There God youre hertes brynge° soone at reste!"　*May God bring your hearts*

Kan I naught seyn, for she bad° hym nought rise,　*asked*
If sorwe it putte out of hire remembraunce,
Or elles that she took it in the wise°　　　　　*as an instance*
970　Of dewete,° as for his observaunce;°　　*duty / (proper) respect*
But wel fynde I she dede° hym this plesaunce,　*did*
That she hym kiste, although she siked° sore,　*sighed*
And bad hym sitte adown withouten more.

Quod Pandarus, "Now wol ye wel bigynne.
975　Now doth hym sitte,° goode nece deere,　　*have him sit down*

6. This is said about those who are not worth two beans (vetches).

Upon youre beddes syde al ther withinne,[7]
That ech of yow the bet may other heere."
And with that word he drow hym° to the feere,°   *withdrew / hearth*
And took a light, and fond his contenaunce,°   *assumed an appearance*
980 As° for to looke upon an old romaunce.°   *As if / romance (book)*

Criseyde, that was Troilus lady right,
And cler° stood on a ground of sikernesse,°   *clear, safe / security*
Al° thoughte she hire servant and hire knyght   *Although*
Ne sholde of right non untrouthe° in hire   *by rights no infidelity*
 gesse,°   *suspect*
985 Yet natheles,° considered° his distresse,   *nevertheless / considering*
And that love is in cause° of swich folie,   *the cause*
Thus to hym spak she of his jalousie:

"Lo, herte myn, as wolde° the excellence   *would have it*
Of love, ayeins the which that no man may—
990 Ne oughte ek—goodly make resistence,
And ek bycause I felte wel and say°   *saw*
Youre grete trouthe° and servise every day,   *fidelity*
And that youre herte al myn was, soth to seyne,
This drof° me for to rewe° upon youre peyne.   *drove / have pity*

995 "And youre goodnesse have I founde alwey yit,°   *ever yet*
Of which, my deere herte and al my knyght,
I thonke it yow,° as fer as I have wit,   *I thank you*
Al° kan I nought as muche as it were right;   *Although*
And I, emforth my connyng° and my might,   *to the extent of my understanding*
1000 Have and ay shal, how sore that me smerte,°   *however sorely it pains me*
Ben to yow trewe and hool° with al myn herte,   *whole, entirely*

"And dredeles,° that shal be founde at preve.°   *doubtless / at the test*
But, herte myn, what al this is to seyne
Shal wel be told, so that ye nought yow greve,[8]
1005 Though I to yow right on youreself compleyne,[9]
For therwith mene° I fynaly the peyne   *mean, intend*
That halt° youre herte and myn in hevynesse   *holds*
Fully to slen,° and every wrong redresse.   *slay*

"My goode myn, noot I for-why ne how[1]
1010 That jalousie, allas, that wikked wyvere,°   *serpent*
Thus causeles is cropen° into yow,   *has crept*
The harm of which I wolde fayn delyvere.°   *gladly eliminate*
Allas, that he, al hool or of hym slyvere,[2]

---

7. All within, that is, within the curtains surrounding the bed.
8. So that you won't grieve (any longer) *or* if you won't take offense.
9. Even though I should complain to you about your own self.
1. My good possession, I don't know why or how. Criseyde uses the possessive pronoun "mine" as a
 noun, "my own one."
2. As a whole or as a sliver of himself.

Shuld han his refut° in so digne° a place;   refuge / worthy
1015 Ther Jove hym sone out of youre herte arace!³

"But O, thow Jove, O auctour° of nature,   author, creator, lord
Is this an honour to thi deyte,°   deity, godhead
That folk ungiltif° suffren hire injure,°   guiltless / their injury
And who that giltif is, al quyt° goth he?   free
1020 O, were it lefull for to pleyn on° the,   permitted to complain about
That undeserved suffrest jalousie,⁴
Of that I wolde upon the° pleyne and crie!   you

"Ek al my wo is this, that folk now usen°   are accustomed
To seyn right thus, 'Ye, jalousie is love!'
1025 And wolde a busshel venym° al excusen,   a bushel of venom
For that o greyn° of love is on it shove.°   one grain / pushed into it
But that woot° heighe God that sit° above,   knows / Who sits
If it be likkere° love, or hate, or grame;°   more like / anger
And after° that, it oughte bere his° name.   in accordance with / to bear its

1030 "But certeyn is, som manere jalousie
Is excusable more than som,° iwys;   another
As whan cause is,° and som swich fantasie   there is cause
With piete° so wel repressed is   piety, a sense of duty
That it unnethe° doth or seyth amys,°   scarcely / amiss
1035 But goodly drynketh up° al his° distresse—   drinks up, endures / its
And that excuse I, for the gentilesse;°   noble restraint

"And som so ful of furie is and despit°   hostility
That it sourmounteth° his repressioun.°   surpasses / restraint
But herte myn, ye be nat in that plit,°   condition
1040 That thonke I God; for which youre passioun
I wol nought calle it but illusioun°   only a fantasy
Of habundaunce° of love and besy cure,°   abundance / anxious care
That doth° youre herte this disese° endure.   causes / distress

"Of which I am right sory but nought wroth;°   angry
1045 But, for my devoir° and youre hertes reste,   sake
Wherso yow list, by ordal or by oth,⁵
By sort,° or in what wise so yow leste,°   drawing lots / it pleases you
For love of God, lat preve it° for the beste;   let it be put to the test
And if that I be giltif, do me deye!°   make me die
1050 Allas, what myght I more don or seye?"

With that a fewe brighte teris° newe   tears
Owt of hire eighen fille,° and thus she seyde,   eyes fell
"Now God, thow woost, in thought ne dede° untrewe   deed
To Troilus was nevere yet Criseyde."

---

3. May Jupiter forthwith root it out of your heart! Here, as commonly (see lines 947, 966 above), the word *Ther* introducing an entreaty or asseveration in the subjunctive mood need not be translated.
4. (You) who permit jealousy of the undeserving. Criseyde continues to address Jupiter, using the familiar thee/thou forms, and verbs ending in *-est*, appropriate for addressing divinities. She and Troilus regularly address each other with the more formal ye/you forms.
5. However it pleases you, by judicial ordeal or purgation by oath-taking.

1055 With that here heed down in the bed she leyde,
And with the sheete it wreigh,° and sighte° soore,   hid / sighed
And held hire pees;° nought o° word spak she more.   peace / one

But now help God to quenchen al this sorwe!
So hope I that he shal, for he best may.°   can
1060 For I have seyn° of a ful misty morwe°   seen / morning
Folowen ful ofte a myrie someris day;
And after wynter foloweth grene May;
Men sen alday,° and reden ek° in stories,   see every day / also read
That after sharpe shoures° ben victories.   battle-assaults

1065 This Troilus, whan he hire wordes herde,
Have ye no care,° hym liste nought to slepe;   Rest assured
For it thoughte hym no° strokes of a yerde°   seemed to him not merely / rod
To heere or seen Criseyde, his lady, wepe;
But wel he felt aboute his herte crepe,
1070 For everi tere which that Criseyde asterte,°   escaped from
The crampe of deth to streyne° hym by the herte.   constrict

And in his mynde he gan the tyme acorse°   curse
That he com there, and that,° that he was born;   that (time)
For now is wikke° torned into worse,   bad
1075 And al that labour he hath don byforn,
He wende° it lost; he thoughte he nas but lorn.°   reckoned / lost
"O Pandarus," thoughte he, "allas, thi wile°   your guile
Serveth of nought, so weylaway the while!"⁶

And therwithal he heng° adown the heed,   hung
1080 And fil on knees, and sorwfully he sighte.°   sighed
What myghte he seyn? He felte he nas but° deed,   was nothing other than
For wroth° was she that sholde his sorwes lighte.°   angry / alleviate
But natheles,° whan that he speken myghte,   nevertheless
Than seyde he thus, "God woot that of this game,°   trickery
1085 Whan al is wist,° than am I nought to blame."   known

Therwith the sorwe so his herte shette°   shut, penned in
That from his eyen fil° there nought a tere,   eyes fell
And every spirit his vigour in knette,⁷
So they astoned° or oppressed were.   stunned
1090 The felyng° of his sorwe, or of his fere,   sensation
Or of aught elles, fled was out of towne;
And down he fel al sodeynly a-swowne.°   in a swoon

This was no litel sorwe for to se;
But al was hust,° and Pandare up as faste;   hushed
1095 "O nece, pes,° or we be lost!" quod he,   peace
"Beth naught agast!"° But certeyn, at the laste,   afraid
For this or that, he into bed hym caste,

6. Is of no use, so alas for the time.
7. And every spirit contracted its force. In medieval physiology three types of spirits—vital, natural,
and animal—course through one's veins, enabling life.

And seyde, "O thef,° is this a mannes herte?"   *thief, wretch*
And of he rente° al to his bare sherte,   *he tore off (Troilus's clothing)*

1100 And seyde, "Nece, but° ye helpe us now,   *unless*
Allas, youre owen Troilus is lorn!"°   *lost*
"Iwis, so wolde I, and I wiste° how,   *if I knew*
Ful fayn,"° quod she. "Allas, that I was born!"   *gladly*
"Yee, nece, wol ye pullen out the thorn
1105 That stiketh in his herte?" quod Pandare.
"Sey 'Al foryeve,' and stynt is al this fare!"[8]

"Ye, that to me," quod she, "ful levere° were   *preferable*
Than al the good the sonne aboute gooth."°   *the sun encircles (in its course)*
And therwithal she swor hym in his ere,°   *ear*
1110 "Iwys, my deere herte, I am nought wroth,
Have here my trouthe!"°—and many an other oth.°   *promise / oath*
"Now speke to me, for it am I, Criseyde!"
But al for nought; yit myght he nought abreyde.°   *he still can't revive*

Therwith his pous° and paumes° of his hondes   *pulse / palms*
1115 They gan to frote,° and wete° his temples tweyne;°   *rub / wet / two*
And to deliveren hym fro bittre bondes°   *bitter bonds (of death)*
She ofte hym kiste; and shortly for to seyne,
Hym to revoken° she did al hire peyne;°   *recall (to consciousness) / effort*
And at the laste, he gan his breth to drawe,
1120 And of his swough° sone after that adawe,°   *swoon / awaken*

And gan bet° mynde and reson to hym take,   *the better*
But wonder soore° he was abayst,° iwis;   *very grievously / abashed*
And with a sik,° whan he gan bet awake,   *sigh*
He seyde, "O mercy, God, what thyng is this?"
1125 "Why do ye with youreselven thus amys?"°   *amiss*
Quod tho Criseyde, "Is this a mannes game?°   *manly behavior*
What, Troilus, wol ye do thus for shame?"

And therwithal hire arm over hym she leyde,°   *laid*
And al foryaf,° and ofte tyme hym keste.°   *forgave / kissed*
1130 He thonked hire, and to hire spak, and seyde
As fil to purpos for his herte reste;[9]
And she to that answerde hym as hire leste,°   *it pleased her*
And with hire goodly wordes hym disporte°   *to cheer him up*
She gan, and ofte his sorwes to comforte.

1135 Quod Pandarus, "For aught I kan aspien,°   *see*
This light, nor I, ne serven here of nought.°   *for anything*
Light is nought good for sike° folkes yën!°   *sick / eyes*
But, for the love of God, syn ye ben brought
In thus good plit,° lat now no hevy thought   *condition*
1140 Ben hangyng in the hertes of yow tweye"—°   *two*
And bar° the candel to the chymeneye.°   *carried / fireplace*

8. Say "All is forgiven" and all this commotion will be stopped.
9. What was to the point for his heart's peace.

Soone after this, though it no nede were,
Whan she swiche othes as hire leste devyse°   *it pleased her to devise*
Hadde of hym take, hire thoughte tho no fere,
1145 Ne cause ek non to bidde hym thennes rise.[1]
Yet lasse° thyng than othes may suffise   *a lesser*
In many a cas, for every wyght, I gesse,
That loveth wel, meneth but gentilesse.

But in effect° she wolde wite anon   *in fact*
1150 Of what man, and ek wheer, and also why
He jalous was, syn° ther was cause non;   *since*
And ek the sygne that he took it by,°   *by which he got it (jealousy)*
She badde hym that to telle hire bisily,°   *promptly*
Or elles, certeyn, she bar hym on honde°   *accused him*
1155 That this was don of malice, hire to fonde.°   *test*

Withouten more, shortly for to seyne,
He most obeye unto his lady heste;°   *lady's behest*
And for the lasse harm, he moste feyne.°   *dissemble*
He seyde hire, whan she was at swich a feste,°   *festival*
1160 She myght on hym han loked at the leste—
Noot I nought what, al deere ynough a rysshe,[2]
As he that nedes most a cause fisshe.°   *needs must hunt up a reason*

And she answerde, "Swete, al were it° so,   *even if it were*
What harm was that, syn° I non yvel mene?°   *since / intend*
1165 For, by that God that bought° us bothe two,   *redeemed (an anachronism)*
In alle thyng° is myn entente cleene.   *things, affairs*
Swiche argumentes° ne ben naught worth a beene.   *disputes, reasonings*
Wol ye the childissh jalous contrefete?°   *jealous one imitate*
Now were it worthi that ye were ybete."°   *beaten*

1170 Tho Troilus gan sorwfully to sike—°   *sigh*
Lest she be wroth, hym thoughte his herte
deyde—°   *it seemed to him his heart died*
And seyde, "Allas, upon my sorwes sike°   *sick*
Have mercy, swete herte myn, Criseyde!
And if that in tho° wordes that I seyde   *those*
1175 Be any wrong, I wol no more trespace.°   *transgress*
Doth what yow list; I am al in youre grace."

And she answerde, "Of gilt misericorde!°   *for (your) offence, mercy*
That is to seyn, that I foryeve° al this,   *forgive*
And evere more on this nyght yow recorde,°   *remember*
1180 And beth wel war ye do namore amys."
"Nay, dere herte myn," quod he, "iwys!"°   *certainly*
"And now," quod she, "that I have don yow smerte,°   *caused you to feel pain*
Foryeve° it me, myn owene swete herte."   *Forgive*

1. There seemed to her then no (occasion for) fear, nor also any cause to ask him to rise from there.
2. I don't know what all; it's all expensive enough at the cost of a rush (i.e., a trifle).

This Troilus, with blisse of that supprised,°   *seized*
1185 Putte al in Goddes hand, as he that mente
Nothing but wel; and sodeynly avysed,°   *determined*
He hire in armes faste to hym hente.°   *took*
And Pandarus with a ful good entente
Leyde hym to slepe,° and seyde, "If ye be wise,   *went to bed*
1190 Swouneth nought now, lest more folk arise!"[3]

What myghte or may the sely° larke seye,   *hapless*
Whan that the sperhauk° hath it in his foot?   *sparrow hawk*
I kan namore; but of thise ilke tweye—°   *same two*
To whom this tale sucre be or soot—°   *be sugar or soot (sweet or bitter)*
1195 Though that I tarie° a yer, somtyme I moot,°   *tarry / must*
After° myn auctour, tellen hire gladnesse,   *Following*
As wel as I have told hire hevynesse.

Criseyde, which that felte hire thus itake,°   *taken, embraced*
As writen clerkes in hire bokes olde,
1200 Right as an aspes° leef she gan to quake,   *aspen*
Whan she hym felte hire in his armes folde.
But Troilus, al hool° of cares colde,   *whole, healed*
Gan thanken tho the bryghte goddes sevene;°   *seven (planetary) gods*
Thus sondry peynes bryngen folk in hevene.

1205 This Troilus in armes gan hire streyne,°   *clasp*
And seyde, "O swete, as evere mot I gon,°   *i.e., as I live and breathe*
Now be ye kaught; now is ther but we tweyne!°   *two*
Now yeldeth yow, for other bote° is non!"   *remedy*
To that Criseyde answerde thus anon,
1210 "Ne hadde I er° now, my swete herte deere,   *before*
Ben yolde,° ywis, I were now nought heere!"   *yielded*

O, sooth° is seyd, that heled° for to be   *truth / healed*
As of a fevre or other gret siknesse,
Men moste drynke, as men may ofte se,
1215 Ful bittre drynke; and for to han gladnesse
Men drynken ofte peyne and gret distresse—
I mene it here, as for this aventure,
That° thorugh a peyne hath founden al his cure.   *(Regarding him) who*

And now swetnesse semeth more swete,
1220 That° bitternesse assaied° was byforn;   *In that / experienced*
For out of wo in blisse now they flete;°   *float*
Non swich they felten sithen° they were born.   *since*
Now is this bet than bothe two be lorn.°   *lost*
For love of God, take every womman heede
1225 To werken thus, if it comth to the neede.

Criseyde, al quyt° from every drede and tene,°   *freed / trouble*
As she that juste cause hadde hym to triste,°   *trust*
Made hym swych feste° it joye was to sene,   *cheer*

3. Chaucer doesn't say that Pandarus left the room, but his return in line 1555 below implies it.

30

Nor did they leave that place before they had a thousand times embraced together with sweet joy and ardent delight, and just as many times and much more did they kiss each other as those who burned with equal fire and who were very dear to each other. But when the welcoming was finished, they mounted the stairs and entered the bedroom.

Whan she his trouthe° and clene entente wiste;°   *fidelity / knew*
1230 And as aboute a tree, with many a twiste,°   *tendril*
Bytrent and writh the swote wodebynde,[4]
Gan ech of hem in armes other wynde.

And as the newe abaysed° nyghtyngale,   *recently startled*
That stynteth° first whan she bygynneth to synge,   *stops*
1235 Whan that she hereth any herde tale,°   *shepherd talk*
Or in the hegges any wyght stirynge,
And after siker° doth hire vois out rynge,   *(feeling) safe*
Right so Criseyde, whan hire drede stente,°   *ceased*
Opned hire herte and tolde hym hire entente.

1240 And right as he that seth° his deth yshapen,°   *sees / destined*
And dyen mot, in ought that he may gesse,
And sodeynly rescous doth° hym escapen,   *rescue causes*
And from his deth is brought in sykernesse,°   *safety*
For al this world, in swych present gladnesse
1245 Was Troilus, and hath his lady swete.
With worse hap° God lat us nevere mete!   *fortune*

Hire armes smale,° hire streghte bak and softe,   *slender*
Hire sydes longe, flesshly, smothe, and white
He gan to stroke, and good thrift bad° ful ofte   *wished blessing upon*
1250 Hire snowissh throte, hire brestes rounde and lite,
Thus in this hevene he gan hym to delite,
And therwithal a thousand tyme hire kiste,
That what to don, for joie unnethe he wiste.°   *he scarcely knew*

Than seyde he thus: "O Love, O Charite!
1255 Thi moder ek, Citheria the swete,[5]
After thiself next heried° be she—   *praised*
Venus mene I, the wel-willy° planete!—   *benevolent*
And next that, Imeneus,° I the grete,°   *Hymen (god of marriage) / greet*
For nevere man was to yow goddes holde°   *(so) beholden*
1260 As I, which° ye han brought fro cares colde.   *whom*

"Benigne Love, thow holy bond of thynges,
Whoso wol grace and list the nought honouren,[6]
Lo, his desir wol fle° withouten wynges;   *fly*
For noldestow of bownte hem socouren[7]
1265 That serven best and most alwey labouren,°   *always strive the most*
Yet were al lost, that dar I wel seyn, certes,
But if° thi grace passed° oure desertes.   *Unless / exceeded*

---

4. Encircles and wreathes the sweet woodbine (honeysuckle).
5. Your mother, also, Citheria (i.e., Venus) the sweet. Venus is Love's (Amor's, Cupid's) mother.
6. Whoever wishes for grace and is not pleased to honor you. The idea of love as a bond is elaborated from Boethius; see lines 1744–71 below. This stanza is adapted from an address to the Virgin Mary as mediator of divine grace, spoken by St. Bernard in Dante's *Paradise* 33.14–18.
7. For if you would not in your kindness succor them.

"And for thow me, that koude leest disserve[8]
Of hem that° noumbred ben unto° thi grace,   *those who / in*
1270 Hast holpen,° ther° I likly was to sterve,°   *(You) have helped / where / die*
And me bistowed in so heigh a place
That thilke boundes° may no blisse pace,°   *those same boundaries / pass*
I kan namore; but laude° and reverence   *honor*
Be to thy bounte° and thyn excellence!"   *goodness*

1275 And therwithal Criseyde anon he kiste,
Of which certein she felte no disese,
And thus seyde he: "Now wolde God I wiste,
Myn herte swete, how I yow myght plese!
What man," quod he, "was evere thus at ese
1280 As I, on which the faireste and the beste
That evere I say deyneth hire herte reste?[9]

"Here may men seen that mercy passeth right;°   *surpasses justice*
Th'experience of that is felt in me,
That am unworthi to° so swete a wight.°   *of / person*
1285 But herte myn, of youre benignite,
So thynketh, though that I unworthi be,
Yet mot I nede amenden in som wyse,
Right thorugh the vertu of youre heigh servyse [1]

"And for the love of God, my lady deere,
1290 Syn God hath wrought° me for° I shall yow serve—   *made / in order that*
As thus I mene: he wol ye be my steere,°   *helm, pilot*
To do° me lyve, if that yow liste,° or sterve—°   *cause / it please you / die*
So techeth me how that I may disserve
Youre thonk,° so that I thorugh myn ignoraunce   *thanks, favorable thought*
1295 Ne do no thyng that yow be displesaunce.°   *a displeasure*

"For certes, fresshe wommanliche wif,[2]
This dar I seye, that trouth° and diligence,   *fidelity*
That shal ye fynden in me al my lif;
N'y wol nat, certein, breken youre defence;°   *violate your prohibition*
1300 And if I do, present or in absence,
For love of God, lat sle me with the dede,°   *with the deed, at once*
If that it like° unto youre wommanhede."   *be pleasing*

"Iwys," quod she, "myn owen hertes list,°   *delight*
My ground of ese, and al myn herte deere,
1305 Gramercy,° for on° that is al my trist!   *Much thanks / in*
But lat us falle awey° fro this matere,°   *turn aside / subject matter*
For it suffiseth, this that seyd is heere,
And at o word, withouten repentaunce,
Welcome, my knyght, my pees,° my suffisaunce!"°   *peace / sufficiency*

---

8. And because you (have helped) me, who least knows how to be deserving.
9. Whom I ever saw deigns to bestow her heart.
1. Yet I must needs grow better in some way through the ennobling effect of your exalted service.
2. Womanly woman, i.e., paragon of womanhood. See line 106 above.

31

Long would it be to recount the joy and impossible to tell the delight which they took together when they came into it; they undressed and got into bed, where the lady, remaining still in her last garment, with pleasing speech said to him, "Shall I strip myself? The newly married are bashful the first night."

32

To whom Troilo said, "My soul, I pray that I may have you naked in my arms as my heart desires." And then she: "See how I free myself of it." And her shift thrown away, she gathered herself quickly into his arms; and straining each other with fervor, they felt the ultimate value of love.

33

O sweet night, and much desired, what were you to the two happy lovers! If the knowledge were given to me that all the poets have had, it could not be described by me. Let him think of it who was ever as much advanced by the grace of love as these were, and he will know in part their delight.

34

They did not leave one another's arms the whole night, and while they held one another embraced, they thought they were taken from each other or that it was not true that they were together, as they were in one another's arms, but they believed they were dreaming that they embraced, and often one asked the other, "Do I have you in my arms, or do I dream, or are you your very self?"

1310 Of hire delit or joies oon the leeste°   *the very least*
Were impossible to my wit to seye;
But juggeth ye that han ben at the feste°   *feast, celebration*
Of swich gladnesse, if that hem liste° pleye!   *it pleased them*
I kan namore, but thus thise ilke tweye°   *same two*
1315 That nyght, bitwixen drede and sikernesse,°   *security*
Felten in love the grete worthynesse.

O blisful nyght, of hem so longe isought,
How blithe unto hem bothe two thow weere!
Why nad I° swich oon with my soule ybought,°   *had I not / purchased*
1320 Ye, or the leeste joie that was theere?
Awey, thow foule daunger° and thow feere,   *aloofness, haughtiness*
And lat hem in this hevene blisse dwelle,
That is so heigh that al ne kan I telle!

But sooth is, though I kan nat tellen al,
1325 As kan myn auctour, of his excellence,
Yet have I seyd, and God toforn,° and shal   *as God is my witness*
In every thyng, al holly his sentence;°   *wholly his meaning*
And if that ich, at Loves reverence,°   *out of reverence for Love*
Have any word in eched° for the beste,   *added*
1330 Doth therwithal right as youreselven leste.°   *it pleases you*

For myne wordes, heere and every part,°   *everywhere*
I speke hem alle under° correccioun   *as liable to*
Of yow that felyng° han in loves art,   *sympathetic understanding*
And putte it al in youre discrecioun
1335 To encresse or maken dymynucioun
Of my langage, and that I yow biseche.
But now to purpos° of my rather° speche.   *to the point / earlier*

Thise ilke° two, that ben in armes laft,°   *same / left*
So loth to hem asonder gon it were,³
1340 That ech from other wenden ben biraft,°   *would think they were bereft*
Or elles—lo, this was hir mooste feere—
That al this thyng but nyce° dremes were;   *foolish*
For which ful ofte ech of hem seyde, "O swete,
Clippe° ich yow thus, or elles I it meete?"°   *Embrace / dream it*

---

3. It was so unpleasant to them to go apart.

35

And they gazed at one another with such desire that they did not turn their eyes from each other, and the one said to the other, "My love, ah! can it be that I am with you?" "Yes, heart of my body, thanks be to God," frequently replied the other. And very often clasping each other closely, they kissed together sweetly.

36

Troilo often kissed the beautiful, amorous eyes of Criseida, saying: "You thrust into my heart the fiery darts of love by which I am all inflamed; you captured me, and I did not hide myself by fleeing as he who fears would do; you hold me and always will hold me in love's net, my beautiful eyes."

37

Then he kissed them and kissed them yet again, and Criseida kissed his also; then he kissed all her face and breast, and never an hour passed without a thousand sighs, not those grieving ones by which one loses color but those devout ones by which was shown the affection which lay in their breast; and after this their delight was renewed.

38

Ah, here let the wretched misers take thought, who blame him who is in love and who has not, as they do, in every way given himself entirely to making money, and consider if, holding it very dearly, as much pleasure was ever given them by it as love renders in a single moment to him to whom by good fortune, love is joined.

39

They will say yes but they will lie. With laughter and with jeers, they will call this love grievous madness, without seeing that they will lose themselves and their money in a single hour without having known in their lives what joy is. May God make them sad and give their gains to lovers.

1345 And Lord! So he gan goodly° on hire se°   intently / look
That nevere his look ne bleynte° from hire face,   turned away
And seyde, "O deere herte, may it be
That it be soth, that ye ben in this place?"
"Yee, herte myn, God thank I of his grace,"
1350 Quod tho Criseyde, and therwithal hym kiste,
That where his spirit was, for joie he nyste.°   did not know

This Troilus ful ofte hire eyen° two   eyes
Gan for to kisse, and seyde, "O eyen clere,
It weren ye that wroughte° me swich wo,   caused
1355 Ye humble nettes° of my lady deere!   modest nets
Though ther be mercy writen in youre cheere,°   countenance
God woot, the text ful hard is, soth, to fynde!
How koude ye° withouten bond me bynde?"   were you able

Therwith he gan hire faste in armes take,
1360 And wel a thousand tymes gan he syke—°   sigh
Naught swiche sorwfull sikes as men make
For wo, or elles when that folk ben sike,
But esy sykes, swiche as ben to like,°   enjoy
That shewed his affeccioun withinne;
1365 Of swiche sikes koude he nought bilynne.°   cease

Soone after this they spake of sondry thynges,
As fel to purpos of° this aventure,°   had to do with / situation
And pleyinge entrechaungeden° hire rynges,   exchanged
Of whiche I kan nought tellen no scripture;°   inscription
1370 But wel I woot, a broche, gold and asure,[4]
In which a ruby set was lik° an herte,   in the shape of
Criseyde hym yaf,° and stak° it on his sherte.   gave / fastened

Lord, trowe ye° a coveytous° or a wrecche,   do you think / covetous one
That blameth love and halt of it despit,
1375 That of tho pens° that he kan mokre and   pence
   kecche°   hoard and grasp after
Was evere yit yyeven° hym swich delit   granted
As is in love, in o poynt, in som plit?°   a single jot, in some situation
Nay, douteles, for also God me save,
So perfit° joie may no nygard° have.   Such perfect / miser

1380 They wol seyn "Yis," but Lord, so they lye,
Tho besy wrecches,° ful of wo and drede!   Those busy wretches
Thei callen love a woodnesse° or folie,   madness
But it shall falle° hem as I shal yow rede:°   befall / counsel
They shal forgon the white and ek the rede,[5]

4. But I know well, a brooch, gold and azure (in color, or, inset with a stone of lapis lazuli). This may
be the same brooch that Troilus later gave Criseyde (see V.1661).
5. They must forgo the white (silver) and also the red (gold). Elsewhere by "the white and the red"
Chaucer means wine. The contemporary poet Gower also uses "the white and the red" to mean
money.

40

Reassured of being together, the two lovers began to talk together and to recount to one another their past laments, their anguish, and their sighs; and all such talk, they often interrupted with fervent kissing, and abandoning past suffering they took delicious joy together.

41

There was no talk of sleeping, but they desired by staying very well awake to keep the night from coming to an end. They could not satiate one another, however much they might do or say what they believed belonged to that act, and without letting the hours run in vain, they used all of them that night.

42

But when near day they heard the cocks crow because of the dawn which was rising, the desire of embracing rekindled itself and they grieved for the hour which must part them and must put them into new suffering, which neither had yet felt, through their being separated, now that they were far more than ever inflamed with love.

1385 And lyve in wo, ther God yeve hem
    meschaunce,°   *may God give them bad luck*
And every lovere in his trouthe avaunce!°   *prosper in his integrity*

As wolde God° tho wrecches that dispise   *Would God that*
Servise of love hadde erys also° longe   *ears just as*
As hadde Mida,° ful of coveytise,°   *Midas / covetousness*
1390 And therto dronken hadde as hoot and stronge°   *hot and strong (a drink)*
As Crassus did for his affectis wronge,[6]
To techen hem that they ben in the vice,°   *wrong*
And loveres nought, although they holde hem nyce.°   *consider them foolish*

Thise ilke two° of whom that I yow seye,°   *same two / tell*
1395 Whan that hire hertes wel assured were,
Tho gonne they to speken and to pleye,
And ek rehercen° how, and whan, and where   *recount*
Thei knewe hem first, and every wo and feere
That passed was; but al swich hevynesse—
1400 I thank it God—was torned to gladnesse.

And evere mo, when that hem fel° to speke   *they happened*
Of any wo of swich a tyme agoon,°   *past*
With kissyng al that tale sholde breke°   *they had to interrupt*
And fallen in a newe joye anoon;
1405 And diden al hire myght, syn they were oon,
For to recoveren° blisse and ben at eise,   *regain*
And passed° wo with joie contrepeise.°   *former / to counterbalance*

Resoun wol nought that I speke of slep,
For it acordeth nought to° my matere.   *doesn't accord with*
1410 God woot, they took of that ful litel kep!°   *care*
But lest this nyght, that was to hem so deere,
Ne sholde in veyn escape in no manere,[7]
It was byset° in joie and bisynesse   *employed*
Of al that souneth into° gentilesse.   *tends toward, conduces to*

1415 But whan the cok, comune° astrologer,   *common, everyman's*
Gan on his brest to bete and after crowe,
And Lucyfer, the dayes messager,[8]
Gan for to rise and out hire bemes throwe,
And estward roos—to hym that koude it knowe—°   *could recognize it*
1420 Fortuna Major,[9] that anoon Criseyde,
With herte soor, to Troilus thus seyde:

---

6. As Crassus did for his wrong desires. In 53 B.C.E. the Roman general Crassus had molten gold poured into his mouth because of his greed.
7. (Lest this night) should in any way slip away in vain.
8. *Lucyfer*, the "Light-Bringer," is the morning star, Venus (with the feminine pronoun *hire*).
9. In *Purgatory* 19.4–5, Dante speaks of *Fortuna Major* (the Greater Fortune) as rising in the east before dawn. Chaucer may have known that Dante refers to a group of six stars located in the constellations of Aquarius and Pisces. Possibly Chaucer thought *Fortuna Major* was the planet Jupiter.

43

When Criseida heard them crow, she said sorrowing: "O my love, now it is time that you must arise, if indeed we wish to hide our desire, but I wish, my love, to embrace you a little before you arise so that I may feel less sorrow at your departure. Ah, embrace me, my sweet life."

44

Almost weeping, Troilo embraced her and, clasping her tightly, kissed her, cursing the day which was coming that so speedily separated them. Then he began saying to her, "The parting grieves me beyond measure: how can I ever part from you, since you, lady, give me the happiness that I feel?

45

"I do not know why I do not die just thinking that I must go away against my will and that already I have been exiled from life, and death mounts to power over me, nor do I know how or when I shall return. O fortune, why do you take me far from such pleasure, which pleases me more than anything else? Why do you take solace and peace away from me?

46

"Ah, what shall I do, if already at the first step the desire to return here so constrains me that life may not bear it, oh wretched me! Alas, why do you come so soon to separate us, O pitiless day? When will you sink low so that I may see you restore us? Alas, that I do not know!" Then he turned to Criseida and kissed her fresh face,

"Myn hertes lif, my trist, al my plesaunce,[1]
That I was born, allas, what me is wo,° — *how sorrowful I am*
That day of us moot make disseveraunce!° — *parting*
1425 For tyme it is to ryse and hennes° go, — *hence*
Or ellis I am lost for evere mo!
O nyght, allas, why nyltow over us hove° — *hover, linger*
As longe as whan Almena lay by Jove?[2]

"O blake nyght, as folk in bokes rede,
1430 That shapen art° by God this world to hide — *You who were created*
At certeyn tymes wyth thi derke wede,° — *garment*
That° under that men myghte in reste abide, — *So that*
Wel oughten bestes pleyne° and folk the chide,° — *complain / chide you*
That there as° day wyth labour wolde us breste,° — *when / break, afflict*
1435 That thow thus fleest, and deynest° us nought reste. — *grant*

"Thow doost, allas, to shortly thyn office,
Thow rakle° nyght! Ther God,° maker of kynde,° — *hasty, rash / May God / nature*
The, for thyn haste and thyn unkynde° vice, — *unnatural*
So faste° ay to oure hemysperie bynde — *tightly*
1440 That nevere more under the ground thow wynde!° — *may you turn*
For now, for thow so hiest° out of Troie, — *hasten*
Have I forgon° thus hastili my joie!" — *lost*

This Troilus, that with tho wordes felte,
As thoughte hym tho,° for piëtous° distresse — *it seemed to him then / pitiful*
1445 The blody teris from his herte melte,
As he that nevere yet swich hevynesse
Assayed° hadde, out of so gret gladnesse, — *Experienced*
Gan therwithal Criseyde, his lady deere,
In armes streyne,° and seyde in this manere: — *hold tight*

1450 "O cruel day, accusour° of the joie — *betrayer*
That nyght and love han stole° and faste iwryen,° — *have stolen / concealed*
Acorsed be thi comyng into Troye,
For every bore° hath oon of thi bryghte yën!° — *opening, chink / eyes*
Envyous day, what list the° so to spien? — *why does it please you*
1455 What hastow lost? Why sekestow° this place? — *do you seek*
Ther God° thi light so quenche, for his grace! — *May God*

"Allas, what° have thise loveris the agylt,° — *how / offended you*
Dispitous day? Thyn be the peyne of helle!
For many a lovere hastow slayn, and wilt;
1460 Thy pourynge° in wol nowher lat hem dwelle. — *staring, poring*
What profrestow° thi light here for to selle? — *Why do you offer*

1. This and the following stanzas of complaint against Night and Day reflect a tradition of lovers'
"dawn-songs," called *aubades*. The principal source of these in medieval Europe was Ovid, *Amores*
1.13. A notable example is John Donne's "The Sun Rising" (1633).
2. Jupiter miraculously extended the length of the night when he lay with Alcmena and Hercules
was conceived.

47

saying, "If I believed, fair lady, that I should remain continually in your mind as I hold you in mine, this would be more dear to me than the Trojan kingdom, and I would be patient at this parting since I come to it against my will, and I would hope to return here at the proper time and place to temper, as now, our fire."

48

Sighing, Criseida answered him while she held him tightly in her arms, "My soul, I have already heard it said long ago, if I remember correctly, that love is an avaricious spirit and when he seizes anything he holds it so strongly clasped and pressed with his claws that counsel as to how to free it is given in vain.

49

"He has seized me in such a manner for you, my dear love, that if I wished to return now to what I was before, do not take it into your head that I could do so. You are always, morning and night, fixed in my mind, and if I believed myself to be so in yours, I should hold myself happier than I could ask.

Go selle it hem that smale selys grave;[3]
We wol the° nought; us nedeth° no day have."   *want you / we need*

   And ek the sonne, Titan,[4] gan he chide,
1465 And seyde, "O fool, wel may men the dispise,
That hast the Dawyng° al nyght by thi syde,   *Dawn*
And suffrest hire° so soone up fro the rise   *permits her*
For to disese° loveris in this wyse.   *discomfort*
What, holde° youre bed ther, thow, and ek thi Morwe!°   *keep to / Morning*
1470 I bidde God, so yeve° yow bothe sorwe!"   *I pray God, may He give*

   Therwith ful soore he syghte,° and thus he seyde: *sighed*
"My lady right, and of my wele° or wo   *well-being*
The welle and roote, O goodly myn Criseyde,
And shal° I rise, allas, and shal I so?   *must*
1475 Now fele I that myn herte moot a-two,°   *(break) in two*
For how sholde I my lif an houre save,
Syn that with yow is al the lif ich have?

   "What shal I don? For, certes, I not° how,   *don't know*
Ne whan, allas, I shal the tyme see
1480 That in this plit° I may ben eft° with yow;   *condition / again*
And of my lif, God woot how that shal be,
Syn that desir right now so streyneth° me   *grips*
That I am ded anon, but° I retourne.   *unless*
How sholde I longe, allas, fro yow sojourne?°   *travel*

1485 "But natheles,° myn owen lady bright,   *nevertheless*
Were it so that I wiste outrely°   *utterly, for sure*
That I, youre humble servant and youre knyght,
Were in youre herte iset so fermely
As ye in myn—the which thyng, trewely,
1490 Me levere were than thise worldes tweyne—[5]
Yet sholde I bet enduren al my peyne."

   To that Criseyde answerde right anon,
And with a sik she seyde, "O herte deere,
The game,° ywys, so ferforth° now is gon   *affair / far*
1495 That first shal Phebus fallen fro his speere,[6]
And everich egle ben the dowves feere,°   *dove's mate*
And everich roche out of his° place sterte,°   *its / leap*
Er Troilus oute° of Criseydes herte.   *Before Troilus shall go out*

   "Ye ben so depe in-with myn herte grave,°   *engraved*
1500 That, though I wolde it torne out of my thought,
As wisly verray God° my soule save,   *As surely as God himself*

3. Go sell it to those who engrave small seals (and would want good light).
4. Titan, the sun, is here merged with Tithonus, the lover of Aurora, the dawn.
5. Would be more desirable to me than these two worlds. The *Filostrato* parallel ("than the Trojan realm") may suggest that Troilus means "than the worlds of Greece and Troy," or he may mean "than two worlds such as this."
6. That first Phoebus (god of the Sun) shall fall from his sphere. This and the following lines reflect the ancient schema of "impossibles," hyperbolic expressions of constancy.

50

"Therefore live certain of my love, which is greater than I have ever felt for another, and if you desire with fervor to return here, I desire it very much more than you, nor will any opportunity be given to me that you will not return here. Heart of my body, to you I commend myself." And this said, sighing, she kissed him.

51

Troilo arose against his will after he had kissed her again a hundred times. But still, seeing what had to be, he dressed himself completely, and then, after many words, said, "I follow your will, I am going from here; act so that your promises are not denied me, and I commend you to God and leave my soul with you."

52

A voice did not come to her for a reply, so much grief constrained her at his departure, but Troilo set out from there with quick steps toward his palace, and he feels indeed that love inflames his desire much more than it did before, so much more had he found Criseida worthy than he had judged her to himself earlier.

The two lovers recall the things they have done, and with such reflection joyous love enkindles itself in them more.

53

After Troilo had returned to the royal palace, he quietly went to bed to sleep a little, if he could, for ease, but sleep could not enter his breast, because new thoughts so disturbed him as he remembered the delights he had left, and he thought to himself how much more worthy the beautiful Criseida was than he had believed.

To dyen in the peyne,° I koude nought.   *Were I to die by torture*
And, for the love of God that us hath wrought,°   *created*
Lat in youre brayn non other fantasie
1505 So crepe that it cause me to dye!

"And that ye me wolde han as faste° in mynde   *firmly*
As I have yow, that wolde I yow biseche;
And if I wiste sothly° that to fynde,   *truly knew*
God myghte nought a poynt° my joies eche.°   *one bit / increase*
1510 But herte myn, withouten more speche,
Beth to me trewe, or ellis were it routhe,°   *a pity*
For I am thyn, by God and by my trouthe!

"Beth glad, forthy,° and lyve in sikernesse!°   *therefore / security*
Thus seyde I nevere er this, ne shal to mo;°   *any others*
1515 And if to yow it were a gret gladnesse
To torne ayeyn° soone after that ye go,   *return*
As fayn° wolde I as ye that it were so,   *gladly*
As wisly° God myn herte brynge at reste!"   *surely*
And hym in armes tok, and ofte keste.°   *kissed*

1520 Agayns his wil, sith° it mot nedes be,   *since*
This Troilus up ros, and faste hym cledde,°   *clothed*
And in his armes took his lady free°   *noble*
An hondred tyme, and on his wey hym spedde;
And with swich voys as though his herte bledde,
1525 He seyde, "Farwel, dere herte swete;
Ther God us graunte sownde° and soone to mete!"   *health*

To which no word for sorwe she answerde,
So soore gan his partyng hire distreyne;°   *distress*
And Troilus unto his paleys ferde,°   *went*
1530 As wo-bygon as she was, soth to seyne.
So harde hym wrong° of sharp desir the peyne   *wrung*
For to ben eft there° he was in plesaunce,   *again where*
That it may nevere out of his remembraunce.

Retorned to his real° paleys soone,   *royal*
1535 He softe into his bed gan for to slynke,°   *creep*
To slepe longe, as he was wont to doone.
But al for nought; he may wel ligge and wynke,°   *lie down and close his eyes*
But slep ne may ther in his herte synke,
Thynkyng how she for whom desir hym brende°   *burned*
1540 A thousand fold was worth more than he wende.°   *thought*

54

He kept turning over in his mind each act and the sophisticated conversation and repeating to himself again the pleasure and sweet jesting. Also he kept feeling for her a far greater love than he had imagined, and with such thoughts he burned more strongly in love, and did not know it.

55

Criseida did likewise to herself, speaking of Troilo in her heart, and rejoicing inwardly in such a lover, she rendered boundless thanks to Love, and it seemed to her a full thousand years before her fond lover would return to her and she would hold him in her arms and kiss him often, as she had done the night before.

And in his thought gan up and down to wynde°   revolve
Hire wordes alle, and every countenaunce,
And fermely impressen in his mynde
The leeste point that to him was plesaunce;
1545   And verraylich° of thilke° remembraunce   truly / that same
Desir al newe hym brende, and lust to brede°   desire to grow
Gan more than erst,° and yet took he non hede.°   before / heed

Criseyde also, right in the same wyse,
Of Troilus gan in hire herte shette°   enclose
1550   His worthynesse, his lust,° his dedes wise,   vigor
His gentilesse, and how she with hym mette,
Thonkyng Love he so wel hire bisette,°   employed
Desiryng eft to han hire herte deere
In swich a plit, she dorste make hym cheere.[7]

1555   Pandare, o-morwe,° which that° comen was   in the morning / who
Unto his nece and gan hire faire grete,
Seyde, "Al this nyght so reyned it, allas,
That al my drede is that ye, nece swete,
Han litel laiser° had to slepe and mete.°   leisure / dream
1560   Al nyght," quod he, "hath reyn so do° me wake,   caused
That som of us, I trowe,° hire hedes ake."°   suppose / ache

And ner° he com, and seyde, "How stant° it now   nearer / stands
This mury morwe?° Nece, how kan ye fare?"   merry morning
Criseyde answerde, "Nevere the bet° for yow,   better
1565   Fox that ye ben! God yeve° youre herte kare!°   give / care, vexation
God help me so, ye caused al this fare,°   to-do
Trowe I," quod she, "for al youre wordes white.°   specious
O, whoso seeth yow knoweth yow ful lite."

With that she gan hire face for to wrye°   cover
1570   With the shete, and wax° for shame al reed;   grew
And Pandarus gan under for to prie,°   peer
And seyde, "Nece, if that I shal be ded,
Have here a swerd and smyteth of° myn hed!"   smite off
With that his arm al sodeynly he thriste°   thrust
1575   Under hire nekke, and at the laste hire kyste.

I passe al that which chargeth nought° to seye.   is not important
What! God foryaf his deth,[8] and she al so
Foryaf, and with here uncle gan to pleye,
For other cause was ther noon than so.
1580   But of this thing right to the effect° to go: point
Whan tyme was, hom til° here hous she wente,   When it was time, home to
And Pandarus hath° fully his entente.   has (obtained)

7. In such a condition that she dared to entertain him.
8. God forgave his death. Ultimately from Luke 23:34, "Father, forgive them, for they know not what they do," and proverbial as an expression of extraordinary forgiving.

Pandaro comes to Troilo, who praises him and Love most highly and talks about Love's unexpected sweetnesses.

56

In the morning Pandaro came to Troilo, who had risen, and greeted him; Troilo returned his salutation and threw himself on his neck with eagerness: "My Pandaro, you are welcome," and he kissed him lovingly on the forehead. "You have put me from Hell into Paradise, as I hope not to be killed.

57

"If I were to die a thousand times a day for you, I should never be able to work so that I might do an atom of what I know clearly would be fitting for you. You have moved me from bitter plaint into joy." And he kissed him anew and then said, "My sweet bliss who makes me happy, when will it be that I shall ever hold you?

58

"The sun, which sees the whole world, does not see so beautiful a lady, nor so pleasing, and, if my words merit belief, so well-mannered, lovely, and attractive as she by whose good grace more than anything else I live truly happy. Praised be love, who has made me hers, and likewise your good service.

59

"Therefore you have not given me a little thing, nor have you given me to a little thing. My life will always be obligated to you, and you shall have it whenever it pleases you; you have raised it from death to life." And here he was silent, more joyful than ever. Pandaro heard him, waited a little, and then light-heartedly replied thus to his words:

60

"If I have, fair sweet friend, done anything that is dear to you, I am very glad, and it is most pleasing to me. But nevertheless I remind you more than ever that you should put a rein to your amorous desire and that you should be prudent so that, where you have taken away torment with delightful joy, you will not return yourself to distress through talking."

Now torne we ayeyn° to Troilus,   *let us turn back*
That resteles ful longe abedde lay,
1585 And pryvely sente after Pandarus,
To hym to com in al the haste he may.
He com anon°—nought ones° seyde he nay— *immediately / once*
And Troilus ful sobrely he grette,°   *greeted*
And down upon his beddes syde hym sette.

1590 This Troilus, with al th'affeccioun
Of frendes love that herte may devyse,
To Pandarus on knowes fil adown,°   *fell down on his knees*
And er that he wolde of the place arise
He gan hym thonken in his beste wise
1595 An hondred sythe,° and gan the tyme blesse *times*
That he° was born, to brynge hym fro destresse. *he (i.e., Pandarus)*

He seyde, "O frend of frendes the alderbeste° *best of all*
That evere was, the sothe for to telle,
Thow hast in hevene ybrought my soule at reste
1600 Fro Flegitoun,⁹ the fery° flood of helle,   *fiery*
That, though I myght a thousand tymes selle° *give*
Upon a day my lif in thi servise,
It myghte naught a moote° in that suffise. *mote, whit*

"The sonne,° which that al the world may se, *sun*
1605 Saugh nevere yet my lif,° that dar I leye,° *in my lifetime / wager*
So inly° fair and goodly as is she   *entirely*
Whos I am al, and shal,° tyl that I deye.   *shall be*
And that I thus am hires, dar I seye,
That° thanked be the heighe worthynesse   *For that*
1610 Of Love, and ek thi kynde bysynesse.

"Thus hastow me no litel thing yyive,°   *given*
For which to the obliged be for ay°   *ever*
My lif. And whi? For thorugh thyn help I lyve,
Or elles ded hadde I ben many a day."
1615 And with that word down in his bed he lay,
And Pandarus ful sobrely hym herde
Tyl al was seyd, and than he thus answerde:

"My deere frend, if I have don for the°   *succeeded for you*
In any cas, God wot, it is me lief,°   *desirable*
1620 And am as glad as man may of it be,
God help me so; but tak now nat a-grief°   *badly*
That° I shal seyn: be war of this meschief, *What*
That, there as° thow now brought art in thy blisse, *seeing that*
That thow thiself ne cause it nat to misse.° *go amiss*

1625 "For of fortunes sharpe adversitee
The worste kynde of infortune is this,
A man to han ben in prosperitee,

9. Phlegethon, a river of fire in Hades (the name means "burning").

61

"I shall act so that it may be to your satisfaction," replied Troilo to his dear friend. Then with the greatest joy, he related to him the happy things which had befallen him and said further: "I tell you truly that I have never been in the toils of love as I am now, and much more than before does the fire which I have drawn from the eyes and face of Criseida burn me.

62

"I burn more than ever, and this new fire I feel is of another quality from the one before. The pleasure refreshes me as I think always in my heart of the beauty which is the cause of it, but it is true that it makes my wishes to return to her amorous arms and to kiss her delicate face a little more burning than they used to be."

63

The young man could not grow weary of talking to Pandaro of the happiness he had felt, and of the delight, and of the comfort given to his woes, and of the perfect love he bore Criseida, in whom alone he had placed his hope, and he had put into oblivion every other matter and great desire.

And it remembren whan it passed is.
Th'art wis ynough; forthi° do nat amys: *therefore*
1630 Be naught to rakel,° theigh thow sitte warme,°   *rash / are well placed*
For if thow be, certeyn it wol the harme.

"Thow art at ese, and hold the° wel therinne;   *maintain yourself*
For also seur° as reed is every fir,   *surely*
As gret a craft is kepe wel as wynne.[1]

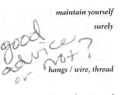

1635 Bridle alwey wel thi speche and thi desir,
For worldly joie halt° nought but by a wir.°   *hangs / wire, thread*
That preveth wel, it brest al day so ofte;[2]
Forthi nede is° to werken with it softe."   *Hence there is need*

Quod Troilus, "I hope, and God toforn,°   *as God is my witness*
1640 My deere frend, that I shal so me beere°   *conduct myself*
That in my gylt° ther shal nothyng be lorn,°   *through my fault / lost*
N'y nyl nought rakle as for to greven heere.[3]
It nedeth naught this matere ofte stere;°   *stir, bring up*
For wystestow° myn herte wel, Pandare,   *if you knew*
1645 God woot, of this thow woldest litel care."

Tho gan he telle hym of his glade nyght,
And wherof first his herte dred,° and how,   *dreaded*
And seyde, "Frend, as I am trewe knyght,
And by that feyth I shal° to God and yow,   *owe*
1650 I hadde it nevere half so hote as now;
And ay the more that desir me biteth
To love hire best, the more it me deliteth.

"I not° myself naught wisly° what it is,   *don't know / certainly*
But now I feele a newe qualitee—
1655 Yee, al another than I dide er° this."   *before*
Pandare answerd, and seyde thus, that "he
That ones° may in hevene blisse be,   *once*
He feleth other weyes, dar I leye,°   *otherwise, I dare wager*
Than thilke° tyme he first herde of it seye."   *that same*

1660 This is o word for al:° this Troilus   *one word for the whole matter*
Was nevere ful to speke° of this matere,   *tired of speaking*
And for to preisen unto Pandarus
The bounte° of his righte lady deere,   *goodness*
And Pandarus to thanke and maken cheere.
1665 This tale ay was span-newe to bygynne,[4]
Til that the nyght departed hem atwynne.°   *apart*

1. It is as great an art to maintain as to acquire.
2. This is well proven (by the fact that) it so often breaks continually.
3. Nor will I (be) so rash as to trouble her.
4. This talk was always starting over as brand-new.

Troilo returns to Criseida by the way used before, and discoursing lovingly, solaces himself with her.

64

After a little time, the happy fortune of Troilo gave an opportunity for his love. When night had grown dark, he went forth alone from his palace without seeing any star in the sky, entered stealthily by the accustomed way to his pleasure, and quietly and secretly placed himself in the usual spot.

65

Just as Criseida had come before, so in due course she came this time, and she followed entirely the manner of the first time. And after they had greeted one another joyously and pleasingly, as much as was suitable, hand in hand with great delight they entered the bedroom together and without any delay they went to bed.

66

When Criseida had Troilo in her arms, she began joyously to speak thus: "What lady ever was there or could there ever be who could feel as much bliss as I do now? Ah, who would restrain himself from wishing to die bit by bit if in order to have only a little of such a great pleasure, it could not be otherwise?"

67

Then she continued: "My sweet love, I do not know what to say, nor should I ever be able to tell the sweetness and the fiery desire which you have placed in my breast, where I should wish to have you completely always, just as I have your image there; nor would I ask more of Jove, if he would grant me this, than that he would keep you always as you are now.

68

"I do not believe that he can ever reduce this fire, as I believed he would do after we had been together a great deal, but I did not see clearly. You have thrown upon it blacksmith's water so that it burns more than it did, and so I have never loved you as much as I love you now, for day and night I desire and long for you."

69

Troilo spoke similar things to her as they both held each other pressed in their arms, and playfully they used all those words which are usually said between one lover and another to arouse such delights, kissing each other's mouth, eyes, and breast, giving to one another salutations which, when they wrote to each other, were passed over in silence.

2 Soon after this, for that Fortune it wolde,
Icomen was the blisful tyme swete
That Troilus was warned that he sholde,
1670 There he was erst,° Criseyde his lady mete,   *formerly*
For which he felte his herte in joie flete°   *float*
And feithfully gan alle the goddes herie.°   *praise*
And lat se now if that he kan be merie!

And holden was the forme° and al the wise°   *propriety / manner*
1675 Of hire commyng, and of his also,
As it was erst, which nedeth nought devyse.°   *recount*
But pleynly to th'effect° right for to go: *point*
In joie and suerte° Pandarus hem two *weird*   *security*
Abedde brought, whan that hem bothe leste,°   *it pleased them both*
1680 And thus they ben in quyete and in reste.

Nought nedeth it to yow, syn they ben met,[5]
To axe at° me if that they blithe were;   *ask of*
For if it erst was wel, tho was it bet
A thousand fold; this nedeth nought enquere.°   *be asked*
1685 Ago° was every sorwe and every feere;   *Gone*
And bothe, ywys, they hadde, and so they wende,°   *thought*
As muche joie as herte may comprende.°   *comprehend, contain*

This is no litel thyng of for to seye;
This passeth° every wit for to devyse;   *surpasses*
1690 For ech of hem gan otheres lust° obeye.   *desire*
Felicite, which that thise clerkes wise
Comenden so, ne may nought here suffise;
This joie may nought writen be with inke; *NARRATOR'S*
This passeth al that herte may bythynke. *CLAIMS*
  HERE

5. There is no need for you, since they have met.

70

But the unfriendly day drew near, as was clearly perceived by signs, which each of them cursed angrily, for it seemed to them that it came much sooner than it usually came, which for a certainty grieved each of them. But since they could not be together any more, then each rose up without delay.

71

The one departed from the other in the usual manner after many sighs, and they planned to pass in the future without delay to those delights so that they could by meeting together temper the sufferings of love and fashion the joyful period of youth while it might last into a well-being so wrought.

The author writes about what Troilo sang because of love and what his life was like and what he delighted in.

72

Troilo was happy and led a life of song and joy. The high beauty and the lovely looks of any other lady—except his Criseida—he did not prize and he believed that all other men lived in sad distress compared to himself, so greatly was his beloved sweet and pleasing to him.

73

At times he took Pandaro by the hand and walked with him in a garden and talked to him first of Criseida, of her worth and courtesy; then joyfully he began to sing to him, entirely removed from melancholy, in such a manner as is here set forth without any change:

1695	But cruel day—so wailaway the stounde!—°	*time*
	Gan for t'aproche, as they by sygnes knewe,	
	For which hem thoughte° feelen dethis° wownde.	*they seemed / death's*
	So wo was hem that chaungen gan hire hewe,°	*hue*
	And day they gonnen to despise al newe,	
1700	Callyng it traitour, envyous, and worse,	
	And bitterly the dayes light thei corse.	

	Quod Troilus, "Allas, now am I war	
	That Piros[6] and tho swifte steedes thre,	
	Which that drawen forth the sonnes char,°	*chariot*
1705	Han gon som bi-path° in dispit of me;	*shortcut*
	That maketh it so soone day to be;	
	And for° the sonne hym hasteth thus to rise,	*because*
	Ne shal I nevere don hire sacrifise."[7]	

	But nedes day departe hem moste soone,[8]	
1710	And whan hire speche don was and hire cheere,°	*pleasantries*
	They twynne° anon, as they were wont to doone,	*part*
	And setten tyme of metyng eft yfeere;°	*again together*
	And many a nyght they wroughte° in this manere,	*conducted*
	And thus Fortune a tyme ledde in joie	
1715	Criseyde and ek this kynges sone of Troie.	

	In suffisaunce, in blisse, and in singynges,	
	This Troilus gan al his lif to lede.	
	He spendeth, jousteth, maketh festeynges;°	*gives feasts*
	He yeveth frely° ofte, and chaungeth wede,°	*gives generously / clothing*
1720	And held aboute hym alwey, out of drede,°	*doubtless*
	A world of folk, as com hym wel of kynde,[9]	
	The fresshest and the beste he koude fynde;	

	That swich a vois was of hym and a stevene,°	*report, fame*
	Thorughout the world, of honour and largesse,	
1725	That it up rong° unto the yate° of hevene;	*resounded / gate*
	And, as in love, he was in swich gladnesse	
	That in his herte he demed,° as I gesse,	*thought*
	That ther nys lovere in this world at ese	
	So wel as he; and thus gan love hym plese.	

1730	The goodlihede° or beaute which that kynde°	*loveliness / nature*
	In any other lady hadde yset	
	Kan nought the montance° of a knotte unbynde	*extent*
	Aboute his herte of al Criseydes net.	
	He was so narwe ymasked and yknet,°	*enmeshed and tied*

---

6. Pyrois is one of the four steeds who draw the sun's chariot, according to Ovid.
7. I shall never perform a sacrifice for them, i.e., the sun-god and his horses.
8. But of necessity the day must soon part them.
9. As well became him by nature; as he was naturally inclined to do.

74

"O eternal light,* whose glad splendor makes fair the third heaven, from which rain on me pleasure, delight, pity, and love; friend of the sun, and daughter of Jove, benign lady of every gentle heart, certain cause of the strength which moves me to the sweet sighs of my well-being, forever praised be your power.

75

"The heavens, the earth, and the sea, and the underworld all feel your power in themselves, O clear light, and if I discern truly, plants, seeds and grass likewise, birds, beasts, and fish, with eternal vapor feel you in the pleasing season, and men and gods, nor has any creature in the world worth or endurance without you.

76

"You first, O beautiful goddess, moved Jove to the high joyous effects by which all things live and are, and often make him gentle toward the harmful works of us mortals, and turn the weeping we merit into glad and delightful rejoicings; and of old you sent him here below in a thousand forms when you wounded him now for one woman and now for another.

77

"At your pleasure you make the fierce Mars benign and humble and drive away every anger; you expel vileness and fill him who sighs because of you, O goddess, with high disdain; you make each one according to his desires worthy and deserving of high dominion; you make each who is in any degree inflamed with your fire courteous and well-mannered.

78

"You, fair goddess, hold houses and cities, kingdoms, and provinces, and all the world in unity; you are the proven cause of friendships and of their precious fruit; you alone know the hidden qualities of things from which you draw such order that you make marvel whoever does not know how to examine your power carefully.

*See *Troilus and Criseyde* III. 1–42.

1735   That it undon on any manere syde,°   *to untie it in any way*
That nyl naught ben, for aught that may bitide.°   *for whatever may happen*

And by the hond ful ofte he wolde take
This Pandarus, and into gardyn lede,
And swich a feste° and swich a proces° make   *celebration / narration*
1740   Hym of Criseyde, and of hire wommanhede,
And of hire beaute, that withouten drede
It was an hevene his wordes for to here;
And thanne he wolde synge in this manere:

Canticus Troili°   *The Song of Troilus*

"Love, that of erthe and se hath governaunce,[1]
1745   Love, that his hestes° hath in hevene hye,   *commandments*
Love, that with an holsom alliaunce
Halt peples joyned, as hym lest hem gye,[2]
Love, that knetteth° lawe of compaignie,°   *knits together / companionship*
And couples doth° in vertu for to dwelle,   *causes*
1750   Bynd° this acord, that I have told and telle.   *Bind (imperative verb)*

"That, that[3] the world with feith which that is stable
Diverseth so his stowndes concordynge,[4]
That elementz that ben so discordable°   *inclined to discord*
Holden a bond perpetuely durynge,°   *enduring*
1755   That Phebus mote° his rosy day forth brynge,   *Phoebus (god of the sun) may*
And that the mone hath lordshipe over the nyghtes:
Al this doth Love, ay heried° be his myghtes!—   *praised*

"That, that the se,° that gredy is to flowen,   *sea*
Constreyneth to a certeyn ende° so   *boundary*
1760   His flodes that so fiersly they ne growen
To drenchen erthe° and al for evere mo;   *drown the earth*
And if that Love aught lete his bridel go,

---

1. See the note to line 3 above. Troilus's song here is drawn from Boethius, *Consolation of Philosophy* 2.m8. Chaucer's own translation:

> That the world with stable feyth varieth accordable chaungynges; that the contrarious qualities of elementz holden among hemself allyaunce perdurable; that Phebus, the sonne, with his goldene chariet bryngeth forth the rosene day; that the moone hath comaundement over the nyghtes, which nyghtes Esperus, the eve-sterre, hath brought; that the see, gredy to flowen, constreyneth with a certain eende his floodes, so that it is nat leveful* to strecche his brode termes or bowndes uppon the erthes (that is to seyn, to coveren al the erthe)—al this accordaunce [and] ordenaunce of thynges is bounde with love, that governeth erthe and see, and hath also comandement to the hevene. And yif this love slakede the bridelis, alle thynges that now loven hem togidres wolden make batayle contynuely, and stryven to fordo the fassoun** of this world, the which they now leden in accordable feith by fayre moevynges. This love halt togidres peples joyned with an hôly bôund, and knytteth oacrement of mariages of chaste loves; and love enditeth lawes to trewe felawes. O weleful were mankynde, yif thilke love that governeth hevene governede yowr corages.

Leveful: "permitted"
**Fassoun*: "fabric."
2. Holds people joined, as it pleases him to guide them.
3. This, namely that. The first conjunction anticipates *this* of line 1757, and the parallel conjunction in line 1758 refers back to the same *this*. Parallel with the second conjunction *that* of line 1751 are the *that's* of lines 1753, 1755, and 1756.
4. So varies its harmonious seasons.

79

"You impose laws on all the universe through which it maintains itself in being; nor is anyone opposed to your son who does not repent of it if he persists in acting so. And I who formerly was opposed to him in my talk, lately, as is fitting, find myself so much enamored that I could never be able to express how much.

80

"I care little about this if anyone happens to find fault with it, because he does not know what he is saying. May the strong Hercules in this defend me, since he could not protect himself from love. It happens that each wise man praises him for it, and he who does not wish to cover himself with fraud will never say that what was formerly right for Hercules is wrong for me.

81

"Therefore, I love, and among your grand effects this one pleases and gratifies me much; this I follow, in which all delights are, if my soul sees correctly, more than in anything else completed and perfected; in contrast with this everything else is diminished; this makes me follow that lady who more than any other is the mistress of virtue.

82

"This induces me now to rejoice and will always do so, if only I am prudent; this induces me, goddess, so much to praise to myself your bright and invigorating ray because of which I bless the fact that no arms defended me from that bright visage in which I saw your virtue depicted and your power bright and distinct.

83

"And I bless the season, the year, and the month, the day, the hour, and the moment that that virtuous, beautiful, graceful, and courteous one first appeared to my eyes; and I bless the son who kindled me by his strength through her power and who has made me a true servant to her, placing my peace in her eyes.

84

"And I bless the fervent sighs which I have driven formerly from my breast for her, and I bless the pains and the torments which perfect love made me have, and I bless the fiery desires drawn by her face more beautiful than any other because they have been the price of an object so lofty and so gracious.

Al that now loveth asondre sholde lepe,
And lost were al that Love halt now to-hepe.°   together

1765 "So wolde God, that auctour is of kynde,
That with his bond Love of his vertu liste
To cerclen hertes alle and faste bynde,
That from his bond no wight the wey out wiste;[5]
And hertes colde, hem wolde I that he twiste°   would wring, constrain
1770 To make hem love, and that hem liste ay rewe°   it please them ever to have pity
On hertes sore, and kepe hem that ben° trewe!"   protect those who are

5. So may God, author of nature, will it that Love by his power may be pleased to encircle all hearts
and bind them fast with his bond, so that from his bond no person may know the way out.
Alternatively, *Love* may be in apposition with *bond* in line 1766: may God encircle hearts with his
bond Love. (Because it is remote from its governing word *wolde*, the infinitive *cerclen* may be
preceded by *To*.)

85

"But above all I bless God, who gave such a dear lady to the world and who in this lower depth still put so much light into my discernment that for her in preference to any other great desire I might burn and in her might take delight. For that the thanks which ought to be rendered never could be rendered by man.

86

"If a hundred tongues, each one speaking, were in my mouth and I might have the skill of every poet in my breast, I should never be able to express the true virtues, the lofty charm and her abundant courtesy; therefore I devoutly pray him who has the power of expression that he lend it to me for a long time and make me know how to use it.

87

"You are the very one, O goddess, who can do it, if only you wish to, and I pray you greatly for it. Who could then call himself happier if you dispose all the time which destiny has allotted me to my pleasure and to hers? Ah, do it, goddess, since I have gathered myself into your arms, which I had left, not knowing well your true power.

88

"Let him who wants to pursue power and riches, arms, horses, wild beasts, dogs, birds, the studies of Pallas, and the valorous deeds of Mars; I wish to spend all my time in gazing at the beautiful eyes of my lady and her true beauties, which are those things which place me above Jove whenever I gaze at them, so much is my heart enamored of her.

89

"I have not the thanks which it would be fitting for me to give to you, O beautiful eternal light; however I would rather be silent than not render them completely. You, clear light, fail not to fulfill my desire; prolong, hide, correct, and govern my ardor and that of her to whom I am given, and make it so that I may never be another's."

90

In the undertakings involved in their war, he was always the first in arms, for he sallied forth from the city upon the Greeks so spirited and so strong and so fierce that everyone was afraid of him, if the story does not err. And Love, of whom he was a faithful servant, lent him this spirit which was much greater than usual.

91

In times of truce he hunted birds, holding falcons, gerfalcons, and eagles; and sometimes he hunted with dogs, pursuing bears, boars, and great lions; all the small animals he disdained. And when he saw Criseida at appointed times he made himself gracious and beautiful like a falcon who comes out from its hood.

92

All his talk was of love or of good manners, and full of courtesy; he greatly praised the honoring of the valiant and likewise the driving away of the wicked. He was also pleased to see young men adorned with graceful modesty, and he considered any man lost without love, of whatever station he might be.

93

And although he was of royal blood and, if he wished, could have had great power, he made himself kind to all alike, although sometimes a man might not deserve it. Thus Love, who is worth everything, wanted him to act to please others; pride, envy, and avarice he held in hatred, and what each of them draws with it.

In alle nedes for the townes werre
He was, and ay,° the first in armes dyght,°   *always / arrayed*
And certeynly, but if that bokes erre,
1775 Save Ector most ydred° of any wight;°   *feared / person*
And this encrees° of hardynesse and myght   *increase*
Com hym of love, his ladies thank° to wynne,   *thanks, favor*
That altered his spirit so withinne.

In tyme of trewe,° on haukyng° wolde he ride,   *truce / a-hawking*
1780 Or elles honte boor, beer, or lyoun;
The smale bestes leet he gon biside.
And whan that he com ridyng into town,
Ful ofte his lady from hire wyndow down,
As fressh as faukoun comen out of muwe,°   *molting pen*
1785 Ful redy was hym goodly to saluwe.°   *greet*

And moost of love and vertu was his speche,
And in despit hadde alle wrecchednesse;°   *meanness*
And douteles, no nede was° hym biseche   *there was no need*
To honouren hem that hadde worthynesse,
1790 And esen° hem that weren in destresse;   *relieve*
And glad was he if any wyght wel ferde,°   *fared well*
That lovere was, whan he it wiste° or herde.   *knew*

For soth to seyne, he lost held° every wyght,   *considered*
But if° he were in Loves heigh servise—   *Unless*
1795 I mene folk that oughte it ben of right.[6]
And over al this, so wel koude he devyse
Of sentement and in so unkouth wise
Al his array, that every lovere thoughte
That al was wel, what so he seyde or wroughte.[7]

1800 And though that he be come of blood roial,
Hym liste of pride at no wight for to chace;[8]
Benigne he was to ech in general,°   *everyone*
For which he gat hym thank° in every place.   *thanks, good will*
Thus wolde Love—yheried° be his grace!—   *praised*
1805 That Pride, Envye, Ire, and Avarice
He gan to fle, and everich other vice.

6. I mean, people who rightfully should be in it (Love's service).
7. And beyond all this, he knew so well how to order all his behavior (*array*) feelingly and in so striking a way (*unkouth wise*) that every lover thought whatever he said or did was well done.
8. It pleased him to persecute no one out of arrogance.

94

But such happiness lasted for a little time, thanks to envious Fortune, who holds nothing stable in this world. She turned toward him her bitter face, by a new event, as it so happened, and turning everything upside down, took from him Criseida and turned his sweet fruit and his joyous love into sad grief.

Thow lady bryght, the doughter to Dyone,°   *Dione's daughter (i.e., Venus)*
Thy blynde and wynged sone ek, daun° Cupide,   *lord*
Yee sustren nyne ek, that by Elicone
1810   In hil Pernaso listen for t'abide,[9]
That ye thus fer han deyned me to gyde—
I kan namore, but syn that ye wol wende,
Ye heried ben for ay withouten ende![1]

Thorugh yow have I seyd fully in my song
1815   Th'effect° and joie of Troilus servise,   *result*
Al be that ther was som disese among,[2]
As to myn auctour listeth° to devise.   *it pleases*
My thridde° bok now ende ich in this wyse,   *third*
And Troilus in lust° and in quiete   *pleasure*
Is with Criseyde, his owen herte swete.

Explicit liber tercius.[3]

Book Four

Incipit prohemium quarti libri.[1]

But al to litel, weylaway the whyle,°   *woe be the time*
Lasteth swich joie, ythonked be Fortune,
That semeth trewest whan she wol bygyle
And kan to fooles so hire song entune°   *sing*
5   That she hem hent and blent,° traitour comune!   *seizes and blinds*
And whan a wight° is from hire whiel ythrowe,   *person*
Than laugheth she, and maketh hym the mowe.°   *makes a face (moue) at him*

From Troilus she gan hire brighte face
Awey to writhe,° and tok of hym non heede,   *twist*
10   But caste hym clene out of his lady° grace,   *lady's*
And on hire whiel she sette up Diomede;
For which myn herte right now gynneth blede,
And now my penne, allas, with which I write,
Quaketh for drede of that I moste endite.°   *set down*

15   For how Criseyde Troilus forsook—
Or at the leeste, how that she was unkynde—
Moot hennesforth° ben matere of my book,   *Must henceforth*
As writen folk thorugh which it is in mynde.°   *by whom it has been recorded*
Allas, that they scholde evere cause fynde

---

9. Are pleased to dwell. Both Mount Helicon and Mount Parnassus were sacred to the nine sisters, the Muses. Chaucer here and elsewhere (and Boccaccio in one place) takes Helicon to be a fountain on Mount Parnassus.
1. In that you have deigned to guide me thus far—I can say no more, but since you wish to depart, may you be praised forever without end.
2. Although there was some distress mixed in.
3. Here ends the third book.
1. Here begins the proem (prologue) of the fourth book.

Part Four

Here begins the fourth part of the "Filostrato," in which is shown in the first place how it happened that Criseida was given back to her father. Calchas requested an exchange of prisoners and Antenor was granted to him; Criseida is asked for; it is decided to give her up. Troilo at first grieves to himself; then he and Pandaro discuss various methods for the consolation of Troilo. The rumor of her coming departure reaches Criseida; ladies visit her; after their departure Criseida weeps. Pandaro arranges with her that Troilo shall go to her that evening; he goes there; she faints; Troilo wishes to kill himself; she revives; they go to bed, weep, and speak of various things; in the end Criseida promises to return on the tenth day; Troilo departs. First of all the Trojans fight and many are captured and killed by the Greeks.

1

While the Greeks held the city bound with a strong siege, Hector, in whose hands was the whole war, made a selection of his friends and also of other Trojans and sallied out valiantly with his chosen men against the Greeks on the broad plains as he had done many other times with various fortunes in the melee.

2

The Greeks came against him, and they consumed all that day in hard battle; but in the end the sally of the Trojans did not turn out well; therefore they all had to take flight with loss and pain, and many of them died in sorrow and grief and many noble kings and other great barons among them were taken prisoner.

20 To speke hire harm! And if they on hire lye,
   Iwis, hemself sholde han the vilanye.[2]

   O ye Herynes, Nyghtes doughtren thre,
   That endeles compleignen evere in pyne,°   *torment*
   Megera, Alete, and ek° Thesiphone,[3]   *also*
25 Thow cruel Mars ek, fader to Quyryne,°   *Quirinus (i.e., Romulus)*
   This ilke° ferthe book me helpeth fyne,°   *same / conclude*
   So that the losse of lyf and love yfeere°   *together*
   Of Troilus be fully shewed heere.

Explicit prohemium quarti libri.[4]

Incipit liber quartus.°   Here begins the fourth book.

   Liggyng in oost,° as I have seyd er this,   *Lying in host, besieging*
30 The Grekys stronge aboute Troie town,
   Byfel° that, whan that Phebus° shynyng is   *It happened / the sun god*
   Upon the brest of Hercules lyoun,[5]
   That Ector, with ful many a bold baroun,
   Caste° on a day with Grekis for to fighte,   *Planned*
35 As he was wont, to greve hem what° he myghte.   *to afflict them however*

   Not I° how longe or short it was bitwene   *I don't know*
   This purpos and that day they issen mente,°   *intended to sally forth*
   But on a day, wel armed, brighte, and shene,°   *gleaming*
   Ector and many a worthi wight out wente,[6]
40 With spere in honde and bigge bowes bente;
   And in the berd,° withouten lenger lette,°   *face to face / delay*
   Hire fomen° in the feld hem faste mette.   *foes*

[handwritten margin note: until this point, war has played a tiny role, but here it is the focus. Love/war]

   The longe day, with speres sharpe igrounde,
   With arwes, dartes, swerdes, maces felle,°   *cruel*
45 They fighte and bringen hors and man to grounde,
   And with hire axes out the braynes quelle.°   *dash*
   But in the laste shour,° soth° for to telle,   *assault / truth*

2. Surely they themselves ought to bear the reproach.
3. Night's three daughters, the Erinyes, are the Furies; cf. the note to I.6 above.
4. Here ends the proem of the fourth book.
5. "Hercules's lion" is the zodiacal sign Leo. The sun was in Leo from mid July to early August; by *brest* ("front"? "center"?) Chaucer may refer to the early or middle part of that period.
6. For a few lines Chaucer imitates the heavy alliteration characteristic of contemporary battle poetry.

3

Among these were the magnificent Antenor, Polydamas his son, and Menestheus, Xanthippus, Sarpedon, Polymnestor, Polites also, and the Trojan Ripheus, and many more whom Hector's prowess was not able to rescue in the disengagement, so that great and bitter lament was made in Troy and it was almost the foreshadowing of a much greater woe.

4

Priam asked for a truce and it was given him, and negotiations began between them about the exchange of prisoners at that time, and about the giving of gold for them in addition. Hearing of this, Calchas, with changed face and with loud lament, came among the Greeks and by hoarse crying brought it about that they listened to him for a little.

The oration of Calchas to the Greeks, in which he explains to them his merits and then asks for some prisoners for whom he may exchange Criseida.

5

"Lords," began Calchas, "I was a Trojan as you all know, and if you remember well, I am he who first brought hope of that for which you are here and told you that you will obtain it at the destined time, that is, victory in your undertaking, for Troy shall be destroyed and burned by you.

6

"The steps and also the method to follow in this you know, for I have shown you. And in order that all your desires might come about in the time I foretold, without trusting in any messenger or in any document open or sealed, I came here to you, as is apparent, to give you in this matter both counsel and aid.

The folk of Troie hemselven so mysledden°   *conducted themselves so poorly*
That with the worse at nyght homward they fledden.

50 At which day was taken Antenore,
Maugre° Polydamas or Monesteo,   *In spite of (the efforts of)*
Santippe, Sarpedoun, Polynestore,
Polite, or ek° the Trojan daun° Rupheo,   *also / lord*
And other lasse° folk as Phebuseo;   *lesser*
55 So that, for harm, that day the folk of Troie
Dredden to lese° a gret part of hire joie.   *Feared they would lose*

Of Priamus was yeve,° at Grek requeste,   *By Priam there was granted*
A tyme of trewe,° and tho they gonnen trete°   *truce / negotiate*
Hire prisoners to chaungen,° meste° and leste,   *exchange / the more important*
60 And for the surplus yeven sommes grete.[7]
This thing anon was couth° in every strete,   *forthwith was known*
Bothe in th'assege,° in town, and everywhere,   *the besieging force*
And with the firste it com to Calkas ere.°   *Calchas's ear*

Whan Calkas knew this tretis sholde holde,°   *negotiation should be held*
65 In consistorie° among the Grekes soone   *council*
He gan in thringe° forth with lordes olde,   *press*
And sette hym there as he was wont to doone;
And with a chaunged° face hem bad a boone,°   *discolored / asked a favor*
For love of God, to don that reverence,
70 To stynte noyse and yeve° hym audience.°   *give / a hearing*

Than seyde he thus: "Lo, lordes myn, ich was
Troian, as it is knowen out of drede;°   *doubtless*
And, if that yow remembre, I am Calkas,
That alderfirst yaf° comfort to youre nede,   *first of all gave*
75 And tolde wel how that ye shulden spede.°   *prosper*
For dredeles,° thorugh yow shal in a stownde°   *doubtless / time, trice*
Ben Troie ybrend° and beten down to grownde.   *burnt*

"And in what forme, or in what manere wise,°   *fashion or manner*
This town to shende,° and al youre lust° t'acheve,   *will be destroyed / desire*
80 Ye han er this wel herd me yow devyse;°   *recount*
This knowe ye, my lordes, as I leve.°   *believe*
And for the Grekis weren me so leeve,°   *dear, beloved*
I com° myself, in my propre persone,°   *came / in (my own) person*
To teche in this how yow was best to doone.

7. And to give great sums for the surplus (of prisoners of one side over the other).

7

"Wishing to do this, I needed to depart craftily and very secretly without making this known to anyone, and, like a traitor, as soon as the bright day turned dark, I went out alone and came here from there quietly and I brought nothing with me but I left all that I had there.

8

"Of this in truth I care little or nothing, except for a young daughter of mine whom I left there. Alas, hard and unfeeling father that I was, would that I had led this little lonely one here in safety! But fear and haste would not permit it. This makes me grieve for what I have left in Troy; this takes from me both gaiety and joy.

9

"Nor have I yet seen a time when I could ask for her back; therefore I have been silent. But now is the time when she could be obtained if I could win this gift from you; and if it may not now be had, never shall I hope to see her more, and henceforth I shall lead my life in desolation without caring more for life than death.

10

"Here with you are noble Trojan barons, and many others, whom you exchange with your enemies for your prisoners. Give me one only of the many of them, in return for whose redemption I may have my daughter. In the name of God, my lords, console this wretched old man, who is void and deprived of any other solace.

11

"And do not let desire to have gold or prisoners draw you from this, for I swear to you by God that every Trojan power, each bit of wealth is certainly in your hands; and if I am not deceived, soon the prowess will fail him who holds shut the gates to the desire of all of you, as will appear by his violent death."

85 "Havyng unto my tresor ne my rente°   *income*
   Right no resport,° to respect of° youre ese,   *regard / in comparison with*
   Thus al my good I lefte and to yow wente,
   Wenyng in° this yow lordes for to plese.   *Thinking by*
   But al that los ne doth me no disese.
90 I vouchesauf, as wisly have I° joie,   *am willing, as surely as I have*
   For yow to lese° al that I have in Troie,   *To lose on your behalf*

   "Save of° a doughter that I lefte, allas,   *Except for*
   Slepyng at hom, whanne out of Troie I sterte.°   *rushed*
   O sterne, O cruel fader that I was!
95 How myghte I have in that so hard an herte?
   Allas, I ne hadde ibrought hire in hire sherte!°   *nightshirt*
   For sorwe of which I wol nought lyve to-morwe,
   But if° ye lordes rewe° upon my sorwe.   *Unless / have pity*

   "For by that cause I say° no tyme er now   *because I saw*
100 Hire to delivere, ich holden have my pees;°   *peace*
   But now or nevere, if that it like° yow,   *please*
   I may hire have right soone, douteles.
   O help and grace amonges al this prees!°   *throng*
   Rewe on this olde caytyf° in destresse,   *wretch*
105 Syn° I thorugh yow have al this hevynesse.   *Since*

   "Ye have now kaught and fetered in prisoun
   Troians ynowe,° and if youre willes be,°   *enough / it be your will*
   My child with° oon may han redempcioun;   *in return for*
   Now for the love of God and of bounte,°   *goodness*
110 Oon of so fele,° allas, so yive° hym me!   *many / give*
   What nede were it this preiere for to werne,°   *deny*
   Syn° ye shul bothe han folk and town as yerne?°   *Since / very soon*

   "On peril of my lif, I shal nat lye;
   Appollo hath me told it feithfully;°   *truthfully*
115 I have ek° founde it be astronomye,   *also*
   By sort, and by augurye ek, trewely,[8]
   And dar wel say, the tyme is faste by°   *near at hand*
   That fire and flaumbe° on al the town shal sprede,   *flame*
   And thus shal Troie torne to asshen dede.°   *dead ashes*

120 "For certein, Phebus° and Neptunus bothe,   *Phoebus Apollo*
   That makeden the walles of the town,
   Ben° with the folk of Troie alwey so wrothe°   *Are / angry*
   That they wol brynge it to confusioun,
   Right in despit of kyng Lameadoun;[9]

---

8. Calchas's prediction is based on the oracle of Apollo, astrological calculation, casting lots, and augury with birds.
9. Benoît (see Introduction) says Neptune built the walls of Troy and Apollo consecrated them. Commonly Apollo was thought to have raised the walls with his music. Ovid tells that King Laomedon, Priam's father, refused to pay Neptune and Apollo their wages.

Antenor was given to Calchas, and in the presence of Troilo Criseida was asked for, and it was decided that she should be rendered up.

12

While saying this the aged priest, humble in speech and looks, constantly streaked his cheeks with tears, and his hoary beard and hard breast were all bathed; nor were his prayers void of piteous effect, for when he stopped speaking, the Greeks all shouted noisily, "Let Antenor be given to him."

13

Thus it was done, and Calchas was content, and he enjoined the business upon the negotiators, who told his desire to King Priam and to his sons and to the lords who were also there, and then a deliberation was held about this, and to the ambassadors they replied briefly: if they were to give up the persons they demanded, their own should be returned to them.

14

Troilo was present at the demand which the Greeks made, and hearing Criseida asked for, he suddenly felt his heart being all transfixed within him and a pain so sharp that he believed himself dying where he sat; but with difficulty he still restrained the love and grief within, as was fitting.

15

And full of anguish and of cruel fear, he began to await what would be replied, with no usual care turning over within himself what he might have to do, if his misfortune were so great that he might hear it decided among his brothers that Criseida should be given up to Calchas, so that he might be able to overturn the decision altogether.

125 Bycause he nolde payen hem here hire,°   *wages*
    The town of Troie shal ben set on-fire."

    Tellyng his tale alwey, this olde greye,°   *graybeard*
    Humble in his speche and in his lokyng° eke,   *countenance*
    The salte teris from his eyen tweye°   *two eyes*
130 Ful faste ronnen down by either cheke.
    So longe he gan of socour hem biseke°   *beseech them*
    That, for to hele° hym of his sorwes soore,   *heal*
    They yave° hym Antenor, withouten moore.°   *gave / further ado*

    But who was glad ynough but Calkas tho?
135 And of this thyng ful soone his nedes leyde°   *urged his business*
    On hem that° sholden for the tretis° go,   *those who / negotiation*
    And hem for Antenor ful ofte preyde
    To bryngen hom kyng Toas° and Criseyde.   *Thoas*
    And whan Priam his save-garde° sente,   *safe conduct*
140 Th'embassadours to Troie streight they wente.

    The cause itold° of hire comyng, the olde   *having been told*
    Priam, the kyng, ful soone in general
    Let her-upon° his parlement to holde,° *Granted herewith / to be held*
    Of which th'effect rehercen° yow I shal.   *recount*
145 Th'embassadours ben answerd for fynal;°   *finally*
    Th'eschaunge of prisoners and al this nede°   *affair*
    Hem liketh° wel, and forth in they procede.   *Please them*

    This Troilus was present in the place
    Whan axed was for Antenor Criseyde,
150 For which ful soone chaungen gan his face,
    As he that° with tho wordes wel neigh deyde.   *one who*
    But natheles° he no word to it seyde,   *nevertheless*
    Lest men sholde his affeccioun espye;
    With mannes herte he gan his sorwes drye,°   *endure*

155 And ful of angwissh and of grisly° drede   *grim*
    Abod° what lordes wolde unto it seye;   *Awaited*
    And if they wolde graunte—as God forbede—°   *God forbid!*
    Th'eschaunge of hire, than° thoughte he thynges tweye:° *then / two*
    First, how to save hire honour, and what weye
160 He myghte best th'eschaunge of hire withstonde.°   *oppose*
    Ful faste he caste° how al this myghte stonde.   *considered*

16

Love made him ready to oppose anything, but on the other side was Reason, which stood against it and which made that noble enterprise very dubious, lest perhaps Criseida might be angry with it because of shame, and in such a manner the timid youth stood between the two courses, wishing and not wishing now this, now that.

17

While he stood suspended in such a way many things were discussed among the barons as to what was needed now in view of the things which had happened, and, as has been said, to those who waited, replies were fully given, and one was that Criseida should be rendered up, who had never been detained there.

Troilo faints hearing that Criseida was surrendered, and straightway leaves the council.

18

As the lily after it has been turned up in the fields by the plough falls and withers through excessive sun and its beautiful color grows changed and pale, so at the words delivered to the Greeks about the counsel decided upon among the Trojans did Troilo under such a weight of affliction and of peril fall there in a swoon, pierced by profound grief.

19

Priam and Hector and his brothers took him in their arms, strongly alarmed at this occurrence, and each worked hard to comfort him and like skilled men they exerted themselves to recover his dead powers, now rubbing his wrists and now often bathing his face, but still their work was of little value.

20

He lay among his kinsmen stretched out and overcome, and he still had a little of the breath of life there. And his face was pallid, deadly pale, and he was all livid, and he seemed a thing more dead than living, marked by affliction in such a manner that it made everyone weep, so severe was the high thunderbolt that assailed him when he heard of the surrender of Criseida.

21

But after his sorrowing soul had wandered for a long time before it would return, it came back quietly; and then, like one who has awakened suddenly, he rose to his feet all bewildered, and before anyone asked him what it was that he had felt, pretending that he had something else to do, he departed from them.

Love hym made al prest to don hire byde,°   *eager to make her stay*
And rather dyen than she sholde go;
But Resoun seyde hym, on that other syde,
165 "Withouten assent of hire ne do nat so,
Lest for thi werk° she wolde be thy fo,   *conduct*
And seyn that thorugh thy medlynge is iblowe°   *blown abroad, made public*
Youre bother° love, ther it was erst° unknowe."   *Of the two of you / formerly*

For which he gan deliberen,° for the beste,   *decide*
170 That though the lordes wolde that she wente,
He wolde lat hem graunte what hem leste,°   *pleased them*
And telle his lady first what that they mente;
And whan that she hadde seyd hym hire entente,
Therafter wolde he werken also blyve,°   *very swiftly*
175 Theigh° al the world ayeyn° it wolde stryve.   *Though / against*

Ector, which that wel the Grekis herde,
For Antenor how they wolde han Criseyde,
Gan it withstonde,° and sobrely answerde: *oppose*
"Syres, she nys no prisonere," he seyde;
180 "I not° on yow who that this charge° leyde,   *don't know / commission*
But, on my part, ye may eftsone° hem telle,   *in reply*
We usen here° no wommen for to selle."   *are not accustomed here*

The noyse of peple up stirte° thanne at ones,   *rose up*
As breme° as blase of straw[1] iset on-fire;   *fiercely*
185 For infortune° it wolde, for the nones,°   *ill fortune / nonce*
They sholden hire confusioun desire.[2]
"Ector," quod they, "what goost° may yow enspyre°   *evil spirit / inspire*
This womman thus to shilde° and don us leese°   *shield / cause us to lose*
Daun° Antenor—a wrong wey now ye chese—°   *Lord / choose*

190 "That° is so wys and ek so bold baroun?   *Who (i.e., Antenor)*
And we han nede to° folk, as men may se.   *of*
He is ek oon the grettest° of this town.   *the very greatest*
O Ector, lat tho fantasies be!
O kyng Priam," quod they, "thus sygge° we,   *say*
195 That al oure vois° is to forgon° Criseyde."   *voice, vote / give up*
And to deliveren Antenor they preyde.

O Juvenal,[3] lord, trewe is thy sentence,
That litel wyten° folk what is to yerne,°   *know / to be desired*
That° they ne fynde in hire desir offence;   *So that*
200 For cloude of errour let hem to discerne°   *keeps them from seeing*
What best is. And lo, here ensample as yerne:°   *an example forthwith*

---

1. The phrase *blase of straw* may, in the context of the *noyse of peple*, refer to the Uprising (Peasants' Revolt) of 1381, one of whose leaders was Jack Straw. Chaucer's contemporary Gower made a similar pun on the name Straw.
2. That they should desire their own ruin. The reference is to the Trojans' desire to redeem Antenor in the exchange of prisoners. See the note to line 205 below.
3. Lines 198–201 draw on the Roman poet Juvenal's *Satires* (early second century C.E.) 10.2–4.

22

And he took himself toward his own palace without listening or turning to anyone, and sighing and dejected as he was, without wishing for anyone's company, he went there into his room, and said that he wished to rest, and so all, friend and servant however dear, went out from there, but they closed the windows first.

The author, who usually calls on his lady for aid, here refuses to, saying that without it he knows through his sorrowing how to recount the sorrows of others.

23

To what follows after, lovely lady, I do not care at all if you are not present because my power of invention by itself, if weak memory does not deceive it, will know how to recount well, without any aid from you, who are the cause of such bitter pain, the heavy sorrow by which, oppressed through your departure, it feels itself sad.

24

Up to here I have happily sung the bliss which Troilo felt through love, although it was mixed with sighs; now it is fitting for me to turn from joy to sorrow. Therefore, if you do not listen to me, I do not care because your heart will be forced to change and make you feel pity for my life which is more sorrowful than any other.

25

But if, however, it ever comes to your ears, I pray you by the love which I bear you that you have some regard for my woes, and by returning, give back to me the comfort which you have taken from me with your departure. And if it would displease you to find me dead, return at once, for short is the life which your departure has left me.

This folk desiren now deliveraunce
Of Antenor, that brought hem to meschaunce,°   *ruin*

For he was after traitour to the town
205   Of Troye.⁴ Allas, they quytte hym out to rathe!°   *released him too hastily*
O nyce° world, lo, thy discrecioun!   *foolish*
Criseyde, which that nevere dide hem scathe,°   *harm*
Shal now no lenger in hire blisse bathe;
But Antenor, he shal com hom to towne,
210   And she shal out;° thus seyden here and howne.⁵   *must (go) out*

For which delibered° was by parlement   *decided*
For Antenor to yelden out° Criseyde,   *give up (in exchange)*
And it pronounced by the president,
Altheigh that Ector "nay" ful ofte preyde.
215   And fynaly, what wight that it withseyde,°   *whoever opposed it*
It was for nought; it moste ben and sholde,°   *must be and would have to be*
For substaunce° of the parlement it wolde.   *the majority*

Departed° out of parlement echone,°   *Having departed / each one*
This Troilus, withouten wordes mo,
220   Unto his chambre spedde hym faste allone,
But if it were a man of his or two   *Unless*
The which he bad° out faste for to go   *requested*
Bycause he wolde slepen, as he seyde,
And hastily upon his bed hym leyde.

225   And as in wynter leves ben biraft,°   *are taken away*
Ech after other, til the tree be bare,
So that ther nys but bark and braunche ilaft,
Lith Troilus, byraft of ech welfare,
Ibounden in the blake bark° of care,   *black bark (of a tree)*
230   Disposed wood out of his wit to breyde,⁶
So sore hym sat° the chaungynge of Criseyde.   *beset*

---

4. Antenor's treason, narrated by Benoît and Guido (see Introduction), was his plot to remove the Palladium, on which depended the preservation of Troy. See I.153–54 above.
5. Thus said master and members of the household alike, i.e., everybody.
6. In a state to go mad out of his mind.

The author describes the lamentations, the anguish, and the griefs of Troilo because of the coming departure of Criseida.

26

Then Troilo, who remained alone in his locked and darkened room, without suspicion of any man or fear of being able to be heard, began to utter the sorrow gathered in his sad breast because of the suddenly occurring misfortune in such a manner that he seemed not a man but a raging beast.

27

The bull does not go leaping otherwise, now here, now there, after he has received the mortal stroke and bellowing in misery makes known what pain he has conceived, than Troilo did, raging against himself and without restraint striking his head against the wall and his face with his hands and his breast and his aching arms with his fists.

28

His wretched eyes for pity of his heart wept sorely, and seemed two fountains which threw water out abundantly; the deep sobs of weeping at the vain words constantly took away his strength, words which, always in strange outbursts, went on begging for nothing else but death, blaspheming and mocking the gods and himself.

29

After his great fury had vented itself and his weeping had moderated itself by length of time, Troilo, enkindled in the fire of sorrow, threw himself upon his bed a little while, not resting however—not even a little moment—from weeping sorely and from sighing so much that his head and breast scarcely sufficed him for such suffering as was given him.

30

Then shortly after, he began to say to himself in his plaint, "O wretched Fortune, what have I done to you that you thus oppose yourself to my every desire? Have you any other business except my suffering? Why have you turned so soon your dark face toward me who formerly loved you far more than any other god as you know well, cruel one?

31

"If my joyous and gracious life was displeasing to you, why did you not throw down the pride of haughty Ilium? Why did you not take from me my father? Why not Hector, in whose valor rests every hope in these grievous times? Why did you not yourself carry off from us Polyxena and why not Paris and Helen also?

He rist hym up,° and every dore he shette;° *[handwritten: hopelessness]*   rises up / shut
And wyndow ek, and tho this sorwful man *[handwritten: Troilus shuts out opportunities]*
Upon his beddes syde adown hym sette,
235 Ful lik a ded ymage, pale and wan;
And in his brest the heped° wo bygan   heaped-up
Out breste,° and he to werken° in this wise   To burst out / conduct himself
In his woodnesse,° as I shal yow devyse.   madness

[handwritten: woodnesse like madness, + all the tree imagery]

Right as the wylde bole° bygynneth sprynge,°   bull (in a sacrifice) / lunge
240 Now her, now ther, idarted° to the herte,   pierced
And of his deth roreth in compleynynge,
Right so gan he aboute the chaumbre sterte,°   lunged
Smytyng his brest ay with his fistes smerte;°   painfully
His hed to the wal, his body to the grounde
245 Ful ofte he swapte,° hymselven to confounde.°   dashed / destroy

His eyen two, for piete° of herte,   the pitiful state
Out stremeden° as swifte welles tweye;°   streamed, flowed / two
The heighe sobbes of his sorwes smerte°   painful
His speche hym refte;° unnethes° myghte he   Robbed him of speech / scarcely
    seye,
250 "O deth, allas, why nyltow do me deye?°   cause me to die
Acorsed be that day which that Nature
Shop° me to ben a lyves° creature!"   Created / living

But after, whan the furie and al the rage,
Which that his herte twiste° and faste threste,°   wrung / oppressed
255 By lengthe of tyme somwhat gan aswage,°   to be assuaged
Upon his bed he leyde hym down to reste.
But tho bygonne his teeris more out breste,°   to burst out
That wonder is the body may suffise
To° half this wo which that I yow devyse.   To (endure)

260 Than seyde he thus: "Fortune, allas the while!
What have I don? What° have I thus agylt?°   How / offended
How myghtestow for rowthe° me bygile?°   pity / deceive, seduce
Is ther no grace, and shal I thus be spilt?°   ruined
Shal thus Criseyde awey, for that thow wilt?°   because you wish it
265 Allas, how maistow in thyn herte fynde
To ben to me thus cruwel and unkynde?

"Have I the nought honoured al my lyve,
As thow wel woost,° above the goddes alle?   As you know well
Whi wiltow me fro joie thus deprive?
270 O Troilus, what may men now the calle

32

"If Criseida alone were left to me, I should not care for any other great loss nor say a word about it. But your arrows always go directly at the things for which the greatest desire is had. The more to show the force of your deception you carry away from me all my comfort. Ah would you had now slain me first!

33

"Alas, Love, sweet and pleasing lord, who knows what lies in my soul, what shall my sorrowing life be, if I lose this bliss, this peace of mine? Alas, gentle Love, who gave my mind consolation once, what shall I do, true lord, if she to whom, by your will, I gave myself completely is taken away from me?

34

"I shall weep and I shall remain ever sorrowful wherever I may be while life shall endure in this suffering body! O soul, wretched and bewildered, why do you not flee from the most unfortunate body that lives? O dejected soul, leave the body and follow Criseida. Why do you not do it? Why do you not vanish?

35

"O sorrowing eyes, whose comfort was all in our Criseida's face, what will you do? Now you will always remain in sad grief since it will be parted from you and your valor will be destroyed, overwhelmed, and conquered by your weeping. In vain will you see other virtue now, if your well-being is taken from you.

But wrecche of wrecches, out of honour falle°   *having fallen*
Into miserie, in which I wol bewaille
Criseyde—allas!—til that the breth me faille?

"Allas, Fortune, if that my lif in joie
275 Displesed hadde unto° thi foule envye,   *Was displeasing to*
Why ne haddestow my fader, kyng of Troye,
Byraft° the lif, or don° my bretheren dye,   *Snatched away / caused*
Or slayn myself, that thus compleyne and crye—
I, combre-world, that may of nothyng serve,⁷
280 But evere dye and nevere fulli sterve.°   *die*

"If that Criseyde allone were me laft,
Nought roughte I whiderward° thow woldest me   *I don't care whither*
   steere;°   *lead*
And hire, allas, than hastow me biraft.
But everemore,° lo, this is thi manere,   *always*
285 To reve° a wight that° most is to hym deere,   *rob from / what*
To preve° in that thi gerful° violence.   *prove, display / changeable*
Thus am I lost; ther helpeth no diffence.°   *remedy*

"O verrey° lord, O Love! O god, allas!   *true*
That knowest best myn herte and al my thought,
290 What shal my sorwful lif don in this cas,
If I forgo that° I so deere° have bought?   *what / at so high a price*
Syn° ye Criseyde and me han fully brought   *Since*
Into youre grace, and bothe oure hertes seled,°   *sealed, legally bound*
How may ye suffre,° allas, it be repeled?°   *allow / to be repealed*

295 "What shal I don? I shal, while I may dure°   *last*
On lyve° in torment and in cruwel peyne,   *Alive*
This infortune or this disaventure,°   *unhappiness*
Allone as I was born, iwys, compleyne;°   *(I shall) surely complain about*
Ne nevere wol I seen it shyne or reyne,
300 But ende I wol, as Edippe,° in derknesse   *Oedipus (who blinded himself)*
My sorwful lif, and dyen in distresse.

"O wery goost, that errest° to and fro,   *wanders*
Why nyltow fleen° out of the wofulleste   *fly*
Body that evere myghte on grounde go?
305 O soule, lurkynge in this wo, unneste,°   *leave your nest*
Fle forth out of myn herte, and lat it breste,°   *burst*
And folowe alwey Criseyde, thi lady dere.
Thi righte place is now no lenger° here.   *longer*

"O woful eyen two, syn youre disport⁶   *pleasure*
310 Was al to sen Criseydes eyen brighte,
What shal ye don but, for my discomfort,
Stonden for naught,⁸ and wepen out youre sighte,
Syn she is queynt° that wont was° yow to lighte?   *quenched / was accustomed*

---

7. I, an encumbrance on the world, who am good for nothing.
8. Be worth nothing, possibly with play on the notion that an eye is shaped like a zero (*naught*).

36

"O my Criseida, O sweet bliss of the sorrowing soul which calls on you, who will give comfort any more to my sufferings? Who will calm my love longing? If you take yourself from here, alas, fitting it is that that weary one who loves you more than himself should die; and I shall die without having deserved it—may the sin belong to the pitiless gods.

37

"Ah, if now your departure might be delayed so that I, poor man, might have learned through long usage to endure it! I do not wish to say that I would not have opposed your going to the utmost of my power, but if, however, I might have seen this coming, your departure, which now seems so grievous to me, might have seemed sweet to me through long habit.

38

"O ill-lived old man, O crazed old man, what fantasy or what disdain moved you to go to the Greeks since you were a Trojan? Was anyone honored in all our kingdom more than you, native or stranger? O wicked counsel, O breast filled with treacheries, deceits, and malices, if only I now had you, as I would wish, in Troy!

39

"If only you had died the day you went from here! If only you had died at the feet of the Greeks when you first opened your mouth to ask for the return of her who enamors me! O how much ill for me that you came into the world! You are the cause of the sorrow which stabs me to the heart. If only Menelaus had driven the lance that pierced Protesilaus into your heart!

40

"If you were dead I should certainly live, since there would be no one to seek Criseida; if you were dead I should not be desolate, and Criseida would not be parted from me; if you were dead, I see very clearly that what now grieves me would not afflict me. Therefore, your life is the sad cause of my death and of my sorrowful lot."

Troilo falls asleep; then he has Pandaro summoned and they sorrow together and they discuss many things relating to Troilo's well-being.

41

A thousand sighs more burning than fire were issuing from his amorous breast mingled with tears and with sorrowing words without giving any respect to one another. And these laments had so overcome him that he

In vayn fro this forth have ich eyen tweye°   *two eyes*
315 Ifourmed,° syn youre vertu° is aweye.   *formed, created / power*

"O my Criseyde, O lady sovereigne
Of thilke° woful soule that thus crieth,   *that same*
Who shal now yeven° comfort to my peyne?   *give*
Allas, no wight. But whan myn herte dieth,
320 My spirit, which that so unto yow hieth,°   *hastens*
Receyve in gree,° for that shal ay° yow serve;   *favorably / always*
Forthi no fors is, though the body sterve.⁹

"O ye loveris, that heigh° upon the whiel   *high*
Ben set of Fortune, in good aventure,°   *stead*
325 God leve° that ye fynde ay love of stiel,°   *grant / steel*
And longe mote° youre lif in joie endure!   *may*
But whan ye comen by my sepulture,
Remembreth that youre felawe resteth there;
For I loved ek, though ich unworthi were.

330 "O oold, unholsom,° and myslyved° man—   *corrupt / wicked*
Calkas I mene—allas, what eiled the°   *ailed you*
To ben a Grek, syn thow art born Troian?
O Calkas, which that wolt my bane° be,   *destruction*
In corsed tyme was thow born for me!
335 As wolde blisful Jove,° for his joie,   *May blessed Jupiter grant*
That I the° hadde wher I wolde, in Troie!"   *you*

A thousand sikes,° hotter than the gleede,°   *sighs / glowing coal*
Out of his brest ech after other wente,
Medled° with pleyntes new, his wo to feede,°   *Mingled / feed, fuel*
340 For which his woful teris nevere stente;°   *ceased*
And shortly, so his peynes hym torente,°   *tore up*
And wex so mat,° that joie nor penaunce°   *defeated / torment*
He feleth non, but lith° forth in a traunce.   *lies*

9. Therefore it doesn't matter even if my body should die.

could not do any more, and so he fell asleep, but he slept scarcely any time before he awoke.

42

And sighing, he rose to his feet, went to the door that he had locked and opened it and said to one of his confidential servants, "Make haste; call Pandaro quickly; make him come to me." And afterwards he took himself sorrowfully into the darkness of his room, full of sighs and all drowsy.

43

Pandaro came. Already he had heard what the Greek ambassadors requested and also how the lords had made the decision to give Criseida back. With his face all disturbed by this, thinking over Troilo's sorrows, he entered the dark and quiet room, nor did he know what word, sad or happy, to say.

44

Troilo, as soon as he saw him, threw himself on his neck, weeping so strongly that no man could easily recount it. When the sorrowing Pandaro heard that, he began to weep, he felt such pity for him, and in such a manner, without doing anything other than weep bitterly, they remained awhile without either one speaking much or little.

45

But when Troilo had recovered his spirit, he began first, "O Pandaro, I am dead. My happiness is turned to pain, O wretched me, and my sweet comfort. Insidious Fortune leads it from here, and together with it my solace and my pleasure. Have you yet heard how my Criseida is to be taken from here by the Greeks?"

[handwritten note: parallel to Troilus' reaction]

Pandare, which that in the parlement
345   Hadde herd what every lord and burgeys° seyde,   *burgess, citizen*
And how ful graunted was by oon assent°   *by one accord, by consensus*
For Antenor to yelden° so Criseyde,   *surrender*
Gan wel neigh wood out of his wit to breyde,[1]
So that for wo he nyste what he mente,°   *he didn't know what he intended*
350   But in a rees° to Troilus he wente.   *rush*

A certeyn knyght that for the tyme kepte
The chambre door undide it hym anon;°   *for him forthwith*
And Pandare, that ful tendreliche wepte,
Into the derke chambre, as stille as ston,
355   Toward the bed gan softely to gon,
So confus that he nyste° what to seye;   *didn't know*
For verray wo his wit was neigh aweye.°   *nearly gone*

And with his chiere and lokyng al totorn°   *face and look all ravaged*
For sorwe of this, and with his armes folden,
360   He stood this woful Troilus byforn,°   *in front of*
And on his pitous° face he gan byholden.   *pitiful*
But Lord, so ofte gan his herte colden,°   *grow cold*
Seyng° his frend in wo, whos hevynesse   *Seeing*
His herte slough,° as thoughte hym, for destresse.   *slew*

365   This woful wight, this Troilus, that felte
His frend Pandare ycomen hym to se,
Gan as the snow ayeyn° the sonne melte;   *facing*
For which this sorwful Pandare, of pitee,
Gan for to wepe as tendreliche as he;
370   And specheles thus ben thise ilke tweye,°   *same two*
That neither myghte o° word for sorwe seye.   *one*

But at the laste this woful Troilus,
Neigh ded for smert, gan bresten out to rore,[2]
And with a sorwful noise he seyde thus,
375   Among hise sobbes and his sikes sore:
"Lo, Pandare, I am ded, withouten more.°   *further ado*

1. Went nearly mad, out of his mind.
2. Nearly dead for the pain, burst out roaring.

46

Pandaro, who was weeping no less sorely, replied, "Yes, if only it were not true! Ah, woe is me! For I did not believe that this time so sweet and untainted would die out soon, nor could I myself see that anything could hurt your perfect bliss except that it should be disclosed; now I see that all our precautions were inadequate.

47

"But why do you give yourself so much anguish? That which you desired you have had; you ought to be content with that alone. Leave both these and other woes to me, who have ever loved and never had a glance from her who undoes me and who alone could give me peace.

48

"And besides that, this city is seen to be full of beautiful and gracious ladies and, if it merits belief that I wish you happiness, there is none of them, the most beautiful you wish, who would not be willing to have pity on you, if you will suffer the pains of love for her; therefore if we lose this lady; we shall find many others.

49

"And as I have often heard said before, the new love always drives away the old. A new pleasure will take away the present suffering from you, if you do what I say. Therefore do not wish to die for her, and do not wish to be your own enemy. Do you think, perhaps, by weeping to regain her or to keep her from going?"

Hastow nat herd at parlement," he seyde,
"For Antenor how lost is my Criseyde?"

This Pandarus, ful ded and pale of hewe,
380 Ful pitously answerde and seyde, "Yis!
As wisly were it° fals as it is trewe,   *Surely would that it were*
That I have herd, and woot° al how it is.   *(I) know*
O mercy, God, who wolde have trowed° this?   *believed*
Who wolde have wend° that in so litel a throwe°   *thought / space of time*
385 Fortune oure joie wold han overthrowe?

"For in this world ther is no creature,
As to my dom, that ever saugh ruyne
Straunger than this, thorugh cas or aventure.°   *chance or happenstance*
But who may al eschue,° or al devyne?°   *avoid / foretell*
390 Swich is this world! Forthi° I thus diffyne:°   *Therefore / conclude*
Ne trust no wight to fynden in Fortune
Ay propretee; hire yiftes ben comune.[3]

"But telle me this: whi thow art now so mad°   *insane*
To sorwen thus? Whi listow° in this wise,   *do you lie down*
395 Syn thi desir al holly° hastow had,   *wholly*
So that, by right, it oughte ynough suffise?°   *to be sufficient*
But I, that nevere felte in my servyse°   *service (as an unrequited lover)*
A frendly cheere or lokyng of an eye,
Lat me thus wepe and wailen til I deye.

400 "And over al this, as thow wel woost thiselve,
This town is ful of ladys al aboute;
And, to my doom,° fairer than swiche twelve°   *in my judgment / twelve such*
As evere she was, shal I fynde in som route—°   *crowd*
Yee, on or two, withouten any doute.
405 Forthi° be glad, myn owen deere brother!   *Therefore*
If she be lost, we shal recovere an other.

"What! God forbede alwey that ech plesaunce°   *every delight*
In o° thyng were and in non other wight!°   *one / person*
If oon kan synge, an other kan wel daunce;
410 If this be goodly, she is glad and light;
And this is fair, and that kan good aright.°   *had good sense indeed*
Ech for his vertu holden is for deere,
Both heroner and faucoun for ryvere.[4]

"And ek, as writ Zanzis,[5] that was ful wys,
415 'The newe love out chaceth ofte the olde';
And upon newe cas lith newe avys.[6]

3. No person trusts ever to find in Fortune one's own possessions (i.e., special favor); her gifts are common to all. In her fickleness, Fortune is evenhanded.
4. Both the falcon for hunting herons and the falcon for hunting waterfowl.
5. *Zanzis* may be Chaucer's (or Pandarus's) invention; in the *Filostrato* the adage is merely what one often hears told. The actual source of the proverb is probably Ovid, *Remedia amoris* 462. Pandarus should not cite Ovid, who lived centuries after the Trojan War.
6. For a new situation new counsel is appropriate.

50

Troilo, hearing Pandaro, began to weep more strongly, afterwards saying, "I pray God that he send me death before I commit such a sin. Although there may be other ladies graceful and well-bred—and I confess it to you—none of them was ever like her to whom I am given, and I am entirely hers.

51

"From her beautiful eyes flew the sparks which inflamed me with the fire of love. Passing through me by the thousands, these gently led love with them inside my heart, where it selected them as it was pleased to, and here they first began the fire whose great heat has been the cause of all my worth.

52

"That I could never extinguish—even though I might wish to (which I do not)—so powerful is it. And if it were still greater, I should not grieve at it, if only Criseida might stay with us for whose departure, not for love, my enamored soul feels affliction within. There is not any other—may it displease no one—who can be in any way equal to her.

53

"How then could love or the consolations of anyone ever turn my desire to another lady? I have enough anguish to sustain in my heart but much more, even up to the extreme woes, would I receive in it before I would set my soul upon any other lady; may Love and God and this world prevent it.

Thenk ek, thi lif to saven artow holde.°   *bound*
Swich fir, by proces, shal of kynde colde,[7]
For syn it is but casuel° plesaunce,   *chance*
420   Som cas° shal putte it out of remembraunce;   *chance happenstance*

"For also seur as° day comth after nyght,   *as sure as*
The newe love, labour, or oother wo,
Or elles selde seynge of a wight,°   *seeing someone seldom*
Don° olde affecciouns alle over-go.°   *Causes / to pass away*
425   And, for thi part, thow shalt have oon of tho°   *one of those (causes)*
T'abregge with° thi bittre peynes smerte;°   *To abbreviate, lessen / sharp*
Absence of hire shal dryve hire out of herte."

Thise wordes seyde he for the nones° alle,   *for the nonce*
To help his frend, lest he for sorwe deyde;
430   For douteles, to don° his wo to falle,   *cause*
He roughte° nought what unthrift° that he seyde.   *heeded / nonsense*
But Troilus, that neigh° for sorwe deyde,   *nearly*
Took litel heede of al that evere he mente—°   *said*
Oon ere° it herde, at tother° out it wente—   *ear / the other*

435   But at the laste answerde, and seyde, "Frend,
This lechecraft,° or heeled thus° to be,   *medicine / healed in this way*
Were wel sittyng,° if that I were a fend—°   *suitable / fiend*
To traysen a wight° that trewe is unto me!   *To betray a person*
I pray God lat this conseil nevere ythe;°   *succeed*
440   But do me rather sterve anon-right° here,   *die forthwith*
Er I thus do as thow me woldest leere!°   *teach*

"She that I serve, iwis,° what so° thow seye,   *indeed / whatever*
To whom myn herte enhabit° is by right,   *devoted*
Shal han me holly° hires til that I deye.   *wholly*
445   For Pandarus, syn I have trouthe hire hight,°   *promised her fidelity*
I wol nat ben untrewe for no wight,
But as hire man I wol ay lyve and sterve,°   *die*
And nevere other creature serve.

"And ther thow seist° thow shalt as faire fynde   *where you say*
450   As she, lat be;° make no comparisoun   *leave off (such talk)*
To creature yformed° here by kynde!°   *created / nature*
O leve° Pandare, in conclusioun,   *dear*
I wol nat ben of thyn opynyoun
Touchyng al this. For which I the biseche,
455   So hold thi pees; thow sleest° me with thi speche!   *you slay*

"Thow biddest° me I shulde love another   *You entreat*
Al fresshly newe, and lat Criseyde go!
It lith nat in my power, leeve brother;
And though° I myght, I wolde nat do so.   *if*
460   But kanstow playen raket,° to and fro,   *racket ball*

---

7. Such fire, in the course of time, shall naturally grow cold.

54

"And death and the tomb alone will be able to take away this firm love of mine, whatever may follow to me from this; these shall lead my soul with my love down to Hell to the ultimate torment. There together they shall weep for Criseida, whose I shall ever be, wherever I may be, if love is not forgotten through death.

55

"Therefore, in God's name, stop saying, Pandaro, that any other lady may come into my heart where I hold Criseida with her proper behavior as a certain emblem of my pleasures, however displeasing her departure—of which there is talk among us, though we do not see her yet carried from here—may now be to my mind which struggles with its pain.

56

"But you speak in logic-chopping terms, as if one should say that it is less pain to lose than never to have had anything. This is clear folly, Pandaro—bear this in mind—because what ill fortune brings to one who has been happy surpasses every sorrow, and he departs from the truth who says otherwise.

57

"But tell me, if my love is of concern to you, since it seems to you so light a thing to change love, as you have been telling me just now, why have you not changed your course? Since your cruel love bears so much harshness for you, why have you not followed another lady who might have made your life peaceful?

58

"If you who are used to living with a vexatious love have not been able to change it to another, how can I, who have lived with it, happy and joyful, thus drive it away as you say? Why do I now see grievous chance suddenly menace me? I am captured in another way which your mind does not distinguish.

59

"Believe me, Pandaro, believe me that love, when it fixes itself through the highest pleasure in anyone's mind, can never be driven out from there though it can well fall away from there in the process of time, if sorrow, or death, or poverty, or not seeing the beloved object cause it to do so, as has happened already to many people.

Nettle in, dok out,[8] now this, now that, Pandare?
Now foule falle hire for thi wo that care![9]

"Thow farest ek by° me, thow Pandarus,   *behave also with regard to*
As he that, whan a wight is wo bygon,°   *woebegone*
465 He cometh to hym a paas° and seith right thus: *apace, speedily*
'Thynk nat on smert,° and thow shalt fele non.'   *pain*
Thow moost me first transmewen in° a ston,   *transmute into*
And reve me° my passiones alle,   *take from me*
Er thow so lightly do° my wo to falle.   *may so easily cause*

470 "The deth may wel out of my brest departe°   *separate, remove*
The lif, so longe may this sorwe myne,°   *undermine, burrow*
But fro my soule shal Criseydes darte
Out° nevere mo; but down with Proserpyne,[1]   *Go out*
Whan I am ded, I wol go wone in pyne,°   *dwell in torment*
475 And ther I wol eternaly compleyne
My wo, and how that twynned° be we tweyne.°   *separated / two*

"Thow hast here made an argument for fyn,°   *finally or to this end*
How that it sholde a lasse° peyne be   *lesser*
Criseyde to forgon, for she was myn
480 And lyved in ese and in felicite,
Whi gabbestow,° that seydest unto me   *do you chatter idly*
That 'hym is wors that is fro wele ythrowe,°   *thrown from well-being*
Than° he hadde erst° noon of that wele yknowe'?   *Than if / formerly*

"But tel me now, syn that the thynketh so light°   *it seems to you so easy*
485 To changen so in love ay to and fro,
Whi hastow nat don bisily thi myght
To chaungen hire that doth the° al thi wo?   *causes you*
Why nyltow lete hire fro thyn herte go?
Whi nyltow love an other lady swete,°   *sweet*
490 That may thyn herte setten in quiete?°   *at rest*

"If thou hast had in love ay yet myschaunce°   *always bad luck so far*
And kanst it not out of thyn herte dryve,
I, that levede yn lust° and in plesaunce   *lived in delight*
With here, as muche as creature on lyve,°   *alive*
495 How sholde I that foryete,° and that so blyve?°   *forget / quickly*
O, where hastow ben hid so longe in muwe,°   *cooped up so long a time*
That kanst so wel and formely° arguwe?   *formally, logically*

"Nay, God wot, nought worth° is al thi red,°   *of no value / counsel*
For which, for what that evere may byfalle,°   *Whence whatever may happen*
500 Withouten wordes mo, I wol be ded.
O deth, that endere art of° sorwes alle,   *you who bring to an end*
Com now, syn I so ofte after the calle;

---

8. The opening of a charm to remove a thorn by rubbing with a dock leaf: "Nettle in, dock out." That is, "Now this, now that."
9. Now may evil befall her who may care about your sorrow!
1. Proserpina, queen of the underworld.

60

"What shall I do then, unhappy unfortunate, if I lose Criseida in such a manner that I have lost her forever because Antenor is exchanged for her? Alas, how much better were death for me or never to have been born! Ah, what shall I do? My heart despairs; ah death, come to me who calls you; ah come, do not let me languish in my love.

61

"Death, you will be as sweet to me as life is to him who leads a joyous one. Already your horrid aspect is not forbidding to me. Come then and end my pain. Ah, do not linger, for this fire has already so set aflame each of my veins that your blow will be a cool refreshment to me. Ah, come now, for my heart really desires you.

62

"Slay me, for God's sake; do not consent that I live so long in this world that I see my heart depart from my body. Ah do it, death, I pray you for it in the name of God. Much more will that grieve me than dying. Satisfy my desire in this respect. You kill so many against their will that you can well do me this pleasure."

63

Thus weeping Troilo grieved, and Pandaro wept likewise, and nevertheless he often comforted him most compassionately as much as he could; but such comfort was of no use, rather the sorrowful lament and the anguish continually increased because he was so unhappy about that matter.

64

Pandaro said to him, "Dear friend, if my arguments are not pleasing to you, and her coming departure to you is as disagreeable as it seems, why do you not take means to protect your life in what way you can and ravish her away? Paris went into Greece and took Helen away from there, the flower of all other ladies.

65

"And will you not dare in your own Troy to ravish a lady who pleases you? You will do this, if you will trust me. Drive away sorrow, drive it away, drive out your anguish and your sorrowful woes; dry the sad tears from your face, and show now your great soul, working so that Criseida may be ours."

For sely° is that deth, soth for to seyne,   *happy*
That, ofte ycleped,° cometh and endeth peyne.   *invoked*

505 "Wel wot I, whil my lyf was in quyete,
Er thow me slowe,° I wolde have yeven hire;°   *slew / paid ransom (to death)*
But now thi comynge is to me so swete
That in this world I nothing so desire.
O deth, syn with this sorwe I am a-fyre,°   *on fire*
510 Thou other do° me anoon yn teris drenche,°   *May you either cause / drown*
Or with thi colde strok myn hete° quenche.   *heat*

[handwritten note:] Troilus is finally speaking some sense to Pandarus

"Syn that thou sleest so fele° in sondry wyse   *slay so many*
Ayens° hire wil, unpreyed,° day and nyght,   *Against / unbesought*
Do me at my requeste this service:
515 Delyvere° now the world—so dostow right—   *Set free*
Of me, that am the wofulleste wyght
That evere was; for tyme is° that I sterve,°   *it's time / die*
Syn in this world of right nought° may I serve."   *rightfully nothing*

This Troylus in teris gan distille,
520 As licour out of a lambyc ful faste;²
And Pandarus gan holde his tunge stille,
And to the ground his eyen doun he caste.
But natheles,° thus thought he at the laste: *nevertheless*
"What! Parde,° rather than my felawe deye,   *By God*
525 Yet shal I somwhat more unto hym seye."

And seyde, "Frend, syn thow hast swych distresse,
And syn the list° myn argumentz to blame,   *it pleases you*
Why nylt thiselven helpen don redresse³
And with thy manhod letten° al this grame?°   *prevent / grief*
530 Go ravysshe° here! Ne kanstow nat, for shame?   *abduct, seize*
And other° lat here out of towne fare,°   *either / go*
Or hold here stille, and leve thi nyce fare.⁴

"Artow in Troie, and hast non hardyment°   *daring*
To take a womman which that loveth the
535 And wolde hireselven ben of thyn assent?°   *in agreement with you*
Now is nat this a nyce° vanitee?   *foolish*
Ris up anon, and lat this wepyng be,

2. This Troilus began quickly to flow in tears like a liquid from an alembic, i.e., a retort used in distilling.
3. Why don't you yourself wish to help to set things right (bring redress).
4. Or hold her motionless (or, continually), and leave off your foolish to-do.

66

Troilo then replied to Pandaro, "Friend, I see well that you devote every ingenuity to taking away my anguished sufferings. Although I weep and abandon myself completely to a sorrow which surpasses every power of mine, so severe has been its great blow, I have thought of what you say and have also devised many other things.

67

"Yet I have not been able in my fervent love to turn my back on the decision the Trojans are bound to. Rather on thinking it over, I have seen myself that the times do not permit such a renunciation. If each of our men were returned right here, and Antenor also, I would not care about breaking faith; rather I would do it, whatever might happen.

68

"Also I fear to tarnish her honor and her reputation with violent abduction, and I do not know for sure that she would be content with it, though indeed I know that she loves me much. Therefore my heart has not dared to make a decision, because, on the one hand, it desires this and, on the other, it fears to displease, for I would not wish to keep her if it were displeasing to her.

69

"I also thought of asking my father for her so that by his grace he might give her to me. But I think that this would be to accuse her and to make known the things already done. I do not hope even then that he would necessarily give her, either because he would not break promised matters or because he would say she was not equal to me, to whom he wishes to give a lady of royal blood.

70

"And so I remain weeping in amorous perplexity, a wretched man, and I don't know what to do since I feel lacking in me the valor of love, if indeed it remains strong, and on each side hope flees and the causes of torment increase. I wish I had been dead the day that such desire was first kindled in me."

And kith° thow art a man; for in this houre   *make known*
I wol ben ded, or she shal bleven oure."°   *remain ours*

540 To this answerde hym Troilus ful softe,
And seyde, "Parde, leve brother deere,
Al this have I myself yet thought ful ofte,
And more thyng than thow devysest° here.   *propose*
But whi this thyng is laft,° thow shalt wel here;   *ignored*
545 And whan thow me hast yeve an audience,
Therafter maystow telle al thi sentence.°   *thoughts*

"First, syn thow woost° this town hath al this werre   *you know*
For ravysshyng of wommen so by myght,[5]
It sholde nought be suffred me to erre,°   *permitted for me to do wrong*
550 As it stant° now, ne don so gret unright.°   *stands / so great a wrong*
I sholde han also blame of every wight,
My fadres graunt if that I so withstoode,[6]   *of = ove*
Syn she is chaunged° for the townes goode.   *exchanged*

"I have ek thought, so it were hire assent,°   *if she agreed*
555 To axe hire at° my fader, of his grace;   *To ask for her from*
Than thynke I this were hire accusement,[7]
Syn wel I woot I may hire nought purchace;°   *obtain*
For syn my fader, in so heigh a place
As parlement hath hire eschaunge enseled,°   *ratified*
560 He nyl for me his lettre be repeled.[8]

"Yet drede I moost hire herte to perturbe
With violence, if I do swich a game;   *excuses, excuses*
For if I wolde it openly desturbe,°   *impede*
It mooste be disclaundre° to hire name.   *slander*
565 And me were levere° ded than hire diffame—°   *I'd rather be / defame*
As nolde God but if I sholde have
Hire honour levere than my lif to save![9]

"Thus am I lost, for aught° that I kan see.   *anything*
For certeyn is, syn that I am hire knyght,
570 I moste° hire honour levere° han than me   *must / dearer*
In every cas,° as lovere ought of right.   *situation, event*
Thus am I with desir and reson twight:°   *torn*
Desir for to destourben hire me redeth,°   *advises*
And reson nyl nat; so myn herte dredeth."

575 Thus wepyng that° he koude nevere cesse,°   *so that / cease*
He seyde, "Allas, how shal I, wrecche, fare?
For wel fele I alwey my love encresse,
And hope is lasse and lasse alway, Pandare.

5. For the abduction of women thus by force. Troilus refers to Paris's abduction of Helen, the cause of the Trojan War. See lines 608–609 below.
6. Blame from everyone if I thus opposed my father's decree.
7. This would be an accusation against her.
8. He will not wish for his decree to be repealed for my sake.
9. God forbid but that I should hold her honor dearer than saving my life!

71

Pandaro then said, "You will do as you please, but if I were burning as greatly as you show yourself to be, however heavy the responsibility might be, had I the power that you have, unless force prevented me, I would do all in my power to carry her off, no matter whom it might displease.

72

"When the enamored mind burns from necessity, Love does not look at subtleties, as it seems that you do. If he harms you as fiercely as you say, follow his will and in manly fashion oppose this cruel torment and choose rather to be blamed somewhat than to die with suffering in sad lament.

73

"You do not have to ravish a lady who is far from your desire, but she is one who will be content with what you do, and if from this there should follow too much evil or blame of you, you have the way of ending it immediately, that is to say, to bring her back again. Fortune aids whoever is bold and rejects the timid.

74

"And even if this thing should displease her, in a short time you will have peace again—although I do not believe that she would be much vexed at it as she is so much pleased by the love you bear her. As for her reputation, that it should be lost is, to tell the truth, less grievous and less displeasing. Let her do without it, as Helen does, provided that she satisfies your full desire.

75

"Therefore take courage, be valorous; love cares not for promise or faith. Show yourself a little spirited now, have mercy upon yourself. I shall be with you in every perilous case as much as my power allows me. Decide indeed to act; then the gods will have to aid us."

Encressen ek° the causes of my care.　　　　　　　　　*Increase also*
580　So weilaway, whi nyl myn herte breste?
For, as in° love, ther is but litel reste."　　　　　　　*with regard to*

Pandare answerde, "Frend, thow maist, for me,
Don as the list; but hadde ich it so hoote,
And thyn estat,[1] she sholde go with me,
585　Though al this town cride on this thyng by note.°　　*in unison*
I nolde sette at al that noys a grote![2]
For whan men han wel cryd, than wol they rowne;°　*quiet down to a whisper*
Ek wonder last° but nyne nyght° nevere in towne.　　*a wonder lasts / nights*

"Devyne° not in resoun ay so depe　　　　　　　　　　*Speculate*
590　Ne preciously,° but help thiself anon.　　　　　　　*scrupulously*
Bet is that othere than thiselven wepe,
And namely,° syn ye two ben al on,°　　　　　　　　*especially / one*
Ris up, for by myn hed, she shal not goon!
And rather be in blame a lite° ifounde　　　　　　　　*little*
595　Than sterve° here as a gnat, withouten wounde.　　　*die*

"It is no rape, in my dom,° ne no vice,　　　　　　　*judgment*
Hire to witholden that ye love moost;
Peraunter° she myghte holde the for nyce°　　　　　　*Perhaps / think you foolish*
To late hire go thus unto the Grekis oost.°　　　　　*host, besieging force*
600　Thenk ek Fortune, as wel thiselven woost,°　　　　　*know*
Helpeth hardy° man unto his enprise,°　　　　　　　　*a brave / undertaking*
And weyveth° wrecches for hire cowardise.　　　　　　*neglects*

"And though thy lady wolde a lite hire greve,
Thow shalt thiself thi pees° hereafter make;　　　　　*peace*
605　But as for me, certeyn, I kan nat leve°　　　　　　　*believe*
That she wolde it as now for yvel take.°　　　　　　　*take it amiss*
Whi sholde thanne of ferd° thyn herte quake?　　　　*for fear*
Thenk ek how Paris hath, that is thi brother,
A love; and whi shaltow nat have another?

610　"And Troilus, o thyng I dar the swere:
That if Criseyde, which that is thi lief,°　　　　　　　*beloved*
Now loveth the as wel as thow dost here,°　　　　　　*her*
God help me so, she nyl nat take a-grief,°　　　　　　*amiss*
Theigh thow do boote° anon in this meschief;°　*provide a remedy / bad business*
615　And if she wilneth fro the° for to passe,　　　　　　*wishes from you*
Thanne is she fals; so love hire wel the lasse.

"Forthi° tak herte, and thynk right as a knyght:　　　*Therefore*
Thorough love is broken al day° every lawe.　　　　　*continually*
Kith° now somwhat thi corage and thi myght;　　　　*Make known*
620　Have mercy on thiself for any awe.°　　　　　　　　*despite any fear*
Lat nat this wrecched wo thyn herte gnawe,

---

1. If I had it so hot, and had your estate, i.e., your princely position and power.
2. I wouldn't value all that noise at a groat's worth. A groat is a coin worth four pence.

76

Troilo felt well the force of Pandaro's remarks and replied, "I am content, but if my flame were a thousand times more burning and my torment greater than it is, I would not, to satisfy myself, do this courteous lady the least displeasure; I would wish to die first; therefore I wish to hear it from her."

77

"Then let us rise up from here and remain no longer. Wash your face, and let us return to court and under a smile let us conceal our sorrow. The people have yet perceived nothing but, by staying here, we make anyone who notices it marvel. Now conduct yourself so that you strongly conceal things and I will contrive a way for you to speak with Criseida this evening."

The news of her departure comes to Criseida, and she is visited by many ladies, not without great vexation to her.

78

Fleetest fame, who reports the false and the true equally, had flown with swiftest wings through all Troy and with a well-directed word had related

But manly sette the world on six and sevene;[3]
And if thow deye a martyr, go to hevene!

625 "I wol myself ben with the at this dede,
Theigh° ich and al my kyn upon a stownde° Though / in a short time
Shulle° in a strete as dogges liggen° dede, Must / lie
Thorugh-girt° with many a wid and blody wownde,° Pierced through
In every cas I wol a frend be founde.
And if the list here sterven° as a wrecche, it please you to die
630 Adieu, the devel spede hym that it recche!"[4]

This Troilus gan with tho wordes quyken,° revive
And seyde, "Frend, graunt mercy,° ich assente. much thanks
But certeynly thow maist nat so me priken,° goad
Ne peyne non ne may me so tormente,
635 That, for no cas,° it is nat myn entente, in any event
At shorte wordes,° though I deyen sholde, To speak briefly
To ravysshe° hire, but if° hireself it wolde." abduct, carry off / unless

"Whi, so mene I," quod Pandare, "al this day.
But telle me thanne, hastow hire wil assayed,° examined
640 That sorwest° thus?" And he answerde hym, "Nay." You who grieve
"Wherof artow,"° quod Pandare, "thanne amayed—° Why are you / dismayed
That nost nat° that she wol ben yvele You who don't know
appayed—° displeased
To ravysshe hire, syn thow hast nought ben there,
But if° that Jove told it in thyn ere?° Unless / ear

645 "Forthi ris up, as nought ne were, anon,[5]
And wassh thi face, and to the kyng thow wende,° may you go
Or he may wondren whider° thow art goon. whither
Thow most with wisdom° hym and othere blende,° prudence / blind, deceive
Or, upon cas,° he may after the sende perchance
650 Er thow be war;° and shortly, brother deere, warned
Be glad, and lat me werke in this matere,

"For I shal shape° it so, that sikerly° arrange / surely
Thow shalt this nyght som tyme, in som manere,
Come speken with thi lady pryvely,° secretly
655 And by hire wordes ek, and by hire cheere,° demeanor
Thow shalt ful sone aperceyve° and wel here° perceive / hear
Al hire entente, and in this cas the beste.° best (to be done)
And far° now wel, for in this point I reste." fare

The swifte Fame, which that false thynges
660 Egal° reporteth lik the thynges trewe, Equally
Was thoroughout Troie yfled with preste° wynges swift
Fro man to man, and made this tale° al newe, brought this report

---

3. But in manly fashion bet the world on a throw of the dice. The precise sense of *on six and sevene*, presumably from the dicing game of hazard, is unknown.
4. Goodbye—may the devil help (i.e., take) whoever may care about it!
5. Therefore get up, as if it were nothing, forthwith.

what and of what nature was the message which had been brought by the Greeks, and that Criseida had been given by the king to the Greeks in exchange for Antenor.

79

When Criseida, who already did not care for her father any more, heard that news, she said to herself, "Alas, my sad heart!" And it strongly grieved her as one who had turned her desire to Troilus, whom she loved more than any other. And for fear that what she heard told might be true, she dared not ask a question.

80

But as we see that it happens that one lady, if she is fond of another lady, goes to visit her when new events affect her, if she wishes her well, so many ladies came to pass the day with Criseida, all full of sympathetic joy, and they began to tell her about the event with its arrangements: how she was being exchanged and with what terms.

81

Said one, "Certainly it pleases me greatly that you will return to your father and are to be with him." Another said, "And it is so with me, but I am not pleased that she is leaving us." Another said, "She will be able to arrange peace for us and to do so with him [Calchas] who, you know, puts into effect, as we have heard, any course of action he wishes to."

82

This, and much other womanly talk, she heard without answering, almost as if she were not there, for she despised it. Nor could her beautiful face hide the arduous high-born thoughts she had of love which came to her when she heard the news. The body was there and the soul was elsewhere, seeking Troilo without knowing where.

83

And these ladies who believed they were giving her consolation through staying, by their excessive talk greatly displeased her as one who felt in her mind quite another passion than the one those who were there thought they saw color her face, and very often in a lady-like manner she dismissed them, such desire she had of being without them.

How Calkas° doughter, with hire brighte hewe,   *Calchas's*
At parlement, withouten wordes more,
665 Ygraunted was in chaunge of° Antenore.   *exchange for*

The whiche tale anon-right as° Criseyde   *as soon as*
Hadde herd, she, which that of hire fader roughte,° *who cared for her father*
As in this cas,° right nought, ne whan he deyde,   *In this matter*
Ful bisily to Jupiter bisoughte
670 Yeve hem meschaunce that this tretis broughte;[6]
But shortly, lest thise tales sothe° were,   *true*
She dorst at no wight asken it,° for fere.   *dared ask nobody about it*

As she that hadde hire herte and al hire mynde
On Troilus iset so wonder faste
675 That al this world ne myghte hire love unbynde,
Ne Troilus out of hire herte caste,
She wol ben his, while that hire lif may laste.
And thus she brenneth° both in love and drede,   *burns*
So that she nyste what was best to reede.°   *advise*

680 But as men seen in towne and al aboute
That wommen usen° frendes to visite,   *are accustomed*
So to Criseyde of wommen com a route,°   *crowd*
For pitous joie, and wenden hire delite;
And with hire tales, deere ynough a myte,[7]
685 Thise wommen, which that in the cite dwelle,
They sette hem down and seyde as I shall telle.

Quod first that oon, "I am glad, trewely,
Bycause of yow, that° shal youre fader see."   *who*
Another seyde, "Ywis,° so nam nat° I,   *Indeed / am not*
690 For al to litel hath she with us be."
Quod tho the thridde, "I hope, ywis, that she
Shal bryngen us the pees° on every syde,   *peace*
That, whan she goth, almyghty God hire gide!"°   *may God guide her*

Tho wordes and tho wommanysshe thynges,
695 She herde hem right as though she thennes° were;   *thence, gone away*
For God it woot, hire herte on othir thyng is.
Although the body sat among hem there,
Hire advertence° is alwey elleswhere,   *attention*
For Troilus ful faste° hire soule soughte;   *very eagerly*
700 Withouten word, on hym alwey she thoughte.

Thise wommen, that thus wenden° hire to plese,   *supposed*
Aboute naught° gonne alle hire tales spende.° *nothing / spend their chatter*
Swich vanyte ne kan don hire non ese,

6. To give those who arranged this treaty misfortune.
7. For compassionate well-wishing, and meant to cheer her up. And with their talk, expensive enough
   at a mite (a small coin)—i.e., worth little.

84

Nor could she restrain every sigh, and sometimes some little tear falling gave sign of the torment by which her soul was constrained. But those stupid ladies who made a circle around her believed that the young woman did this from sorrow because she had to leave those who were her usual companions.

85

And each one wished to comfort her only for things that were not grievous to her. Many words they spoke to console her for the leave which she had to take of them, but they were only scratching her heels when her head itched, since she took no thought of them but only of Troilo, whom she was leaving.

When the ladies have gone, Criseida weeps and sorrows for the coming separation from Troilo.

86

But after much chirping in vain, such as most women make, they took their leave and went away, and she, gradually overcome and oppressed by bitter sorrow, entered into her room weeping softly, and without seeking remedy for her great evil with any counsel, she made such weeping that never was the like made.

87

The grieving woman had thrown herself prone upon her bed, weeping so strongly that it could not be told. And often she beat her white breast, calling on death to slay her, since she was obliged by cruel fate to leave her delight, and plucking her blonde hair, she tore it, and a thousand times she continuously called on death.

As she that al this mene while brende°   *burned*
705 Of other passioun than that they wende,
So that she felte almost hire herte dye
For wo and wery° of that compaignie. *weariness or (she felt) weary*

For which no lenger myghte she restreyne
Hir teeris, so they gonnen up to welle,
710 That yaven° signes of the bittre peyne   *gave*
In which hir spirit was, and moste dwelle,° *must remain*
Remembryng hir, fro heven into which° helle *what sort of*
She fallen was, syn she forgoth° the syghte *since she does without*
Of Troilus, and sorwfully she sighte.°   *sighed*

715 And thilke° fooles sittynge hire aboute   *those same*
Wenden° that she wepte and siked° sore *Supposed / sighed*
Bycause that she sholde° out of that route° *must / company*
Departe, and nevere pleye with hem more.
And they that hadde yknowen hire of yore° *for some time*
720 Seigh° hire so wepe and thoughte it kyndenesse,° *Saw / natural affection*
And ech of hem wepte ek for hire destresse.

And bisyly they gonnen hire comforten
Of thyng, God woot, on which she litel thoughte;
And with hire tales wenden hire disporten,° *thought to entertain her*
725 And to be glad they often hire bysoughte;
But swich an ese° therwith they hire wroughte,° *comfort / brought her*
Right as a man is esed for to feele
For ache of hed to clawen° hym on his heele! *scratch*

But after al this nyce vanyte°   *silly chatter*
730 They toke hire leve,° and hom they wenten alle. *their leave*
Criseyde, ful of sorwful piete,°   *piteousness*
Into hire chambre up went out of the halle,
And on hire bed she gan for ded to falle,
In purpos° nevere thennes° for to rise; *Intending / thence*
735 And thus she wroughte,° as I shal yow devyse. *behaved*

Hire ownded° heer, that sonnyssh° was of hewe, *wavy / sunlike*
She rente,° and ek hire fyngeres longe and smale° *tore / slender*
She wrong° ful ofte, and bad° God on hire rewe,° *wrung / asked / to have pity*
And with the deth to doon boote on hire bale.[8]
740 Hire hewe, whilom° bright, that tho° was pale, *formerly / then*
Bar° witnesse of hire wo and hire constreynte;° *Bore / distress*
And thus she spak, sobbyng in hire compleynte:

---

8. And with death to bring remedy for her ruin.

88

She said: "Alas, unfortunate woman, wretched, sorrowing me, where am I going? O poor me, who was born in an evil moment, where do I leave you, my sweet love? Ah, if only I had been drowned at birth or had never seen you, my sweet desire, since wicked fate now steals both me from you and you from me.

89

"What shall I do, my sorrowful life, when I cannot see you any more? What shall I do when I am parted from you, Troilo? Certainly I do not believe I shall ever eat or drink, and if by itself the bewildered soul does not leave the body, to the utmost of my power I shall drive it out with starvation, because I see that I shall henceforth always go from bad to worse.

90

"Now I shall in truth be a widow, since I am obliged to part from you, heart of my body, and the black attire will be a true testimony of my sufferings. O me, alas, what a cruel thought is that in which the parting holds me! O me, how shall I be able to endure seeing myself parted from you, Troilo?

"Allas," quod she, "out of this regioun
I, woful wrecche and infortuned° wight,   *ill-fortuned*
745 And born in corsed constellacioun,⁹
Moot° goon and thus departen fro my knyght!   *Must*
Wo worth,° allas, that ilke° dayes light   *Woe betide / same*
On which I saugh hym first with eyen tweyne,°   *my two eyes*
That causeth me, and ich hym, al this peyne!"

750 Therwith the teris from hire eyen two
Down fille, as shour° in Aperil ful swithe;°   *a shower / swiftly*
Hire white brest she bet,° and for the wo   *beat*
After the deth she cryed a thousand sithe,°   *times*
Syn he that wont hire wo was for to lithe
755 She moot forgon;¹ for which disaventure
She held hireself a forlost° creature.   *utterly lost*

She seyde, "How shal he don, and ich also?
How sholde I lyve if that I from hym twynne?°   *separate*
O deere herte eke, that I love so,
760 Who shal that sorwe slen° that ye ben inne?   *slay*
O Calkas, fader, thyn be al this synne!
O moder myn, that cleped° were Argyve,   *named*
Wo worth° that day that thow me bere on lyve!°   *May woe befall / bore to life*

"To what fyn° sholde I lyve and sorwen thus?   *end, purpose*
765 How sholde a fissh withouten water dure?°   *endure*
What is Criseyde worth, from Troilus?
How sholde a plaunte or lyves° creature   *living*
Lyve withouten his kynde noriture?°   *natural nourishment*
For which ful ofte a by-word° here I seye,   *proverb*
770 That 'rooteles moot grene° soone deye.'   *must a green (plant)*

"I shal doon thus—syn neither swerd ne darte°   *spear*
Dar I noon handle, for the crueltee—
That ilke° day that I from yow departe,   *same*
If sorwe of that nyl nat my bane° be: *destruction*
775 Thanne shal no mete or drynke come in me
Til I my soule out of my breste unshethe,°   *unsheathe*
And thus myselven wol I don to dethe.

"And, Troilus, my clothes everychon
Shul blake ben in tokenyng,° herte swete,   *as a sign*
780 That I am as out of this world agon,
That wont was° yow to setten in quiete;   *Who was accustomed*
And of myn ordre,° ay til deth me mete,°   *(religious) order / meet*

---

9. And (I who was) born in an unfavorable array of the planets—i.e., am star-crossed.
1. Since she had to do without him who was accustomed to alleviate her woe.

91

"How shall I be able to exist without a soul? It will remain here for a certainty with our love and with you to lament the sorrowful parting which we are obliged to make as a reward for such good love. O me, my Troilo, will you now endure seeing me go from you? Why do you not strive to retain me by love or by force?

92

"I shall go from here, and I do not know if I shall ever see you again, my sweet love, but you who so much love me, what will you do? Ah, can you sustain such sorrow? I shall certainly not bear it, since excessive woes will break my heart. Ah, if only it were soon, because afterwards I shall be beyond this heavy sorrow.

93

"Oh, my father, iniquitous and disloyal to your fatherland, may that moment be accursed when such evil came into your breast that you wished to join the Greeks and to leave the Trojans! Would God you were dead in the infernal vale, you wicked old man, who in the last years of your life have practiced such deception.

94

"Ah me, alas, wretched and sorrowful, for I must bear the penance of the sin, I who did not deserve such a painful life for my failings. O truth of heaven, light of pity, how do you permit such a judgment that one person sins and the other weeps as I do, who did not sin and am undone with grief?"

Pandaro finds Criseida, who is weeping, speaks somewhat with her and arranges for the coming of Troilo.

95

Who could ever tell fully what Criseida said in her weeping? Certainly not I, since speech falls short of fact, so cruel and fierce was her pain. But while such laments were being made, Pandaro, to whom no door was ever closed, came and entered the room where she was making her cruel lament.

The observance evere, in youre absence,
Shal sorwe ben, compleynt, and abstinence.[2]

785 "Myn herte and ek the woful goost therinne
Byquethe I with youre spirit to compleyne
Eternaly, for they shal nevere twynne;°   *separate*
For though in erthe ytwynned be we tweyne,°   *we two are separated*
Yet in the feld° of pite, out of peyne,   *field*
790 That highte° Elisos, shal we ben yfeere,°   *is named / together*
As Orpheus and Erudice, his fere.[3]

"Thus, herte myn, for Antenor, allas,
I soone shal be chaunged,° as I wene.°   *exchanged / suppose*
But how shul ye don in this sorwful cas?°   *situation*
795 How shal youre tendre herte this sustene?°   *sustain, endure*
But, herte myn, foryete° this sorwe and tene,°   *forget / trouble*
And me also; for sothly for to seye,
So ye wel fare, I recche naught to deye."[4]

How myghte it evere yred° ben or ysonge,   *read*
800 The pleynte that she made in hire destresse?
I not;° but, as for me, my litel tonge,   *I don't know*
If I discryven° wolde hire hevynesse,   *describe*
It sholde make hire sorwe seme lesse
Than that° it was, and childisshly deface   *what*
805 Hire heigh compleynte, and therfore ich it pace.°   *pass over*

Pandare, which that sent from Troilus
Was to Criseyde—as ye han herd devyse°   *heard it described*
That for the beste it was acorded° thus,   *agreed*
And he ful glad to doon hym that servyse—
810 Unto Criseyde, in a ful secree° wise,   *secret*

2. Criseyde intends to withdraw from the world as if a nun, wearing black and maintaining the *observance*, the rituals and rules, of a religious order.
3. The "field of pity," Elysium, is the counterpart of heaven in Hades, where Orpheus and his mate (*fere*), Eurydice, dwell.
4. As long as you fare well, I don't care about dying.

96

He saw her on her bed wrapped in sobs, tears, and sighs, and he saw all her breast and her face bathed in tears and with her eyes welling with desire to weep, and she herself disheveled, giving a true indication of her bitter torments. When she saw him, she hid her face in her arms for shame.

97

"Cruel was that moment," Pandaro began to say, "in which I arose, for wherever I go today, it seems to me I hear everywhere sorrow, torments, weeping, anguish, and loud woes, sighs, pain, and bitter lamentation. O Jove, what are you about to do? I believe that you pour tears from Heaven because our deeds are so repugnant to you.

98

"And you, my disconsolate sister, what do you propose to do? Do you think you will fight against the fates? Why disfigure your beautiful self with such cruel and unmeasured weeping? Rise up and turn and speak; lift up your face and dry your inconsolable eyes a bit, and hear what I, who am sent by your sweet friend, say to you."

Ther as she lay in torment and in rage,°   *passionate grieving*
Com hire to telle al hoolly° his message,   *wholly*

And fond° that she hireselven gan to trete°   *found / behaved*
Ful pitously, for with hire salte teris
815   Hire brest, hire face, ybathed was ful wete;
The myghty tresses of hire sonnysshe° heeris   *sunlike*
Unbroiden° hangen al aboute hire eeris,°   *unbraided / ears*
Which yaf hym verray signal of martire°   *sign of martyrdom*
Of deth, which that hire herte gan desire.

820   Whan she hym saugh, she gan for shame anon
Hire tery face atwixe° hire armes hide;   *between*
For which this Pandare is so wo-bygon
That in the hous he myghte unnethe abyde,°   *scarcely stand to stay*
As he that pite felt on every syde;
825   For if Criseyde hadde erst° compleyned soore,   *formerly*
Tho gan she pleyne a thousand tymes more.

And in hire aspre° pleynte thus she seyde: *bitter*
"Pandare first of joies mo than two
Was cause causyng° unto me, Criseyde,   *the primary cause (in logic)*
830   That now transmewed ben in° cruel wo.   *am transmuted into*
Wher⁵ shal I seye to yow welcom or no,
That alderfirst° me broughte unto servyse   *Who first of all*
Of love—allas!—that endeth in swich wise?°   *such a manner*

"Endeth than° love in wo? Ye, or men lieth,°   *then / people lie*
835   And alle worldly blisse, as thynketh me.°   *it seems to me*
The ende of blisse ay sorwe it occupieth.
And whoso troweth° nat that it so be,   *believes*
Lat° hym upon me, woful wrecche, ysee,°   *Let / look*
That myself hate and ay my burthe acorse,°   *continually curse my birth*
840   Felyng alwey fro wikke° I go to worse.   *bad*

"Whoso me seeth, he seeth sorwe al atonys—°   *at once, together with it*
Peyne, torment, pleynte, wo, distresse!
Out of my woful body harm ther noon is,⁶
As angwissh, langour,° cruel bitternesse,   *suffering*
845   Anoy,° smert,° drede, fury, and ek siknesse.   *Vexation / pain*
I trowe,° ywys, from hevene teeris reyne°   *believe / rain down*
For pite of myn aspre° and cruel peyne."   *bitter*

"And thow, my suster, ful of discomfort,"
Quod Pandarus, "what thynkestow° to do?   *do you intend*
850   Whi ne hastow to thyselven som resport?°   *regard*
Whi wiltow thus thiself, allas, fordo?°   *destroy*
Leef al this werk,° and tak now heede to   *business, pain*
That° I shal seyn; and herkne° of good entente   *What / listen*
This which by me thi Troilus the sente."

5. *Wher*, whether, introducing a pair of alternatives and not to be translated.
6. There is no hurt outside of my woeful body—i.e., all pains reside in me.

99

Then Criseida turned, making such weeping as could not be told, and gazed at Pandaro saying, "Oh wretched me, what does my soul wish, whom I must abandon in tears, not knowing if it will ever be that I shall see him again? Does he want sighs, or tears, or what does he ask? I have many of them if he sends for these."

100

She had the look of one who is carried to the grave, and her face, made in Paradise, was seen to be transfigured overall; its beauty and its pleasing smile had abandoned it in flight and around her eyes a purple circle gave a true sign of her suffering.

101

When Pandaro, who had wept all day long with Troilo, saw that, he could not withhold his sorrowing tears, but likewise began to weep sorrowfully with her, letting go what he wished to say; but when they had done this together for a time, Pandaro first moderated his weeping.

102

And he said, "Lady, I believe you have heard—but I am not certain of it—how you are asked for by your father, and already the decision to surrender you has been made by the king, so that you must go from here during this week, if I have heard the truth. And it could not be fully told how grievous this thing is to Troilo, who desires wholly to die from grief for it.

103

"And he and I have wept so much today that it is a marvel where the weeping has come from. Now at last by my counsel he has somewhat restrained himself from weeping and it seems that he has a desire to be with you, and so as it pleased him, I have come to tell you of it before you separate in order that you may together vent your sorrow somewhat."

855 Tornede hire tho° Criseyde, a wo makynge   *Then turned*
   So gret that it a deth was for to see.
   "Allas," quod she, "what wordes may ye brynge?
   What wol my deere herte seyn to me,
   Which that° I drede nevere mo to see?   *Whom*
860 Wol he han pleynte or teris er I wende?°   *before I go away*
   I have ynough, if he therafter sende!"

   She was right swich to seen in hire visage
   As is that wight that men on beere° bynde;   *funeral bier*
   Hire face, lik of Paradys the ymage,
865 Was al ychaunged in another kynde.
   The pleye, the laughter, men was wont° to fynde   *people were accustomed*
   On° hire, and ek hire joies everichone,   *In*
   Ben fled; and thus lith° now Criseyde allone.   *lies*

   Aboute hire eyen two a purpre° ryng   *purple*
870 Bytrent,° in sothfast tokenyng° of hire peyne,   *Encircles / a true sign*
   That to biholde it was a dedly thyng;
   For which Pandare myghte nat restreyne
   The teeris from his eighen° for to reyne;°   *eyes / rain down*
   But natheles,° as he best myghte, he seyde   *nevertheless*
875 From Troilus thise wordes to Criseyde:

   "Lo, nece, I trowe° ye han herd al how   *suppose*
   The kyng with othere lordes, for the beste,
   Hath mad eschaunge of Antenor and yow,
   That cause is of this sorwe and this unreste.
880 But how this cas dooth Troilus moleste,°   *causes harm to Troilus*
   That may non erthly mannes tonge seye—
   As he that shortly shapith hym° to deye.   *prepares*

   "For which we han so sorwed, he and I,
   That into litel° bothe it hadde us slawe;°   *nearly (?) too soon (?) / slain*
885 But thorugh my conseyl this day finaly
   He somwhat is fro wepynge now withdrawe,
   And semeth me° that he desireth fawe°   *it seems to me / eagerly*
   With yow to ben al nyght, for to devyse
   Remedie in this, if ther were any wyse.°   *way (to do it)*

890 "This, short and pleyn, th'effect° of my message,   *purport*
   As ferforth as° my wit kan comprehende,   *As far as*
   For ye that ben of torment in swich rage°   *passionate grieving*
   May to no long prologe as now entende.°   *attend, listen*
   And hereupon ye may answere hym sende;
895 And for the love of God, my nece deere,
   So lef° this wo er Troilus be here!"   *leave off*

104

"Great is my sorrow," said Criseida, "as of one who loves him more than herself, but his sorrow is much greater to me when I hear that he longs for death because of me. Now my heart will break, if ever a heart should break because of fierce grief; now hostile Fortune satisfies its hunger with my losses; now I know its hidden deceits.

105

"Grievous to me is the departure, God knows it, but it is more grievous to me to see Troilo afflicted, and so very insupportable that without some respite I shall die of it. And I wish to die without hope of grace since I see my Troilo so wounded. Tell him to come when he wishes; this will be to me the greatest comfort in my anguish."

106

And this said, she fell back prone; then with her face upon her arms she began again to weep. To her Pandaro said, "Alas, wretched woman, what will you do now? Will you not take some little comfort, thinking that the hour is already so near when he whom you love so much will take you in his arms? Rise up, compose yourself that he may not find you so disarranged.

107

"If he knew that you were acting this way, he would kill himself, and nobody could restrain him from it; and if I believed that you would remain like this, believe me, he would not set foot here if I could prevent it, for I know that his life would be endangered by it. Therefore rise up, refresh yourself so that you may lighten and not increase his woe."

"Gret is my wo," quod she, and sighte° soore   *sighed*
As she that feleth dedly sharp distresse;
"But yit to me his sorwe is muchel more,
900 That° love hym bet than he hymself, I gesse.   *I who*
Allas, for me hath he swich hevynesse?°   *grief*
Kan he for me so pitously° compleyne?   *piteously, pityingly*
Iwis, his sorwe doubleth al my peyne.

"Grevous to me, God woot, is for to twynne,"°   *separate*
905 Quod she, "but yet it harder is to me
To sen° that sorwe which that he is inne;   *see*
For wel I woot it wol my bane° be,   *death*
And deye I wol in certeyn," tho quod she;
"But bid° hym come, er deth, that thus me threteth,°   *ask / threatens*
910 Dryve out that goost° which in myn herte beteth."   *(vital) spirit*

Thise wordes seyd, she on hire armes two
Fil gruf,° and gan to wepen pitously.   *face down*
Quod Pandarus, "Allas, whi do ye so,
Syn wel ye woot the tyme is faste° by   *near*
915 That he shal come? Aris up hastily,
That he yow nat bywopen° thus ne fynde,   *bewept, disfigured with tears*
But° ye wole have hym wood° out of his mynde.   *Unless / mad*

"For wiste he° that ye ferde° in this manere,   *if he knew / were behaving*
He wolde hymselven sle;° and if I wende°   *slay / had thought*
920 To han this fare,° he sholde nat come here   *conduct*
For al the good° that Priam may dispende.°   *wealth / distribute*
For to what fyn° he wolde anon pretende,°   *goal / aim*
That knowe ich wel; and forthi yet° I seye: *therefore still*
So lef° this sorwe, or platly° he wol deye.   *leave off / plainly*

925 "And shapeth yow° his sorwe for t'abregge,°   *prepare / alleviate*
And nought encresse, leeve nece swete!°   *dear sweet niece*
Beth rather to hym cause of flat than egge,⁷
And with som wisdom ye his sorwe bete.°   *assuage*
What helpeth it to wepen ful a strete,°   *a streetful*
930 Or though ye° bothe in salte teeris dreynte?°   *Or for you / to have drowned*
Bet is a tyme of cure ay than of pleynte.

"I mene thus: whan ich hym hider° brynge,   *hither*
Syn ye be wise and bothe of oon assent,°   *accord*
So shapeth° how destourbe° youre goynge,   *plan / to impede*
935 Or come ayeyn soon after ye be went.°   *you have gone*
Women ben wise in short avysement;°   *with brief deliberation*
And lat sen how youre wit shal now availle,°   *help*
And that that° I may helpe, it shal nat faille."   *that with which*

7. Be for him the cause of the flat rather than the edge (of the sword)—as swords were sometimes thought to heal, the sense is "of healing rather than wounding."

108

"Go," Criseida said. "I promise you, my Pandaro, I shall exert myself to do it. When you have left, I shall rise from my bed without any delay, and my woe and my lost delight I shall hold completely locked in my heart. Let him come then and in the usual way, for he will find the door ajar as it usually is."

Pandaro comforts Troilo once again and tells him that he may go to Criseida that night, and he does so.

109

Pandaro found Troilo again deep in thought and so strongly downcast in appearance that for pity he became sorrowful for it, saying to him, "Now, brave youth, have you become such a coward as you appear? Your love has not yet departed from you. Why do you still upset yourself so much that your eyes already seem dead in your head?

"Go," quod Criseyde, "and uncle, trewely,
940 I shal don al my myght me to restreyne
From wepyng in his sighte, and bisily
Hym for to glade° I shal don al my peyne,   *gladden*
And in myn herte seken every veyne.°   *vein, i.e., place*
If to° his sore ther may be fonden salve,   *for*
945 It shal nat lakke,° certeyn, on my halve."°   *be lacking / on my part*

Goth Pandarus, and Troilus he soughte
Til in a temple he fond hym al allone,
As he that of his lif no lenger roughte;°   *longer cared*
But to the pitouse° goddes everichone   *pitying*
950 Ful tendrely he preyde and made his mone,° *moan, complaint*
To doon hym sone out of this world to pace,° *pass*
For wel he thoughte ther was non other grace.

And shortly, al the sothe for to seye,
He was so fallen in despeir that day,
955 That outrely° he shop hym° for to deye. *utterly, entirely / was prepared*
For right thus was his argument alway:
He seyde he nas but lorn,° weylaway!   *lost*
"For al that comth, comth by necessitee:[8]
Thus to ben lorn, it is my destinee.

960 "For certeynly, this wot I wel," he seyde,
"That forsight of divine purveyaunce°   *providence, foreseeing*
Hath seyn° alwey me to forgon° Criseyde,   *(fore-)seen / that I would lose*
Syn God seeth every thyng, out of doutaunce,° *doubt*
And hem disponyth,° thorugh his ordinaunce, *disposes them*
965 In hire merites° sothly for to be,   *According to their deserts*
As they shul comen by predestyne.°   *predestination*

"But natheles,° allas, whom shal I leeve?° *nevertheless / believe*
For ther ben grete clerkes many oon°   *scholars many a one*
That destyne thorugh argumentes preve;
970 And som men seyn that nedely° ther is noon, *necessarily*
But that fre chois is yeven° us everychon. *given*
O, welaway! So sleighe arn° clerkes olde *sly, cunning are*
That I not° whos opynyoun I may holde. *don't know*

"For som men seyn, if God seth al biforn—
975 Ne God may nat deceyved ben, parde—°   *indeed*
Than moot it fallen, theigh men hadde it sworn,[9]
That° purveiance hath seyn before to be. *That which*
Wherfore I sey, that from eterne° if he   *eternity*
Hath wist° byforn oure thought ek as oure dede,° *known / deeds*
980 We han no fre chois, as thise clerkes rede.° *advise, argue*

---

8. Troilus's tangled meditation on the old problem of divine foreknowledge, predestination, and free will is drawn from Boethius, *Consolation of Philosophy*, 5.pr.2 and 3. Troilus breaks off the argument without presenting Boethius's defense of free will.
9. Then it must happen, even though people had sworn (that it wouldn't happen).

"For other thought, nor other dede also,
Myghte nevere ben, but swich as purveyaunce,
Which may nat ben deceyved nevere mo,
Hath feled° byforn, withouten ignoraunce.   *sensed, seen*
985 For yf ther myghte ben a variaunce°   *variation (i.e., loophole)*
To writhen° out fro Goddis purveyinge,   *wriggle*
Ther nere no prescience° of thyng comynge,   *would be no foreknowledge*

"But it were rather an opynyoun
Uncerteyn, and no stedfast forseynge;°   *secure foresight*
990 And certes, that were an abusioun,°   *error, absurdity*
That God sholde han no parfit cler wytynge°   *perfect clear knowledge*
More than we men that han doutous wenynge.°   *unreliable opinion*
But swich an errour upon God to gesse°   *to imagine of God*
Were fals and foul, and wikked corsednesse.

995 "Ek this is an opynyoun of some
That han hire top ful heighe and smothe yshore:[1]
They seyn right thus, that thyng is nat to come
For that the prescience hath seyn byfore
That it shal come; but they seyn that therfore°   *because*
1000 That it shal come, therfore the purveyaunce
Woot it byforn, withouten ignoraunce;

"And in this manere this necessite
Retorneth in his part contrarie agayn.
For nedfully byhoveth it nat to bee
1005 That thilke thynges fallen in certayn
That ben purveyed; but nedly, as they sayn,
Byhoveth it that thynges whiche that falle,
That they in certayn ben purveyed alle.[2]

"I mene as though I laboured me in° this   *I took pains about*
1010 To enqueren which thyng cause of which thyng be:
As wheither that the prescience of God is
The certeyn cause of the necessite
Of thynges that to comen ben, parde,°   *by God, indeed*
Or if necessite of thyng comynge
1015 Be cause certeyn of the purveyinge.°   *foreseeing*

"But now n'enforce I me nat° in shewynge   *I don't trouble myself*
How the ordre of causes stant;° but wel woot I   *stands*
That it byhoveth° that the byfallynge°   *is necessary / occurrence*
Of thynges wist° byfore certeynly   *known*
1020 Be necessario, al seme it° nat therby   *although it may not seem*
That prescience put fallynge necessaire°   *make the occurrence necessary*
To thyng to come, al falle it foule or faire.[3]

---

1. That have very prominent and smoothly shaved crowns of their heads. The learned clerkes who could write about predestination and free will would be churchmen with shaved (tonsured) heads.
2. And in this way this necessity turns back on itself, since it is not necessary that things that have been foreseen will certainly happen. But, as they say, it necessarily is the case that all the things that do happen have certainly been foreseen (i.e., by God).
3. Of things to come, whether it turn out bad or good.

"For if ther sitte a man yond on a see,°   *seat*
Than by necessite bihoveth it
1025 That, certes, thyn opynyoun sooth° be   *true*
That wenest or conjectest that he sit.[4]
And further over° now ayeynward° yit,   *moreover / on the other hand*
Lo, right so is it of the part contrarie,°   *on the other side*
As thus—now herkne,° for I wol nat tarie:°   *listen / tarry*

1030 "I sey that if the opynyoun of the°   *your opinion*
Be soth, for that he sitte,° than sey I this: *because he is sitting*
That he mot° sitten by necessite;   *must*
And thus necessite in eyther° is.   *both of you*
For in hym, nede of sittynge is, ywys,
1035 And in the,° nede of soth; and thus, forsothe,   *you*
There mot necessite ben in yow bothe.

"But thow mayst seyn, the man sit nat therfore°   *for this reason*
That thyn opynyoun of his sittynge soth is,
But rather, for the man sit ther byfore,[5]
1040 Therfore is thyn opynyoun soth, ywis.
And I seye, though the cause of soth of this
Comth of his sittyng, yet necessite
Is entrechaunged,° both in hym and the.   *mutual, reciprocal*

"Thus in this same wise, out of doutaunce,°   *doubt*
1045 I may wel maken, as it semeth me,
My resonyng of Goddes purveyaunce°   *providence, foreseeing*
And of the thynges that to comen be;°   *are to come (in the future)*
By which resoun men may wel yse
That thilke thynges that in erthe falle,°   *happen*
1050 That by necessite they comen alle.

"For although that for° thyng shal come, ywys,   *because*
Therfore is it purveyed,° certeynly—   *foreseen*
Nat that it comth for° it purveyed is—   *because*
Yet natheles, bihoveth it nedfully[6]
1055 That thing to come be purveyd, trewely,
Or elles,° thynges that purveyed be,   *else*
That they bitiden° by necessite.   *(It must be) that they happen*

"And this suffiseth right ynough, certeyn,
For to destruye oure fre chois every del.°   *free will entirely*
1060 But now is this abusioun,° to seyn   *an error, a falsehood*
That fallyng° of the thynges temporel°   *the occurrence / worldly*
Is cause of Goddes prescience eternel.
Now trewely, that is a fals sentence,°   *idea*
That thyng to come° sholde cause his   *things to come (in the future)*
prescience.

---

4. You who think or conjecture that he is sitting.
5. But rather because the man is sitting in front of you.
6. Yet nevertheless, it is necessarily the case.

110

"You have lived long without her; doesn't your heart give you the power to still live? Were you born into the world only for her? Show yourself somewhat a man and take heart; drive away these sorrows and these laments, at least in part. I have not stopped any place, except here with you, since I spoke to her and was with her a long time.

111

"And it seems to me that you do not feel half the pain that your sorrowing lady does, for this departure so displeases her that her sighs are so burning that they surpass yours twenty to one. Therefore, give yourself some peace, since at least you can know in this bitter case how dear you are to her,

1065 "What myght I wene,° and° I hadde swich a thought,   *think / if*
But that God purveyeth thyng that is to come
For that° it is to come, and ellis° nought?   *Because / otherwise*
So myghte I wene that thynges alle and some°   *every one*
That whilom ben byfalle and overcome⁷
1070 Ben cause of thilke sovereyne° purveyaunce   *sovereign (i.e., divine)*
That forwoot° al withouten ignoraunce.   *foreknows*

"And over° al this, yet sey I more herto:°   *beyond / about this*
That right as whan I wot ther is a thyng,
Iwys, that thyng moot nedfully° be so;   *must necessarily*
1075 Ek right so, whan I woot a thyng comyng,°   *future event*
So mot it come; and thus the bifallyng
Of thynges that ben wist bifore the tyde,°   *time (of their occurrence)*
They mowe nat ben eschued on no syde."°   *avoided in any way*

Thanne seyde he thus: "Almyghty Jove in trone,°   *throne*
1080 That woost of al thys thyng the sothfastnesse,°   *truth*
Rewe° on my sorwe: or do° me deyen sone,   *Have pity / either cause*
Or bryng Criseyde and me fro this destresse!"
And whil he was in al this hevynesse,
Disputyng with hymself in this matere,
1085 Com Pandare in, and seyde as ye may here:

"O myghty God," quod Pandarus, "in trone,°   *throne*
I!° Who say evere a wis man faren° so?   *Ah! / behave*
Whi, Troilus, what thinkestow to doone?
Hastow swich lust° to ben thyn owen fo?   *such a desire*
1090 What, parde,° yet is nat Criseyde ago!°   *by God / gone*
Whi list the so thiself fordoon° for drede   *ruin*
That in thyn hed thyne eyen semen° dede?   *eyes seem*

"Hastow nat lyved many a yer byforn°   *year beforehand*
Withouten hire, and ferd° ful wel at ese?   *fared*
1095 Artow° for hire and for noon other born?   *Are you*
Hath Kynde° the wrought al only hire to plese?   *Nature*
Lat be, and thynk right thus in thi disese:
That, in the dees° right as ther fallen chaunces,°   *dice / winning throws*
Right so in love ther come and gon plesaunces.

1100 "And yet this is a wonder most of alle,
Whi thow thus sorwest, syn thow nost nat° yit,   *you don't know*
Touchyng° hire goyng, how that it shal falle,°   *With regard to / turn out*
Ne yif° she kan hireself destourben° it.   *if / forestall*
Thow hast nat yet assayed° al hire wit.   *examined*
1105 A man may al bytyme° his nekke beede▪   *soon enough / offer*
Whan it shal of,° and sorwen at the nede.   *must (be cut) off*

---

7. That formerly have occurred and finished happening.

112

"I have just now arranged with her that you will go to her and be with her tonight, and what you have already planned you will show her in the best way you can. You will see right away what will be entirely pleasing to her. Perhaps the two of you will find the means for great alleviations of your ills."

113

Sighing, Troilo replied: "You speak well, and I wish to do thus." And many other things he said. But when it appeared time to go, Pandaro left him thinking about matters and went away. And it seemed to him a thousand years before he would be in the arms of his dear comfort, whom Fortune afterwards wrongly took from him.

Criseida swoons in Troilo's arms who, believing her dead, intends to kill himself with his drawn sword.

114

When the hour and moment had come, Criseida came to him with a lighted torch as she always did and received him in her arms, and he, oppressed with heavy sorrow, took her in his, and the silent pair could not conceal their wounded hearts, but, having embraced without saying a word, they began a great and torrential weeping.

115

And both pressed each other tightly together, entirely bathed in tears, and, though they wished to speak, they could not, for anguished weeping and sobs and sighs prevented them, and nevertheless they kissed each other sometimes and drank the falling tears without care that they were bitter beyond their nature.

"Forthi° tak hede of that that I shal seye: *Therefore*
I have with hire yspoke and longe ybe,°   *been (with her)*
So as acorded° was bitwixe us tweye;°   *agreed / two*
1110 And evere mor me thynketh thus, that she
Hath somwhat in hire hertes privete°   *private space*
Wherwith° she kan, if I shal right arede,°   *The means by which / reckon*
Destourbe° al this of which thow art in drede.   *Forestall*

"For which my counseil is, whan it is nyght
1115 Thow to hire go and make of this an ende;
And blisful Juno thorugh hire grete myght
Shal, as I hope,° hire grace unto us sende.   *hope, expect*
Myn herte seyth, 'Certeyn, she shal nat wende.'°   *go*
And forthi° put thyn herte a while in reste,   *therefore*
1120 And hold this purpos, for it is the beste."

This Troilus answerd, and sighte° soore: *sighed*
"Thow seist° right wel, and I wol don right so."   *speak*
And what hym liste,° he seyde unto it more.°   *as he pleased / more about it*
And whan that it was tyme for to go,
1125 Ful pryvely° hymself, withouten mo,°   *secretly / more (ado) or others*
Unto hire com, as he was wont to doone;
And how they wroughte,° I shal yow tellen soone.   *conducted things*

Soth is, that whan they gonnen first to mete,
So gan the peyne hire hertes for to twiste
1130 That neyther of hem other myghte grete,
But hem° in armes toke, and after kiste.   *each other*
The lasse° woful of hem bothe nyste°   *less / didn't know*
Wher that he was, ne myghte o° word out brynge,   *one*
As I seyde erst, for wo and for sobbynge.

1135 The woful teeris that they leten falle
As bittre weren, out of teris kynde,°   *unlike the nature of tears*
For peyne, as is ligne aloes or galle—[8]
So bittre teeris weep° nought, as I fynde,   *wept*
The woful Mirra thorugh the bark and rynde—[9]
1140 That° in this world ther nys so hard an herte   *So that*
That nolde han rewed° on hire peynes smerte.°   *taken pity / sharp*

8. Medicinal *ligne aloes* is, like gall, bitter.
9. Myrrha, transmuted into a tree, wept (through the bark and cortex) tears of myrrh.

116

But after their spirits, exhausted by the anguish of tears and sighs, had returned to their places through the slackening of their bitter pains, Criseida, having raised her sorrowful eyes with their cruel yearnings to Troilo, said in a broken voice, "O my lord, who takes me from you, and where do I go from here?"

117

Then she fell back fainting with her face on his breast, and her strength left her, with so much grief was her heart oppressed, and her spirit exerted itself to take flight. And Troilo gazed into her face and called her and felt that she did not hear. And her veiled eyes and her falling gave him the impression that she might be dead.

118

When Troilo saw that, distressed by a double sorrow, he laid her down, often kissing her tearful face, seeking if he might see in her any sign of life, and sorrowfully he tried each part, and weeping he said that it seemed to him she had passed from this wretched life.

119

She was cold and without any feeling as far as Troilo could tell. And this seemed to him a true argument that she had finished her days. Therefore, after a very long lament, before he proceeded to any other act, he dried her face and composed her body as men are accustomed to do with the dead.

But whan hire woful weri goostes tweyne°   *two spirits*
Retourned ben ther as hem oughte dwelle,
And that somwhat to wayken° gan the peyne *weaken*
1145 By lengthe of pleynte, and ebben gan the welle
Of hire teeris, and the herte unswelle,° *reduce its swelling*
With broken vois, al hoors forshright,° *hoarse from too much shrieking*
Criseyde
To Troilus thise ilke° wordes seyde: *same*

"O Jove, I deye, and mercy I beseche!
1150 Help, Troilus!" And therwithal hire face
Upon his brest she leyde and loste speche—
Hire woful spirit from his propre° place, *its proper*
Right with the word, alwey o poynt to pace.° *at the point of passing away*
And thus she lith with hewes° pale and grene, *complexion*
1155 That whilom° fressh and fairest was to sene. *formerly*

This Troilus, that on hire gan biholde,
Clepyng° hire name—and she lay as for ded— *Calling*
Without answere, and felte hire lymes° colde, *limbs*
Hire eyen throwen upward to° hire hed, *in*
1160 This sorwful man kan° now noon other red,° *knows / counsel*
But ofte tyme hire colde mowth he kiste.
Wher hym was wo,° God and hymself it wiste! *Whether he had sorrow*

He rist hym° up, and long streght° he hire leyde; *rose / stretched at length*
For signe of lif, for aught° he kan or may, *anything*
1165 Kan he non fynde in nothyng° on Criseyde, *anywhere*
For which his song ful ofte is "weylaway!"
But whan he saugh that specheles she lay,
With sorweful vois and herte of blisse al bare,
He seyde how she was fro this world yfare.° *gone*

1170 So after that he longe hadde hire compleyned,
His hondes wrong, and seyd that was to seye,° *what was (fitting) to say*
And with his teeris salt hire brest byreyned,° *rained on*
He gan tho teeris wypen of° ful dreye,° *off / dry*
And pitously gan for the soule preye,
1175 And seyde, "O Lord, that set art in thi trone,° *throne*
Rewe ek° on me, for I shal folwe hire sone!" *Have pity also*

She cold was, and withouten sentement° *sensation*
For aught he woot,° for breth ne felte he non, *all he knew*
And this was hym a pregnant argument
1180 That she was forth out of this world agon.° *gone*
And whan he say ther was non other woon,° *resource*
He gan hire lymes dresse° in swich manere *arrange her limbs*
As men don hem that shal ben layd on beere.° *a bier*

120

And this done, with a firm mind, he drew his own sword from its sheath, completely disposed to lay hold of death so that his spirit might follow that of his lady in so sad a fate and might live with her in the Underworld, since bitter Fortune and harsh love were driving him from this life.

121

But first he said, burning with noble disdain, "O cruel Jove, and you, wicked Fortune, behold I come to do what you wish. You have taken from me my Criseida, whom I thought you were destined to take from me with another device, and where she may be now I do not know but I see her body here most wrongly killed by you.

122

"And I shall leave the world and follow her with my spirit since it pleases you. Perhaps I shall have better luck there with her when I have peace from my sighs, if one loves there as I have heard it sometimes said that one does. Since you do not wish to see me alive, at least place my soul with her.

123

"And you, city, which I leave at war, and you, Priam, and you, dear brothers, God be with you, for I am going beneath the ground after the fair eyes of Criseida. And you for whom sorrow seizes me so much and who divides my soul from the body, receive me"—Criseida he meant to say, holding his sword already at his breast to die,

124

when she, recovering her senses, heaved a very great sigh, calling on Troilo. To her he said, "My sweet desire, do you still live now?" And weeping he took her again in his arms, and as best he could, alleviating her suffering with words, he comforted her, and her straying soul returned to her heart from where it had taken flight.

And after this, with sterne and cruel herte,
His swerd anon out of his shethe he twighte°   *drew*
Hymself to slen,° how° sore that hym smerte,°   *slay / however / pained*
So that his soule hire soule folwen myghte
Ther as the doom of Mynos wolde it dighte,[1]
Syn Love and cruel Fortune it ne wolde°   *didn't wish it*
That in this world he lenger lyven sholde.

Than seyde he thus, fulfild of heigh desdayn:°   *filled with high disdain*
"O cruel Jove, and thow, Fortune adverse,
This al and som:° that falsly have ye slayn   *This is the sum of it*
Criseyde, and syn° ye may do me no werse,   *since*
Fy on youre myght and werkes so dyverse!°   *perverse*
Thus cowardly ye shul me nevere wynne;°   *defeat*
Ther shal no deth me fro my lady twynne.°   *separate*

"For I this world, syn ye have slayn hire thus,
Wol lete° and folwe hire spirit low or hye.°   *abandon / high*
Shal nevere lovere seyn that Troilus
Dar nat for fere with his lady dye;
For certeyn I wol beere° hire compaignie   *bear, keep*
But syn° ye wol nat suffre us lyven here,   *since*
Yet suffreth that oure soules ben yfere.°   *together*

"And thow, cite,° which that I leve° in wo,   *city / abandon*
And thow, Priam, and bretheren alle yfeere,°   *together*
And thow, my moder, farwel, for I go;
And Atropos,[2] make redy thow my beere;°   *bier*
And thow, Criseyde, o swete herte deere,
Receyve now my spirit!" wolde he seye,
With swerd at herte, al redy for to deye.

But as God wolde, of swough° therwith sh'abreyde,°   *(her) swoon / woke*
And gan to sike,° and "Troilus" she cride;   *sigh*
And he answerde, "Lady myn, Criseyde,
Lyve ye yet?" and leet his swerd down glide.
"Ye, herte myn, that thonked be Cipride!"°   *Cyprian Venus*
Quod she; and therwithal she soore syghte,°   *sighed*
And he bigan conforte hire as he myghte,

Took hire in armes two, and kiste hire ofte,
And hire to glade° he did al his entente;°   *gladden / effort*
For which hire goost, that flikered ay o-lofte,°   *fluttered ever aloft*
Into hire woful herte ayeyn° it wente.   *again*
But at the laste, as that hire eye glente°   *glanced*
Asyde, anon she gan his swerd espie,
As it lay bare, and gan for fere crye,

1. Where the judgment of Minos wished to direct it. Minos was judge of the dead in Hades.
2. Atropos, one of the three Fates, cuts the thread of life.

The two lovers take themselves to bed and there sigh, weep, and discuss various things, and in the morning they arise.

125

And being for a while all distraught, she was silent; and then seeing the sword, she began, "Why was that drawn from the sheath?" To whom Troilo tearfully related what might have happened to his life. At that she said, "What is this I hear? So, if I had remained a little longer, you would have killed yourself in this place!

126

"Ah, me, what dreadful thing have you said to me? I would never have remained alive after you, but through my breast I would have driven it. Now we have much to praise God for; however, let us now go to bed. There we shall talk of our woes. If I consider the consumed torch, there is already a great part of the night gone."

127

As at other times their embraces had been close, so they were now, but these were more bitter with tears than the pleasing ones had formerly been sweet. And the sad discussion commenced without delay between them. And Criseida began: "Sweet friend, listen very attentively to what I say.

128

"After I heard the sad news of my wicked father's treachery—as God may preserve your fair face for me—no woman ever felt as much distress as I felt then like one who does not care for gold, city, or palace but only to remain always with you in joy and in pleasure, and you with me.

129

"And I wished to despair entirely, not believing that I would ever see you again, but since you have seen my soul wander off and return back, I feel certain thoughts pass through my mind, which may perhaps be useful, and which I wish to be clear to you before we lament any further since perhaps we can still have good hope.

And asked hym, whi he it hadde out drawe.
And Troilus anon the cause hire tolde,
And how hymself therwith he wolde han slawe;°   *slain*
For which Criseyde upon hym gan biholde,
1230   And gan hym in hire armes faste folde,
And seyde, "O mercy, God! Lo, which° a dede!   *what*
Allas, how neigh° we weren bothe dede!   *near*

"Than° if I nadde° spoken, as grace was,   *Then / had not*
Ye wolde han slayn youreself anon?" quod she.
1235   "Yee, douteles"; and she answerde, "Allas,
For by that ilke° Lord that made me,   *same*
I nolde a forlong wey on lyve have be³
After youre deth, to han ben° crowned queene   *(even) to have been*
Of al that lond the sonne on shyneth sheene.°   *brightly*

1240   "But with this selve° swerd, which that here is,   *same*
Myselve I wolde han slawe,"° quod she tho.   *slain*
"But hoo,° for we han° right ynough of this,   *stop / have had*
And lat us rise, and streght° to bedde go,   *straightway*
And there lat us speken of oure wo;
1245   For, by the morter° which that I se brenne,°   *wick-lamp or candle / burn*
Knowe I ful wel that day is nat far henne."°   *hence*

Whan they were in hire bed, in armes folde,
Naught was it lik tho nyghtes here-byforn.
For pitously ech other gan byholde,
1250   As they that hadden al hire blisse ylorn,°   *lost*
Bywaylinge ay the day that they were born;
Til at the laste this sorwful wight, Criseyde,
To Troilus thise ilke° wordes seyde: *same*

"Lo, herte myn, wel woot ye this," quod she,
1255   "That if a wight alwey his wo compleyne
And seketh nought how holpen for to be,°   *how to be helped*
It nys but folie and encrees° of peyne;   *an increase*
And syn that here assembled be we tweyne°   *two*
To fynde boote° of wo that we ben inne,   *a remedy*
1260   It were al tyme soone to bygynne.

"I am a womman, as ful wel ye woot,
And as I am avysed sodeynly,°   *precipitously resolved*
So wol I telle yow, whil it is hoot.
Me thynketh° thus: that nouther° ye nor I   *It seems to me / neither*
1265   Ought half this wo to maken, skilfully;°   *in reason*
For ther is art° ynough for to redresse   *are means*
That° yet is mys,° and slen° this hevynesse.   *What / amiss / to slay*

"Soth is, the wo, the which that we ben inne,
For aught I woot,° for nothyng ellis° is   *know / else*

---

3. I wouldn't wish to have been alive a furlong way. A *forlong wey* is the time it takes to walk a furlong (one-eighth mile), two or three minutes.

130

"You see that my father requests me, whom I would not obey by going from here if the king did not force me, whose faith must be kept, as you should know; therefore I must go with Diomede, who has been the negotiator of these cruel pacts, whenever he returns: may God wish that neither he nor that cruel moment ever come.

1270 But for the cause that we sholden twynne.°   *separate*
    Considered al,° ther nys namore amys.   *All things considered*
    But what is thanne a remede unto this,
    But that we shape us° soone for to meete?   *arrange*
    This al and som,° my deere herte sweete.   *This is the whole matter*

1275 "Now, that I shal wel bryngen it aboute
    To come ayeyn,° soone after that I go,   *back*
    Therof am I no manere thyng° in doute;   *in no way*
    For, dredeles,° withinne a wowke° or two   *doubtless / week*
    I shal ben here; and that it may be so
1280 By alle right° and in a wordes fewe,   *In all justice*
    I shal yow wel an heep of weyes° shewe.   *heap of ways (i.e., reasons)*

    "For which I wol nat make long sermoun—°   *speech*
    For tyme ylost may nought recovered be—
    But I wol gon to my conclusioun,
1285 And to the beste,° in aught that I kan see.   *to what is best*
    And for the love of God, foryeve° it me   *forgive*
    If I speke aught ayeyns° youre hertes reste;   *against*
    For trewely, I speke it for the beste,

    "Makyng alwey a protestacioun
1290 That now thise wordes which that I shal seye
    Nis but° to shewen yow my mocioun°   *are only / inclination*
    To fynde unto oure help the beste weye;
    And taketh it non other wise, I preye,
    For in effect, what so ye me comaunde,
1295 That wol I don, for that is no demaunde.°   *there is no question of that*

    "Now herkneth this: ye han wel understonde
    My goyng graunted is by parlement
    So ferforth° that it may nat be withstonde°   *conclusively / opposed*
    For al this world, as by my jugement.
1300 And syn ther helpeth non avisement°   *counsel*
    To letten° it, lat it passe out of mynde,   *prevent*
    And lat us shape° a bettre wey to fynde.   *plan*

    "The soth is this: the twynnyng of us tweyne°   *separation of us two*
    Wol us disese and cruelich anoye,°   *distress*
1305 But hym byhoveth° somtyme han a peyne   *it behooves him*
    That° serveth Love, if that he wol have joye.   *Who*
    And syn I shal no ferther out of Troie
    Than I may ride ayeyn° on half a morwe,°   *back / morning*
    It oughte lesse° causen us to sorwe;   *the less*

1310 "So as° I shal not so ben hid in muwe,°   *Seeing that / cooped up*
    That day by day, myn owne herte deere—
    Syn wel ye woot that it is now a trewe—°   *there is now a truce*
    Ye shal ful wel al myn estat yheere.°   *hear about my condition*
    And er that trewe is doon, I shal ben heere;

131

"But you know that every relative of mine is here except my father, and each of my things still remains here, and if I remember rightly, there is continual talk between you and the Greeks of an end to this perilous war, and if Menelaus' wife is given back to him, I believe you will have it, and I know that you are already close to it.

132

"I shall return here if you effect it, since I do not have anywhere else to go. And if perchance you do not effect it, I shall have cause for coming here in times of truce, for you know that it is not customary to deny such entrances to women, and my relatives will gladly see me here and will invite me here.

133

"Then we shall be able to have some solace, though the waiting may be a heavy grievance. But one must prepare to sustain some hardship if he wishes joy to come to him with greater pleasure afterwards. I see indeed that while we live in Troy we must sometimes pass many a day in anguished suffering without seeing each other.

134

"And besides this, a greater hope of returning here, peace or no, springs up in me. My father now has this desire, and perhaps he imagines that because of his wrongdoing I cannot remain here without fear of being subjected to violence or blame here. When he knows that I am honored here, he will not care any more about my returning.

1315 And thanne have ye both Antenore ywonne
And me also. Beth glad now, if ye konne,°   *can*

"And thenk right thus: 'Criseyde is now agon.°   *gone*
But what, she shal come hastiliche ayeyn!'
And whanne, allas? By God, lo, right anon,
1320 Er° dayes ten, this dar I saufly° seyn.   *Before / safely*
And than at erste° shal we be so feyn,°   *for the first time / glad*
So as° we shal togideres evere dwelle,   *In that*
That al this world ne myghte oure blisse telle.

"I se that oft-tyme, there as we ben now,°   *in our present situation*
1325 That for the beste, oure counseyl° for to hide,   *plan*
Ye speke nat with me, nor I with yow
In fourtenyght, ne se yow go ne ride.⁴
May ye naught ten dayes thanne abide,°   *wait*
For myn honour, in swich an aventure?°   *such a happenstance*
1330 Iwys, ye mowen ellis lite endure!⁵

"Ye knowe ek how that al my kyn is heere,
But if that onliche° it my fader be,   *Unless only*
And ek myn othere thynges° alle yfeere,°   *goods / together*
And nameliche,° my deere herte, ye,   *especially*
1335 Whom that I nolde leven for to se°   *leave off seeing*
For al this world, as wyd as it hath space,
Or ellis se ich nevere° Joves face!   *may I never see*

"Whi trowe° ye my fader in this wise   *think*
Coveyteth° so to se me, but for drede   *Desires*
1340 Lest in this town that folkes me despise
Because of hym, for his unhappy° dede?   *ill-fated*

4. For a fortnight (two weeks), nor (should I) see you walk or ride.
5. Indeed, you can otherwise endure but little!

135

"And for what purpose should he hold me among the Greeks who, as you see, are always in arms? And if he would not keep me there, I do not see where else he could send me. And even if he could, I believe he would not, since he would not wish to trust me to the Greeks. Therefore, it is suitable to send me back here, nor do I see anything clearly against it.

136

"He is, as you know, old and avaricious, and he has here property which needs his action and his voice. As he holds this dear, I shall tell him of it in order to make him more easily return me here, showing him how I can provide a remedy for anything that might happen unexpectedly; and he, through avarice, will take delight in my return."

What woot my fader what lif that I lede?⁶
For if he wiste in Troie how wel I fare,
Us neded° for my wendyng° nought to care.   *We would need / departure*

1345 "Ye sen that every day ek, more and more,
Men trete of pees,° and it supposid is   *negotiate about peace*
That men the queene Eleyne shal restore,°   *restore (to her Greek husband)*
And Grekis us restoren that is mys;°   *what is lost*
So, though ther nere comfort non° but this,   *there were no comfort*
1350 That men purposen° pees on every syde,   *propose*
Ye may the bettre at ese of herte abyde.°   *wait*

"For if that it be pees, myn herte deere,
The nature of the pees moot nedes dryve°   *must needs require*
That men moost entrecomunen yfeere,°   *communicate together*
1355 And to and fro ek ride and gon as blyve°   *quickly*
Alday as thikke as been fleen° from an hyve,   *bees fly*
And every wight han liberte to bleve°   *remain*
Whereas hym liste the bet, withouten leve.⁷

"And though so be that pees ther may be non,
1360 Yet hider,° though° ther nevere pees ne were,   *hither / even if*
I moste° come; for whider sholde I gon,   *must*
Or how, meschaunce,° sholde I dwelle there   *worse luck*
Among tho men of armes evere in feere?
For which, as wisly God my soule rede,°   *may God surely direct my soul*
1365 I kan nat sen wherof ye sholden drede.°   *why you should be afraid*

"Have here another wey, if it so be
That al this thyng ne may yow nat suffise:
My fader, as ye knowen wel, parde,°   *by God*
Is old, and elde° is ful of coveytise,°   *old age / covetousness*
1370 And I right now have founden al the gise,°   *means*
Withouten net, wherwith I shal hym hente.°   *catch*
And herkeneth how, if that ye wol° assente: *will*

"Lo, Troilus, men seyn that hard it is
The wolf ful and the wether hool to have;⁸
1375 This is to seyn, that men ful ofte, iwys,
Mote spenden part the remenant for to save;°   *to save the remainder*
For ay with gold men may the herte grave°   *make an impression on*
Of hym that set is upon coveytise;
And how I mene, I shal it yow devyse:

1380 "The moeble° which that I have in this town   *movable property*
Unto my fader shal I take, and seye
That right for trust and for savacioun°   *safekeeping*
It sent is from a frend of his or tweye,°   *two*
The whiche frendes ferventliche hym preye

6. What does my father know about the life I lead?
7. Where it best may please him, without permission.
8. To have both the wolf full and the wether whole (i.e., the sheep uneaten).

137

Attentively Troilo listened to the lady and her speech impressed his mind, and it seemed to him almost probable that what she said with certainty was so, ought to be so. But because he loved her very much, only slowly did he put faith in it. However, at last, like one who was eager to believe, searching his own mind, he brought himself to believe it.

1385 To senden after more, and that in hie,[9]
　　Whil that this town stant° thus in jupartie.　　　　　　　　　*stands*

　　"And that shal ben an huge quantite—
　　Thus shal I seyn—but lest it folk espide,°　　　　　*people should spy it*
　　This may be sent by no wyght but by me.
1390 I shal ek shewen hym, yf pees bytyde,°　　　　　　*should occur*
　　What frendes that ich have on every syde
　　Toward° the court, to don the wrathe pace°　　*At / cause the anger to pass*
　　Of Priamus and don hym stonde in grace.°　　*bring him (Calchas) into favor*

　　"So what for o thyng and for other, swete,
1395 I shal hym so enchaunten with my sawes°　　　　　　*speeches*
　　That right in hevene his sowle is, shal he mete;°　　　　　*dream*
　　For al Appollo, or his clerkes lawes,°　　　　　*learned precepts*
　　Or calkullynge, avayleth nought thre hawes;[1]
　　Desir of gold shal so his soule blende°　　　　　*blind, deceive*
1400 That, as me lyst,° I shal wel make an ende.　　　　　*as it pleases me*

　　"And yf he wolde ought by hys sort it preve[2]
　　If that I lye, in certayn I shal fonde°　　　　　　　　　*try*
　　Distorben° hym and plukke hym by the sleve,　　　　*To disturb*
　　Makynge his sort, and beren hym on honde[3]
1405 He hath not wel the goddes understonde;°　　*understood the gods*
　　For goddes speken in amphibologies,°　　　　　*ambiguities*
　　And for o° soth they tellen twenty lyes.　　　　　　　*one*

　　"Ek, 'Drede fond first goddes, I suppose'—[4]
　　Thus shal I seyn—and that his coward herte
1410 Made hym amys° the goddes text to glose,°　　*erroneously / interpret*
　　Whan he for fered out of Delphos sterte.[5]
　　And but° I make hym soone to converte　　　　　　*unless*
　　And don my red° withinne a day or tweye,　　*execute my plan*
　　I wol to yow oblige me° to deye."　　　　　　*pledge myself*

1415 And treweliche, as writen wel I fynde
　　That al this thyng was seyd of good entente,°　　　*in good faith*
　　And that hire herte trewe was and kynde
　　Towardes hym, and spak right as she mente,°　　*just as she thought*
　　And that she starf° for wo neigh° whan she wente,　　*died / nearly*
1420 And was in purpos evere to be trewe:
　　Thus writen they that of hire werkes knewe.

　　This Troilus, with herte and erys spradde,°　　*ears spread, wide open*
　　Herde al this thyng devysen° to and fro,　　　　　*being planned*
　　And verrayliche° him semed that he hadde　　　　　*truly*

---

9. That they may send more thereafter, and that in haste.
1. Or (Calchas's) calculating (i.e., divination) is not worth three hawthorn berries. Calchas would consult Apollo's oracle for information about the future.
2. And if he wished at all to test by sortilege (divination by drawing lots).
3. While he is engaged in his sortilege, and lead him to believe.
4. Also, "Fear first invented gods, I suppose." The saying is ancient and widespread.
5. When he for fear moved quickly out of (Apollo's oracle at) Delphi.

138

Thus part of their heavy grief departed from them and hope returned. And becoming then less bitter in feeling, they began again the game of love. And just as a bird in the spring season takes delight in his song from leaf to leaf, so did they, in speaking to each other of many things.

139

But because the thought that she must depart could not pass from the heart of Troilo, he began to speak in this manner: "O my Criseida, very much more beloved than any other goddess and more to be honored by me, who just now intended to kill myself believing you dead, what kind of life will be mine do you think, if you do not return quickly?

140

"Rest assured that it is as certain as death that I would kill myself if you should delay returning here a little bit too long. And I don't see clearly yet how I might manage without sorrowful and bitter languishing, knowing that you are elsewhere, and a new fear comes to me that Calchas may keep you and that what you say may not happen.

141

"I do not know if peace shall ever be between us, but peace or not, I scarcely believe that Calchas will ever wish to return here, for he would not believe that he could remain here without the infamy of his crime which was great, if we do not wish to deceive ourselves in this matter. And if with so much insistence he asks for your return, I scarcely have faith that he will send you back.

1425 The selve wit;° but yet to late° hire go   *same idea / let*
His herte mysforyaf hym° evere mo;   *had misgivings*
But fynaly, he gan his herte wreste°   *constrain*
To trusten hire, and took it for the beste.

For which° the grete furie of his penaunce°   *Whence / torment*
1430 Was queynt with° hope, and therwith hem bitwene   *quenched by*
Bigan for joie th'amorouse daunce;°   *amorous dance, lovemaking*
And as the briddes,° whanne the sonne is shene,°   *birds / shining*
Deliten in hire song in leves° grene,   *leaves*
Right so the wordes that they spake yfeere°   *together*
1435 Delited hem, and made hire hertes clere.°   *bright*

But natheles,° the wendyng° of Criseyde,   *nevertheless / departing*
For al this world, may nat out° of his mynde,   *pass out*
For which ful ofte he pitously hire preyde
That of hire heste° he myghte hire trewe fynde,   *promise*
1440 And seyde hire, "Certes, if ye be unkynde,
And but° ye come at day set° into Troye,   *unless / the appointed day*
Ne shal I nevere have hele,° honour, ne joye.   *health*

"For also soth as sonne uprist o-morwe—
And God so wisly thow me, woful wrecche,
1445 To reste brynge⁶ out of this cruel sorwe!—
I wol myselven sle° if that ye drecche.°   *slay / delay*
But of my deeth though litel be to recche,°   *care about*
Yet, er that ye me causen so to smerte,°   *feel pain*
Dwelle° rather here, myn owen swete herte.   *Remain*

1450 "For trewely, myn owne lady deere,
Tho sleghtes° yet that I have herd yow stere°   *Those stratagems / propose*
Ful shaply° ben to faylen alle yfeere.°   *Very likely / together*
For thus men seyth 'That on thenketh the beere,°   *The bear thinks one thing*
But al another thenketh his ledere.'°   *leader, trainer*
1455 Youre syre° is wys; and seyd is,° out of drede,°   *father / it is said / doubtless*
'Men may the wise atrenne,° and naught atrede.'°   *outrun / outwit*

"It is ful hard to halten unespied°   *limp undetected*
Byfore a crepel,° for he kan° the craft;   *cripple / knows*
Youre fader is in sleght as Argus eyed;⁷
1460 For al be that his moeble° is hym biraft,°   *movable property / stolen*
His olde sleighte° is yet so with hym laft   *cunning*
Ye° shal nat blende° hym for youre wommanhede,   *That you / blind, deceive*
Ne feyne aright;° and that is al my drede.   *dissimulate successfully*

"I not° if pees shal evere mo bitide;°   *don't know / occur*
1465 But pees or no, for ernest ne for game,
I woot, syn Calkas on the Grekis syde

6. For as certainly as the sun rises up in the morning—and God, may you thus surely bring me,
woeful wretch, to rest.
7. Your father is provided with eyes like Argus in matters of deception. The giant Argus had a hundred
eyes.

142

"He will give you a husband among the Greeks, and he will show you that in being besieged there is fear of coming to an evil end. He will flatter you and make you honored by the Greeks, and he is revered there, as I understand, and his power is valued there greatly; therefore, not without distress, I fear that you will never return to Troy.

143

"And to think this is so grievous to me that I could not tell you about it, beautiful soul; and you alone have in your hands the key of my life and death, and I know that you can make the former wretched or sweet as it pleases you, O bright star by which I voyage to a gracious port; if you forsake me, remember that I shall die.

144

"Therefore, in God's name, let us find a way and a cause that you may not go, if it can be found. Let us go from here into another place, and let us not care if the king's promises become voided as long as we are able to flee his anger; far from here there are people who will be glad to see us and who will, besides, have us always for their lords.

Hath ones ben and lost so foule his name,[8]
He dar nomore come here ayeyn for shame;
For which that wey,° for aught I kan espie,°   *way, plan / see*
1470 To trusten on nys but a fantasie.

"Ye shal ek sen, youre fader shal yow glose°   *cajole*
To ben a wif; and as he kan wel preche,
He shal som Grek so preyse and wel alose°   *commend*
That ravysshen he shal yow with his speche,
1475 Or do yow don° by force as he shal teche;   *make you do*
And Troilus, of whom ye nyl han routhe,°   *won't have pity*
Shal causeles so sterven° in his trouthe!   *thus die*

"And over al this,° youre fader shal despise   *furthermore*
Us alle, and seyn this cite° nys but lorn,°   *city / lost*
1480 And that th'assege° nevere shal aryse,°   *siege / be lifted*
For-whi° the Grekis han it alle sworn,   *Because*
Til we be slayn and down oure walles torn.
And thus he shal yow with his wordes fere,°   *frighten*
That ay drede I that ye wol bleven° there.   *remain*

1485 "Ye shal ek seen so many a lusty knyght
Among the Grekis, ful of worthynesse,
And ech of hem with herte, wit, and myght
To plesen yow don al his bisynesse,°   *take every pain*
That ye shul dullen of the rudenesse°   *tire of the boorishness*
1490 Of us sely° Troians, but if routhe°   *simple / unless pity*
Remorde yow, or vertu of youre trouthe.[9]

"And this to me so grevous is to thynke
That fro my brest it wol my soule rende;°   *tear*
Ne dredeles,° in me ther may nat synke°   *doubtless / sink, be impressed*
1495 A good opynyoun,° if that ye wende,°   *expectation / depart*
For whi° youre fadres sleghte wol us shende.°   *Because / ruin*
And if ye gon, as I have told yow yore,°   *said to you long ago*
So thenk I n'am but ded, withoute more.

"For which, with humble, trewe, and pitous herte,
1500 A thousand tymes mercy I yow preye;
So rueth° on myn aspre° peynes smerte,   *have pity / bitter*
And doth somwhat as that I shal yow seye,
And lat us stele° awey bitwixe us tweye;°   *steal / we two together*
And thynk that folie is, whan man may chese,°   *one may choose*
1505 For accident his substaunce ay to lese.[1]

---

8. I know that, since Calchas has once gone over to the Greeks' side and lost his reputation so disgracefully.
9. Should cause you remorse, or the power of your fidelity.
1. Ever to lose his substance (the essential thing) for an accident (a mere attribute, inessential characteristic). The terms derive from elementary logic. Troilus goes on (line 1513) to play on the sense of *substaunce* as one's wealth; he also plays on the sense of *accident* as unfortunate occurrence, "uncertainty" as opposed to *sikernesse* (line 1512).

145

"So let us fly from here secretly, and let us go there together, you and I, and what time we have left to live in the world, heart of my body, let us live it together in delight. This I would wish, and this I desire if you agree to it, and this is safer, and every other course of action seems to me difficult."

146

Sighing, Criseida answered him, "My dear joy and delight of my heart, all those things could happen and even more, in the way which you have described; but I swear to you, by those arrows of love which entered my breast because of you, that commands, flatteries, or a husband will not ever turn my desire from you.

"I mene thus: that syn we mowe er° day   *can before*
Wel stele awey and ben togidere so,
What wit° were it to putten in assay,°   *cleverness / to the test*
In cas° ye sholden to youre fader go,   *In case, Assuming*
1510 If that° ye myghten come ayeyn or no?   *Whether*
Thus mene I: that it were a gret folie
To putte that sikernesse in jupertie.°   *certainty in jeopardy*

"And vulgarly to speken of substaunce
Of tresour,[2] may we bothe with us lede°   *bring*
1515 Inough to lyve in honour and plesaunce
Til into° tyme that we shal ben dede;   *Until*
And thus we may eschuen° al this drede.°   *avoid / uncertainty*
For everich other wey ye kan recorde,°   *bring to mind*
Myn herte, ywys, may therwith naught acorde.°   *agree*

1520 "And hardily, ne dredeth no poverte,°   *fear no poverty*
For I have kyn and frendes elleswhere
That, though we comen in oure bare sherte,°   *shirt*
Us sholde neyther lakken gold ne gere,[3]
But ben honured while we dwelten there.
1525 And go we anon;° for as in myn entente,°   *let's go forthwith / understanding*
This is the beste, if that ye wole assente."

Criseyde, with a sik,° right in this wise   *sigh*
Answerde, "Ywys, my deere herte trewe,
We may wel stele° awey, as ye devyse,°   *steal / propose*
1530 And fynden swich unthrifty weyes° newe,   *profitless ways*
But afterward ful soore it wol us rewe.°   *we will regret it*
And helpe me God so at my mooste nede,
As causeles° ye suffren al this drede!   *For no reason*

"For thilke° day that I for cherisynge°   *that same / cherishing*
1535 Or drede of fader, or for other wight,
Or for estat,° delit, or for weddynge,   *estate, status, wealth*
Be fals to yow, my Troilus, my knyght,
Saturnes doughter, Juno, thorugh hire myght,
As wood° as Athamante do° me dwelle   *mad / cause*
1540 Eternalich in Stix, the put° of helle![4]   *pit*

"And this on every god celestial
I swere it yow, and ek on ech goddesse,
On every nymphe and deite° infernal,   *deity*
On satiry and fawny more and lesse,[5]
1545 That halve goddes ben° of wildernesse;   *Who are demigods*

2. And to speak, in common parlance, of the "substance" of one's wealth.
3. Neither gold nor possessions would have to be lacking for us.
4. Juno persuaded the fury Tisiphone to haunt Athamas and drive him mad. Though the Styx is usually a river or marsh in the underworld, in some medieval accounts it was a pit.
5. (I swear) by greater and lesser satyrs and fauns.

147

"But what you said about going away is not, it seems to me, wise advice. One must take thought in these grave times, and you should take care of yourself and yours. If we went away from here, as you were saying, you could see three dire things: one would come from broken faith which brings more ill than others believe.

148

"And this would be perilous to your relatives, for seeing themselves left because of a woman without your aid and counsel, they would make others afraid of betrayals. And, if I consider rightly, you would be much blamed for it, nor would the truth about you ever be believed by anyone who had seen only this act.

149

"And if any time demands faith or loyalty, it seems to be the time of war, since no one has so much power that he can long stand by himself alone. Many join together in the hope that what they give for others may be given for them, since, if they put their trust in property and person, then they lose hope.

150

"On the other hand, what do you think would be said among the people about your departure? They would not say that love with his hot darts had led you to such a course, but fear and baseness. Therefore keep yourself from such a thought, should it ever enter your heart, if your reputation, which rings so clearly with your valor, is at all dear to you.

151

"Then think how much my honor and my chastity, held in the highest, would be stained with infamy, would even be completely undone and lost to me; and they would never be raised up again by any excuse or by any power which I would be able to use, whatever I should do, if I were to remain alive a hundred thousand years.

And Attropos[6] my thred of lif tobreste°   *may (you) burst, cut*
If I be fals! Now trowe° me if yow leste!°   *believe / it please you*

"And thow, Symois, that as an arwe clere°   *clear*
Thorugh Troie rennest° downward to the se,°   *run / sea*
1550 Ber witnesse of this word that seyd is here:[7]
That thilke° day that ich untrewe be   *that same*
To Troilus, myn owene herte fre,°   *noble beloved*
That thow retourne bakward to thi welle,°   *source*
And I with body and soule synke in helle!

1555 "But that ye speke,° awey thus for to go   *insofar as you suggest*
And leten° alle youre frendes, God forbede°   *abandon / forbid*
For° any womman that ye sholden so,°   *For the sake of / do so*
And namely syn° Troie hath now swich° nede   *especially since / such*
Of help. And ek of o° thyng taketh hede: *one*
1560 If this were wist,° my lif lay° in balaunce,   *known / would lie*
And youre honour; God shilde° us fro meschaunce!°   *shield / misfortune*

"And if so be that pees heere-after take,°   *take place (?), take effect (?)*
As alday happeth° after anger game,°   *regularly occurs / pleasantness*
Whi, Lord, the sorwe and wo ye wolden make,
1565 That ye ne dorste come ayeyn° for shame!   *would dare not come back*
And er that ye juparten° so youre name,   *put in jeopardy*
Beth naught to hastif in this hoote fare,°   *rash conduct*
For hastif man ne wanteth° nevere care.   *lacks*

"What trowe ye° the peple ek al aboute *to read*   *do you think*
1570 Wolde of it seye? It is ful light t'arede.°   *easy to suppose*
They wolden seye, and swere it out of doute,°   *beyond a doubt*
That love ne drof° yow naught to don this dede,   *drove*
But lust voluptuous and coward drede.°   *cowardly fear*
Thus were al lost, ywys,° myn herte deere,   *for certain*
1575 Youre honour, which that now shyneth so clere.

"And also thynketh on myn honeste,°   *reputation for decency*
That floureth° yet, how foule° I sholde it shende,^   *flourishes / vilely / destroy*
And with what filthe it spotted sholde be,
If in this forme° I sholde with yow wende.°   *manner / depart*

---

6. See line 1208 and accompanying note above.
7. Using the traditional figure of the "impossible," Criseyde calls to witness the river Simois that, if she should be untrue to Troilus, the river would run backward to its source, and that she would descend to hell, body and soul.

152

"And beside this I wish you to consider carefully what happens in almost every case. There is nothing so vile that does not, if it is guarded well, make itself painfully desired, and the more you yearn to possess it, the sooner loathing comes into your heart if full power of seeing it is given to you, and also of keeping it.

153

"Our love, which pleases you so much, does so because it is necessary for you to act furtively and to seldom come to this peace. But if you will possess me freely, soon the burning torch will be extinguished which now enkindles you and me likewise. For if we wish our love to last, as we now do, it must always be stolen.

154

"Therefore take comfort, and by turning your back on Fortune, vanquish her and tire her out. No person in whom she might find a free soul was ever a subject to her. Let us follow her course. In the meantime make up some journey and lessen your sighs undertaking that, for on the tenth day I will make my return here without fail."

155

"If you," said Troilo then, "are here on the tenth day, I am content. But in the meantime from whom will my sorrowful sighs have any relief? I cannot now, as you know, pass an hour without great torment if I do not see you; how can I pass ten days until you return?

156

"Ah, for God's sake, find a way to remain; ah, do not go if you see any way. I know you are quick-witted, if I understand correctly what I hear from you, and if you love me, you can see clearly that I am all consumed with this thought only, namely, that you are going away from here; and if you go, you can see what my life will be then."

1580 Ne though I lyved unto the werldes ende,
My name sholde I nevere ayeynward wynne;°   win back
Thus were I lost, and that were routhe° and synne.   a pity

"And forthi sle° with resoun al this hete!°   slay / heat, impetuousness
Men seyn, 'The suffrant° overcomith,' parde;°   patient one / by God
1585 Ek 'Whoso wol han lief,° he lief moot lete.'°   a dear thing / must give up
Thus maketh vertu of necessite
By pacience, and thynk that lord is he
Of Fortune ay° that naught wole of hire recche,°   always / be concerned
And she ne daunteth no wight but a wrecche.

1590 "And trusteth this: that certes, herte swete,
Er Phebus suster, Lucina the sheene,
The Leoun passe out of this Ariete,⁸
I wol ben here, withouten any wene.°   doubt
I mene, as helpe me Juno, hevenes quene,
1595 The tenthe day, but if that deth m'assaile,°   unless death should attack me
I wol yow sen withouten any faille."°   without fail

"And now, so° this be soth," quod Troilus,   as long as
"I shal wel suffre unto° the tenthe day,   be patient until
Syn that I se that nede it mot be° thus.   it must needs be
1600 But for the love of God, if it be may,°   may be
So late us stelen priveliche° away;   steal secretly
For evere in oon,° as for to lyve in reste,   For always
Myn herte seyth that it wol be the beste."

8. Before Phoebus's (the sun's) sister, the bright Lucina (the moon), may pass out of the zodiacal sign Aries (the Ram), in which it now is, and through the three intermediate signs (Taurus, Gemini, Cancer) to a position beyond the Lion (Leo), Criseyde intends to be back in Troy. As the moon makes its circuit of the skies every twenty-eight days, its passing by four and more of the twelve signs of the zodiac would be some ten days.

157

"Ah me," said Criseida, "you slay me, and more than you know, you give me too much sadness, for I see that you do not trust my promise as much as I thought. Ah my dear sweet, why are you so mistrustful? Why do you take from yourself the power over yourself? Who would believe that a man so strong in arms could not endure ten days' waiting?

158

"I believe it may be far better to take the course of action that I have told you of. Be content with it, my sweet lord, and take it for certain in your breast that the spirit in my heart weeps at my removal from your sweet sight, perhaps more than you believe or think; I feel it strongly through all my senses.

159

"To spend time is useful sometimes to gain time, my soul. I am not, as you contend, taken from you because I am given back to my father. And do not insist in your heart that I am so stupid that I do not know how to find both the means and the way to return to you, whom I desire more than my life and whom I love far too much.

160

"And so, I pray you, if my prayer avails, both by the great love which you bear for me and by that which I bear for you, which is just as much, that you comfort yourself in regard to this departure, since, if you were to know how much it hurts me to see the tears and the strong sighs which you give vent to, it would cause you regret, and it would grieve you to make so many.

not worthy dishonored life

"O mercy, God, what lif is this?" quod she.
1605 "Allas, ye sle° me thus for verray tene!°   slay / vexation
I se wel now that ye mystrusten me,
For by youre wordes it is wel yseene.
Now for the love of Cinthia the sheene,°   the bright Cynthia, the moon
Mistrust me nought thus causeles, for routhe,°   without cause, for pity
1610 Syn to be trewe I have yow plight my trouthe.°   pledged my truthfulness

"And thynketh wel that somtyme it is wit
To spende a tyme, a tyme for to wynne;°   acquire
Ne, parde, lorn° am I naught fro yow yit,   lost
Though that we ben a day or two atwynne.°   separated
1615 Drif out the fantasies yow withinne,
And trusteth me, and leveth ek° youre sorwe,   also abandon
Or here my trouthe:° I wol naught lyve tyl morwe.° hear my pledge / morning

"For if ye wiste how soore° it doth me smerte,°   sorely / pain
Ye wolde cesse of this; for, God, thow wost,
1620 The pure° spirit wepeth in myn herte   very
To se yow wepen that° I love most,   weep whom
And that I mot° gon to the Grekis oost.   must
Ye, nere it that I wiste° remedie   were it not that I knew
To come ayeyn, right here I wolde dye!

1625 "But certes,° I am naught so nyce° a wight   surely / foolish
That I ne kan ymaginen a wey
To come ayeyn that day that I have hight.°   promised
For who may holde a thing that wol awey?°   wishes (to fly) away
My fader naught, for al his queynte° pley!   clever
1630 And by my thrift,° my wendyng° out of Troie   as I may prosper / going
Another day shal torne us alle to joie.

"Forthi° with al myn herte I yow biseke,   Therefore
If that yow list don ought for my preyere,⁹
And for that love which that° I love yow eke,   with which
1635 That er that I departe fro yow here,
That of so good a confort and a cheere

9. If it pleases you to do anything in response to my entreaty.

161

"For you in joy and in delight I hope to live and to return quickly and to find a way to your desire and mine. Do bring it about that I may see you composed in such a way, before I depart from you, that I may have no more sorrow than that which a too ardent love has placed in my mind. Do this, I pray you, my sweet repose.

162

"And I pray you, while I am afar, that you do not let yourself be taken by pleasure for any woman or by any extraordinary beauty, for if I should know of it, you must take it for certain that I would kill myself like an insane woman, complaining of you who, breaking the bounds of propriety, would leave me for another, you who know that I love you more than a man might ever love a woman."

163

To this last part Troilo answered sighing, "If I wished to do this which you now touch on with suspicion, I cannot see how I ever could, because love for you has seized me so strongly through loving. Nor can I see how this love which I bear you can cease during life, and I shall explain to you the reason in a few words.

164

"Beauty, which will often ensnare others, did not impel me to love you; gentle breeding, which will catch the desire of the noble, did not draw me to love you; nor yet did grace, nor wealth—in all of which you are more abundant than any other lady given to love ever might be—make me feel love for you in my heart.

I may yow sen that ye may brynge at reste
Myn herte, which that is o poynt to breste.°   *at the point of bursting*

"And over al this I prey yow," quod she tho,
1640 "Myn owene hertes sothfast° suffisaunce,   *true, steadfast*
Syn I am thyn al hol,° withouten mo,°   *whole / more*
That whil that I am absent, no plesaunce
Of oother do me° fro youre remembraunce;   *Of others cause me (to pass)*
For I am evere agast,° forwhy men rede°   *terrified / whence they say*
1645 That love is thyng ay ful of bisy drede.°   *anxious fear*

"For in this world ther lyveth lady non,
If that ye were untrewe—as God defende!—°   *may God forbid it*
That so bitraised° were or wo-bigon   *betrayed*
As I, that alle trouthe in yow entende,°   *perceive*
1650 And douteles, if that ich other wende,°   *supposed otherwise*
I ner but° ded; and er° ye cause fynde,   *would only be / before*
For Goddes love, so beth me naught° unkynde!"   *don't be to me*

To this answerde Troilus and seyde,
"Now God, to whom ther nys no cause ywrye,°   *hidden*
1655 Me glade,° as wys° I nevere unto Criseyde,   *gladden / surely*
Syn thilke° day I saugh hire first with yë,°   *that same / eye*
Was fals, ne nevere shal° til that I dye.   *shall be*
At shorte wordes,° wel ye may me leve.°   *In short / believe*
I kan na more; it shal be founde at preve."°   *when put to the test*

1660 "Grant mercy,° goode myn, iwys!" quod she,   *Great thanks*
"And blisful Venus lat me nevere sterve°   *die*
Er I may stonde of plesaunce in degree°   *in so happy a situation*
To quyte° hym wel that so wel kan deserve;   *requite*
And while that God my wit wol me conserve,°   *preserve for me*
1665 I shal so don, so trewe I have yow founde,
That ay honour to me-ward° shal rebounde.°   *toward me / return*

"For trusteth wel that youre estat roial,
Ne veyn delit, nor only° worthinesse   *the unique*
Of yow in werre° or torney marcial,°   *war / martial tourney*
1670 Ne pompe, array, nobleye,° or ek richesse°   *nobility / also wealth*
Ne made me to rewe° on youre destresse,   *pity*
But moral vertu, grounded upon trouthe—
That was the cause I first hadde on yow routhe!°   *pity*

165

"But your high and noble acts, your excellence and your courtly speech, your manners more well-bred than any other lady's, and your charming ladylike disdain, by which every vulgar appetite and action seemed to be base to you, have put you with love in my mind. Such are you to me, O my sovereign lady.

166

"And the years cannot take away these things with fickle Fortune; and so with more anguish and greater suffering I hope in my desire to have you always. Ah me, alas! what will be the redemption for my loss if you go away, my sweet love? Certainly none, if not death at last; this alone will be the end of my woes."

167

After they had talked much and wept together, as dawn was already near, they left off that and embraced one another closely. But when the cocks had long crowed, after fully a thousand kisses, each arose, the one commending himself to the other, and thus they separated weeping.

"Eke gentil° herte and manhod that ye hadde,   noble
1675 And that ye hadde, as me thoughte, in despit°   scorn
Every thyng that souned into° badde,   tended toward
As rudenesse and poeplissh appetit,°   vulgar desire
And that youre resoun bridlede° youre delit,°   reined in / pleasure
This made, aboven every creature,
1680 That I was youre, and shal° while I may dure.°   shall be / live

"And this may lengthe of yeres naught fordo,°   destroy
Ne remuable° Fortune deface.   changeable
But Juppiter, that of his myght may do°   cause
The sorwful to be glad, so yeve° us grace   give
1685 Or° nyghtes ten to meten in this place,   Before
So that it may youre herte and myn suffise!
And fareth now wel, for tyme is that ye rise."

And after that they longe ypleyned hadde,
And ofte ykist, and streite° in armes folde,°   tightly / embraced
1690 The day gan rise, and Troilus hym cladde,°   clothed himself
And rewfullich° his lady gan byholde,   piteously
As he that felte dethes cares colde,
And to hire grace he gan hym recomaunde.
Wher hym was wo, this holde I no demaunde.[1]

1695 For mannes hed ymagynen ne kan,
N'entendement° considere, ne tonge telle   Nor understanding
The cruele peynes of this sorwful man,
That passen° every torment down in helle.   Which surpass
For whan he saugh that she ne myghte dwelle,
1700 Which that his soule out of his herte rente,°   tore
Withouten more out of the chaumbre he wente.

Explicit liber quartus.[2]

Book Five

Incipit liber quintus.°   Here begins the fifth book

Aprochen gan the fatal destyne
That Joves° hath in disposicioun,°   Jupiter / at his disposal
And to yow, angry Parcas, sustren thre,
Committeth to don execucioun;[1]
5 For which Criseyde moste out° of the town,   must go out
Troilus shal dwellen forth in pyne°   torment
Til Lachesis his thred no lenger twyne.°   may spin no longer

1. Whether he was sorrowful, I consider this no question.
2. Here ends the fourth book.
1. And to you, angry Parcae, sisters three, (Jupiter) entrusts the task of executing (the fatal destiny). The Parcae are the three Fates. Lachesis (line 7) is usually the Fate who measures out the thread of life, while Clotho spins it.

Part Five

Here begins the fifth part of the "Filostrato," in which Criseida is given back. Troilo accompanies her, returns to Troy, weeps alone and afterwards with Pandaro, through whose counsel they go to spend some days with Sarpedon. They return to Troy, where each place reminds Troilo of Criseida, and to mitigate his sorrows, he sings of them, waiting until the tenth day passes. And first of all to Diomede is given back Criseida whom Troilo accompanies as far as the outside of the city, and having parted from him, she is joyfully received by her father.

1

That same day Diomede was there for the purpose of giving Antenor to the Trojans; therefore Priam gave to him Criseida, so full of sighs, of tears, and of sorrow that it causes anyone who sees her grief. On the other side was her lover, in such sadness that no one ever saw the like.

2

It is true that with great force he marvelously concealed within his sad breast the great battle which he had with sighs and tears, and in his face little or nothing yet appeared, though he looked forward to being alone and then to weeping and to lamenting and to venting himself at great length.

3

O how many things came to his noble mind when he saw Criseida given to her father! Likewise, raging all over with anger and suffering, he was consumed and said softly, "O sorrowing wretch, now what do I wait for? Is it not better to die at once than to live and languish ever in tears?

4

"Why do I not break up these pacts with arms? Why do I not kill Diomede here? Why do I not cut down the old man who has made them? Why do I not defy all my brothers? Would that they were now all destroyed! Why do I not set Troy in lamentation and in sorrowing outcry? Why do I not ravish Criseida now and heal myself?

The gold-tressed Phebus heighe on-lofte[2]
Thries° hadde alle with his bemes cleene°
10 The snowes molte,° and Zepherus° as ofte
Ibrought ayeyn° the tendre leves grene,
Syn° that the sone of Ecuba° the queene
Bigan to love hire first for whom his sorwe
Was al, that she departe sholde a-morwe.°

15 Ful redy was at prime° Diomede   *about 6 to 9 A.M.*
Criseyde unto the Grekis oost° to lede,   *host*
For sorwe of which she felt hire herte blede,
As she° that nyste what was best to rede.°   *Like a woman / advise*
And trewely, as men in bokes rede,
20 Men wiste nevere womman han the care,°   *to have (such) distress*
Ne was so loth° out of a town to fare.°   *loath, reluctant / go*

This Troilus, withouten reed or loore,°   *counsel or instruction*
As man that hath his joies ek forlore,°   *wholly lost*
Was waytyng° on his lady evere more   *attending*
25 As she that was the sothfast crop and more°   *foliage and root, i.e., entirety*
Of al his lust° or joies heretofore.   *desire*
But Troilus, now far-wel al thi joie,
For shaltow nevere sen hire eft° in Troie!   *again*

Soth is that while he bood° in this manere,   *waited*
30 He gan his wo ful manly for to hide,
That wel unnethe° it sene was in his chere;°   *scarcely / face*
But at the yate° ther she sholde° out ride,   *gate / had (to)*
With certeyn folk he hoved° hire t'abide,°   *lingered / wait*
So wo-bigon, al° wolde he naught hym pleyne,   *although*
35 That on his hors unnethe he sat for peyne.

For ire° he quook,° so gan his herte gnawe,°   *anger / quaked / consume itself*
Whan Diomede on horse gan hym dresse,°   *mount*
And seyde to hymself this ilke sawe:°   *same speech*
"Allas," quod he, "thus foul a wrecchednesse,
40 Whi suffre ich it? Whi nyl ich it redresse?°   *set it right*
Were it nat bet atones° for to dye   *at once*
Than evere more in langour thus to drye?°   *suffer*

"Whi nyl I make atones riche and poro
To have inough to doone er that she go?[3]
45 Why nyl I brynge al Troie upon a roore?°   *uproar*

2. The golden-haired Phoebus (the sun) high aloft. The elaborate marking of time lets us know that
    we are in spring of the third year of the lovers' affair.
3. Why won't I at once make rich and poor alike (i.e., everyone) have enough to do (in defending
    themselves from me) before she would go.

5

"Who will forbid it, if I shall indeed want to do it? Why do I not approach the Greeks and see if they might wish to give Criseida to me? Ah, why do I wait longer, why not run there at once and make them give her to me?" But fear lest Criseida might be killed in such an attempt made him give up so bold and daring a plan.

6

When Criseida saw that, sorrowful though she was, she must depart with the company which had to leave, she mounted her horse and began to say to herself angrily, "Ah, cruel Jove and grievous Fortune, where do you bear me from here against my will? Why is my sorrow so pleasing to you?

7

"Cruel and pitiless, you take me away from the pleasure which was dearest to my heart. Perhaps you believe I will humbly present you with a sacrifice or honor, but you are deceived: I shall always sorrow to your vituperation and dishonor until I return to see again the fair face of Troilo."

8

Here she turned herself disdainfully to Diomede and said, "Let us go from here now; we have shown ourselves long enough to these people who can now hope for a remedy for their woes if they consider carefully the honorable exchange which you have made, who have given up for a woman so great and so feared a king."

9

And this said, she gave spurs to her horse without saying anything except farewell to her servants. And the king and his barons clearly recognized the lady's scorn. Forth she went without listening to leave-taking or speeches or looking at anyone, and she departed from Troy, destined nevermore to return there or to be with Troilo.

10

By way of courtesy Troilo, with many companions, mounted his horse with a falcon on his fist and accompanied her outside the walls and willingly would have gone all the way even to her lodging, but it would have been too open and also would have been considered indiscreet.

Whi nyl I slen° this Diomede also?   *slay*
Why nyl I rather with a man or two
Stele° hire away? Whi wol I this endure?   *steal*
Whi nyl I helpen to myn owen cure?"°   *remedy, relief*

50 But why he nolde don so fel° a dede,   *violent*
But shal I seyn, and whi hym liste it spare:°   *it pleased him to hold off*
He hadde in herte alweyes a manere° drede   *kind of*
Lest that Criseyde, in rumour of this fare,°   *the tumult of this activity*
Sholde han ben slayn; lo, this was al his care.
55 And ellis,° certeyn, as I seyde yore,°   *otherwise / earlier*
He hadde it don,° withouten wordes more.   *He would have done it*

Criseyde, whan she redy was to ride,
Ful sorwfully she sighte,° and seyde "Allas!"   *sighed*
But forth she moot,° for aught that may bitide;°   *had to go / happen*
60 Ther is non other remedie in this cas.
And forth she rit° ful sorwfully a pas.°   *rides / at a walk*
What wonder is, though that hire sore smerte,°   *it pained her sorely*
Whan she forgoth hire owen swete herte?

This Troilus, in wise° of curteysie,   *the manner*
65 With hauk on honde° and with an huge route°   *a hawk on his fist / crowd*
Of knyghtes, rood and did° hire companye,   *kept*
Passyng al the valeye fer withoute,

11

Antenor, surrendered by the Greeks, had already come among them, and the young Trojans had received him with great rejoicing and honor; and although this return was very painful to Troilo's heart because of Criseida's surrender, still he received him with a good face and made him ride before him with Pandaro.

12

And being already about to take leave, he and Criseida stopped a moment and they gazed into one another's eyes, and the lady could not restrain her tears. And then they took each other by the right hand and toward her Troilo then drew so near that she could hear him speaking softly, and he said, "Return, do not make me die."

13

And without anything further, having turned his steed, with his face all overcast, he said nothing to Diomede. And of such action Diomede alone took note and saw well the love between the two, and in his thoughts he established it with various reasonings. And while he whispered to himself about this, he was secretly taken with her.

And ferther wolde han riden, out of doute,
Ful fayn,° and wo was hym to gon so sone;°
70 But torne he moste, and it was ek to done.⁴

And right with that was Antenor ycome
Out of the Grekis oost,° and every wight   *host*
Was of it glad, and seyde he was welcome.
And Troilus, al nere his herte° light,   *though his heart was not*
75 He peyned hym° with al his fulle myght   *took pains*
Hym to withholde of wepyng atte leeste,°   *at the least*
And Antenor he kiste and made feste.°   *greeted warmly*

And therwithal he moste° his leve take,   *was obliged*
And caste his eye upon hire pitously,
80 And neer° he rood, his cause for to make,°   *nearer / plead*
To take hire by the honde al sobrely.
And Lord, so she gan wepen tendrely!
And he ful softe and sleighly° gan hire seye,   *secretly*
"Now holde youre day,° and do° me nat to   *keep your appointment / cause*
    deye."

85 With that his courser torned he aboute
With face pale, and unto Diomede
No word he spak, ne non of al his route;°   *company*
Of which the sone of Tideus° took hede,   *Diomede's father*
As he that koude more than the crede⁵
90 In swich a craft, and by the reyne hire hente;°   *took her by the reins*
And Troilus to Troie homward he wente.

This Diomede, that ledde hire by the bridel,
Whan that he saugh the folk of Troie aweye,
Thoughte, "Al my labour shal nat ben on ydel,°   *in vain*
95 If that I may, for somwhat shal I seye,
For at the werste° it may yet shorte oure weye.°   *worst / shorten our journey*
I have herd seyd ek tymes twyes° twelve,   *twice*
'He is a fool that wol foryete hymselve.' "°   *ignore his own advantage*

But natheles,° this thoughte he wel ynough,   *nevertheless*
100 That "Certeynlich I am aboute nought,°   *I am acting pointlessly*
If that I speke of love or make it tough;°   *behave too forwardly*
For douteles, if she have in hire thought
Hym that I gesse, he may nat ben ybrought
So soon awey; but I shal fynde a meene°   *means*
105 That she naught wite° as yet shal what I mene."   *will not know*

This Diomede, as he that koude his good,°   *knew what was best for him*
Whan tyme was, gan fallen forth in speche
Of this and that, and axed° whi she stood   *asked*
In swich disese,° and gan hire ek biseche   *distress*
110 That if that he encresse myghte or eche°   *might increase or augment*

4. But he had to turn back, and also it had to be done.
5. Like one who knew more than the creed, i.e., the fundamentals.

With any thyng hire ese,° that she sholde   *comfort*
Comaunde it hym, and seyde° he don it wolde.   *(he) said*

For treweliche he swor hire as a knyght
That ther nas thyng° with which he myghte hire plese,   *was nothing*
115 That he nolde don his peyne° and al his myght   *expend his effort*
To don it, for to don° hire herte an ese;   *bring*
And preyede hire she wolde hire sorwe apese,°   *assuage*
And seyde, "Iwis,° we Grekis kan have joie   *Certainly*
To honouren° yow as wel as folk of Troie."   *In honoring*

120 He seyde ek thus: "I woot yow thynketh straunge—
Ne wonder is, for it is to yow newe—
Th'aquayntaunce of thise Troianis to chaunge°   *exchange*
For folk of Grece, that ye nevere knewe.
But wolde nevere God but if° as trewe   *but that*
125 A Grek ye sholde among us alle fynde
As any Troian is, and ek as kynde.

"And by the cause° I swor yow right, lo, now,   *because*
To ben youre frend, and helply,° to my myght,   *helpful*
And for that° more aquayntaunce ek of yow   *because*
130 Have ich had than another straunger wight,°   *foreign person*
So fro this forth,° I pray yow, day and nyght   *this time forth*
Comaundeth me, how soore that me smerte,°   *however sorely it may pain me*
To don al that may like° unto youre herte;   *be pleasing*

"And that ye me wolde as youre brother trete,°   *treat*
135 And taketh naught my frendshipe in despit;°   *scornfully*
And though youre sorwes be for thynges grete—
Not I nat whi—but out of more respit[6]
Myn herte hath for t'amende it gret delit;
And if I may youre harmes nat redresse,°   *set right*
140 I am right sory for youre hevynesse,°   *sorrow*

"For though ye Troians with us Grekes wrothe°   *angry*
Han many a day ben, alwey yet, parde,°   *by God*
O° god of Love in soth° we serven bothe.   *One / truth*
And for the love of God, my lady fre,°   *noble*
145 Whomso° ye hate, as beth nat wroth with me,   *Whomever*
For trewely, ther kan no wyght yow serve
That half so loth° youre wratthe wold disserve.°   *loath, reluctantly / deserve*

"And nere it° that we ben so neigh° the tente   *were it not / near*
Of Calcas, which that° sen us bothe may,   *who*
150 I wolde of this yow telle al myn entente—°   *meaning, intentions*
But this enseled° til anothir day.   *this is sealed up*
Yeve° me youre hond; I am, and shal ben ay,°   *Give / ever*
God helpe me so, while that my lyf may dure,°   *last*
Youre owene aboven every creature.

---

6. I don't know why—but without further delay.

14

Her father received her with great rejoicing, although such love weighed heavy on her. She remained silent and shy, wholly consuming herself with heavy sorrow and in a wretched state, still having her heart fixed on Troilo, which was soon to change and to forsake him for a new lover.

155 "Thus seyde I nevere er° now to womman born,   *before*
    For God myn herte as wisly glade° so,   *may (God) surely gladden*
    I loved never womman here-biforn
    As paramours, ne nevere shal no mo.[7]
    And for the love of God, beth nat my fo,
160 Al kan I naught to yow, my lady deere,
    Compleyne aright, for I am yet to leere.°   *to be taught*

    "And wondreth nought, myn owen lady bright,
    Though that I speke of love to yow thus blyve;°   *quickly*
    For I have herd er this of many a wight,
165 Hath loved thyng he nevere saigh his lyve.°   *saw in his life*
    Ek° I am nat of power for to stryve   *Also*
    Ayeyns° the god of Love, but hym obeye   *Against*
    I wole alwey; and mercy I yow preye.

    "Ther ben so° worthi knyghtes in this place,   *such*
170 And ye so fayr, that everich of hem alle
    Wol peynen hym° to stonden in youre grace.   *take pains*
    But myghte me so faire a grace falle,[8]
    That ye me for youre servant wolde calle,
    So lowely° ne so trewely yow serve   *humbly*
175 Nil non of hem° as I shal til I sterve."°   *None of them will / die*

    Criseyde unto that purpos lite° answerde,   *on this subject little*
    As she that° was with sorwe oppressed so   *Like a woman who*
    That, in effect, she naught his tales herde
    But here and ther, now here a word or two.
180 Hire thoughte° hire sorwful herte brast° a-two,   *It seemed to her / burst*
    For whan she gan hire fader fer espie°   *see far off*
    Wel neigh° down of hire hors she gan to sye.°   *nigh / sink*

    But natheles° she thonketh Diomede   *nevertheless*
    Of al his travaile° and his goode cheere,°   *effort / demeanor*
185 And that hym list° his frendshipe hire to bede;°   *it pleased him / offer*
    And she accepteth it in good manere,
    And wol do fayn° that is hym lief° and dere,   *gladly / pleasing*
    And tristen° hym she wolde, and wel she myghte,   *trust*
    As seyde she; and from hire hors sh'alighte.°   *dismounted*

190 Hire fader hath hire in his armes nome,°   *taken*
    And twenty tyme he kiste his doughter sweete,
    And seyde, "O deere doughter myn, welcome!"
    She seyde ek she was fayn° with hym to mete,   *glad*
    And stood forth muwet,° milde, and mansuete.°   *mute / meek*
195 But here I leve hire with hire fader dwelle,
    And forth I wol of Troilus yow telle.

---

7. By way of passionate love, nor shall I ever any more (i.e., love any other woman).
8. But should so lovely a favor befall me.

Troilo, having returned to Troy, sighs and weeps, and grieving he recalls the delights enjoyed with Criseida.

15

Troilo returned to Troy, sad and distressed as much as anyone ever was, and wrathful and impassioned in countenance, he did not stop before he reached his palace. Dismounting there, very much more thoughtful than he had ever been before, he allowed no one to say anything to him but entered his room alone.

16

There he gave free vent to the grief which he had restrained, calling on death, and he kept on weeping for his happiness, which seemed to him lost, and crying out so strongly that he was afraid of being heard by those who were going about through the courtyard. And he remained the whole day in such weeping that neither servant nor friend saw him.

17

If the day was passed in grief, the night, already dark, did not lessen it, but his weeping and his great sorrow were redoubled; thus did his misfortune control him. He cursed the day that he was born and the gods and goddesses and Nature and his father and those who had given their word that Criseida would be surrendered.

18

He also cursed himself that he had let her so depart and that he had not carried out the alternative that he had favored, that is, to want to fly with her, and bitterly he repented this, and he wished to die of sorrow for it, or because he had not at least asked for her, since she might perhaps have been given to him.

19

And turning himself in his bed, now here and now there without finding a resting place, he said to himself sometimes weeping, "What a night this is, when I compare it to the night that is past, if I think of the hour it is now! Now I kissed the white breast, the mouth, the eyes, and the lovely face of my lady and closely embraced her.

20

"She was kissing me, and we had a glad and gracious good time talking. Now I find myself alone, alas, and weeping, in fear whether such a joyous night is destined ever to come again. Now I keep embracing the pillow, and I feel the amorous flame growing greater, and hope growing less through the grief which overcomes it.

To Troie is come this woful Troilus,
In sorwe aboven alle sorwes smerte,°   *painful*
With feloun° look and face dispitous.°   *hostile / cruel*
200 Tho sodeynly° doun from his hors he sterte,°   *Then suddenly / leapt*
And thorugh his paleis,° with a swollen herte,   *palace*
To chaumbre he wente; of nothyng took he hede,°   *heed*
Ne non to hym dar speke a word for drede.

And ther his sorwes that he spared° hadde   *restrained*
205 He yaf an issue large,° and "Deth!" he criede;   *gave full vent to*
And in his throwes frenetik° and madde   *frantic throes*
He corseth Jove, Appollo, and ek Cupide;
He corseth Ceres, Bacus, and Cipride,⁹
His burthe, hymself, his fate, and ek nature,
210 And, save° his lady, every creature.   *except for*

To bedde he goth, and walwith° ther and torneth   *wallows*
In furie, as doth he Ixion in helle,¹
And in this wise° he neigh° til day sojorneth.°   *state / near / remains*
But tho° bigan his herte a lite unswelle   *then*
215 Thorugh teris, which that gonnen up to welle,°   *to well up*
And pitously he cryde upon Criseyde,
And to hymself right thus he spak, and seyde,

"Wher is myn owene lady, lief° and deere?   *beloved*
Wher is hire white brest? Wher is it, where?

9. Ceres (goddess of agriculture), Bacchus (god of wine), and *Cipride*, i.e., Venus (goddess of Love),
were commonly associated in a saying as old as the playwright Terence (second century B.C.E.),
that "without Ceres and Bacchus, Venus is cold."
1. Jupiter had Ixion chained to an eternally revolving wheel in the underworld.

21

"What shall I do then, sorrowing wretch? I shall wait, provided that I can do so. But if my mind is thus saddened by her departure, how do I hope to be able to persevere? He who loves well has no power at all to rest." For that reason he did the same thing the following night and the day that passed before it.

220 Wher ben hire armes and hire eyen cleere
That yesternyght this tyme° with me were?   *at this time last night*
Now may I wepe allone many a teere,
And graspe° aboute I may, but in this place,   *grope*
Save a pilowe, I fynde naught t'enbrace.

225 "How shal I do? Whan shal she come ayeyn?°   *again, back*
I not,° allas, whi lete ich hire to go;   *don't know*
As wolde God ich hadde as tho ben sleyn!
O herte myn, Criseyde, O swete fo!°   *sweet enemy*
O lady myn, that I love and na mo,°   *no others*
230 To whom for evermo myn herte I dowe,°   *endow, grant*
Se how I dey, ye nyl° me nat rescowe!°   *if you will / rescue*

"Who seth yow now, my righte lode-sterre?°   *guiding star*
Who sit° right now or stant° in youre presence?   *sits / stands*
Who kan conforten now youre hertes werre?°   *war, disturbance*
235 Now I am gon, whom yeve ye° audience?   *do you give*
Who speketh for me right now in myn absence?
Allas, no wight; and that is al my care,
For wel woot I, as yvele as I ye fare.°   *you're doing as badly as I am*

"How sholde I thus ten dayes ful endure,
240 Whan I the firste nyght have al this tene?°   *affliction*
How shal she don ek, sorwful creature?
For tendernesse, how shal she sustene°   *sustain, endure*
Swich wo for me? O pitous, pale, grene°   *with a greenish pallor*
Shal ben youre fresshe, wommanliche face
245 For langour, er ye torne° unto this place."   *before you return*

And whan he fil in any slomberynges,
Anon° bygynne he sholde° for to grone   *Immediately / would*
And dremen of the dredefulleste thynges
That myghte ben; as mete° he were allone   *such as to dream*
250 In place horrible makyng ay his mone,°   *moan, complaint*
Or meten° that he was amonges alle   *dream*
His enemys, and in hire° hondes falle.   *their*

And therwithal his body sholde sterte,°   *would start, move suddenly*
And with the stert al sodeynliche awake,
255 And swich a tremour fele aboute his herte
That of the fere° his body sholde° quake;   *fear / would*
And therwithal he sholde a noyse make,
And seme as though he sholde falle depe
From heighe o-lofte;° and thanne he wolde wepe,   *from high aloft*

260 And rewen° on hymself so pitously   *have pity*
That wonder was to here his fantasie.°   *hear his imaginings*
Another tyme he sholde myghtyly
Conforte hymself, and sein° it was folie   *say*
So causeles swich drede for to drye;°   *suffer*
265 And eft° bygynne his aspre° sorwes newe,   *again / bitter*
That° every man myght on his sorwes rewe.°   *So that / take pity*

Sorrowing, Troilo relates what kind of night he had had to Pandaro, who reprimands him and encourages him to go away somewhere.

22

Neither Pandaro nor any other was able to come to him that day; so, when morning came, Troilo had him called at once, so that he could relieve his wretched heart by speaking of Criseida. Pandaro came there and had truly guessed what he had done that night and also what he desired.

23

"O my Pandaro," said Troilo, hoarse from his crying and his long weeping, "what shall I do, since the fire of love thus embraces me within so much that I cannot rest much or little? What shall I do in my sorrow, since Fortune has been so hostile to me that I have lost my sweet friend?

24

"I do not believe that I shall ever see her again; and so I wish I had fallen dead when I let her part from me yesterday! O sweet bliss, O my dear delight, O beautiful lady to whom I gave myself, O my sweet soul, O only comfort of my sad eyes turned to rivers, alas, do you see that I am dying? Why don't you help me?

25

"Who sees you now, fair sweet soul? Who sits with you, heart of my body? Who listens to you now, who talks with you? Ah me, not I who am more miserable than any other man! Ah, what are you doing? Do you have any thought of me now, or have you forgotten me for your old father who now has you, making me thereby live in such grievous pain?

26

"As you hear me now, Pandaro, so have I carried on all night, and this love-suffering has not let me sleep; or indeed if any sleep has found a

Who koude telle aright or ful discryve° — *describe*
His wo, his pleynt, his langour, and his pyne?° — *torment*
Naught alle the men that han or ben on lyve.° — *have been or are alive*
270 Thow, redere, maist thiself ful wel devyne° — *divine, suppose*
That swich a wo my wit kan nat diffyne;° — *define, represent*
On ydel° for to write it sholde I swynke,° — *In vain / toil*
Whan that my wit is wery it to thynke.° — *thinking about it*

On hevene yet the sterres weren seene,
275 Although ful pale ywoxen° was the moone, — *grown*
And whiten° gan the orisonte shene° — *to grow white / bright horizon*
Al estward, as it wont° is for to doone; — *accustomed*
And Phebus° with his rosy carte soone — *Phoebus, god of the sun*
Gan after that to dresse hym up to fare° — *prepare to rise*
280 Whan Troilus hath sent after Pandare.

[marginal note: sunrise]

This Pandarus,[2] that of° al the day biforn — *on*
Ne myghte han comen° Troilus to se, — *Couldn't come*
Although he on his hed° it hadde sworn— — *by his head (a mild oath)*
For with the kyng Priam al day was he,
285 So that it lay nought in his libertee
Nowher° to gon—but on the morwe° he wente — *Anywhere / morning*
To Troilus, whan that he for hym sente.

For in his herte he koude wel devyne° — *suppose*
That Troilus al nyght for sorwe wook;° — *kept awake*
290 And that he wolde telle hym of his pyne,° — *torment*
This knew he wel ynough, withoute book.
For which to chaumbre streght the wey he took,
And Troilus tho sobrelich he grette,° — *greeted*
And on the bed ful sone he gan hym sette.

295 "My Pandarus," quod Troilus, "the sorwe
Which that I drye° I may nat longe endure. — *suffer*
I trowe° I shal nat lyven til to-morwe. — *believe*
For which I wolde alweys, on aventure,[3]
To the devysen° of my sepulture° — *describe / burial*
300 The forme; and of my moeble° thow dispone° — *movable goods / dispose*
Right as the° semeth best is for to done. — *to you*

"But of the fir and flaumbe funeral
In which my body brennen° shal to glede,° — *burn / embers*
And of the feste and pleyes palestral° — *(funeral) athletic games*
305 At my vigile,° I prey the, tak good hede — *wake*
That that be wel;° and offre Mars my steede, — *That it be well done*

---

2. In colloquial fashion, this sentence has no predicate.
3. For which reason I wish in any event, for that occasion (of my death).

place in my languishing, it is to no avail because when I sleep, I dream of flight or of being alone in fearful places or in the hands of fierce enemies.

27

"And it is such a distress to me to see this and such terror is in my heart that it were better for me to lie awake and grieve. Oftentimes there comes to me a trembling, which shakes and wakes me and makes it seem that I am falling from on high into the depths, and awakened I call loudly upon Love together with Criseida, now praying for mercy and now for death.

28

"To such a point as you hear, have I, poor wretch, come, and I grieve for myself and for the parting more than I ever believed I would do. Oh me, I confess that I should still hope for help and that the beautiful lady will still be coming back with it, but the heart which loves her does not allow me and always calls to her."

29

After he had spoken and talked in such a manner for a long time, Pandaro, sorrowing for this heavy and distressing wretchedness, said, "Pray tell me, Troilo, if this sadness is ever to have a respite or an end. Don't you think that others besides you may have felt the blow of love or have been forced to part?

30

"Truly there are others as much in love as you are; by Pallas I swear it to you! And it seems to me certain that there are also some who are more unfortunate than you who have not, however, given themselves as completely as you have to living so wretchedly, but, when their sorrow presses on them too much, they try hard to alleviate it with hope.

330

My swerd, myn helm; and, leve° brother deere,
My sheld to Pallas yef, that shyneth cleere.⁴

"The poudre° in which myn herte ybrend° shal to
310   That preye I the thow take and it conserve
In a vessell that men clepeth° an urne,
Of gold, and to my lady that I serve,
For love of whom thus pitouslich I sterve,°   *pitifully I die*
So yeve° it hire, and do me this plesaunce,°   *give / favor*
315   To preyen hire kepe it for a remembraunce.

"For wele I fele, by my maladie⁵
And by my dremes now and yore ago,°   *formerly*
Al certeynly that I mot nedes° dye.   *must needs*
The owle ek, which that hette Escaphilo,⁶
320   Hath after me shright° al thise nyghtes two.   *screeched*
And god Mercurye,⁷ of me now, woful wrecche,
The soule gyde,° and whan the liste,° it fecche!"   *guide / it please you*

Pandare answerde and seyde, "Troilus,
My deere frend, as I have told the yore,°   *you before*
325   That it is folye for to sorwen thus,
And causeles, for which I kan namore.°   *I can't do (i.e., say) more*
But whoso wil nought trowen reed ne loore,°   *believe advice or instruction*
I kan nat sen in hym no remedie,
But lat hym worthen° with his fantasie.   *be, live*

330   "But, Troilus, I prey the, tel me now
If that thow trowe er this that° any wight   *believe that before this*
Hath loved paramours° as wel as thow?   *passionately*
Ye, God woot, and fro many a worthi knyght
Hath his lady gon a fourtenyght,°   *fortnight*
335   And he nat yet made halvendel the fare.°   *half the fuss*
What nede is the° to maken al this care?°   *it for you / lamentation*

"Syn day by day thow maist thiselven se
That from his love, or ellis from his wif,
A man mot twynnen° of necessite—   *separate*
340   Ye, though he love hire as his owene lif—
Yet nyl he with hymself thus maken strif.°   *thus quarrel*
For wel thou woost,° my leve brother deere,   *you know*
That alwey frendes may nat ben yfeere.°   *together*

"How don this folk that seen hire loves wedded
345   By frendes myght, as it bitit ful ofte,⁸

4. Offer my shield to Pallas (Athena), who shines brightly. One could possibly construe it that the
   shield shines brightly.
5. For indeed I sense, because of my illness.
6. Also the owl that is named Ascalaphus (whom Proserpine changed into an owl). In the *Legend of
   Good Women* Chaucer writes that the owl *prophete is of wo and of myschaunce.*
7. Mercury is traditionally the guide of the souls of the deceased, the psychopomp.
8. How do these people behave, who see their beloveds wedded by their relatives' force (i.e., in an
   arranged marriage), as it happens quite often?

31

"And you should do the same. You say that she has promised you to return here within ten days. This is not so long a period that you should not be able to wait without becoming sad and being like a grouch. How could you suffer the torment if the separation had to be for a year?

32

"Dispel your dreams and fears; let them go with the winds, for that's all they are. They proceed from melancholy, and they make you see what you fear. Only God knows the truth of what will be, and the dreams and the auguries to which stupid people pay attention do not amount to a trifle and have no bearing on the future, great or little.

33

"Therefore, in God's name, spare yourself; leave off this grief that's so fierce. Do me this favor, give me this gift, rise up, lighten your thoughts, and talk to me of past joys and prepare your noble soul for future joys, which will return in a very short time; therefore, hoping well, take comfort.

And sen hem in hire spouses bed ybedded?
God woot, they take it wisly,° faire, and softe,   *prudently*
Forwhi° good hope halt° up hire herte o-lofte.°   *Because / holds / aloft*
And for° they kan a tyme of sorwe endure,   *because*
350 As tyme hem hurt, a tyme doth hem cure.

"So shuldestow endure, and laten slide°   *let slip by*
The tyme, and fonde° to ben glad and light.   *try*
Ten dayes nys so longe nought t'abide.°   *to wait*
And syn° she the° to comen hath bihyght,°   *since / to you / promised*
355 She nyl hire heste° breken for no wight.°   *promise / any person*
For dred the° nat that she nyl fynden weye   *fear*
To come ayein; my lif that dorste I leye.°   *I dare wager on that*

"Thi swevnes ek° and al swich fantasie°   *dreams also / imagining*
Drif out and lat hem faren to meschaunce,°   *go to misfortune, to the devil*
360 For they procede of° thi malencolie   *issue from*
That doth° the fele in slep al this penaunce.°   *causes / suffering*
A straw for alle swevenes signifiaunce!9
God helpe me so, I counte hem nought a bene!°   *(as worth) not a bean*
Ther woot no man aright° what dremes mene.   *correctly*

365 "For prestes° of the temple tellen this,   *priests*
That dremes ben the revelaciouns
Of goddes, and as wel° they telle, ywis,   *as well, furthermore*
That they ben infernals illusiouns;
And leches seyn that of complexiouns
370 Proceden they,1 or fast,° or glotonye.   *fasting*
Who woot in soth° thus what thei signifie?   *truth*

"Ek oother seyn that thorugh impressiouns,
As if a wight hath faste° a thyng in mynde,   *fixed*
That therof cometh swiche avysiouns;°   *visions*
375 And other seyn, as they in bokes fynde,
That after tymes of the yer, by kynde,2
Men dreme, and that th'effect goth by° the moone.   *proceeds according to*
But leve° no drem, for it is nought to doone.°   *believe / to be done*

"Wel worthe of dremes ay thise olde wives,3
380 And treweliche ek augurye° of thise fowles,°   *divination / birds*
For fere of which men wenen lese° here lyves,   *believe they will lose*
As revenes qualm,° or shrichyng° of thise owles.   *ravens' croak / screeching*
To trowen° on it bothe fals and foul is.   *believe*
Allas, allas, so noble a creature
385 As is a man shal dreden swich ordure!°   *filth, nonsense*

"For which with al myn herte I the biseche,
Unto thiself that al this thow foryyve;4

9. A straw for (i.e., To heck with) all dreams' significance.
1. And physicians say that they proceed from *complexiouns*, i.e., the particular balance of such bodily humors as *malencolie*.
2. That according to the seasons of the year, by natural process.
3. May it always be well with these old women concerning dreams—i.e., leave dreams to old women.
4. That you abandon for yourself all this (nonsensical belief in dreams and auguries).

34

"This city is great and full of delight, and now, as you know, there is a truce; let us go to some pleasant place far from here, and there you shall stay with one of these kings and shall share with him your grievous life while you undergo the terms which the fair lady has given who has wounded your heart.

35

"Ah do it, I pray you; rise up! Sorrowing as you are is not a noble act, and lying down is indeed just the same. And if your stupid and eccentric ways should be known outside, you would be ashamed, and men would say that you were weeping, like a coward, for the adverse times and not for love, or that you were pretending to be ill."

36

"Ah me, he who loses much weeps much, nor can he who has not experienced it know what that happiness is which I am letting go; therefore I should not be blamed if I never did anything except weep. But because you, my friend, have asked me, I shall comfort myself with all my power in order to serve you and in order to please you.

37

"May God send us soon the tenth day so that I may become again as joyful as I was when it was agreed to give her up. Never was a rose in the sweet spring as beautiful as I am disposed to become again when I shall see the fresh complexion of that lady who is to me the cause of torment and of joy returned to Troy.

And ris now up withowten more speche,
And lat us caste how forth may best be dryve
390 This tyme,[5] and ek how fresshly° we may lyve   *joyously*
Whan that she comth, the which shal be right soone.
God helpe me so, the beste is thus to doone.

"Ris, lat us speke of lusty° lif in Troie   *the happy*
That we han led, and forth the tyme dryve;
395 And ek of tyme comyng us rejoie,°   *rejoice*
That bryngen shal oure blisse now so blyve;°   *quickly*
And langour° of thise twyes° dayes fyve   *sorrow / twice*
We shal therwith so foryete or oppresse°   *forget or suppress*
That wel unneth it don shal us duresse.[6]

400 "This town is ful of lordes al aboute,
And trewes° lasten al this mene while.   *truces*
Go we pleye us in som lusty route
To Sarpedoun, nat hennes but a myle;[7]
And thus thow shalt the tyme wel bygile,°   *beguile, wile away*
405 And dryve it forth unto that blisful morwe°   *morning*
That thow hire se, that° cause is of thi sorwe.   *who*

"Now ris, my deere brother Troilus,
For certes it non honour is to the
To wepe and in thi bedde to jouken° thus;   *roost (as a falcon), rest*
410 For trewelich, of o° thyng trust to me: *one*
If thow thus ligge° a day, or two, or thre,   *lie*
The folk wol seyn that thow for cowardise
The feynest° sik, and that thow darst nat rise!"   *Pretend yourself to be*

This Troilus answerde, "O brother deere,
415 This knowen folk that han ysuffred peyne,
That though he wepe and make sorwful cheere
That feleth° harm and smert° in every veyne,   *(He) who feels / pain*
No wonder is; and though ich evere pleyne,°   *always complain*
Or alwey wepe, I am no thyng° to blame,   *in no way*
420 Syn° I have lost the cause of al my game.°   *Since / happiness*

"But syn of fyne force I mot arise,[8]
I shal arise as soone as evere I may;
And God, to whom myn herte I sacrifice,
So sende° us hastely the tenthe day!   *May (He) send*
425 For was ther nevere fowel° so fayn° of May   *bird / glad*
As I shal ben whan that she comth in Troie
That° cause is of my torment and my joie.   *(She) who*

---

5. And let us plan how this interval of time may best be spent. *Drive forth* (of time), "spend, pass."
6. That scarcely will it bring us hardship.
7. Let's go to Sarpedon's, only a mile from here, to amuse ourselves in some gallant company. Sarpedon was king of Licia and ally of Troy.
8. But since from sheer compulsion I must arise.

38

"But where can we go for diversion, as you suggest? Shall we go to Sarpedon? And how can I stay there? I shall always have in my soul the question whether she might perhaps be able to return before the given day for some reason. For I would not, if that might happen, be absent for all that the world has or could have of marvelous things."

39

"Ah, if she returns, I shall arrange it that someone shall come for me without delay," replied Pandaro. "I shall place someone here for this purpose alone so that it shall be well known to us. I wish it were now! No one would wish it as much as I. So do not for this reason give up the idea of going away; let us go where you suggested to me just now."

Troilo and Pandaro together go to Sarpedon, where Troilo was scarcely able to endure a stay of five days.

40

The two companions started on the way and after about four miles had passed, they arrived where Sarpedon was, who when he knew it, came joyfully toward Troilo and received him very lovingly. Although they were weary from much sighing, they still enjoyed a great festivity with the powerful baron.

41

He, as one who was more noble-hearted in everything than any other, showed marvelous honor to each, now with hunts, now with the gracious company of beautiful and very worthy ladies, with songs and music, and always with the splendid grandeur of banquets, so many and of such sort that their equal had never been given in Troy.

42

But what help were these celebrations to the faithful Troilo, who had no heart for them? He was where the desire formed in his thoughts often drew him, and with the eyes of his mind he constantly saw Criseida as his god, imagining now one thing, now another about her, and often sighing for love.

"But whider is thi reed,"[9] quod Troilus,
"That we may pleye us° best in al this town?"   *amuse ourselves*
430 "By God, my conseil is," quod Pandarus,
"To ride and pleye us with kyng Sarpedoun."
So longe° of this they speken up and down   *for a long time*
Til Troilus gan at the laste assente
To rise, and forth to Sarpedoun they wente.

435 This Sarpedoun, as he that honourable
Was evere his lyve,° and ful of heigh largesse,°   *throughout his life / generosity*
With al that myghte yserved ben on table
That deynte° was, al° coste it gret richesse,   *choice, delicious / although*
He fedde hem day by day, that swich noblesse,
440 As seyden bothe the mooste and ek the leeste,[1]
Was nevere er that day wist° at any feste.   *known*

Nor in this world ther is non instrument
Delicious,° thorugh wynd or touche of corde,°   *Delightful / string*
As fer° as any wight hath evere ywent,°   *far / supposed*
445 That tonge telle or herte may recorde,
That at that feste it nas wel herd acorde;°   *heard to harmonize*
Ne of ladys ek so fair a compaignie
On daunce, er tho,° was nevere iseye with ië.°   *before then / seen with eye*

But what availeth this to° Troilus,   *how does this help*
450 That for his sorwe nothyng of it roughte?°   *cared*
For evere in oon° his herte pietous°   *continually / pitiful*

<hr>

9. But where is (it, according to) your advice.
1. As both the greatest and the least people (i.e., everyone) said.

43

Any other lady, although she might be worthy and beautiful, was grievous for him to see. Any solace, any sweet song, was vexatious to him, since he did not see her into whose hands Love had placed the key to his wretched life. And he had happiness only when he could think of her, letting every other matter go.

44

Not an evening or morning passed that he did not cry out with sighs, "O beautiful light, O morning star!" Then, as if she were present listening, a thousand times and more calling her a thorn rose, he always felt it necessary that she should greet him before he would stop, and his salutation ended with sighing.

45

Not an hour of the day passed that he did not call her by name a thousand times; her name was always in his mouth, and he pictured her beautiful face and her graceful words in his heart and mind. The letters sent to him by her he turned over fully a hundred times a day, so much did it please him to see them again.

46

They had not stayed there three days when Troilo began to say to Pandaro, "Why should we stay here any longer? Are we duty-bound to live and die here? Are we waiting to be dismissed? To tell you the truth, I want to go away. Please let's go away, for God's sake; we have been long enough with Sarpedon and have been gladly received."

47

Pandaro said to him, "Now, have we come here just for a little warmth or has the tenth day come? Please restrain yourself a little longer since going from here now would seem a rudeness. Where will you go now? In what place could you enjoy a more pleasant visit? Please let's stay two days longer; then we shall go away, and, if you wish, we'll return home."

Ful bisyly° Criseyde, his lady, soughte.   *anxiously*
On hire was evere al that his herte thoughte,
Now this, now that, so faste° ymagenynge   *much*
455 That glade, iwis, kan hym no festeyinge.²

Thise ladies ek that at this feste ben,
Syn that° he saugh his lady was aweye,   *Because*
It was his sorwe upon hem for to sen,°   *look*
Or for to here° on instrumentes pleye.   *hear*
460 For° she that of his herte berth° the keye   *Because / bears, keeps*
Was absent, lo, this was his fantasie—°   *whim, fancy*
That no wight sholde° maken melodie.   *ought to*

Nor ther nas houre° in al the day or nyght,   *Nor was there an hour*
Whan he was there as° no wight myghte hym heere,   *where*
465 That he ne seyde, "O lufsom° lady bryght,   *lovely*
How have ye faren syn that° ye were here?   *since*
Welcome, ywis, myn owne lady deere!"
But weylaway, al this° nat but a maze.°   *this is / delusion*
Fortune his howve entended bet to glaze!³

470 The lettres ek that she of olde tyme
Hadde hym ysent, he wolde allone rede
An hondred sithe atwixen noon and prime,⁴
Refiguryng° hire shap,° hire wommanhede,   *Representing again / shape*
Withinne his herte, and every word or dede
475 That passed was; and thus he drof t'an ende°   *passed to the end*
The ferthe day, and seyde he wolde wende.°   *wished to depart*

And seyde, "Leve° brother Pandarus,   *Dear*
Intendestow that we shal here bleve°   *remain*
Til Sarpedoun wol forth congeyen us?°   *bid us good-bye, dismiss us*
480 Yet were it fairer that we toke oure leve.
For Goddes love, lat us now soone° at eve   *promptly*
Oure leve take, and homward lat us torne,
For treweliche, I nyl nat° thus sojourne."°   *I do not wish / to remain*

Pandare answerde, "Be we comen hider
485 To fecchen fir and rennen hom ayein?⁵
God help me so, I kan nat tellen whider°   *where*
We myghte gon, if I shal sothly seyn,°   *speak truly*
Ther° any wight is of us more feyn°   *Where / happier with us*
Than Sarpedoun; and if we hennes hye°   *hasten from here*
490 Thus sodeynly, I holde it vilanye.°   *discourtesy*

---

2. That indeed no festivity can gladden him.
3. (The goddess) Fortune intended to make him a better hood of glass, i.e., to delude him even further.
4. A hundred times between noon and prime, i.e., between 12 to 3 P.M. and 6 to 9 A.M.—all afternoon and night.
5. To fetch fire and run back home? A man who borrows hot coals to start his fire must hurry home with them.

48

Although Troilo stayed against his will, he remained in his usual thoughts. Nor was anything that Pandaro might say to him important. But after the fifth day, having taken their leave, although it was displeasing to Sarpedon, they returned to their homes, Troilo saying along the road, "O God, shall I find my love returned?"

49

But Pandaro, like one who indeed knew the whole intention of Calchas, spoke otherwise very softly to himself: "This wish of yours, so fiery and fierce, will be able to cool itself if what I heard during the time when she was here does not deceive me, for I believe that the tenth day and month and year will pass before you see her again."

Returned to Troy, Troilo goes to see Criseida's house, and each place he sees where he used to see her recalls her.

50

After they had returned home, they both went into a room and seated themselves and talked much of Criseida, without Troilo giving way to his inflamed sighs. But after a while they arose, Troilo saying: "Let us go, and so we shall at least see the house, since we can do nothing else."

51

And this said, he took Pandaro by the hand and he covered his face a little with a false smile, and he descended from the palace, and he feigned various reasons to the others who were with him in order to conceal the injuries of love which he felt. But when he had sought out with his eyes the closed palace of Criseida, he felt a new agitation,

"Syn that° we seyden that we wolde bleve°   *Since / remain*
With hym a wowke,° and now, thus sodeynly,   *week*
The ferthe day to take of hym owre leve—
He wolde wondren on it, trewely!
495 Lat us holden forth° oure purpos fermely;   *maintain*
And syn that ye bihighten° hym to bide,°   *promised / remain*
Holde forward° now, and after lat us ride."   *Keep your agreement*

Thus Pandarus, with alle peyne and wo,
Made hym to dwelle; and at the wikes° ende   *week's*
500 Of Sarpedoun they toke hire leve tho,°   *then*
And on hire wey they spedden hem to wende.°   *hastened to depart*
Quod Troilus, "Now Lord me grace sende,
That I may fynden at myn hom-comynge
Criseyde comen!"° And therwith gan he synge.   *to have arrived*

505 "Ye, haselwode!"[6] thoughte this Pandare,
And to hymself ful softeliche he seyde,
"God woot, refreyden° may this hote fare,°   *cool off / passionate affair*
Er Calkas sende Troilus Criseyde!"
But natheles,° he japed° thus, and pleyde,   *nevertheless / joked*
510 And swor, ywys, his herte hym wel bihighte°   *assured*
She wolde come as soone as evere she myghte.

Whan they unto the paleys° were ycomen   *palace*
Of Troilus, they doun of hors alighte,
And to the chambre hire wey than han they nomen;°   *taken*
515 And into tyme° that it gan to nyghte°   *up to the time / grow dark*
They spaken° of Criseÿde the brighte;   *spoke*
And after this, whan that hem bothe leste,°   *when it pleased them both*
They spedde hem fro the soper unto reste.

On morwe,° as soone as day bygan to clere,°   *the morning / brighten*
520 This Troilus gan of his slep t'abrayde,°   *wake*
And to Pandare, his owen brother deere,
"For love of God," ful pitously he sayde,
"As go we sen° the palais° of Criseyde;   *Let's go see / palace*
For syn° we yet may have namore feste,°   *since / happiness*
525 So lat us sen hire paleys atte leeste."

And therwithal, his meyne for to blende,°   *to deceive his retinue*
A cause he fond° in towne for to go,   *contrived*
And to Criseydes hous they gonnen wende.°   *go*
But Lord, this sely° Troilus was wo!   *hapless*
530 Hym thoughte his sorwful herte braste° a-two.   *would burst*
For whan he saugh hire dores spered° alle,   *barred*
Wel neigh° for sorwe adoun he gan to falle.   *nigh*

6. The sense of "hazelwood" here is not entirely clear, but in context the expression seems to imply an attitude of incredulity approaching a mocking skepticism.

52

It seemed that his heart would break when he saw the door locked and the windows, and so much did the newly born suffering draw him from himself that he didn't know if he stood or if he walked, and his completely changed face would have given a manifest sign of it to anyone who might have glanced at him even cursorily.

53

Filled with sorrow, he spoke with Pandaro as he was best able concerning his new anguish. Then he said, "Alas, how luminous and pleasing you were, O place, when that beautiful one resided in you who bore my peace entirely within her eyes. Now you are left dark without her, and I do not know whether you will ever have her again."

54

When he went riding through Troy alone, he remembered every place; of these places he would go about speaking to himself: "Here I saw her laugh joyfully, here I saw her glancing toward me, here she graciously greeted me, here I saw her rejoice and here stay thoughtful, here I saw her full of pity for my sighs.

55

"There she was when her fair and beautiful eyes captured my love; there she was when she kindled my heart with a sigh of the greatest fire; there she was when through her womanly worth she graciously pleased me; there I saw her disdainful; and there my gentle lady showed herself submissive to me."

Therwith, whan he was war° and gan biholde   *aware*
How shet° was every wyndow of the place,   *shut*
535 As frost, hym thoughte, his herte gan to colde;°   *grow cold*
For which with chaunged dedlich pale face,
Withouten word, he forthby gan to pace,°   *rode by it*
And as God wolde, he gan so faste ride
That no wight of his contenance espide.

540 Than seide he thus: "O paleys desolat,°   *deserted*
O hous of houses whilom best ihight,[7]
O paleys empty and disconsolat,
O thow lanterne of which queynt° is the light,   *quenched*
O paleys, whilom° day, that now art nyght,   *formerly*
545 Wel oughtestow to falle, and I to dye,
Syn she is went° that wont° was us to gye!°   *has gone / accustomed / guide*

"O paleis, whilom crowne of houses alle,   *crown of all houses*
Enlumyned with sonne° of alle blisse!   *Sun of all happiness*   *Illuminated with the sun*
O ryng, fro which the ruby is out falle,
550 O cause of wo, that cause hast ben of lisse!°   *joy*
Yet, syn I may no bet,° fayn° wolde I kisse   *can do no better / gladly*
Thy colde dores, dorste I° for this route;°   *if I dared / crowd*
And farwel shryne, of which the seynt° is oute!"   *saint*
Troilus kept by the croud

Therwith he caste on Pandarus his yë,
555 With chaunged face, and pitous to biholde;
And whan he myghte his tyme aright aspie,°   *see a good opportunity*
Ay as he rood to Pandarus he tolde
His newe sorwe and ek his joies olde,
So pitously and with so ded an hewe°   *deadly a hue*
560 That every wight myghte on his sorwe rewe.°   *take pity*

Fro thennesforth he rideth up and down,
And every thyng com hym to remembraunce
As he rood forby° places of the town   *rode by*
In which he whilom° hadde al his plesaunce.   *formerly*
565 "Lo, yonder saugh ich last my lady daunce;
And in that temple, with hire eyen° cleere,   *eyes*
Me kaughte first my righte lady dere.

"And yonder have I herd ful lustyly°   *heartily*
My dere herte laugh; and yonder pleye
570 Saugh ich hire ones ek° ful blisfully;   *once also*
And yonder ones to me gan she seye,
'Now goode swete, love me wel, I preye';
And yond so goodly gan she me biholde
That to the deth myn herte is to hire holde.°   *bound, obligated*

7. O house of houses, formerly called the best.

56

Then thinking of this, he went on to add: "Long, O Love, have you made my chronicle if I do not wish to deceive myself, and memory well repeats the truth to me. Wherever I walk or pause, if I look carefully, I observe fully a thousand signs of your victory which you have had triumphing over me who formerly scorned every lover.

57

"Well have you avenged the insult done you, powerful and much to be feared lord. But since my soul has given itself entirely to serve you, as you can clearly see, let it not die disconsolate; return it to its first pleasure; force Criseida, as you do me, so that she may return to put an end to my woes."

58

He went sometimes to the gate through which his lady had departed. "From here she went forth who comforts me, from here went forth my sweet life; as far as there I escorted her, and there I made my parting from her, and there, alas, I touched her hand," he said to himself continuing slowly.

59

"Here you went away, heart of my body; when will it be that you will return from there, my dear welfare and my sweet desire? Truly I do not know, but these ten days will be more than a thousand years! Ah, shall I never see you return to cheer me with your delightful ways just as you have promised? Ah, will it ever be? Ah, I wish it were just now!"

575 "And at that corner, in the yonder hous,
Herde I myn alderlevest° lady deere   *dearest of all*
So wommanly, with vois melodious,
Syngen so wel, so goodly, and so cleere
That in my soule yet me thynketh° ich here   *it seems to me*
580 The blisful sown;° and in that yonder place   *sound*
My lady first me took unto hire grace."°   *good graces, favor*

Thanne thoughte he thus: "O blisful lord Cupide,
Whan I the proces have in my memorie
How thow me hast wereyed° on every syde,   *assaulted*
585 Men myght a book make of it, lik a storie.
What nede is the° to seke on me° victorie,   *for you / from me*
Syn° I am thyn and holly° at thi wille?   *Since / wholly*
What joie hastow thyn owen folk to spille?°   *destroy*

"Wel hastow, lord, ywroke° on me thyn ire,   *avenged*
590 Thow myghty god, and dredefull° for to greve!°   *fearsome / offend*
Now mercy, lord! Thow woost° wel I desire   *you know*
Thi grace moost of alle lustes leeve,°   *dear pleasures*
And lyve and dye I wol in thy byleve;°   *belief, religion*
For which I n'axe in guerdoun but o bone—[8]
595 That thow Criseyde ayein me sende sone.°   *soon*

"Destreyne° hire herte as faste to retorne   *Constrain*
As thow doost myn to longen hire to see;
Than woot I wel that she nyl naught sojorne.°   *delay*
Now blisful lord, so cruel thow ne be
600 Unto the blood of Troie, I preye the,
As Juno was unto the blood Thebane,
For which the folk of Thebes caughte hire bane."[9]

And after this he to the yates° wente   *gates*
Ther as Criseyde out rood a ful good paas,°   *distance*
605 And up and down ther made he many a wente,°   *passage, turn*
And to hymself ful ofte he seyde, "Allas,
Fro hennes° rood my blisse and my solas!°   *From here / solace, comfort*
As wolde° blisful God now, for his joie,   *May (God) wish*
I myghte hire sen ayein° come into Troie!   *again, back*

610 "And to the yonder hille I gan hire gyde,°   *escort*
Allas, and ther I took of hire my leve!
And yond I saugh hire to hire fader ride,
For sorwe of which myn herte shal tocleve;°   *split in two*
And hider hom I com° whan it was eve,   *came*
615 And here I dwelle out cast from alle joie,
And shal, til I may sen hire eft° in Troie."   *see her again*

8. In return for which I ask as a reward but one gift.
9. For which (cruelty) the people of Thebes received their destruction. Jealous of her husband Jupiter's affairs with Theban women, Juno exerted her wrath against Thebes.

Troilo, having considered with himself his own condition, sings what his life may be.

60

It seemed to him that there was less color than usual in his face, and this gave him the idea of being pointed at many times, as if men said, "Why has Troilo become so stricken and so distraught?" There was no one who pointed at him, but he who knows the truth is suspicious.

61

Therefore it pleased him to show in verse who was the cause of it, and sighing when he was tired of grieving, as if giving some respite to his sorrow while he waited during the adverse time, he went about singing to himself of this in a low voice and refreshing his soul, which was subdued by an excess of love, in this manner:

62

"The sweet sight and the fair gentle look of the most beautiful eyes that were ever seen, which I have lost, make my life seem so grievous that I go about heaving sighs. And they have led me to such a point already that, instead of the light and joyous sighs which I used to give, I bear desires for death because of your departure, so strongly does it pain me.

63

"Alas, Love, why at the first step did you not wound me so that I might have died? Why did you not separate from my wretched self the anguished spirit which I bear, because I now see myself brought from high to low? There is no comfort, Love, for my sorrow except death when I find myself parted from those beautiful eyes where I have formerly seen you.

64

"When for a gentle act of salutation I turn my eyes somewhat toward a beautiful lady, so completely is my strength undone that I cannot hold my weeping within me. The wounds of love make me not like this when I remember my lady from the sight of whom—O woe is me—I am so far that, if Love should will it, I would wish to die.

65

"Since my fortune is so cruel that what my eyes see saddens me more and more, for God's sake, Love, let your hand close them now that they

And of hymself ymagened he ofte
To ben defet,° and pale, and waxen lesse°   *disfigured / grown smaller*
Than he was wont,° and that men seyden softe,°   *used to being / quietly*
620   "What may it be? Who kan the sothe gesse°   *guess the truth*
Whi Troilus hath al this hevynesse?"
And al this nas but° his malencolie,   *was only*
That he hadde of hymself swich fantasie.°   *imaginings*

Another tyme ymaginen he wolde
625   That every wight that wente by the weye
Hadde of hym routhe,° and that they seyen sholde,   *pity*
"I am right sory Troilus wol deye."
And thus he drof° a day yet forth or tweye,°   *passed / two*
As ye have herd; swich lif right gan he lede
630   As he that stood bitwixen° hope and drede.   *between*

For which hym likede° in his songes shewe   *it pleased him*
Th'enchesoun° of his wo, as he best myghte;   *occasion, cause*
And made a song of wordes but a fewe,
Somwhat his woful herte for to lighte;°   *cheer*
635   And whan he was from° every mannes syghte,   *away from*
With softe vois he of his lady deere,
That absent was, gan synge as ye may heere:

... I think Troilus might want Criseyde to come back to Troy ... maybe

Canticus Troili°   *Song of Troilus*

"O sterre, of which I lost have al the light,
With herte soor wel oughte I to biwaille°   *lament*
640   That evere derk in torment, nyght by nyght,
Toward my deth with wynd in steere° I saille;   *at my back / astern*
For which the tenthe nyght, if that I faille°   *lack*
The gydyng° of thi bemes bright an houre,   *guidance*
My ship and me Caribdis wol devoure."[1]

1. Charybdis (the legendary whirlpool-monster opposite the rock Scylla between Sicily and mainland Italy) will devour my ship and me.

have lost the sight they loved to see. Leave my flesh denuded, O love, because when life is acquired through death, dying ought to be joyous, and you know well where my soul should go from here.

66

"It will go to those fair arms from which ill fortune has cast the body. Do you not see that I am already marked in my face with death's color? See the anguish, which drives my soul from me, draw it forth, and bear it to the bosom most beloved by it, where it expects peace, because already every other thing displeases it."

67

When he had spoken thus in his singing, he turned to his old sighing. When going about by day and when in bed at night, he thought always of his Criseida, nor did he take delight in scarcely any other thing. And he often counted the days which had passed, thinking never to arrive at the tenth, when Criseida should return to him from the Greeks.

68

Beyond the usual fashion, the days seemed long to him and the nights more so. He measured from the first morning light until when the stars appeared, and he said that the sun had embarked on new wanderings and the horses did not run as they formerly did. Of the night he said the same, and one, two . . . he counted all the stars.

69

The old moon was already horned at the departure of Criseida and he had seen it in the morning when he left her; therefore he often said to himself, "When it has sprouted its new horns, just as it did when our lady went away, then my soul will have returned here."

645 This song whan he thus songen hadde, soone
He fil° ayeyn into his sikes° olde;   *fell / sighs*
And every nyght, as was his wone° to doone,   *custom*
He stood the brighte moone to byholde,
And al his sorwe he to the moone tolde,
650 And seyde, "Ywis, whan thow art horned newe,[2]
I shal be glad, if al the world be trewe!

"I saugh thyn hornes olde ek by the morwe°   *in the morning*
Whan hennes° rood my righte lady dere   *hence*
That cause is of my torment and my sorwe;
655 For which, O brighte Latona[3] the clere,
For love of God, ren° faste aboute thy spere!°   *run / sphere*
For whan thyne hornes newe gynnen sprynge,
Than shal she come that may my blisse brynge."

The dayes moore and lenger every nyght
660 Than they ben wont° to be, hym thoughte° tho,   *accustomed / it seemed to him*
And that the sonne went° his cours unright°   *sun traveled / awry*
By lenger weye than it was wont to do;
And seyde, "Ywis, me dredeth° evere mo   *I fear*
The sonnes sone, Pheton,[4] be on lyve,°   *alive*
665 And that his fader carte° amys he dryve."   *his father's (Phoebus's) chariot*

2. Indeed, when you are horned anew, i.e., when the new moon will appear as a crescent. Criseyde
departed when the horns were *olde* (line 652), in the moon's last phase.
3. Latona is Diana's (the moon's) mother. The error may have been induced by Latin poets' reference
to the moon as Latonia (offspring of Latona).
4. That the sun's son, Phaeton. Phaeton drove the sun-god's chariot one day and lost control of it,
scorching the earth.

70

He gazed at the Greeks tented before Troy, and where he formerly used to be disturbed on seeing them, now they were gazed at with delight. And he used to give himself to believe that the breezes which he felt blowing in his face were sighs sent from Criseida, often saying, "Either here or there is my gracious lady."

71

In this manner and in many other ways, he passed the time sighing. And Pandaro was always with him, who comforted him often while he was doing this, and into glad and gay conversation Pandaro endeavored, as best he could, to draw him, always giving him good hope of his beautiful and worthy love.

Part Six

Here begins the sixth part of the "Filostrato" in which first of all Criseida, while at her father's, grieves at being far from Troilo. Diomede comes to her, talks, disparages Troy and the Trojans and then discloses his love to her, to whom she replies and leaves him in doubt if he pleases her or not and, otherwise grown lukewarm toward Troilo, she begins to forget him. And to begin with, Criseida, weeping, sorrows at being far from Troilo.

1

On the other side by the seashore, with few women, among armed men, was Criseida. She spent the nights in bitter tears since it was more fitting for her to be on her guard by day. For that reason her fresh and delicate cheeks had grown pale and thin, far from her usual fine health.

Upon the walles faste ek° wolde he walke,   *resolutely also*
And on the Grekis oost° he wolde se;°   *host / look*
And to hymself right thus he wolde talke:
"Lo, yonder is myn owene lady free,°   *noble*
670 Or ellis yonder, ther tho° tentes be;   *where those*
And thennes° comth this eyr,° that is so soote° *thence / air, breeze / sweet*
That in my soule I fele it doth me boote.°   *good, a remedy*

"And hardily,° this wynd that more and moore   *surely*
Thus stoundemele° encresseth in my face *hour by hour, gradually*
675 Is of my ladys depe sikes° soore.   *sighs*
I preve° it thus: for in noon other place   *prove*
Of al this town, save onliche° in this space,   *except only*
Fele I no wynd that sowneth° so lik peyne;°   *sounds / pain*
It seyth, 'Allas! Whi twynned° be we tweyne?' "° *separated / two*

680 This longe tyme he dryveth forth right thus
Til fully passed was the nynthe nyght;
And ay bisyde hym was this Pandarus,
That bisily did al his fulle myght
Hym to conforte and make his herte light,
685 Yevyng° hym hope alwey the tenthe morwe° *Giving / morning*
That she shal come and stynten° al his sorwe.   *put a stop to*

Upon that other syde ek was Criseyde,
With wommen fewe, among the Grekis stronge,
For which ful ofte a day° "Allas," she seyde,   *often by day*
690 "That I was born! Wel may myn herte longe
After° my deth, for now lyve I to° longe.   *For / too*
Allas, and I ne may it nat amende,
For now is wors than evere yet I wende!°   *had supposed*

"My fader nyl for nothyng do me grace°   *allow me*
695 To gon ayeyn, for naught I kan hym queme;°   *please*
And if so be that I my terme pace,°   *miss my appointment*
My Troilus shal in his herte deme°   *think*
That I am fals, and so it may wel seme:
Thus shal ich have unthonk° on every side—   *ill will, blame*
700 That I was born so weilaway the tide!°   *alas for the time*

"And if that I me putte in jupartie°   *jeopardy*
To stele° awey by nyght, and it bifalle   *steal*
That I be kaught, I shal be holde a spie;°   *considered a spy*
Or elles—lo, this drede I moost of alle—
705 If in the hondes of som wrecche° I falle,   *villain*
I nam but lost, al° be myn herte trewe.   *although*
Now, myghty God, thow on my sorwe rewe!"°   *take pity*

2

She kept on weeping when she recalled the pleasure she had formerly enjoyed with Troilo, and she kept on describing all the acts which had happened between them, and she kept on recalling to herself each and every word whenever she had the time or the power. Therefore seeing herself far from him, she made a bitter fountain of her eyes.

3

Nor would anyone be so pitiless that, hearing her sorrowing lament he could restrain himself from weeping with her. She wept so bitterly when a moment of time was given her that it could not be entirely described, and what afflicted her more than anything else was that she had no one with whom to grieve.

4

She would gaze upon the walls of Troy, and the palaces, the towers, and the fortresses, and she would say to herself, "Ah me, how much joy, how much pleasure, and how much sweetness I once had within them! And now in sad misery do I consume my precious beauty here. Ah me, my Troilo, what are you doing now? Do you still remember anything of me?

5

"O, wretched me! Now if only I had believed you, and we had both gone together wherever and to whatever kingdom it had pleased you! For now I would not feel sorrows, nor would so much good time be lost! Afterwards, we would have returned, when it might have been possible, and who would then have spoken evilly of me because I had gone away with such a man?

6

"O, wretched me, for I perceive too late that my judgment now turns enemy to me! I fled the bad and followed the worse, and so my heart is a beggar of joy; and in vain do I call upon death for comfort since I cannot see you, O sweet friend, and I fear I shall never see you again; may the Greeks be soon or devastated!

Ful pale ywoxen° was hire brighte face,   *grown*
Hire lymes lene,° as she that al the day   *lean, withered*
710 Stood, whan she dorste,° and loked on the place   *dared*
Ther she was born, and ther she dwelt hadde ay;
And al the nyght wepyng, allas, she lay.
And thus despeired,° out of alle cure,°   *despairing / beyond all remedy*
She ladde° hire lif, this woful creature.   *led*

715 Ful ofte a day she sighte° ek for destresse,   *sighed*
And in hireself she wente ay purtraynge°   *portraying*
Of Troilus the grete worthynesse,
And al his goodly wordes recordynge°   *calling to mind*
Syn first that day hire love bigan to springe.
720 And thus she sette hire woful herte afire
Thorugh remembraunce of that° she gan desire.   *what*

In al this world ther nys so cruel herte
That hire hadde herd compleynen in hire sorwe
That nolde han wepen° for hire peynes smerte,°   *wouldn't have wept / sharp*
725 So tendrely she weep,° bothe eve and morwe.   *wept*
Hire nedede° no teris for to borwe!°   *she needed / borrow*
And this was yet the werste of al hire peyne:
Ther was no wight to whom she dorste hire pleyne.°   *complain*

Ful rewfully° she loked upon Troie,   *piteously*
730 Biheld the toures heigh° and ek the halles;   *high towers*
"Allas," quod she, "the plesance and the joie,
The which that now al torned into galle° is,   *gall, bitterness*
Have ich had ofte withinne yonder walles!
O Troilus, what dostow° now?" she seyde.   *are you doing*
735 "Lord, wheyther thow yet thenke° upon Criseyde?   *do you still think*

"Allas, I ne hadde trowed on youre loore⁵
And went with yow, as ye me redde° er this!   *advised*
Than hadde I now nat siked° half so soore.   *sighed*
Who myghte han seyd that I hadde don amys
740 To stele awey with swich oon as he ys.
But al to late comth the letuarie°   *medicine*
Whan men the cors° unto the grave carie.   *corpse*

"To late is now to speke of that matere.
Prudence, allas, oon of thyne eyen thre⁶
745 Me lakked° alwey, er that I come here!   *I lacked*
On tyme ypassed° wel remembred me,°   *past / I remembered*
And present tyme ek koud ich wel ise,°   *see*
But future tyme, er I was in the snare,
Koude° I nat sen; that causeth now my care.   *Could*

5. Alas, that I hadn't believed in your instruction.
6. One of your three eyes. The notion that Prudence has three eyes to see time past, present, and future probably derives from a passage in Dante (*Purgatory* 29.130–32) and its commentaries.

7

"But I shall do my utmost to flee from here, if I am not permitted to come to you in any other way, and to return to you as I promised, and the smoke may go where it may wish to go and what can occur to me from this can occur, for rather than wishing to die of sorrow, I wish that he will speak and bark about me who may wish to."

8

But from so high and great an intent, a new lover soon diverted her. Now Diomede tried every argument that he could in order to enter her heart. Nor did his purpose fail him at his time, and in a brief space he expelled Troilo and Troy and every other thought of him which was in her, either false or true.

How Diomede speaks to Criseida of various things and at last discloses to her the love which he bears for her.

9

She had not been there the fourth day after the bitter departure when Diomede found an honorable reason to come to her. He found her weeping alone and almost a transformed woman from the day when riding with her he had led her there from Troy; this seemed a great marvel to him.

10

And he said to himself at first sight, "I believe my labor will be vain. This lady is, as I see, sad for the love of another, full of sighs and devotion. One would have to be too much the sovereign artist who could drive away the first in order that he might enter there. O me, it was a bad thing for me to go to Troy when I brought her here!"

750 "But natheles, bityde what bityde,[7]
I shal to-morwe at nyght, by est or west,
Out of this oost° stele in som manere syde,°   host / on one side or the other
And gon with Troilus where as hym lest.°
This purpos wol ich holde, and this is best.
755 No fors of wikked tonges janglerie,[8]
For evere on love han wrecches had envye.

"For whoso wol of every word take hede,°   heed
Or reulen hym° by every wightes wit,°   govern himself / understanding
Ne shal he nevere thryven,° out of drede;°   prosper / beyond a doubt
760 For that that° som men blamen evere yit,   that which
Lo, other manere folk comenden it.
And as for me, for al swich variaunce,
Felicite clepe I my suffisaunce.[9]

"For which, withouten any wordes mo,
765 To Troie I wole,° as for conclusioun."   will go
But God it wot,° er fully monthes two,   knows
She was ful fer fro that entencioun!
For bothe Troilus and Troie town
Shal knotteles thoroughout hire herte slide;[1]
770 For she wol take a purpos for t'abide.°   remain (with the Greeks)

This Diomede, of whom yow telle I gan,
Goth now withinne hymself ay arguynge,
With al the sleghte° and al that evere he kan,°   cunning / knows, is able
How he may best, with shortest taryinge,
775 Into his net Criseydes herte brynge.
To this entent° he koude nevere fyne;°   aim / cease, leave off
To fisshen hire° he leyde out hook and lyne.   fish for her

But natheles,° wel in his herte he thoughte   nevertheless
That she nas nat withoute a love in Troie,
780 For nevere sythen° he hire thennes° broughte   since / from there
Ne koude he sen hire laughe or maken joie.
He nyst° how best hire herte for t'acoye;°   didn't know / soothe
"But for t'asay,"° he seyde, "it naught n'agreveth,°   attempt (something) / harms
For he that naught n'asaieth naught n'acheveth."

---

7. But nevertheless, let happen what may happen—come what may.
8. With regard to wicked tongues' chatter/gossip, it is of no importance.
9. I call felicity sufficient for me.
1. Shall slide (like a thread through a needle) through her heart without a knot.

11

But as one who had great daring and a bold heart, he took resolve, since he had come there to show her, even if he must certainly die for it, the fierce onslaughts which Love was making him feel because of her and how he had been first kindled for her; and having seated himself he drew indirectly to his desires.

785 Yet seyde he to hymself upon a nyght,
"Now am I nat a fool, that woot° wel how   *who know*
Hire wo for love is of another wight,
And hereupon to gon assaye hire now?[2]
I may wel wite° it nyl nat ben my prow,°   *know / to my profit*
790 For wise folk in bookes it expresse,
'Men shal nat wowe° a wight in hevynesse.'°   *woo / grief*

"But whoso myghte wynnen swich a flour°   *flower*
From hym for whom she morneth° nyght and day,   *mourns*
He myghte seyn he were a conquerour."
795 And right anon, as he that bold was ay,
Thoughte in his herte, "Happe how happe may,°   *Whatever may happen*
Al° sholde I dye, I wol hire herte seche!°   *Although / seek*
I shal namore lesen° but my speche."   *lose, forfeit*

This Diomede, as bokes us declare,[3]
800 Was in his nedes prest and corageous,[4]
With sterne vois and myghty lymes square,°   *solid limbs*
Hardy, testif,° strong, and chivalrous   *testy, impetuous*
Of dedes, lik his fader Tideus,
And som men seyn he was of tonge large;°   *free with his tongue*
805 And heir he was of Calydoigne and Arge.[5]

Criseyde mene° was of hire stature;°   *middling / height*
Therto° of shap, of face, and ek of cheere,   *Further, Also*
Ther myghte ben no fairer creature.
And ofte tymes this was hire manere:
810 To gon ytressed° with hire heres clere°   *braided, coiffured / bright*
Doun by hire coler° at hire bak byhynde,   *collar*
Which with a thred of gold she wolde bynde;

And, save° hire browes joyneden yfeere,°   *except / together*
Ther nas no lak, in aught I kan espien.°   *lack, defect / observe*
815 But for to speken of hire eyen° cleere,   *eyes*
Lo, trewely, they writen that hire syen°   *who saw her*
That Paradis stood formed in hire yën.
And with hire riche beaute evere more
Strof° love in hire ay,° which of hem was more.   *Strove, Vied / always*

820 She sobre was, ek symple,° and wys withal,   *unaffected*
The best ynorisshed° ek that myghte be,   *brought up*
And goodly of hire speche in general,
Charitable, estatlich, lusty, fre;°   *dignified and lively and noble*

2. And in light of this to go to make an attempt at her now?
3. The following portraits of Diomede, Criseyde, and Troilus are drawn from a Latin poem of the late twelfth century, the *Ylias* (i.e., *Iliad*) *of Dares the Phrygian* by Joseph of Exeter. Joseph's poem was based on the *History of the Destruction of Troy* by Dares; see the Introduction. The *Ylias* was commonly known in the late Middle Ages as *Dares*.
4. Was in times of crisis (*or* in his affairs) ready/vigorous and spirited/brave.
5. Tideus's realms (see line 934 below), Calydon in Aetolia (Asia Minor) and Argos in the Peloponnesus.

12

And first he began to speak of the cruel war between his people and the Trojans, asking her what she thought about it, whether she believed their intention frivolous or vain. From this he passed on then to ask if the ways of the Greeks seemed strange to her. Nor did he long keep himself from asking her why Calchas refrained from marrying her off.

13

Criseida, who still had her soul fixed on her sweet lover in Troy, did not perceive his cunning, but replied to Diomede as it pleased her master Love. And many times she pierced his heart with grievous pain and sometimes she gave joyous hope of what he sought.

Ne nevere mo ne lakked hire° pite;   *she lacked*
825 Tendre-herted, slydynge of corage;⁶
But trewely, I kan nat telle hire age.

And Troilus wel woxen° was in highte,   *grown*
And complet° formed by proporcioun°   *perfectly / in proportion*
So wel that kynde it nought amenden myghte;°   *nature couldn't amend it*
830 Yong, fressh, strong, and hardy as lyoun;°   *brave as a lion*
Trewe as stiel in ech condicioun;°   *circumstance or quality*
Oon of the beste entecched° creature   *endowed*
That is or shal whil that the world may dure.°   *last*

And certeynly in storye it is yfounde
835 That Troilus was nevere unto no wight,
As in his tyme, in no degree secounde°   *in no way second*
In durryng don that longeth to a knyght.⁷
Al° myghte a geant° passen° hym of myght,   *Although / giant / surpass*
His herte ay with the first and with the beste
840 Stood paregal,° to durre don that hym leste.°   *fully equal / what pleased him*

But for to tellen forth of Diomede:
It fel° that after, on the tenthe day   *happened*
Syn that° Criseyde out of the citee yede,°   *Since / went*
This Diomede, as fressh as braunche in May,
845 Com to the tente ther as° Calkas lay,°   *where / lodged*
And feyned hym° with Calkas han° to doone;   *pretended / to have (business)*
But what he mente, I shal yow tellen soone.

Criseyde, at shorte wordes for to telle,
Welcomed hym and down hym by hire sette—
850 And he was ethe° ynough to maken dwelle!°   *easy / stay*
And after this, withouten longe lette,°   *delay*
The spices° and the wyn men forth hem fette;°   *spiced cakes / fetched*
And forth they speke of this and that yfeere,°   *together*
As frendes don, of which som shal ye heere.

855 He gan first fallen of the werre in speche⁸
Bitwixe° hem and the folk of Troie town;   *Between*
And of th'assege° he gan hire ek biseche   *siege*
To telle hym what was hire opynyoun;
Fro that demaunde° he so descendeth down°   *request / passed on*
860 To axen hire if that hire straunge thoughte°   *(they) seemed strange to her*
The Grekis gise° and werkes that they wroughte;°   *manners / performed*

And whi hire fader tarieth° so longe   *delays*
To wedden hire unto som worthy wight.
Criseyde, that was in hire peynes stronge°   *grievously suffering*
865 For love of Troilus, hire owen knyght,

---

6. Benoît writes of her "mais sis corages li changot" (but her purpose/intention wavered in her), and
Guido writes "animi constantiam non servasset" (she had not kept constancy of mind). Chaucer's
phrase means "slippery/changeable/wavering of spirit/resolution/mood/heart."
7. In the daring to do (derring-do) that is appropriate for a knight.
8. He first fell into talk about the war.

14

As he became reassured about her, he began to say, "Youthful lady, if I have looked well at that angelic face, which is more pleasing than any other I have ever seen, it seems to me to appear transformed by cruel suffering from that day on which we started from Troy and, as you know, came here.

15

"Nor do I know what can be the cause, unless it is love, which, if you are wise, you will cast away, when you hear the reason, because you ought to do as I say. The Trojans are, one can say, held by us in prison, as you see, for we are not disposed to leave without destroying Troy with sword or with fire.

16

"Do not believe that anyone who is in Troy will ever find pity from us. Never did anyone commit such another outrage or shall commit it, even if the world were everlasting, that the punishment which we shall give to Paris, if we can, for the deed done by him will not be a very shining example to him either here among the living or among the dead in Hell.

17

"And if there were indeed a dozen Hectors, as there is only one, and six times as many brothers, if Calchas does not lead us here by ambiguities and by errors, we shall have the desired honors equally over them, however many they may be, and soon. And their death, which shall come shortly, will give us certainty that our hope is not false.

18

"And do not believe that Calchas would have demanded you back with such insistency if he had not foreseen what I say. I discussed this matter well with him before he did it and examined all the circumstances. And so, in order to save you from such peril, he took my advice to return you here.

As ferforth° as she konnyng° hadde or myght   *far / understanding*
Answerde hym tho; but as of his entente,°   *as for his intentions/meaning*
It semed nat she wiste° what he mente.   *that she knew not*

But natheles,° this ilke° Diomede   *nevertheless / same*
870   Gan in hymself assure,° and thus he seyde: *have confidence*
"If ich aright have taken of yow hede,°   *heed*
Me thynketh° thus, O lady myn, Criseyde,   *It seems to me*
That syn I first hond on youre bridel leyde,
Whan ye out come of Troie by the morwe,°   *in the morning*
875   Ne koude I nevere sen yow but° in sorwe.   *except*

"Kan I nat seyn what may the cause be,
But if° for love of som Troian it were,   *Unless*
The which right sore wolde athynken° me   *displease*
That ye for any wight that dwelleth there
880   Sholden spille a quarter of a tere°   *tear*
Or pitously° youreselven so bigile—°   *pitifully / delude*
For dredeles,° it is nought worth the while.   *doubtless*

"The folk of Troie, as who seyth,° alle and some   *so to speak*
In prisoun ben, as ye youreselven se;
885   Nor thennes° shal nat oon on-lyve° come   *from there / alive*
For al the gold atwixen° sonne and se.   *between*
Trusteth wel, and understondeth me,
Ther shal nat oon to mercy gon° on-lyve,   *obtain mercy*
Al° were he lord of worldes twiës° fyve!   *Though / twice*

890   "Swich wreche° on hem for fecchynge° of   *vengeance / abduction*
Eleyne°   *Helen*
Ther shal ben take, er that we hennes wende,°   *go hence*
That Manes,° which that goddes ben of peyne,   *the shades of the underworld*
Shal ben agast° that Grekes wol hem shende,°   *terrified / destroy*
And men shul drede, unto the worldes ende,
895   From hennesforth to ravysshen° any queene,   *ravish, abduct*
So cruel shal oure wreche on hem be seene.

"And but if Calkas lede us with ambages—⁹
That is to seyn, with double wordes slye,
Swiche as men clepen° a word with two   *call*
visages—°   *faces (i.e., meanings)*
900   Ye shal wel knowen that I naught ne lie,
And al this thyng right sen it with youre yë,°   *eye*
And that anon,° ye nyl nat trowe° how sone;   *forthwith / believe*
Now taketh hede,° for it is for to doone.°   *heed / to be done, inevitable*

"What! Wene ye° youre wise fader wolde   *Do you suppose*
905   Han yeven° Antenor for yow anon,   *given*
If he ne wiste that the cite sholde
Destroied ben? Whi, nay, so mote I gon!°   *so may I walk (mild oath)*
He knew ful wel ther shal nat scapen° oon   *escape*

9. And unless Calchas is leading us on with ambiguities.

19

"And I encouraged him in it, hearing of your admirable virtues and noble qualities; and learning that Antenor was to be given to them for you, I offered myself as a negotiator, and he laid upon me the task of doing it, knowing full well my faithfulness. Nor were the goings and comings to see you, speak to you, hear you, and know you tiring to me.

20

"Therefore I wish to say to you then, beautiful and dear lady, abandon the deluding love of the Trojans, drive away this bitter hope which makes you now sigh in vain, and call back the bright beauty which more than any other pleases one who is discriminating, for to such a condition has Troy now come that any hope that man has there is lost.

21

"And if it were indeed to stand forever, still the king and his sons and the inhabitants are barbarous and ill-mannered and little to be valued in respect to the Greeks, who can go before any other nation in noble customs and in refined appearance. You are now among well-bred men, where before you were among senseless brutes.

22

"And do not believe that among the Greeks love may not be more noble and more perfect than among the Trojans, for your great worth, your great beauty, and your angelic appearance will find here a very worthy lover, if it pleases you to accept him, and if it should not displease you, I would be that one more gladly than be the king of Greece now."

23

And having said this he became as red as fire in his face, and his voice trembled somewhat, and he lowered his eyelids toward the ground, turning his eyes somewhat from her. But then he turned with sudden thought, more alert than he had been, and with fluent speech continued, "Let it not be disturbing to you: I am as gentle born as any man in Troy.

24

"If my father Tydeus had lived—he died fighting at Thebes—I should have been king of Calydon and Argos, as even yet I intend to be, and I did not come into the kingdom a stranger but known, of ancient and revered lineage and, if it can be believed, descended from a god, so that I am not of the least importance among the Greeks.

That Troian is; and for the grete feere
910 He dorste nat° ye dwelte lenger there.   *dared not*

"What wol ye more, lufsom° lady deere?   *lovely*
Lat Troie and Troian fro youre herte pace!°   *pass*
Drif° out that bittre hope, and make good cheere,   *Drive*
And clepe ayeyn° the beaute of youre face   *recall*
915 That ye with salte teris° so deface,   *tears*
For Troie is brought in swich a jupartie°   *jeopardy*
That it to save is now no remedie.

"And thenketh wel, ye shal in° Grekis fynde   *among*
A moore parfit love, er it be nyght,
920 Than any Troian is, and more kynde,
And bet to serven yow wol don his myght.¹
And if ye vouchesauf,° my lady bright,   *agree*
I wol ben he to serven yow myselve,
Yee, levere° than be kyng of Greces twelve!"   *Yea rather*

925 And with that word he gan to waxen° red,   *grow*
And in his speche a litel wight° he quok,°   *bit / quavered*
And caste° asyde a litel wight his hed,   *turned*
And stynte° a while; and afterward he wok,°   *stopped / roused himself*
And sobreliche on hire he threw his lok,
930 And seyde, "I am, al be it° yow no joie,   *although it may be*
As gentil man° as any wight in Troie.   *well-born a man*

"For if my fader Tideus," he seyde,
"Ilyved hadde, ich hadde ben er this
Of Calydoyne and Arge a kyng, Criseyde!
935 And so hope I that I shal yet, iwis.
But he was slayn—allas, the more harm is!—
Unhappily° at Thebes al to rathe,°   *Unluckily / quickly*
Polymyte and many a man to scathe.²

1. And (a Greek who) will exert his power the better to serve you.
2. To the harm of Polynices and many a man. Tideus fought on the side of Polynices in the struggle
of the *Seven Against Thebes*; see lines 1485–1510 below.

25

"I pray you then, if my prayer avails, that you drive away any melancholy and that you take me into your service if I appear to you of as much worth and quality as befits your sovereignty. I shall be what your honor and your noble beauty, which I see in you more than in any other, demand so that you in return will hold Diomede dear."

Marveling at his boldness, Criseida replies in accordance with the arguments advanced.

26

Criseida listened and replied with a few words and at intervals, shame-faced according as his speech demanded; but then, hearing this last matter, she said to herself that his boldness was great, eyeing him askance, full of anger, so much did Troilo have power in her, and thus in a low voice she said,

27

"I love, Diomede, that land in which I grew up and was raised, and her war grieves me as much as it can and gladly would I see her free. And if cruel fate shuts me out from there, this makes me disturbed with good reason. But for any suffering received through me, I pray that a good recompense may be rendered you.

28

"I know well that the Greeks are of high worth and well-mannered, as you say, but the high worth of the Trojans is not less on that account; and their qualities have appeared in the work of Hector's hands. Nor do I believe it is good sense to disparage others because of quarrels or because of some other reason and then to praise oneself above the others.

29

"I have not known love since the man died to whom I gave it loyally as my husband and lord. Nor did I ever care for any other, Greek or Trojan, in such fashion; nor do I desire to care for any, nor ever shall. I readily believe that you are descended of royal blood, since I have indeed heard it.

"But herte myn, syn that I am youre man—
940 And ben° the first of whom I seche grace—   *(you) are*
To serve° yow as hertely° as I kan,   *Serving / earnestly*
And evere shal whil I to lyve have space,°   *space of time*
So,° er that I departe out of this place,   *As long as*
Ye wol me graunte that I may to-morwe,
945 At bettre leyser,° telle yow my sorwe."   *With more leisure*

What° sholde I telle his wordes that he seyde?   *Why*
He spak inough for o° day at the meeste.°   *one / most*
It preveth° wel; he spak so that Criseyde   *turns out*
Graunted on the morwe, at his requeste,
950 For to speken with hym at the leeste—°   *least*
So that° he nolde speke of swich matere.   *So long as*
And thus to hym she seyde, as ye may here,

As she that° hadde hire herte on Troilus   *As a woman who*
So faste° that ther may it non arace;°   *firmly / uproot*
955 And strangely° she spak, and seyde thus: *distantly, coldly*
"O Diomede, I love that ilke° place   *same*
Ther° I was born; and Joves, for his grace,   *Where*
Delyvere it soone of al that doth it care!°   *afflict*
God, for thy myght, so leve° it wel to fare!   *allow*

960 "That Grekis wolde hire wrath on Troie wreke,°   *avenge*
If that they myght, I knowe it wel, iwis;
But it shal naught byfallen° as ye speke,   *fall out, happen*
And God toforn!° And forther over this,°   *God willing! / furthermore*
I woot my fader wys and redy° is,   *well-advised, resourceful*
965 And that he me hath bought,° as ye me tolde,   *redeemed*
So deere,° I am the more unto hym holde.°   *At so high a price / beholden*

"That Grekis ben of heigh condicioun°   *noble status*
I woot ek wel; but certeyn, men shal fynde
As worthi folk withinne Troie town,
970 As konnyng,° and as parfit, and as kynde,   *intelligent*
As ben bitwixen Orkades and Inde;³
And that ye koude° wel yowre lady serve,   *knew how*
I trowe° ek wel, hire thank° for to deserve.   *believe / her thanks*

"But as to speke° of love, ywis," she seyde,   *as for speaking*
975 "I hadde a lord, to whom I wedded was,
The whos myn herte al was, til that he deyde;⁴
And other love, as help me now Pallas,°   *Pallas Athena*
Ther in myn herte nys, ne nevere was.

---

3. As there are between the Orkneys (at the western extremity of the world) and India (at the eastern).
4. To whom my heart entirely belonged, until he died.

30

"And this makes me greatly wonder that you can give your heart to a mere woman of lower rank as I am. The beautiful Helen would be suitable for you. I have tribulations, and I am not disposed to hear such news. Certainly, I do not say for that reason that I am sorry to be loved by you.

31

"The times are cruel and you are in arms. Let the victory which you expect come; then I shall know much better what to do. Perhaps the pleasures which are not congenial now will be more pleasing to me, and you will be able to speak to me again, and perhaps your words will be dearer to me than they are now. A man must consider the time and the season when he wishes to capture another."

32

This last speech was very pleasing to Diomede, and it seemed to him that he could still hope for mercy, such as he had afterward to his pleasure, and he replied to her, "Lady, I pledge you the greatest faith I can, that I am and will be ever at your command." And he said some other things and after this went away.

33

He was tall and handsome in person, young, fresh, and very pleasing, and strong and proud, as men say, and as smooth-tongued as ever any other Greek, and he had a nature prone to love—things that Criseida in her woes kept considering to herself, after he had left, in doubt whether to approach or to flee from him.

And that ye ben of noble and heigh kynrede,°   *kindred*
980   I have wel herd it tellen, out of drede.°   *beyond a doubt*

"And that doth° me to han so gret a wonder   *causes*
That ye wol scornen° any womman so,   *treat disrespectfully*
Ek, God woot, love and I ben fer ysonder!°   *far apart*
I am disposed bet, so mot I go,⁵
985   Unto my deth, to pleyne° and maken wo.   *lament*
What I shal after° don I kan nat seye;   *afterwards*
But trewelich, as yet me list nat° pleye.   *it pleases me not*

"Myn herte is now in tribulacioun,
And ye in armes bisy day by day.
990   Herafter, whan ye wonnen han° the town,   *have conquered*
Peraventure° so it happen may   *Perhaps*
That whan I se that° nevere yit I say°.   *what / saw*
Than wol I werke that I nevere wroughte!°   *what I never did*
This word to yow ynough suffisen oughte.°   *should suffice*

995   "To-morwe ek wol I speken with yow fayn,°   *gladly*
So that° ye touchen naught of this matere.   *So long as*
And whan yow list,° ye may come here ayayn;°   *it pleases you / again*
And er ye gon, thus muche I sey° yow here: *tell*
As help me Pallas with hire heres clere,°   *bright hair*
1000   If that I sholde of any Grek han routhe,°   *pity*
It sholde be youreselven, by my trouthe!

"I say nat therfore that I wol yow love,
N'y say nat nay;° but in conclusioun,   *Nor do I say nay*
I mene° wel, by God that sit° above!"   *mean, intend / Who sits*
1005   And therwithal she caste hire eyen° down,   *eyes*
And gan to sike,° and seyde, "O Troie town,   *sigh*
Yet bidde° I God in quiete and in reste   *pray*
I may yow sen, or do° myn herte breste."°   *make / burst*

But in effect,° and shortly for to seye,   *But actually*
1010   This Diomede al fresshly newe ayeyn°   *again*
Gan pressen on, and faste hire mercy preye;°   *eagerly beg for her favor*
And after this, the sothe for to seyn,
Hire glove he took, of which he was ful feyn;°   *glad*
And finaly, whan it was woxen eve°   *had reaching evening*
1015   And al was wel, he roos and tok his leve.

The brighte Venus folwede and ay taughte°   *showed*
The wey ther brode° Phebus down alighte;°   *broad / set*
And Cynthea hire char-hors overraughte°   *leaned over her chariot horses*
To whirle out of the Leoun, if she myghte;
1020   And Signifer his candels sheweth brighte⁶

5. I am more inclined, so may I walk (a mild oath).
6. Venus as the evening star follows the sun (Phoebus) and thus shows where it set. The sun seems broad as it nears the horizon. Cynthia, the moon, reaches out over the horses that draw her chariot to urge them, if she can, to wheel out of the sign Leo. See IV.1591–93. The Signifer (Zodiac) displays its bright candles, i.e., stars.

34

These things cooled the warm thoughts which she had of wishing only to return. These things bent her whole heart, which had been set on Troilo, and turned her desire away, and a new hope somewhat put to flight her severe torment. And it happened that, moved by these reasons, she did not keep her promise to Troilo.

Whan that Criseyde unto hire bedde wente
Inwith° hire fadres faire brighte tente,   *Within*

Retornyng in hire soule° ay up and down   *Turning over in her mind*
The wordes of this sodeyn° Diomede,   *impetuous*
His grete estat, and perel° of the town,   *the peril*
And that she was allone and hadde nede
Of frendes help; and thus bygan to brede°   *breed, grow*
The cause whi, the sothe for to telle,
That she took fully purpos for to dwelle.[7]

The morwen° com, and gostly° for to speke,   *morning / figuratively or truly*
This Diomede is come unto Criseyde;
And shortly, lest that ye my tale breke,°   *interrupt*
So wel he for hymselven spak° and seyde   *spoke*
That alle hire sikes° soore adown he leyde;   *sighs*
And finaly, the sothe for to seyne,
He refte° hire of the grete° of al hire peyne.   *took from / main part*

And after this the storie telleth us
That she hym yaf° the faire baye stede°   *gave / steed*
The which he ones wan of Troilus;[8]
And ek a broche—and that was litel nede—°   *there was little need for that*
That Troilus° was, she yaf this Diomede.   *Troilus's*
And ek, the bet from sorwe hym to releve,°   *relieve*
She made hym were a pencel of hire sleve.[9]

I fynde ek in stories elleswhere,
Whan thorugh the body hurt was Diomede
Of Troilus, tho° wep she many a teere   *then*
Whan that she saugh his wyde wowndes blede,
And that she took, to kepen° hym, good hede;°   *tend to / much care*
And for to helen hym of his sorwes smerte,°   *painful*
Men seyn—I not°—that she yaf hym hire herte.   *I don't know / gave*

But trewely, the storie telleth us,
Ther made nevere womman moore wo°   *lamentation*
Than she, whan that she falsed° Troilus.   *was false to*
She seyde, "Allas, for now is clene ago°   *completely gone*
My name of trouthe° in love, for everemo!   *fidelity*
For I have falsed oon the gentileste°   *the very noblest*
That evere was, and oon the worthieste!

"Allas, of me, unto the worldes ende,
Shal neyther ben ywriten nor ysonge
No good word, for thise bokes wol me shende."°   *reproach*
O, rolled shal I ben on many a tonge!

---

7. That she wholly intended to remain (with the Greeks).
8. Which he once won from Troilus. Apparently (as Benoît writes) Diomede had given the horse to Criseyde, and she returned it.
9. She made him wear a pennon made from her sleeve (a common motif of chivalric romance).

Thorughout the world my belle shal be ronge![1]
And wommen moost wol haten me of alle.
Allas, that swich a cas° me sholde falle!°   *fate / befall*

1065 "Thei wol seyn, in as muche as in me is,[2]
I have hem don dishonour, weylaway!
Al be I nat° the first that dide amys,°   *Although I'm not / amiss, wrong*
What helpeth that to don° my blame awey?   *take*
But syn I se ther is no bettre way,
1070 And that to° late is now for me to rewe,°   *too / regret it, repent*
To Diomede algate° I wol be trewe.   *at any rate*

"But, Troilus, syn I no bettre may,°   *since I can do no better*
And syn that thus departen° ye and I,   *separate*
Yet prey I God, so yeve° yow right good day,   *may He give*
1075 As for the gentileste, trewely,
That evere I say,° to serven° feythfully,   *saw / serving*
And best° kan ay his lady° honour kepe."   *(he who) best / lady's*
And with that word she brast° anon to wepe.°   *burst out / weeping*

"And certes° yow ne haten shal I nevere;   *certainly*
1080 And frendes° love, that shal ye han of me,   *a friend's*
And my good word, al sholde I lyven evere.°   *though I should live forever*
And trewely I wolde sory be
For to seen yow in adversitee;
And gilteles, I woot wel, I yow leve.°   *believe*
1085 But al shal passe; and thus take I my leve."

But trewely, how longe it was bytwene
That she forsok hym for this Diomede,
Ther is non auctour telleth it, I wene.°   *think*
Take every man now to° his bokes heede,   *of*
1090 He shal no terme° fynden, out of drede.°   *span of time / doubt*
For though that he bigan to wowe° hire soone,   *woo*
Er° he hire wan, yet was ther more to doone.   *Before*

Ne me ne list° this sely° womman chyde   *it doesn't please / hapless*
Forther than the storye wol devyse.°   *describe*
1095 Hire name, allas, is publysshed so wide
That for hire gilt it oughte ynough suffise.
And if I myghte excuse hire any wise,°   *in any way*
For she so sory was for hire untrouthe,°   *infidelity*
Iwis,° I wolde excuse hire yet for routhe.°   *Indeed / pity*

1. My bell will be rung, i.e., my story will be the subject of defamation.
2. They will say, inasmuch as it is my fault.

Part Seven

Here begins the seventh part of the "Filostrato," in which first of all Troilo on the tenth day waits for Criseida at the gate. When she does not come, he excuses her and returns there the eleventh day and many others, and when she does not come, he goes back to his tears. Troilo consumes himself with sorrow; Priam asks him the reason; Troilo is silent about it; Troilo dreams Criseida has been taken from him; he tells it to Pandaro and wishes to kill himself; Pandaro restrains him and dissuades him from this; he writes to Criseida; Deiphebo perceives his affliction; while he is lying in bed, ladies visit him; Cassandra reprimands him and he reprimands her. And in the first place when the tenth day has arrived, Troilo and Pandaro await Criseida at the gate.

1

Troilo, as it has been said above, was passing the time awaiting the appointed day, which came indeed after long waiting. Then, making show of other doings, he went alone toward the gate, speaking much of this with Pandaro. And they went toward the Greek camp, gazing attentively to see whether they might spy anyone coming toward Troy.

2

And everyone who was seen by them coming toward them, alone or accompanied, was believed to be Criseida until they had approached so closely to them that they might be clearly recognized. And thus they remained until past midday, fooled often by their beliefs as experience afterwards showed.

3

Troilo said, "From what I can see, she would not come now before meal-time. She will find it very difficult to get herself away from her old father—more than she wishes. What will you say for my advice? I really believe that she would have come, if she had been able to come, and if she had not stayed to eat with him.

4

Pandaro said, "I believe you say the truth, but let us go away and later we shall return here." This was agreeable to Troilo in the end, and so they did it. And the time that they remained before they returned was very little, but their hope, as it appeared, deceived them and they found it empty because this gentle lady had not come, and already the ninth hour was far gone.

1100 This Troilus, as I byfore have told,
Thus driveth forth,° as wel as he hath myght;   *endures*
But often was his herte hoot and cold,
And namely° that ilke° nynthe nyght,   *especially / same*
Which on the morwe she hadde hym bihight³
1105 To com ayeyn. God woot, ful litel reste
Hadde he that nyght—nothyng to slepe hym leste.⁴

The laurer-crowned Phebus° with his heete   *laurel-crowned Phoebus*
Gan, in his cours ay upward as he wente,
To warmen of the est se the wawes weete,°   *the wet waves of the east sea*
1110 And Nysus doughter song with fressh entente,⁵
Whan Troilus his Pandare after sente;
And on the walles of the town they pleyde,°   *passed the time*
To loke if they kan sen° aught of Criseyde.   *see whether they can see*

Tyl it was noon they stoden° for to se   *stood*
1115 Who that ther come, and every maner wight°   *sort of person*
That com fro fer, they seyden it was she—
Til that thei koude knowen° hym aright.   *could recognize*
Now was his herte dul, now was it light.
And thus byjaped° stonden for to stare   *deluded*
1120 Aboute naught° this Troilus and Pandare.   *For nothing*

To Pandarus this Troilus tho seyde,
"For aught I woot, byfor noon, sikirly,°   *certainly*
Into this town ne comth nat here Criseyde.
She hath ynough to doone, hardyly,°   *assuredly*
1125 To wynnen° from hire fader, so trowe° I.   *get away / believe*
Hire olde fader wol yet make hire dyne°   *dine*
Er that she go—God yeve° hys herte pyne!"°   *may God give / torment*

Pandare answerede, "It may wel be, certeyn.
And forthi° lat us dyne, I the byseche,   *therefore*
1130 And after noon than maystow come ayeyn."°   *you may come again*
And hom they go, withoute more speche,
And comen ayeyn—but longe may they seche°   *seek*
Er that they fynde that they after cape.°   *what they are gazing toward*
Fortune hem bothe thenketh for to jape!°   *mock*

3. After which she had promised him in the morning.
4. Not at all did it please him to sleep.
5. And Nysus's daughter sang with renewed purpose. In Ovid's account the daughter, Scylla, betrayed her father and was changed into a bird.

5

Troilo said, "Perhaps her father has impeded her and wishes that she remain until vespers, and therefore her return will now be late. Let us remain outside so that she may have a quick entrance, because oftentimes these guards are used to holding in talk whoever comes, without distinguishing for whom it is fitting."

6

Twilight came and then came the evening, and many persons deceived Troilo who stood ever in suspense, trained toward the camp, and he gazed at all who came from the direction of the shore to Troy, and he gathered nothing of what he asked for.

7

Therefore he turned to Pandaro saying, "This lady has acted wisely if I understand her ways rightly. She wants to come secretly; therefore she waits for the night, and I commend it. She will not wish to make people wonder or say, 'Has she who was asked for in return for Antenor come back here so soon?'

8

"Therefore, do not let the waiting be distasteful to you, my Pandaro; I pray you for God's sake. We do not have anything else to do now. Let it not weigh heavily on you to follow my desire and, if I am not mistaken, it seems to me I see her. Ah, look down there, do you not see what I do?" "No," said Pandaro. "If I open my eyes really wide, what you show me seems to me a cart."

9

"Ah me, you say the truth!" Troilo said. "As things are, what I wish would now happen transports me very much!" Already the light of the sun had grown pale and some stars seemed to be appearing in the sky when Troilo said, "Some sweet thought comforts me in my desire; be certain that she must come from there now."

10

Pandaro laughed to himself at what Troilo said, but silently, and understood clearly the reason which moved him to say it, and in order not to make him more sorrowful than he was, he made a semblance of believing him and said, "This poor wretch waits for a wind from Mongibello [Mount Etna]!"

1135 Quod Troilus, "I se wel now that she
Is taried° with hire olde fader so,   *Has tarried*
That er she come, it wol neigh even° be.   *nearly evening*
Com forth; I wol unto the yate° go.   *gate*
Thise porters° ben unkonnyng° evere mo,   *gatekeepers / inept*
1140 And I wol don hem° holden up the yate   *have them*
As naught ne were,° although she come late." *As if nothing were the matter*

The day goth faste, and after that com eve,
And yet com nought to Troilus Criseyde.
He loketh forth by hegge,° by tre, by greve,°   *hedge / grove*
1145 And fer° his hed over the wal he leyde;°   *far / put*
And at the laste he torned hym° and seyde,   *turned*
"By God, I woot hire menyng° now, Pandare! *grasp her meaning*
Almoost, ywys, al newe was my care.°   *renewed was my sorrow*

"Now douteles, this lady kan hire good;° *knows what's good for her*
1150 I woot she meneth riden pryvely.°   *secretly*
I comende hire wisdom, by myn hood!
She wol nat maken peple nycely°   *foolishly*
Gaure on° hire whan she comth, but softely° *To stare at / quietly*
By nyghte into the town she thenketh ride.°   *means to ride*
1155 And, deere brother, thynk nat longe t'abide.°   *wait*

"We han naught elles for to don,° ywis.   *nothing else to do*
And Pandarus, now woltow trowen° me?   *believe*
Have here my trouthe,° I se hire! Yond she is. *pledge*
Heve° up thyn eyen,° man! Maistow° nat se?" *Lift / eyes / Can you*
1160 Pandare answerede, "Nay, so mote I the!° *as I may prosper*
Al wrong, by God! What saistow,° man? Where *are you saying*
arte?°   *are you*
That I se yond nys but a fare-carte."°   *cart for hauling*

"Allas, thow seyst right soth," quod Troilus.
"But, hardily, it is naught al for nought
1165 That in myn herte I now rejoysse thus;
It is ayeyns° som good I have a thought. *in anticipation of*
Not I nat° how, but syn that I was wrought° *I don't know / made*
Ne felte I swich a comfort, dar I seye;
She comth to-nyght, my lif that dorste I leye!"° *pledge*

1170 Pandare answerde, "It may be, wel ynough,"
And held° with hym of al that evere he seyde. *agreed*
But in his herte he thoughte, and softe lough,° *laughed quietly*
And to hymself ful sobreliche he seyde,
"From haselwode, there° joly Robyn pleyde,[6] *where*

---

6. On hazelwood as expressing skepticism see line 505 above. Robin was a common name for a shepherd or rustic. "What you're waiting for will come from never-never-land." Likewise the *Filostrato* parallel—this fellow expects a (cool) wind from Mongibello, i.e., from fiery Etna!

11

The waiting was for nothing, and the sentries above the gate were making a great noise calling citizens and strangers within, whoever might not wish to remain without, and also all the peasants with their beasts; but Troilo delayed the sentries more than two hours. At last when the sky was all starry, with Pandaro he returned within.

12

And although he had deceived himself many times during the day, now with one hope, now with another, Love wished indeed, however, that he might give credit to one of those less foolish hopes. Therefore he directed his speech anew to Pandaro, saying, "We are foolish because we have waited for her this day.

13

"She told me she would remain ten days with her father, not any more, and after that she would return to Troy. The end of the period is this present day; therefore she ought to return tomorrow, if we count straight; and we have stayed here the whole day, since desire made us so unmindful.

14

"Early tomorrow morning, Pandaro, we must return here." And they did so, but their looking up and down availed little, for to another she had already directed her thoughts so that, after much looking attentively, they returned within, as they had done the day before, when night had already come. But this was to Troilus excessively bitter.

15

And the glad hope that he had, had almost nothing more to fasten itself to. For that reason he grieved much within himself and began to lament strongly both about her and about Love, and it seemed wrong to him that she should delay so long in returning for any reason after she had faithfully promised him to return.

16

But, after the tenth day had already passed, Troilo waited the third and the fourth and the fifth and the sixth days with sighs, hoping for, and despairing of, her return. And after this a longer respite yet was obtained of hope and all in vain; she still did not return, and so Troilo pined because of it.

1175 Shal come al that that° thow abidest° heere.   *which / await*
    Ye, fare wel al the snow of ferne yere!"[7]

    The warden° of the yates° gan to calle   *guardian / gates*
    The folk which that withoute° the yates were,   *outside*
    And bad° hem dryven in hire bestes° alle,   *bade / animals*
1180 Or all the nyght they moste bleven° there.   *remain*
    And fer withinne the nyght, with many a teere,
    This Troilus gan homward for to ride,
    For wel he seth it helpeth naught t'abide.°   *remain*

    But natheles,° he gladed hym° in this: *nevertheless / cheered himself*
1185 He thought he misacounted° hadde his day,   *miscounted*
    And seyde, "I understonde have al amys.
    For thilke° nyght I last Criseyde say,°   *that same / saw*
    She seyde, 'I shal ben here, if that I may,
    Er that the moone, O deere herte swete,
1190 The Leoun passe, out of this Ariete.'[8]

    "For which she may yet holde al hire byheste."°   *entirely keep her promise*
    And on the morwe° unto the yate he wente,   *morning*
    And up and down, by west and ek by este,
    Upon the walles made he many a wente.°   *turn*
1195 But al for nought; his hope alwey hym blente.°   *blinded, deceived*
    For which at nyght, in sorwe and sikes° sore,   *sighs*
    He wente hym hom, withouten any more.

    His hope al clene out of his herte fledde;
    He nath wheron now lenger for to honge;[9]
1200 But for the peyne hym thoughte° his herte bledde,   *it seemed to him*
    So were his throwes° sharpe and wonder° stronge;   *throes / wondrously*
    For whan he saugh° that she abood° so longe,   *saw / delayed*
    He nyste what he juggen of it myghte,[1]
    Syn° she hath broken that she hym bihighte.°   *Since / promised*

1205 The thridde, ferthe, fifte, sexte day
    After tho dayes ten of whlch I toldc,
    Bitwixen hope and drede his herte lay,
    Yet somwhat trustyng on hire hestes° olde.   *promises*

7. Yea, farewell all the snow of yesteryear! Former years' snow was a common symbol of the irrevocable past.
8. See IV.1592.
9. Now he no longer has that on which he may support himself.
1. He didn't know what he might think of it.

17

The tears, which had lessened through the comfortings of Pandaro, and the sighs returned without his having recalled them, his fiery desires forcing a way for them, and those tears which hope had spared, came out doubled by the sufferings which were heated in him, cheated as he was, more than they had been before, indeed twenty for one.

18

In him each old standing desire returned anew and on top of that the deceit which it seemed to him he was enduring and the hostile spirit of jealousy, a suffering which was more grievous than any other and which begged for rest, as they know who have already experienced it. And so he wept day and night as much as his eyes and he had the capacity to weep.

19

He almost did not eat or drink, so full of anguish was his sad breast, and beside this he could not sleep unless overcome by sighing, and he held himself and his life completely in contempt, and he fled from delight as from fire, and every festivity, and every company he likewise fled as much as he could.

20

And in his face he had become such that he seemed a beast rather than a man; nor would anyone have recognized him, so pale and so upset was his appearance. All strength had left his body, and there was scarcely enough vitality in his limbs to sustain him, and he did not wish to take any comfort that anyone might give him.

Priam and his sons marvel at seeing Troilo so disfigured, and cannot learn from him what may be the reason.

21

Priam, who saw him so upset, sometimes called to him, saying, "Son, what have you felt? What matter is it that grieves you so much? You do not seem the same; you are so pallid. What is the reason for this wretched condition? Tell me, son. You do not support yourself, and if I perceive rightly, you are quite faint."

22

Hector, Paris, and the other brothers and sisters said the same to him and asked where he had got such a great sorrow and from what cruel events. And to all of them he said that he felt a pain in his heart, but

But whan he saugh she nolde hire terme° holde,   *appointed time*
1210 He kan now sen non other remedie
But for to shape hym° soone for to dye.   *prepare himself*

Therwith the wikked spirit, God us blesse,
Which that men clepeth woode° jalousie,   *insane*
Gan in hym crepe,° in al this hevynesse;°   *creep / grief*
1215 For which, by cause he wolde° soone dye,   *because he wished*
He ne et° ne drank, for his malencolye,   *ate*
And ek from every compaignye he fledde:
This was the lif that al the tyme he ledde.

He so defet° was, that no manere man   *disfigured*
1220 Unneth° hym myghte knowen ther° he wente;   *Scarcely / where*
So was he lene, and therto pale and wan,
And feble, that he walketh by potente;°   *with a crutch*
And with his ire° he thus hymselve shente.°   *rage / harmed*
But whoso axed hym wherof hym smerte,°   *he was hurting*
1225 He seyde his harm was al aboute his herte.

Priam ful ofte, and ek his moder° deere,   *mother*
His bretheren and his sustren gonne hym freyne°   *ask*
Whi he so sorwful was in al his cheere,°   *demeanor*
And what thyng was the cause of al his peyne;
1230 But al for naught. He nolde° his cause pleyne,°   *would not / lament*
But seyde he felte a grevous maladie
Aboute his herte, and fayn° he wolde dye.   *gladly*

what that might be none could question him so closely that he could learn more of it from him.

Troilo sees in a dream Criseida being taken from him; he complains of her to Pandaro and wishes to kill himself, and with great difficulty is restrained by him.

23

One day, all melancholy because of the broken pledge, Troilo had gone to sleep, and in a dream he saw the perilous sin of her who made him languish. For he seemed to hear within a shady wood a great and unpleasant crashing; at that, when he raised his head, he seemed to see a great charging boar.

24

And then afterward he seemed to see Criseida underneath its feet, from whom it drew her heart with its snout and it appeared to him that Criseida was not concerned by such a great hurt but almost took pleasure in what the animal did, which made him so strongly indignant that it broke his feeble sleep.

25

When he was awake he began to think over what he had seen in his dream, and he seemed clearly to discern what this which had appeared to him meant. And quickly he had Pandaro called; to whom, when he had come to him, weeping he began, "My Pandaro, my life is no longer pleasing to God.

26

"Your Criseida, alas, in whom I trusted more than in any other, has deceived me. She has given her love to another, which grieves me much more than death. The gods have shown it to me in a dream." And then he told him all the dream; then he began to tell what such a dream meant, and thus he said to him,

27

"This boar which I saw is Diomede, since his grandfather slew the boar of Calydon, if we can believe our ancestors, and ever afterward his descendants have carried the swine for a crest. Ah me, bitter and true dream! He will have taken her heart, that is her love, with his speech.

28

"This man holds her, ah, my sorrowing life, as you also can plainly see; this man alone prevents her return. If it were not this, surely she had

So on a day he leyde hym doun to slepe,
And so byfel° that yn his slep hym thoughte°   *it happened / it seemed to him*
1235 That in a forest faste° he welk° to wepe   *thick / walked*
For love of here° that hym these peynes wroughte;°   *her / caused*
And up and doun as he the forest soughte,°   *explored*
He mette he saugh a bor° with tuskes grete,   *dreamed he saw a boar*
That slepte ayeyn° the bryghte sonnes hete.   *under*

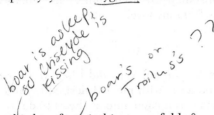

1240 And by this bor, faste in his armes folde,°   *embraced*
Lay, kyssyng ay, his lady bryght, Criseyde.
For sorwe of which, whan he it gan byholde,
And for despit,° out of his slep he breyde,°   *resentment / started*
And loude he cride on° Pandarus, and seyde: *to*
1245 "O Pandarus, now know I crop and roote.°   *foliage and root (i.e., all)*
I n'am but ded; ther nys noon other bote.°   *remedy*

"My lady bryght, Criseyde, hath me bytrayed,
In whom I trusted most of ony wight.°   *any person*
She elliswhere hath now here herte apayed.°   *pleased, satisfied*
1250 The blysful goddes thorugh here grete myght
Han° in my drem yshewed° it ful right.   *have / shown*
Thus yn my drem Criseyde have I byholde"—
And al this thing to Pandarus he tolde.

the power to return, and neither her aged father nor any other care would have impeded her. And so in my belief I am deceived and mocked, awaiting her in vain.

29

"Alas, Criseida, what subtle ingenuity, what new pleasure, what delightful beauty, what anger against me, what just disdain, what failing of mine or what cruel aberration have been able to bring your noble soul to another aim? Alas, constancy promised to me, alas, fidelity and loyalty, who has cast you away from my love?

30

"O me, why did I ever let you go? Why did I believe your bad advice? Why did I not carry you away with me as I desired to, alas? Why did I not break the pacts made, as it came into my heart to do so, when I saw you surrendered? You would not now be disloyal and false, nor I sad.

31

"I believed you and I hoped for certain that your faith would be sacred and your words a truth most certain and more open than the light of the sun to living men. And you spoke to me ambiguously and slyly as it now appears in your follies, for not only have you not returned to me but you are in love with another man.

32

"What shall I do, Pandaro? I feel strongly in my mind such a newly kindled fire that I find no place in my thought for rest. I wish to seize death with my hands, for to remain longer in life would not be a pleasure. Since Fortune has brought me to such a wicked fate, dying will be a delight where living would be distress and offense."

33

And this said, he ran to a sharp knife which hung in the room and would have stabbed himself in the breast if it were not that he was restrained by Pandaro, who seized the wretched youth when he saw him despairing in the words he used with sighs and with tears shed.

34

Troilo cried out: "Ah do not hold me, my dear friend, by God I pray you; since I am disposed to such a wish, let me follow my savage desire; let me go if you do not wish to know first what the death may be to which I hasten; let me go, Pandaro, for I will wound you if you do not let me go, and then I will slay myself.

"O my Criseyde, allas, what subtilte,°   *ingenious argument*
1255 What newe lust,° what beaute, what science,°   *desire / knowledge*
What wratthe of° juste cause have ye to me?   *with*
What gilt of me,° what fel° experience   *guilt of mine / terrible*
Hath fro me raft,° allas, thyn advertence?°   *taken / attention*
O trust, O feyth, O depe asseuraunce!°   *assurance*
1260 Who hath me reft° Criseyde, al my plesaunce?   *snatched from me*

"Allas, whi leet° I you from hennes° go,   *allowed / hence*
For which wel neigh° out of my wit I breyde?°   *nearly / went*
Who shal now trowe° on any othes mo?°   *believe / more oaths*
God wot, I wende,° O lady bright, Criseyde,   *thought*
1265 That every word was gospel° that ye seyde!   *the gospel truth*
But who may bet bigile,° yf hym lyste,°   *better deceive / it please him*
Than he on whom men weneth best to triste?°   *one thinks it best to trust*

"What shal I don, my Pandarus, allas?
I fele now so sharp a newe peyne,
1270 Syn° that ther lith° no remedye in this cas,   *Since / lies, is*
That bet° were it I with myn hondes tweyne°   *better / two*
Myselven slowh alwey than thus to pleyne;[2]
For thorugh the deth my wo sholde han an ende,
Ther° every day with lyf myself I shende."°   *Seeing that / destroy*

2. That I slew myself at any rate rather than to lament thus.

35

"Let me remove from the world the most sorrowing body that lives; let me, by dying, make your deceitful lady content, whom I shall still go on following through the dark shadows in the sorrowful realm; let me kill myself since a languishing life is worse than death." And so saying, he strove for the knife which Pandaro denied him.

36

Pandaro also cried out as he held him firmly, and if it had not been that Troilo was weak, Pandaro's strength would have been overcome, such spasms did Troilo make aided by fury. Yet in the end Pandaro removed the blade from his hand and made him against his will sit weeping with him.

37

And after bitter weeping he turned toward him pitifully with such words: "Troilo, I have always believed that your devotion to me was such that, if I might have dared to demand that you would kill yourself for me or for another, you would have done it without delay, courageously, as I would do it for you in any situation.

38

"And at my asking you have not been willing to shun a foul and displeasing death, and if I had not now been stronger than you, I should have seen you die here. I did not believe it, and I see you fail in the promises given to me, although you can still amend this if you note effectively what I say to you.

39

"Through what appears to me, you have conceived that Criseida may be Diomede's, and, if I have well understood what you have said, no other thing gives you faith in this save the dream, which you suspect through the animal which wounds with its tusks, and without wishing to think more about it first, you wished to end your sad weeping with death.

40

"I have told you on another occasion that it was folly to regard dreams too closely. No one has been, nor is, nor ever will be alive who can interpret with certainty what the fancy can show to others in sleep with varying forms, and many indeed have believed one thing while another has happened opposite and contrary.

1275 Pandare answerde and seyde, "Allas the while°   *time*
That I was born! Have I nat seyd er this,
That dremes many a maner° man bigile?°   *sort of / deceive*
And whi? For folk expounden hem amys.°   *them wrongly*
How darstow seyn° that fals thy lady ys   *dare you say*
1280 For° any drem, right for° thyn owene drede?°   *Because of / because of / fear*
Lat be° this thought: thow kanst no dremes rede.°   *Dismiss / interpret*

41

"So it might come about with this. Perhaps where you interpret the animal as hostile to your love, it will be beneficial to you and will not do you injury as you suppose. Does it seem to you an honorable act for any man, let alone a royal one as you are, to kill himself with his own hands and to make such howling on account of love?

42

"This matter was to be handled in quite another manner than you were doing it. First, you had to find out in a subtle way if it was true, as you could have, and if you had found it false and not entirely true, then you had to raise yourself from faith in dreams and from deception by them, which are harmful to you.

43

"If you had found it true that you had been abandoned by Criseida for another, you should not deliberately determine to die as the only course of action, for I do not know by whom it was ever anything but blamed, but the desirable decision would be to scorn her as she has scorned you.

44

"And even if heavy thoughts press you to die in order to feel a lesser grief, you should not have done what you did, for there is another way to accomplish such a wish and your depraved thoughts should have shown it to you, since the Greeks, who are before the threshold of the gates of Troy, will kill you without asking pardon.

45

"Let us go together, then, armed against the Greeks when you wish to die; here as honored youths let us fight against them and kill them like men; we shall die avenged and certainly I shall not forbid you from doing so, provided that I perceive that a just cause moves you to wish to die in such a trial of arms."

46

Troilo, who still raged enkindled with anger, listened to him as much as his sorrow permitted, and when he had heard him for a long time, he wept like one still sorrowful. He turned toward him who was waiting to see if he had changed from his mad enterprise, and in this way, weeping he spoke to him, always breaking his speech with sobs:

"Peraunter,° ther° thow dremest of this boor,   *Perhaps / whereas*
It may so be that it may signifie
Hire fader, which that old is and ek hoor,°   *hoar, gray-haired*
1285   Ayeyn the sonne lith o poynt to dye,[3]
And she for sorwe gynneth wepe and crie,
And kisseth hym, ther he lith on the grounde:
Thus sholdestow thi drem aright expounde!"

---

3. Under the sun lies at the point of dying.

47

"Pandaro, live certain of this, that I am completely yours in whatever I can be, and it will not be hard for me to live and die as it shall be pleasing to you, and if I was through fury beyond wise counsel a little before when you seized me for my own welfare, your virtue ought not to wonder at it.

48

"Sudden belief in the deplorable dream made me fall into such error. Now, less full of anger, I see clearly my great delusion and my mad desire. But if you see by what test I can perceive the truth of this suspicion, tell it; in God's name I ask you for it because I am upset and do not see it by myself!"

49

To him Pandaro said: "It seems to me that she is to be tested by writing; since if she does not care for you any longer, I do not believe we shall have a reply from her, or, if we do have one, we shall be able to see clearly through the written words if you ought to hope any more for her return or if she is in love with another man.

50

"Since she left, you have never written to her nor she to you, and she could have such a reason for her staying that you would say that she might well have cause to stay. And it could be such that you would reproach her for timidity more than for any other offense. Therefore, write to her, because if you indeed do it, you will see clearly what you are searching for."

51

Troilo was already feeling regret; so he believed him willingly, and having drawn apart, he commanded that writing materials should be given to him immediately, and it was done. Then, having thought over somewhat what he ought to write, he began, not as one deranged, and without delay wrote to his lady and in this manner:

"How° myghte I than don," quod Troilus,   *What*
1290 "To knowe of this, yee, were it nevere so lite?"[4]
"Now seystow° wisly," quod this Pandarus;   *you speak*
"My red° is this: syn thow kanst wel endite,°   *advice / compose*
That hastily a lettre thow hire write,
Thorugh which thow shalt wel bryngyn it aboute
1295 To know a soth of that thow art in doute.[5]

"And se now whi: for this I dar wel seyn,
That if so is that she untrewe be,
I kan nat trowen° that she wol write ayeyn.°   *believe / in return*
And if she write, thow shalt ful sone yse
1300 As wheither she hath any liberte
To come ayeyn; or ellis in som clause,
If she be let,° she wol assigne a cause.   *hindered*

"Thow hast nat writen hire syn that° she wente,   *since*
Nor she to the; and this I dorste laye,°   *wager*
1305 Ther may swich cause ben in hire entente°   *state of mind*
That hardily° thow wolt thiselven saye   *surely*
That hire abod° the best is for yow twaye.°   *delay / two*
Now writ hire thanne, and thow shalt feele° sone   *perceive*
A soth of al.° Ther is namore to done."   *The truth about everything.*

1310 Acorded° ben to this conclusioun,   *Agreed*
And that anon, thise ilke° lordes two;   *same*
And hastily sit° Troilus adown,   *sits*
And rolleth° in his herte to and fro   *rolls, turns over*
How he may best discryven hire° his wo.   *describe to her*
1315 And to Criseyde, his owen lady deere,
He wrot right thus, and seyde as ye may here:°   *hear*

---

4. To be sure of this, indeed, even if it were ever so small a matter.
5. To know the truth about that of which you are in doubt.

Troilo writes to Criseida of what it is that sustains his life and prays her that she should return as she promised.

52

"Youthful lady, to whom Love gave me and holds me yours and, while I shall be in life, will always hold me with complete faith, ever since you by your departure left me here in greater misery than anyone believes, my bewildered soul commends itself to your great virtue and cannot send you any other salutation.

53

"Although you have almost become a Greek, my letter ought not yet be rejected by you, since, in a short time, so long a love is not forgotten as that which holds and has held our friendship together, which, I pray, may be eternal, and therefore please take it and read it until its end.

54

"If in any case the servant might complain of his superior, perhaps I would be right if I were to complain of you, considering the faith I gave to your devoted affection and to the many promises and to the oath to every god that you would return by the tenth day—and yet you have not made your return by the fortieth.

55

"But since it is fitting that whatever pleases you should please me, I dare not complain, but as humbly as I can, more burning with love than ever, I write to you of my view and likewise of my fervid longing and of my life also, full of desire to know what your life has been since you were transported among the Greeks.

56

"It seems to me, if I well understand what is in your mind, that your father's flatteries have influenced you, or a new love has entered your

Litera Troili° — The Letter of Troilus

"Right fresshe flour, whos I ben have and shal,° — shall be
Withouten part of elleswhere servyse,[6]
With herte, body, lif, lust, thought, and al,
1320 I, woful wyght, in everich humble wise° — manner
That tonge telle or herte may devyse,
As ofte as matere occupieth place,[7]
Me recomaunde unto youre noble grace. — I commend myself

"Liketh yow to witen,° swete herte, — May it please you to know
1325 As ye wel knowe, how longe tyme agon° — ago
That ye me lefte in aspre° peynes smerte,° — bitter / sharp
Whan that ye wente, of which yet boote non° — still no remedy
Have I non had, but evere wors bigon° — worse off
Fro day to day am I, and so mot dwelle,
1330 While it yow list, of wele and wo my welle.[8]

"For which to yow, with dredful° herte trewe, — reverent
I write, as he that sorwe drifth° to write, — drives, compels
My wo, that everich houre encresseth newe,
Compleynyng, as I dar or kan endite.° — compose
1335 And that defaced is,° that may ye wite° — that it is defaced / blame (on)
The teris which that fro myn eyen reyne,° — rain
That wolden speke, if that they koude, and pleyne.° — complain, lament

"Yow first biseche I, that youre eyen clere
To loke on this defouled ye nat holde;[9]
1340 And over al this,° that ye, my lady deere, — Moreover
Wol vouchesauf° this lettre to byholde; — grant
And by the cause ek° of my cares colde — because also
That sleth my wit, if aught amys m'asterte,[1]
Foryeve° it me, myn owen swete herte! — Forgive

1345 "If any servant dorste or oughte of right° — dared or rightly should
Upon his lady pitously compleyne,
Thanne wene° I that ich oughte be that wight, — think
Considered° this, that ye thise monthes tweyne° — Considering / two
Han taried, ther ye seyden,° soth to seyne, — whereas you said
1350 But dayes ten ye nolde in oost sojourne—° — remain in the (Greek) host
But in two monthes yet ye nat retourne.

"But for as muche as me moot nedes like° — it must needs please me
Al that yow liste,° I dar nat pleyne moore, — pleases you
But humblely, with sorwful sikes sike,° — sick sighs
1355 Yow write ich myn unresty° sorwes soore, — unquiet

6. With no share of my service given elsewhere.
7. As often as matter occupies space, i.e., always. As elsewhere (e.g., IV.960–1078, IV.1505), Troilus displays a knowledge of the topics of philosophy, here the issue of whether a true void can exist (whether nature abhors a vacuum).
8. And so (I) must remain as long as it pleases you, source of my well-being and sorrow.
9. That you don't consider your clear eyes to be defiled by looking at this (letter).
1. Which destroy my intelligence, if anything issues from me wrongly (i.e., if I write anything improper).

mind, or—what rarely shows itself among us, an old man become generous—that the grasping Calchas may be liberal [i.e., no longer cares about his possessions in Troy], though your innermost intention [to beguile your father by appealing to his greed] led me to believe the contrary at our last bitter weeping together.

57

"Besides you have remained very far beyond our agreement when, according to your promises, you should have returned very soon. If it were the first or third cause, you should have indicated it to me, since you know that I do, and did, agree to what you wished, for patiently I should have borne it although it might be very grievous to me.

58

"But I fear strongly that a new love may be the cause of your long stay which, if it were, would be to me a greater sorrow than any that I have yet experienced, and if my fervor has deserved betrayal, you should not have known it by now. Wretchedly I live in such fear of this that it steals from me delight and hope.

59

"This fear makes me utter cries full of pain when I want to rest. This fear alone overcomes my thoughts so that I don't know what to do. This fear, O wretched me, kills me, and I do not know how to defend myself from it, nor can I. This fear has brought me to the point where I am useful neither to Venus nor to Mars.

60

"My sorrowing eyes after your departure never ceased weeping. I could not then eat or drink, rest or sleep; but always I have uttered moans and what can be heard most from my lips is the constant naming of you and calling either on you or on love for comfort. I believe that because of this alone I am not dead.

61

"You can easily imagine what I would do if I were certain of what I fear. Certainly I believe that I would kill myself if I knew you had made such a betrayal. And to what end should I live here afterwards, when I have lost hope of you, my soul, from whom I, living in tears, wait for my only peace?

62

"The sweet songs and the pleasant gatherings of friends, the birds and dogs and going about enjoying myself, the beautiful ladies, the temples and the great festivals, which in the past I used to go seeking, I now all shun, and they are, alas, hateful to me whenever I think to myself that you now dwell far from here, my sweet well-being and my sovereign hope.

Fro day to day desiryng evere moore
To knowen fully, if youre wille it weere,
How ye han ferd° and don whil ye be theere;   *have fared*

"The whos welfare and hele ek God encresse²
1360 In honour swich° that upward in degree°   *such / in its development*
It growe alwey, so that it nevere cesse.
Right as youre herte ay kan, my lady free,
Devyse, I prey to God so moot° it be,   *may*
And graunte it that ye soone upon me rewe,°   *take pity*
1365 As wisly° as in al I am yow° trewe.   *surely / to you*

"And if yow liketh° knowen of the fare°   *it pleases you / condition*
Of me, whos wo ther may no wit discryve,
I kan namore but, chiste of every care,°   *receptacle of every sorrow*
At wrytyng of this lettre I was on-lyve,°   *alive*
1370 Al redy out my woful gost° to dryve,   *spirit, life*
Which I delaye, and holde hym yet in honde,
Upon the sighte of matere of youre sonde.³

"Myn eyen two, in veyn° with which I se,   *vain*
Of sorwful teris salte arn waxen welles;°   *have become wells*
1375 My song, in pleynte° of myn adversitee;   *(has turned) into a lament*
My good, in harm; myn ese ek woxen helle is.°   *also has become hell*
My joie, in wo; I kan sey yow naught ellis,
But torned is—for which° my lif I warie—°   *for which reason / curse*
Everich joie or ese in his° contrarie;   *into its*

1380 "Which with youre comyng hom ayeyn to Troie
Ye may redresse, and more a thousand sithe°   *times*
Than evere ich hadde encressen° in me joie.   *increase*
For was ther nevere herte yet so blithe
To han his lif as I shal ben as swithe°   *soon*
1385 As I yow see; and though no manere routhe°   *kind of pity*
Commeve° yow, yet thynketh on youre trouthe.°   *May move / pledge*

2. Whose (i.e., your) welfare and health may God also increase.
3. Which (driving out of life) I delay, and still cajole him (i.e., his *gost*) with false promises, in anticipation of my seeing the subject matter of your message.

63

"The painted flowers and the new grass which make the fields fully a thousand colors cannot entrance my soul, O lady, which is gripped by you in the heat of love. Only that part of the heavens delights me under which I now believe that you live; I look at that and say, 'That now sees her from whom I hope for grace.'

64

"I gaze at the mountains which stand round about the place which holds you hidden from me, and sighing, I say, 'They have, without knowing it, the love-inspiring view of the beautiful eyes for which I grieve, far from them in a very distressful life. Now I wish I were one of them, or I wish I were dwelling upon one of them so that I might see her.'

65

"I gaze upon the waves descending to the sea near which you now dwell and say, 'Those, after flowing somewhat, will come where the divine light of my eyes has gone to stay and will be seen by her; ah me, wretched life of mine, why can I not go in their place as they do?'

66

"If the sun sets, I behold it with envy because it seems to me that longing for my joy—that is, drawn on by desire of you—he comes to see you again sooner than usual, and after some sighing, I come to hate him and my sorrows increase. So, fearing that he may take you from me, I pray the night that it will make him go down quickly.

67

"Hearing sometimes the place where you live named or seeing sometimes someone who has come from there rekindles the fire in my heart, which is worn out by too much sorrow, and it seems that I feel some hidden joy in my soul, bound by the pleasure of love, and I say to myself, 'I wish I might go from here to where he comes from, O my sweet desire!'

68

"But what do you do among armed knights, among the warlike men and among the clamor, under the tents in the midst of ambushes, often frightened by the rages, by the sound of arms, and by the storms of the sea near which you now dwell? Is it not, my lady, a grievous distress to you, who used to live so pleasantly in Troy?

69

"I have in truth, as I ought to, more compassion for you than I have for myself. Return, therefore, and keep all your promises before I fall into a worse condition. I pardon you any hurt done to me by your remaining,

"And if so be my gilt hath deth deserved,
Or if yow list° namore upon me se,°   *it pleases you / to look*
In guerdoun° yet of that I have yow served,   *As a reward*
1390 Byseche I yow, myn owen lady free,°   *noble, gracious*
That hereupon ye wolden write me,
For love of God, my righte lode-sterre,°   *guiding star*
That deth may make an ende of al my werre;°   *war, struggle*

"If other cause aught doth° yow for to dwelle,°   *causes / remain*
1395 That° with youre lettre ye me recomforte;°   *(I beseech you) That / encourage*
For though to me youre absence is an helle,
With pacience I wol my wo comporte,°   *bear up under my grief*
And with youre lettre of hope I wol desporte.°   *cheer up*
Now writeth, swete, and lat me thus nat pleyne;
1400 With hope, or deth, delivereth me fro peyne.

"Iwis, myne owene deere herte trewe,
I woot that whan ye next upon me se,
So lost have I myn hele° and ek myn hewe,°   *health / color*
Criseyde shal nought konne° knowen me.   *be able*
1405 Iwys, myn hertes day, my lady free,
So thursteth° ay myn herte to byholde   *thirsts*
Youre beute,° that my lif unnethe I holde.°   *beauty / I scarcely sustain.*

and I ask no amends for it except the sight of your beautiful face, in which alone is all my Paradise.

70

"Ah, I pray you for it by that desire which formerly seized me for you and you for me, and likewise by that sweetness which kindled our hearts equally, and moreover by that beauty which you possess, my gracious lady, by the sighs and by the piteous laments which we formerly made, so many of them together.

71

"By the sweet kisses and by that embrace which once held us so tightly together, by the great joy and the sweet discourse which made our delight more joyous, by that pledge also which it pleased you to give once in tearful words when we parted the last time and then afterwards did not come back together again,

72

"I pray that you remember me and that you return, and if it happens that you are prevented, tell me who has detained you from making a return here after the tenth day. Ah, let it not be irksome to your polished speech; in this at least make my life happy and tell me if, from now on, I should hope any more to have you, my sweet love.

73

"If you will give me hope, I shall wait, although it may be grievous to me beyond measure; if you take it from me, I shall slay myself and make an end of my hard life. But although the injury may be mine, let the shame be yours, for to such an inglorious end you will have led a subject of yours who has not committed any fault.

74

"Pardon me if in the order of writing I have erred, and if perchance you see the letter which I send covered with stains, for my suffering is the greater cause of one and of the other since I live and abide in tears, and no occurrence checks them in me. Therefore these spots, which are so frequent, are tears of sorrow.

75

"Although there still remains a great deal for me to say, I do not say more except 'do come'; ah, do it, my soul, for you will be able to if you will apply yourself to it as much as you know how to. Ah me, for you will not recognize me, I am so changed in my malignant sorrows! Nor do I say any more to you except that God be with you and make you soon to be with me."

"I say namore, al° have I for to seye   *although*
To yow wel more than I telle may;
1410   But wheither that ye do° me lyve or deye,   *cause*
Yet praye I God, so yeve° yow right good day!   *may He give*
And fareth wel, goodly, faire, fresshe may,°   *maiden*
As she that° lif or deth may me comande!   *As a woman who*
And to youre trouthe° ay I me recomande,°   *fidelity / commend myself*

76

Then he gave it sealed to Pandaro who sent it. And the reply was awaited by them in vain for many days. And so the more than human sorrow of Troilo persevered, and the opinion of his maddening dream was reaffirmed for him, not so much however that he did not hope that Criseida might love him yet.

Deiphebo perceives the cause of Troilo's sorrow, incites him to future battle, and makes known to his brothers what he has heard.

77

From day to day his sorrow increased as hope died out; so he needed to lie down, for he could do no more. But one day, only by chance, Deiphebo, for whom he had much love, came to see him. Not seeing him in his sorrow, he began to say softly, "Ah, Criseida, do not make me die by sorrowing so much."

78

Deiphebo perceived then what it was that constrained him and, making an appearance of not having heard him, he said, "Brother, why do you not comfort your sad soul? The gay season comes and manifests its beauty, the meadows grow green again and make themselves a joyous sight, and the day has already come when the term of the truce is completed.

79

"So in the customary way we shall be able to make our valor in arms felt by the Greeks: do you not wish to come any more with us in arms, for you used to be the first to strike and as a valiant fighter to be so feared by them that you used to make all fly before you? Hector has already urged us to be with him tomorrow outside the moats."

80

As a famished lion who rests himself wearied with searching for prey suddenly starts up, shaking his mane, if he perceives a stag, or a bull, or any other thing which stimulates his appetite, desiring only that, such was Troilo when he heard that the dubious war was to begin again; vigor suddenly ran through his inflamed heart.

81

And raising his head, he said, "My brother, I am in truth somewhat weak, but I have such a desire for war that I shall arise immediately from this

1415 "With hele° swich that, but ye yeven° me   *health / unless you give*
      The same hele, I shal non hele have.
      In yow lith,° whan yow liste° that it so be,   *lies / it please you*
      The day in which me clothen° shal my grave;   *clothe, cover*
      In yow my lif, in yow myght for to save
1420 Me fro disese of alle peynes smerte;°   *sharp pains*
      And far now wel, myn owen swete herte!
              Le vostre T."°   *Your T.*

      This lettre forth was sent unto Criseyde,
      Of which hire answere in effect was this:
      Ful pitously she wroot ayeyn,° and seyde,   *in return*
1425 That also sone° as that she myghte, ywys,   *as soon*
      She wolde come, and mende al that was mys.°   *amiss*
      And fynaly she wroot and seyde hym thenne,
      She wolde come, ye, but she nyste° whenne.   *didn't know*

      But in hire lettre made she swich festes°   *pleasantries, compliments*
1430 That wonder was, and swerth° she loveth hym best,   *(she) swears*
      Of which he fond° but botmeles bihestes.°   *found / ungrounded promises*
      But Troilus, thow maist now, est or west,
      Pipe in an ivy lef, if that the lest!⁴
      Thus goth the world. God childe° us fro meschaunce,   *shield*
1435 And every wight that meneth trouthe avaunce!⁵

      Encressen° gan the wo fro day to nyght   *To increase*
      Of Troilus, for tarying of Criseyde;
      And lessen° gan his hope and ek his myght,   *diminish*
      For which al down he in his bed hym leyde.°   *laid himself*
1440 He ne eet,° ne dronk, ne slep, ne word seyde,   *ate*
      Ymagynyng ay that she was unkynde,
      For which wel neigh° he wex° out of his mynde.   *nigh / went*

---

4. Pipe in an ivy leaf, if it pleases you—i.e., go whistle, act in vain. Blowing on the edge of a leaf makes a shrieking sound.
5. And (may God) further every person who means (i.e., holds to) the truth.

bed reinvigorated, and I swear to you, if I ever fought with a hard and strong heart against the Greeks, now I will fight harder than before because I hold them in so great a hatred."

82

Deiphebo understood well what those words were aimed at, and he comforted him greatly, saying to him that they would wait for him; therefore, for Troilo's comfort he would not stay longer now, and they said farewell to each other. Troilo remained with his usual woes; Deiphebo went quickly to his brothers and told them the whole matter.

83

This they readily believed because of actions already seen, and in order not to make him sad about this, they decided among themselves not to say anything about it and to aid him. Therefore they sent word immediately to their ladies that each of them should go to visit him with songs and singers and make an entertainment for him so that he might forget his troubled life.

The royal Trojan ladies visit Troilo, whom Cassandra rebukes, and he, praising Criseida, strongly reproves her.

84

In a little time the room was full of ladies and of music and of songs. On one side of him was Polyxena, who seemed like an angel in looks; on the other sat the beautiful Helen; Cassandra also stood in front of him; Hecuba was there and Andromache, and many of his sisters-in-law and relatives were gathered.

85

Each one comforted him as best she could, and someone asked him how he felt. He did not reply but gazed now at one, now at another, and in his devoted mind he remembered his Criseida, nor did he disclose this more than with sighing, and yet he felt a certain amount of delight both through the music and through their beauty.

86

Cassandra, who by chance had heard what Deiphebo had said to his brothers, as if mocking one who showed himself and appeared so distressed, said, "Brother, as I perceive, you have felt harm from accursed love by which we must be undone, as we can see if we wish to.

87

"And since indeed it had to be this way, would that you loved a noble lady! But you are led to waste away by the daughter of a wicked priest, of ill life and of small importance. Behold the honored son of a noble king who leads his life in sorrow and in weeping because Criseida has departed from him!"

This drem, of which I told have ek byforn,°   *also before*
May nevere outen° of his remembraunce.   *go out*
1445 He thought ay wel he hadde his lady lorn,°   *lost*
And that Joves of his purveyaunce°   *providence, foreknowledge*
Hym shewed hadde in slep the signifiaunce
Of hire untrouthe and his disaventure,°   *misfortune*
And that the boor° was shewed hym in figure.°   *boar / symbolically*

1450 For which he for Sibille his suster sente,
That called was Cassandre ek al aboute,[6]
And al his drem he tolde hire er he stente,°   *before he stopped*
And hire bisoughte assoilen hym° the doute   *resolve for him*
Of the stronge boor with tuskes stoute;
1455 And fynaly, withinne a litel stounde,°   *while*
Cassandre hym gan right thus his drem expounde:

She gan first smyle, and seyde, "O brother deere,
If thow a soth of this desirest knowe,

---

6. The Sybil was called Cassandra all around (the region). Chaucer takes the common noun "Sybil," or "prophetess," to be a proper noun, a name for the prophetess Cassandra.

88

Troilo was disturbed when he heard these remarks, both because he heard her disparaged whom he loved most, and because, perceiving that his secret had come to her ears—not knowing how—he thought that she might know it through the response of the gods. Nevertheless he said, "This might appear true if I were silent."

Thow most a fewe of olde stories heere,
1460 To purpos° how that Fortune overthrowe°   *Pertaining to / overthrown*
Hath lordes olde, thorugh which, withinne a throwe,°   *short time*
Thow wel this boor shalt knowe, and of what kynde°   *lineage*
He comen is, as men in bokes fynde.

"Diane,° which that wroth° was and in ire   *(The goddess) Diana / angry*
1465 For° Grekis nolde don° hire sacrifice,   *Because / wouldn't perform*
Ne encens° upon hire auter° sette afire,   *incense / altar*
She, for that Grekis gonne hire so despise,
Wrak hire° in a wonder cruel wise;°   *Avenged herself / manner*
For with a boor as gret as ox in stalle
1470 She made up frete hire corn° and vynes alle.   *caused their grain to be devoured*

"To sle° this boor was al the contre raysed,°   *slay / rallied*
Amonges which ther com, this boor to se,
A mayde,° oon of this world the beste   *maiden (Atalanta)*
ypreysed;°   *most praised*
And Meleagre,° lord of that contree,   *Meleager, prince of Calydon*
1475 He loved so this fresshe mayden free°   *noble*
That with his manhod, er he wolde stente,°   *cease*
This boor he slough,° and hire the hed he sente;   *slew*

"Of which, as olde bokes tellen us,
Ther ros a contek° and a gret envye;°   *strife / enmity*
1480 And of° this lord descended Tideus°   *from / Tydeus, Diomede's father*
By ligne,° or ellis olde bookes lye.   *By lineage*
But how this Meleagre gan to dye
Thorugh° his moder, wol I yow naught telle,   *By the agency of*
For al to longe it were for to dwelle."

1485 She tolde ek how Tideus, er she stente,°   *stopped*
Unto the stronge citee of Thebes,
To cleymen kyngdom of the citee, wente,
For° his felawe, daun Polymytes,[7]   *For the sake of*
Of which the brother, daun° Ethiocles,   *lord*
1490 Ful wrongfully of Thebes held the strengthe;
This tolde she by proces, al by lengthe.°   *successively at full length*

She tolde ek how Hemonydes asterte,°   *escaped*
Whan Tideus slough fifty knyghtes stoute.[8]
She tolde ek alle the prophecyes by herte,
1495 And how that seven kynges with hire route°   *their armies*

---

7. Cassandra tells of the war of the Seven Against Thebes, which explains how the boar of Troilus's dream (like that killed by Diomede's ancestor Meleager) represents Diomede. Polynices (*Polymytes*), son of Oedipus, was to alternate with his brother Eteocles (*Ethiocles*) as ruler of Thebes. When Eteocles refused to give up the kingship, Polynices gathered six champions, including Tydeus, to gain the city. The others of the Seven were Adrastus (king of Argos, father-in-law of Polynices), Amphiaraus (*Amphiorax*), Capaneus, Hippomedon (*Ypomedoun*), and Parthenopaeus (*Parthonope*). All of the Seven except Adrastus were slain, and Creon, who seized control of Thebes, refused them burial. This led to the expedition of Theseus, king of Athens, which is mentioned at the beginning of the Knight's Tale in the *Canterbury Tales*. This epic precursor to the Trojan War is the same story that Criseyde was listening to in II.81–105.
8. Eteocles sent *Hemonydes* (the son of Haemon, i.e., Maeon) with forty-nine others to kill Tydeus. Tydeus single-handedly slew all but Maeon.

89

And he began, "Cassandra, your desire to guess with your imaginings every secret more than other people, has already caused you sorrow many times. Perhaps it would be wiser for you to be silent than to speak so wildly. You cast your discourses in front of all, nor do I know what you mean about Criseida.

90

"Therefore, seeing that you talk too much, I wish to do what I have not done yet, that is, to show your foolishness. You say that excessive love for Criseida makes me pale and you wish to make me greatly ashamed, but thus far your Apollo, whom you say you mocked, has not clearly revealed the truth to you.

91

"Criseida never pleased me with such love, nor do I believe that there may be, or that there ever was, anyone in the world who would dare to maintain this lie. And if, as you go on saying, it were true, I swear by my faith I would never have let her go from here unless Priam had slain me.

Bysegeden° the citee al aboute;   *Besieged*
And of the holy serpent, and the welle,
And of the furies, al she gan hym telle;[9]

Of Archymoris brennynge and the pleyes,[1]
1500 And how Amphiorax fil thorugh the grounde,[2]
How Tideus was sleyn, lord of Argeyes,°   *Argives, people of Argos*
And how Ypomedoun° in litel stounde°   *Hippomedon / while*
Was dreynt,° and ded Parthonope° of wownde;   *drowned / Parthenopaeus*
And also how Capaneus the proude
1505 With thonder-dynt was slayn, that cride loude.[3]

She gan ek telle hym how that eyther° brother,   *either (i.e., both)*
Ethiocles and Polymyte also,
At a scarmuche° ech of hem slough° other,   *skirmish / slew*
And of Argyves[4] wepynge and hire wo;
1510 And how the town was brent,° she tolde ek tho;°   *burned / also then*
And so descendeth down from gestes° olde   *stories*
To Diomede, and thus she spak and tolde:

"This ilke boor bitokneth° Diomede,   *same boar signifies*
Tideus sone,° that down descended is   *son of Tydeus*
1515 Fro Meleagre, that° made the boor to blede;°   *who / bleed*
And thy lady, wherso° she be, ywis,   *wherever*
This Diomede hire herte hath, and she his.
Wep if thow wolt, or lef,° for out of doute,   *leave off*
This Diomede is inne, and thow art oute."

1520 "Thow seyst nat soth,"° quod he, "thow sorceresse,   *the truth*
With al thy false goost° of prophecye!   *spirit*
Thow wenest ben a gret devyneresse!
Now sestow nat this fool of fantasie[5]
Peyneth hire° on ladys for to lye?°   *Takes pains / lie, slander*
1525 Awey!" quod he. "Ther Joves yeve° the sorwe!   *May Jove give*
Thow shalt be fals, peraunter,° yet tomorwe!   *perhaps*

9. A *serpent* sent by Jove stung and killed the infant Archemorus (Opheltes) while his nurse was away guiding the army of the Seven toward a stream (*the welle*). Incited by the *furies*, the women of Lemnos killed all but one of the island's males.
    After line 1498 all but two of the manuscripts of *Troilus* have a twelve-verse Latin summary of Statius's Latin epic, the *Thebaid* (ca. 91 C.E.), a principal source of the Theban material in Chaucer's poem. The summary is not Chaucer's work, though he probably included it here. It may have circulated as a mnemonic. In translation:
    "The first [book] associates the exiled Polynices with Tydeus; the second tells of the embassy of Tydeus and of the ambush [by Eteocles]; the third sings of Haemonides [Maeon] and of the secretive seers; the fourth has the seven kings going into battle; then in the fifth the Furies of Lemnos and the serpent are told of; in the sixth the cremation of Archemorus and the games are read about; the seventh brings the Greeks to Thebes and the seer [Amphiaraus] to the shades; in the eighth fell Tydeus, the hope, the life of the Pelasgians; in the ninth Hippomedon dies along with Parthenopaeus; struck by lightning, Capaneus is overcome in the tenth; in the eleventh the brothers [Eteocles and Polynices] kill one another with wounds; the twelfth tells about the weeping Argia [Argiva] and the fire."
1. Of Archemorus's cremation and the (funeral) games—i.e., the Nemean Games instituted here.
2. Amphiaraus was swallowed by the earth. See II.184–85.
3. Capaneus boasted (*cride loude*) that even Zeus could not stop his attack, whereupon he was "slain by a thunderbolt."
4. Argia, wife of Polynices; the form *Argiva* appears in the last line of the *Thebaid* summary.
5. You think you're a great prophetess! Now don't you (other people listening) see this victim of delusions (Cassandra)?

92

"Not that I believe that he would have allowed it the way he allowed Paris to ravish Helen, from which we now have such recompense; so check your ready tongue. But let us suppose, however, that it might indeed be so, that I am in this grievous suffering for her, why is Criseida not in every act worthy of any great man, whoever you may wish him to be?

93

"I do not wish to speak of her beauty, which in the judgment of everyone surpasses that of the very highest, because the fallen flower is soon brown. But let us come merely to her gentility, which you disparaged so much, and in this matter let everyone agree to the truth if I tell it, and if another denies it, I pray him that he produce the reason why.

94

"Gentility exists wherever virtue is; this no one who understands it will deny, and all the virtues are seen in her if the cause may be argued from the effect. But indeed one must arrive at such a conclusion point by point only in order to satisfy this woman who says so much of every gentle person without knowing what it is she chatters about.

95

"If my sight, and what others say of her, does not greatly deceive me, no one is more chaste, nor ever has been, than she. And if I hear the truth, she is discreet and modest beyond others, and certainly her appearance shows it, and likewise she is silent and retiring where it is suitable, which in a lady is a sign of noble nature.

96

"Her discretion appears in her actions and in her speech, which is very sound and sensitive and full of all reason, and I saw this year in part how much it might be in the excuse she made for her father's treason. And in her weeping she gave a sign with fitting words of her high-minded and very real scorn.

97

"Her behavior is very well known, and therefore it seems to me that it has no need to be defended either by me or by others. Nor do I believe there is any knight in this land—be there as many courteous ones as you wish—whom she would not mate in the middle of the chessboard in courtesy and in liberality, if only she should have sufficient means to do so.

"As wel thow myghtest lien on° Alceste,[6]   *lie about*
That was of creatures, but° men lye,   *unless*
That evere weren, kyndest and the beste!
1530 For whan hire housbonde was in jupertye°   *jeopardy*
To dye hymself but if° she wolde dye,   *unless*
She ches° for hym to dye and gon to helle,   *chose*
And starf anon,° as us the bokes telle."   *died immediately*

6. Alceste, heroine of the Prologue to Chaucer's *Legend of Good Women*. The Fates promised to deliver her husband, Admetus, from death if his father, mother, or wife would die for him.

98

"And I know this because I have already been where she has honored me and others so nobly that on royal thrones sit many who would seem to have been inconvenienced to do it and would have omitted it negligently like low-born men. Her praiseworthy renown may declare whether she has always been modest here.

99

"What more, Cassandra, do you now demand in a lady? Your royal blood? Not all those on whom you see a crown or scepter or an imperial robe are kings. Many times have you already heard, a king is he who is worthy through virtue, not through power. And if this lady were able to, do you not believe that she would rule as well as you?

100

"She would know much better than you how to wear it, the crown I mean, if you understand me. Nor would she be, as you are, a silly woman who takes a bite at every person. Would that God had made me worthy of having her as my lady, as it is rumored among you, so that I might hold in the highest esteem what Lady Cassandra holds in disrepute.

101

"Now go away with mischance, since you do not know how to talk rationally. Spin, and reform your moral ugliness, and leave the virtue of others alone. Here is a sorry thing; here is a new calamity—that a madwoman through her vanity wishes to abuse what is to be praised, and if she is not listened to, it grieves her."

102

Cassandra was silent and gladly would have wished to be elsewhere that moment, and she mingled among the other ladies without saying any more, and when she had gone from his sight, she went at once to the royal palace, nor did he ever give her another opportunity to visit him. She was not so well regarded and listened to in that place.

103

Hecuba, Helen, and the others commended what Troilo had said, and after a little they all comforted him pleasingly with words, with mirth, and with play. And then they all went away together, each returning to her place. And afterwards they visited him again many times while he stayed enfeebled in his bed.

104

Through so continuing to be in grief, Troilo became strong enough to bear it with patience, and so also through the ardent desire which he had to demonstrate his prowess against the Greeks, he soon regained the strength which he had lost through the too bitter pains he had sustained.

105

And besides this, Criseida had written to him and said that she loved him more than ever, and she had presented many false excuses for having remained so long without returning and had asked still another delay for her return, which was never to be, and he had granted it, hoping to see her again, but he knew not when.

106

And in many battles then fought with his adversaries, he showed how much he was worth in arms. And his sighs and the other bitter laments which he had through their actions he sold to them dearly, beyond any estimation, not, however, as much as his anger desired. But afterwards death, which obliterates everything, brought peace to love and its strife.

Part Eight

Here begins the eight part of the "Filostrato" in which first of all Troilo with letters and with messages again tests Criseida, who deceives him with her words. Soon, through a garment taken by Deiphebo from Diomede, Troilo recognizes from a brooch which was on it that Criseida was Diomede's. Troilo grieves with Pandaro and completely despairs. Last of all, slain by Achilles, his sorrows end. And first of all Troilo with letters and with messages again tests the faith and love of Criseida.

1

He was, as has been said, already accustomed to suffering, and it made the deep sorrow stronger in him, that could never be told by anyone, which his father, and himself, and his brothers had through the death of Hector, in whose supreme courage the forts and the walls and the gates of Troy trusted. This held them for a long time in tears and in tribulation.

Cassandre goth, and he with cruel herte
1535 Foryat° his wo, for angre of hire speche;   *Forgot*
And from his bed al sodeynly he sterte,°   *started up*
As though al hool hym hadde ymad a leche.[7]
And day by day he gan enquere and seche°   *seek*
A sooth of° this with al his fulle cure;°   *The truth about / diligence*
1540 And thus he drieth forth his aventure.°   *endures his lot*

Fortune, which that permutacioun°   *the changes*
Of thynges hath, as it is hire° comitted   *to her*
Thorugh purveyaunce and disposicioun
Of heighe Jove, as regnes shal be flitted
1545 Fro folk in folk, or when they shal be smytted,[8]   *struck down*
Gan pulle awey the fetheres brighte of Troie
Fro day to day, til they ben bare of joie.

Among al this, the fyn of the parodie[9]
Of Ector gan aprochen wonder blyve.°   *wondrously quickly*
1550 The fate wolde° his soule sholde unbodye,   *willed it that*
And shapen hadde a mene° it out to dryve,   *had arranged a means*
Ayeyns which fate hym helpeth° nat to stryve;   *it helps him*
But on a day to fighten gan he wende,°   *go*
At which—allas!—he caughte his lyves ende.

1555 For which me thynketh° every manere wight°   *it seems to me / sort of person*
That haunteth° armes oughte to biwaille   *practices*
The deth of hym that was so noble a knyght;
For as he drough a kyng by th'aventaille,
Unwar of this, Achilles thorugh the maille[1]
1560 And thorugh the body gan hym for to ryve;°   *pierce*
And thus this worthi knyght was brought of lyve.°   *from life*

For whom, as olde bokes tellen us,
Was mad swich wo that tonge it may nat telle,
And namely,° the sorwe of Troilus,   *especially*
1565 That next hym° was of worthynesse welle;°   *to him / the source*

---

7. As if a physician had made him all whole.
8. Through the providence and disposition of high Jove, as (when) realms must be transferred from people to people, or when they must be struck down. *Smytted* may mean "sullied" (as if "smutted") rather than "smitten."
9. Meanwhile, the end of the period (of life).
1. For as he dragged a king by the *aventaille* (the chain-mail neck guard attached to the helmet), unaware of this (what was coming), Achilles through his mail (armor).

2

But he did not because of this separate himself from love although hope had largely died out; rather he sought in every fashion and way, as lovers are accustomed to do, to be able to have again, as he used to have before, his sweet and only beloved, always excusing her for not returning, thinking this to be because of her not being able to.

3

He sent her more letters, writing what he felt for her night and day, recalling to mind the sweet time and the promised pledge to return, and reproving courteously her long stay. Numerous times also he sent Pandaro over there whenever any truce or pact was granted between them.

4

And likewise many times he also had in mind the wish to go there in the light habit of a pilgrim. But he did not know how to disguise himself so that the truth would seem to him sufficiently concealed, nor did he know how to find a credible excuse if he were to have been recognized in such a wretched garb.

And in this wo gan Troilus to dwelle
That, what for sorwe, and love, and for unreste,
Ful ofte a day he bad° his herte breste.°   *bade / to burst*

But natheles,° though he gan hym dispaire,   *nevertheless*
1570 And dradde° ay that his lady was untrewe,   *dreaded*
Yet ay on hire his herte gan repaire.°   *return*
And as thise lovers don, he soughte ay newe°   *ever anew*
To gete ayeyn° Criseyde, brighte of hewe;   *get back*
And in his herte he wente° hire excusynge,   *went on*
1575 That Calkas caused al hire tariynge.

And ofte tyme he was in purpos grete°   *fully resolved*
Hymselven lik a pilgrym to desgise
To seen hire; but he may nat contrefete°   *dissemble*
To ben unknowen of folk that weren wise,
1580 Ne fynde excuse aright that may suffise
If he among the Grekis knowen° were;   *recognized*
For which he wep° ful ofte and many a tere.   *wept*

To hire he wroot yet ofte tyme al newe
Ful pitously—he lefte° it nought for slouthe—°   *neglected / sloth*
1585 Bisechyng hire that sithen° he was trewe,   *since*
That she wol come ayeyn and holde hire trouthe.°   *fulfill her pledge*
For which Criseyde upon a day, for routhe—°   *pity*
I take it so—touchyng° al this matere,   *with regard to*
Wrot hym ayeyn,° and seyde as ye may here: *in return*

Litera Criseydis°   *Criseyde's Letter*

1590 "Cupides sone, ensample° of goodlyheede,   *example, model*
O swerd° of knyghthod, sours° of gentilesse,   *sword / source*
How myght a wight in torment and in drede
And heleles,° yow sende as yet° gladnesse?   *without health / nevertheless*
I herteles,° I sik,° I in destresse!   *dispirited / sick*
1595 Syn ye with me, nor I with yow, may dele,°   *Since / deal, interact*
Yow neyther sende ich herte may nor hele.°   *health*

"Youre lettres ful, the papir al ypleynted,°   *filled with laments*
Conceyved hath myn hertes pitee,²
I have ek seyn with teris al depeynted°   *stained*
1600 Youre lettre, and how that ye requeren° me   *ask*
To come ayeyn, which yet ne may nat be;
But whi, lest that this lettre founden were,
No mencioun ne make I now, for feere.

2. My heart's pity has comprehended. Or, if *papir* is construed as the (singular) subject, "has engendered my heart's pity."

5

He did not have from her anything but fair words and grand promises without effect, and so he began to presume that they were all idle tales and to become suspicious of what was the truth, as is often likely to happen to someone who considers the facts he has at hand without ignoring any; for his suspicion was not an empty one.

6

And well he knew that a new love was the cause of such lies and so many of them, affirming to himself that neither paternal flatteries nor devoted caresses would ever have had so much strength in her heart. Nor was there an opportunity for him to see by what ways he might become more certain of what his foreboding dream had already shown him.

7

Love had much lessened his faith in the dream, just as it happens that he who loves believes reluctantly, while loving, something which increases his pain. But an occurrence not long after gave him faith that

"Grevous to me, God woot, is youre unreste,
1605 Youre haste, and that the goddes ordinaunce°   *ordinance, decree*
It semeth nat ye take it for the beste.
Nor other thyng nys in youre remembraunce,°   *mind*
As thynketh me,° but only youre plesaunce.   *it seems to me*
But beth nat wroth,° and that I yow biseche;   *angry*
1610 For that° I tarie is al for wikked speche.°   *The reason that / wicked gossip*

"For I have herd wel moore than I wende,°   *had thought*
Touchyng° us two, how thynges han ystonde,°   *With regard to / stood*
Which I shal with dissymelyng° amende.   *dissembling*
And beth nat wroth, I have ek understonde
1615 How ye ne do but holden me in honde.°
But now no force.° I kan nat in yow gesse°   *no matter / imagine*
But alle trouthe and alle gentilesse.

"Come I wole; but yet in swich disjoynte°   *such a predicament*
I stonde as now that what yer or what day
1620 That this shal be, that kan I naught apoynte.°   *appoint, specify*
But in effect° I pray yow, as I may,   *finally, essentially*
Of youre good word and of youre frendship ay;
For trewely, while that my lif may dure,°   *last*
As for a frend ye may in me assure.°   *trust, be assured*

1625 "Yet preye ich yow, on yvel ye ne take°   *that you take it not amiss*
That it is short which that I to yow write;
I dar nat, ther° I am, wel lettres make,   *where*
Ne nevere yet ne koude I wel endite.°   *compose*
Ek gret effect° men write in place lite;°   *significance / a small space*
1630 Th'entente° is al, and nat the lettres space.°   *One's intention / length*
And fareth now wel. God have yow in his grace!
La vostre C."°   *Your C.*

This Troilus this lettre thoughte al straunge°   *distant, cold*
Whan he it saugh, and sorwfullich he sighte;°   *sighed*
Hym thoughte it lik a kalendes° of chaunge.   *first day, harbinger*
1635 But fynaly, he ful ne trowen myghte°   *couldn't entirely believe*
That she ne wolde hym holden that she hyghte;°   *keep what she promised*
For with ful yvel wille list hym to leve
That loveth wel, in swich cas, though hym greve.[4]

But natheles° men seyen that at the laste,   *nevertheless*
1640 For° any thyng, men° shal the soothe se;   *Despite / a person*
And swich a cas bitidde,° and that as faste,°   *happened / very soon*
That Troilus wel understod that she
Nas nought° so kynde as that hire oughte be.°   *Was not / she ought to be*
And fynaly, he woot° now out of doute   *knew*
1645 That al is lost that he hath ben aboute.°   *engaged in*

---

3. How you do nothing but cajole me with false promises.
4. For very reluctantly it pleases one who loves much to leave off (loving) in such a case, though it may cause him sorrow.

it was indeed true of Diomede, as he at first suspected, and took from him any excuse and turned him to believing it.

Deiphebo displays through Troy a garment taken by him in battle from Diomede, on which Troilo recognizes a brooch given by him to Criseida.

8

Fearful and in suspense because of his love, Troilo was not without torment when he heard that Deiphebo, after a very prolonged combat between the Trojans and the Greeks, had returned with an ornamented garment taken from the seriously wounded Diomede, and was proud of such booty and very pleased with himself.

9

And while Deiphebo was having it carried before him through Troy, Troilo came up unexpectedly and commended him greatly among all the people, and in order to see it better, he held it somewhat and while he gazed—his eyes wandering now there, now there, all around—it happened that he saw on the breast a brooch of gold, placed there perhaps for a buckle.

10

Since he had given it to Criseida when, sorrowing, he took leave of her the morning after the last time he had spent the night with her, he recognized it at once. And so he said, "I see indeed that my dream, my suspicion, and my thought are true."

Troilo sorrows together with Pandaro over the deceit of Criseida, which is clearly known.

11

Having left there, Troilo sent for Pandaro, to whom, when he had come to him, he began with weeping to lament the long love which he had held for his Criseida, and he began to show him clearly the treachery he had been dealt, sorrowing for it strongly, calling upon death alone for relief.

12

And weeping he began to say thus: "O my Criseida, where is the faith, where is the love, where is the desire now, where is the grace so sworn by you to God, ah me, at your departure? Diomede possesses everything and I, who loved you more, am left through your deceit in weeping and in distress.

Stood on a day in his malencolie
This Troilus, and in suspecioun
Of hire for whom he wende° for to dye.   *thought*
And so bifel° that thorughout Troye town,   *it happened*
1650 As was the gise,° iborn° was up and down   *custom / carried*
A manere cote-armure,[5] as seith the storie,
Byforn Deiphebe,° in signe of his victorie;   *In front of Deiphebus*

The whiche cote, as telleth Lollius,°   *Lollius, supposed author*
Deiphebe it hadde rent° fro Diomede   *torn*
1655 The same day. And whan this Troilus
It saugh,° he gan to taken of it hede,°   *saw / heed*
Avysyng° of the lengthe and of the brede,°   *Taking note / breadth*
And al the werk;° but as he gan byholde,   *workmanship*
Ful sodeynly his herte gan to colde,°   *grow cold*

1660 As he that on the coler° fond withinne   *collar*
A broch that he Criseyde yaf that morwe°   *gave on that morning*
That she from Troie moste nedes twynne,°   *had to separate*
In remembraunce of hym and of his sorwe.
And she hym leyde° ayeyn hire feith to borwe°   *laid, offered / as a pledge*
1665 To kepe it ay!° But now ful wel he wiste,   *keep (her faith) always*
His lady nas no lenger on to triste.°   *to be relied on*

He goth hym hom and gan ful soone sende
For Pandarus, and al this newe chaunce,°   *happenstance*
And of this broche, he tolde hym word and ende,°   *beginning (= ord) and end*
1670 Compleynyng of hire hertes variaunce,°   *fickleness*
His longe love, his trouthe, and his penaunce.°   *suffering*
And after° deth, withouten wordes moore,   *to*
Ful faste he cride, his reste hym to restore.

aesthetic beauty hiding flaws or terrible (& ugly) truth (s) [handwritten annotation]

Than spak he thus, "O lady myn, Criseyde,
1675 Where is youre feith, and where is youre biheste?°   *promise*
Where is youre love? Where is youre trouthe?" he seyde.
"Of Diomede have ye now al this feeste!°   *pleasure*
Allas, I wolde han trowed atte leeste°   *believed at the least*

---

5. A kind of coat-armor—i.e., a coat of arms, a tunic emblazoned with an identifying heraldic device, often worn over armor by a warring knight.

broach: T → C → D → T [handwritten annotation]
Troy victory; Troilus defeat [handwritten annotation]

13

"Who will ever believe in any oath, who in love, who in a woman ever, when he regards your false perjury well? Ah me, that I don't know. I never thought that you had a heart so rigid and hard that because of another man I should ever depart from your soul, since I loved you more than myself, and, deceived, I waited for you always.

14

"Now did you not have another jewel that you could give to your new lover, I mean to Diomede, except that one which I had given to you with so many tears to remind you of poor, wretched me while you were staying with Calchas? Nothing else made you do it except spite and to show very clearly your mind.

15

"I see that you have driven me completely out of your breast, and against my will I still hold your beautiful face as an effigy in mine with excruciating grief. O poor me, that I was born in an evil hour! This thought kills me and robs me of any hope of future joy and is the cause to me of anguish and distress.

16

"You have wrongfully driven me from your mind, where I thought I would dwell always, and in my place you have falsely put Diomede, but by the goddess Venus, I swear to you I shall make you sorrow for it soon with my sword in the first melee if I can happen to find him, provided that I can overcome him in strength.

17

"Or else he will slay me, and it will be dear to you, but I hope indeed that divine justice will have regard for my bitter sorrow and likewise for your great iniquity. O highest Jove, in whom I know that the right has a sure refuge and from whom radiates all the noble virtue through which man lives and moves, are your just eyes turned elsewhere?

18

"What are your flaming thunderbolts doing? Are they reposing or do you no more hold your eyes turned upon the defects of the human race? O true light, O bright heavens by which earthly minds are cheered, do away with her in whose breast are lies and deceits and betrayals, and do not make her ever worthy of pardon.

That syn° ye nolde in trouthe to me stonde,°   *since / stand, remain*
1680 That ye thus nolde han holden me in honde!°   *cajoled me with false promises*

"Who shal now trowe° on any othes mo?°   *believe / other oaths*
Allas, I nevere wolde han wend,° er this,   *thought*
That ye, Criseyde, koude han chaunged so;
Ne, but I hadde agilt° and don amys,°   *been guilty / amiss*
1685 So cruel wende° I nought youre herte, ywis,   *thought*
To sle° me thus! Allas, youre name of trouthe°   *slay / reputation for integrity*
Is now fordon,° and that is al my routhe.°   *destroyed / regret*

"Was ther non other broch yow liste lete°   *it pleased you to give up*
To feffe with° youre newe love," quod he,   *enfeoff, endow*
1690 "But thilke° broch that I, with teris wete,   *that same*
Yow yaf° as for a remembraunce of me?   *Gave you*
Non other cause, allas, ne hadde ye
But for despit,° and ek for that ye mente°   *spite / because you meant*
Al outrely° to shewen youre entente.°   *utterly, plainly / state of mind*

1695 "Thorugh which I se that clene out of youre mynde
Ye han me cast—and I ne kan nor may,
For al this world, withinne myn herte fynde
To unloven yow a quarter of a day!
In corsed tyme I born was, weilaway,
1700 That yow, that doon° me al this wo endure,   *cause*
Yet love I best of any creature!

"Now God," quod he, "me sende yet the grace
That I may meten° with this Diomede!   *meet*
And trewely, if I have myght and space,°   *opportunity*
1705 Yet shal I make, I hope, his sydes blede.°   *bleed*
O God," quod he, "that oughtest taken heede
To fortheren° trouthe, and wronges to punyce,°   *further, advance / punish*
Whi nyltow don° a vengeaunce of this vice?   *bring about*

19

"O my Pandaro, who has blamed me with so much insistence for having faith in dreams, now you can see what may be seen through them; your Criseida gives you proof of it. The gods have pity upon us mortals and in diverse ways make clear to us what is unknown to us, very often making it known for our good.

20

"And what sometimes manifests itself in sleep is one of the ways; I remember having perceived it many times before. Now I wish that I had died then, since in the future I expect no solace, joy, pleasure, nor delight, but through your counsel I am willing to wait, to die in arms with my enemies.

21

"May God send Diomede in front the first time that I go to battle; this I desire among my great woes so that I may make him test how my sword cuts and may make him die with lamentations in the field, and then it does not matter to me that someone may kill me, if only I may die and find him in misery in the dark kingdom."

22

Pandaro listened to all with sorrow, and, perceiving the truth, he did not know what to say. On the one hand, love of his friend drew him to stay here; on the other, shame for Criseida's sin invited him many times to depart. And he did not know how to decide what he ought to do; both the one and the other grieved him sorely.

23

At last, weeping, he said, "Troilo, I do not know what I ought to say to you. If it is as you say, the more I can, the more I shall blame her, and for her great transgression I do not intend to put forward any excuse, nor do I wish to go any more where she may be. What I did formerly, I did for your love, putting aside all honor of mine.

24

"And if I pleased you, it makes me very glad. In what has now been done I can make no change, and like you I am enraged by it. And if I saw any way of amending it, be certain I would be eager for it; may God, who can, bring about that which may square matters. I pray Him as much as I can that He punish her so that she may not sin more in such a way."

"O Pandarus, that in dremes for to triste°   *for believing in dreams*
1710 Me blamed hast, and wont art oft upbreyde,°   *are often wont to reproach (me)*
Now maistow sen thiself, if that the liste,°   *it please you*
How trewe is now thi nece,° bright Criseyde!   *niece*
In sondry formes, God it woot," he seyde,
"The goddes shewen° bothe joie and tene°   *reveal / grief*
1715 In slep, and by my drem it is now sene.°   *seen*

"And certeynly, withouten moore speche,
From hennesforth, as ferforth° as I may,   *far*
Myn owen deth in armes wol I seche;°   *seek out*
I recche° nat how soone be the day!   *care*
1720 But trewely, Criseyde, swete may,°   *maid*
Whom I have ay with al my myght yserved,
That ye thus doon, I have it nat deserved."

This Pandarus, that al thise thynges herde,
And wiste° wel he seyde a soth of° this,   *knew / the truth about*
1725 He nought a word ayeyn° to hym answerde;   *in return*
For sory of his frendes sorwe he is,
And shamed for his nece hath don amys,
And stant,° astoned of° thise causes tweye,°   *stands / astounded by / two*
As stille as ston; a word ne kowde° he seye.   *could*

1730 But at the laste thus he spak, and seyde:
"My brother deer, I may do the namore.°   *no more for you*
What sholde I seyen? I hate, ywys,° Cryseyde;   *indeed*
And, God woot, I wol hate hire evermore!
And that thow me bisoughtest don of yoore,[6]
1735 Havyng unto myn honour ne my reste°   *comfort*
Right no reward,° I dide al that the leste.°   *regard / pleased you*

"If I dide aught that myghte liken the,°   *have pleased you*
It is me lief;° and of this tresoun now,   *pleasing to me*
God woot that it a sorwe is unto me!
1740 And dredeles, for hertes ese of yow,°   *for your heart's ease*
Right fayn° I wolde amende it, wiste I° how,   *gladly / if I knew*
And fro this world, almyghty God I preye
Delivere hire soon! I kan namore seye."

6. And that which you requested me to do in earlier times.

Troilo seeks Diomede in battle; they insult each other, and at last Troilo is slain by Achilles.

25

Great were the laments and the regrets but still Fortune ran her course. She loved Diomede with all her heart and Troilo wept. Diomede praised God, and Troilo, on the contrary, grieved. Troilo always entered into battle, and more than others he sought Diomede.

26

And many times they came together face to face with vile and rude taunts, and great blows they gave each other, sometimes charging and sometimes heaving swords in hand, intemperately selling each other their love very dear. But Fortune had not disposed that the one should be dealt with as the other proposed.

Gret was the sorwe and pleynte° of Troilus,   *lament*
1745 But forth hire cours Fortune ay gan to holde.
Criseyde loveth the sone of Tideus,
And Troilus moot wepe in cares colde.
Swich is this world, whoso° it kan byholde;   *whoever*
In ech estat° is litel hertes reste.   *station in life*
1750 God leve° us for to take it for the beste!   *grant*

In many cruel bataille, out of drede,°   *beyond a doubt*
Of Troilus, this ilke° noble knyght,   *same*
As men may in thise olde bokes rede,
Was seen his knyghthod and his grete myght;
1755 And dredeles,° his ire, day and nyght,   *doubtless*
Ful cruwely the Grekis ay aboughte;°   *always paid for, suffered*
And alwey moost this Diomede he soughte.

And ofte tyme, I fynde that they mette°   *met*
With blody strokes and with wordes grete,
1760 Assayinge° how hire speres weren whette;°   *Testing / sharpened*
And, God it woot, with many a cruel hete°   *heat, rage*
Gan Troilus upon his helm to bete!°   *beat*
But natheles, Fortune it naught ne wolde
Of oothers° hond that eyther deyen sholde.°   *the other's / had to die*

1765 And if I hadde ytaken° for to write   *undertaken*
The armes° of this ilke° worthi man,   *feats of arms / same*
Than wolde ich of his batailles endite;°   *compose*
But for that I to writen first bigan
Of his love, I have seyd as I kan—
1770 His worthi dedes, whoso list hem heere,
Rede Dares,[7] he kan telle hem alle ifeere—°   *together*

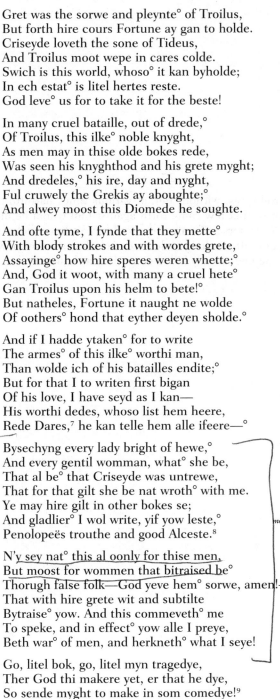

Bysechyng every lady bright of hewe,°   *color*
And every gentil womman, what° she be,   *whoever*
That al be° that Criseyde was untrewe,   *although it is the case*
1775 That for that gilt she be nat wroth° with me.   *angry*
Ye may hire gilt in other bokes se;
And gladlier° I wol write, yif yow leste,°   *more happily / if it please you*
Penolopeës trouthe and good Alceste.[8]

N'y sey nat° this al oonly for thise men,   *I don't say*
1780 But moost for wommen that bitraised be°   *who have been betrayed*
Thorugh false folk—God yeve hem° sorwe, amen!—   *give them*
That with hire grete wit and subtilte
Bytraise° yow. And this commeveth° me   *Betray / moves*
To speke, and in effect° yow alle I preye,   *in essence*
1785 Beth war° of men, and herkneth° what I seye!   *Beware / listen to*

Go, litel bok, go, litel myn tragedye,
Ther God thi makere yet, er that he dye,
So sende myght to make in som comedye![9]

---

7. On Dares Phrygius, historian of the Trojan War, see the Introduction and the note to line 799 above.
8. About the fidelity of Penelope and good Alceste. Odysseus's wife Penelope waited chastely for his homecoming for twenty years. On Alceste see lines 1527–33 above.
9. May God send your author yet, before he dies, power to compose some comedy.

27

The wrath of Troilo was, without fail, at various times harmful to the Greeks, so much so that few came forth against him whom he did not hurl dead from their horses if only they would await him, such wicked blows he dealt, and after a long stalemate, Achilles one day slew him wretchedly after he had already killed more than a thousand.

But litel book, no makyng° thow n'envie,°   writing / envy or rival
1790 But subgit° be to alle poesye;   subject
And kis the steppes° where as thow seest pace°   footprints / walk
Virgile, Ovide, Omer, Lucan, and Stace.[1]

And for° ther is so gret diversite   because
In Englissh and in writyng of oure tonge,
1795 So prey I God that non myswrite the,
Ne the mysmetre for defaute of tonge;[2]
And red wherso thow be,° or elles songe,   wherever you are read
That thow be understonde, God I biseche!
But yet to purpos° of my rather° speche: the point / earlier

1800 The wrath, as I bigan yow for to seye,
Of Troilus[3] the Grekis boughten deere,°   paid for dearly
For thousandes his hondes maden deye,°   caused to die
As he that was withouten any peere,°   peer, equal
Save Ector,° in his tyme, as I kan heere.   Except for Hector
1805 But—weilawey, save only Goddes wille,[4]
Despitously° hym slough° the fierse Achille.   cruelly, disdainfully / slew

And whan that he was slayn in this manere,[5]
His lighte goost° ful blisfully is went°   spirit, soul / went
Up to the holughnesse of the eighthe spere,
1810 In convers letyng everich element;[6]
And ther he saugh with ful avysement°   deliberation, contemplation
The erratik sterres, herkenyng armonye[7]
With sownes° ful of hevenyssh° melodie.   sounds / celestial

And down from thennes faste he gan avyse°   behold, contemplate
1815 This litel spot of erthe that with the se°   sea
Embraced is, and fully gan despise
This wrecched world, and held° al vanite   considered
To respect of the pleyn felicite[8]
That is in hevene above; and at the laste,
1820 Ther° he was slayn his lokyng° down he caste,   Where / gaze

---

1. Vergil, Ovid, Homer, Lucan (author of the *Civil War*), and Statius (author of the *Thebaid*), all ancient and authoritative poets.
2. I pray to God that no one copy you erroneously, or ruin your meter because of a deficiency of language. Chaucer refers to the diversity of dialects in English, whose confusion can lead to the scribal corruption of poetic texts in such matters as the pronunciation of final -e.
3. The allusion here to the opening of the *Iliad* ("the wrath of Achilles") follows one (lines 1755–56 above) to the opening of Vergil's *Aeneid* ("arms and the man I sing"). Chaucer knew Vergil directly; he could have known of Homer's opening lines through (Latin) quotation in grammar books.
4. Alas, except that it was God's will.
5. Lines 1807–27 are drawn from Boccaccio's *Teseide*, which describes the flight of Arcite's soul. Chaucer omits the account in his redaction of the *Teseide* in the Knight's Tale of the *Canterbury Tales*. Both Boccaccio and Chaucer draw likewise from Dante, Lucan, Cicero's *Dream of Scipio* (and Macrobius's commentary on it), and Boethius.
6. Up to the hollowness/concavity of the eighth sphere, leaving on the other side every element. The details are controversial, but probably the sphere is that of the fixed stars (rather than the moon), from which Dante also looked back at the earth, and *everich element* probably means "every movable astral body (the planets, sun, and moon)" rather than each of the four elements (earth, water, air, fire).
7. The wandering stars (i.e., planets, sun, and moon), listening to the harmony—i.e., the "harmony of the spheres."
8. With respect to (In comparison with) the full/perfect happiness.

28

Such an end had the ill-conceived love of Troilo for Criseida, and such an end had his wretched sorrow, to which none other was ever equal. Such an end had the bright splendor which he would have brought to the royal throne; such was the end of Troilo's vain hope in the base Criseida.

The author speaks to young lovers very briefly, showing that love is to be placed more in mature women than in young ones.

29

O youths in whom amorous desire comes surging with age, I pray you for the sake of God that you restrain your ready steps to the evil appetite and that you mirror yourselves in Troilo's love which my verses have displayed above because, if you will read them in the right spirit, you will not lightly have trust in all women.

30

A young woman is both fickle and desirous of many lovers, and she esteems her beauty greater than the mirror shows, and puffed up she has the vainglory of her youth, which is more pleasing and attractive the more she appraises it to herself. She does not feel virtue or reason, unsteady always as a leaf in the wind.

31

And many women also, because they are descended from noble lineage and know how to count their ancestors, believe that they ought to have an advantage over others in loving and think that civility is an outrage and that they should turn up their noses and go about with a scornful manner. Shun these and regard them as base, for they are beasts; they are not noble ladies.

32

The perfect lady has a stronger desire to be loved and takes delight in loving; she discerns and sees what is to be avoided, she picks and chooses prudently, and she fulfills her promises. These are to be followed, but one ought not, however, to choose in haste, for all are not sensible even though they may be older, and those are worthless.

And in hymself he lough° right at the wo · · · · · · · · · · · *laughed*
Of hem that wepten° for his deth so faste, · · · · · · · · · · *wept*
And dampned° al oure werk that foloweth so · · · *damned, condemned*
The blynde lust,° the which that may nat laste, · · · · · · *desire*
1825 And sholden° al oure herte on heven caste;° *(when we) should / turn heavenward*
And forth he wente, shortly for to telle,
Ther as Mercurye sorted hym to dwelle.[9]

Swich fyn° hath, lo, this Troilus for love! · · · · · · · *Such an end*
Swich fyn hath al his grete worthynesse!
1830 Swich fyn hath his estat real° above! · · · · · · · · · *royal estate*
Swich fyn his lust,° swich fyn hath his noblesse! · · *desire, pleasure*
Swych fyn hath false worldes brotelnesse!° · · *brittleness, insecurity*
And thus bigan his lovyng of Criseyde,
As I have told, and in this wise° he deyde. · · · · · · · · · *manner*

1835 O yonge, fresshe folkes, he or she,
In which that° love up groweth with youre age, · · · · · *In whom*
. Repeyreth hom° fro worldly vanyte, · · · · · *Return home (to heaven)*
And of youre herte up casteth the visage° · · · · · · *turn up the face*
To thilke° God that after his ymage · · · · · · · · · · · *that same*
1840 Yow made, and thynketh al nys but a faire,[1]
This world that passeth soone as floures° faire. · · · · · *flowers*

And loveth hym the which that° right for love · · · · · · *Him Who*
Upon a crois,° oure soules for to beye,° · · · · · · *cross / redeem*
First starf,° and roos, and sit° in hevene above; · · · · *died / sits*
1845 For he nyl falsen° no wight, dar I seye, · · · · · · · *be false to*
That° wol his herte al holly° on hym leye.° · *Who / wholly / lay, entrust*
And syn° he best to love is, and most meke, · · · · · · · · *since*
What nedeth feynede° loves for to seke? · · · · · · *feigned, false*

Lo here, of payens° corsed olde rites! · · · · · · · · · *pagans'*
1850 Lo here, what alle hire goddes may availle!° · · · · *be good for*
Lo here, thise wrecched worldes appetites!
Lo here, the fyn and guerdoun° for travaille° · · *reward / toil, service*
Of Jove, Appollo, of Mars, of swich rascaille!° · · · · · *rabble*
Lo here, the forme of olde clerkis speche[2]
1855 In poetrie, if ye hire bokes seche.° · · · · · · · · · · · *search*

O moral Gower, this book I directe
To the and to the, philosophical Strode,[3]

9. Where Mercury allotted him to dwell. Mercury is the pagan guide of souls in the afterlife.
1. And understand that all is but a fair—i.e., a marketplace like the cherry fair at cherry harvest time, a "Vanity Fair."
2. The form (substance, essential [pagan] principle *or* literary form, style) of the speech of ancient clerks (i.e., learned authors).
3. John Gower was a friend of Chaucer's and a fellow poet. Strode is probably Ralph (or Randolph) Strode, an Oxford philosopher also known as a poet; he seems to be the same person as a London lawyer who lived near Chaucer.

33

Therefore be prudent and have compassion upon Troilo and yourself at the same time, and it will be well done. And piously make a prayer for him to Love that he may repose in peace in the region where he dwells and that he kindly grant you the grace to love so wisely that in the end you will not die for an evil woman.

Part Nine

Here begins the ninth and last part of the "Filostrato" in which the author speaks to his work and commands it to whom and with whom it ought to go, and what it ought to do, and then he ends.

1

My piteous song, happy times are usually the occasion of sweet verses, but in my heavy affliction love has drawn you unnaturally from my sorrowing soul, nor do I know the reason for it unless it may have come from a hidden power inspired and moved in my transfixed heart by the supreme excellence of our lady.

2

She, as I know, for I often feel it, can make me nothing or make me do much more than I have the skill to do, and from this I believe may arise the reason for the occasion of your long speaking and I am glad that it may have come more from this than from bitter sorrow. But whatever it may have been, we are at the end desired by me.

3

We have come to the port which we were seeking, now going among rocks and now sailing through open sea with zephyr and with storm, following over the uncertain sea the noble light and the revered sign of that star which makes each of my thoughts expert in achieving its proper end and which then brought it about that this end was made known to me.

4

I judge, therefore, that the anchors are to be cast here and an end made to the journey, and those thanks which the grateful pilgrim ought to render to the one who has guided him, we shall here render with full heart. And upon the shore, which is now nearby, we shall place on the ship garlands and other honors befitting our love.

To vouchen sauf, ther nede is,° to correcte,   *grant where there is need*
Of youre benignites and zeles goode.[4]
1860 And to that sothfast Crist, that starf on rode,[5]
With al myn herte of° mercy evere I preye,   *for*
And to the Lord right thus I speke and seye:[6]

Thow oon, and two, and thre, eterne on lyve,°   *eternally alive*
That regnest ay° in thre, and two, and oon,   *(the Trinity) that reigns ever*
1865 Uncircumscript,° and al maist circumscrive,°   *Limitless / circumscribe*
Us from visible and invisible foon°   *foes*
Defende, and to thy mercy, everichon,
So make us, Jesus, for thi mercy, digne,
For love of mayde and moder thyn benigne.[7]
Amen.

Explicit liber Troili et Criseydis.[8]

---

4. Out of your benevolence and good zeal (i.e., kind eagerness to help).
5. And to Christ, firm in truth, Who died on the cross.
6. Lines 1863–65 closely follow Dante, *Paradise* 14.28–30.
7. And in your mercy, Jesus, make us every one worthy of your mercy, for the love of your benevolent mother the Virgin.
8. Here ends the Book of Troilus and Criseyde.

5

Then you, somewhat rested, will betake yourself to the noble lady of my thoughts. O happy you who will see her which I, sorrowing wretch, cannot do! And when with joy you have been received in her hands, humbly commend me to her high worth, which alone can give me salvation.

6

And in the nearly tearful habit in which you are, I pray you to tell her about my wretched life through the miseries of another, the woes and the sighs and the bitter laments in which I have been, and am, sorrowful since the bright rays of her beautiful eyes were hidden from me by her departure, for I lived happy only in their presence.

7

If while she is listening to you, you see that her angelic face shows a little charity or she sighs for my toil, pray her as much as you can that it may please her to return here now or to command my soul to take itself away from me because, wherever it must go from here, death is much better for me than such a life.

8

But look that you do not make such a high embassy without Love, for you might perhaps be very ill received, and also without him you would not know what is good to do; if you go with him you will, I believe, be honored. Now go, for I pray Apollo that he lend you so much grace that you may be listened to and she may send you to me with a joyful reply.

THE TESTAMENT
OF CRESSEID
by Robert Henryson

The Testament of Cresseid
by Robert Henryson†

Introduction

Robert Henryson has traditionally been classed with a group of Scottish poets including William Dunbar and Gavin Douglas, in the fifteenth and sixteenth centuries, who because of their obvious debt to Chaucer's style were called (rather condescendingly) Scottish Chaucerians. Little is known of his life. He may have taken a degree in law, and he was a schoolmaster and notary public in the important royal burgh of Dumfermline in Scotland. He is mourned in William Dunbar's "Lament for the Makaris" and hence was dead before 1506. Apart from the *Testament of Cresseid* and a few short poems he is best known for his poetic collection of Aesopian fables, *The Morall Fabillis*, and for his poem on *Orpheus and Eurydice*.

The *Testament of Cresseid* was in circulation by 1492; its date is otherwise unknown. Because it was included in Thynne's 1532 edition of the works of Chaucer it became very widely known and was in fact for many years assumed to be Chaucer's own work, in spite of the obvious internal evidence that it was not. Modern editions are based on the edition printed by Henry Charteris in Edinburgh in 1593.

As Chaucer devised a fictional source, Lollius, for *Troilus and Criseyde*, so Henryson claims that he draws the story of the final fate of Cresseid from *ane uther quair* (line 61), "another small book," apart from Chaucer's own poem. This second source is very likely fictitious. After an introduction reminiscent of Chaucer's minor poems, representing the narrator's own condition, Henryson builds the poem around a series of elaborated motifs: the parade and court of the planets (146–343), Cresseid's two complaints (407–69, 546–74), and her testament itself (577–591). The leprosy that Henryson depicts accords with medieval descriptions of the disease, not an uncommon one in the Middle Ages. Leprosy was thought to be a sexually transmitted disease, and was also ritually unclean in biblical thought.

Henryson's Middle Scots dialect differs little from Chaucer's Middle English. The most noticeable difference is the spelling *qu* for southern *w*: *quhen*, "when"; *quhisling*, "whistling." The ending *-and* corresponds to southern *-ing*, and *-ait* to *-ed*, and *-is* to *-es*.

---

† The text of the poem presented here, derived from the Charteris print, reprints by permission the text edited by Robert L. Kindrick, *The Poems of Robert Henryson* (Kalamazoo, MI: TEAMS, Medieval Institute Publications, 1997), 156–74.

Many words can be deciphered by sometimes substituting Chaucerian spellings for Scottish ones (which often in fact represented different sounds):

For Henryson's *ch*, read Chaucerian *gh*: *richt, micht, brocht.*
For *a*, read *o*: *ane, fra* (from), *sa, quha, cald, twa, sang, nane, fand* (found).
For *ai*, read *o* or *a*: *maist, raid, baith, wrait, sair, mair, hait; cair, maid.*
For *au* read *o*: *auld, cauld.*
For *ei* read *ea* or *ee* or *i*: *greit, eirdly, leine, speir; sleip, leif; seiknes, leif* (life).
For *ui*, read *u* or *oo*: *luifis* (love's); *buik, tuik.*

A few frequent words with unfamiliar senses or spelling:

be: by, when
cair(full): sorrow(ful)
can, past tense *culd*:
   know (how), be able; (as auxil.)
   did
ene: eyes
hes: has
ilk: each
lipper: leper(s), leprous
nocht: not

quhilk: which
sal: shall
scho: she
sic: such
suld: should
thir: these
til(l): to, until
uther: other(s)
wes: was

The Testament of Cresseid

Ane doolie sessoun° to ane cairfull dyte°	*A dismal season / sad poem*
Suld correspond and be equivalent:°	*congruous*
Richt sa it wes quhen I began to wryte	
This tragedie; the wedder° richt fervent,°	*weather / hot*
5 Quhen Aries, in middis of the Lent,[1]	
Schouris° of haill gart fra° the north discend,	*Showers / caused from*
That scantlie° fra the cauld I micht defend.°	*scarcely / could defend (myself)*

Yit nevertheles within myne oratur°	*oratory, study*
I stude,° quhen Titan[2] had his bemis° bricht	*stood / beams*
10 Withdrawin doun and sylit under cure,°	*concealed under a cover*
And fair Venus, the bewtie° of the nicht,	*beauty*
Uprais° and set unto the west full richt	*Rose up*
Hir goldin face, in oppositioun	
Of God Phebus, direct discending doun.[3]	

15 Throwout the glas° hir bemis brast° sa fair	*window / burst forth*
That I micht se on everie syde me by;	
The northin wind had purifyit° the air	*cleared*
And sched° the mistie cloudis fra the sky;	*dispersed*
The froist freisit,° the blastis bitterly	*cold became frozen*
20 Fra Pole Artick come quhisling loud and schill,°	*shrill*
And causit me remufe° aganis my will.	*to move away*

For I traistit° that Venus, luifis° quene,	*trusted / love's*
To quhome sum tyme I hecht° obedience,	*promised*
My faidit° hart of lufe scho° wald mak grene,	*faded, pale / she*
25 And therupon with humbill reverence	
I thocht° to pray hir hie° magnificence;	*intended / high*
Bot for greit cald as than I lattit° was	*hindered*
And in my chalmer° to the fyre can pas.°	*chamber / passed*

Thocht lufe be hait,° yit in ane man of age	*Though love is hot*
30 It kendillis nocht sa sone as in youtheid,	
Of quhome the blude is flowing in ane rage;	
And in the auld the curage doif° and deid	*libido is dull*

1. When Aries, in the middle of Lent. The sun enters the sign of Aries (the Ram) at the vernal equinox. *Lent* is often the equivalent of "spring."
2. Titan (= Latin *Titanius*), like Phoebus, god of the sun. Like Chaucer, Henryson often uses a god's name for the deity and the astral body simultaneously.
3. The planet and goddess Venus rising in the east set her golden face completely opposite the sun as it descended in the west. Such an opposition would be malevolent, though in fact it is astronomically impossible.

Of quhilk° the fyre outward is best remeid:°   *Of which / remedy*
To help be phisike° quhair that nature faillit°   *from medicine / failed*
35 I am expert,° for baith° I have assaillit.°   *experienced / both / tried*

I mend° the fyre and beikit me° about,   *tended / warmed myself*
Than tuik° ane drink, my spreitis° to comfort,   *took / spirits*
And armit me weill fra the cauld thairout.°   *outside*
To cut° the winter nicht and mak it schort   *shorten, alleviate*
40 I tuik ane quair⁴—and left all uther sport°—   *other amusement*
Writtin be° worthie Chaucer glorious   *by*
Of fair Creisseid and worthie Troylus.

And thair I fand,° efter that Diomeid⁵   *found*
Ressavit° had that lady bricht of hew,°   *Received / countenance*
45 How Troilus neir° out of wit abraid°   *nearly / went*
And weipit soir° with visage paill° of hew;   *wept grievously / pale*
For quhilk wanhope° his teiris can renew,°   *which despair / did renew*
Quhill esperance rejoisit° him agane: *Until hope cheered*
Thus quhyle° in joy he levit,° quhyle in pane.°   *sometimes / lived / pain*

50 Of hir behest° he had greit comforting,   *promise*
Traisting° to Troy that scho suld mak retour,   *Trusting*
Quhilk he desyrit maist of eirdly° thing,   *earthly*
For quhy° scho was his only paramour.°   *Because / lover*
Bot quhen he saw passit baith° day and hour   *to have passed both*
55 Of hir ganecome,° than sorrow can oppres   *return*
His wofull hart in cair° and hevines.°   *grief / sadness*

Of his distres me neidis° nocht reheirs,°   *I need / repeat*
For worthie Chauceir in the samin buik,°   *same book*
In gudelie° termis and in joly veirs,°   *goodly / verses*
60 Compylit hes his cairis, quha will luik.⁶
To brek my sleip ane uther quair I tuik,⁷
In quhilk° I fand° the fatall destenie°   *which / found / fated destiny*
Of fair Cresseid, that° endit wretchitlie.   *who*

Quha wait gif° all that Chauceir wrait° was trew?   *Who knows whether / wrote*
65 Nor I wait nocht gif this narratioun
Be authoreist,° or fenyeit of the new°   *authoritative / newly concocted*
Be° sum poeit, throw his inventioun   *By*
Maid° to report the lamentatioun   *Made, composed*
And wofull end of this lustie° Creisseid,   *beautiful, passionate*
70 And quhat distres scho thoillit,° and quhat deid.°   *suffered / what death*

Quhen Diomeid had all his appetyte,
And mair,° fulfillit of° this fair ladie,   *more / satisfied with*
Upon ane uther° he set his haill° delyte   *other / whole*

4. I took a little book (quire). Henryson may refer to the whole of *Troilus and Criseyde* or only to its fifth book.
5. Diomede, Criseyde's lover after she forsook Troilus.
6. Has compiled his sorrows, whoever wishes to look at it.
7. To defer my sleep I took up another little book. Like Chaucer, Henryson refers to a source that doesn't in fact exist.

And send to hir ane lybell of repudie[8]
75 And hir excludit fra his companie.
Than desolait scho walkit up and doun,
And sum men sayis into the court commoun.[9]

O fair Creisseid, the flour and A per se[1]
Of Troy and Grece, how was thow fortunait° *how was it destined for you*
80 To change in° filth all thy feminitie, *into*
And be with fleschelie lust sa maculait,° *defiled*
And go° amang the Greikis air and lait,° *to go / early and late*
Sa giglotlike takand° thy foull plesance! *wantonly taking*
I have pietie thow suld fall sic mischance!²

—doesn't sound like it

85 Yit nevertheles, quhat ever men deme° or say *think*
In scornefull langage of thy brukkilnes,° *frailty*
I sall excuse als far furth° as I may *as far*
Thy womanheid, thy wisdome and fairnes,
The quhilk fortoun hes put to° sic distres *Which Fortune has set in*
90 As hir pleisit,° and nathing throw the gilt *As pleased her (Fortune)*
Of the°—throw wickit langage to be spilt!° *Of yours / ruined*

This fair lady, in this wyse° destitute *manner*
Of all comfort and consolatioun,
Richt privelie,° but fellowschip on fute,³ *secretly*
95 Disagysit passit° far out of the toun *Passed disguised*
Ane myle or twa, unto ane mansioun
Beildit full gay,° quhair° hir father Calchas *Well constructed / where (was)*
Quhilk° than amang the Greikis dwelland was. *Who*

Quhen he hir saw, the caus he can° inquyre *did*
100 Of hir cumming: scho said, siching full soir,° *sighing very sadly*
"Fra° Diomeid had gottin his desyre *As soon as*
He wox° werie and wald° of me no moir." *grew / desired*
Quod Calchas, "Douchter, weip thow not thairfoir;
Peraventure° all cummis for the best. *Perhaps*
105 Welcum to me; thow art full deir ane gest!"° *dear a guest*

This auld Calchas, efter° the law was tho,° *according as / then*
Wes keiper of the tempill as ane preist
In quhilk° Venus and hir sone Cupido *which*
War honourit, and his chalmer was neist;⁴
110 To quhilk Cresseid, with baill aneuch in breist,° *enough anguish in her breast*
Usit to pas,° hir prayeris for to say, *Used to resort*
Quhill° at the last, upon ane solempne day, *Until*

8. And sent to her a bill of divorce (though there is no reason to think that Diomeid legally married Cresseid).
9. And some people say (she walked) into the (royal) court as a common woman, i.e., a whore.
1. The flour and the letter A in itself, i.e., the first of all, the paragon.
2. I have pity that such misfortune should befall you.
3. Lacking (any) fellowship on foot.
4. Were worshiped, and his dwelling was nearest (to it).

As custome was, the pepill far and neir
Befoir the none° unto the tempill went   *noon*
115 With sacrifice, devoit° in thair maneir.   *devout*
Bot still Cresseid, hevie in hir intent,°   *sorrowful of mind*
Into the kirk wald° not hir self present,   *church wished*
For° giving of the pepill ony deming°   *Because of / inkling*
Of hir expuls° fra Diomeid the king,   *expulsion*

120 Bot past° into ane secreit orature,°   *(she) passed / oratory*
Quhair scho micht weip° hir wofull desteny.   *Where she could bemoan*
Behind hir bak scho cloisit fast the dure°   *shut fast the door*
And on hir kneis bair° fell doun in hy;°   *bare knees / haste*
Upon Venus and Cupide angerly°   *sorrowfully*
125 Scho cryit out, and said on this same wyse,°   *manner*
"Allace, that ever I maid yow sacrifice!

"Ye gave me anis° ane devine responsaill°   *once / response*
That I suld be the flour of luif° in Troy;   *flower of love*
Now am I maid ane unworthie outwaill,°   *outcast*
130 And all in cair translatit° is my joy.   *into grief transformed*
Quha sall me gyde? Quha sall me now convoy,°   *escort, protect*
Sen° I fra Diomeid and nobill Troylus   *Since*
Am clene° excludit, as abject° odious?   *completely / a castoff*

"O fals Cupide, is nane to wyte° bot thow   *there is no one to blame*
135 And thy mother, of lufe° the blind goddes!°   *love / goddess*
Ye causit me alwayis understand and trow°   *to believe*
The seid° of lufe was sawin° in my face,   *seed / sown*
And ay° grew grene throw your supplie° and grace. *always / support*
Bot now, allace, that seid with froist° is slane,   *frost*
140 And I fra luifferis left,° and all forlane."°   *cast away / abandoned*

Quhen this was said, doun in ane extasie,
Ravischit in spreit,° intill° ane dreame scho fell,   *spirit / into*
And be apperance hard,° quhair scho did ly,   *heard by an apparition*
Cupide the king ringand ane silver bell,
145 Quhilk men micht heir° fra hevin unto hell;   *Which one could hear*
At quhais sound° befoir Cupide appeiris   *At the sound of which*
The sevin planetis, discending fra thair spheiris;

Quhilk hes° power of all thing generabill,°   *Which have / generated, created*
To reull and steir° be thair greit influence   *rule and direct*
150 Wedder and wind, and coursis variabill:
And first of all Saturne gave his sentence,°   *opinion*
Quhilk° gave to Cupide litill reverence,   *Who*
Bot as ane busteous° churle on his maneli   *rude, violent*
Come crabitlie with auster luik and cheir.[5]

155 His face fronsit,° his lyre° was lyke the leid,° *wrinkled / complexion / lead*
His teith chatterit and cheverit° with the chin,   *quivered*

5. Came crabbedly (with bad temper), with austere look and bearing. Henryson's account of the planet gods follows an elaborate classical and medieval tradition of their iconography.

His ene drowpit,° how sonkin° in his heid,   *drooped / deeply sunk*
Out of his nois° the meldrop° fast can rin,°   *nose / snot / ran*
With lippis bla° and cheikis leine° and thin;   *livid, blue / lean*
160 The ice schoklis° that fra his hair doun hang   *icicles*
Was wonder greit,° and as ane speir° als lang: *Were wondrously large / spear*

Atouir° his belt his lyart lokkis° lay   *Over / gray locks*
Felterit unfair, ovirfret with froistis hoir,[6]
His garmound° and his gyis° full of gray,   *clothing / attire*
165 His widderit weid fra him the wind out woir,[7]
Ane busteous° bow within his hand he boir,°   *A strong / bore*
Under his girdill ane flasche of felloun flanis[8]
Fedderit° with ice and heidit° with hailstanis.   *Feathered / headed*

Than Juppiter, richt fair and amiabill,
170 God of the starnis° in the firmament   *stars*
And nureis° to all thing generabill;°   *nurturer / created*
Fra his father Saturne far different,
With burelie° face and browis bricht and brent,°   *handsome / smooth or lofty*
Upon his heid ane garland wonder gay
175 Of flouris° fair, as it had bene° in May.   *flowers / as if it were*

His voice was cleir, as cristall wer his ene,°   *eyes*
As goldin wyre sa glitterand was his hair,
His garmound and his gyis full of grene
With goldin listis gilt on everie gair;[9]
180 Ane burelie brand° about his middill bair,°   *strong sword / (he) bore*
In his richt hand he had ane groundin speir,
Of his father the wraith° fra us to weir.°   *wrath / fend off*

Nixt efter him come Mars the god of ire,
Of strife, debait,° and all dissensioun,   *contention*
185 To chide and fecht,° als feirs° as ony fyre,   *quarrel and fight / as fierce*
In hard harnes, hewmound, and habirgeoun,
And on his hanche ane roustie fell fachioun,[1]
And in his hand he had ane roustie sword,
Wrything° his face with mony angrie word.   *Contorting*

190 Schaikand° his sword, befoir Cupide he come,   *Shaking, brandishing*
With reid° visage and grislie glowrand ene,°   *red / grisly glowering eyes*
And at his mouth ane bullar stude of fome,°   *a fleck of foam hung*
Lyke to ane bair° quhetting his tuskis kene;   *boar*
Richt tuilyeour lyke,° but° temperance in tene,°   *like a brawler / lacking / rage*
195 Ane horne he blew with mony bosteous brag,°   *violent blast*
Quhilk all this warld with weir° hes maid to wag.°   *war / shake*

6. Matted in an ugly manner, embellished with hoary frost.
7. The wind lifted out (caused to flutter) his withered clothing.
8. Under his belt a sheaf of cruel arrows.
9. Denton Fox (1981) translates: "With golden hems or edges gilded on every gore." A gore is a triangular piece of cloth inserted into a garment.
1. In tough equipment, helmet, and coat of mail, and on his hip a rusty cruel falchion (a short, broad sword). *Roustie* here may mean "bloody," or simply "red," the color assigned to Mars (as gray to Saturn and green and gold to Jupiter).

Than fair Phebus, lanterne and lamp of licht,
Of man and beist, baith° frute and flourisching,°   *both / flowering*
Tender nureis,° and banischer of nicht;   *nurturer*
200 And of the warld causing, be° his moving   *by*
And influence, lyfe in all eirdlie thing,°   *earthly things*
Without comfort of quhome, of force to nocht°   *necessarily to nothing*
Must all ga die° that in this warld is wrocht.°   *go to die / created*

As king royall he raid° upon his chair,°   *rode / chariot*
205 The quhilk Phaeton gydit sum tyme unricht;[2]
The brichtnes of his face quhen it was bair°   *bare, uncovered*
Nane micht behald for peirsing of his sicht;[3]
This goldin cart with fyrie° bemis bricht   *fiery*
Four yokkit steidis[4] full different of hew
210 But bait° or tyring throw the spheiris drew.   *Without abatement*

The first was soyr,° with mane als reid as rois,°   *sorrel / rose*
Callit Eoye, into the orient;°   *(prominent) in the east*
The secund steid to name hecht° Ethios,   *was named*
Quhitlie and paill,° and sum deill ascendent;°   *pale / somewhat rising up*
215 The thrid Peros, richt hait° and richt fervent;°   *hot / burning*
The feird was blak, callit Philogié,
Quhilk rollis Phebus doun into the sey.°   *sea*

Venus was thair present, that goddes° gay,   *goddess*
Hir sonnis querrell° for to defend, and mak   *son's (Cupid's) complaint, suit*
220 Hir awin complaint, cled in ane nyce° array,   *extravagant*
The ane half grene, the uther half sabill blak,
With hair as gold kemmit and sched° abak;   *parted*
Bot in hir face semit° greit variance,   *there seemed*
Quhyles° perfyte treuth and quhyles inconstance.   *Sometimes*

225 Under smyling scho was dissimulait,°   *dissembling*
Provocative° with blenkis° amorous,   *Flirting / glances*
And suddanely changit and alterait,
Angrie as ony serpent vennemous,
Richt pungitive° with wordis odious;°   *stinging / hateful*
230 Thus variant scho was, quha list tak keip:°   *whoever is pleased to notice*
With ane eye lauch,° and with the uther weip,°   *laughing / weeping*

In taikning that all fleschelie paramour,[5]
Quhilk Venus hes in reull° and governance,   *under her rule*
Is sum tyme sweit, sum tyme bitter and sour,
235 Richt unstabill and full of variance,
Mingit° with cairfull° joy and fals plesance,   *Mingled / sorrowful*
Now hait,° now cauld, now blyth, now full of wo,   *hot*
Now grene as leif, now widderit° and ago.°   *withered / passed away*

2. Which Phaeton at one time steered wrong. See *Troilus and Criseyde* 5.664–65.
3. None could gaze at because of its (the sun's) piercing of his sight (i.e., eyes).
4. The four steeds yoked to the sun's chariot were named in Ovid's *Metamorphoses* (2.153–54) and with variations by medieval writers. Four regions of the sky—the east, rising higher, the heat of the day, the setting—were assigned to the horses.
5. Signifying that all fleshly love affairs.

With buik in hand than come Mercurius,[6]
240 Richt eloquent and full of rethorie,°   *rhetoric*
With polite° termis and delicious,°   *polished / delightful*
With pen and ink to report all reddie,°   *all ready to record*
Setting° sangis and singand merilie;   *Composing*
His hude° was reid, heklit atovir° his croun,   *hood / fringed over*
245 Lyke to ane poeit of the auld fassoun.°   *old fashion*

Boxis he bair° with fyne electuairis,°   *bore / medicines*
And sugerit syropis for digestioun,
Spycis belangand to the pothecairis,°   *apothecaries, pharmacists*
With mony hailsum° sweit confectioun;   *many a wholesome*
250 Doctour in phisick,° cled° in ane skarlot goun,°   *medicine / clad / gown*
And furrit weill,° as sic ane aucht° to be;   *well furred / such a one ought*
Honest and gude, and not ane word culd lie.°   *did lie*

Nixt efter him come lady Cynthia,°   *Cynthia, the moon*
The last of all and swiftest in hir spheir;
255 Of colour blak, buskit° with hornis twa,   *arrayed*
And in the nicht scho listis° best appeir;   *is pleased*
Haw° as the leid,° of colour nathing cleir,   *Pale / lead*
For all hir licht scho borrowis at hir brother
Titan, for of hir self scho hes nane uther.°   *has no other (light)*

260 Hir gyse° was gray and full of spottis blak,   *attire*
And on hir breist ane churle[7] paintit full evin°   *depicted very exactly*
Beirand° ane bunche of thornis on his bak,   *Carrying*
Quhilk for his thift micht clim na nar the hevin.[8]
Thus quhen thay gadderit war thir° goddes sevin,   *these*
265 Mercurius thay cheisit° with ane assent   *chose*
To be foirspeikar° in the parliament.   *the speaker*

Quha had bene thair and liken for to heir[9]
His facound° toung and termis exquisite,   *eloquent*
Of rethorick the prettick° he micht leir,°   *practice / learn*
270 In breif sermone° ane pregnant sentence° wryte.   *speech / pithy discourse*
Befoir Cupide veiling° his cap alyte,°   *doffing / a little*
Speiris° the caus of that vocatioun,°   *(He) asks / convocation*
And he anone schew his intentioun.[1]

"Lo," quod Cupide, "quha will blaspheme the name
275 Of his awin° god, outher° in word or deid,   *own / either*
To all goddis he dois baith lak° and schame,   *defamation*
And suld have bitter panis to his meid.°   *pains for his reward*
I say this by yone wretchit Cresseid,

6. Mercury with book in hand was traditionally god of eloquence, music, medicine, and thieving and lying (see the ironic line 252).
7. In medieval legend the man in the moon was a peasant (*churle*) and a thief who carried a stolen bundle of thorns.
8. Who, because of his theft, could climb no nearer to the heavens. Beyond the sphere of the moon existed no such corrupt things as thieves.
9. Whoever may have been there and taking delight in hearing.
1. And he forthwith revealed his accusation.

The quhilk throw me° was sum tyme flour of
   lufe,°   *by my agency / flower of love*
280 Me and my mother starklie can reprufe,°   *rebuked severely*

"Saying of hir greit infelicitie
I was the caus, and my mother Venus,
Ane blind goddes hir cald that micht not se,[2]
With sclander and defame injurious.°   *unlawful, harmful*
285 Thus hir leving° unclene and lecherous   *living, conduct*
Scho wald returne in° me and my mother,   *turn back to (i.e., blame on)*
To quhome I schew my grace abone° all uther.   *above*

"And sen° ye ar all sevin deificait,°   *since / deified*
Participant° of devyne sapience,   *Partaking*
290 This greit injure° done to our hie° estait   *lawless act, injury / high*
Me think with pane we suld mak recompence;[3]
Was never to goddes done sic° violence: *such*
As weill for yow as for my self I say,°   *speak*
Thairfoir ga° help to revenge, I yow pray!"   *go*

295 Mercurius to Cupide gave answeir
And said, "Schir° King, my counsall is that ye   *Sir*
Refer yow to the hiest° planeit heir   *highest*
And tak° to him the lawest° of degré   *add / lowest*
The pane° of Cresseid for to modifie:°   *punishment / determine*
300 As God Saturne, with him tak Cynthia."
"I am content," quod he, "to tak thay twa."°   *those two*

Than thus proceidit Saturne and the Mone
Quhen thay the mater rypelie° had degest:°   *wisely / considered*
For the dispyte° to Cupide scho had done   *insult*
305 And to Venus, oppin° and manifest,   *overt*
In all hir lyfe with pane° to be opprest,   *pain*
And torment sair° with seiknes° incurabill,   *sore, fierce / sickness*
And to all lovers be abhominabill.

This dulefull° sentence Saturne tuik on° hand,   *dismal / took in*
310 And passit doun quhair cairfull° Cresseid lay,   *sorrowful*
And on hir heid he laid ane frostie wand;
Than lawfullie° on this wyse° can he say,   *legalistically / manner*
"Thy greit fairnes and all thy bewtie gay,
Thy wantoun blude° and eik° thy goldin hair,   *unruly blood, passion / also*
315 Heir I exclude fra the for evermair.

"I change thy mirth into melancholy,
Quhilk is the mother of all pensivenes;°   *sorrowful thought*
Thy moisture and thy heit in cald and dry;[4]
Thyne insolence, thy play and wantones,
320 To greit diseis;° thy pomp and thy riches°   *Into great disease / wealth*

---

2. Called her a blind goddess who could not see.
3. It seems to me we ought to make recompense (for this injury) with punishment.
4. (I change) your moisture and your heat into cold and dry. Of the four humors, the "melancholy"
   had the qualities of coldness and dryness, and was taken as the cause of leprosy.

In mortall neid;° and greit penuritie°   *need, crisis / penury*
Thow suffer sall, and as ane beggar die."

O cruell Saturne, fraward° and angrie,   *froward, aggressive*
Hard is thy dome° and to° malitious!   *judgment / too*
325 On fair Cresseid quhy hes thow° na mercie,   *have you*
Quhilk was sa sweit, gentill and amorous?°   *amiable*
Withdraw thy sentence and be gracious—
As thow was never; sa schawis through thy deid,⁵
Ane wraikfull° sentence gevin on° fair Cresseid.   *vengeful / given to*

330 Than Cynthia, quhen Saturne past° away,   *passed*
Out of hir sait° discendit doun belyve,°   *seat / quickly*
And red ane bill° on Cresseid quhair scho lay,   *verdict*
Contening this sentence diffinityve:°   *final*
"Fra heit° of bodie I the now depryve,   *heat*
335 And to thy seiknes sall be na recure°   *remedy*
Bot in dolour° thy dayis to indure.   *pain*

"Thy cristall ene mingit° with blude I mak,   *spotted with*
Thy voice sa cleir unplesand, hoir, and hace,°   *grating and hoarse*
Thy lustie lyre° ovirspred with spottis blak,   *lovely face*
340 And lumpis haw° appeirand in thy face: *pale, livid*
Quhair thow cummis, ilk° man sall fle the place.   *each*
This° sall thow go begging fra hous to hous   *Thus*
With cop and clapper lyke ane lazarous."⁶

This doolie° dreame, this uglye visioun   *dismal*
345 Brocht to ane end, Cresseid fra it awoik,°   *awoke*
And all that court and convocatioun
Vanischit away: than rais° scho up and tuik°   *rose / took*
Ane poleist glas, and hir schaddow culd luik;⁷
And quhen scho saw hir face sa deformait,
350 Gif° scho in hart was wa aneuch,° God wait!°   *If / woeful enough / knows*

Weiping full sair,° "Lo, quhat it is," quod sche,   *grievously*
"With fraward° langage for to mufe and steir°   *froward, rash / move and arouse*
Our craibit° goddis; and sa is sene on° me!   *ill-tempered / so it is seen with*
My blaspheming now have I bocht full deir;°   *bought at a high price*
355 All eirdlie° joy and mirth I set areir.°   *earthly / behind*
Allace, this day; allace, this wofull tyde°   *time*
Quhen I began with my goddis for to chyde!"°   *dispute*

Be° this was said, ane chyld come fra the hall   *When*
To warne Cresseid the supper was reddy;
360 First knokkit at the dure, and syne culd call,°   *afterwards called*
"Madame, your father biddis yow cum in hy:°   *haste*

5. As you never were—so it is evident from your deed.
6. Lepers, "lazars," traditionally begged for a living, carrying a cup to receive alms and a clapper (a rattle, wooden bell, or the lid of a clap-dish) to warn people of their approach, as they were ritually unclean (see Leviticus 13:45) and potentially contagious.
7. A polished mirror, and looked at her image. Here as elsewhere *culd* is an auxiliary verb meaning "did."

He hes merwell sa lang on grouf ye ly,[8]
And sayis your beedes° bene to lang sum deill;°   *prayers / somewhat*
The goddis wait° all your intent full weill."   *know*

365 Quod scho, "Fair chyld, ga to my father deir
And pray him cum to speik with me anone."°   *forthwith*
And sa he did, and said, "Douchter, quhat cheir?"°   *how are you*
"Allace!" quod scho, "Father, my mirth is gone!"
"How sa?" quod he, and scho can all expone,°   *expound*
370 As I have tauld, the vengeance and the wraik°   *revenge*
For hir trespas Cupide on hir culd tak.°   *took*

He luikit° on hir uglye lipper° face,   *looked / leprous*
The quhylk° befor was quhite as lillie flour;   *Which*
Wringand his handis, oftymes he said allace
375 That he had levit° to se that wofull hour;   *lived*
For he knew weill that thair was na succour
To hir seiknes,° and that dowblit his pane;°   *sickness / doubled his pain*
Thus was thair cair aneuch betuix thame twane.[9]

Quhen thay togidder murnit° had full lang,   *mourned*
380 Quod Cresseid, "Father, I wald not be kend;°   *wish not to be recognized*
Thairfoir in secreit wyse ye let me gang°   *manner may you let me go*
To yone° hospitall at the tounis end,   *yonder*
And thidder sum meit° for cheritie me send   *food*
To leif° upon, for all mirth in this eird°   *live / earth*
385 Is fra me gane; sic is my wickit weird!"°   *such is my wicked fate*

Than in ane mantill and ane bawer° hat,   *beaver*
With cop and clapper, wonder prively,°   *wondrously secretly*
He opnit ane secreit get° and out thair at   *gate*
Convoyit° hir, that° na man suld espy,   *Escorted / so that*
390 Unto° ane village half ane myle thairby;°   *To / from there*
Delyverit hir in at the spittaill hous,°   *hospital, lepers' house*
And daylie sent hir part of his almous.°   *alms*

Sum knew hir weill, and sum had na knawledge
Of hir becaus scho was sa deformait,
395 With bylis° blak ovirspred in hir visage,   *boils*
And hir fair colour faidit and alterait.
Yit thay presumit, for hir hie regrait°   *great lamentation*
And still murning,° scho was of nobill kin;   *continual grieving*
With better will thairfoir they tuik hir in.

400 The day passit and Phebus went to rest,
The cloudis blak ouerheled° all the sky.   *covered over*
God wait gif° Cresseid was ane sorrowfull gest,   *knows whether*
Seing that uncouth fair and harbery!°   *unpleasant food and lodging*
⌐ it meit° or drink scho dressit hir to ly°   *Without food / prepared to lie*

rvels that you lie prostrate for so long.
vas there sorrow enough between the two of them.

405 In ane dark corner of the hous allone,
And on this wyse,° weiping, scho maid hir mone.°   *manner / lament*

The Complaint of Cresseid[1]

"O sop° of sorrow, sonkin into cair,   *bread soaked in a liquid*
O cative° Creisseid, for now and ever mair   *wretched*
Gane° is thy joy and all thy mirth in eird;°   *Gone / on earth*
410 Of all blyithnes now art thou blaiknit bair[2]
Thair is na salve° may saif° the of thy sair!°   *medicine / heal / sore*
Fell° is thy fortoun, wickit is thy weird,°   *Cruel / fate*
Thy blys is baneist° and thy ball on breird!°   *banished / bale sprouting*
Under the eirth, God gif I gravin wer,°   *God grant that I were buried*
415 Quhair nane of Grece nor yit of Troy micht heird!°   *could hear (of it)*

"Quhair is thy chalmer wantounlie besene;°   *chamber pleasantly furnished*
With burely bed and bankouris browderit bene;[3]
Spycis and wyne to thy collatioun,°   *snack before retiring*
The cowpis° all of gold and silver schene,°   *cups / bright*
420 Thy sweit meitis° servit in plaittis clene   *foods*
With saipheron sals° of ane gude sessoun;°   *saffron sauce / seasoning, flavor*
Thy gay garmentis with mony gudely° goun   *a goodly*
Thy plesand lawn° pinnit with goldin prene°   *linen / brooch*
All is areir,° thy greit royall renoun!   *lost*

425 "Quhair is thy garding° with thir greissis° gay   *garden / these herbs*
And fresche flowris, quhilk the quene Floray°   *Flora, goddess of flowers*
Had paintit° plesandly in everie pane,°   *painted / part*
Quhair thou was wont° full merilye in May   *you were accustomed*
To walk and tak the dew be° it was day,[4]   *when*
430 And heir° the merle° and mawis° mony ane,   *hear / blackbird / thrush*
With ladyis fair in carrolling to gane°   *go*
And se the royall rinkis° in thair array,   *warriors*
In garmentis gay garnischit° on everie grane?°   *adorned / particular*

"Thy greit triumphand fame and hie° honour,   *high*
435 Quhair thou was callit of eirdlye wichtis flour,°   *flower of earthly people*
All is decayit, thy weird° is welterit° so;   *fate / tossed about*
Thy hie estait is turnit in darknes dour;°   *harsh, gloomy*
This lipper ludge° tak for thy burelie bour,°   *lepers' lodge / lovely chamber*
And for thy bed tak now ane bunche of stro,°   *straw*
440 For waillit° wyne and meitis° thou had tho°   *choice / food / then*
Tak mowlit breid, peirrie and ceder sour;[5]
Bot° cop and clapper now is all ago.[6]   *Except for / gone*

---

1. Chaucer composed his *Anelida and Arcite* in rhyme royal, and included in it an elaborate complaint written mainly in nine-line stanzas rhyming *aabaabbab*. Henryson adopts both forms.
2. Bare (forlorn) of all your happiness now you are made pale.
3. Fox (1981) translates: "With excellent bed and handsomely embroidered tapestry furniture-coverings."
4. The custom, especially in Scotland, was for girls to beautify themselves by washing their faces with dew early (when it was day) on May Day.
5. Take moldy bread, pear juice, and sour cider.

"My cleir voice and courtlie carrolling,
Quhair I was wont with ladyis for to sing,
445 Is rawk as ruik, full hiddeous, hoir and hace;[6]
My plesand port,° all utheris precelling,°   *looks / excelling*
Of lustines° I was hald maist conding—°   *beauty / worthy*
Now is deformit the figour of my face;
To luik on it na leid° now lyking hes.°   *person / has*
450 Sowpit in syte, I say with sair siching,[7]
Ludgeit° amang the lipper leid,° 'Allace!'   *Lodged / leprous people*

"O ladyis fair of Troy and Grece, attend°   *behold*
My miserie, quhilk nane may comprehend,
My frivoll fortoun,° my infelicitie,   *fickle fortune*
455 My greit mischeif, quhilk na man can amend.
Be war in tyme, approchis neir the end,°   *the end comes nearer*
And in your mynd ane mirrour mak of me:
As I am now, peradventure° that ye   *perhaps*
For all your micht may cum to that same end,
460 Or ellis war° gif ony war° may be.   *else beware / worse*

"Nocht is your fairnes bot ane faiding flour,
Nocht is your famous laud° and hie° honour   *praise / high*
Bot wind inflat in° uther mennis eiris,°   *blown into / ears*
Your roising reid to rotting sall retour;[8]
465 Exempill mak of me in your memour°   *memory*
Quhilk° of sic thingis wofull witnes beiris.°   *Which / bears sad witness*
All welth in eird,° away as wind it weiris;°   *on earth / goes to waste*
Be war thairfoir, approchis neir° your hour;   *nearer*
Fortoun is fikkill quhen scho beginnis and steiris."°   *stirs, is aroused*

470 Thus chydand° with hir drerie destenye,   *quarreling*
Weiping scho woik° the nicht fra end to end;   *stayed awake through*
Bot all in vane; hir dule,° hir cairfull° cry,   *grief / sorrowful*
Micht not remeid,° nor yit hir murning mend.°   *be remedied / abate*
Ane lipper° lady rais° and till hir wend,°   *leprous / rose up / went*
475 And said, "Quhy spurnis thow° aganis the wall   *do you kick*
To sla° thy self and mend nathing at all?   *slay*

"Sen° thy weiping dowbillis bot° thy wo,   *Since / only doubles*
I counsall the mak vertew of ane neid;°   *necessity*
Go leir° to clap thy clapper to and fro,   *learn*
480 And leif° efter the law of lipper leid."°   *live / leprous folk*
Thair was na buit,° bot furth with thame scho yeid°   *remedy (for it) / went*
Fra place to place, quhill cauld and hounger sair°   *grievous*
Compellit hir to be ane rank° beggair.   *pure, gross*

That samin tyme, of Troy the garnisoun,°   *garrison, defending force*
485 Quhilk had to chiftane° worthie Troylus,   *as chief*
Throw jeopardie of weir° had strikken doun   *a risky operation in battle*

6. Is as raucous as a rook's, very hideous, grating, and hoarse.
7. Sopped (immersed) in sorrow, I say with grievous sighing.
8. Your rosy redness (complexion) shall turn into a rotten one.

Knichtis of Grece in number mervellous;
With greit tryumphe and laude° victorious   *praise*
Agane° to Troy richt royallie thay raid°   *Back / rode*
490 The way quhair Cresseid with the lipper baid.°   *lepers dwelled*

Seing that companie, all with ane stevin°   *voice*
Thay gaif ane cry, and schuik coppis gude speid,° *shook their cups briskly*
"Worthie lordis, for Goddis lufe° of hevin,   *love*
To us lipper part° of your almous deid!"°   *share / almsgiving*
495 Than to thair cry nobill Troylus tuik heid,°   *took heed*
Having pietie, neir by the place can pas°   *passed*
Quhair Cresseid sat, not witting quhat° scho was. *who*

Than upon him scho kest° up baith hir ene,°   *cast / eyes*
And with ane blenk° it come into his thocht   *glance*
500 That he sumtime hir face befoir had sene,
Bot scho was in sic plye° he knew hir nocht;   *such a plight, condition*
Yit than hir luik into his mynd it brocht
The sweit visage and amorous blenking°   *loving looks*
Of fair Cresseid, sumtyme his awin° darling.   *own*

505 Na wonder was, suppois in mynd that he
Tuik hir figure sa sone,[9] and lo, now quhy·
The idole° of ane thing in cace° may be   *image / a (given) situation*
Sa deip imprentit° in the fantasy°   *imprinted / phantasia, memory*
That it deludis the wittis outwardly,°   *the (five) outer senses*
510 And sa appeiris in forme and lyke estait°   *similar condition or bodily form*
Within the mynd° as it was figurait.   *memory*

Ane spark of lufe° than till° his hart culd° spring *love / to / did*
And kendlit° all his bodie in ane fyre;   *kindled*
With hait fewir,° ane sweit° and trimbling   *hot fever / sweat*
515 Him tuik,° quhill° he was reddie to expyre;   *took / until*
To beir his scheild his breist began to tyre;°   *grow weary*
Within ane quhyle he changit mony hew;°   *many a hue*
And nevertheles not ane ane uther knew.°   *neither knew the other*

For knichtlie pietie° and memoriall°   *pity / in honor of the memory*
520 Of fair Cresseid, ane gyrdill can° he tak,   *did*
Ane purs of gold, and mony gay jowall,°   *many a lovely jewel*
And in the skirt of Cresseid doun can swak;°   *he tossed*
Than raid° away and not ane word he spak,   *rode*
Pensiwe° in hart, quhill° he come to the toun,   *Pensive / until*
525 And for greit cair° oft syis° almaist fell doun. *sorrow / times*

The lipper folk to Cresseid than can draw
To se the equall distributioun
Of the almous,° bot quhen the gold thay saw,   *alms*
Ilk° ane to uther prewelie can roun,°   *Each / privately whispered*
530 And said, "yone° lord hes mair° affectioun,   *yonder / has more*

---

9. Fox (1981) translates: "It was no wonder, even if he in his mind conceived her image so quickly."

How ever it be, unto yone lazarous°   *the leper over there*
Than to us all; we knaw be° his almous."   *by*

"Quhat lord is yone," quod scho, "have ye na feill,°   *knowledge*
Hes° done to us so greit humanitie?"°   *Who has / humane kindness*
535   "Yes," quod a lipper man, "I knaw him weill;
Schir° Troylus it is, gentill and fre."°   *Sir / noble*
Quhen Cresseid understude that it was he,
Stiffer than steill thair stert ane bitter stound[1]
Throwout hir hart, and fell° doun to the ground.   *(she) fell*

540   Quhen scho ouircome,° with siching sair° and sad, *came to / grievous sighing*
With mony cairfull° cry and cald ochane:°   *sorrowful / cold lament*
"Now is my breist with stormie stoundis stad,°   *beset by violent pangs*
Wrappit in wo, ane wretch full will of wane!"°   *bewildered or hopeless*
Than fel in swoun full oft or° ever scho fane,°   *before / ceased*
545   And ever in hir swouning cryit scho thus,
"O fals Cresseid and trew knicht Troylus!

"Thy lufe,° thy lawtie,° and thy gentilnes   *love / loyalty*
I countit small in my prosperitie,
Sa efflated° I was in wantones,   *puffed up*
550   And clam upon the fickill quheill sa hie.[2]
All faith and lufe I promissit to the
Was in the self° fickill and frivolous: *itself*
O fals Cresseid and trew knicht Troilus!

"For lufe of me thow keipt continence,°   *maintained self-restraint*
555   Honest and chaist° in conversatioun;°   *decent and chaste / conduct*
Of all wemen protectour and defence
Thou was, and helpit thair opinioun;°   *furthered their reputation*
My mynd in fleschelie foull affectioun
Was inclynit to lustis lecherous:
560   Fy, fals Cresseid; O trew knicht Troylus!

"Lovers be war and tak gude heid about°   *pay close attention concerning*
Quhome that ye lufe, for quhome ye suffer paine.
I lat yow wit,° thair is richt few thairout°   *I'm letting you know / abroad*
Quhome ye may traist° to have trew lufe agane;°   *trust / love in return*
565   Preif° quhen ye will, your labour is in vaine.   *Put it to the test*
Thairfoir I reid° ye tak thame as ye find,   *counsel*
For thay ar sad° as widdercok in wind.   *as steadfast*

"Becaus I knaw the greit unstabilnes,
Brukkill° as glas, into° my self, I say—   *Frail / within*
570   Traisting in uther als° greit untaithfulnes,   *Expecting (to find) in others as*
Als° unconstant, and als untrew of fay—°   *(And to find them) as / faith*
Thocht° sum be trew, I wait° richt few ar thay;   *Though / know*
Quha findis treuth, lat him his lady ruse;°   *praise*
Nane but my self as now I will accuse."

1. A bitter pain, sharper than a steel edge, started up there.
2. And I climbed so high on the fickle wheel (of Fortune).

575 Quhen this was said, with paper scho sat doun,
And on° this maneir maid hir testament: *in*
"Heir° I beteiche° my corps and carioun°   *Here / yield up / dead body*
With wormis and with taidis° to be rent;°   *toads / torn*
My cop and clapper, and myne ornament,
580 And all my gold the lipper folk sall have,
Quhen I am deid, to burie me in grave.

"This royall ring, set with this rubie reid,
Quhilk Troylus in drowrie° to me send,   *as a love token*
To him agane I leif° it quhen I am deid,   *in return I bequeath*
585 To mak my cairful deid° unto him kend.°   *sorrowful death / known*
Thus I conclude schortlie and mak ane end:
My spreit° I leif to Diane° quhair scho dwellis, *soul / Diana, goddess of chastity*
To walk with hir in waist woddis° and wellis.°   *wild woods / streams*

"O Diomeid, thou hes baith broche° and belt   *brooch*
590 Quhilk Troylus gave me in takning°   *as a token*
Of his trew lufe," and with that word scho swelt.°   *died*
And sone ane lipper° man tuik of° the ring,   *leprous / took off*
Syne° buryit hir withouttin tarying;   *Then*
To Troylus furthwith the ring he bair,
595 And of Cresseid the deith he can° declair.   *did*

Quhen he had hard° hir greit infirmitie,   *heard about*
Hir legacie and lamentatioun,
And how scho endit in sic° povertie,   *such*
He swelt° for wo and fell doun in ane swoun;   *fainted*
600 For greit sorrow his hart to brist° was boun;°   *burst / ready*
Siching° full sadlie, said, "I can° no moir;   *Sighing / know or can do*
Scho was untrew and wo is me thairfoir."

Sum said he maid ane tomb of merbell° gray,   *marble*
And wrait° hir name and superscriptioun,°   *wrote / epitaph*
605 And laid it on hir grave quhair that scho lay,
In goldin letteris, conteining this ressoun:°   *statement*
"Lo, fair ladyis, Cresseid of Troy the toun,
Sumtyme countit° the flour of womanheid,   *reckoned*
Under this stane, lait lipper,° lyis deid."   *lately a leper*

610 Now, worthie wemen, in this ballet° schort,   *ballad, ditty*
Maid for your worschip and instructioun,[3]
Of° cheritie, I monische° and exhort,   *Out of / admonish (you)*
Ming° not your lufe with fals deceptioun: *Mingle*
Beir in your mynd this schort conclusioun
615 Of fair Cresseid, as I have said befoir.
Sen scho is deid I speik of hir no moir.

---

3. Made to honor you and for your instruction.

CRITICISM

C. S. LEWIS

What Chaucer Really Did to *Il Filostrato*†

A great deal of attention has deservedly been given to the relation between the *Book of Troilus* and its original, *Il Filostrato*, and Rossetti's collation placed a knowledge of the subject within the reach even of undergraduate inquirers.[1] It is, of course, entirely right and proper that the greater part of this attention has been devoted to such points as specially illustrate the individual genius of Chaucer as a dramatist and a psychologist. But such studies, without any disgrace to themselves, often leave singularly undefined the historical position and affinities of a book; and if pursued intemperately they may leave us with a preposterous picture of the author as that abstraction, a *pure* individual, bound to no time nor place, or even obeying in the fourteenth century the aesthetics of the twentieth. It is possible that a good deal of misunderstanding still exists, even among instructed people, as to the real significance of the liberties that Chaucer took with his source. M. Legouis, in his study of Chaucer to which we all owe so much, remarks that Chaucer's additions 'implied a wider and more varied conception' than those of Boccaccio; and again 'Chaucer's aim was not like Boccaccio's to paint sentimentality alone, but to reflect life'. I do not wish to contradict either statement, but I am convinced that both are capable of conveying a false impression. What follows may be regarded as a cautionary gloss on M. Legouis's text. I shall endeavour to show that the process which *Il Filostrato* underwent at Chaucer's hands was first and foremost a process of *medievalization*. One aspect of this process has received some attention from scholars,[2] but its importance appears to me to be still insufficiently stressed. In what follows I shall, therefore, restate this aspect in my own terms while endeavouring to replace it in its context.

Chaucer had never heard of a renaissance; and I think it would be difficult to translate either into the English or the Latin of his day our distinction between sentimental or conventional art on the one hand, and art which paints 'Life'—whatever this means—on the other. When first a manuscript beginning with the words *Alcun di giove sogliono il favore* came into his hands, he was, no doubt, aware of a difference between its contents and those of certain English and French manuscripts which he had read before. That some of the differences did not please him is apparent from his treatment. We may be sure, however, that he noticed and approved the new use of stanzas, instead of octosyllabic couplets, for narrative. He certainly thought the story a good story; he may even have thought it a story better told than any that he had yet read. But there was also, for Chaucer, a special reason why he

† From *Essays and Studies* 17 (1932): 56–75. Reprinted by permission of the publishers, The English Association.
1. Lewis refers to William M. Rossetti's parallel text, Chaucer Society, First Series, Nos. 44 and 65 (London: Trübner, 1873, 1883) [*Editor*].
2. v. Dodd, *Courtly Love in Chaucer and Gower*, 1913.

should choose this story for his own retelling; and that reason largely determined the alterations that he made.

He was not yet the Chaucer of the *Canterbury Tales*: he was the *grant translateur* of the *Roman de la Rose*, the author of the *Book of the Duchesse*, and probably of 'many a song and many a lecherous lay'.[3] In other words he was the great living interpreter in English of *l'amour courtois*. Even in 1390, when Gower produced the first version of his *Confessio Amantis*, such faithful interpretation of the love tradition was still regarded as the typical and essential function of Chaucer: he is Venus' 'disciple' and 'poete', with whose 'ditees and songes glade . . . the lond fulfild is overal'. And Gower still has hopes that Chaucer's existing treatments of *Frauendienst* are only the preludes to some great 'testament' which will 'sette an ende of alle his werk'.[4] These expectations were, of course, disappointed; and it is possibly to that disappointment, rather than to a hypothetical quarrel (for which only the most ridiculous grounds have been assigned), that we should attribute Gower's removal of this passage from the second text of the *Confessio Amantis*. It had become apparent that Chaucer was following a different line of development, and the reference made to him by Venus had ceased to be appropriate.

It was, then, as a poet of courtly love that Chaucer approached *Il Filostrato*. There is no sign as yet that he wished to desert the courtly tradition; on the contrary, there is ample evidence that he still regarded himself as its exponent. But the narrative bent of his genius was already urging him, not to desert this tradition, but to pass from its doctrinal treatment (as in the *Romance of the Rose*) to its narrative treatment. Having preached it, and sung it, he would now exemplify it: he would show the code put into action in the course of a story—without prejudice (as we shall see) to a good deal of doctrine and pointing of the amorous moral by the way. The thing represents a curious return upon itself of literary history. If Chaucer had lived earlier he would, we may be sure, have found just the model that he desired in Chrestien de Troyes. But by Chaucer's time certain elements, which Chrestien had held together in unity, had come apart and taken an independent life. Chrestien had combined, magnificently, the interest of the story, and the interest of erotic doctrine and psychology. His successors had been unable or unwilling to achieve this union. Perhaps, indeed, the two things had to separate in order that each might grow to maturity; and in many of Chrestien's psychological passages one sees the embryonic allegory struggling to be born.[5] Whatever the reason may be, such a separation took place. The story sets up on its own in the prose romances—the 'French book' of Malory: the doctrine and psychology set up on their own in the *Romance of the Rose*. In this situation if a poet arose who accepted the doctrines and also had a narrative genius, then *a priori* such a poet might be expected to combine again the two elements—now fully grown—which, in their rudimentary form, had lain together in Chrestien. But this is exactly the sort of poet that Chaucer was; and this

---

3. *C.T.*, I 1086.
4. *Conf. Am.* viii. 2941–58.
5. v. *Lancelot*, 369–81, 2844–61; *Yvain*, 6001 et seq., 2639 et. seq.: *Cligès*, 5855 et seq.

(as we shall see) is what Chaucer did. The *Book of Troilus* shows, in fact, the very peculiar literary phenomenon of Chaucer groping back, unknowingly, through the very slightly medieval work of Boccaccio, to the genuinely medieval formula of Chrestien. We may be thankful that Chaucer did not live in the high noon of Chrestien's celebrity; for, if he had, we should probably have lost much of the originality of Troilus. He would had less motive for altering Chrestien than for altering Boccaccio, and probably would have altered him less.

Approaching *Il Filostrato* from this angle, Chaucer, we may be sure, while feeling the charm of its narrative power, would have found himself, at many passages, uttering the Middle English equivalent of 'This will never do!' In such places he did not hesitate, as he might have said, to *amenden* and to *reducen* what was *amis* in his author. The majority of his modifications are corrections of errors which Boccaccio had committed against the code of courtly love; and modifications of this kind have not been entirely neglected by criticism. It has not, however, been sufficiently observed that these are only part and parcel of a general process of medievalization. They are, indeed, the most instructive part of that process, and even in the present discussion must claim the chief place; but in order to restore them to their proper setting it will be convenient to make a division of the different capacities in which Chaucer approached his original. These will, of course, be found to overlap in the concrete; but that is no reason for not plucking them ideally apart in the interests of clarity.

I. Chaucer approached his work as an 'Historical' poet contributing to the story of Troy. I do not mean that he necessarily believed his tale to be wholly or partly a record of fact, but his attitude towards it in this respect is different from Boccaccio's. Boccaccio, we may surmise, wrote for an audience who were beginning to look at poetry in our own way. For them *Il Filostrato* was mainly, though not entirely, 'a new poem by Boccaccio'. Chaucer wrote for an audience who still looked at poetry in the medieval fashion—a fashion for which the real literary units were 'matters', 'stories', and the like, rather than individual authors. For them the *Book of Troilus* was partly, though of course only partly, 'a new bit of the Troy story', or even 'a new bit of the matter of Rome'. Hence Chaucer expects them to be interested not only in the personal drama between his little group of characters but in that whole world of story which makes this drama's context: like children looking at a landscape picture and wanting to know what happens to the road after it disappears into the frame. For the same reason they will want to know his authorities. Passages in which Chaucer has departed from his original to meet this demand will easily occur to the memory. Thus, in i. 141 et seq., he excuses himself for not telling us more about the military history of the Trojan war, and adds what is almost a footnote to tell his audience where they can find that missing part of the story—'in Omer, or in Dares, or in Dyte'. Boccaccio had merely sketched in, in the preceding stanza, a general picture of war sufficient to provide the background for his own story—much as a dramatist might put *Alarums within* in a stage direction: he has in view an audience fully conscious that all this is mere necessary 'setting' or hypothesis. Thus again, in iv. 120 et seq., Chaucer inserts into the speech of *Calkas* an account of the quarrel between *Phebus* and *Neptunus* and *Lameadoun*. This is not dramatically necessary. All that was needed for *Calkas's* argument has already been given in lines 111 and 112 (cf. *Filostrato*, iv. xi). The Greek leaders did not need to be told about Laomedon; but Chaucer is not thinking of the Greek leaders; he is thinking of his audience who will gladly learn, or be reminded, of that part of the cycle. At lines 204 et seq. he inserts a note on the later history of *Antenor* for the same reason. In the fifth book he inserts unnecessarily lines 1464–1510 from the story of Thebes. The spirit in which this is done is aptly expressed in his own words:

> And so descendeth down from gestes olde
> To Diomede.
>
> (v. 1511, 1512)

The whole 'matter of Rome' is still a unity, with a structure and life of its own. That part of it which the poem in hand is treating, which is, so to speak, in focus, must be seen fading gradually away into its 'historial' surroundings. The method is the antithesis of that which produces the 'framed' story of a modern writer: it is a method which romance largely took over from the epic.

II. Chaucer approached his work as a pupil of the rhetoricians and a firm believer in the good, old, and now neglected maxim of Dante: *omnis qui versificatur suos versus exornare debet in quantum potest*. This side of Chaucer's poetry has been illustrated by Mr. Manly[6] so well that most readers will not now be in danger of neglecting it. A detailed application of this new study to the *Book of Troilus* would here detain us too long, but a cursory glance shows that Chaucer found his original too short and proceeded in many places to 'amplify' it. He began by abandoning the device—that of invoking his lady instead of the Muses—whereby Boccaccio had given a lyrical instead of a rhetorical turn to the invocation, and substituted an address to *Thesiphone* (*Filostrato*, I. i–v, cf. *Troilus*, i. 1–14). He added at the beginning of his second book an invocation of *Cleo* and an apology of the usual medieval type, for the defects of his work (ii. 15–21). Almost immediately afterwards he inserted a *descriptio* of the month of a May (an innovation which concerned him as poet of courtly love no less than as rhetorician) which is extremely beautiful and appropriate, but which follows, none the less, conventional lines. The season is fixed by astronomical references, and *Proigne* and *Tereus* appear just where we should expect them (ii. 50–6, 64–70). In the third book the scene of the morning parting between the two lovers affords a complicated example of Chaucer's medievalization. In his original (III. xlii) Chaucer read

> Ma poich' e galli presso al giorno udiro
> Cantar per l'aurora che surgea.

He proceeded to amplify this, first by the device of *Circuitio* or *Circumlocutio; galli*, with the aid of Alanus de Insulis, became 'the cok, comune astrologer'. Not content with this, he then repeated the sense of that

---

6. *Chaucer and the Rhetoricians*, Warton Lecture XVII, 1926.

whole phrase by the device *Expolitio*, of which the formula is *Multiplice forma Dissimuletur idem: varius sis et tamen idem*,[7] and the theme 'Dawn came' is varied with *Lucifer* and *Fortuna Minor*, till it fills a whole stanza (iii. 1415–21). In the next stanza of Boccaccio he found a short speech by *Criseida*, expressing her sorrow at the parting which dawn necessitated: but this was not enough for him. As poet of love he wanted his *alba*; as rhetorician he wanted his *apostropha*. He therefore inserted sixteen lines of address to Night (1427–42), during which he secured the additional advantage, from the medieval point of view, of 'som doctryne' (1429–32). In lines 1452–70 he inserted antiphonally Troilus's *alba*, for which the only basis in Boccaccio was the line *Il giorno che venia maledicendo* (III. xliv). The passage is an object lesson for those who tend to identify the traditional with the dull. Its matter goes back to the ancient sources of medieval love poetry, notably to Ovid, *Amores*, i. 13, and it has been handled often before, and better handled, by the Provençals. Yet it is responsible for one of the most vivid and beautiful expressions that Chaucer ever used.

> Accursed be thy coming into Troye
> For every bore hath oon of thy bright eyen.

A detailed study of the *Book of Troilus* would reveal this 'rhetoricization', if I may coin an ugly word, as the common quality of many of Chaucer's additions. As examples of *Apostropha* alone I may mention, before leaving this part of the subject, iii. 301 et seq. (*O tonge*), 617 et seq. (*But o Fortune*), 715 et seq. (*O Venus*), and 813 et seq. where Chaucer is following Boethius.

III. Chaucer approached his work as a poet of *doctryne* and sentence. This is a side of his literary character which twentieth-century fashions encourage us to overlook, but, of course, no honest historian can deny it. His contemporaries and immediate successors did not. His own creatures, the pilgrims, regarded *mirthe* and *doctryne*,[8] or, as it is elsewhere expressed, *sentence* and *solas*,[9] as the two alternative, and equally welcome, excellences of a story. In the same spirit Hoccleve praises Chaucer as the *mirour of fructuous entendement* and the universal *fadir in science*[1]—a passage, by the by, to be recommended to those who are astonished that the fifteenth century should imitate those elements of Chaucer's genius which it enjoyed instead of those which we enjoy. In respect of *doctryne*, then, Chaucer found his original deficient, and *amended* it. The example which will leap to every one's mind is the Boethian discussion on free will (iv. 946–1078). To Boccaccio, I suspect, this would have seemed as much an excrescence as it does to the modern reader; to the unjaded appetites of Chaucer's audience mere thickness in a wad of manuscript was a merit. If the author was so 'courteous beyond covenant' as to give you an extra bit of *doctryne* (or of story), who would be so churlish as to refuse it on the pedantic ground of irrelevance? But this passage is only one of many in which Chaucer departs

---

7. Geoffroi de Vinsauf, *Poetr. Nov.* 220–5.
8. *Canterbury Tales*, B 2125.
9. Ibid., A 798.
1. *Regement*, 1963 et seq.

from his original for the sake of giving his readers interesting general knowledge or philosophical doctrine. In iii. 1387 et seq., finding Boccaccio's attack upon *gli avari* a little bare and unsupported, he throws out, as a species of buttress, the *exempla* of *Myda* and *Crassus*.[2] In the same book he has to deal with the second assignation of Troilus and Cressida. Boccaccio gave him three stanzas of dialogue (*Filostrato*, III. lxvi–lxviii), but Chaucer rejected them and preferred—in curious anticipation of Falstaff's thesis about pitch—to assure his readers, on the authority of *thise clerkes wyse* (iii. 1691) that *felicitee* is felicitous, though *Troilus* and *Criseyde* enjoyed something better than *felicitee*. In the same stanza he also intends, I think, an allusion to the *sententia* that occurs elsewhere in the Franklin's Tale.[3] In iv. 197–203, immediately before his *historical* insertion about Antenor, he introduces a *sentence* from Juvenal, partly for its own sake, partly in order that the story of Antenor may thus acquire an exemplary, as well as a *historial* value. In iv. 323–8 he inserts a passage on the great *locus communis* of Fortune and her wheel.

In the light of this sententious bias, Chaucer's treatment of Pandarus should be reconsidered, and it is here that a somewhat subtle exercise of the historical imagination becomes necessary. On the one hand, he would be a dull reader, and the victim rather than the pupil of history, who would take all the doctrinal passages in Chaucer seriously: that the speeches of Chauntecleer and Pertelote and of the Wyf of Bath not only *are* funny by reason of their sententiousness and learning, but are intended to be funny, and funny by that reason, is indisputable. On the other hand, to assume that sententiousness became funny for Chaucer's readers as easily as it becomes funny for us, is to misunderstand the fourteenth century: such an assumption will lead us to the preposterous view that *Melibee* (or even the Parson's Tale) is a comic work—a view not much mended by Mr. Mackail's suggestion that there are some jokes *too* funny to excite laughter and that *Melibee* is one of these. A clear recognition that our own age is quite abnormally sensitive to the funny side of sententiousness, to possible hypocrisy, and to dulness, is absolutely necessary for any one who wishes to understand the past. We must face the fact that Chaucer's audience could listen with gravity and interest to edifying matter which would set a modern audience sleeping or sniggering. The application of this to Pandarus is a delicate business. Every reader must interpret Pandarus for himself, and I can only put forward my own interpretation very tentatively. I believe that Pandarus is meant to be a comic character, but not, by many degrees, so broadly comic as he appears to some modern readers. There is, for me, no doubt that Chaucer intended us to smile when he made Troilus exclaim

What knowe I of the queene Niobe?
Lat be thyne olde ensaumples, I thee preye.

(I. 759)

2. This might equally well have been treated above in our rhetorical section. The instructed reader will recognize that a final distinction between *doctrinal* and *rhetorical* aspects, is not possible in the Middle Ages.
3. C.T., F 762.

But I question if he intended just that sort of smile which we actually give him. For me the fun lies in the fact that poor Troilus says what I have been wishing to say for some time. For Chaucer's hearers the point was a little different. The suddenness of the gap thus revealed between Troilus's state of mind and Pandarus's words cast a faintly ludicrous air on what had gone before: it made the theorizing and the *exempla* a little funny in retrospect. But it is quite probable that they had not been funny till then: the discourse on contraries (i. 631–44), the *exemplum* of Paris and Oenone, leading up to the theme 'Physician heal thyself' (652–72), the doctrine of the Mean applied to secrecy in love (687–93), the *sentences* from Solomon (695) and elsewhere (708), are all of them the sort of thing that can be found in admittedly serious passages,[4] and it may well be that Chaucer 'had it both ways'. His readers were to be, first of all, edified by the doctrine for its own sake, and then (slightly) amused by the contrast between this edification and Troilus's obstinate attitude of the plain man. If this view be accepted it will have the consequence that Chaucer intended an effect of more subtility than that which we ordinarily receive. We get the broadly comic effect—a loquacious and unscrupulous old uncle talks solemn platitude at interminable length. For Chaucer, a *textuel* man talked excellent doctrine which we enjoy and by which we are edified: but at the same time we see that this 'has its funny side'. Ours is the crude joke of laughing at admitted rubbish: Chaucer's the much more lasting joke of laughing at 'the funny side' of that which, even while we laugh, we admire. To the present writer this reading of Pandarus does not appear doubtful; but it depends, to some extent, on a mere 'impression' about the quality of the Middle Ages, an impression hard to correct, if it is an error, and hard to teach, if it is a truth. For this reason I do not insist on my interpretation. If, however, it is accepted, many of the speeches of Pandarus which are commonly regarded as having a purely dramatic significance will have to be classed among the examples of Chaucer's doctrinal or sententious insertions.[5]

IV. Finally, Chaucer approached his work as the poet of courtly love. He not only modified his story so as to make it a more accurate representation in action of the orthodox erotic code, but he also went out of his way to emphasize its didactic element. Andreas Capellanus had given instructions to lovers; Guillaume de Lorris had given instructions veiled and decorated by allegory; Chaucer carries the process a stage further and gives instruction by example in the course of a concrete story. But he does not forget the instructional side of his work. In the following paragraphs I shall sometimes quote parallels to Chaucer's innovations from the earlier love literature, but it must not be thought that I suppose my quotations to represent Chaucer's immediate source.

1. Boccaccio in his induction, after invoking his mistress instead of the Muses, inserts (I. vi) a short request for lovers in general that they will pray for him. The prayer itself is disposed of in a single line.

> Per me vi prego ch'amore preghiate.

---

4. Cf. *C.T.*, I 140–155.
5. From another point of view Pandarus can be regarded as the *Vekke* of the *R. R.* (cf. Thessala in *Cligès*) taken out of allegory into drama and changed in sex so as to 'double' the roles of *Vekke* and *Frend*.

This is little more than a conceit, abandoned as soon as it is used: a modern poet could almost do the like. Chaucer devotes four stanzas (i. 22–49) to this prayer. If we make an abstract of both passages, Boccaccio will run 'Pray for me to Love', while Chaucer will run 'Remember, all lovers, your old unhappiness, and pray, for the unsuccessful, that they may come to solace; for me, that I may be enabled to tell this story; for those in despair, that they may die; for the fortunate, that they may persevere, and please their ladies in such manner as may advance the glory of Love'. The important point here is not so much that Chaucer expands his original, as that he renders it more liturgical: his prayer, with its careful discriminations in intercession for the various recognized stages of the amorous life, and its final reference *ad Amoris majorem gloriam*, is a collect. Chaucer is emphasizing that parody, or imitation, or rivalry—I know not which to call it—of the Christian religion which was inherent in traditional *Frauendienst*. The thing can be traced back to Ovid's purely ironical worship of Venus and Amor in the *De Arte Amatoria*. The idea of a love religion is taken up and worked out, though still with equal flippancy, in terms of medieval Christianity, by the twelfth-century poet of the *Concilium Romaricimontis*,[6] where Love is given Cardinals (female), the power of visitation, and the power of cursing. Andreas Capellanus carried the process a stage further and gave Love the power of distributing reward and punishment after death. But while his hell of cruel beauties (*Siccitas*), his purgatory of beauties promiscuously kind (*Humiditas*), and his heaven of true lovers (*Amoenitas*)[7] can hardly be other than playful, Andreas deals with the love religion much more seriously than the author of the *Concilium*. The lover's qualification is *morum probitas*: he must be truthful and modest, a good Catholic, clean in his speech, hospitable, and ready to return good for evil. There is nothing in *saeculo bonum* which is not derived from love:[8] it may even be said in virtue of its severe standard of constancy, to be 'a kind of chastity'—*reddit hominem castitatis quasi virtute decoratum*.[9]

In all this we are far removed from the tittering nuns and *clerici* of the *Concilium*. In Chrestien, the scene in which Lancelot kneels and adores the bed of Guinevere (as if before a *corseynt*)[1] is, I think, certainly intended to be read seriously: what mental reservations the poet himself had on the whole business is another question. In Dante the love religion has become wholly and unequivocally serious by fusing with the real religion: the distance between the *Amor deus omnium quotquot sunt amantium* of the *Concilium*, and the *segnore di pauroso aspetto* of the *Vita Nuova*,[2] is the measure of the tradition's real flexibility and universality. It is this quasi-religious element in the content, and this liturgical element in the diction, which Chaucer found lacking in his original at the very opening of the book, and which he supplied. The line

---

6. *Zeitschrift für Deutsches Alterthum*, vii, pp. 160 et seq.
7. Andreas Capellanus, *De Arte Honeste Amandi*, ed. Troejel, i. 6 D² (pp. 91–108).
8. Ibid., i. 6 A (p. 28).
9. Ibid., i. 4 (p. 10).
1. *Lancelot*, 4670, 4734 et seq.
2. *Vit. Nuov.* iii.

That Love hem bringe in hevene to solas

is particularly instructive.

2. In the Temple scene (Chaucer, i. 155–315. *Filostrato*, I. xix–xxxii) Chaucer found a stanza which it was very necessary to *reducen*. It was Boccaccio's twenty-third, in which Troilus, after indulging in his 'cooling card for lovers', mentions that he has himself been singed with that fire, and even hints that he has had his successes; but the pleasures were not worth the pains. The whole passage is a typical example of that Latin spirit, which in all ages (except perhaps our own) has made Englishmen a little uncomfortable; the hero must be a lady-killer from the very beginning, or the audience will think him a milksop and a booby. To have abashed, however temporarily, these strutting Latinisms, is not least among the virtues of medieval *Frauendienst*: and for Chaucer as its poet, this stanza was emphatically one of those that 'would never do'. He drops it quietly out of its place, and thus brings the course of his story nearer to that of the *Romance of the Rose*. The parallelism is so far intact. Troilus, an unattached young member of the courtly world, wandering idly about the Temple, is smitten with Love. In the same way the Dreamer having been admitted by Ydelnesse into the garden goes 'pleying along ful merily'[3] until he looks in the fatal well. If he had already met Love outside the garden the whole allegory would have to be reconstructed.

3. A few lines lower Chaucer found in his original the words

il quale amor trafisse
Più ch'alcun altro, pria del tempio uscisse.

(I. xxv)

Amor trafisse in Boccaccio is hardly more than a literary variant for 'he fell in love': the allegory has shrunk into a metaphor and even that metaphor is almost unconscious and fossilized. Over such a passage one can imagine Chaucer exclaiming, *tantamne rem tam negligenter?* He at once goes back through the metaphor to the allegory that begot it, and gives us his own thirtieth stanza (I. 204–10) on the god of Love in anger bending his bow. The image is very ancient and goes back at least as far as Apollonius Rhodius.[4] Ovid was probably the intermediary who conveyed it to the Middle Ages. Chrestien uses it, with particular emphasis on Love as the avenger of contempt.[5] But Chaucer need not have gone further to find it than to the *Romance of the Rose*,[6] with which, here again, he brings his story into line.

4. But even this was not enough. Boccaccio's *Amor trafisse* had occurred in a stanza where the author apostrophizes the *Cecità delle mondane menti*, and reflects on the familiar contrast between human expectations and the actual course of events. But this general contrast seemed weak to the poet of courtly love: what he wanted was the explicit erotic *moral* based on the special contrast between the ὕβρις of the young scoffer and the complete surrender which the offended deity soon

3. *R. R.* 1329 (English Version).
4. *Argonaut*, iii. 275 et seq.
5. *Cligès*, 460; cf. 770.
6. *R. R.* 1330 et seq.; 1715 et seq.

afterwards extracted from him. This conception, again, owes much to Ovid; but between Ovid and the Middle Ages comes the later practice of the ancient Epithalamium during the decline of antiquity and the Dark Ages: to which, as I hope to show elsewhere, the system of courtly love as a whole is heavily indebted. Thus in the fifth century Sidonius Apollinarus, in an Epithalamium, makes the bridegroom just such another as Troilus: a proud scoffer humbled by Love. Amor brings to Venus the triumphant news

> Nova gaudia porta
> Felicis praedae, genetrix. Calet ille *superbus*
> Ruricius.[7]

Venus replies

> gaudemus nate, *rebellem*
> Quod vincis.

In a much stranger poem, by the Bishop Ennodius, it is not the ὕβρις of a single youth, but of the world, that has stung the deities of love into retributive action. Cupid and Venus are introduced deploring the present state of Europe.

> Frigida consumens multorum possidet artus
> Virginitas.[8]

and Venus meets the situation by a threat that she'll 'larn 'em':

> Discant populi tunc crescere divam
> Cum neglecta iace.[9]

They conclude by attacking one Maximus and thus bringing about the marriage which the poem was written to celebrate. Venantius Fortunatus, in his Epithalamium for Brunchild, reproduces, together with Ennodius's spring morning, Ennodius's boastful Cupid, and makes the god, after an exhibition of his archery, announce to his mother, *mihi vincitur alter Achilles*.[1] In Chrestien the role of tamed rebel is transferred to the woman. In *Cligès* Soredamours confesses that Love has humbled her pride by force, and doubts whether such extorted service will find favour.[2] In strict obedience to this tradition Chaucer inserts his lines 214–31, emphasizing the dangers of ὕβρις against Love and the certainty of its ultimate failure; and we may be thankful that he did, since it gives us the lively and touching simile of *proude Bayard*. Then, mindful of his instructional purpose, he adds four stanzas more (239–66), in which he directly exhorts his readers to avoid the error of Troilus, and that for two reasons: firstly, because Love *cannot* be resisted (this is the policeman's argument—we may as well 'come quiet'); and secondly because Love is a thing 'so vertuous in kinde'. The second argument, of course, follows traditional lines, and recalls Andreas's theory of Love as the source of all secular virtue.

7. *Sid. Apoll.* Carm. xi. 61.
8. Ennodius Carm. I, iv. 57.
9. Ibid. 84.
1. Venant. Fort. VI, i.
2. *Cligès*, 682, 241.

5. In lines 330–50 Chaucer again returns to Troilus's scoffing—a scoffing this time assumed as a disguise. I do not wish to press the possibility that Chaucer in this passage is attempting, in virtue of his instructional purpose, to stress the lover's virtue of secrecy more than he found it stressed in his original; for Boccaccio, probably for different reasons, does not leave that side of the subject untouched. But it is interesting to note a difference in the content between this scoffing and that of Boccaccio (*Filostrato* I. xxi, xxii). Boccaccio's is based on contempt for women, fickle as wind, and heartless. Chaucer's is based on the hardships of love's *lay* or religion: hardships arising from the uncertainty of the most orthodox *observances*, which may lead to various kinds of harm and may be taken amiss by the lady. Boccaccio dethrones the deity: Chaucer complains of the severity of the cult. It is the difference between an atheist and a man who humorously insists that he 'is not of religioun'.

6. In the first dialogue between Troilus and Pandarus the difference between Chaucer and his original can best be shown by an abstract. Boccaccio (II. vi–xxviii) would run roughly as follows:

т. Well, if you must know, I am in love. But don't ask me with whom (vi–viii).
p. Why did you not tell me long ago? I could have helped you (ix).
т. What use would *you* be? Your own suit never succeeded (ix).
p. A man can often guide others better than himself (x).
т. I can't tell you, because it is a relation of yours (xv).
p. A fig for relations! Who is it? (xvi).
т. (after a pause) Griseida.
p. Splendid! Love has fixed your heart in a good place. She is an admirable person. The only trouble is that she is rather *pie* (*onesta*): but I'll soon see to that (xxiii). Every woman is amorous at heart: they are only anxious to save their reputations (xxvii). I'll do all I can for you (xxviii).

Chaucer (I. 603–1008) would be more like this:

т. Well, if you must know, I am in love. But don't ask me with whom (603–16).
p. Why did you not tell me long ago? I could have helped you (617–20).
т. What use would *you* be? Your own suit never succeeded (621–3).
p. A man can often guide others better than himself, as we see from the analogy of the whetstone. Remember the doctrine of contraries, and what Oenone said. As regards secrecy, remember that all virtue is a mean between two extremes (624–700).
т. Do leave me alone (760).
p. If you die, how will she interpret it? Many lovers have served for twenty years without a single kiss. But should they despair? No, they should think it a guerdon even to serve (761–819).
т. (much moved by this argument, 820–6) What shall I do? Fortune is my foe (827–40).

P. Her wheel is always turning. Tell me who your mistress is. If it were my sister, you should have her (841–61).

T. (after a pause)—My sweet foe is Criseyde (870–5).

P. Splendid: Love has fixed your heart in a good place. This ought to gladden you, firstly, because to love such a lady is nothing but good: secondly, because if she has all these virtues, she must have Pity too. You are very fortunate that Love has treated you so well, considering your previous scorn of him. You must repent at once (874–935).

T. (kneeling) Mea Culpa! (936–8).

P. Good. All will now come right. Govern yourself properly: you know that a divided heart can have no grace. I have reasons for being hopeful. No man or woman was ever born who was not apt for love, either natural or celestial: and celestial love is not fitted to Criseyde's years. I will do all I can for you. Love converted you of his goodness. Now that you are converted, you will be as conspicuous among his saints as you formerly were among the sinners against him (939–1008).

In this passage it is safe to say that every single alteration by Chaucer is an alteration in the direction of medievalism. The Whetstone, Oenone, Fortune, and the like we have already discussed: the significance of the remaining innovations may now be briefly indicated. In Boccaccio the reason for Troilus's hesitation in giving the name is Criseida's relationship to Pandaro: and like a flash comes back Pandaro's startling answer. In Chaucer his hesitation is due to the courtly lover's certainty that 'she nil to noon suich wrecche as I be wonne' (778) and that 'full harde it wer to helpen in this cas' (836). Pandaro's original

> Se quella ch'ami fosse mia sorella
> A mio potere avrai tuo piacer d'ella
>
> (xvi)

is reproduced in the English, but by removing the words that provoked it in the Italian (E tua parenta, xv) Chaucer makes it merely a general protestation of boundless friendship in love, instead of a cynical defiance of scruples already raised (Chaucer 861). Boccaccio had delighted to bring the purities of family life and the profligacy of his young man about town into collision, and to show the triumph of the latter. Chaucer keeps all the time within the charmed circle of *Frauendienst* and allows no conflict but that of the lover's hopes and fears. Again, Boccaccio's Pandaro has no argument to use against Troilo's silence, but the argument 'I may help you'. Chaucer's Pandarus, on finding that this argument fails, proceeds to expound the code. The fear of dishonour in the lady's eyes, the duty of humble but not despairing service in the face of all discouragement, and the acceptance of this service as its own reward, form the substance of six stanzas in the English text (lines 768–819): at least, if we accept four lines very characteristically devoted to 'Ticius' and what 'bokes telle' of him. Even more remarkable is the difference between the behaviour of the two Pandars after the lady's name has been disclosed. Boccaccio's, cynical as ever, encourages Troilo by the reflection that female virtue is not really a serious obstacle: Chaucer's makes the virtue of the lady itself the ground for hope—arguing scholastically that the *genus* of virtue implies that *species* thereof which is *Pitee* (897–900). In what follows, Pandarus, while continuing to advise, becomes an adviser of a slightly different sort. He instructs Troilus not so much on his relationship to the Lady as on his relationship to Love. He endeavours to awaken in Troilus a devout sense of his previous sins against that deity (904–30) and is not satisfied without confession (931–8), briefly enumerates the commandments (953–9), and warns his penitent of the dangers of a divided heart.

In establishing such a case as mine, the author who transfers relentlessly to his article all the passages listed in his private notes can expect nothing but weariness from the reader. If I am criticized, I am prepared to produce for my contention many more evidential passages of the same kind. I am prepared to show how many of the beauties introduced by Chaucer, such as the song of Antigone or the riding past of Troilus, are introduced to explain and mitigate and delay the surrender of the heroine, who showed in Boccaccio a facility condemned by the courtly code.[3] I am prepared to show how Chaucer never forgets his erotically didactic purpose; and how, anticipating criticism as a teacher of love, he guards himself by reminding us that

> For to winne love in sondry ages
> In sondry londes, sondry ben usages.[4]
>
> (ii, 27)

But the reader whose stomach is limited would be tired, and he who is interested may safely be left to follow the clue for himself. Only one point, and that a point of principle, remains to be treated in full. Do I, or do I not, lie open to the criticism of Professor Abercrombie's 'Liberty of Interpreting'?[5]

The Professor *quem honoris causa nomino* urges us not to turn from the known effect which an ancient poem has upon us to speculation about the effect which the poet intended it to have. The application of this criticism which may be directed against me would run as follows: 'If Chaucer's *Troilus* actually produces on us an effect of greater realism and nature and freedom than its original, why should we assume that this effect was accidentally produced in the attempt to conform to an outworn convention?' If the charge is grounded, it is, to my mind, a very grave one. My reply is that such a charge begs the very question which I have most at heart in this paper, and but for which I should regard my analysis as the aimless burrowings of a thesismonger. I would retort upon my imagined critic with another question. This poem is more lively and of deeper human appeal than its original. I grant it. This poem conforms more closely than its original to the system of courtly love. I claim to prove it. What then is the natural conclusion to draw? Surely, that courtly love itself, in spite of all its shabby origins and pedantic rules, is

---

3. A particularly instructive comparison could be drawn between the Chaucerian Cresseide's determination to yield, yet to seem to yield by force and deception, and Bialacoil's behaviour. *R. R.* 12607–88: specially 12682, 3.
4. Cf. ii. 1023 et seq.
5. *Proceedings of Brit. Acad.*, vol. xvi, Shakespeare Lecture, 1930.

at bottom more agreeable to those elements in human, or at least in European, nature, which last longest, than the cynical Latin gallantries of Boccaccio? The world of Chrestien, of Guillaume de Lorris, and of Chaucer, is nearer to the world universal, is less of a closed system, than the world of Ovid, of Congreve, of Anatole France.

This is doctrine little palatable to the age in which we live: and it carries with it another doctrine that may seem no less paradoxical— namely, that certain medieval things are more universal, in that sense more classical, can claim more confidently a *securus judicat*, than certain things of the Renaissance. To make Herod your villain is more human than to make Tamburlaine your hero. The politics of Machiavelli are provincial and temporary beside the doctrine of the *jus gentium*. The love-lore of Andreas, though a narrow stream, is a stream tending to the universal sea. Its waters move. For real stagnancy and isolation we must turn to the decorative lakes dug out far inland at such a mighty cost by Mr. George Moore; to the more popular corporation swimming-baths of Dr. Marie Stopes; or to the teeming marshlands of the late D. H. Lawrence, whose depth the wisest knows not and on whose bank the hart gives up his life rather than plunge in:

> Þær mæg nihta gehwæm niðwundor seon
> Fyr on flode!

MORTON W. BLOOMFIELD

Distance and Predestination in *Troilus and Criseyde*†

> For we are but of yesterday.
> —Job viii.9

In *Troilus and Criseyde* Chaucer as commentator occupies an unusual role. It is indeed common for authors to enter their own works in many ways. Writers as diverse as Homer, Virgil, Dante, Cervantes, Fielding, Thackeray, and George Eliot all do so. Sometimes, as with Fielding, the author may keep a distance between himself and his story; sometimes, as with Dante, he may penetrate into his story as a major or the major character; and sometimes, as with Homer, he may both enter and withdraw at will. When Homer directly addresses one of his characters, he is deliberately breaking down, for artistic reasons, the aloofness to which he generally holds.

Chaucer also frequently appears in his own works, usually as one of his dramatis personae, and participates in the action.[1] Although he is not always an important or major character, his actions or dreams within

---

† From *PMLA* 72 (1957): 14–26. Reprinted by permission of the publisher.
1. On this point in connection with the *Canterbury Tales* see Donaldson's stimulating "Chaucer the Pilgrim," *PMLA*, LXIX (1954), 928–936. I am indebted to Professor Donaldson for several suggestions made orally to me which I have woven into this article—notably the root idea of n. 5 at the end of this essay.

the work frequently provide the occasion for, or give a supposed rationale to, his literary creations. Chaucer the character's decision to go on a pilgrimage to Canterbury provides the ostensible justification for the *Canterbury Tales*. His dreams as a character, following a great medieval literary convention, give rise to the *Parlement of Foules* and the *Hous of Fame*.

In *Troilus and Criseyde* Chaucer plays his artistic role with a striking difference. Here he conceives of himself as the narrator of a history, of a true event as the Middle Ages conceived it, which happened in the past; and as historian he meticulously maintains a distance between himself and the events in the story. His aloofness is similar to and yet different from Fielding's in *Tom Jones* or Thackeray's in *Vanity Fair*. In these works the authors look upon their puppets from their omniscient, ironical, humorous, and at times melancholy point of view and make comments on them or their predicaments, using them as excuses for brief essays or paragraphs on different subjects. In *Troilus* Chaucer does not look upon his characters as his creations. His assumed role is primarily descriptive and expository. Though we are continually reminded of the presence of Chaucer the historian, narrator, and commentator, at the same time we are never allowed to forget that he is separate from the events he is recording.

Troilus is not a dream vision nor is it a contemporary event. It is the past made extremely vivid by the extensive use of dialogue, but still the past. Chaucer cannot change the elements of his story. As God cannot violate His own rationality, Chaucer cannot violate his data. Bound by his self-imposed task of historian, he both implies and says directly that he cannot do other than report his tale.

If we assume that Chaucer is a painstaking artist—and it is impossible not to—it is clear that the nature of the role he assumes has an extremely important meaning in the economy and plan of the poem. Why, we must ask, does Chaucer as character-narrator continually remind us of his aloofness from and impotence in the face of the events he is narrating? An historian takes for granted what Chaucer does not take for granted. A Gibbon does not tell us constantly that the events of the decline and fall of the Roman Empire are beyond his control. That is an assumption that anyone reading a true history makes at the outset. Chaucer introduces just this assumption into his body of his work, continually reminding us of what seems, in the context of a supposed history, most obvious. What is normally outside the historical work, a presupposition of it, is in the history of Troilus and Criseyde brought into the poem and made much of. This unusual creative act calls for examination.

We must also wonder at the quantitative bulk of Chaucer's comments on the story. Frequently, even in the midst of the action of the inner story, we are reminded of the presence of the narrator—sometimes, it is true, by only a word or two. We cannot dismiss these numerous comments merely as remarks necessary to establish rapport with the audience under conditions of oral delivery. The few remarks of this nature are easy to pick out. If we compare the simple comments made by the narrator in, say *Havelock the Dane* or any other medieval romance with those made by the *Troilus* narrator, I think the difference is plain.

Although many stanzas belong completely to the commentator *in propria persona* and others pertain to the events of the tale, so many are partly one or the other, or merely suggest the presence of a narrator, that a mathematical table which could reveal the actual percentage of commentator stanzas or lines would be misleading and inaccurate.[2] Anyone who has read the poem must be aware of the presence of the commentator most of the time; one is rarely allowed to forget it for long. And even more impressive than the number of comments are the times and nature of the author's intervention. At all the great moments he is there directing us, speaking in his own person close to us and far from the events of the tragedy which he is presenting to us within the bounds of historical fact.

This sense of distance between Chaucer as character and his story is conveyed to us in what may be designated as temporal, spatial, aesthetic, and religious ways, each reinforcing the other and overlapping. For the sake of clarity, however, we may examine each in turn as a separate kind of aloofness.

The aspect of temporal distance is the one most constantly emphasized throughout the poem. Chaucer again and again tells us that the events he is recording are historical and past. He lets us know that customs have changed since the time when Pandarus, Troilus, and Criseyde lived. The characters are pagans who go to temples to worship strange gods and are caught up in one of the great cataclysms of history. Their ways of living are different from ours. Their love-making varies from the modern style. They lived a long time ago, and Chaucer, to tell their story, is forced to rely on the historians. In order to understand their actions, we must make an effort in comprehension. Yet, says Chaucer, diversity of custom is natural. At times, it is true, Chaucer is very anachronistic, but he still succeeds in giving his readers (or listeners) a feeling for the pastness of his characters and their sad story and for what we today call cultural relativity.[3]

Throughout, Chaucer tries to give us a sense of the great sweep of time which moves down to the present and into the future and back beyond Troy, deepening our sense of the temporal dimension. He tells us that speech and customs change within a thousand years (ii.22 ff.) and that this work he is writing is also subject to linguistic variability (v.1793 ff.). Kingdoms and power pass away too; the *translatio regni*(or *imperii*) is inexorable—"regnes shal be flitted / Fro folk in folk" (v.1544–45). The characters themselves reach even farther backward in time. Criseyde and her ladies read of another siege, the fall of Thebes, which

---

2. For what they are worth, I give the following statistics on the first book. All Chaucer quotations are from the edn. of F. N. Robinson, Boston, 1933. The following passages seem to me to belong wholly or partially to the narrator as commentator: ll. 1–56 (proem), 57–63, 100, 133, 141–147, 155, 211–217, 252–266, 377–378, 393–399, 450–451 (a direct rapport remark), 492–497, 737–749 (doubtful), 1086–92. Excluding ll. 737–749, we find that 141 lines out of 1092 may be said to be comments by the author as commentator. Roughly 12% of the lines of the first book (one line in 8⅓ lines) belong to the commentator. Even allowing for subjective impressions, 10% would certainly be fair. This is a remarkably high percentage I should say. The proem I shall analyze below. The other remarks bear on his sources, moralize, establish a mood of acceptance, indicate distance and pastness and refer to fate and destiny. For overt references to fate and providence in the poem, see the list in Eugene E. Slaughter, "Love and Grace in Chaucer's *Troilus*," *Essays in Honor of Walter Clyde Curry* (Nashville, 1955), p. 63, n. 8.
3. See Morton W. Bloomfield, "Chaucer's Sense of History," *JEGP*, li (1952), 301–313.

took place long before the siege of Troy (II.81 ff.). Cassandra, in her interpretation of Troilus' dream (v.1450–1519), goes into ancient history to explain Diomede's lineage. We are all part of time's kingdom, and we are never allowed to forget it.

Yet, as I have already mentioned, Chaucer vividly reconstructs, especially in his use of dialogue, the day-by-day living of his chief characters. This precision of detail and liveliness of conversation only serve to weight the contrast between himself in the present and his story in the past, to make the present even more evanescent in the sweep of inexorable change. It is the other side of the coin. These inner events are in the past and in a sense dead, but when they occurred they were just as vivid as the events that are happening now. The strong reality and, in a sense, nearness of the past makes meaningful its disappearance and emphasizes paradoxically its distance. If there are no strong unique facts, there is nothing to lament. We cannot escape into the web of myth and cycle; the uniqueness of the past is the guarantee of its own transience. This is the true historical view and this is Chaucer's view. For him, however, even unique events have meaning, but only in the framework of a world view which can put history into its proper place.

Not frequently used, yet most important when it is, is the sense of spatial distance which Chaucer arouses in his readers. The events of the poem take place in faraway Asia Minor. Chaucer creates a sense of spatial distance by giving us a shifting sense of nearness and farness. At times we seem to be seeing the Trojan events as if from a great distance and at others we seem to be set down among the characters. This sense of varying distance is most subtly illustrated in the fifth book when Chaucer, after creating a most vivid sense of intimacy and closeness in describing the wooing of Criseyde by Diomede, suddenly moves to objectivity and distance in introducing the portraits of the two lovers and his heroine (799 ff.)—a device taken from Dares. With the approach of the hour of betrayal, as we become emotionally wrought up and closely involved, Chaucer the narrator brings us sharply back to his all-seeing eye and to a distance. The same technique may also be seen elsewhere in the poem. This continual inversion of the telescope increases our sense of space and gives us a kind of literary equivalent to the perspective of depth in painting.

Chaucer, in his insistence on cultural relativity, not only emphasizes chronological but also geographic variability. "Ek for to wynnen love in sondry ages, / In sondry londes, sondry been usages" (II.27–28). Above all we get this sense of spatial distance in the final ascent of Troilus to the ogdoad, the eighth sphere,[4] where in a sense he joins Chaucer in

---

4. Although irrelevant to the point I am making about the sense of distance in the journey to or through the spheres, there is some question as to the reading and meaning here (v.1809). I follow Robinson and Root who take the reading "eighth" rather than "seventh" as in most manuscripts. Boccaccio uses "eighth," and there is a long tradition extending back to classical antiquity which mades the ogdoad the resting place of souls (see Morton W. Bloomfield, *The Seven Deadly Sins*, East Lansing, 1952, pp. 16–17 ff.). Cf., however, Jackson I. Cope, "Chaucer, Venus and the 'Seventhe Spere'," *MLN*, LXVII (1952), 245–246. (Cope is unaware of the ogdoad tradition and also assumes that Troilus is a Christian.) There is also the problem of the order in which the spheres are numbered. If the highest is the first then the eighth sphere is that of the moon, the one nearest the earth. Root believes Chaucer is following this arrangement. However, as Cope points out, Chaucer in the opening stanza of Bk. III names "Venus as the informing power of the

looking down on this "litel spot of erthe" and can even contemplate his own death with equanimity.

The sense of aesthetic distance[5] is evoked by the continual distinction Chaucer makes between the story and the commentator, between the framework and the inner events. Although his basic "facts" are given, Chaucer never lets the reader doubt for long that he is the narrator and interpreter of the story. Once, at least, he adopts a humorous attitude towards his dilemma. He insists that he is giving his readers Troilus' song of love (1.400 ff.), "Naught only the sentence" as reported by Lollius but "save oure tonges difference" "every word right thus." This attitude is, however, rare. But it is not unusual for Chaucer to insist upon his bondage to the facts. Yet he strains against the snare of true events in which he is caught. Indeed Chaucer tries again and again, especially where the betrayal of Criseyde is involved, to fight against the truth of the events he is "recording." He never hides his partiality for that "hevennysh perfit creature" (1.104), and in this attitude as in others he notifies us of the narrow latitude which is allowed him. As he approaches the actual betrayal, he slows down; and with evident reluctance, as his reiterated, "the storie telleth us" (v.1037), "I fynde ek in the stories elleswhere" (v.1044), "men seyn—I not" (v.1050) show, he struggles against the predestined climax. The piling up of these phrases here emphasizes the struggle of the artist-narrator against the brutality of the facts to which he cannot give a good turn. As a faithful historian, he cannot evade the rigidity of decisive events—the given. Criseyde's reception of Diomede cannot be glossed over.[6] All this makes us more aware of Chaucer the narrator than ordinarily and increases our sense of aesthetic distance between the reporter and what is reported, between the frame and what is framed.

Finally we may call certain aspects of Chaucerian distance religious. Troilus, Pandarus, and Criseyde are pagans who lived "while men loved the lawe of kinde" (*Book of the Duchess*, l. 56)—under natural law. The great barrier of God's revelation at Sinai and in Christ separates Chaucer and us from them. Chaucer portrays them consciously as pagans, for he never puts Christian sentiments into their mouths.[7] He may violate our

---

third sphere" and therefore must be using the opposite numbering system. Troilus then goes to the highest sphere, that of the fixed stars.

E. J. Dobson ("Some Notes on Middle English Texts," *Eng. and Ger. Stud.*, Univ. of Birmingham, I [1947–48], 61–62) points out that Dante, *Paradiso* xxii, 100–154, which is Boccaccio's (and hence Chaucer's) source for this passage in the *Teseide*, makes clear that the emendation to "eighth" is justified.

5. Needless to say I am not using this phrase in the sense given it by Edward Bullough in his " 'Psychical Distance' as a Factor in Art and an Aesthetic Principle," *Brit. Jour. of Psychol.*, v (1913), reprinted in *A Modern Book of Esthetics, An Anthology*, ed. Melvin Rader, rev. ed. (New York, 1952) pp. 401–428, He refers to "distance" between the art object on the one hand and the artist or audience in the other. The distance here referred to is within the poem, between the character-narrator Chaucer and the events.

6. Chaucer sets himself the problem of interpreting Criseyde's action here by his sympathetic portrayal of her character and by his unblinking acceptance of the "facts" of his history. Boccaccio evades it by his pre-eminent interest in Troilus. Henryson gives Troilus an "unhistorical" revenge. Shakespeare has blackened Cressida's character throughout. Christopher Hassall, in his libretto for William Walton's opera on the subject, makes Criseyde a victim of a mechanical circumstance and completely blameless. Only Chaucer, by a strict allegiance to the "historical" point of view, poses the almost unbearable dilemma of the betrayal of Troilus by a charming and essentially sympathetic Criseyde.

7. The only exception is to be found in the Robinson text where at III. 1165 we find the reading in a speech by Criseyde "by that God that bought us both two." I am convinced that the Root reading

historic sense by making the lovers act according to the medieval courtly love code, but not by making them worship Christ. They are reasonable pagans who can attain to the truths of natural law—to the concept of a God, a creator, and to the rational moral law but never to the truths of revealed Christian religion. Chaucer is very clear on this point and in the great peroration to the poem he expressly says

> Lo here, of payens corsed olde rites,
> Lo here, what alle hire goddes may availle;
> Lo here, thise wrecched worldes appetites;
> Lo here, the fyn and guerdoun for travaille
> Of Jove, Appollo, of Mars, of swich rascaille!   (v. 1849–53)

In general, until the end of the poem, Chaucer, as we shall see, plays down his own Christianity for good reason. He even, at times and in consonance with the epic tradition which came down to him, calls upon the pagan Muses and Furies, but he does not avoid the Christian point of view when he feels it necessary to be expressed. Although the religious barrier is not emphasized until the conclusion, we are left in no doubt throughout as to its separating Chaucer from his characters. This sense of religious distance becomes at the end a vital part of the author's interpretation of his story.

A close study of Chaucer's proems written as prefaces to the first four books bears out the analysis offered here. In these Chaucer speaks out, and from his emphases and invocations we may gain some clues as to his intentions. At the beginning of the first proem, we are told of the subject of the work and of its unhappy fatal end. Chaucer does not allow us to remain in suspense at all. He exercises his role as historical commentator immediately at the outset. Tesiphone, one of the Furies, is invoked as an aid. She is a sorrowing Fury, as Dante had taught Chaucer to view her. She is responsible for the torment of humans, but she weeps for her actions. She is also in a sense the invoker himself who puts himself in his poem in a similar role. Chaucer is also a sorrowing tormenter who is retelling a true tale, the predestined end of which he cannot alter. Though ultimately he is to conquer it through religion, Chaucer the commentator is throughout most of the poem a victim of the historical determinism of his own poem. Although it is set down in the introduction to the poem, we may not understand the full meaning of Chaucer's entanglement and the escape provided by Christianity until we reach its end. There the Christian solution to the dilemma of the first proem is again presented but deepened by our knowledge of Troilus' fate and by a greater emphasis. Then, we shall have followed through the sad story under Chaucer the commentator's guidance and the answer is plain. In the proem, on the first reading, however, the problem

---

"wrought" for "bought" is correct. It would be perfectly possible for pagans to use "wrought" but not "bought." If we admit "bought" it would be the only Christian allusion put into the mouths of the Trojan characters and would conflict with the expressedly pagan attitude of these figures. I now take a stronger position on the matter than I allowed myself to express in "Chaucer's Sense of History," *JEGP*, LI (1952), 308, n. 17. Various references to grace, the devil (I.805), a bishop (II. 104), saints' lives (II. 118) and celestial love (I. 979) need not, from Chaucer's point of view of antiquity, be taken as Christian.

and the solution cannot be clear in spite of Chaucer's open words. We too must discover the answer.

On the other hand, in the first prologue, he does tell us, so that we may understand, that he the conductor and recorder of his story is like Troilus after the betrayal, unhappy in love. In the *Book of the Duchess*, the dreamer's unhappiness in love is assuaged within the dream and inner story by the grief of the man in black, whose loss of his beloved foreshadows what would have happened to the dreamer's love in one form or another, for all earthly love is transitory. Death is worse than unhappiness in love. Chaucer the *Troilus* narrator who dares not pray to love "for myn unliklynesse" is also going to learn in his tale that the love of the Eternal is the only true love. Actually Chaucer, because he conceives of himself as historian, has already learned before he begins. Hence, it is not quite accurate to say as above that he is going to learn, for he already knows. The reader, however, unless he is extraordinarily acute, remains in ignorance until he finishes the whole work. He discovers in the course of the experience of the history what Chaucer already knows and has really told him in the beginning, for Chaucer concludes his first proem by calling on all lovers both successful and unsuccessful to join him in prayer for Troilus. It is, he says, only in heaven, in the *patria* of medieval theology, that we can find lasting happiness. Troilus will find a pagan equivalent for this in his pagan heaven at the end. One cannot, however, quite believe Chaucer here until one reads the poem and finds that he is deadly serious when he prays that God "graunte" unhappy lovers "soone owt of this world to pace" (1.41). It is the love of God which is the answer to the love of woman and of all earthly things.

In other words, Chaucer in his introduction to the poem indicates his bondage to historical fact, his own grief at his position, the problem of the unhappiness in this world which he, like Troilus and all unhappy lovers, must face, and the only true solution for all the lovers of this world.

The second proem appeals to Clio, the Muse of history, and alludes to the diversity of human custom and language. The sense of history and cultural relativity manifested here emphasizes the distance in time which temporal barriers impose. "For every wight which that to Rome went / Halt not o path, or alwey o manere" (11.36–37).

The opening of Book III calls upon Venus, goddess of love, and, although it makes other points as well, underlines again the pagan quality of the history. Venus in her symbolic, astrological, and divine role conquers the whole world and binds its dissonances and discords together. It is she who understands the mysteries of love and who explains the apparent irrationality of love. The proem closes with a brief reference to Calliope, Muse of epic poetry, as Chaucer wishes to be worthy, as an artist, of his great theme of love.

Finally, in the last proem, we have an appeal to Fortune the great presiding deity of the sublunar world. Here as always she suggests instability and transience. Chaucer then alludes to the binding power of his sources. He closes his prologue with an invocation to all the Furies and to Mars with overtones suggesting his unhappy role as commentator and the paganness of the story he is unfolding.

These proems cannot be completely explained in terms of my interpretation, for they are also, especially the third and fourth, appropriate artistically to the theme of the books they serve to introduce and the various stages of the narrative. In general they emphasize the tragic end of the tale, the unwilling Fury-like role Chaucer has to play, the historical bonds which shackle him, the pity of it all, the aloofness and distance between the Chaucer of the poem and the history itself he is telling, and the one possible solution to the unhappiness of the world. Nor are these sentiments confined to the prefaces. They occur again and again throughout the body of the poem.[8] Chaucer takes pains to create himself as a character in his poem and also to dissociate this character continually from his story.

The attitude of Chaucer the character throughout makes it possible for us to understand the crucial importance of the concept of predestination in the poem. In the past there has been much debate in Chaucerian criticism over the question of predestination in *Troilus*. We know that Chaucer was profoundly interested in this question and that it was a preoccupation of his age. It seems to me that, if we regard the framework of the poem—the role that Chaucer sets himself as commentator—as a meaningful part of the poem and if we consider the various references to fate and destiny in the text, we can only come to the conclusion that the Chaucerian sense of distance and aloofness is the artistic correlative to the concept of predestination. *Troilus and Criseyde* is a medieval tragedy of predestination because the reader is continually forced by the commentator to look upon the story from the point of view of its end and from a distance. The crux of the problem of predestination is knowledge. So long as the future is not known to the participants in action, they can act as if they were free. But once a position of distance from the action is taken, then all can be seen as inevitable. And it is just this position which Chaucer the commentator takes and forces upon us from the very beginning. As John of Salisbury writes, "however, when you have entered a place, it is impossible that you have not entered it; when a thing has been done it is impossible that it be classed with things not done; and there is no recalling to non-existence a thing of the past."[9] All this presupposes knowledge which is impossible *in media re*. It is just this knowledge that Chaucer the commentator-historian gives us as he reconstructs the past. Hence we are forced into an awareness of the inevitability of the tragedy and get our future and our present at the same time, as it were.

Bound by the distance of time and space, of art and religion, Chaucer sits above his creation and foresees, even as God foresees, the doom of his own creatures: God, the *Deus artifex* who is in medieval philosophy the supreme artist and whose masterpiece is the created world.[1] But Chaucer is like God only insofar as he can know the outcome, not as

8. See n. 2 above.
9. *Policraticus*, ii, 22, ed. C. C. I. Webb (Oxford, 1909), i, 126. The translation is by Joseph B. Pike, *Frivolities of Courtiers* (Minneapolis, 1938), p. 111. Incidentally it should be noted that Calchas' foreknowledge through divination is on a basic level the cause of the tragedy.
1. "We are looking on at a tragedy that we are powerless to check or avert. Chaucer himself conveys the impression of telling the tale under a kind of duress" (G. L. Kittredge, *Chaucer and his Poetry*, Cambridge, 1915, p. 113).

creator. Analogically, because he is dealing with history, and, we must remember, to the medieval Englishman his own history, he can parallel somewhat his Maker. He is not the creator of the events and personages he is presenting to us; hence he cannot change the results. On the other hand God is the creator of His creatures; but He is bound by His own rationality and His foreknowledge. The sense of distance that Chaucer enforces on us accentuates the parallel with God and His providential predestination. We cannot leap the barriers which life imposes on us, but in the companionship of an historian we can imitate God *in parvo*. As God with His complete knowledge of future contingents sees the world laid out before Him all in the twinkling of an eye, so, in the case of history, with a guide, we share in small measure a similar experience. The guide is with us all the way, pointing to the end and to the pity of it. We must take our history from his point of view.

It is, of course, as hazardous to attribute opinions to Chaucer as it is to Shakespeare. Yet I suspect both were predestinarians—insofar as Christianity allows one to be. It is curious that all the great speeches on freedom of the will in Shakespeare's plays are put into the mouths of his villains—Edmund in *Lear*, Iago in *Othello*, and Cassius in *Julius Caesar*. This is not the place to discuss the relation of Chaucer to fourteenth-century thinking or to predestination, but I think he stands with Bishop Bradwardine who, when Chaucer was still very young, thundered against the libertarians and voluntarists because they depreciated God at the expense of His creatures and elevated man almost to the level of his Creator. Even the title of his masterpiece *De causa Dei* reveals clearly his bias. God's ways are not our ways and His grace must not be denied. His power (i.e., manifest in predestination) must be defended. Chaucer is probably with him and others on this issue and in the quarrel over future contingents which became the chief issue[2]—a reduction of the problem to logic and epistemology as befitted a century fascinated by logic and its problems. Regardless of Chaucer's personal opinion, however, I think I have shown that one of the main sources of the inner tensions of *Troilus* is this sense of necessity of an historian who knows the outcome in conflict with his sympathies as an artist and man, a conflict which gives rise to a futile struggle until the final leap which elevates the issue into a new and satisfactory context. This conflict causes the pity, the grief, the tears—and in a sense the ridiculousness and even the humor of it all.

Yet, throughout, the maturity of Chaucer's attitude is especially noteworthy. Predestination which envelops natural man implicates us all. Only from a Christian point of view can we be superior to Troilus and Criseyde and that is not due to any merit of our own, but to grace. As natural men and women we too are subject to our destiny whatever it may be. Chaucer links himself (and us) with his far-off characters, thereby strengthening the human bond over the centuries and increasing the objectivity and irony of his vision. We are made to feel that this is reality, that we are looking at it as it is and even from our distance participate in it.

2. On this dispute in the 14th century, see L. Baudry, *La querelle des futurs contingents* (Paris, 1950), and Paul Vignaux, *Justification et prédestination au XIVe siècle* (Paris, 1934).

There is no escape from the past if one chooses to reconstruct artistically, as Chaucer does, the past from the vantage ground of the present. Chaucer's creation of himself in *Troilus* as historian-narrator and his emphasis on the distance between him and his characters repeat, in the wider frame of the present and in the panorama of complete knowledge, the helplessness and turmoil of the lovers in the inner story. The fact that Chaucer regards his story as true history does not, of course, make his point of view predestinarian; in that case all historians would be committed to a philosophy of predestination. The point is that the author creates a character—himself—to guide us through his historical narrative, to emphasize the pitiful end throughout, to keep a deliberate distance suggested and stated in various ways between him and us and the characters of the inner story. He makes his chief character awake to the fact of predestination towards the end of the story and at the conclusion has this character join, as it were, us and Chaucer the character—in space instead of time—in seeing his own story through the perspective of distance. It is all this which gives us the clue. The outer frame is not merely a perspective of omniscience but also of impotence and is in fact another level of the story. It serves as the realm of Mount Ida in the *Iliad*—a wider cadre which enables us to put the humans involved into their proper place.

Every age has its polarities and dichotomies, some more basic than others. To believing medieval man, the fundamental division is between the created and the uncreated. God as the uncreated Creator is the unchanging norm against which all His creatures must be set and the norm which gives the created world its true objectivity. The true Christian was bound to keep the universe in perspective: it was only one of the poles of this fundamental polarity. The city of God gives meanings to the city of the world.

The impasse of the characters can only be solved on this other level and in this wider cadre. Actually for Troilus and Criseyde there is no final but merely a temporary solution—the consolation of philosophy— from which only the betrayed lover can benefit. Troilus begins to approach his narrator's viewpoint as he struggles against his fate beginning in the fourth book. The political events have taken a turn against him, and he tries to extricate himself and his beloved. But he is trapped and, what is even worse, long before Criseyde leaves he becomes aware of his mistake in consenting to let her go. In spite of her optimistic chatter, he predicts almost exactly what will happen when she joins her father. And he tells her so (IV.1450 ff.) Yet like one fascinated by his own doom he lets her go. He struggles but, in spite of his premonitions, seems unable to do anything about it.

It has long been recognized that Troilus' speech in favor of predestination (IV.958 ff.) is an important element in the poem.[3] It certainly

---

3. I am aware, of course, that this famous speech was added only in the second or final version of the poem as Root has clearly shown. I do not think that this point has much relevance to my argument one way or another. Inasmuch as we can probably never know why Chaucer added the passage, one explanation is as good as another. We must take the poem in its final form as our object for analysis. My case, which is admittedly subjective, does not rest on this passage. It may be that Chaucer felt that by adding this speech he was making clearer a point he already had in mind. Or it is possible that it was only on his second revision that he saw the full implications of his argument. Or finally it may have occurred to him that by bringing Troilus closer to his own

indicates that Troilus believes in predestination, and I think in the light of what we have been saying here represents a stage in Troilus' approach to Chaucer. When, in the pagan temple, he finally becomes aware of destiny,[4] he is making an attempt to look at his own fate as Chaucer the commentator all along has been looking at it. The outer and inner stories are beginning to join each other. This movement of narrator and character towards each other in the last two books culminates in the ascent through the spheres at the end where Troilus gets as close to Chaucer (and us) as is possible in observing events in their proper perspective— *sub specie aeternitatis*. As Boethius writes in the *Consolation of Philosophy*

> Huc [Nunc] omnes pariter uenite capti
> Quos fallax ligat improbis catenis
> Terrenas habitans libido mentes,
> Haec erit uobis requies laborum,
> Hic portus placida manens quiete,
> Hoc patens unum miseris asylum.   (III, metrum x)

Or as Chaucer himself translates these lines

> Cometh alle to gidre now, ye that ben ykaught and ybounde
> with wikkide cheynes by the desceyvable delyt of erthly
> thynges enhabitynge in your thought! Her schal ben the
> reste of your labours, her is the havene stable in pesible
> quiete; this allone is the open refut to wreches.

From this vantage point all falls into its place and proper proportion. Troilus now has Chaucer's sense of distance and joins with his author in finding what peace can be found in a pagan heaven.

Just before this soul journey, Chaucer has even consigned his very poem to time and put it in its place along with all terrestrial things (v. 1793 ff.) in the kingdom of mutability and change. As Chaucer can slough off his earthly attachments and prides, even the very poem in which he is aware of their transitory nature, Troilus his hero can also do so.

Thus towards the end, in the last two books, we see the hero beginning to imitate his narrator and the narrator, his hero, and the distance set up between the two begins to lessen and almost disappear. A dialectic of distance and closeness which has been from the beginning more than implicit in the poem between God, Chaucer the commentator-narrator, and the characters—notably Troilus—of the inner story, becomes sharply poised, with the triangle shrinking as the three approach each other.[5] A final shift of depth and distance, however, takes place at the

---

position before the end, he would deepen the significance of what he wished to say. These explanations for the addition are at least as plausible and possible as any other.

4. The location of this speech is not, I think, without significance. The end of pagan or purely natural religion is blind necessity, and in its "church" this truth can best be seen.

5. Another triangle has its apex in Pandarus who is, of course, the artist of the inner story as Chaucer is of the outer one and as God is of the created world. Pandarus works on his material—Troilus and especially Criseyde—as his "opposite numbers" do with their materials. All are to some extent limited—Pandarus by the characters of his friend and niece and by political events; Chaucer by his knowledge and by history; God by His rationality. All this is another story, however; my interest here is primarily in the triangle with Troilus as apex.

end. The poem does not come to a close with Troilus joining Chaucer. A further last leap is to establish again, even as at the beginning, a new distance. Beyond the consolation of philosophy, the only consolation open to Troilus is the consolation of Christianity. In the last stanzas, Chaucer the narrator escapes from Troilus to where the pagan cannot follow him; he escapes into the contemplation of the mysteries of the Passion and of the Trinity, the supreme paradox of all truth, which is the only possible way for a believing Christian to face the facts of his story. The artist and the historian who have been struggling in the breast of Chaucer can finally be reconciled. Here free will and predestination, human dignity and human pettiness, joy and sorrow, in short all human and terrestrial contradictions, are reconciled in the pattern of all reconciliation: the God who becomes man and whose trinity is unity and whose unity is trinity. Here the author-historian can finally find his peace at another distance and leave behind forever the unhappy and importunate Troilus, the unbearable grief of Criseyde's betrayal, the perplexities of time and space, and the tyranny of history and predestination.

E. TALBOT DONALDSON

The Ending of *Troilus*†

One of Chaucer's familiar pretenses is that he is a versifier utterly devoted to simplicity of meaning—for the reason that he considers himself, apparently, utterly incapable of complexity. He defines his poetic mission as the reporting of facts in tolerable verse, and he implies that that's hard enough to do. True poetry may, for all of him, do something much better but it is not clear to Chaucer exactly what it is or how it does it. He and *ars poetica* are, to be sure, on parallel roads, moving in the same direction; but the roads are a long way apart and are destined to meet, perhaps, not even in infinity. On the one hand, Chaucer, reciting his simple stories 'in swich Englissh as he can'; on the other, poetry, penetrating regions of complex significance far beyond the grasp of a simple straightforward versifier.

Chaucer's pretended inferiority complex on the subject of poetry must have stemmed from something real in his own life probably connected with his being a bourgeois writing for highborn members of the royal court. What interests me now however, is not the origin of the pose, but its literary value. For I think that Chaucer discovered in the medieval modesty convention a way of poetic life: that, by constantly assuring us, both through direct statement and through implication, of his inability to write anything but the simplest kind of verse, Chaucer creates just that poetry of complex significance that he disclaims striving for. In this

† First published in *Early English and Norse Studies, presented to Hugh Smith* . . . , ed. Arthur Brown and Peter Foote (London: Methuen, 1963) and reprinted by permission of The Continuum International Publishing Group. The text here is taken from the slightly revised version printed in E. Talbot Donaldson, *Speaking of Chaucer* (New York: W. W. Norton & Company 1970; London: Athlone, 1970), pp. 84–101.

paper I shall focus attention on the last stanzas of *Troilus*, where it seems to me that a kind of dramatization of his poetic ineptitude achieves for him a poetic success that not many poets in any language have attained. But I shall first consider briefly some characteristic Chaucerian 'ineptitudes' in his other works.

Modesty is endemic both with Chaucer in his own first person—whoever that is—and with his dramatic creations: none of them can do much in the way of poetry. Like the Squire, they cannot climb over so high a stile, or, like his father, they set out to plough, God wot, a large field with weak oxen; or, if they are not ploughing a field, they're gleaning it, like the author of the Prologue to the *Legend of Good Women*, and are full glad of any kernel that their talented predecessors have missed. Or else, like the Prioress, they are so afflicted by infantilism that they speak no better than a child of twelvemonth old, or less. Like the Merchant and the Franklin, they are rude men, 'burel' men, they cannot glose, they have no rhetoric, they call a spade a spade; they come after even such second-rate poets as that fellow Chaucer, bearing only *hawe bake*—pig food—and are reduced to prose, like the Man of Law in his Prologue. They can't even get the data down in the right order, like the Monk or like the narrator of the Prologue to the *Canterbury Tales*. Or, worst of all, as in the case of the pilgrim who recites the romance of Sir Thopas, their inability to frame a story of their own makes them resort to 'a rim I lerned longe agoon', and when that is shot down in mid-flight, they have to take refuge in one of the most anaesthetic sermons that ever mortified a reader. If it is dramatically appropriate that they be capable rhetoricians, like the Clerk, they comply at once with a decree that declares high style to be inappropriate to their audience. In short, they seldom admit to more than a nodding acquaintance with the Muse.

The normal function of the modesty convention is, I suppose, to prepare a pleasant surprise for the reader when the poem turns out better than he has been led to expect, or, at worst, to save him disappointment when the implied warning is fulfilled. This latter alternative is perhaps valid in some of Chaucer's tales, notably the Monk's. But the really important function of the modesty convention in Chaucer is to prepare a soil in which complexity of meaning may grow most fruitfully. That is, the narrator's assertion, implicit or explicit, of his devotion to the principle of simplicity, his denial of regard for possible complexity, results, by a curious paradox, *in* complexity; for the harder he tries to simplify issues, the less amenable to simplification they become, and, in artistic terms, the more complex and suggestive the poem becomes. To epitomize, the typical Chaucerian narrator begins by assuring you, either by a modesty prologue or by the notable simplicity of his manner—sometimes by both—that in what you are about to hear there will be nothing but the most straightforward presentation of reality: the narrator's feet are firmly on the ground, but he is no poet, and his control of anything but fact is weak. Subsequently the poet Chaucer, working from behind the narrator, causes to arise from this hard ground a complex of possible meanings, endlessly dynamic and interactive, amplifying, qualifying, even denying the simple statement: these draw much of their vitality from the fact that they exist—or seem to exist—either, unknown to or in spite of the narrator; indeed, the latter sometimes betrays an uneasy awareness that the poem has got out of hand and is saying something he doesn't approve of or at least didn't intend, and his resistance to this meaning may well become an important part of it. That is, the ultimate significance of the poem derives much from the tension between the narrator's simple statement and the complex of implications that have arisen to qualify it.

The Chaucer who tells of the pilgrimage to Canterbury provides an obvious example of this tension between the simple and the complex. At the very beginning of the Prologue he lets us know exactly what we may expect of his narrative—namely what he saw with his own two eyes, and not an adverb more. And, as I have tried to show elsewhere,[1] his prospectus itself is a miracle of stylistic simplicity, its pedestrian matter-of-factness supporting by example the limited poetic ideal that it is expressing. Yet it is because he has succeeded in persuading the reader to expect no more than meets the eye that, when he comes to the portrait of the Prioress,[2] the poet is able to reveal to us the profoundest depths of that rather shallow lady. The narrator, to be sure, describes her flatly as he saw her, and what he saw was attractive, and it attracted the warm fervour of his love; but what he did not see was that everything he did see amounted to a well-indexed catalogue of the Prioress's shortcomings, which seen coldly would produce a kind of travesty of a Prioress. But because of his love for the woman, he is unaware of the satirical potential of his portrait, so that this potential, while always imminent, is never actually realized. One feels that if any one had pointed it out to the narrator, he would have been horrified, as, indeed, the Prioress would have been horrified if any one had pointed it out to her—and as even today certain readers are horrified when one points it out to them. And quite rightly, too, because of the great love that permeates the simple description. But the effect achieved by means of a narrator who resists complexity is of a highly complex strife between love and satire, between wholehearted approval and heartless criticism. These are factors which in logic would cancel one another, as a negative cancels a positive; but in poetry they exist forever side by side—as they also do in reality wherever there are ladies at once so attractive and so fallible as the Prioress. Indeed, the two factors, love and satire, unite with one another to form a third meaning—one which both qualifies and enhances the Prioress's own motto, *amor vincit omnia*, by suggesting something of the complex way in which love does conquer all. This occurs because the narrator, incapable of complexity, adheres rigorously to the presentation of simple fact.

The ways in which Chaucerian narrators enhance the meaning of their stories by missing the point of them are various. Occasionally, indeed, a narrator will rise up in the pulpit sententiously to point *out* or at least to point *to* what he takes to be his real meaning. The only trouble is that his aim is likely to be poor: he will suggest a meaning which, while it bears some logical relation to the ultimate significance, is at best no

---

1. See 'The Masculine Narrator and Four Women of Style', in *Speaking of Chaucer* (New York, 1970), pp. 46–47.
2. For further discussion of this portrait, see *Speaking of Chaucer*, pp. 3–4 and 59–64.

more than gross over-simplification. For instance, the Nun's Priest, at the end of his remarkably verbose epic of Chauntecleer, solemnly addresses his audience:

> Lo, swich it is for to be reccheless
> And necligent, and truste on flaterye.
> But ye that holden this tale a folye,
> As of a fox, or of a cok and hen,
> Taketh the moralitee, goode men. (B²3736–40)

He then goes on to quote St Paul in a way that suggests that doctrine is produced every time a pen inscribes words on paper—a thought most comforting to an author hard put to determine his own meaning. With Pauline authority on his side, the Nun's Priest exhorts us:

> Taketh the fruit, and lat the chaf be stille. (B²3443)

Now all this certainly bids us find a simple moral in the story; but, so far as I know, no two critics have ever found the same moral: most agree only in rejecting the Nun's Priest's stated moral about negligence and flattery. The reason for this disagreement is, as I have tried to suggest elsewhere,[3] that the real moral of the Tale is in the chaff—the rhetorical amplifications which make of Chauntecleer a good representative of western man trying to maintain his precarious dignity in the face of a universe and of a basic avian (or human) nature which fail to co-operate with him. But the Nun's Priest, characteristically, suggests this moral only by pointing towards another which satisfies nobody.

Another Canterbury narrator, the Knight, similarly asks us to take a simple view of a story which is really very complex. After describing the languishing of Arcite in Theban exile and of Palamon in Athenian prison, both of them quite out of the running in their race for Emily, the narrator finishes off the first part of his poem with a *demande d'amour*:

> You loveres axe I now this questioun:
> Who hath the worse, Arcite or Palamoun? (A1347–8)

With this tidy rhetorical flourish the Knight suggests that his story is a simple one about a rivalry in love. The question invites the reader to take sides in this rivalry, to feel sorrier for one youth than the other, and hence to choose a favourite for the contest that is to come. He appeals, that is, to our sense of justice. Until recently, the majority of Chaucerian critics put their money on Palamon; and since at the end of the story Providence accords him Emily and lets him live happily ever after, while it buries Arcite, this majority have naturally felt that justice has operated in an exemplary manner, and nothing is pleasanter than to see justice behave itself. Yet there has always been a noisy group—with whom I deeply sympathize—who feel that Arcite is very badly treated by the story. This disagreement represents a kind of protracted response to the Knight's rhetorical question.

---

3. See E. T. Donaldson, ed., *Chaucer's Poetry*, pp. 940–4; also 'Patristic Exegesis in the Criticism of Medieval Literature: The Opposition', *Selected Papers from the English Institute, 1958–1959,* repr. in *Speaking of Chaucer*, pp. 146–50.

The lack of critical agreement, however, once again suggests that there is something wrong both about the question and about the debate. If intelligent readers cannot agree on which of the two young men is the more deserving, then there is probably not much difference between them. And indeed, the way the poem carefully balances their claims bears this out. On temperamental grounds you may prefer a man who mistakes his lady for Venus to a man who knows a woman when he sees one, or you may not; but such preference has no moral validity. The poem concerns something larger than the young men's relative deserts, though it is something closely related to that question. Recognition of their equality leads to the conclusion that the poem does not assert the simple triumph of justice when Palamon ends up with Emily, nor the triumph of a malignant anti-justice when Arcite ends up in his cold grave, alone. What is does suggest—and I think with every syllable of its being—is that Providence is not working justly, so far as we can see, when it kills Arcite, nor, so far as we can see, unjustly when it lets Palamon live happily ever after. For no matter how hard we look, we cannot hope to see why Providence behaves as it does; all we can do is our best, making a virtue of necessity, enjoying what is good, and remaining cheerful.

But to most of us this is an unpalatable moral, far less appealing than the one which will result if only we can promote Palamon into an unchallenged position of deserving; and it is a very stale bit of cold cabbage indeed unless it is as hard-won as the Knight's own battles. The experience by which the individual attains the Knight's tempered view of life is an important part of that view, and renders it, if not palatable, digestible and nourishing. This experience must include our questioning of relative values, our desire to discover that even-handed justice does prevail in the universe, and our resistance to the conclusion that justice, so far as we can see, operates at best with only one hand. The emotional history of the ultimate conclusion makes it valid; and the way the Knight's question is framed, pointing at what we should like to believe, and through that at what we shall have to believe, causes us to share in that experience—leads us through the simple to the complex.

It is at the end of *Troilus* that Chaucer, employing the kind of devices I have been discussing, achieves his most complex poetic effect. His narrator has worked hard, from the very beginning, to persuade us of his simplicity, though from the very beginning his simplicity has been compromised by the fact that, apparently unknown to himself, he wavers between two quite different—though equally simple—attitudes towards his story. It is the saddest story in the world, and it is the gladdest story in the world. This double attitude appears strongly in the opening stanzas, when he tells us that his motive for writing is, paradoxically, to bring honour to Love and gladden lovers with a love story so sad that his verses shed tears while he writes them and that Tisiphone is his only appropriate Muse. Yet though he starts out firmly resolved to relate the double sorrow of Troilus

> . . . in loving of Criseide,
> And how that she forsook him er she deide,   (*TC* I. 55–6)

as the story progresses he seems to forget all about the second sorrow. The historical perspective, which sees before and after and knows the sad ending, gives way to the limited, immediate view of one who loves the actors in the story, and in his love pines for what is not so desperately that he almost brings it into being. The scholar's motive for telling a sad story simply because it is true finds itself at war with the sentimentalist's motive of telling a love story simply because it is happy and beautiful. The optimism that one acquires when one lives with people so attractive makes a gay future for all seem inevitable. Once launched upon the love story, the narrator refuses to look forward to a future that the scholar in him knows to be already sadly past; at moments when the memory of that sad future breaks in on him, he is likely to deny his own sources, and to suggest that, despite the historical evidence to the contrary, Criseide was, perhaps, not unfaithful at all—men have been lying about her.[4]

For the greater part of the poem the intimately concerned, optimistic narrator is in full control of the story—or rather, the story is in full control of him, and persuades him that a world that has such people in it is not only the best of all possible worlds, but the most possible. When in the fifth book the facts of history force him back towards the historical perspective, which has always known that his happiness and that of the lovers were transitory, illusory, he does his best to resist the implications arising from his ruined story—tries to circumvent them, denies them, slides off them. Thus an extraordinary feeling of tension, even of dislocation, develops from the strife in the narrator's mind between what should be and what was—and hence what is. This tension is the emotional storm-centre which causes the narrator's various shifts and turns in his handling of the ending, and which also determines the great complexity of the poem's ultimate meaning.

So skilfully has Chaucer mirrored his narrator's internal warfare—a kind of nervous breakdown in poetry—that many a critic has concluded that Chaucer himself was bewildered by his poem. One, indeed, roundly condemns the whole fifth book, saying that it reads like 'an earlier draft . . . which its author lacked sufficient interest to revise'. According to this critic, Chaucer 'cannot bring himself to any real enthusiasm for a plot from which the bright lady of his own creation has vanished'. And, elsewhere, 'What had happened to the unhappy Criseyde and to her equally unhappy creator was that the story in which they were involved had betrayed them both'.[5] Now this is, in a rather sad way, the ultimate triumph of Chaucer's method. The critic responds with perfect sympathy to the narrator's bewilderment, even to the extent of seeming to suggest that the poet had written four-fifths of his story before he discovered how it came out. But in fact Chaucer's warmly sympathetic narrator has blinded the critic's eyes as effectively as he had blinded his own. It is not true that the bright lady of Chaucer's creation has vanished—Criseide is still very much present in book five. What has vanished is the bright dream of the enduring power of human love, and in a burst of creative power that it is not easy to match elsewhere.

For the *moralitee* of *Troilus and Criseide* (and by morality I do not

4. *TC* IV. 20–1.
5. Marchette Chute, *Geoffrey Chaucer of England* (London, 1946), pp. 179, 180, and 178.

mean 'ultimate meaning') is simply this: that human love, and by a sorry corollary everything human, is unstable and illusory. I give the moral so flatly now because in the remainder of this paper I shall be following the narrator in his endeavour to avoid it, and indeed shall be eagerly abetting him in trying to avoid it, and even pushing him away when he finally accepts it. I hope in this way to suggest how Chaucer, by manipulating his narrator, achieves an objective image of the poem's significance that at once greatly qualifies and enhances this moral, and one that is, of course, far more profound and less absolute than my flatfooted statement. The meaning of the poem is not the moral, but a complex qualification of the moral.

Let us turn now to that part of the poem, containing the last eighteen stanzas, which is often referred to by modern scholars, though not by the manuscripts, as the Epilogue. I object to the term because it implies that this passage was tacked on to the poem after the poet had really finished his work, so that it is critically if not physically detachable from what has gone before.[6] And while I must admit that the nature of this passage, its curious twists and turns, its occasional air of fecklessness, set it off from what has gone before, it also seems to me to be the head of the whole body of the poem.[7]

The last intimately observed scene of the action is the final, anticlimactic interview between Troilus and Pandarus, wherein the latter is driven by the sad logic of his loyalty and of his pragmatism to express hatred of his niece, and to wish her dead. Pandarus's last words are, 'I can namore saye', and it is now up to the narrator, who is as heart-broken as Troilus and Pandarus, to express the significance of his story. His first reaction is to take the epic high road; by means of the exalted style to reinvest Troilus with the human dignity that his unhappy love has taken from him. The narrator starts off boldly enough:

> Greet was the sorwe and plainte of Troilus;
> But forth hire cours Fortune ay gan to holde.
> Criseide loveth the sone of Tydeüs,
> And Troilus moot weepe in cares colde.   (*TC* v. 1744–7)

But though the manner is epic, the subject is not: an Aeneas in Dido's pathetic plight is no fit subject for Virgilian style. And the narrator, overcome by the pathos of his story, takes refuge in moralization:

> Swich is this world, whoso it can biholde:
> In eech estaat is litel hertes reste—
> God leve us for to take it for the beste!

How true! And how supremely, brilliantly, inadequate! It has been said that all experience does no more than prove some platitude or other, but one hopes that poetic experience will do more, or in any case that poetry will not go from pathos to bathos. This moral, the trite moral of the

<hr />

6. The extreme exponent of detachability is W. C. Curry in his well-known essay, 'Destiny in *Troilus and Criseyde*', *PMLA*, xlv (1930), 129 ff., reprinted in his *Chaucer and the Mediaeval Sciences* (second revised and enlarged ed., 1960): see especially pp. 294–8.
7. I believe that this is the opinion of many Chaucerians. See, e.g., Dorothy Everett, *Essays on Middle English Literature* (1955), pp. 134–8, and Dorothy Bethurum, 'Chaucer's Point of View as Narrator', *PMLA*, lxxiv (1959), 516–18.

Monk's Tale—Isn't life awful?—which the Monk arrives at—again and again—*a priori* would be accepted by many a medieval man as a worthy moral for the *Troilus*, and the narrator is a medieval man. But the poet behind the narrator is aware that an experience that has been intimately shared—not merely viewed historically, as are the Monk's tragedies—requires not a moral, but a meaning arrived at *a posteriori*, something earned, and in a sense new. Moreover, the narrator seems still to be asking the question, Can nothing be salvaged from the wreck of the story? For he goes on once more to have recourse to epic enhancement of his hero, more successfully this time, since it is the martial heroism of Troilus, rather than his unhappy love, that is the subject: there follow two militant stanzas recounting his prowess and his encounters with Diomede. But again the epic impulse fails, for the narrator's real subject is not war but unhappy love, for which epic values will still do nothing—will neither salvage the dignity of Troilus nor endow his experience with meaning. In a wistful stanza, the narrator faces his failure to do by epic style what he desires to have done:

> And if I hadde ytaken for to write
> The armes of this ilke worthy man, [But, unfortunately, *arma virumque non cano*]
> Than wolde ich of his batailes endite;
> But for that I to writen first bigan
> Of his love, I have said as I can—
> His worthy deedes whoso list hem heere,
> Rede Dares—he can telle hem alle yfere.   (1765–71)

This sudden turn from objective description to introspection mirrors the narrator's quandary. Unable to get out of his hopeless predicament, he does what we all tend to do when we are similarly placed: he begins to wonder why he ever got himself into it. The sequel of this unprofitable speculation is likely to be panic, and the narrator very nearly panics when he sees staring him in the face another possible moral for the love poem he has somehow been unwise enough to recite. The moral that is staring him in the face is written in the faces of the ladies of his audience, the anti-feminist moral which is at once obvious and, from a court poet, unacceptable:

> Biseeching every lady bright of hewe,
> And every gentil womman what she be,
> That al be that Criseide was untrewe,
> That for that gilt she nat be wroth with me.
> Ye may hir giltes in othere bookes see;
> And gladlier I wol write, if you leste,
> Penelopeës trouthe and good Alceste.

While anticipating the ladies' objections, the narrator has, with that relief only a true coward can appreciate, glimpsed a possible way out: denial of responsibility for what the poem says. He didn't write it in the first place, it has nothing to do with him, and anyhow he would much rather have written about faithful women. These excuses are, of course, very much in the comic mood of the Prologue to the *Legend of Good*

Women where Alceste, about whom he would prefer to have written, defends him from Love's wrath on the grounds that, being no more than a translator, he wrote about Criseide 'from innocence, and knew not what he said'. And if he can acquit himself of responsibility for Criseide by pleading permanent inanity, there is no reason why he cannot get rid of all his present tensions by funneling them into a joke against himself. This he tries to do by turning upside down the anti-feminist moral of the story:

> N'I saye nat this al only for thise men,
> But most for wommen that bitraised be . . .

And I haven't recited this exclusively for men, but also, or rather but mostly, for women who are betrayed

> Thrugh false folk—God yive hem sorwe, amen!—
> That with hir grete wit and subtiltee
> Bitraise you; and this commeveth me
> To speke, and in effect you alle I praye,
> Beeth war of men, and herkneth what I saye.

The last excursion into farce—in a poem that contains a good deal of farce—is this outrageous inversion of morals, which even so has a grotesque relevance if all human love, both male and female, is in the end to be adjudged unstable. With the narrator's recourse to comedy the poem threatens to end. At any rate, he asks it to go away:

> Go, litel book, go, litel myn tragedye,
> Ther God thy makere yit, er that he die,
> So sende might to make in som comedye. . . .

(Presumably a comedy will not blow up in his face as this story has, and will let him end on a note like the one he has just sounded.) There follows the celebrated injunction of the poet to his book not to vie with other poetry, but humbly to kiss the steps of Virgil, Ovid, Homer, Lucan, and Statius. This is the modesty convention again, but transmuted, I believe, into something close to arrogance. Perhaps the poem is not to be classed with the works of these great poets, but I do not feel that the narrator succeeds in belittling his work by mentioning it in connection with them; there is such a thing as inviting comparison by eschewing comparison. It seems that the narrator has abandoned his joke, and is taking his 'little book'—of more than 8,000 lines—seriously. Increasing gravity characterizes the next stanza, which begins with the hope that the text will not be miswritten nor mismetred by scribes and lesser breeds without the law of final -e. Then come two lines of emphatic prayer:

> And red wherso thou be, or elles songe,
> That thou be understonde, God I biseeche.

It is perhaps inconsiderate of the narrator to implore us to take his sense when he has been so irresolute about defining his sense. But the movement of the verse now becomes sure and strong, instead of uncertain and aimless, as the narrator moves confidently towards a meaning.

For in the next stanza, Troilus meets his death. This begins—once again—in the epic style, with perhaps a glance at the *Iliad*:

> The wratthe, as I bigan you for to saye,
> Of Troilus the Greekes boughten dere.

Such dignity as the high style can give is thus, for the last time, proffered Troilus. But for him there is to be no last great battle in the West, and both the stanza, and Troilus's life, end in pathos:

> But wailaway, save only Goddes wille:
> Despitously him slow the fierse Achille.

Troilus's spirit at once ascends into the upper spheres whence he looks down upon this little earth and holds all vanity as compared with the full felicity of heaven. The three stanzas describing Troilus's afterlife afford him that reward which medieval Christianity allowed to the righteous heathen. And in so doing, they salvage from the human wreck of the story the human qualities of Troilus that are of enduring value—most notably, his *trouthe*, the integrity for which he is distinguished. Moreover, this recognition by the plot that some human values transcend human life seems to enable the narrator to come to a definition of the poem's meaning which he has hitherto been unwilling to make. Still close to his characters, he witnesses Troilus's rejection of earthly values, and then, apparently satisfied, now that the mortal good in Troilus has been given immortal reward, he is willing to make that rejection of *all* mortal goods towards which the poem has, despite his resistance, been driving him. His rejection occurs—most unexpectedly—in the third of these stanzas. Troilus, gazing down at the earth and laughing within himself at those who mourn his death,

> . . . dampned al oure werk that folweth so
> The blinde lust, the which that may nat laste,
> And sholden al oure herte on hevene caste.

Up until the last line Troilus has been the subject of every main verb in the entire passage; but after he has damned all *our* work, by one of those syntactical ellipses that make Middle English so fluid a language, Troilus's thought is extended to include both narrator and reader: in the last line, *And sholden al oure herte on hevene caste*, the plural verb *sholden* requires the subject *we*; but this subject is omitted, because to the narrator the sequence of the sense is, at last, overpoweringly clear. When, after all his attempts not to have to reject the values inherent in his love story, he finally does reject them, he does so with breath-taking ease.

He does so, indeed, with dangerous ease. Having taken up arms against the world and the flesh, he lays on with a will:

> Swich fin hath, lo, this Troilus for love;
> Swich fin hath al his grete worthinesse;
> Swich fin hath his estaat real above;
> Swich fin his lust, swich fin hath his noblesse;
> Swich fin hath false worldes brotelnesse:
> And thus bigan his loving of Criseide,
> As I have told, and in this wise he deide.

But impressive as this stanza is, its movement is curious. The first five lines express, with increasing force, disgust for a world in which everything—not only what merely *seems* good, but also what really *is* good—comes to nothing in the end. Yet the last two lines,

> And thus bigan his loving of Criseide,
> As I have told, and in this wise he deide,

have, I think, a sweetness of tone that contrasts strangely with the emphatic disgust that precedes them. They seem to express a deep sadness for a doomed potential—as if the narrator, while forced by the evidence to condemn everything his poem has stood for, cannot really quite believe that it has come to nothing. The whole lovely aspiration of the previous action is momentarily recreated in the spare summary of this couplet.

The sweetness of tone carries over into the next two stanzas, the much-quoted ones beginning.

> O yonge, freshe folkes, he or she,
> In which that love up groweth with youre age,
> Repaireth hoom fro worldly vanitee,
> And of youre herte up casteth the visage
> To thilke God that after his image
> You made; and thinketh al nis but a faire
> This world that passeth soone as flowres faire.

The sweetness here adheres not only to what is being rejected, but also to what is being sought in its stead, and this marks a development in the narrator. For he does not now seem so much to be fleeing away, in despair and disgust, from an ugly world—the world of the Monk's Tale—as he seems to be moving voluntarily through this world *towards* something infinitely better. And while this world is a wretched one—ultimately—in which all love is *feined*, 'pretended' and 'shirked', it is also a world full of the young potential of human love—'In which that love up groweth with *oure* age'; a world which, while it passes soon, passes soon as flowers fair. All the illusory loveliness of a world which is man's only reality is expressed in the very lines that reject that loveliness.

In these stanzas the narrator has been brought to the most mature and complex expression of what is involved in the Christian rejection of the world that seems to be, and indeed is, man's home, even though he knows there is a better one. But the narrator himself remains dedicated to simplicity, and makes one last effort to resolve the tension in his mind between loving a world he ought to hate and hating a world he cannot help loving; he endeavors to root out the love:

> Lo, here of payens cursed olde rites;
> Lo, here what alle hir goddes may availe;
> Lo, here thise wrecched worldes appetites;
> Lo, here the fin and guerdon for travaile
> Of Jove, Appollo, of Mars, of swich rascaile;
> Lo, here the forme of olde clerkes speeche
> In poetrye, if ye hir bookes seeche.

For the second time within a few stanzas a couplet has undone the work of the five lines preceding it. In them is harsh, excessively harsh, condemnation of the world of the poem, including gods and rites that have played no great part in it. In brilliant contrast to the tone of these lines is the exhausted calm of the last two:

> Lo, here the forme of olde clerkes speeche
> In poetrye, if ye hir bookes seeche.

There is a large imprecision about the point of reference of this couplet. I do not know whether its *Lo here* refers to the five preceding lines or to the poem as a whole, but I suppose it refers to the poem as a whole, as the other four *Lo here*'s do. If this is so, then the form of *olde clerkes speeche* is being damned as well as the *payens cursed olde rites*—by parataxis, at least. Yet it is not, for the couplet lacks the heavy, fussy indignation of the earlier lines: instead of indignation there is, indeed, dignity. I suggest that the couplet once more reasserts, in its simplicity, all the implicit and explicit human values that the poem has dealt with, even though these are, to a medieval Christian, ultimately insignificant. The form of old clerks' speech in poetry is the sad story that human history tells. It is sad, it is true, it is lovely, and it is significant, for it is poetry.

This is the last but one of the narrator's searches for a resolution for his poem. I have tried to show how at the end of *Troilus* Chaucer has manipulated a narrator capable of only a simple view of reality in such a way as to achieve the poetic expression of an extraordinarily complex one. The narrator, moved by his simple devotion to Troilus, to Pandarus, above all to Criseide, has been vastly reluctant to find that their story, so full of the illusion of happiness, comes to nothing—that the potential of humanity comes to nothing. To avoid this—seemingly simple—conclusion he has done everything he could. He has tried the epic high road; he has tried the broad highway of trite moralization; he has tried to eschew responsibility; he has tried to turn it all into a joke; and all these devices have failed. Finally, with every other means of egress closed, he has subscribed to Troilus's rejection of his own story, though only when, like Gregory when he wept for Trajan, he has seen his desire for his hero's salvation confirmed. Once having made the rejection, he has thrown himself into world-hating with enthusiasm. But now the counterbalance asserts its power. For the same strong love of the world of his story that prevented him from reaching the Christian rejection permeates and qualifies his expression of the rejection. Having painfully climbed close to the top of the ridge he did not want to climb, he cannot help looking back with longing at the darkening but still fair valley in which he lived; and every resolute thrust forward ends with a glance backward. In having his narrator behave thus, Chaucer has achieved a meaning only great poetry can achieve. The world he knows and the heaven he believes in grow ever farther and farther apart as the woeful contrast between them is developed, and ever closer and closer together as the narrator blindly unites them in the common bond of his love. Every false start he has made has amounted, not to a negative, but to a positive; has been a necessary part of the experience without which the moral of the poem would be as meaningless and unprofitable as in the form I gave it a little while ago. The poem states, what much of Chaucer's poetry states, the necessity under which men lie of living in, making the best of, enjoying, and loving a world from which they must remain detached and which they must ultimately hate: a little spot of earth that with the sea embraced is, as in Book Three Criseide was embraced by Troilus.

For this paradox there is no logical resolution. In the last two stanzas of the poem Chaucer, after asking Gower and Strode for correction, invokes the power that, being supra-logical itself, can alone resolve paradox. He echoes Dante's mighty prayer to the Trinity, 'that al maist circumscrive', and concludes with the lines:

> So make us, Jesus, for thy mercy digne,
> For love of Maide and Moder thyn benigne.

The poem has concerned a mortal woman whose power to love failed, and it ends with the one mortal woman whose power to love is everlasting. I think it is significant that the prayer of the poem's ending leads up, not to Christ, son of God, but to his mother, daughter of Eve— towards heaven, indeed, but towards heaven through human experience.

SHEILA DELANY

Techniques of Alienation in *Troilus and Criseyde*†

The principle of alienation in art, or esthetic distancing, has been in our time most clearly articulated by the German communist poet and playwright Bertolt Brecht. Brecht wrote frequently about alienation (A-effect) in art, and one of his most succinct definitions of it comes from a brief essay on acting:

> The A-effect consists in turning the object of which one is to be made aware, to which one's attention is to be drawn, from something ordinary, familiar, immediately accessible, into something peculiar, striking, and unexpected. What is obvious is in a certain sense made incomprehensible, but this is only in order that it may then be made all the easier to comprehend. Before familiarity can turn into awareness the familiar must be stripped of its inconspicuousness; we must give up assuming that the object in question needs no explanation. However frequently recurrent, modest, vulgar it may be it will now be labelled as something unusual.[1]

Yet alienation in art was not invented by Brecht. It was rather a discovery or even a recovery, for deliberate esthetic distancing has been practiced in various arts of different historical periods. There is nothing specifically twentieth-century about it, though it will be in any given period a "mod-

† From *The Uses of Criticism*, ed. A. P. Foulkes, Literaturwissenschaftliche Texte, Theorie und Kritik 3 (Bern: Peter Lang, 1976); 77–95. Reprinted by permission.
1. "Short Description of a New Technique of Acting which Produces an Alienation Effect" (1940); in *Brecht on Theatre*, trans. and ed. John Willett (New York: Hill and Wang, 1974), 143–44.

ern" technique. It will be useful to any artist in any medium who wants his or her work to be actively evaluated rather than passively received according to formal convention.

Indeed the purpose of alienation technique can be said to be: to undercut the conventional forms on which an audience habitually relies as a cue to response. The danger in automatic or habitual response (and it is of course culturally conditioned) is that the audience may fail to understand two things about the work of art. First, the audience may neglect substantive intellectual issues—whether moral, religious or political issues—which the artist considers essential to the work. Second, the audience may ignore or minimize the degree of deliberate shaping that informs the work, its individual, made quality. Hence techniques of alienation call into question both the received forms and the responses that are usually adequate to them. By jolting the audience out of easy reliance on received forms, alienation reasserts the importance of consciousness. The primacy of the artist's conscious aim is reasserted, and so is the necessity for the audience to understand the work of art through an act of conscious will. The desired response is not a passionate swoon, but a passionately correct esthetic and moral judgment.

I should like to give a few examples of how A-effect operates in a given work of art. Afterward I shall offer a reading of *Troilus and Criseyde* as a work in which Chaucer uses A-effect in order to goad the audience toward critical judgment of the conventions of medieval romance, and of character and action in the poem. Such judgment is not, of course, an end in itself, but the means toward an ideological end: that the audience should understand and accept the rigorous Augustinian doctrine which Chaucer makes explicit in the so-called "epilogue" but which has been adumbrated all along precisely by alienation techniques. Chaucer uses devices which, in Brechtian terms, "[turn] the object . . . from something ordinary, familiar, immediately accessible, into something peculiar, striking, and unexpected." The ordinary is made for the moment incomprehensible, but only so that another viewpoint, the orthodox Christian, may enter and eventually dominate: once we permit that to happen, comprehension is restored, albeit on a new level. I hope that the non-Chaucerian examples I give will expand my reader's notion of A-effect so that Chaucer's esthetic purpose will become the more apparent.

For Brecht, one of the best exemplars of A-effect was the traditional Chinese theatre. Here a number of devices were used to create an impression of strangeness. Among them is the decorous, controlled and ritualistic quality of the acting, an apparent coldness which "comes from the actor's holding himself remote from the character portrayed." This style of acting contrasts with the conventional western mode where the actor tries to become the figure he portrays, tries to lose himself in the dramatic character. Another alienation device in Chinese theatre is the candor of stage business. Props are handed the actor while he performs, the setting is changed in full view of the audience. There is no attempt to "create an illusion," hence no fear of breaking one. And above all, Brecht writes, the Chinese artist never acts as if there were a fourth wall besides the three surrounding him. He expresses his awareness of being watched . . . The audience identifies itself with the actor as being an observer, and accordingly develops his attitude of observing or looking on.[2]

It is beyond the scope of this paper to discuss the ideological purpose of these devices in the Chinese theatre itself, but in western theatre the dramatic function of A-effect, in Brecht's view, is to reveal the abnormality of the normal—that is, of life under capitalism—and to make it impossible for the audience to accept as natural or inevitable the events they see on stage.

Brecht was also alert to A-effect in painting, especially in the works of Breughel, who, as Brecht remarks, "deals in contradictions." Breughel is able to explore the fullest meaning of the events he depicts not by presenting them in magnificent, sentimental and unrealistic isolation but rather by locating those events very solidly in the real world where they occurred. Thus

> In *The Fall of Icarus* the catastrophe breaks into the idyll in such a way that it is clearly set apart from it and valuable insights into the idyll can be gained. He doesn't allow the catastrophe to alter the idyll; the latter rather remains unaltered and survives undestroyed, merely disturbed. . . . The characters turn their backs on the incident. Lovely picture of the concentration needed for plowing. The man fishing in the right foreground, and his particular relationship to the water. . . . Special beauty and gaiety of the landscape during the frightful event.[3]

Similarly with Breughel's painting *The Tower of Babel* (158–59):

> The tower has been put up askew. . . . Delivery of the building materials is a very laborious business; the effort is obviously wasted. . . . Powerful oppression prevails, the attitude of the men bringing up the building materials is extremely servile, the builder is guarded by armed men.

What Breughel forces us to acknowledge, then, is the depth and the dialectical complexity of human existence at any given moment: its physical, social and mythic components and the often disjunctive relation among them.

Let us turn to literature, in fact to medieval romance, for Chaucer was by no means the only poet to exercise a critical perspective on courtly love and romance. When Gottfried von Strassburg composed his great verse romance *Tristan* during the first few years of the thirteenth century, he stressed two intentions. One was to follow the old authoritative source of the Tristan legend as closely as possible; the other was to show Tristan and Isolde not as fairy-tale creatures but as real flesh-and-blood lovers in a hostile society. Unfortunately the two aims were not always consistent, for early versions of the romance contained motifs that

2. "Alienation Effects in Chinese Acting," ibid., 91–92.
3. "Alienation Effects in the Narrative Pictures of the Elder Breughel," ibid., 157.

caused Gottfried some discomfort. Among them was the motif of the
dragon that must be killed in order to obtain the hand of the princess
Isolde. Gottfried permits himself the dragon, but at the same time he
exposes the absurdity of promising one's daughter to whoever kills a
dragon. He does this mainly through dialogue, especially in such an
exchange as the one that occurs between Isolde and her mother when a
false steward claims to have killed the dragon:

> "Oh, no, my pretty daughter. Gently," her mother Isolde said to
> her, "do not take it so to heart! For whether it was done by fair
> means or foul, we shall see that nothing comes of it! . . ."
> "Oh, mother," said the lovely girl, "my lady, do not dishonor your
> high birth and person! Before I comply, I will stab a knife through
> my heart! I shall take my own life before he has his pleasure of
> me! . . ."
> "No, sweet daughter, have no fear of that. Whatever he or any-
> body says, it is of no importance at all. He shall never be your hus-
> band, not if all the world had sworn it!"

And when it comes to the old motif of a swallow bringing one of Isolde's
golden hairs back to England, Gottfried rejects it outright:

> Did ever a swallow nest at such inconvenience that, despite the
> abundance in its own country, it went ranging overseas into strange
> lands in search of nesting materials? I swear the tale grows fantastic,
> the story is talking nonsense here! It is absurd, too, for anyone to
> say that Tristan, with a company, sailed the seas at random and
> failed to attend to how long he was sailing or where he was bound
> for, nor even knew whom he was seeking!—What old score was he
> settling with the book, who had this written and recited? The whole
> lot of them, the King, who sent his council abroad, and his envoys
> (had they gone on a mission in this style) would have been dolts and
> fools.[4]

In short, Gottfried asks us all along to decide: not to be taken in auto-
matically by romance conventions and motifs, but to retain the same
critical perspective that he does. As befits his artistic self-consciousness,
however, Gottfried does not hesitate to employ such an "unrealistic"
motif as the little multicolored dog Petitcrieu as a polysemous symbol.
The principle Gottfried argues for, then, is the artist's freedom to choose,
reject or manipulate material for his own conscious aims.[5]

Closer to home, the music of Pharaoh Sanders shows a powerful and
witty use of A-effect. His saxophone speaks like a voice or blows like
wind. The artist as shaman conjures spirits down from the sky or up
from earth with bells, makes the ancient ram's horn shriek, exorcises.

4. *Tristan*, trans. A. D. Hatto (Middlesex: Penguin, 1960), 154–55: Chapter 11, "The Wooing Expe-
dition."
5. It should be added, though, that eventually Gottfried fails to sustain his dual purpose, for the
conscious critical perspective he turns on romance is turned more and more searchingly on Tristan
and Isolde themselves. In showing us their human reality Gottfried also demonstrates their capac-
ity to be vicious, manipulative and opportunistic. By the end of his work (and it is unfinished) the
reader finds it difficult to admire Tristan and Isolde at all.

You are entirely caught up in the power of the ceremony, its eros and thanatos—until eventually the band breaks into a facile waltz: the old English tune "Greensleeves." Everyone is stunned for a moment, the audience laugh, they are surprised and restored. The artist has taken you out of the work as masterfully as he put you into it. Partly the shock of contrast and perspective shows us how far we had entered into the shamanistic experience; it demands that we know why, and what it means about our lives. But the contrast also says something about the innocuous, familiar "Greensleeves" as well: that it too is art; as much as the ram's horn, it is material to be used by someone who has the genius to use it new.

I would suggest, then, that there are four general hallmarks of alienation effect in literature. First, the audience is discouraged from identifying with the central characters, and is encouraged instead to evaluate them, their actions and their opinions as correct or incorrect. Second, the work of art tries to illuminate the peculiarity of the everyday by offering a different point of view from the one usually adequate to the particular medium or form. Third, there is on the artist's part a clear awareness of his or her own role and of the artificiality of medium or form. Fourth, the crucial questions are not asked, nor the crucial statements made, subtly or indirectly at the risk of their being ignored or minimized; they are asked or stated openly and directly, whether by artist, narrator, or *dramatis personae*.

Let me turn now to *Troilus* to show how Chaucer deliberately introduces these techniques of alienation into his version of the medieval romance. Many of the stylistic features of *Troilus* that I shall use have already been noticed, listed, and in varying degrees of thoroughness discussed by other writers. I shall not retrace their steps in detail, but instead will attempt to show that there is a connection between the many stylistic peculiarities of *Troilus*, for the poem does indeed make sense as an esthetic whole if we apply appropriate esthetic standards. Nor do I intend to give an exhaustive reading: *Troilus* is a work of staggering richness, and I hope here to add another way of approaching it, as valid and as partial as any other.

1. *The audience is not encouraged to identify with the central characters, but is encouraged to evaluate their actions and opinions as correct or incorrect.*

It has long been one of the commonplaces of Chaucer criticism that Chaucer is "half in love with Criseyde"—much as Alexander Pope, according to Cleanth Brooks, is charmed with Belinda in the *Rape of the Lock*.[6] I believe that Chaucer is tougher on his heroine than many

6. See "The Case of Miss Arabella Fermor" in *The Well-Wrought Urn* (New York: Harcourt Brace, 1947). I have argued against Brooks's position in "Sex and Politics in the *Rape of the Lock*," *ESC* 1 (1975): 46–60, reprinted in *Weapons of Criticism: Marxism in America and the Literary Tradition*, ed. Norman Rudich (Palo Alto: Ramparts Press, 1975), and in my *Writing Woman: Women Writers and Women in Literature, Medieval to Modern* (New York: Schocken Books, 1983).

This is not to say that the Narrator may not be charmed by Criseyde. The crucial distinction between Chaucer and his narrator is kept before us especially by E. T. Donaldson; see "Chaucer the Pilgrim," "Four Women of Style," and "Criseyde and Her Narrator," all reprinted in *Speaking of Chaucer*; see also his commentary on *Troilus* in *Chaucer's Poetry*.

critics acknowledge, and that if we sympathize with her or Troilus by the end of the poem it is despite Chaucer's best efforts to disengage us. It seems to me that both figures become, during the course of the poem, increasingly lucid and, simultaneously, more difficult to accept in their own terms as Chaucer pushes them to act out the furthest implications of their characters and opinions, placing them (in Turgenev's phrase) in relations that bring them out.

In the delineation of character Chaucer uses several means to distance us from his hero and heroine. One aspect of style that helps to provide a critical perspective is the imagery associated with them, particularly the two prominent and sustained image-clusters of animals and of fire or heat. Lists of these images have been compiled by others, and I shall not repeat the effort:[7] more to the point here is the effect of imagery. Both image clusters are associated predominantly, though not only, with Troilus; both imply a view of him which is at odds with, and belittles, his own professions of noble motives and good intentions. If Troilus is as proud as a peacock (1.210), timid as a snail (1.300) or a mouse (3.736), as needy of control as Bayard the horse (1.218–24), trapped like a bird (1.353), as frustrated as a bear gnawing its chain (1.509), as unresponsive to reason as an ass to the harp (1.731), if he is an ape of God like every other lover (1.913)—all this suggests the animal nature of Troilus and of mankind; that aspect of his nature which he wilfully ignores but which is forcefully brought home to us. Nor is the point conveyed only indirectly, but in a narrative interjection:

> But O Fortune, executrice of wyrdes!
> O influences of thise hevens hye!
> Soth is, that under God ye ben oure hierdes,
> Though to us bestes ben the causes wrie.   3.617–20

The image anticipates a line from Chaucer's later lyric "Truth"—"Forth, beste, out of thy stal!"—a lyric which develops the Christian ideology implicit throughout *Troilus* and stated clearly in the "epilogue."

We may consider too a more ironic use of imagery:

> What myghte or may the sely larke seye,
> Whan that the sperhauk hath it in his foot?   3.1191–92

7. For example, Beryl Rowland, "The Horse and Rider Figure in Chaucer's Works," *UTQ* 35 (1966): 246–59, and "Aspects of Chaucer's Use of Animals," *Archiv* 201 (1964): 110–14. The most thorough compilation is in Meech, *Design*. Since Meech's primary concern is with overall structure and patterns of design, he rarely gives a close analysis of the images he lists. Though this doesn't diminish the importance of his work, I would suggest that a close reading sometimes leads to a conclusion at odds with Meech's own position, which is that Chaucer "means to build sympathy for [Troilus] and even admiration" (404). Even without a close reading of imagery, however, Meech's view of Troilus seems inconsistent. On the same page he writes that Chaucer, in giving freedom of will to Troilus, renders him, like the other characters, "praise or blameworthy." But if Troilus can be judged blameworthy, in what sense is he sympathetic or admirable? These responses to Troilus are not necessarily mutually exclusive, but the categories do require some further adjustment.

For other comments on Chaucer's animal imagery, see John Spiers on the Fox in *Chaucer the Maker* (London: Faber and Faber, 1951), 67; Mary Griffin, "The Pekok . . ." in *Studies on Chaucer and His Audience* (Hull, Quebec: Les Éditions 'L'Éclair', 1956); and D. W. Robertson's illuminating discussions of animal iconography in his *Preface*.

As Meech points out, "The instances of figurative linkage with animals in the *Troilus* not only outnumber those in the *Filostrato* but are more diverse than they and more vividly particular" (323). Images of fire are fewer than in Boccaccio, and used somewhat differently (353).

The next stanza tells us that it is Criseyde who "felte hire thus itake" (1198). Yet the lines occur just after the extremely awkward and nearly pornographic prelude to the lovers' union. It is a section of the narrative in which Troilus has swooned from either sorrow or fear; he has been accused of cowardice by both Pandarus and Criseyde, and Criseyde has had to take the physical initiative. By the time we come to the conventional image of pursuer and prey we wonder who is the hawk and who the sely lark. Since Chaucer's management of the narrative has virtually destroyed the conventional romance (and social!) sex-role allocation, the image is exposed as rigid and trite; simultaneously, it exposes the deficiencies of human reality.

The imagery of fire seems to serve a similar purpose. The fire of lust and the fires of hell are too intimate a part of the medieval imagination and the medieval iconographic tradition to be irrelevant here: again they suggest, however indirectly, a system of values against which Troilus must be weighed and found wanting.

Another means of alienating the characters appears with the portraits of Troilus, Criseyde and Diomede that are placed so oddly near the end of the poem (5.799–840). The portraits have drawn assorted critical comment, some writers viewing them as belated and inept, others as entirely appropriate.[8] My view is that they are both their placement is awkward and unexpected from the point of view of conventional romance narrative, and the descriptions are jarringly formal in contrast with the psychological depth and realism to which the poem has accustomed us; nonetheless they are appropriate to Chaucer's aim. They force us suddenly to see the three from afar, no longer living persons but static iconographical figures in a stained-glass window, as they will go down in tradition. This abrupt perspective prepares us for the cosmic distancing and the moral placement that become explicit at the end of the poem.

Finally, the behavior of Troilus and Criseyde provides the most direct and powerful means by which Chaucer encourages a critical view of his characters. It is somewhat inaccurate to call this process a progressive degradation or degeneration of character, as this implies a radical decline from some earlier peak of virtue. I tend here to agree with Arthur Mizener when he writes,

> Chaucer's characters do not change or develop under the impact of experience; they display various aspects of an established set of characteristics as the progress of the narrative places them in varying circumstances.[9]

Pandarus offers little difficulty to most critics: the immorality implicit in his cynicism is revealed when he approves Troilus's love though it were adulterous and incestuous (1.676–79); when he offers Troilus his sister (1.860–61); when he slanders Poliphete in order to bring Troilus

8. Meech (448n7) gives a brief resumé of the controversy. For his own view see pages 112–13; also A. C. Spearing, "Chaucer as Novelist" in *Criticism and Medieval Poetry* (London: Edward Arnold, Ltd., 1964), 98; Claes Schaar, *The Golden Mirror* (Lund: Gleerup; reprinted 1967), 191–92; and Donaldson, *Speaking*, 57–58.
9. "Character and Action in the Case of Criseyde," reprinted in Chaucer, *Modern Essays in Criticism*, ed. Edward Wagenknecht (New York: Oxford Univ. Press, 1959), 351.

and Criseyde together (2.1615–21); confesses himself to be a pander (3.253–55); and lies to Criseyde (3.786–91 and elsewhere).

With Troilus, self-pity, self-deception and passivity become more and more prominent traits of character, to the point where his taking to bed after hearing of Criseyde's exchange for Antenor comes across as a piece of comedy—a predictable reflex, like a nervous tic. As J. S. P. Tatlock noted, "A modern man is excusable for thinking him a poor stick who gets from Criseyde when she is exposed to Diomed, no more than his deserts."[1] It may be difficult (even Tatlock finds it difficult) to extend such traits into a critical judgment. But when Troilus descends to Pandarus's level by offering any one of his sisters in exchange for services rendered (3.407–13), we can scarcely avoid such a judgment. Similarly we can only feel that something is seriously amiss when Troilus wishes his father, brothers or himself dead rather than Criseyde exchanged (4.274–80).

With Criseyde, the problem of evaluation is somewhat more difficult. I cannot help thinking that part of the difficulty comes from a subtle kind of sexism: that gentlemanly critics, seeing in Criseyde qualities they are taught to accept as "feminine," are as reluctant to deplore these qualities in Criseyde as they would be with any real woman. But Criseyde's character—her very "femininity"—includes conscious and manipulative self-presentation, coyness, calculation, egocentricity, self-pity, self-deception, fear and passivity. To be sure, these traits are understandable in context of Criseyde's tenuous social position, just as they are understandable today in real women for the same reasons. What is the weight of social circumstance relative to individual will? No Catholic can afford to privilege the former so heavily that it outweighs the latter: nor does Chaucer. For him, finally, as for any Catholic, the moral will is determinative and (though we might not agree) in some sense untouched by circumstance. If we want a sense of what Chaucer considers an ideal of femininity we have only to read his portrait of "good fair White" in *Book of the Duchess*: a woman governed not by fear but by prudence, self-confidence, honesty and the conscious choice of virtue.

A few passages will suffice, I hope, to indicate the basis of my response to Criseyde. When Pandarus first comes to Criseyde she employs a flirtatious feminine strategy: the claim that she has only recently dreamt of her visitor (2.89–90). It is the same strategy that the Wife of Bath's gossip advised her to use in order to entrap the young clerk Jankin. Criseyde continues to play up to Pandarus's superior masculine knowledge of the affairs of war, but when she asserts "I am of Grekes so fered that I deye" (2.124) I become rather uncomfortable with her milking the feminine role. When Pandarus begins to speak of love, "With that she gan hire eighen down to cast"—another bit of conscious self-presentation. In defending her morality Criseyde says to her uncle that surely he would have chastised her had she loved "outher hym [Troilus] or Achilles, / Ector, or any mannes creature" (2.416–17). Hector and [Troilus] yes—but Achilles, an enemy hero? Does she know herself already so opportunistic, or is she merely thoughtless?

1. "The People in Chaucer's *Troilus*," in Wagenknecht, 336.

Criseyde's egocentricity emerges as she continually credits herself with power of life and death over Troilus—if she refuses to love him he will surely die of sorrow or commit suicide. Repeatedly she uses this misperception to justify her action (e.g., 2.459–60, 663–65, 1590–94). Pandarus is able to play on this idea, so flattering to any woman's concept of herself (cf. 2.1127, 1279–81 and 1736); and when the same motive is given for her wish to comfort Diomede (5.1042), though he has displayed no sorrow, its shallowness is at last painfully obvious.

The famous line "Who yaf me drynke?" (2.651) has been made to yield assorted fruit. I see in it another instance of Criseyde's passivity, and a theatrical assumption of the posture of the traditional romance heroine. In his parodistic balade, "To Rosemounde," Chaucer presents himself as a lovelorn "trewe Tristan the secounde." Criseyde has just been reading a romance with her women; perhaps her reference to a love-potion is meant to identify her as a new Isolde.

Like Pandarus, Criseyde can talk up any argument that serves her purpose; if it serves her purpose to slander her father (4.1366–1407), so be it. And, like her uncle, she is always prepared to find reasons after the fact for her actions: reasons for loving Troilus (2.701ff.), reasons for leaving Troy (4.1528ff.) and finally reasons for not returning to Troy (5.689–707, 1023–29).

As I read the poem, then, Chaucer has taken some pains to distance us from Troilus and Criseyde. Of course there must be in any great literature some sense on the spectator's part of *sua res agitur*. Yet it is not always through consistent positive identification that this is best accomplished. Nor is some degree of identification incompatible with moral judgment if the author's aim is to enable us to judge ourselves. I am by no means immune from empathy with the story of Troilus and Criseyde, yet the net effect, I feel, is well conveyed by a statement that Brecht made about two of his plays:

> The spectator's "splendid isolation" is left intact; . . . he is not fobbed off with an invitation to feel sympathetically, to fuse with the hero and seem significant and indestructible. . . . A higher type of interest can be got from making comparisons, from whatever is different, amazing, impossible to take in as a whole.[2]

2. *The work of art tries to illuminate the peculiarity of the everyday by offering a different point of view from the one usually adequate to the medium or form.*

In an essay on acting, Brecht writes that

> The object of the A-effect is to alienate [that is, to externalize or objectify] the social gest underlying every incident. By social gest is meant the mimetic and gestural expression of the social relationships prevailing between people of a given period.[3]

To which one can add that it is precisely in exposing the underlying social gest that the so-called normality—the real peculiarity and relativ-

2. Notebook entry on *Baal* and *Dickicht*, Willett, 9.
3. "Short Description," in Willett, 139.

ity—of a given action or opinion becomes apparent. As the *Troilus* is not a drama but a narrative poem, exposure is achieved through the resources of style. Chaucer's main vehicle here is his narrative persona, but he is also able to use equivocal language and religious imagery with devastating effect, and to give the work a sociopolitical background which provides a constant touchstone for evaluation.

E. Talbot Donaldson's phrase "deliberate mystification" best summarizes Chaucer's narrative stance in the *Troilus*: a device whereby the Narrator's questions or assertions force us to challenge what we would otherwise have taken for granted or accepted as a normal convention of romance. Some of these *loci* have been analyzed by Donaldson, primarily in relation to Criseyde: I shall consider a few others. One is the Narrator's comment after he describes Criseyde's social status:

> But wheither that she children hadde or noon,
> I rede it naught, therfore I late it goon. 1.132–33

To this point we have naturally assumed that Criseyde had no children. Yet she is a widow, we are reminded, and might have had children. If so, where are they; if not, why not? It is of course easiest for narrative purposes to have Criseyde childless; if this is the reason why she is traditionally childless, then we are forcibly reminded of the artificiality of romance itself—its freedom from the encumbrances of normal social life.

Or again, when Troilus suffers the pangs of unrequited love and claims to have a fever, the Narrator remarks:

> But how it was, certeyn, kan I nat seye,
> If that his lady understood nat this,
> Of feynede hire she nyste, oon of the tweye;
> But wel I rede that, by no manere weye,
> Ne semed it as that she of hym roughte,
> Or of his peyne, or whatsoevere he thoughte.   1.492–97

It would scarcely have occurred to us to think that Criseyde knew of Troilus's love before her interview with Pandarus in Book 2. But the Narrator raises that possibility under guise of denying it—or at least of judging by appearances—and with it the possibility of a Criseyde as capable of manipulating Pandarus as she is of being manipulated by him.

After Criseyde's interview with Pandarus, the latter requests a more private conversation:

> And everi wight that was aboute hem tho,
> That herde that, gan fer awey to stonde,
> Whil they two hadde al that hem liste in honde.   2.215–17

What is "al that hem liste"? Why do we need to be excluded from the conversation along with the women in waiting, especially when we have heard every detail of what has just preceded? The Narrator tells us in the next stanza that the subject of their conversation was "hire estat and hire governaunce"—but why is special privacy suddenly required, and what is the particular meaning here of "estate" and of "governance": social position merely, or moral conduct? And what is the relation between uncle and niece anyway: how frequent a visitor is he, has he been a lover, why does Criseyde flirt with him?

After Criseyde and Troilus have been brought together, but before their union is consummated, the Narrator tells us that she was no longer afraid—"I mene, as fer as oughte ben requered" (3.483). But what, precisely, is the requisite degree of fear in such a case? Chaucer deftly allows his Narrator to remind us that there is another stage to the romance; and while Criseyde may feel no fear at the moment, she is of course virtuous and modest enough to feel some fear of the potential sexual bond if she should think of it. The technique resembles that in an earlier passage where, assuring us that Criseyde did not fall in love too quickly (2.666ff.), the Narrator causes us to wonder whether she did not, after all, do exactly that. How consciously does Criseyde participate in her own deception? Two further examples suggest that she may have been a willing victim. The Narrator does not know whether Criseyde believed Pandarus's lie about Troilus being out of town (3.575–81), nor can he say with any certainty whether, in the bedroom scene, she tolerated Troilus's familiarity out of sorrow or social obligation or some other motive (3.967–73).

Besides the ambiguity of the narrative voice, the entire linguistic texture of the *Troilus* abounds with equivocation. A general syntactic ambiguity pervades the poem, as in stanza two of the first book:

> To the clepe I, thow goddesse of torment,
> Thow cruwel Furie, sorwynge evere yn peyne,
> Help me, that am the sorwful instrument,
> That helpeth loveres, as I kan, to pleyne.   2.8–11

The phrase "sorwynge evere yn peyne" could apply, syntactically, either to "thow" or to "I"; "to pleyne" could be attached to "help me" or to "that helpeth lovers"; "kan" means either can or know. 1.623 depends heavily on punctuation, hence on editorial discretion, for its meaning: "how devel maistow brynge me to blisse?" or "How, devel, maistow brynge me to blisse?" with emphasis on the ironic contrast between devil and bliss. When Criseyde first looks at Troilus, armed and mounted, from her window, we are told that he had "a body and a myght / To don that thing" (2.633–34). The verb is not specified, presumably it is to fight, for he is just come from battle; or is it to make love, inasmuch as Troilus is being observed by Criseyde as her future lover? Soon after, we learn that Troilus wrote frequently to Criseyde:

> Fro day to day he leet it nought refreyde,
> That by Pandare he wroot somwhat or seyde.   2.1343–44

What is the exact weight of "by Pandare he wroot"—that the letter was delivered by Pandarus, or that the letter was composed by Pandarus, or both? Still further on, Pandarus exhorts Criseyde:

> "Sle naught this man, that hath for yow this peyne!
> Fy on the devel! thynk which one he is,
> And in what plite he lith; com of anon!
> Thynk al swich taried tyde but lost it nys.
> That wol ye bothe seyn, whan ye ben oon."   2.1736–40

The first "he" has an indefinite antecedent (devil/man), though the sense of the next line makes clear that the subject is Troilus; "seyn" can be read as either see or say; "oon" may mean either when the pair is alone together or when they are sexually united.

Donaldson notes another linguistic habit of the narrator: his use of the qualifier "as":

> All but the very simplest uses of *as* to express equivalence cause a distancing between the things compared. . . . But in the last two books of *Troilus* Chaucer rarely if ever permits the narrator to say in his own person, and in so many words, that Criseyde loved Troilus. There is always a distancing device, if only one so seemingly negligible as the little *as*. Yet the cumulative effect of such devices may well weaken one's confidence that what is said to be real is real.[4]

Similar in effect to syntactic ambiguity and qualifiers is another form of equivocal language: pun. Again it isn't my purpose to compile an exhaustive list of puns in Troilus,[5] but rather to indicate a stylistic tendency. Probably the two best-known puns in Troilus occur when we see the "makeless" (Matchless/unmated, 1.172) Criseyde, and when Troilus apostrophizes the house of the absent Criseyde as a lantern "of which queynt is the light" (quenched/cunt, 5.543). To these we may add the "stuwe" (closet/brothel, 3.601) in which Troilus is concealed at Pandarus's house; the narrator's indignation at anyone who might "lye on" (tell lies about/be recumbent upon, 4.20) Criseyde; his regret for the laughter "men" (people/males, 4.866) used to find in Criseyde; and Troilus's agonized self-interrogation about why he does not help to his own "cure" (benefit/salvation, 5.49).

All of these stylistic features are confusing on the surface and are intended to be so; my argument is that they illuminate by confusion, thus leading deeper than the surface. Through pun, ambiguity and the rest, the familiar becomes unfamiliar, the reliable phrase, feeling or concept becomes unreliable, the inconspicuous word becomes conspicuous, and a conventional idea is made to yield unconventional associations. Once again the reader is jolted out of easy expectations and made to confront other possibilities. It is a technique favored by the French surrealists too—to use language in such a way as to demonstrate the artificiality of our conditioned expectations. While I am far from claiming Chaucer as a proto-surrealist, I would suggest he had a similar purpose in mind.

That same process of illumination by confusion is evident in Chaucer's handling of religious imagery in *Troilus*. Early on in the poem the religious imagery seems quite in the tradition of courtly lyric and romance as Chaucer develops the "religion of love" in scrupulous detail with its god, its prayers, its servants, saints and martyrs, its heaven, its

---

4. *Speaking*, 71.
5. Some of Chaucer's puns have been listed by H. Kökeritz, "Rhetorical Word-Play in Chaucer," *PMLA* 69 (1954): 937–52, and by Paul F. Baum, "Chaucer's Puns," *PMLA* 71 (1956): 225–46, and "Chaucer's Puns: A Supplementary List," *PMLA* 73 (1958): 167–70. For others in *Troilus*, and a more detailed discussion, see Sheila Delany, "Anatomy of the Resisting Reader," *Exemplaria* 4 (1992): 7–34.

hope, despair and grace (1.15–51). He allows Troilus to develop it further in baiting lovers, just after his own "conversion" (1.330–50). But gradually the congruence dissolves. The juxtaposition of religion and love becomes so strained, incompatible and finally outrageous—"yoked by violence together" as Dr. Johnson remarked of Donne's imagery—that we must see the two value systems as finally hostile. The following sequence will illustrate this development.

The first intrusive note is sounded when Pandarus, describing the valor of Troilus, calls him "shield and life for us": there is the briefest disjunction in which we remind ourselves that it is not a prayer, nor is Jesus being described, but Troilus. The gap widens when we find that Troilus trivializes religious devotion by using it as his cover for amorous pursuit (3.533–46). Later, Criseyde's body is referred to as "this hevene" (3.1251). Apart from the obvious January-like overtones of the image, the phrase occurs after we have been nearly stifled by the sultry atmosphere of this first consummation, with its voyeurism, reversal of sex-roles, petulance and manipulation and near-pornography: an atmosphere resembling that of the Temple of Venus in the *Parliament of Fowls*: and this is Troilus's heaven. But the climax of bad taste is reached with the Narrator's comment on Criseyde's attitude toward Pandarus's interference: "What! God foryaf his deth, and she al so / Foryaf . . ." (3.1577 78). Here it is no longer possible to hold the two systems in equilibrium; they have parted company for good.

The social dimension provided by the Trojan background also offers a perspective on the love-story: not only as an allegorical parallel to it, as John McCall shows[6] but also as a larger reality which Troilus and Criseyde are willing to trivialize for their own needs, much as they trivialize religion. Pandarus does it first, when the arrival of a Greek spy provides the occasion (or excuse) for Pandarus to deliver Troilus's first letter to Criseyde (2.1111–15); Troilus repeats it by reducing the war and negotiations as nothing more than a backdrop to their romance (4.1286–1358). We discover via Calkas that the fate of Troy is sealed in its origins: a labor dispute (albeit with the gods): "Bycause he [King Lameadoun] nolde payen hem here hire, / The town of Troie shal ben set on-fire" (4.125–26). And the tragic history of Thebes is also kept before us in the romance read by Criseyde's ladies, as well as in Diomede's antecedents. These, the historical, political and economic realities, Troilus and Criseyde try to insulate themselves from. By conventional romance standards they are perfectly justified in doing so, but in offering this touchstone of judgment Chaucer again exposes not only the artificiality of romance convention but also what Brecht calls "the underlying social gest."

3. *There is on the artist's part an explicitly stated awareness of his/her own role and of the artificiality of medium or genre.*

Here again narrative voice is the primary vehicle conveying the awareness of the artist observing himself being observed, or, in Robert O.

6. John P. McCall, "The Trojan Scene in Chaucer's *Troilus*," *ELH* 29 (1962): 263–75.

Payne's formulation, "art so unconcealed as to demand the reader's con-
tinual consciousness of it as a process symbolic of its own content."[7]
Though it is naturally in the four prologues that the artist-narrator is
most explicitly conscious of his role, his voice intrudes throughout the
poem, whether he is establishing his personal relation to love (1.8–56,
3.1319–20), or reminding us of the painstaking scrupulosity with which
he uses old material (1.393–99, 4.1415–21, 5.799, 834, 1044, 1051).
He may call our attention to the artificiality of rhetoric by translating it
for us into everyday terms: "The dayes honour, and the hevenes yë, / The
nyghtes foo—al this clepe I the sonne" (2.904–5). Sometimes he
reminds us of the mechanics, the bare bones, of his narrative (1.1086,
3.491–505, 531–32, 4.1127). Or, using the conventional modesty trope,
he may assert his incompetence to do justice to a particularly moving
scene (4.799–805, 5.267–73).

Perhaps the most striking use of A-effect through authorial interven-
tion occurs in five stanzas toward the very end of the poem (5.1765–
99). Having just told us of Troilus's death, the poet proceeds to remind
us that his real subject is love, not war; sends us to the relevant sources
if we wish to pursue the theme of war; sends us to other books treating
of Criseyde; restates his purpose and defines his audience; apostrophizes
his book; and concludes with a brief digression on the condition of the
English language and its potentially destructive effect on his work. This
remarkable passage forces us to see, if we have not already absorbed the
point, that the story could have been told differently, and that the pres-
ent version is the result of conscious effort and selection. The passage
also distances us in another way. By reminding us of deliberate craft, it
reintroduces an intellectual perspective. This not only helps us to over-
come the nearly unbearable tension and pathos of the last book, but also
prepares us for the *moralitas* with which the poem ends.

4. *Crucial questions are asked, and statements made, directly, whether by
artist, narrator or* dramatis personae.

Not every question in a work of art constitutes an effort toward A-
effect. Questions play an important role, for instance, in Wolfram's *Par-
zival*, as an index to the hero's naiveté; and "Who's there?"—the opening
words of *Hamlet*—poses the problems of mistrust and mistaken identity
that are so important in the play. Such questions as these do not exist
for the sake of their answers, but rather for what they mean in them-
selves. I am speaking here, however, of questions that transcend the
immediate literary context—indeed that transcend art itself, leaping out
of the work of art as permanently important questions about why we live
as we do. These questions, moreover, are not only answerable, they are
answered in the work of art.

An example of such questions appears in the rice-merchant's "Song
of Supply and Demand" from Brecht's *The Measures Taken*:

> Down the river there is rice
> In the provinces up the river people need rice:

7. Payne, *Key*, 217.

If we leave the rice in the warehouses
The rice will cost them more.
Those who pole the rice-barge will then get less rice
And rice will be even cheaper for me.
What is rice actually?
Do I know what rice is?
God knows what rice is!
I don't know what rice is
I only know its price.

. . . . . .

What is a man actually?
Do I know what a man is?
God knows what a man is!
I don't know what a man is
I only know his price.

The series of questions and answers takes us through a rapid course in basic dialectics: not only supply and demand, but theory of value, labor-power as commodity, alienation and class consciousness.

In *Troilus* there is an infrastructure of precisely such heavily charged questions and their eventual answers. "If no love is," asks Troilus,

"O God, what fele I so?
And if love is, what thing and which is he?
If love be good, from whennes cometh my woo?"   1.400–402

Though there are specific passages that could be taken as answers to this group of questions about love (e.g., 3.1744–71), the fullest answer is the entire poem with epilogue, for only on finishing the poem do we learn what love is in its human and divine manifestations, and whence comes Troilus's woe.

Rather petulantly, Criseyde asks another key question just before her first sexual encounter with Troilus: "Is this a mannes game?" (3.1126). The subject of manliness or manhood is raised several times in the poem, at four different levels of meaning. In the courtly-love tradition, Troilus is "her man"—the devoted servant of his mistress (as in 1.468 and 4.447). Criseyde's question suggests three other levels as well. Its surface reference is to courage ("be a man"), while the obvious ironic reference is to sexuality. At the same time we can ask the question "What is it to be a man?" of any person, humanity at large (as it is used, e.g., in 2.1501 and 3.10). Thus Criseyde's question leads far beyond its immediate dramatic context and invites us to consider what it is, after all, to be most fully human. This question, like the other, has a dual aspect which requires for its real answer both the dramatic action and the epilogue: Troilus's fear, weakness and lust truly express the limitations of human nature, while his eventual transcendence expresses what humanity is capable of at its Christian best.

Troilus poses a third question, which strikes at the heart of the poem: "Whi nyl I helpen to myn owen cure?" (5.49). In the immediate context Troilus is contemplating some drastic action to rescue Criseyde. Yet the question opens almost dizzying vistas of meaning—the paralytic disease of his own character, human nature at large, the question how far our will is free, the abuse of free will if we have it, etc. It then contracts as rapidly again as we are deftly returned to the dramatic context.

Probably the most important question in the poem—the tropological question "Quo tendas?" ("Where are you heading?")—is asked thrice by Criseyde. It is couched in at least twenty occurrences throughout the poem of the word "fyn" (goal or purpose), so that the questions themselves emerge with startling clarity to illuminate more than their immediate narrative context. Reproaching Pandarus for suggesting the idea of loving Troilus, Criseyde says, "Is al this paynted proces seyd, allas! / Right for this fyn?" (2.424–25). It is not the only "painted process" we encounter in the poem: her question might as well apply to the words of Troilus or Diomede, or to her own professions of love: what are, after all, the real aims or motives of the speakers? Just after Criseyde has decided to love Troilus she repeats the question: "To what fyn lyve I thus?" and a few lines later confesses her ignorance of ultimate ends: "To what fyn is swich love I kan nat see" (2.794). Later, lamenting her departure from Troy she exclaims, "To what fyn sholde I lyve and sorwen thus?" (4.764). To what end—her love, her life, anyone's life, human life. With Troilus's ironic laughter in the eighth sphere, the answer finally appears in the magnificently orchestrated stanza that concludes the narrative proper:

> Swich fyn hath, lo, this Troilus for love!
> Swich fyn hath al his grete worthynesse!
> Swich fyn hath his estat real above,
> Swich fyn his lust, swich fyn hath his noblesse!
> Swich fyn hath false worldes brotelnesse!   5.1828–32

Though the reading of *Troilus* that I have just presented is not specifically a Marxist reading, it has some methodological relevance for those who are committed to Marxist, historicist or other contemporary criticism and esthetics. If I have succeeded it indicates, first of all, that the application of modern critical categories to older literature is not necessarily a Procrustean effort. On the contrary, the validity of a theory like Brecht's lies precisely in its ability to illuminate art for which it was not specifically designed: the art of earlier periods and of other cultures. Much of this work remains to be done, though we may look for examples to the pioneering studies of Max Raphael on prehistoric cave painting, of George Thomson on Greek tragedy, or of Norman O. Brown on the evolution of Greek myth. In short, alterity, too, has its limits.

This is perhaps my most evident theoretical conclusion, but I want to mention two others. First, I think we can agree that alienation is a subversive technique inasmuch as it undercuts traditional art forms, conventional responses or associations, and some received ideas. In this sense it is legitimate to consider Chaucer a "subversive" poet. Yet the case of *Troilus* shows that subversive art, as technique, is not necessarily subversive in the ideological sense, for it may subvert a current art form in order to revalidate an obsolescent ideology. What Chaucer shows us in *Troilus* is the subversion of courtly romance, in the service of a Christian ideology which had already begun to crumble under the weight of history. The failure of the Crusade movement, the great schism in the

Church, the impact of Aristotelian rationalism and the development of nominalism in Europe had begun the process that would be continued in the revolutionary religious movements of eastern Europe, especially the Hussite and Taborite movements in Bohemia. It would culminate a century after Chaucer's death in the Anabaptist movement and, afterward, the Protestant Reformation. A similar case in our own century is Ezra Pound. Pound was a brilliant and innovative poet, not least in his subversion of conventional poetic technique in the *Cantos*, yet the subversion returns us to Renaissance bourgeois concepts of order, national unity and individual heroism. Style and ideology are not necessarily isomorphic in any period: innovation in the one guarantees nothing in the other.

Second, it is hardly necessary at this stage in the development of Chaucer scholarship to be reminded once again of Chaucer's conscious sophistication. More to the point is our willingness or ability to see Chaucer as a poet who reflects the stress and contradictions of his time. The ambivalence of Chaucer's narrator is something we have all experienced, and if we can no longer look to Christian ideology to resolve it, we can perhaps find in the work of revolutionary poets like Brecht a resolution more appropriate to ourselves. In the tradition of medieval writing about love, *Troilus and Criseyde* is a devastating attack on *La Vita Nuova*, on the conviction that human love can lead to divine love. In love Troilus and Criseyde find their object of worship, and in each other. To this Chaucer says no, because God sits in judgment in heaven; whereas if we are moved to deny *La Vita Nuova* it is because for us god is nowhere.

DAVIS TAYLOR

The Terms of Love: A Study of Troilus's Style†

In Chaucerian criticism it is now a truism to say that Troilus speaks like a courtly lover or, more exactly, like a great number of lovers in medieval poems, but although it is a truism, or perhaps because it is a truism, no one has closely described those conventions in medieval poetry which form the basis of Troilus's style. Charles Muscatine comes closest in his book *Chaucer and the French Tradition*. He is helpful in the early chapters where he surveys in some detail the courtly idiom of French poetry, and he is also convincing when he looks at the ironic oppositions in Chaucer's long poem, but his actual description of Troilus's style is disappointing, partly because he fails to use specific terms, mentioning only such things as Troilus's "fine, lyric expression," the "courtly choiceness of [his] idiom," and the "patterned, symbolic business of the high style," and partly because he fails to correlate specific features of Troilus's speech with his behavior, saying only that Troilus's speech is conven-

† From *Speculum* 51 (1976): 69–90. Reprinted from the revised text in *Chaucer's Troilus: Essays in Criticism*, ed. Stephen A. Barney (Hamden: Archon Books, 1980), 231–56. Reprinted by permission.

tional and his behavior equally conventional, impractical, and idealistic.[1] By a more detailed study of Troilus's style, I hope to show how Chaucer uses specific medieval conventions to create Troilus's speech and how an understanding of them can sharpen one's evaluation of some central issues in the poem.

Other than Muscatine's early chapters on the French tradition, two articles, one by Leo Spitzer and the other by Paul Zumthor, provide a helpful survey of stylistic conventions in medieval love poetry.[2] Using their work as a point of departure, I have centered on three recurrent conventions which distinguish medieval love poetry. The first of these is the use of superlatives to characterize the speaker and his beloved.

In Spitzer's analysis of the English lyric "Blow, Northerne Wynde," he shows how superlatives and a range of constructions which have the force of superlatives are used to characterize the lady as the best of all women, the summation of all value, and the man as the most sorrowful of all lovers, just as unworthy as the mud which drops from the lady's boot.[3] This extreme relationship is, of course, typical of medieval love lyrics, and therein lies a problem, at least to the logically minded reader, for if every woman is most worthy, every man most unworthy, how is any one of them distinguishable, much less superlative? Fortunately, this problem exists more on a logical than experiential plane. As Spitzer notes, when we read the best lyrics, we are swayed by the cumulative power of the superlatives and by the details of the poem to grant lover and beloved a unique individuality. We are convinced by the convention. Another dilemma, however, also arises from the superlatives: no matter how eloquently the man pleads, his cruel mistress cannot yield, for if she does, she ceases to be perfectly virtuous (the basis of her identity) and he to be utterly unworthy (the basis of his identity). Any progress toward sexual consummation thus undermines the poem's characterization as well as its pathos and morality. The solution, clearly, is to put

1. Charles Muscatine, *Chaucer and the French Tradition* (Berkeley, 1964), pp. 124–65, quotations from pp. 134, 135, 148.
2. Leo Spitzer, *Essays in English and American Literature*, ed. Anna Hatcher (Princeton, 1962), pp. 192–247; Paul Zumthor, "Style and Expressive Register in Medieval Poetry," in *Literary Style, A Symposium*, ed. Seymour Chatman (New York, 1971), pp. 263–84. These articles helped me focus on certain stylistic traits, but my indebtedness by no means ends with them. My greatest debt is to my dissertation adviser at Yale University, Marie Borroff, who helped me develop the methods of stylistic analysis used in this paper. Stephen Barney read my dissertation and encouraged me to continue my work. His article, "Troilus Bound," *Speculum* 48 (1972), 445–58, complements mine and is one of several important studies which emphasize Troilus's imagery. These include: Sanford B. Meech, *Design in Chaucer's Troilus* (Syracuse, 1959); Peter Dronke, "L'Amor che move il sole e l'altre stelle," *Studi Medievali* 6 (1965), 389–422), and "The Conclusion of *Troilus and Criseyde,*" *Medium Aevum* 33 (1964), 47–52; P. M. Kean, *Chaucer and the Making of English Poetry,* 1 (London, 1972), 112–178; D. W. Robertson, Jr., *A Preface to Chaucer* (Princeton, 1963); Ida Gordon, *The Double Sorrow of Troilus* (Oxford, 1970). I have not particularly emphasized the figures in Troilus's speech because the above authors have covered this field with considerable thoroughness even though they often disagree in their conclusions.
3. These medieval constructions include negative comparisons which exclude the possibility of any equal in time or space. "For nevere man was to yow goddes holde / As I" (III, 1259–60), and metaphoric identifications with an object representing a superlative degree of excellence, "U swerd of knyghthod" (V, 1591). Spitzer mentions other superlative phrases which do not occur in Chaucer's *Troilus* (*Essays,* pp. 198–99), and to his list, one can add a particular genitive construction which occurs twice in Troilus's speech, first when he thinks of himself as, "wrecche of wrecches" (IV, 271), and second when he calls Criseyde's house, "O hous of houses" (V, 541). This construction is probably modeled on Latin genitives, like *servus servorum* and *sanctus sanctorum,* which themselves are modeled on Hebrew partitive genitives. For a further description of this construction, the reader can refer to my dissertation, "Style and Character in Chaucer's *Troilus,*" Yale University, 1969, pp. 25–26. Throughout this article, I have referred to the above constructions simply as superlatives, not as superlative phrases.

the demands of convention over those of nature and to celebrate as sacred the very distance between lover and beloved. As Joseph Bédier affirms of *amour courtois*: "Ce qui lui est propre, c'est d'avoir conçu l'amour comme un culte qui s'adresse à un objet excellent et se fonde, comme l'amour chrétien, sur l'infinie disproportion du merite au désir."[4] Medieval love lyrics, in much the same way as Keats's "Ode on a Grecian Urn," thus offer a suspended realm where perfection depends on immobility and incompletion, a world far more appropriate for lyric than narrative poetry.

A second stylistic trait, which is also discussed by Spitzer, is the frequent occurrence of quantitative terms, like *al, ful,* and *hele,* in the lover's statements of commitment to his lady—he will love her best of *all,* for *all* time, and with *all* his heart. Such absolute commitments are traditionally demanded by the god of love. In "Blow, Northerne Wynde," for example, the god of love bids the lover to offer the "hord of [his] huerte hele," with the implication that only such a treasure might satisfy the lady, and in the *Roman de la Rose,* Amors makes the command:

> Vueil je e comant que tu aies
> En un seul leu tot ton cuer mis,
> Si qu'il n'i soit mie demis,
> Mais toz entiers, senz tricherie,
> Car je n'aim pas moitelerle.[5] (2240–44)

In these and other poems, the lover seeks his lady's approval and his own salvation through his total commitment, although by the fourteenth century, at least in French court poetry, the lady's approval, or, more exactly, the extent of her approval and any moral implications which might thereby be raised, are far less important than the pathetic tone of the poems. What is emphasized is not the possibility but the impossibility of love, not the joy of the lovers but their martyrdom.

A third stylistic characteristic of medieval love poetry is the recurrence of long internal monologues filled with invocations and complaints. These were immensely popular in French literature, and from the time of Jean de Meun onwards they tended to dwarf the narrative. In Machaut's *Remede de Fortune,* for example, a young man attacks love for seizing his will and placing him at the mercy of his lady and of fortune. His attack takes up half the poem, for Machaut is less interested in the outcome of the man's love than in his psychology, how he changes from the naïve bliss of innocence to the painful recognition that his love might not be returned. Stylistically, these monologues are characterized by repeated elements and by balanced as well as extended phrasing. The poet is in no hurry to reach a conclusion, even the conclusion of a sentence. He wants to keep the emotion suspended, which is the rhythm of both pathos and romance.

One can find other stylistic traits which characterize medieval love poems, but the three noted above—recurrent superlatives, absolute

---

4. "Les Fêtes de mai et les commencements de la poesie lyrique au Moyen Age," *Revue des deux mondes* (mai, 1897), p. 172.
5. Guillaume de Lorris and Jean de Meun, *Le Roman de la Rose,* ed. Ernest Langlois, 5 vols., SATF (Paris, 1914–24), 2:115.

commitments, and extended monologues—occur frequently throughout medieval poetry and form the rhetorical basis for Chaucer's elevated love poems, including the complaints as well as portions of *The Book of the Duchess* and *Anelida and Arcite.* Chaucer knew how to combine these characteristics to achieve the greatest degree of pathos. When he came to writing *Troilus and Criseyde,* he changed Boccaccio's *Filostrato*—as C. S. Lewis has said so aptly, he "medievalized" it[6]—not only by making Troilus a more innocent lover, which is Lewis's point, but also by giving him a more characteristically medieval style.

The extent to which he medievalized Troilus's style can be seen by comparing Troilus's use of these traits with Troiolo's. To look first at superlatives, one can find ten subjects defined by unqualified superlatives in Troiolo's speech in the *Filostrato,* eight in the narrator's speech, seven in Pandaro's, and three in Criseida's,[7] but since Troiolo has almost twice as many lines as Pandaro and three times as many as Criseida, their proportional use of superlatives is just about equal. In Chaucer's poem, on the other hand, Troilus describes twenty-one subjects by unqualified superlatives, the narrator twenty-two, Pandarus nine, and Criseyde four;[8] and if one thinks of them all speaking the same number of lines as Pandarus, the proportional figures are Troilus twenty-six, the narrator eleven, Pandarus nine, and Criseyde six. Nineteen of Troilus's twenty-one superlatives, moreover, Chaucer has added in his reworking of Boccaccio's poem, partly because a considerable number of Troiolo's superlatives occur in passages which Chaucer has not translated or has given to the narrator in the Prohemium to Book III.

Not only does Troilus use more superlatives than Troiolo or his fellow characters in Chaucer's poem, he uses them in particularly medieval ways. Boccaccio's Troiolo, for example, praises Criseida's beauty and good manners in superlative terms but not her goodness or virtue. The closest he comes to such general praise is in his defense of Criseida before Cassandra, where he begins by denying his love (since he is embarrassed to admit it before Cassandra and her companions) and then qualifies his praise with conditionals, like the following:

> Ed elle sono in lei tutte vedute
> Se dall'opra l'effetto s'argomenta.   (VII, 94)

6. "What Chaucer Really Did to *Il Filostrato,*" *Essays and Studies by Members of the English Association* 17 (1932), 56.

7. The term "unqualified superlative" refers to superlatives which are not qualified in one of the following ways: by the specification of a limited place or time, by the indication of a clearly subjective opinion, or by the use of a conditional, future, or interrogative verb that calls into doubt the firmness of the statement. The stanza references given below are to Vittore Branca, *Tutte le opere di Giovanni Boccaccio,* 2 (Verona, 1967), and those in italics designate superlatives where the character is referring to himself. Troiolo: I, 50, 55; III, 58, 81, 81, 84; IV, 50, 164; V, 62; VII, 93. Narrator: I, 17, 19, 25; III, 90; IV, 86; V, 1, 41; VIII, 28. Pandaro: II, 22, 23, 41, 42, 44, 54; IV, 64. Criseida: III, 66; IV, 128, 162.

8. Quotations and references for Chaucer are to the second edition of F. N. Robinson, *The Works of Geoffrey Chaucer* (Boston, 1957). Each line reference below indicates a subject which, in one or more aspects, is designated as superlative without limiting qualification, and the italics are used as in note 7 above. Troilus: I, 331, 339, *514, 534,* 603; III, *417, 1259, 1268, 1271, 1279, 1280,* 1597, 1604; IV, *270, 288, 304,* 449, *516;* V, 541, 547, 1527. Narrator: I, 152, 171, 174, 230, 241, 243, 247, 248, 283, 566, 1079; II, 450; III, 488; V, 20, 198, 247, 439, 447, 808, 821, 1565, 1847. Pandarus: I, 1002; II, 177, 204, 293, 348, 1030, 1150; III, 781, 1626. Criseyde: II, 729, 740, 761; V, 1591.

Se non m'inganna forte la veduta,
E quel ch'altri ne dice, più onesta
Di costei nulla ne fia o è suta.   (VII, 95)

In this context, his conditional praise betrays his worldly bitterness and duplicity. Troilus, on the other hand, does not hesitate to praise both Criseyde's beauty and her virtue, finding her the fairest and the best (III, 1280, IV, 449); and when he answers Cassandra, he praises Criseyde without qualification, comparing her to Alceste. One might argue that this comparison cannot be considered truthful since Troilus, by this point in the poem, clearly suspects that Criseyde is false, but if there is a lie in this comparison, it is a subconscious lie which Troilus says not to fool others but to fool himself.

Troilus's praise of Criseyde, moreover, contrasts markedly with her praise of him. On one occasion, she starts to think of him as the worthiest but then she checks herself: "For out and out he is the worthieste, / Save only Ector, which that is the beste" (II, 739–40). Twenty lines later, she calls Troilus, "this knyght, that is the worthieste," but that rhyme between "worthieste" and "Ector . . . the beste" lingers in the reader's ear as it probably does in hers. By placing Troilus second to Hector among Trojan knights, she shows the same guarded as well as traditional appraisal which one finds in both Pandarus and the narrator (II, 178, IV, 1565). The narrator is particularly careful in his praise. Christ is best, then Hector, then Troilus, whom he praises for distinct qualities, like his desire for worthiness and his friendly behavior (I, 566, 1079). He sees Pandarus not as, "O frend of frendes the alderbeste / That evere was" (III, 1597–98), which is Troilus's appraisal, but as he who is best at doing those services needed by a friend, a statement which might be taken ironically (III, 489). Chaucer thus establishes a definite hierarchy among the knights, with Christ firmly placed at the top, although explicitly placed there only at the end of the poem, and by this hierarchy, he calls into question Troilus's less realistic praise.

Troilus can also be distinguished from Troiolo by his use of superlatives to characterize himself. While Troiolo uses only two, and both of these early in the poem, Troilus uses eight. Some are self-deprecatory; others express his overwhelming sense of love or sorrow. More significantly, Troilus is the only character in Chaucer's poem to individualize himself in this conventional, medieval way.

Similar patterns can be found in the characters' statements of absolute commitment—that is, to love someone best of *all*, for *all* time, or with *all* one's heart. Chaucer's Troilus makes twenty-nine such statements, Boccaccio's Troiolo only seven,[9] and while Troilus's final statement of love is made in absolute terms (V, 1696–1701), Troiolo's is hedged with qualifications. He says that he no longer wants to love but has no choice

9. Citations for Chaucer are to the first line of each minimal terminal unit (t-unit) containing a commitment. A t-unit is an independent clause with its modifying dependent clauses and phrases, and in modern punctuation, a t-unit might properly be separated from other t-units by periods. Troilus: I, 427, 535, 1053, 1055; III, 100, 131, 141, 390, 417, 712, 1297, 1604, 1611; IV, 320, 442, 447, 472, 1654; V, 229, 573, 586, 593, 1317, 1364, 1412, 1414, 1417, 1696, 1699. Criseyde: III, 999, 1494, 1499. Pandarus: I, 593, 988; IV, 624. Citations for Boccaccio are to stanzas in Branca's text. Troiolo: I, 38; III, 36, 59; IV, 50, 54; VII, 47, 52. Criseida: III, 49, 50. Pandaro: none. Narrator: I, 4.

since Criseida's image has not left his heart (VIII, 15). In these statements, Chaucer again contrasts Troilus's style with Criseyde's. Criseyde makes only three absolute commitments and these on only two occasions, just before and after making love, when her commitments are obviously influenced by her passion (III, 999, 1494, 1499). Normally, she prefers conditional commitments, in which the love of one of them depends on that of the other. In her first conversation with Troilus, she asks Pandarus to beseech Troilus: "for Goddes love, that he / Wolde, in honour of trouthe and gentilesse, / As I wel mene, eke menen wel to me" (III, 162–64); after making love, she says that since she is true to him, he should be true to her (III, 1511–12). In these conditional statements, she suggests that she sees love not as an absolute and eternal state but as one that depends on a particular person and time.

Finally, Troilus's style is conventional because of his frequent long monologues. Troilus's monologues extend for 477 lines, Criseyde's for 248 lines, and Pandarus's for sixteen lines. While Troilus tends to consider philosophic subjects, like love and destiny, Criseyde considers practical ones, like the consequences of loving Troilus or Diomede. In these monologues, Troilus frequently invokes classical gods, personified objects, and absent persons in expressions which are more extended and formal than common oaths. To show the comparative prevalence of these invocations in his speech, I counted after formal apostrophes all imperative and interrogative verbs. I counted only imperatives and interrogatives to limit the examples to the most emphatic, and I counted the verbs inflected rather than the nouns apostrophized because to invoke or question one god several times normally represents a more sustained effort than to invoke or question several gods one time. Troilus uses ninety-six such verbs, Criseyde sixteen, and Pandarus three, and all the verbs in Pandarus's speech occur when he gives Criseyde an example of how well Troilus can speak on love.[1] Pandarus obviously associates these expressions with the conventional language of love. Monologues and invocations are also prevalent in Troiolo's speech in the *Filostrato*, but Chaucer has increased the philosophic and medieval cast of Troilus's monologues by giving him two long passages from *The Consolation of Philosophy*, the hymn to love and the discourse on destiny. Through such passages, Chaucer raises central questions about the value of love and the existence of freedom with an insistence which Boccaccio avoids, perhaps because Boccaccio is far more interested in appealing to his mistress than in questioning love.

Chaucer thus uses conventional traits—superlatives, commitments, and monologues—to fashion Troilus's style. He reworks Boccaccio's poem to emphasize these traits; he distinguishes Troilus's style from that of the other characters by them. He thus protrays a conventional lover but not, we must add, in a lyric poem. Rather, he puts Troilus in the midst of a narrative with the result that the very action of the narrative challenges the static ideals of the lyric. How well Troilus survives, first from a moral, then from a realistic perspective, is the next focus of this paper.

1. For line references, see Taylor, "Style and Character," pp. 287–88.

Troilus tends, as we have noted, to use absolute statements, both in his superlative praise of Criseyde and in his total commitment to her. The narrative clearly shows that his praise is neither a helpful nor an accurate judgment, for Criseyde proves unfaithful. It also calls into question his commitment, for although his commitment may bring him one moment of bliss, it later intensifies his suffering. The narrative suggests, in brief, that anyone who puts his trust in this world will be disappointed since this world and all within it are changeable, mortal, and imperfect. This suggestion is made explicit at the poem's end where the narrator calls on young lovers to love Christ, since He is "best" to love.

Chaucer's criticism of Troilus's love, however, is not completely condemning. Even when one emphasizes the narrative, one can find patterns which reaffirm the moral values underlying Troilus's conventional language. One of these values is truth, the keeping of a commitment, and Troilus's truth to Criseyde seems all the more valuable if one notes that the major action in the poem, both political and personal, turns on the faithfulness or lack of faithfulness of the characters. In the political action, the poem opens when Calkas steals privily out of Troy to the Greek host. Since he is a Trojan, he should, as Troilus later points out, be truthful to Troy, but Calkas lacks Troilus's courage to be faithful when he can foresee that such faithfulness may lead to death. The next breach of faith occurs when the parliament supervenes Hector's promise to Criseyde and treats her not as a citizen but as a prisoner of war to be traded for Antenor. By this breach of faith, the people of Troy bring about their own destruction since Antenor later opens the gates to the wooden horse. Chaucer's argument is that a civilization's existence depends on the faithfulness of its citizens.[2]

If one turns from the political to the personal sphere, one finds much the same point, a linking of truth with existence. E. Talbot Donaldson in his commentary on the poem notes this linking when he praises Troilus's truth:

> [His] integrity, the quality that he will not surrender even to keep Criseyde with him, is the one human value the poem leaves entirely unquestioned: it is because of it that Troilus is granted his ultimate vision. It places him, of course, in sharp contrast with Criseyde and her *untrouthe*, and since one of the meanings of *trouthe* is reality, he emerges as more real than she.[3]

In fact, we question Troilus's reality only at those moments when he is not perfectly truthful—for example, when Criseyde asks Troilus how he came to be jealous and the narrator tells us:

> Withouten more, shortly for to seyne,
> He most obeye unto his lady heste;
> And for the lasse harm, he moste feyne.
> He seyde hire, whan she was at swich a feste,
> She myght on hym han loked at the leste,—

2. See, e.g., W. F. Bolton, "Treason in *Troilus*," *Archiv* 203 (1967), 255–62.
3. E. Talbot Donaldson, *Chaucer's Poetry, An Anthology for the Modern Reader* (New York, 1958), p. 974.

Noot I nought what, al deere ynough a rysshe,
As he that nedes most a cause fisshe.　　　　(III, 1156–62)

Here, Troilus slips out of focus, for neither the narrator nor the reader can imagine exactly what he would say; but such moments are rare, and Troilus, because he remains essentially true to Criseyde, remains at the center of the narrative, the action following him even beyond his death to his ascension, where he is associated with the truth and reality of heaven. Criseyde, on the other hand, grows increasingly unfaithful, and as she does so, the action slips away from her. Her ultimate reality, as she recognizes, will be associated only with fiction: "O, rolled shal I ben on many a tonge! / Thorughout the world my belle shal be ronge!" (V, 1061–62). She becomes the subject of our judgment, not, like Troilus, judging us from heaven.

Several readers do not accept this emphasis on faithfulness as an important virtue in the poem. Although they would agree that Troilus is faithful, they discount his faithfulness by claiming that Troilus is faithful to an evil passion, that is, to cupidinous love. Taking this line of reasoning, D. W. Robertson finds Troilus the most culpable of all the characters in the poem:

> Neither Criseyde nor Diomede, both of whom seek momentary footholds on the slippery way of the world, is capable of the idolatry of which Troilus is guilty, or of the depths to which he descends.[4]

I certainly agree with Robertson that Troilus's love is misplaced, but I cannot accept his extreme condemnation of either Troilus or of secular love.

Although Troilus and Criseyde's love ends far from happily, the narrative still suggests that love itself is a positive, natural force, for it is love which takes Troilus out of his original self-absorption and changes him from an arrogant, mocking adolescent into a much more mature person, one who sees in a moment of bliss that love controls the world and one who later learns, when Criseyde must leave, that human love depends on personal choice, that all earthly love is transitory, and that Criseyde, far from being the best, is unfaithful. I do not wish to argue that Troilus's love is rational or perfect, for it is far too centered on Criseyde and far too dependent on her physical presence for such praise, but it is still the one force which connects him with the outer world. In fact, Troilus's behavior is most foolish and destructive when he is farthest from love's influence. One can point to the first two books where, before he really knows Criseyde or anything about love, his passion is primarily a self-construction, or to the first half of the fifth book, where his attention again spins back on himself and, caught between hope and dread, he can even mistake a "fare carte" for Criseyde herself. The end of the narrative would be totally bleak if it did not show Troilus, once more moved by love, turning outwards, first to praise Criseyde before Cassandra, then to reassert his love for her to Pandarus. Since love is the one force which connects Troilus with the outer world, one can

4. D. W. Robertson, Jr., *A Preface to Chaucer: Studies in Medieval Perspectives* (Princeton, 1962), p. 499.

further argue that it together with his faithfulness is responsible for his final ascension and vision. Not until then, because he is a pagan, can Troilus see the truth. Perfected by his love, he is finally like the good soul in Boethius "that hath in itself science of gode werkes" and "beynge in hevene rejoyseth that it is exempt fro alle erthly thynges" (*Consolation*, Bk. II, prose 7, 151–57).

From a moral point of view, the narrative thus affirms the central values of secular love poetry: first, its emphasis on total commitment and faithfulness, without which a lover is hopelessly lost, even ceases to be; second, its promise of perfection, for although the lady may not herself be perfect, her association with perfection is fitting because love takes the individual beyond himself even to God. The poem's affirmation of these conventional values can be further illustrated by looking at some stylistic features in the characters' speech and at some general patterns in the imagery.

Although the following stylistic features may seem rather trivial, some important statements can be drawn from them. For example, Troilus never uses common idioms like *ich mente wel* or *I non yvel mene* while Pandarus and Criseyde use these expressions frequently, especially when they want to conceal the moral significance of a statement by avowing their good intentions.[5] A shocking example occurs at the end of Criseyde's letter where she says, "Th'entente is al, and nat the lettres space" (V, 1630), an avowal which reduces all the truth of language to the intention behind it. Troilus's avoidance of these idioms suggests that he has faith in his truthfulness and therefore does not think to distinguish between his meaning and intention. His inherent truthfulness can also be seen by his infrequent use of the oath, *by my trouthe*, which is one of Pandarus's favorites.[6] Pandarus probably uses this oath so frequently because he feels a continuing need to affirm as true what he suspects is false. Troilus, furthermore, does not pun, he does not mix terms of highly varied qualitative force to blur the moral implications of his statements, and he does not change his definition of various abstracts, like fortune or love, to fit the occasion.[7] For him, love cannot slide, as it does for Pandarus, from a gift of grace (I, 896) to a casual pleasure (IV, 419). By these small traits, one can see that Troilus is an absolutist not only in his commitment to Criseyde but also in his sense of language. He accepts the meaning of words, their integrity, just as he accepts the integrity of other people. These details show that Chaucer is concerned with the moral implications of everyday speech—that is, with the relation between habitual language patterns and habitual behavior. On this level, Troilus is not, as Robertson states, the lowest character in the poem; rather, he is the most praiseworthy.

5. Expressions with the verb, *menen*, like *Ich mente wel*: Pandarus, II, 364, 438, 581, 592, 721; III, 337; Criseyde, III, 164, 1164; V, 1004. Expressions with the nouns, *entente* and *entencioun*, like *And sith I speke of good entencioun*: Pandarus, I, 683; II, 295, 363, 580; Criseyde, III, 1166; V, 1630.
6. This expression occurs thirteen times in Pandarus's speech and twice in Troilus's speech.
7. For Pandarus's puns, see II, 1238–39, 1319–20, 1638. Troilus's word play consists of a rhetorical repetition of sounds, in which the meaning of the words is not changed. See his letter to Criseyde (V, 1354–55). For passages where Pandarus mixes terms of highly varied qualitative strength, see II, 430–35, III, 913, IV, 596–97. For Pandarus's conflicting comments on Fortune, see I, 848–49, where he emphasizes the turning of the wheel, and III, 1630–31, where he suggests that if one sits very still, the wheel will stop.

The imagery of the poem, moreover, works against Robertson's polar distinctions between cupidity and charity, for it suggests that all love is part of God's love, that sexuality and charity are in one continuum.[8] In the Prohemium to Book III, for example, Venus is described both as the divine force of life itself, the "vapour eterne" which is normally associated with the Holy Spirit, and immediately afterwards as the sexual force behind the amorous exploits of Jove. Because Chaucer adds to Boccaccio the explicitly sexual reference to Jove, his intention is clear: he wants to include the sacred and physical under the influence of Venus. He thus sets up a pattern continued throughout Book III.

After Troilus and Criseyde first make love, Troilus praises love in the following stanza:

> "Benigne Love, thow holy bond of thynges,
> Whoso wol grace, and list the nought honouren,
> Lo, his desir wol fle withouten wynges.
> For noldestow of bownte hem socouren
> That serven best and most alwey labouren,
> Yet were al lost, that dar I wel seyn certes,
> But if thi grace passed oure desertes."   (III, 1261–67)

The passage is surprising, for Troilus, although he has just experienced the physical delight of love, emphasizes not the physical but the spiritual. He invokes love as "thow holy bond of thynges," a phrase which recalls Boethius, and then uses an image taken from Dante's final Canto in the *Paradiso*, where Dante praises the Blessed Virgin Mary for so ennobling human nature that God, man's Creator, did not disdain to become His creation. The parallel is significant because Mary is the mortal link which joins God and man and because Mary, throughout the *Divina Comedia*, represents woman's pity and love. She first urges Beatrice to have pity on Dante (*Inferno* II, 94–99). What Chaucer has done in this stanza and the one preceding it, where Troilus praises the planet Venus as "O Love, O Charite," is to bring together a wide range of references traditionally associated with love. These references give a spiritual significance to Troilus and Criseyde's love.

One can sense this same combination of physical and spiritual love in a stanza at the end of the poem. The narrator is admonishing young lovers to return home from worldly vanity and love Christ:

> the which that right for love
> Upon a crois, oure soules for to beye,
> First starf, and roos, and sit in hevene above;
> For he nyl falsen no wight, dar I seye,
> That wol his herte al holly on hym leye.
> And syn he best to love is, and most meke,
> What nedeth feynede loves for to seke?   (V, 1842–48)

Although the main purpose of this stanza is not to remind us of Troilus, the narrator's superlative to describe Christ, "syn he best to love is," and his quantitative intensifiers to describe the perfect lover, who "wol his herte al holly on hym leye," do recall Troilus and his conventional lan-

---

8. See Kean's and Dronke's works cited above for a more complete treatment of this subject.

guage. The language of secular love, "the olde clerkis spech / In poetrie," is thus shifted to describe the perfect Christian love, a shift suggesting that the old speech is not ultimately opposed to the God of love, just as the Old Law is not ultimately opposed to the New.[9] The Old is imperfect but it promises the New. Troilus's love is imperfect, particularly because it is misplaced, but in his faithfulness and commitment he represents an essentially heroic and worthy lover.

One can make similar moral evaluations without all the work of stylistic criticism, but the stylistic criticism does show Chaucer's explicit concern for the language patterns of lyric poetry and for the values inherent in them. An attention to Troilus's style can also lead into another area of criticism, one concerned less with an evaluation of moral issues than with an understanding of Troilus's believability as a character. At the turn of the century, many critics were delighted with *Troilus and Criseyde* because they found it like a novel, calling it, in fact, "the first novel in the modern sense," and they praised in particular the realism of the character motivation.[1] More modern critics have backed away from this interpretation by arguing that Troilus, in any case, could not be considered as a realistic character. Instead, they have viewed him as the type of the idolator or the conventional lover. My emphasis up to now has been on Troilus as a conventional lover, and I do not want to transform him into a purely realistic character who can be understood by the rules of the nineteenth-century novel or Freudian psychology. I do want, however, to change my emphasis and consider him from a more realistic point of view. From this point of view, Troilus often looks helpless or absurd.[2] He is the static, lyric protagonist who is incapable of action and therefore the butt of many jokes. It is important to recognize Troilus's absurdity, for Chaucer questions not only the moral but also the practical implications of his language and behavior. I think Troilus's stature survives all the irony and jokes, but before coming to his defense, let me again clarify the extent to which Chaucer challenges him.

Irony occurs particularly when the realistic demands of the narrative call into question Troilus's idealism. For example, early in the poem Troilus pictures Criseyde as the cruel lady of traditional poetry:

9. In *Troilus and Criseyde*, what has often been called courtly love is set in a pagan world, and Christian ideas, like sin and forgiveness, are associated with pagan gods, like Venus, Cupid, Jove, Mars, and Fortune. Chaucer is thus bringing together two worlds, the medieval courtly and the classical pagan, or, more exactly, he is associating the courtly with the pagan. When he refers to the "olde clerkis" in the phrase, "olde clerkis speche," he is probably continuing this association of pagan and courtly and may thus be referring to both classical writers, like Statius, Lucan, and Ovid, and to medieval Christian writers in the French tradition. The "olde clerkis speche" would thus include the secular love language which has been described in this paper. The relationships between Christian and pagan worlds are treated at greater length by Donald R. Howard, *The Three Temptations, Medieval Man in Search of the World* (Princeton, 1966), pp. 111–18.
1. For examples of this criticism, see Thomas R. Price, "*Troilus and Criseyde*: A Study in Chaucer's Method of Narration," *PMLA* 11 (1896), 307–22, and George Lyman Kittredge, *Chaucer and his Poetry* (Cambridge, Mass., 1960), especially p. 112, from which I have quoted above. A list of articles treating *T&C* as a novel is given by Karl Young, "Chaucer's *Troilus and Criseyde* as Romance," *PMLA* 53 (1938), 38–39. For a survey of more recent criticism, see Alfred David, "The Hero of Troilus," *Speculum* 37 (1962), 566–69.
2. R. K. Root emphasizes his helplessness, Charles Muscatine his absurdity, although Muscatine also feels that Troilus keeps his dignity even in comic situations. My own position is close to Muscatine's. See R. K. Root, *The Poetry of Chaucer*, 2nd ed. (Boston, 1922), p. 117, and Muscatine, *Chaucer*, pp. 136–39, 150–53.

> "But also cold in love towardes the
> Thi lady is, as frost in wynter moone,
> And thow fordon, as snow in fire is soone."   (I, 523–25)

Although the poetry may be effective, this description of Criseyde is ridiculously inaccurate, partly because Troilus has never spoken with her. The narrator, however, does not raise this objection so that he can raise an even more obvious one:

> All was for nought: she herde nat his pleynte;
> And whan that he bythought on that folie,
> A thousand fold his wo gan multiplie.   (I, 544–46)

One has the distinct impression that if it were not for Pandarus, Troilus would wear out his life in woeful verses.

Once Pandarus comes into the poem, he takes up the ironic role. He particularly deflates Troilus's long invocations. Before the meeting with Criseyde at Pandarus's house, Troilus appeals to all the gods of Olympus, much to the frustration of Pandarus who wants to bring him and Criseyde together. Pandarus finally interrupts, "Thow wrecched mouses herte, / Artow agast so that she wol the bite?" (III, 736–37). Pandarus shows the same frustration at the end of Troilus's monologue on predestination where he mocks Troilus's invocation, "Almyghty Jove in trone, / That woost of al this thyng the sothfastnesse . . . ," with his own, "O myghty God . . . in trone, / I! who say evere a wis man faren so?" (IV, 1079–80, 86–87). His reply is brilliant because he radically changes the perspective from the heavens to the earth. Pandarus sees Troilus's logical errors clearly. Troilus has forgotten that he lives in time, that time gives man freedom, and that Criseyde, quite simply, has not yet gone. In effect, he has confused his foresight with God's foresight.

Through Pandarus's and the narrator's comments, Chaucer keeps in the foreground the impracticality of Troilus's speech and action. Troilus's long monologues and invocations are dismissed as retreats; his conventional praise of Criseyde is undercut by his ignorance. Chaucer particularly questions Troilus's absolute commitments and the meaning of his repeated adverbial intensifiers. When Pandarus says to Criseyde,

> "Ther were nevere two so wel ymet,
> Whan ye ben his al hool, as he is youre . . ."

Criseyde understands all the sexual implications,

> "Nay, therof spak I nought, ha, ha!" quod she;
> "As helpe me God, ye shenden every deel!"   (II, 586–90)

But when Troilus uses similar intensifiers in his vows of service,

> "God woot, for I have,
> As ferforthly as I have had konnynge,
> Ben youres al, God so my soule save . . ."

Criseyde is understandably confused,

> "Now thanne thus," quod she, "I wolde hym preye
> To telle me the fyn of his entente.

Yet wist I nevere wel what that he mente."
                                    (III, 100–102, 124–26)

By such comparisons, Chaucer is obviously poking fun at conventional language. What *does* it mean to commit oneself totally to another person, to say, I am all yours? The speaker in a lyric poem does not need to worry about the realistic implications of such commitments—he exists outside of time and the statement is all—but Troilus does have to worry because his statements about love, unless realized in action, will not satisfy his desire. His problem is that of all conventional lovers: he wants Criseyde to remain an idealized object whom he can worship in a thousand selfless and acceptable acts, but he also wants her as a woman in bed, and this problem is only resolved when Pandarus hefts him into Criseyde's bed. Troilus, I think, seems most foolish in the first three books, since it is in these that Chaucer particularly makes fun of the impractical idealism inherent in the traditional love poetry.

If one stresses only the irony, then Troilus begins to look like a caricature of a lover. Such an interpretation, however, misses his strength. Troilus is a far more convincing character partly, as has been suggested, because he remains faithful but also because his speech implies a coherent sense of the world and has a peculiar force and energy.

When the conventional traits in Troilus's speech are considered together, the emerging patterns are surprisingly consistent. For example, Troilus is the one character who uses unqualified superlatives to describe himself. In these he separates himself from others either as someone who is unique in all time, "For nevere man was to yow goddes holde / As I, which ye han brought fro cares colde" (III, 1259–60), or as someone who is unique in a group of people, "O Troilus, what may men now the calle / But wrecche of wrecches, out of honour falle" (IV, 270–71). In the second example, he increases his feelings of separateness by worrying what the world will say. He has the same fear just after he falls in love:

> "What wol now every lovere seyn of the,
> If this be wist? but evere in thin absence
> Laughen in scorn, and seyn, 'Loo, ther goth he
> That held us loveres leest in reverence.'"   (I, 512–16)

Later, when he thinks about disobeying his father's decree, he fears the "blame of every wight" (IV, 551), and, in Book V, he believes that he has become so woe-begone that "every wight" looks on him as they pass him by (V, 625). Even when he is happy, he thinks that he is being watched and thus accuses the sun: "For every bore hath oon of thi bryghte yën!" (III, 1453). In these expressions, he shows an unusual degree of self-consciousness, which one does not find in the other characters, not even in Criseyde. She also fears the blame of others and even, at the end of the poem, worries that her name will be rolled on every tongue, but she does not think of herself as unique, for she finds consolation in the thought that she is not the first to do amiss (V, 1061–67). Others may place her in a separate category; she refuses to do so herself.

Troilus's tendency to think of himself as unique is also clear in another conventional feature of his language, his infrequent use of proverbs.[3] One might dismiss this infrequency as an accident of style—courtly lovers do not tend to use proverbs—but Chaucer has made it an obvious part of Troilus's personality by showing how Troilus, early in the poem, consciously rejects Pandarus's proverbial wisdom:

> ". . . Now pees, and crye namore,
> For I have herd thi wordes and thi lore;
> But suffre me my meschief to bywaille,
> For thi proverbes may me naught availle." (I, 753–56)

In effect, Troilus does not want to be consoled with proverbs. On other occasions, he used them only to mock Pandarus's and Criseyde's own proverbial statements or to single out a highly specific feature of some person or event. He implicitly rejects their basic assumption: that he and everyone else are always alike. Reta Anderson Madsen, in an unpublished dissertation on rhetorical figures in Chaucer, does not discuss Troilus's tendency to isolate himself, but she does draw an important conclusion from his rejection of proverbs:

> He confronts reality much more nakedly than Pandarus or even Criseyde. Neither his emotions nor his reactions are dulled by the recognition that others have felt and reacted in the same way and with predictable results. . . . Paradoxically, he is a basically conventional character who cannot be comforted by conventions, while the more realistic characters of the poem draw much of their strength from their recognition of and use of the power of convention.[4]

In stressing the conventionality of Troilus's language, I have implied that he is similar to most medieval lovers. It is true that he is similar, but not true that he is exactly the same, for he is far more insistent about his unique and special fate than most lovers. Typically, lovers in Machaut and Froissart commit themselves, then draw back to think about love and fortune. In their monologues on these subjects, they compare themselves with others. Mars in Chaucer's *Compleynt of Mars* goes through the same pattern. After an early commitment, he thinks of his hopeless fate, ironically questions love, and then finds some consolation in the recognition: "So fareth hyt by lovers and by me." Similar statements can be found in Anelida's complaints from *Anelida and Arcite*

3. A full discussion of proverbial statements in Chaucer is given by Bartlett Jere Whiting, *Chaucer's Use of Proverbs*, Harvard Studies in Comparative Literature 11 (Cambridge, Mass., 1934). Using his references, I have considered all proverbial statements which give or support instruction, thus implying a standard behavior for everyone, and all those which make comparisons between someone and a proverbial person or animal, thus implying that everyone is alike. Troilus makes ten such comments, but four of these occur on two occasions when he is obviously impatient with Pandarus's and Criseyde's proverbs (IV, 463–69, 1450–59). Of the other six, two occur in his early and rather adolescent pronouncements on love (I, 202, 509), and three stress the singularity of some quality in himself or another (II, 985, IV, 1459, V, 426). On one occasion, he uses a proverbial statement to generalize about life, but on that occasion, he makes from his experience a proverb. He does not use a pre-existent proverb to understand his experience (III, 1282). Pandarus uses sixty-one proverbial comments that fall into the above categories, Criseyde twenty-eight, and the narrator twenty-five, seventeen of which occur in Book I and the Prohemium to Book II. As Troilus's experience in love deepens, the narrator seems to feel less and less confident that life can be understood or directed from a proverbial point of view.
4. "Some Functions of Medieval Rhetoric in Chaucer's Verse Narratives," Diss. Yale University, 1967, p. 207. The dissertation is listed at Yale University under her maiden name, Reta Margaret Anderson, and it is quoted with the permission of the author.

and in Criseyde's complaints. Only after doubts and comparisons do the above lovers recommit themselves to love. Troilus also has his doubts about love, especially before he commits himself to Criseyde, and about fortune, especially in Books IV and V, but once he commits himself, he does not equate his experience with that of others. Even in his three long complaints about fortune, he always thinks of himself as unique. In the first, he calls himself the most wretched person who has ever lived (IV, 270–71); in the second, he appeals to lovers who are at the top of Fortune's wheel to come and look down at his sepulture (IV, 323–39); in the third, he carries on a running argument between what some clerks would say and what he would say (IV, 958–1078).

Troilus's instinctive tendency to separate himself from others, to think of himself as unique, and to think of his destiny as determined helps to explain why he experiences life with such a singular intensity. In the context, his extreme language, including his superlative praise, his total commitments, even his highly rhetorical complaints, becomes more realistic and believable, since only this language has sufficient intensity to fit his sense of himself and his destiny. In fashioning the character of Troilus, Chaucer thus uses conventional rhetoric, but he increases it moral significance and its realism by giving it to a lover whose behavior and self-consciousness are consistent.

Troilus's strength and intelligence are also implied by the rhythm and energy of his syntax. When reading the poem, one tends to think of Troilus's style as opposed to Pandarus's style. Troilus's style is courtly and lyric and therefore, one assumes, artificial, while Pandarus's style is naturalistic and life-like and therefore convincing, but one has to guard against too easy an acceptance of this distinction because, in fact, all the characters share basically the same language and can use a wide range of styles from the most courtly to the most naturalistic. When Troilus loses his temper with Pandarus, he can sound just as colloquial as Pandarus (I, 621–24, 752–56); when Pandarus must beg a favor of Deiphebus, he employs all the conditional verbs and balanced phrases which one expects when Troilus is addressing Criseyde (II, 1430–42). One has to recognize that Pandarus and Troilus are flexible in their speech, that they are not caricatures locked into a single idiom. To make this reservation, however, is not to deny that Pandarus tends to speak one way, Troilus another, as can be shown by a comparison of two passages. In the first, Pandarus is telling Troilus to accept the wisdom of his experience, even if he, Pandarus, has not been all that successful in love:

> "A wheston is no kervyng instrument,
> But yet it maketh sharppe kervyng tolis.
> And there thow woost that I have aught myswent,
> Eschuw thow that, for swich thing to the scole is;
> Thus often wise men ben war by foolys.
> If thow do so, thi wit is wel bewared;
> By his contrarie is every thyng declared.
>
> "For how myghte evere swetnesse han ben knowe
> To him that nevere tasted bitternesse?

Ne no man may ben inly glad, I trowe,
That nevere was in sorwe or som destresse.
Eke whit by blak, by shame ek worthinesse,
Ech set by other, more for other semeth,
As men may se, and so the wyse it demeth."   (I, 631–44)

The overall impression of these two stanzas is that one pithy phrase is added to the next with the meaning of each statement contained within a line or a couplet. The number of t-units (independent clauses plus their modifiers) is high, nine for fourteen lines, and the co-ordination from one clause to the next is either done by parataxis or by co-ordinating conjunction. The movement is one of addition, not of subordination. There is some verb suspension for rhetorical emphasis, as in the last two lines where the suspension is neatly parallel. There is also some padding with conversational tags, like "I trowe" and "as men may see." Finally, there are nineteen finite verbs in a total of 113 words for a finite verb percentage of 16.8%. The percentage of finite verbs in a passage can be an indication both of the level of style (that is, the more finite verbs, the more informal the style), and of the argumentative force-fulness of the language (the more finite verbs, the more forceful).[5] Pandarus's average finite verb percentage is 14.7%. Troilus's is 13.5%, which is not remarkably lower but an indication of his tendency on a serious or uncomfortable occasion to use a more periodic and formal style. Troilus particularly uses this more formal style with Criseyde. With her, his finite verb percentage is 11.7%.

The following passage is spoken by Troilus when he promises that he shall never reveal his love for Criseyde:

"Thow woost how longe ich it [Criseyde's name] forbar to seye
To the, that art the man that I best triste;
And peril non was it to the bywreye,
That wist I wel, but telle me, if the liste,
Sith I so loth was that thiself it wiste,
How dorst I mo tellen of this matere,
That quake now, and no wight may us here?

"But natheles, by that God I the swere,
That, as hym list, may al this world governe,—
And, if I lye, Achilles with his spere
Myn herte cleve, al were my lif eterne,
As I am mortal, if I late or yerne
Wolde it bewreye, or dorst, or sholde konne,
For al the good that God made under sonne—

"That rather deye I wolde, and determyne,
As thynketh me, now stokked in prisoun,
In wrecchidnesse, in filthe, and in vermyne,
Caytif to cruel kyng Agamenoun:
And this in all the temples of this town

---

5. Professor Marie Borroff first directed my attention to both t-units and finite verb percentages as significant measures of syntactic complexity. For a fuller discussion of F-V percentages in Chaucer, please see Appendix.

Upon the goddes alle, I wol the swere
To-morwe day, if that it like the here."   (III. 365–85)

The syntax of the first stanza is relatively simple, but it contains two examples of a construction which occurs frequently in Troilus's speech. These are the embedded clauses, "If the liste" and "Sith I so loth was that thiself it wiste," which come between the imperative, "telle," and its complement, "How dorst I mo tellen. . . ."

The syntax of the next two stanzas is far more complex, primarily because of such embedded clauses. The stanzas can be simplified by omissions and re-arrangements and the change of an *if* to a *than* to read in Modern English: I swear by God, I would rather die and come to an end in prison [than] reveal your secret, and if I lie, let Achilles end my life, even if my life were as eternal as it is mortal. I have changed the *if* to *than* since *rather* in both Middle and Modern English calls for the latter conjunction.[6] A major difference between the original and my re-arrangement is that in the original one can feel Troilus's energy as he works through all kinds of contingent materials, like God's creation of the world, to his emphatic conclusion, his readiness to die in prison. The passage shows his habit of exploring all sides and possibilities, even though his explorations seldom, if ever, change his original feelings. One can indicate the syntactic involutions in the passage by pointing out that the number of t-units is fairly low, six in twenty-one lines, and the number of embedded clauses extremely high, ten for the same number of lines. (There were nine t-units and two embedded clauses in Pandarus's passage of fourteen lines.)[7] Given this syntactic involvement, one might

6. Troilus could follow the clause, "If I reveal it," with a main clause, "let me die." He uses instead the clause, "I would rather die," a change which suggests that he has somewhat lost his original train of thought, but the sentence does not radically break apart, as in an anacoluthon where a new construction takes over before an old one is completed. I have found only one anacoluthon in Troilus's speech (III, 361) but ten in Pandarus's speech (I, 659–62, 806–09; II, 337–43, 379–80, 1279–81; III, 771–77; IV, 397–99, 1086–87; V, 324–26, 337–41). While Troilus's sentences often show emotional strain, they do not fall apart from casual thoughtlessness. His syntax is more strict and formal, while Pandarus's syntax is more open and colloquial. For a full discussion of colloquial traits in Chaucer's verse, see Margaret Schlauch, "Chaucer's Colloquial English: its Structural Traits," *PMLA* 67 (1952), 1103–16, and for a fuller application of her criteria to *Troilus and Criseyde*, see Taylor, "Style and Character," pp. 78–88.
7. To provide further statistical support, I have chosen in a random though even distribution several passages, which add up to at least 700 lines for each speaker, and counted within them both t-units and embedded clauses. I have defined an embedded clause as a clause which occurs somewhere between the subject, verb, and complement of another clause, regardless of the order of those elements. In the following passage,

> "Love, ayeins the which whoso defendeth
> Hymselven most, hym alderlest avaylleth,
> With disespeyr so sorwfulli me offendeth,
> That streight unto the deth myn herte sailleth,   (I, 603–06)

the entire clause, "ayeins the which whoso defendeth / Hymselven most, hym alderlest avaylleth," is considered an embedded clause because it occurs between the subject of the main clause, "Love," and the complement of that clause, "With disespeyr so sorwfulli me offendeth." The noun clause, "Whoso defendeth / Hymselven most," is not counted as a separate embedded clause since it is the subject of its clause and not a separate interruption. The final clause in the passage is not self-embedded but right-branching and therefore not counted. Finally, I have excepted those embedded clauses which are common idioms and do not add new information but merely enforce what has already been said, idioms like the oath, "God helpe me so," and the tag, "that is to seyn." I made this exception since Pandarus frequently uses such idioms, and if they were counted as equal to the interruptions in Troilus's speech, they would have blurred the statistics.

	Occurrence / 1,000 lines	
	Troilus	Pandarus
Embedded phrases:	140	45
t-units	435	526

expect that the finite verb percentage would also be low, indicating a high degree of nominal elements; but, in fact, the percentage is rather high, 16.2%, and in the first two stanzas, extremely high, 19.7%, for here Troilus's thought is most active and complex. In the last stanza, where he is moving to a rhetorical conclusion, the percentage drops to 8%, and the syntax also becomes more additive and balanced, as shown by the repeated prepositional phrases. These two extremes, either of syntactical complexity or of rhetorical balance, are frequent in Troilus's verse and sometimes occur together, as in this passage. He either puzzles over an argument or seeks a rhetorically balanced statement. To gain this balance in other passages, he uses such figures as anaphora (the repetition of opening words or phrases) and *similiter cadens* (the repetition of concluding sounds in one part of speech), or he repeats larger sentence units, like introductory dependent clauses or short independent and interrogative clauses.[8]

Although it is dangerous to make general statements about a character merely by looking at his syntax, I think one can use syntactic evidence to reinforce and re-evaluate statements based on other criteria. For example, one can argue that the involved movement in Troilus's argumentative passages and the heavy repetition in his rhetorical conclusions—his tendency to twist, turn, and repeat before he concludes a sentence—that these interruptions suggest a desire for stasis, a desire to stop the movement of time in order to understand. The syntactic evidence thus reinforces what we have already observed: namely, that Troilus, a lyric protagonist, constantly wants to withdraw from the narrative. This evidence, however, can also lead to a re-evaluation. I think we tend to assume that a character who constantly withdraws must be yielding and passive, but after noting the energy in Troilus's syntax, one must qualify this assumption. Troilus may decide that an action is impossible—for example, in the predestination speech where he begins with the wrong premises—but his decision is marked by the most vigorous argument. Throughout the poem, he struggles with words, seeking the best expression for his ideas and feelings. In this struggle, he is quite unlike Boccaccio's Troiolo, whose language tends to have an almost slick self-assurance as well as an evenness of pace which Troilus's language almost never assumes.[9]

An examination of syntax can likewise lead to both a reinforcement and a re-evaluation of our observations on Pandarus. If we tend to think of Troilus as passive, we also tend to think of Pandarus as active. He is always busy, jumping and leaping, and his language, with its colloquial diction and pat phrases, bustles with life. The syntactic evidence—Pandarus's use of an accumulative, open, and co-ordinate style—reinforces these basic impressions. Pandarus's language flows along as Pandarus flows along, with an easy and assured acceptance of time. Perhaps, how-

---

8. For examples of anaphora, see III, 1744–64; IV, 1206–10; V, 565–81, 610–16. For *similiter cadens*, see I, 603–09. For repeated sentence units, see III, 328–47, 1454–63; IV, 260–66; V, 39–50, 218–45, 1254–68, 1674–76.
9. The differences in the syntax and style of Troilus's and Troiolo's speech can most easily be seen by comparing their letters to Criseyde, especially the two stanzas which begin, "If any servant dorste or oughte of right" (V. 1345), and, "Se 'l serviodore in caso alcun potesse" (VII, 54). For a full discussion of these passages, see Taylor, "Style and Character," pp. 52–57.

ever, the very easiness of his language can lead to a re-evaluation of our original impressions, and even if we cannot deny his *bysynesse*, we can question its quality, especially when recognizing that his language and thoughts, although often perceptive, tend to be lazy. Unlike Troilus, he does not seek an original expression for his thoughts or feelings. Instead, he relies on the most convenient idioms or proverbs and seldom varies his syntax. In brief, Pandarus accepts language as it comes, and it comes easily to him, while Troilus, although he uses many conventional images, never gives the impression that such language is automatic or natural. He is always examining, always thinking or feeling as shown by his dense syntax. The energy of his expression as much as anything else convinces the reader that he must not be dismissed merely as a caricature of a lover.

In this paper, I have concentrated on Troilus's style, not because it is the most distinctive in the poem, but because it leads to the poem's central issues. One responds to the moral issues as one responds to Troilus. If one finds Troilus foolish, then I think one tends to find the whole poem and all the praise of love foolish (or perhaps ironic); but if one finds Troilus heroic, even in a limited way, then the poem also has a serious stature and Troilus's values seem worthy of respect. In his conclusion, Chaucer bids his poem to be subject to all great poetry and to "kis the steppes, where as thow seest pace / Virgile, Ovide, Omer, Lucan, and Stace" (V, 1791–92). For all his humility in this prayer, Chaucer is still placing his poem in the most esteemed poetic company of his time and thereby asking us to consider it as a highly serious work. The irony in the poem is there, but Troilus is also there—stubborn, consistent, and faithful. About Troilus's style, one can say that it is conventional but not that it is artificially conventional, since it is perfectly consistent with his character even to the extent of revealing some subtle aspects of his motivation. One can also say that his style is sometimes foolish but not foolish for the same reasons that Pandarus's and Criseyde's styles are foolish, not because he is shifting vaguely from one issue to the next or swearing profusely by his good intentions. His arguments may be unconvincing but his energy is convincing. Finally, although the poem questions all the values of Troilus's style, the narrator at the end uses the same style to describe the perfect Christian love. Chaucer does not renounce the traditional values of the "olde clerkis speche." Instead, he embodies them in Troilus, who is second only to Hector in all Troy.

APPENDIX: FINITE VERB PERCENTAGES IN CHAUCER

Finite verb percentages provide an accurate indication for the level of speech, from formal to colloquial, throughout Chaucer's poetry, and fairly small differences in percentage can show appreciable difference in style. The sensitivity of F-V percentages as an indicator derives from Chaucer's decasyllabic line. In passages which are neutral in level of formality, Chaucer uses about one finite verb per line, and since the number of words per line averages out at 7.8, the F-V percentage is just over 12.5%. Chaucer's normal narrative, in fact, shows a slightly lower

F-V percentage since about one line in four or five will not have a finite verb. Chaucer gains variety by using either a series of infinitives which have been introduced by a modal verb, a series of present participles, or even a few lines without verbal elements. In conversational passages, the F-V percentage rises above 12.5% since the speakers use more short clauses and more common idioms. The following F-V percentages for Chaucerian narrators in *The Canterbury Tales* have been computed on passages totalling at least 1,000 words, except for the Summoner and Friar, where the base is 500 words. The percentages indicate the general levels of formality and clearly distinguish between the fairly formal narrators, like the Friar and the Clerk, and the clearly informal ones, like the Canon's Yeoman and the Wife of Bath: Friar 11.0%, Clerk 11.3%, Nun's Priest 11.3%, Knight 11.6%, Pardoner 11.7%, narrator of General Prologue 11.8%, Miller 12.4%, Summoner 12.8%, Canon's Yeoman 13.2%, Wife of Bath 14.4%.

The following percentages for various characters in the tales themselves are based on passages of 500 words or more: in The Knight's Tale, Arcita 12.4%, Palamon 12.4%, Theseus (in the Chain of Love speech) 12.4%, Theseus (at the end of Book II) 13.6%; in The Nun's Priest's Tale, Chauntecleer 14.2%; in The Friar's Tale, the Summoner and the Fiend 14.2%; in the Miller's Tale, Nicholas 14.8%.

The following percentages for *Troilus and Criseyde* are from passages totalling 6,000 words or more: the narrator 12.2%, Criseyde 13.2%, Troilus 13.5%, and Pandarus 14.7%. It is interesting to note that Pandarus's percentages do not vary with auditor, an indication that his level of style remains pretty much the same. He averages 14.7% when speaking with Troilus and 14.6% with Criseyde, while Troilus's F-V percentages show considerable variation, 14.1% with Pandarus, 14.0% in monologues, and 11.7% with Criseyde. Criseyde's percentages also vary. She is most colloquial, perhaps because she is most at ease, in her monologues where the F-V percentage is 14.1%. With Pandarus, it is 13.5% and with Troilus, 12.6%.

RICHARD F. GREEN

Troilus and the Game of Love†

"Women of quality are so civil, you can hardly distinguish love from good breeding, and a man is often mistaken."
WYCHERLEY, *The Country Wife* (I, i).

John Benton, in his enlightening discussion of "medieval love," is careful to distinguish between the *love of friendship* ("in courtly circles it could be accepted as reasonable and appropriate to kiss a lady, to give her presents, to declare that one had become a better man through her

---

† From *The Chaucer Review* 13 (1979): 201–20. Reprinted by permission.

friendship")[1] and the *love of concupiscence*. By its failure to distinguish between social and sexual intercourse, Benton suggests, modern scholarship has foisted upon the Middle Ages an anachronistic and misleading hybrid, to which it has given the name "courtly love": "We therefore create nothing but confusion for ourselves if we apply one technical term, other than the ambiguous word 'love,' to both forms of loving. In particular I see no justification for combining aspects of one form of loving with aspects of the other and calling our creation 'courtly love.' While some authors wrote ambiguously about love, the literature I have read does not convince me that medieval people themselves inadvertently confused the categories and could not tell the difference between love which was concupiscent and that which was not" (p. 31). This is a beguiling hypothesis (if only because it appears to confirm what many scholars have long suggested—that the term "courtly love" has very little real meaning), but closer inspection reveals that it may, in fact, be substituting for an unhelpful critical oversimplification an equally difficult sociological one.

It is true that courtly society in the late Middle Ages was far more flamboyant than our own, that its gestures were more expansive, its rituals more overtly elaborate; but are we therefore to conclude that every public demonstration of mutual respect between members of the opposite sex was unambiguously blameless? Benton himself allows that "a person might use the language of friendship with concupiscent desires in his heart" (p. 30), without apparently asking himself why, if for "medieval people" this language was completely free of ambiguity, the concupiscent-at-heart should have bothered to use it. Must we really believe that no courtier or lady ever bestowed a public kiss in a spirit other than that of friendly courtesy, that the outward and visible forms of good-mannered gentility always cloaked quite unexceptionable motives, that no medieval husband would ever have felt a pang of jealousy at the extravagant compliments paid to his wife?

Of course, in the language of friendship all women are paragons of virtue, and we should always be prepared to find a degree of disingenuousness in medieval expressions of confidence in the wholesomeness of friendly love. No Frenchman, says Gontier Col, would dream of slapping, or even chiding, his wife for kissing another man—but then in Italy, or so he has heard, even an ill-advised glance would be enough to send a husband off to the poison cabinet.[2] Though he cannot imagine what reason there might be for it, says the Menagier of Paris, it is reported that the queens of France, after their marriage, are not permitted to kiss any other man save their husband.[3] Of course, men *may* kiss women merely to make them good cheer, says the wife of the Knight

---

1. "Clio and Venus: an Historical View of Medieval Love," in the *Meaning of Courtly Love*, ed. F. X. Newman (Albany: State Univ. of New York Press, 1968), p. 30.
2. "Pareillement di je qu'un regart fait par la fourme [?] ou la famme d'ung Rommain ou Ytalyen donra occasion au mary, comme j'ay oy dire, de l'empoisonner et ainssy la murdrier mauuaisement, la ou ung baisier en France ne donroit pas occasion de tenser sa famme ou au mains la ferir," *Epistles on the Romance of the Rose and Other Documents in the Debate*, ed. C. F. Ward, Diss. Univ. of Chicago, 1911), p. 70.
3. "Les Roynes depuis qu'elles sont mariées, jamais elles ne baiseront homme, ne père, ne frère, ne parent, fors que le Roy, tant comme il vivra; pour quoi elles s'en abstiennent, ne se c'est vray, je ne sçay," *Le Menagier de Paris*, ed. J. Pichon (1847; rpt. Geneva: Slatkine Reprints [1965?], p. 76.

of the Tower Landry; but then, with admirable maternal prudence, she adds, "but as for my doughters whiche ben here present I defende and withsaye to them the kyssyng and alle suche maners of disportes."[4] Clearly, in the Middle Ages, as now, the distinction between complimentary flirtation and outright seduction (even perhaps for those actually engaged in such pursuits) was a fine one, and none but the most socially naïve can have felt absolute confidence that every show of friendly love sprang from only the purest of motives.

In one sense the social reflexes of the medieval noblewoman, at least in the late Middle Ages, needed to be far sharper than her modern counterpart's if she were to maintain the precarious balance between courtesy and propriety. The language of friendship, the medium of polite intercourse between the sexes, was evidently highly stylized; it depended for its effect on an esoteric knowledge of acceptable forms, and its purpose, doubtless, was to serve as a way of marking off the well-bred from the churlish. Its inevitable moral ambiguity was, however, compounded by its heavy dependence upon formulae drawn from the metaphorical language of erotic verse. If a man showed his respect for a woman by ostensibly (in the nineteenth-century sense of the words) "making love" to her, how was she to know whether he might not possibly be in earnest? When Charles d'Orléans was met at Gravelines by the Duchess of Burgundy, who played a significant part in bringing to an end the poet's long imprisonment in England, he is said to have remarked: "Madam, in view of your efforts for my deliverance, I surrender myself as your prisoner."[5] This is an urbane and charming speech; that it draws on the conventional metaphor of the lover as prisoner of his mistress in no way need imply an element of concupiscence in the speaker's attitude. In another context, however, the same metaphor might become highly ambiguous; the Knight of the Tower reports a conversation he had once had with a young lady whom he contemplated marrying: "& so we fill in spekyng of prysoners / And thenne I said to her / damoysell I wold wel and had leuer be youre prysoner than ony others / & I thenke that youre pryson shold not be so hard ne cruell, as is the pryson of englisshe men / And she ansuerd me that she had late sene such one / that she wold wel that he were her prysoner / & I demanded her, yf she wold yeue hym euyl pryson / & she answerd me nay / but that she wold kepe hym as derworthely as her owne body" (p. 27). The social nuances of this interchange have inevitably become blurred with time, but there was clearly something in the lady's reply which, in the Knight's eyes, overstepped the bounds of propriety: "the ouer grete malepertnes & the lyght manere that me semed to see in her, discouraged me so that I maryed not with her" (p. 28).[6]

The activity which both Charles and the Knight of the Tower are here engaged in was that to which the Gawain-poet gives the name "luf-talkyng."[7] Whether public, as in the duke's case, or private, as in the

4. William Caxton, trans., *The Book of the Knight of the Tower*, ed. M. Y. Offord, EETS, SS 2 (London: Oxford Univ. Press, 1971), p. 175.
5. "Madame, vu ce que vous avez fait pour ma délivrance, je me rends votre prisonnier," quoted by P. Champion, *Vie de Charles d'Orléans* (Paris: Honoré Champion, 1911), p. 313.
6. The Knight of the Tower's wife alludes to this episode and discusses its implications later in the work (see p. 168 of *The Book of the Knight of the Tower*).
7. *Sir Gawain and the Green Knight*, ed. J. R. R. Tolkien and E. V. Gordon, rev. ed. (Oxford: Clarendon Press, 1967), l. 927.

knight's, it depended for its effect upon a sophisticated appreciation of the intricacies of erotic metaphor and convention; in Huizinga's words, "a whole system of amatory conceptions and usages was current in aristocratic conversation of those times. What signs and figures of love which later ages have dropped!"[8] Whilst the courtier might engage in love-talking from motives of pure *politesse* (as Castiglione says, "not onlye whan he is stirred thereto by some passion, but often times also to do honour to the woman he talketh withall, seemynge to him that to declare to love her is a witnes that she is woorthie of it"),[9] he might equally well make use of this particular polite accomplishment to achieve undeniably sensual ends. The author of the English poems of Charles d'Orléans, echoing an aphorism in the *Miller's Tale*, says that, while the love of a *bourgeoise* may be won with gifts and that of a peasant girl with blows, a noblewoman will succumb only to "goodly speche and curteys countenaunce."[1] Love-talking is, it seems to me, the very cornerstone of that elaborate social structure to which John Stevens has given the name "the game of love";[2] it is the vehicle for almost all the romantic play-acting of the late medieval aristocracy, and the importance of attuning the ear to its subtleties as we read the courtly verse of the period can hardly be over-stressed.

Just how far the verbal extravagances of romantic play might be taken can be illustrated by reference to one of the commonest and most exaggerated of all erotic fictions in the Middle Ages—the notion that a man might die of unrequited love. Here at least, we may feel, we can tread with some confidence in this murky no-man's-land separating art and life. "Men have died from time to time and worms have eaten them, but not for love." The notion is patently hyperbolical and only the most obtuse literalism could possibly lift it out of the realm of metaphor. True, the "loveris maladye of hereos" does find its way into sober medical textbooks, but we may doubt that, in practice, its victims caused medieval doctors any great concern: Valescus of Taranta, for example, remarks, "firstly, it should be recognized that few, if any, are nowadays slain by hereos," and John of Gaddesden, reflecting the proverbial avarice of his profession, includes hereos amongst a list of ailments upon which he does not propose to spend much time, "since the doctor rarely gets much money by them."[3] When, therefore, we find the heroine of Chartier's *Belle Dame Sans Mercy* rebutting her unwelcome suitor with the words, "This sicknesse is right esy to endure, / But fewe people it causeth for to dy" (293–94),[4] we are unlikely to be ready to credit her with unusual

8. J. Huizinga, *The Waning of the Middle Ages*, trans. F. Hopman (London: Edward Arnold, 1924), p. 107.
9. *The Book of the Courtier*, trans. Sir Thomas Hoby, Tudor Translations, 23 (London: David Nutt, 1900), p. 267.
1. Charles of Orleans, *English Poems*, ed. R. Steele and Mabel Day, EETS, OS 215 and 220, rpt. with supp. (London: Oxford Univ. Press, 1970), pp. 5–6 (II. 140–53); cf. *Miller's Tale*, 3381–82 and the gloss in B. L. MS. Egerton 2864: "Vnde Ouidius Ictibus agrestem ciuilem munere vince Colloquio nobilem comoditate loci."
2. See *Music and Poetry in the Early Tudor Court* (London: Methuen, 1961), pp. 154ff.
3. "Primo sciendum quod pauci vel nulli nunc efficiuntur heroici," and, "quia raro medicus lucratur pecuniam cum eis," J. L. Lowes, "The Loveres Maladye of Hereos," *MP*, 11 (1914), 507 and 503.
4. Trans. Sir Richard Ros, in *Chaucerian and Other Pieces* (Supp. to the *Complete Works of Geoffrey Chaucer*, 6 vols.), ed. W. W. Skeat (Oxford: Clarendon Press, 1897), p. 308.

powers of perception; no lady, we would imagine, however refined her romantic sensibilities, could ever have supposed otherwise.

It is therefore something of a shock to discover that unscrupulous medieval seducers apparently found it worth their while to counterfeit love-sickness. If Chartier's *belle dame* was not to be taken in, evidently there were others who were. The Knight of the Tower's wife, at any rate, saw fit to warn her daughters against those who "gyue oute of theyr brestes grete and fayned syghes / And make as they were thynkynge and Melancolyous / And after they cast a fals loke / And thenne the good and debonayr wymmen that sene them / supposen / that they be esprysed of trewe and feythfull loue / but al suche maner of folke / whiche vsen to make suche semblaunt / ben but deceyours or begylers of the ladyes and damoysels" (p. 166). Christine de Pisan, a professed champion of female honour, paints a similar picture of masculine duplicity:

> Hir wordes spoken been so sighyngly,
> And with so pitous cheere and contenance,
> That euery wight þat meeneth trewely
> Deemeth / þat they in herte han swich greuance:
> They seyn / so importable is hir penance,
> Þat, but hir lady / list to shewe hem grace,
> They right anoon moot steruen in the place.
> (22–28)[5]

Her translator, Thomas Hoccleve, expands the point:

> By procees / wommen meeued of pitee,
> weenyng al thyng were / as þat tho men seye,
> Granten hem grace of hir benignitee,
> For they nat sholden for hir sake deye.
> (43–46)

Most striking of all (in that it provides the strongest evidence that we are here concerned with an actual historical phenomenon) is a passage from *Jacob's Well*; in a list of the attributes of *luxuria* the author includes: "Also leccherouse woordys, and in groping, felyng, in syngynge leccherous songys, in daunsyng, in wowyng, in delyzt of leccherous songys, in feynyng þe seke for loue. . . ."[6]

Clearly, then, the notion of a man's dying for love had become, by the end of the fourteenth century, a social fiction as well as a literary one; for, as these quotations show, feigned love-sickness was a well-used weapon in the armoury of the unscrupulous seducer, and the very fact that such deception could be practiced suggests that the idea had some kind of general social currency. Obviously we are here in a world of elaborate make-believe, where the distinctions between art and life, illusion and reality, game and earnest, have become strangely blurred. Whilst medieval noblemen may have been in as little danger of dying from thwarted passion as ourselves, they seem to have felt that they

5. "Lepistre de Cupide," trans. Thomas Hoccleve, in *Hoccleve's Works*, ed. F. J. Furnivall & I. Gollancz, rev. A. I. Doyle, EETS, ES 61 and 73, rpt. in one vol. (London: Oxford Univ. Press, 1970), p. 294.
6. *Jacob's Well*, Pt. I, ed. A. Brandeis, EETS, OS 115 (London: K. Paul, French, Trübner & Co., 1900), p. 158.

should at least *appear* capable of the kind of elevated emotion such a fate implies. At the very heart of the game of love there lies, I suspect, a simple matter of social ostentation. The capacity to experience exalted human love (by definition, in the Middle Ages, an exclusively aristocratic phenomenon) had come to be regarded as one of the distinguishing features of gentility, and the conventions through which such love was defined, originally pure literary hyperbole, had become part of the code of polite manners. In order to prove himself a gentleman, the courtier had to show himself a lover—to assume the elaborate mask of "trewe Tristram the secounde."

To return, then, to Benton's distinction between the *love of friendship* and the *love of concupiscence,* it was inevitable that, for the late Middle Ages at least, the two categories should have become confused.[7] When the former, which was in essence merely a display of good breeding, depended for its expression on conventions drawn from the latter, only by penetrating the secret recesses of the heart could one ever be sure which was which. Here, for instance, is a striking passage from Gwilym ap Daffyd, Chaucer's great Welsh contemporary: "Such is the pining of a furtive lover that secret love is best for one while we are among crowds—I and my girl, a wanton couple—and no one suspects that we talk together through this our amorous speech."[8] There was, of course, another side of the coin: " 'Come, sit down here, my dear sweet friend,' " says the lady in *Guillaume au Faucon,* and the narrator adds, "[she] was not aware of the state of William's heart when she called him her dear friend; for if she had known it she would never have spoken thus."[9] No wonder that feminists like Christine de Pisan and moralists like the author of *Jacob's Well* found such a state of affairs disturbing; even that resolute defender of "loue peramours," the Knight of the Tower, is forced to shake his head and admit that "the world is hard to knowe and moche merueyllous" (p. 163).

The one thing which prevented the social game turning into moral anarchy was the good faith, the integrity, the "trouthe" of the players. This fact, I believe, helps to account for the prominence given to this particular quality in the courtly literature of the period—as Arveragus' famous line expresses it: "trouthe is the hyeste thyng that man may kepe."[1] In the *Cent Ballades,* written by Boucicault and his noble friends, there is a dramatized conflict between painful loyalty in love and frivolous self-indulgence; we might suppose that no medieval nobleman would, in public at least, espouse the latter, and it is something of a shock to find the Duc de Berri (that great patron of literature and the

---

7. A striking illustration of the fineness of the line dividing them is to be found in Castiglione's *Courtier:* "In case you will needes write or speake to her, do it with such sober moode, and so warilye, that the woordes maye firste attempt the minde, and so doubtfullye touch her entent and will, that they maye leave her a way and a certain issue to feine the understandinge that those woordes conteine love: to the entent if he finde anye daunger, he maye draw backe and make wise to have to spoken or written it to an other ende, to enjoye these familiar cherishinges and daliances with assuraunce, that oftentimes women showe to suche as shoulde take them for frendshippe, afterwarde denye them assone as they perceyve they are taken for tokens of love" (p. 277).
8. Trans. K. H. Jackson, *A Celtic Miscellany* (Harmondsworth: Penguin Books, 1971), p. 99.
9. Trans. R. Hellman and R. O'Gorman, *Fabliaux* (New York: Thomas Crowell, 1965), p. 84.
1. *Franklin's Tale,* 1479, *The Works of Geoffrey Chaucer,* ed. F. N. Robinson, 2nd ed. (Boston: Houghton Mifflin, 1957). All quotations from Chaucer are from this edition. See also John Burrow, *A Reading of Sir Gawain and the Green Knight* (London: Routledge and Kegan Paul, 1965), pp. 42–51.

arts) writing: "they [faithful lovers] would do better to pick a lady every-where—not just one, but three or four pair of them—and to all, in order to win their grace, one can say one thing but one should do another."[2] Even more striking is the cynicism of the Lord of Chambrillac, a royal chamberlain: "I am quite familiar with Troilus, handsome and of high rank, who was faithful to Briseide and wished no other love; all the good he got by it was that he was left without a mistress, for when she left Troilus, Diomede took over; this story teaches me to refrain from setting my heart in one place only."[3] No doubt it was the prevalence of such sentiments as these that led to the Lady of the Tower's warning: "I charge yow doughters / that ye be no players" (p. 175).

This has been, I am fully aware, a "long preamble of a tale," but an understanding of the phenomenon I have been discussing—the paradox that life, or at least its social accoutrements, appears to have imitated art—seems to me vital for a proper appreciation of the best courtly poetry of the period.[4] What is, for our purposes, most significant about the romantic play-acting of the late medieval nobleman is the fact that it seems to have spawned its own literature. If life initially imitated art, art in its turn sought inspiration in this imitation. Just as, on a social level, the distinction between genuine and playful love-talking, between earnest and game, cannot always have been clear-cut even for those involved, so, in literary terms, it is not always obvious whether the poet is taking for his model the idealized love of imaginative fiction or the social expression of this ideal in romantic play. In the hands of a skilful poet, this ambiguity inherent in his material might become a fruitful source of irony; it provided him with ample raw material for mannered comedy, and, at a deeper level, allowed him to explore the inevitable and pathetic inability of the human to contain the ideal.

In order to see *Troilus and Criseyde* in its proper perspective, we must first consider Chaucer's original audience and the attitude he takes to it. That the "yonge, fresshe folkes" addressed in the epilogue were, in the first instance, the fashionable courtiers who surrounded King Rich-ard on the eve of the Appellants' rebellion can hardly be doubted; only for this close-knit group of elegant *familiares* dressed in the "newe guise of Beawme,"[5] so vividly captured in the frontispiece to the Corpus Christi manuscript of the poem,[6] could Chaucer's well-turned compli-

2. "Mieux leur vausist par tout dame choisir, / Non pas une, mais trois ou iiii paire, / Et a toutes, pour leur grace acquerir, / On peut l'un dire, et l'autre doit on faire" (27–30), *Les Cent Ballades*, ed. G. Raynaud, SATF (Paris: Firmin-Didot, 1905), p. 214.
3. "Bien ay oÿ de Troÿluz / Le beau, le preux de hault pouoir, / Qui a Brisaÿda fu druz, / Ne d'autre amer n'ot nul vouloir. / Le bien qu'il en pot recevoir / Fu qu'il demoura sans amie; / Car quant de Troie fu partie, / Dyomèdes en fu saisiz: / Sa dame fu, il ses amis. / Cela m'aprent que je m'atieigne / Qu'en lieu seul soit mon cuer assiz" (13–23), *Cent Ballades*, pp. 203–04.
4. For a discussion of the same phenomenon in the sphere of chivalric literature, see L. D. Benson, *Malory's Morte Darthur* (Cambridge, Mass.: Harvard Univ. Press, 1976), pp. 137–86.
5. John Gower, *Confessio Amantis*, VIII, 2470, ed. G. C. Macaulay, 2 vols., EETS, ES 81 and 82 (London: Clarendon Press, 1900–1901), II, 453.
6. D. A. Pearsall, "The *Troilus* Frontispiece and Chaucer's Audience," *Yearbook of English Studies*, 7 (1977), 68–74, argues effectively against a too facile identification of the details of this frontis-piece with the historical court of Richard II; he concedes, however, that "it represents as a reality the myth of delivery that Chaucer cultivates so assiduously in the poem, with its references to 'al this compaignye' of lovers 'in this place' " (p. 70). That this "myth" must have had some basis in Chaucer's actual audience, from whatever quarter of the court it may have been drawn, can hardly be denied.

ment to Queen Anne, "right as oure firste lettre is now an A" (I, 171), have had much point. He is writing for those confident in their position as the arbiters of polite society, fully cognizant of the intricacies of the sophisticated game of love, and his tone is accordingly deferential. Not without irony, he assumes the role of the uninitiated observer:

> Ek though I speeke of love unfelyngly,
> No wondre is, for it nothyng of newe is;
> A blynd man kan nat juggen wel in hewis.
> (II, 19–21)

He protests that he is an amateur amongst professionals, and that their knowledge of the finer points of the game far outweighs his. He is afraid that he will bore them with obvious details: "this, trowe I, knoweth al this compaignye" (I, 450), or, "reherce it nedeth nought, for ye ben wise" (II, 917); he appeals to them for confirmation: "But now to yow, ye loveres that ben here, / Was Troilus nought in a kankedort . . . ?" (II, 1751–52) and he begs them to make allowances for his inevitable *gaucherie*:

> For myne wordes, heere and every part,
> I speke hem all under correccioun
> Of yow that felyng han in loves art. . . .
> (III, 1331 33)

Troilus and Criseyde was clearly written for an audience whose sensibilities were very much in tune with that spirit of self-conscious play which I have suggested was so congenial to the late medieval aristocracy, and only when we have made the imaginative effort to set the poem in such a context can we begin to respond to its richly ironic vein of social comedy.

There is much in Chaucer's picture of the life of the Trojan nobility that would have seemed familiar to the Ricardian courtiers, but nothing more so than the game of love itself and its manifestation in the intricate artifices of love-talking; the play-mode pervades the poem and provides a frame for the central love affair. The *magister ludi* is, of course, Pandarus, and for much of the poem we see the interaction of the two main characters only against the background of his expertise. He professes himself a lover, but does not seem to take his role very seriously; he is determined, at any rate, not to allow the lover's conventional indifference to food to spoil a good dinner:

> Therwith she lough, and seyde, "Go we dyne."
> And he gan at hymself to jape faste,
> And seyde, "Nece, I have so gret a pyne
> For love, that everich other day I faste—"
> (II, 1163–66)[7]

He sees no reason to keep the name of his mistress secret; indeed, he implies that it is common knowledge (I, 717). We may assume that

---

7. Cf. Charles d'Orléans' complaint, "Also where ye say ye wisshe eche othir day / To ben with me o welaway y cry" (1297–98), *English Poems*, p. 44; and the nineteenth statute in a cynical list in the *Court of Love*, "Mete and drink forgete: / Ech othir day, see that thou fast for love" (484–85), Skeat, *Chaucerian Pieces*, p. 422.

Pandarus regards his love affair as a convenient social fiction, maintained with the style that befits a nobleman, but very much a part of the game world. Criseyde at one point belittles his emotional commitment—"ye hadde nevere thyng so lief" (III, 870)—and there is little to lead us to disagree with her. Though Pandarus' love is frequently in his own mouth, the narrator mentions it only once:

> That Pandarus, for al his wise speche,
> Felt ek his part of loves shotes keene,
> That, koude he nevere so wel of lovyng preche,
> It made his hewe a-day ful ofte greene.
>
> (II, 57–60)

It is important to recognize, however, that, whilst Pandarus is clearly incapable of the depths of emotion experienced by his protégé Troilus, he is no mere shallow hypocrite, ready to turn his familiarity with the rules of the game to his own advantage. The concern he feels for his niece's honour (III, 260–343) and his subsequent disillusionment at her infidelity (V, 1723–43) are obviously genuine, and the moral ambiguity of the role he finds himself playing "bitwixen game and ernest" (III, 254) is manifestly disturbing to him.

With Criseyde Pandarus maintains an affectionate flirtation, rendered only slightly ludicrous by their kinship and the difference in their ages. His harmless love-talking gains point from the fact that she herself, as he recognizes, is no novice in the art:

> Ne I nevere saugh a more bountevous
> Of hire estat, n'a gladder, ne of speche
> A frendlyer, n'a more gracious
> For to do wel, ne lasse hadde nede to seche
> What for to don. . . .
>
> (I, 883–87)

On his frequent visits to his niece he seems at times to come very close to "playing the lover" with her:

> "But I am sory that I have yow let
> To herken of youre book ye preysen thus.
> For Goddes love, what seith it? telle it us!
> Is it of love? O, som good ye me leere!"
> "Uncle," quod she, "youre maistresse is nat here."
> With that thei gonnen laughe. . . .
>
> (II, 94–99)

Is it not, perhaps, an amusing ambiguity in Criseyde's rejoinder (with its secondary implication, "I am not your mistress") that sets them both laughing? In a later scene, Pandarus presses his supper invitation on his niece with a metaphor drawn straight from the conventional language of love—that of the hunter:

> Whan he was com, he gan anon to pleye
> As he was wont, and of hymself to jape;
> And finaly he swor and gan hire seye,

> By this and that, she sholde hym nought escape,
> Ne lenger don hym after hire to cape. . . .
>
> (III, 554–58)

For such passages as these the context is one of laughter, game, and "japing," and this mood of playful familiarity reaches its climax with the interview between the two after the lovers' first night together:

> "Nece, if that I shal be ded,
> Have here a swerd and smyteth of myn hed!"
> With that his arm al sodeynly he thriste
> Under hire nekke, and at the laste hire kyste.
>
> (III, 1572–75)

That Pandarus, with his prying beneath the sheets, seems to come very close to overstepping the bounds of play in this scene may serve to remind us of the ambiguous nature of all games of love, however trivial.

The scenes between Pandarus and Criseyde do not provide the only examples of sociable love-talking in the poem. There is, for instance, Eleyne's "wommanly" playing with Troilus when he is feigning sickness (her injunction, "beth al hool, I preye" [II, 1670], is, I fancy, a playful suggestion that she, as his lady, can heal him with her grace—significantly enough, Criseyde uses exactly these words to Troilus less than two hundred lines later [III, 168]), and, above all, there is the unscrupulous glibness of Diomede. His cynical ensnaring of Criseyde provides a perfect illustration of the way in which the courtier's art might be abused; clearly, he is of the same persuasion as those "many gentylle men whiche," the Lady of the Tower suggests, "ben so fals and deceyuable that they requyre euery gentylle woman that they may fynde" (p. 166):

> Happe how happe may,
> Al sholde I dye, I wol hire herte seche!
> I shal namore lesen but my speche.
>
> (V, 796–98)

Speech is something Diomede can afford to lose, for he has an abundance of it. The address to Criseyde with which he thinks to "shorte oure weye" (V, 96) is a masterpiece of controlled and polished love-talking; in the space of some fifty lines, he moves from formal politeness—for at first he takes care not to "speke of love or make it tough" (V, 101)—through the ambiguities of urbane social intercourse, to a thinly veiled offer of service. "And wondreth nought, myn owen lady bright, / Though that I speke of love to yow thus blyve" (V, 162–63), he concludes disingenuously, yet there is hardly anything about his speech, except perhaps too great a presumption on their short acquaintance, that Criseyde need take exception to. Such is the ambiguity inherent in the game of love that the whole elaborate structure can be accepted by Criseyde as mere social pleasantry. Later on, when Diomede's suit becomes more persistent, Chaucer cuts short an attempt to reproduce the intricacies of his plea in detail:

> What sholde I telle his wordes that he seyde?
> He spak inough, for o day at the meeste.

It preveth wel, he spak so that Criseyde
Graunted, on the morwe, at his requeste,
For to speken with hym at the leeste,
So that he nolde speke of swich matere.
(V, 946–51)

Clearly, he is a highly articulate exponent of the art of love-talking—a
Trojan Sir Gawain; unlike the hero of *Gawain and the Green Knight*,
however, he lacks the basic integrity, the "trouthe," without which court-
liness turns sour. Criseyde's faithlessness to Troilus cannot be defended,
but, in itself, her capitulation to the force of Diomede's eloquence is
hardly to be wondered at:

So wel he for hymselven spak and seyde,
That alle hire sikes soore adown he leyde.
And finaly, the sothe for to seyne,
He refte hire of the grete of al hire peyne.
(V, 1033–36)

Where, then, does Troilus himself stand in this world of elaborate
artificiality? He is, after all, the hero of the poem—the man whose "dou-
ble sorwe" Chaucer sets out to tell. We have been told by C. S. Lewis
that he is an "embodiment of the medieval ideal of lover and warrior,"[8]
yet the Ricardian courtiers who made up Chaucer's original audience
needed to be warned, it seems, that they might find his courtship of
Criseyde unconventional:

if it happe in any wyse,
That here be any lovere in this place
That herkneth, as the storie wol devise,
How Troilus com to his lady grace,
And thenketh, "so nold I nat love purchace,"
Or wondreth on his speche or his doynge,
I noot; but it is me no wonderynge.
(II, 29–35)

Lewis probably expresses the most common critical reaction to Troilus
as a lover, and even John Stevens, sensitive as he generally is to the
nuances of the game of love, finds nothing exceptionable about the abil-
ities of Chaucer's hero as a love-talker.[9] Charles Muscatine comes far
closer, it seems to me, when he writes that, "as medieval romance goes,
as the 'code' goes, Troilus is too perfect a courtly lover."[1] In fact, the
uncompromising purity of his emotion is what sets him apart from the
game-world of the poem; he represents the "thing itself," of which
courtly play is but a pale reflection. It is no wonder that he is so hope-
lessly out of place in the Trojan *beau monde* and that his attempts to
come to terms with it are a source of comic inspiration. He is first shown
as a mocker of Love's followers, not merely that his own subsequent

---

8. *The Allegory of Love* (1936; rpt. New York: Oxford Univ. Press, 1958), p. 195.
9. Commenting on Criseyde's question, "kan he wel speke of love . . . I preye?" Stevens writes, "Troi-
   lus can, and frequently does," *Music and Poetry*, p. 159.
1. *Chaucer and the French Tradition* (Berkeley: Univ. of California Press, 1957), p. 137; one might
   usefully compare Gabriel Josipovici's perceptive comment, "for a long time readers have dismissed
   Troilus's extravagance as belonging *to* the courtly code, and have thought that to recognize this is
   to account for it" *The World and the Book* (1971; rpt. St. Albans: Paladin, 1973), p. 81.

subjugation may satisfy our sense of poetic justice, but because this position furnishes the only possible explanation (other than low birth) of his manifest ignorance of the game of love. His total incomprehension of its intricacies leads to a preposterous dependence upon the worldly-wise Pandarus, and to a courtship which, in its naïve clumsiness, turns at times into high farce.

When Troilus first finds himself in Love's power, his immediate reaction to the code is depreciatory. He sees it as a matter of trivial etiquette:

> In nouncerteyn ben alle youre observaunces,
> But it a sely fewe pointes be;
> Ne no thing asketh so gret attendaunces
> As doth youre lay. . . .
>
> (I, 337–40)

This attack is, of course, an attempt to disguise his own new emotion, but its object is revealing; Troilus disparages that very aspect of the lover's experience which he himself neither understands nor considers important—its embodiment in ritual play. It is for Pandarus to teach him how ineffectual a thing is naked emotion lacking a proper vehicle for its formal expression. Presumably, were it not for Pandarus and his "painted proces," Troilus would continue to wallow and weep in private (I, 699) indefinitely, and, as the narrator quietly points out, "al was for nought: she herde nat his pleynte . . ." (I, 544).

Troilus' sentimental education at the hands of his friend must start from absolute fundamentals; Pandarus is hard-pressed to find a common ground upon which to discuss love with Troilus, for he can presume on no shared experience of the game. Troilus knows nothing, and cares still less, about the instructive example of Niobe (I, 759), and Oenone's letter, which has evidently been passed around the Trojan court, has never reached him: " 'Yee say the lettre that she wrot, I gesse.' 'Nay nevere yet, ywys,' quod Troilus" (I, 656–57). That Pandarus' instructions should be so detailed when Troilus himself comes to write a love-letter (II, 1023–43) is hardly surprising. Love-letters were an important element in the game of love,[2] and Criseyde would presumably know a good letter when she saw one; Pandarus' anxious "kan he theron?" (II, 1197) to Criseyde betrays a certain lack of confidence in his protégé's progress.

As the proem to Book II suggests ("so nold I nat love purchace"), Troilus' attempts to master the subtle art of love-talking are doomed to a singular lack of success. Chaucer's disclaimer of authorial freedom of action here—"for as myn auctour seyde, so sey I" (II, 18)—reminds one of his similarly phrased disavowal of the Miller's obscenities, and indeed his purpose is much the same in both cases: to draw attention to the comic possibilities and to heighten his audience's anticipation. As long as the love-affair is carried on by proxy, Criseyde has no way of knowing the answer to her leading question, "kan he wel speke of love?" (II, 503).

---

2. See, for example: "leccherous maners, as kyssynges, felynges, dern syngynges, gay aray, nyce chere, leccherous songys of loue paramour, & letterys of loue!" *Jacob's Well*, p. 164; and the story reported by the Menagier of Paris that French queens, after their marriage, were allowed to read only their husbands' letters in private: "elles ne lisent jamais seules lettres closes, se elles ne sont escriptes de la propre main de leur mary, si comme l'en dit, et celles lisent-elles toutes seules, et aux autres elles appellent compaignie et les font lire par autres devant elles" (p. 75).

Not until the elaborate charade put on for her benefit at Deiphebus' house does she have a chance to find out at first hand.

The second book ends on a note of eager anticipation. Pandarus has decoyed Eleyne and Deiphebus into the garden, Criseyde is at the door, and at long last Troilus' schooling in the game of love is to be put to the test: "And was the firste tyme he shulde hire preye / Of love; O myghty God, what shal he seye?" (II, 1756–57). The action is suspended for a moment for the elevated sentiments of the proem to Book III, and we are kept on tenterhooks a moment longer as Troilus runs over his speech:

> "Mafay," thoughte he, "thus wol I sey, and thus;
> Thus wol I pleyne unto my lady dere;
> That word is good, and this shal be my cheere;
> This nyl I nought foryeten in no wise."
>
> (III, 52–55)

Then comes the high comedy of his first bathetic utterance to his lady: "Therwith it semed as he wepte almost. / 'Ha, a,' quod Troilus so reufully . . ." (III, 64–65). All this elaborate preparation has produced, not a well-turned phrase, but an inarticulate groan—heart-felt perhaps, but hardly the opening gambit of an experienced love-talker. Criseyde's response is immediate and sympathetic, and this proves too much for Troilus:

> But, Lord, so he wex sodeynliche red,
> And sire, his lessoun, that he wende konne
> To preyen hire, is thorugh his wit ironne.
>
> (III, 82–84)

There is a certain disingenuousness about the "sire" dropped carelessly into the line which, as in the ballad of the Derby Ram, serves to underline the comic incongruity of the situation. Troilus recovers sufficiently to cry "mercy, mercy, swete herte!" not once but twice (III, 98), and to offer to kill himself if that is what Criseyde wants, and then follows an awkward silence. Pandarus pokes his niece, but she is not to be won so easily. For all the world like two doctors discussing a helpless hospital patient, they wrangle over the prostrate Troilus, and Criseyde finally states her conditions—she wishes her prospective lover to give a better account of himself than he has so far managed to do:

> "Now thanne thus," quod she, "I wolde hym preye
> To telle me the fyn of his entente.
> Yet wist I nevere wel what that he mente."
>
> (III, 124–26)

This is Troilus' cue, and like a man transformed he launches into three balade-like stanzas which, in their elegant formal artifice, give a strong impression of having been got up in advance for just such an eventuality. There is nothing of Diomede's smooth changes of tone here. The interview reaches a satisfactory conclusion, thanks largely to Criseyde's social tact, but, though Pandarus' promise of the pleasures of a future meeting, "and lat se which of yow shal bere the belle, / To speke of love aright!" (III, 198–99), may be intended by him as a waggish euphemism, in the context it is not without irony.

The contrast with Diomede throughout this scene is very marked. Skilled love-talking demands a certain ironic detachment; strong emotion and genuine feelings, as Guillaume de Lorris suggests, render a man inarticulate, and only the "faus amant" can "content lor verve"—say one thing and think another.[3] It is therefore to Troilus' credit that he is here, like the Black Knight in the *Book of the Duchess* in a similar position (1218–20), struck dumb. This fact does not lessen the comedy of the situation however: "Ek scarsly ben ther in this place thre / That have in love seid lik, and don in al . . ." (II, 43–44). *Troilus and Criseyde* is not a rarified dream-vision; Chaucer knows that the solidity of his setting is bound to raise very different expectations in his audience, to heighten the incongruous juxtaposition of the ideal world with the actual, to lead to the reflection, "so nold nat I love purchace."

Troilus' comic ineptitude as a love-talker is symptomatic of his general social inflexibility; he plays the lover with a literal-mindedness which at times borders on the ludicrous. As Muscatine says, "he is *too* perfect." In his inability to distinguish game from earnest, his constant insensitivity to the ironies and ambiguities woven into the very fabric of the game of love, he exhibits just that "mechanical inelasticity" which Bergson has claimed to lie at the very heart of comedy. The feigned sickness, for instance, by which the first meeting at Deiphebus' house is engineered, exploits the common metaphor of love as a disease (and, as we have seen, such exploitation would have been familiar enough to the fourteenth-century audience from life, as well as literature), but there is a certain air of absurdity about the owlish solemnity with which Troilus insists that, in his case, the sickness is genuine: "For I am sik in ernest, douteles, / So that wel neigh I sterve for the peyne" (II, 1529–30). The game is no less a game merely because one of the players is incapable of seeing it as such, and one feels that Troilus well deserves Pandarus' laconic rejoinder:

> Thow shalt the bettre pleyne,
> And hast the lasse nede to countrefete,
> For hym men demen hoot that men seen swete.
> (II, 1531–33)

Two important instances of Troilus' literal-mindedness in the affairs of love remain to be cited; the first precipitates the farcical climax of the poem's first major movement, the second contributes significantly to the pathos of its tragic conclusion.

The scene in which Troilus is finally brought to his mistress' bed is one of sustained comic invention; in the solidity of its physical setting and in the string of misadventures which threaten to rob the action of its natural consummation, it reminds one more of a fabliau than an "old romaunce." Whether or not Criseyde believes her uncle's story about

3. *Le Roman de la Rose*, II, ed. E. Langlois, SATF (Paris: Firmin-Didot, 1920), p. 123 (l. 2406); cf. Andreas Capellanus: "there are men who in the presence of ladies so lose their power of speech that they forget the things they have carefully thought out and arranged in their minds; they cannot say anything coherent, and it seems proper to reprove their foolishness, for it is not fitting that any man, unless he be bold and well instructed, should enter into a conversation with ladies" *The Art of Courtly Love*, trans. J. J. Parry (1941; rpt. New York: W. W. Norton and Company, 1969), p. 36.

Horaste, we need not suppose that the lecture on the evils of jealousy which she reads her trembling lover is intended as anything other than a slightly theatrical assertion of her sovereignty. She concludes on a softer note, "of which I am right sory, but nought wroth" (III, 1044), and a more sophisticated lover than Troilus, alerted by her tone of conciliation, would have had little difficulty in winning back her grace. Troilus' social reflexes, however, are woefully inadequate for any such response; he sees only that he has unwittingly displeased her, and his bewilderment is appropriately expressed through the metaphor of a beaten schoolboy (III, 1067–68). He has been left alone to play a part in a game which he no longer understands, and in his frustration he turns against his absent mentor: " 'O Pandarus,' thoughte he, 'allas, thi wile / Serveth of nought, so weylaway the while!' " (III, 1077–78). Finally, he gives up the unequal struggle and swoons. Immediately the bedroom is filled with vigorous and farcical action, as Pandarus bundles his protégé into bed and strips off his clothes, whilst Criseyde "frots" his hands and temples. Few great love scenes can have had so inauspicious a beginning, and few great fictional lovers can have been shown in so undignified a position. The farcical elements should not, however, be allowed to obscure the important fact that it is Troilus' artless naïvety and not, ironically, Pandarus' legerdemain which, in the final analysis, opens up the way to Criseyde's bed.

A far less happy result of Troilus' insensitivity to the subtleties of the game of love arises from his very literal interpretation of the lover's duty of obedience to his lady. The absolute sovereignty of the mistress was a polite fiction of aristocratic courtship, but in an age whose theories of male superiority were stronger than our own, it must have seemed far more appropriate to the hall than the bedroom; the Wife of Bath's longing for "housbondes meeke . . . and fressh abedde" (1259) is, after all, a pipe-dream based upon a quite unresolvable contradiction in terms.[4] Troilus' inevitable sexual dominance over Criseyde is expressed in a memorable image: "What myghte or may the sely larke seye, / Whan that the sperhauk hath it in his foot?" (III, 1191–92). Such a situation should abrogate, or at least modify, all Criseyde's previous claims to lordship, yet, faced with her determination to leave Troy, Troilus duly acquiesces, against his better judgment, Pandarus' advice, and, as she later recognizes (V, 736–49), her own best interests. Though we may find the aspersions which are cast on Troilus' manliness (III, 1098 and 1126) comic in the context of the bedroom scene, there is a certain pathos in his later inability, in the face of a far more serious challenge, to "manly sette the world on six and sevene" (IV, 622). With a short-sightedness which is almost admirable, he sticks doggedly to the rules of a game which has ceased to have any further meaning, and refuses stubbornly to compromise with the demands of a larger world.

The picture of Troilus which I have drawn is not, I am aware, a very sympathetic one, and were there no more to him than this he would appear a scarcely more satisfactory lover for Criseyde than Diomede. *Troilus and Criseyde*, if it is not a tragedy in the full Aristotelian sense,

4. See R. E. Kaske, "Chaucer's Marriage Group," p. 48, in *Chaucer the Love Poet*, ed. J. Mitchell and W. Provost (Athens: Univ. of Georgia Press, 1973), pp. 45–65.

is at least generally recognized to be a serious poem, and that its hero should be no more than a socially inept buffoon is inconceivable. However mechanistic the medieval conception of tragedy, it does seem to have demanded a certain dignity in its heroes (when Midas finds his way into the *Fall of Princes* he leaves his furry ears behind), and Troilus is no exception.

What raises Troilus above the other players of the game is not style but integrity. For the Trojan nobility (or that of Westminster, Sheen, and Eltham, for that matter) love provides an amusing diversion: saying is one thing, doing, quite another (II, 43–44). For Troilus, it is an absolute code demanding his complete fidelity. Whilst sophisticated courtiers talk of dying for love (although, as Charles d'Orléans' English mistress remarks, "their graves are passing hard to spy"),[5] Troilus does so without duplicity; even after he has won his lady (when, for his less scrupulous counterparts there would be little point in maintaining the fiction), he can say to Pandarus:

> Thus hastow me no litel thing yyive.
> For which to the obliged be for ay
> My lif, and whi? For thorough thyn help I lyve,
> Or elles ded hade I ben many a day.
> (III, 1611–14)

Whilst glib love-talkers claim that they have been ennobled by their mistresses' love (although, as the Lady of the Tower remarks, "they done it only for to enhaunce them self / and for to drawe vnto them the grace and vayne glory of the world" [p. 164]), Troilus is clearly quite serious when he says:

> I not myself naught wisly what it is;
> But now I feele a newe qualitee,
> Yee, al another than I dide er this.
> (III, 1653–55)

What, above all, Troilus embodies is the quality of "trouthe," the one quality which, as we have said, prevents the game turning into anarchy. He was, the narrator tells us, "trewe as stiel in ech condicioun" (V, 831), and for his "moral vertu, grounded upon trouthe" (IV, 1672), Criseyde gave him her heart:

> Criseyde, al quyt from every drede and tene,
> As she that juste cause hadde hym to triste,
> Made hym swich feste, it joye was to seene,
> Whan she his trouthe and clene entente wiste;
> And as aboute a tree, with many a twiste,
> Bytrent and writh the swote wodebynde,
> Gan ech of hem in armes other wynde.
> (III, 1226–32)

Even when he can no longer hide from himself the brutal fact of Criseyde's treachery, Troilus cannot find it in his heart to "unloven" her a

---

5. "But many suche as ye in wordis dy / That passyng hard ther graffis ar to spy" *English Poems*, p. 177 (II. 5294–95).

quarter of a day (V, 1695–98). Like Don Quixote, Troilus lives in a fantasy world which comes to seem more real than the welter of meaningless trivia which surrounds it. Troilus is "sely" not merely in the sense that John the Carpenter is "sely," but with something of the innocence of the Prioress' "litel clergeoun." His innocence in a world of elaborate artificiality, his "trouthe" albeit to an illusion, are what win him the reward of laughter at the end of the poem.

Troilus' laugh from the eighth sphere is, at least in part, the laugh of one who has learnt by long experience the ephemeral nature of the game of love. It is a laugh of mature tolerance, far nobler than the worldly cynicism of a Pandarus or a Diomede. It is akin to the rueful smile of the narrator of the *Confessio Amantis*, who, having learnt at long last all the intricacies of the craft of love from his confessor Genius, looks in the glass and sees himself an old man:

> I stod amasid for a while,
> And in my self y gan to smyle
> Thenkende uppon the bedis blake,
> And how they weren me betake,
> For that y shulde bidde and preie.
> (VII, 2957–61)

The elegance and order of the game of love, truly played, is an attractive alternative to the chaos of a fallen world; that Troilus learns finally to relinquish it in favour of a higher order is an appropriate reminder to the "yonge, fresshe folkes" of Richard's court not to take the game, or themselves, too seriously.

KARLA TAYLOR

Proverbs and the Authentication of Convention in *Troilus and Criseyde*†

Writers have long found it natural to associate poets and lovers. Socrates links them in the *Phaedrus*, as does Theseus in *A Midsummer Night's Dream*. Petrarch's *rime* intertwine poetics and love and exhaust the implications of their relationship through the elusive figure of Laura. In his dream visions, Chaucer more often contrasts the two through the oft-noted duality of books and experience, as when *The House of Fame's* eagle chides him for being too "daswed" from reading to know anything about the world of love outside his library. In *The Parlement of Foules*, he again appears to separate books and love, the garden of love unfolding only after the book falls closed. Despite structural juxtaposition of the two spheres of concern, however, Chaucer on a subtler level conflates love and poetics from the opening line, which describes love with an

† From *Chaucer's Troilus: Essays in Criticism*, ed. Stephen A. Barney (Hamden: Archon Books, 1980), 277–96. Copyright © 1980 by Karla Taylor; all rights reserved. Reprinted by permission.

aphorism generally applied to the craft of poetry. The dream results directly from his reading,

> For out of olde feldes, as men seyth,
> Cometh al this newe corn from yer to yere,
> And out of olde bokes, in good feyth,
> Cometh al this newe science that men lere[1]

and the theme of poetics thus also invades the garden of love. In the debate, the cacaphony of avian perspectives raises questions *The Parlement* chooses not to answer, ultimately creating a disjunction between artistic and thematic resolution when the final roundel imposes an artificial veneer of harmony over the birds' dissension. This unsettling thematic irresolution, at odds with satisfying artistic closure, has led Robert Payne to note that Chaucer turns "the form and the substance of a poem into a mutual critique . . . consequently making of the whole an essay in poetics as well as a poem about its subject."[2]

The theme of poetics similarly pervades Chaucer's great love poem, *Troilus and Criseyde*. The poet often intrudes into his text to direct our attention to the process of composition ("translation"). Less overtly, he also weaves poetics into the fabric of the love story, as when Pandarus conceives the nascent love affair in words from Geoffrey of Vinsauf's *Poetria Nova*,[3] or advises Troilus in the craft of writing love epistles There is a vast difference in tone, but none at all in premeditated rhetorical design, between "Biblotte it with thi teris ek a lite" (II. 1027) and "Thise woful vers, that wepen as I write" (I. 7). So many of the lines which refer most immediately to the love affair also comment on the poem itself that this conflation of love and poetics constitutes an important aspect of the "idea" of *Troilus and Criseyde*.

The disjunction between artistic and thematic resolution we find in *The Parlement* is, if anything, more powerfully present and unsettling here. The poem's ending especially requires an act of faith so rigorously that it breaks the illusion, forcing us to reexamine the entire poem. My own search for resolution has led me to explore *Troilus and Criseyde*'s attitude toward language and the manner in which its self-conscious poetic informs and comments upon its treatment of love.

Mutability is the name of *Troilus and Criseyde*; hence, I will concentrate on matters of change and stability in its language. As in *The Parlement of Foules*—as well as in romance generally[4]—Chaucer moves to fix his poem in the continuous literary tradition embodied in his revered "olde bokes." He invokes the passage of time in order to lend history's authenticity to his story, and simultaneously attempts to overcome time by renewing Lollius's old book for his present audience. In *Troilus and Criseyde* more than anywhere else,[5] Chaucer also employs the country cousins of literary tradition, proverbs, which ordinarily reach us through

---

1. *Parlement of Foules*, II. 22–25. References are to *The Complete Works of Geoffrey Chaucer*, ed. F. N. Robinson, 2nd ed. (Boston: Houghton Mifflin, 1957).
2. Robert Payne, *The Key of Remembrance* (New Haven: Yale University Press, 1963), p. 144.
3. Robinson, notes, p. 818.
4. See Larry Benson's discussion of romance authentication in *Art and Tradition in Sir Gawain and the Green Knight* (New Brunswick, N.J.: Rutgers University Press, 1965), pp. 1–10.
5. B. J. Whiting, *Chaucer's Use of Proverbs*, Harvard Studies in Comparative Literature, Vol. XI (Cambridge, Mass.: Harvard University Press, 1934), p. 49.

the *Volksmund* rather than through transmission in written form. Conventional modes of oral expression can provide the same kind of stay against time and change as can written texts, and because proverbs represent an extreme form of convention, so petrified in form that they seem immutable, their treatment in the poem can illuminate the use of other traditional modes as well.

Past studies of *Troilus and Criseyde*'s proverbs, which concentrate on them as means of characterization, define the term so broadly as to include nearly any *sententia*.[6] Such breadth of definition, however, obscures the special linguistic phenomenon I wish to single out. Following more recent attempts to define *proverb*, I will focus not on the whole range of traditional sententious utterances, but on a narrower class, those *sententiae* involving metaphor, enabling them to comment by analogy on their contexts.[7]

Proverbs are crystallized statements of traditional wisdom which posit a logical relationship "mediating between two aspects of reality, two levels of classification."[8] They possess a peculiar linguistic status derived from the fact that, although they are syntagms whose content appears specific and unambiguous, they cannot be treated as such without comic effect or reduced meaning. Each term in a proverb—for example, *leopard* in "the leopard cannot change his spots"—is stable with respect to the rest of the sequence, and cannot be substituted for by any ordinarily available lexical alternative. The equally possible syntagm "the Holstein cow cannot change her spots" communicates a good deal less, in part because it lacks the weight of traditional use.[9] A proverb must be treated as a single significant unit, frozen and selected whole from the lexicon of all complete proverbial statements, rather than as an ordinary syntagm produced by the combinative freedom of the speaker. As a stereotypically fixed articulation, the proverb thus wavers on the threshold between speech and language, syntagm and system,[1] and its comforting authoritativeness stems from this ambiguous linguistic character. Because it is a syntagm, individual speakers "invent" a proverb each time they articulate it; but because the same articulation recurs frequently, it appears to describe a universal truth of nature which many have observed and remarked upon. Once selected, a proverb issues automatically, and hence seems outside human influence and more objective than ordinary sentences.

Nonetheless, proverbs do allow a certain amount of combinative freedom. Because they belong to the language system independent of their articulation in any specific instance, a speaker can allude to them in the same way he "alludes" to a noun with a pronoun. Thus he might say,

6. Whiting, pp. 48–75, and Robert M. Lumiansky, "The Function of Proverbial Monitory Elements in Chaucer's *Troilus and Criseyde*," *Tulane Studies in English*, 2 (1950): 5–48.
7. Barbara Kirshenblatt-Gimblett, "Toward a Theory of Proverb Meaning," *Proverbium*, 22 (1973), 821.
8. Nigel Barley, "A Structural Approach to the Proverb and Maxim, With Special Reference to the Anglo-Saxon Corpus," *Proverbium*, 20 (1972): 737.
9. Barley, p. 741, suggests that the entire proverb can be translated onto another level of diction, as for example, "birds of a feather flock together," or "fowl of similar plumage congregate together." Nonetheless, it seems to me that such a change considerably weakens the proverb's power, here by eliminating the poetic, pointed language of the original. See, however, below in this essay.
1. Roland Barthes, *Elements of Semiology*, trans. Annette Lavers and Colin Smith (New York: Hill and Wang, 1967, reprint ed., 1977), p. 19.

"You know about the leopard's spots," and although he does not state the proverb in its complete form, this does not inhibit its "automatic issue" as an essential underlying element. The full significance of his statement depends on a double mediation, for although he refers directly only to the proverb, the proverb in turn supplies the metaphoric analogy he wishes to make. Even the statement "the Holstein cow . . ." can acquire a significance beyond the literal, if speaker and listener understand it as an allusion to the traditional proverb whose structure is so similar. A proverb's form can change within certain limits as long as both parties understand it as the realization of a shared concept. The immutability in a proverb's form resides at the level of deep structure, a systemic concept which individual "performances" more or less realize—if less, then the speaker invokes the proverb by way of allusion, or as a proverbial phrase.

Despite a proverb's immutability at the level of deep structure, its meaning is not immutable. This results from its character as a specific, metaphoric statement describing another situation by analogy, a character distinguished from that of a maxim, which is a general, literal *sententia*. Both maxims and proverbs can comment on the same situation, as in the following example from Nigel Barley: Albert Smith, previously convicted of theft, has been caught stealing again. We can either invoke the general maxim "once a thief, always a thief," dispensing with metaphoric mediation, or we can comment, "The leopard cannot change his spots." The logical relationship the proverb posits is: leopard is to Albert Smith as spots are to criminality.[2] It acquires its authority by inviting us to derive, from two examples, a general law of nature. Proverb and maxim demand different responses; if we accord both formulations the same treatment, we react to the proverb as Judy Holliday did in *Born Yesterday*: "Of course not—they're right there, in his fur!" This comic failure to acknowledge the analogy disrupts the proverb's power, reducing it to a literal, purely syntagmatic statement which is not only too obvious for words, but also irrelevant.

In this example, both maxim and proverb apply equally well to the recidivist thief Albert Smith. However, if we take the case of Kate Thomas, an unregenerate slob who has once again failed in her New Year's resolution to reform her slovenly habits, we can no longer say, "Once a thief, always a thief." The maxim's general statement refers only to those it describes literally—thieves. But we can still shake our heads and say, "The leopard cannot change his spots;" the same proverb easily encompasses both situations, even with the change in gender. This is possible because, although we can manipulate a proverb's form only within limits, its meaning depends on the context which evokes it.

Conversely, a proverb may create as well as describe a situation, since it exists in the language prior to any particular articulation. Albert Smith may relapse into thievery because he has already identified himself as the leopard incapable of changing his spots. Or if he is in fact innocent, falsely accused on the basis of incriminating circumstantial evidence, the proverb offers a convenient, familiar—and prejudicial—framework

2. Barley, pp. 739–40.

conditioning the observer's perceptions. Though Smith is innocent, belief in the proverb may cause justice to light upon him as the likely suspect, and his subsequent conviction circularly confirms the authority of the old saying which influenced it. The proverb thus becomes a self-fulfilling expectation.

Since a proverb varies its meaning according to context, it betrays slightly the stability promised by its fixed form. Because, then, a sort of treachery inheres in proverbs, when we find them—as we do in *Troilus and Criseyde*—"as 'slydyng of corage' as ever Criseyde was,"[3] it is not Chaucer's peculiar invention. Proverbs by their nature betray the expectations of stability they arouse, and the regularity with which they do so here bespeaks the poet's perception and exploitation of proverbial language's semantic slippage in order to comment on language in general. In transmitting traditional forms of expression, Chaucer seeks not only to validate "truth by finding it in the past and making it live in the present,"[4] but also to warn us of the limitations of this endeavor.

Chaucer exploits this semantic slippage most clearly in the variations on a single proverb, and on a set of catalogues expressed in proverbial language. My first example appears at I. 257–58: "The yerde is bet that bowen wole and wynde / Than that that brest." These words, or allusions to the proverb they represent, recur so frequently that they become a *Leitmotif* in the poem. Here the poet, considering the inescapable power of Love, offers two possible descriptions of the shortly to be smitten Troilus. He can be either the wood that breaks, if he tries to withstand Love's inexorable attack, or the flexible wood that survives by bending, if he succumbs. The second alternative is clearly more desirable, and because Troilus does indeed succumb, he defines himself here as the wood that bends.

The next reference to the proverb changes the image slightly, but not the fundamental structure or concept:

> And reed that boweth down for every blast,
> Ful lightly, cesse wynd, it wol aryse;
> But so nyl nought an ook, whan it is cast . . .
>
> (II. 1387–89)

The comparison between a flexible survivor and a stiff victim remains, although a reed and an oak tree replace the two "yerdes." More important, however, the contextual reference has shifted as well as the desirable alternative, for the image offers two descriptions of Criseyde. She can either bend but never break, never yielding to Troilus's advances; or she can seem unbending until she finally gives way altogether, becoming Troilus's mistress. Up to this point Troilus has met with little success in breeching the lady's defenses, and Pandarus wants the second alternative to assure his friend that, if he perseveres, Criseyde will eventually capitulate. Combining this with the first realization of the proverb, we can see a developing distinction: Troilus is the reed (or "yerde") that bends and Criseyde is the oak that falls.

Thus Pandarus. But the poet begins to have other ideas which com-

---

3. Payne, p. 211.
4. Payne, p. 175.

plicate the facile distinction I have just made. Shortly before Pandarus defines Criseyde in such comforting—and wishful—terms, the poet describes the growth of Troilus's desire with several proverbial analogies, including:

> Or as an ook comth of a litel spir,
> So thorugh this lettre, which that she hym sente,
> Encressen gan desir, of which he brente.   (II. 1335–37)

This is our familiar "Great oaks from little acorns grow," modulated slightly to sustain the basic opposition between a great stiff stick and a small flexible one. But here Troilus is an oak grown out of his former sapling state, and through the juxtaposition of "Thorugh more wode or col, the more fir" (II. 1332), he is an oak threatened with conflagration. Chaucer thus qualifies the optimistic reference to Criseyde as an oak ripe for the axe before Pandarus makes it.

As one would expect of a central image, our opposed pair reappears at the consummation in Book III:

> And as aboute a tree, with many a twiste,
> Bytrent and writh the swote wodebynde,
> Gan ech of hem in armes other wynde.   (III. 1230–32)

Though this is not precisely an allusion to the original proverb, the diction—tree, wode-, -bynde, wynde—forces us to connect it to the other related images I have cited. Here at the moment of stasis, the zenith before the poem's declining action, the image also reaches a state of equilibrium. Unlike earlier instances, it makes no opposed identifications. Instead it is a picture of mutuality, sustaining the ambiguity which arose when Troilus grew into an oak, not sixty lines before Criseyde became one too.

The final transformation of the proverb occurs in Book IV. When Troilus returns from the parliamentary decision to exchange Criseyde for Antenor, the poet describes him with an image from Dante:[5]

> And as in wynter leves ben biraft,
> Ech after other, til the tree be bare,
> So that ther nys but bark and braunche ilaft,
> Lith Troilus, byraft of ech welfare,
> Ibounden in the blake bark of care . . .   (IV. 225–29)

Again, the image alludes to rather than states the proverb, but when Troilus is thus clearly bound in a tree, it supplies a new reference for the matrix of language originally invoked by "The yerde is bet that bowen wole and wynde / Than that that brest." If Troilus has finally put down roots, then Criseyde, although the poem does not state it in so many words, finally becomes the bending reed, surviving each storm because of her lack of firmness. But what are we to do with the proverb, which seemed so clear and authoritative when it first appeared? Its clarity depends on isolating a moment in the narrative, but we cannot choose

---

5. Robinson, in his note to these lines, p. 828, cites the first three as an allusion to the *Inferno*, iii. 12 ff. But the last two lines also recall the Pier della Vigne episode in xiii, where the Emperor's councillor is metamorphosed into a tree because of his despair.

to see the analogy as the characters do, in terms of action in time. For us, as for the poet, the entire cumulative text—beginning, middle, and end—exists simultaneously, transcending the gradual unfolding of meaning. The transformations in reference the proverb undergoes cause us to distrust it, wherever it appears, as a figure pretending to stability, calling upon a venerable tradition which crystallizes its structure—but not its meaning. It is an example of a failed attempt to secure stability through traditional language.

Both the attempt to secure stability through traditional language and the failure of that attempt are aspects of a deliberate poetic strategy in *Troilus and Criseyde*. When Chaucer bids his poem farewell, he includes a plea for the preservation of his text: "So prey I God that non myswrite the, / Ne the mysmetre for defaute of tonge" (V. 1795–96). Exact transmission and order of a poetic text are crucial to its meaning, but the act of making such a plea implies a recognition that change and instability in language are likely.[6] The poet demonstrates the importance of order to meaning with a set of catalogues, once again expressed in proverbial language, which seek to establish in metaphor a relationship between fixed natural phenomena and the course of the love affair. Each catalogue comments optimistically on the ascending action, but Chaucer realizes its potential for reversal when he transposes the order of terms or shifts the context in the descending action of the last two books. In the midst of Troilus's first sorrow, his lovesickness for Criseyde, Pandarus attempts to exorcise despair with:

> "For thilke grownd that bereth the wedes wikke
> Bereth ek thise holsom herbes, as ful ofte
> Next the foule netle, rough and thikke,
> The rose waxeth swoote and smothe and softe;
> And next the valeye is the hil o-lofte;
> And next the derke nyght the glade morwe;
> And also joie is next the fyn of sorwe." (I. 946–52)

Immediately before Troilus faints in Book III, the poet anticipates the imminent transformation of abject failure into success with a similar list:

> But now help God to quenchen al this sorwe!
> So hope I that he shal, for he best may.
> For I have seyn, of a ful misty morwe
> Folowen ful ofte a myrie someris day;
> And after wynter foloweth grene May.
> Men sen alday, and reden ek in stories,
> That after sharpe shoures ben victories. (III. 1058–64)

By offering the cycles of nature as metaphors for the course of the love affair, this string of proverbs makes the reversal of fortune seem inevi-

---

6. Perhaps we can divide the conflicting impulses and attribute the attempt to fix language to Chaucer in his pose as the redactor of Lollius, and the sober recognition of futility to Chaucer *in propria persona*; but I think such a distinction would be too facile. What are we to do with passages such as this one in which both impulses are simultaneously present, one implying the other, and indeed so intertwined that it is impossible to separate them? The difficulty of making such a distinction has led me in this argument to equate poet and narrator; although I am in general agreement with the now traditional separation between Chaucer and his narrative *personae*, it does not seem pertinent here.

table. A low point is but a prelude to a high one. But once again, proverbial language proves treacherous; by invoking cycles as analogues to the story, the words also imply their own inversion. It is equally true that after day comes night, winter follows summer, and victories often evaporate in the renewal of strife. What transpires later in *Troilus and Criseyde* serves only to emphasize the double potential of these proverbs. Their apparent fixity of meaning is compromised in Book IV, when Pandarus, offering his ineffectual consolations "for the nones alle" (IV. 428), uses the same words to convey precisely the opposite advice:

> "For also seur as day comth after nyght,
> The newe love, labour, or oother wo,
> Or elles selde seynge of a wight,
> Don olde affecciouns alle over-go."
>
> (IV. 421–25)

Proverbs cannot transfer the stability of fixed natural cycles to the love affair—a metaphorical analogy is after all nothing more than a verbal act—but they succeed in arousing Troilus's expectation of the immutability they seem to promise. Promising so much, they must inevitably disappoint, and when Chaucer puts an end to the illusion he himself perpetrated, its unreality is starkly evident:

> The day goth faste, and after that com eve,
> And yet com nought to Troilus Criseyde.   (V. 1142–43)

After these lines, we can no longer deny that analogies first proposed by verbal fiat can be disposed of in the same manner. Proverbs are apt not to describe reality as it is, but only as we wish it to be. They operate in the optative mode, for the relationship Chaucer reveals in them, taking with one hand what he gives with the other, is not that between love and nature, but that between love and the element of desire implicit in the language we use to formulate reality.

In this context, let us return for a moment to the point at which Criseyde becomes an oak, a passage extraordinary for the conspicuousness of its rhetoric:

> "Peraunter thynkestow: though it be so,
> That Kynde wolde don hire to bygynne
> To have a manere routhe upon my woo,
> Seyth Daunger, 'Nay, thow shalt me nevere wynne!'
> So reulith hire hir hertes gost withinne,
> That though she bende, yeet she stant on roote;
> What in effect is this unto my boote?
>
> "Thenk here-ayeins: whan that the stordy ook,
> On which men hakketh ofte, for the nones,
> Receyved hath the happy fallyng strook,
> The greete sweigh doth it come al at ones,
> As don thise rokkes or thise milnestones;
> For swifter course comth thyng that is of wighte,
> Whan it descendeth, than doth don thynges lighte.

"And reed that boweth down for every blast,
Ful lightly, cesse wynd, it wol aryse;
But so nyl nought an ook, whan it is cast;
It nedeth me nought the longe to forbise."   (II. 1373–90)

By introducing the first half of the proverbial comparison with "peraun-
ter," Pandarus identifies it as a rhetorical "opposite" to be discarded
when he proposes the second half. This kind of rhetorical structure
arouses strong expectations; as soon as we read "peraunter," we know
that "thenk here-ayeins" will eventually follow. When Cicero writes "*non
solo*," one can rest assured that "*sed etiam*" will complete his thought,
and when a sonneteer begins his octave with "when," one expects the
sestet to begin with "then." A poet can play with these expectations. An
excellent example is Shakespeare's Sonnet 29, in which he postpones
"then" until a line and a half into the sestet, thus bringing the reader's
desire for rhetorical fulfillment to such a pitch that when it finally comes,
his spirit, out of pure relief, soars "like to the lark at break of day arising."
Here, Pandarus arouses the same expectations in Troilus, and strength-
ens his rhetorical structure with proverbial language, which itself con-
tains a strong element of desire. What prevents the argument from
convincing absolutely is its purely verbal nature. In addition to the
emphatic rhetorical structure, Pandarus adorns the argument with per-
sonifications. And curiously, amidst all the words, Criseyde disappears.
The bending-reed-opposite clearly refers to her, but thereafter, not even
a pronoun connects her to rhetorical fulfillment. Formally, structure and
proverb mime arousal and fulfillment of desire, but this verbal process
can be extended to reality outside words only by an act of faith. Pandarus
does not say, "Criseyde *is* an oak," he merely suggests, "Think of it rather
this way." Troilus believes because he wants to, but Chaucer, by stress-
ing the fictive, rhetorical nature of the passage, asks us to consider
whether its formal fulfillment can be extended beyond words. And in an
act parallel to his retraction of a relationship between natural cycles and
the love affair, he shows that there is no necessary connection when he
makes Criseyde ultimately more similar to a bending reed than a sturdy
oak.

To summarize: the stability proverbial language promises is doubly
deceptive, because the same words can mean various things in various
contexts, and because the relationship to reality they propose is not
direct, but mediated by desire. Chaucer stresses the same elements in
other conventional manners of speaking, especially the poetic words of
love, which seek to fix experience by supplying a stable context of verbal
tradition. These traditions constitute a lexicon like that of proverbs, and
the inherent mutability of proverbs also marks the conventions which
appropriate the language of religion and the hunt to describe the love
affair between Troilus and Criseyde.

Pandarus, who knows the "olde daunce," teaches Troilus the words
which portray love as a religious experience. But he finds himself sud-
denly out of control just as his schemes verge on success. As Troilus
waits in the secret stew, Pandarus bids him make ready, "For thow shalt
in to hevene blisse wende" (III. 704), then adding, "this nyght shal I

make it weel, / Or casten al the gruwel in the fire" (III. 710–11). Troilus's response, a prayer for "hevene blisse," shows how thoroughly the parodic language of religion has shaped his conception of love. In Troilus's eyes, Criseyde is a goddess who bestows grace, and whose presence defines the meaning of his entire world. Love becomes the Beatific Vision in his hymn at III. 1261ff., a passage imitated from Bernard's prayer in the *Paradiso* (Canto xxxiii). Pandarus understands the nature of *amour courtois*: its conventions are fiction, or literally lies.[7] Only figuratively can a mortal woman be a goddess, and when a lover expresses his feelings in such terms, he refracts objective reality through the prism of his desire. But Troilus does not use the conventions merely in a manner of speaking; believing, as it appears, in a natural link between *res* and *verbum*, he treats the two as commutative terms. However, he is a character in a poem where this relationship is problematic, where language as convention rather than ideal is a theme.[8] In his desire for transcendence, he reifies the fiction and confounds words with the reality they only indirectly represent.

Attempting to create a reality to match the verbal image, Troilus creates instead a burden too heavy for any mortal love to bear. His religious language is a convention abstracted from its original context, and as we know from proverbs, contextual shift signals mutability. Although Troilus tries thereby to make his love transcendent of time and place, to seize the day and fix it eternally, the unfixed nature of his language— along with his blind trust—betrays him. In a sense, this traditional form of love discourse causes the tragic end of the story by arousing expectations it cannot fulfill. Through his language Troilus seeks to achieve the stability of the ideal; instead, he makes the comparative inadequacy of the real stand out the more sharply.

The same reversal—poetic description confounded with the thing described—is also at work in another convention, love as the hunt. By shaping action and response after its own image, this convention creates rather than describes the course of events. Troilus is a bird of prey, a noble falcon who catches his victim; and "What myghte or may the sely larke seye, / Whan that the sperhauk hath it in his foot?" (III. 1191–92). Much of what goes wrong in the love affair can be traced to this attitude toward love, arising out of the conventions of artistic language. Hunt imagery determines that the men pursue Criseyde without much regard for her desires and fears, and she responds like a chased animal, postponing the inevitable for as long as possible.

In Criseyde's second courtship, Chaucer again exploits the duplicity of conventional language by reusing the same elements in a different

7. Norman E. Eliason, *The Language of Chaucer's Poetry: An Appraisal of the Verse, Style and Structure*, Anglistica 17 (Copenhagen: Rosenhild and Bagger, 1972), pp. 126–34.
8. Susan Schibanoff, in "Argus and Argive: Etymology and Characterization in Chaucer's *Troilus*," *Speculum* 51 (1976): 657, says: "In his *Troilus*, a poem which consists much more of words than of action, Chaucer seems preoccupied with the conventional aspects of language, and with the attempts of the two lovers to probe the realities behind the words which had, by common usage and agreement, become the highly codified language of love. That words fail miserably to communicate realities, or that the people of *Troilus* fail miserably to detect the truths they represent, is poignantly symbolized in the lover's realization that Criseyde's absence will be permanent: Troilus accepts the fact that Criseyde's 'name of trouthe/Is now fordon' (V. 1686–687) not because of Cassandra's words, but because of the undeniable implications of a material object—Criseyde's brooch torn from Diomede's cloak."

context. We are alerted to the lexical similarities by repetition of a maxim, previously uttered by Pandarus: "Unknowe, unkist, and lost, that is unsought" (I. 809), and by Criseyde: "He which that nothing undertaketh, / Nothyng n'acheveth" (II. 807–808). Diomede's version echoes Criseyde's: "For he that naught n'assaieth, naught n'acheveth" (V. 784). The poet recalls the convention of love as hunt when Diomede considers

> How he may best, with shortest taryinge,
> Into his net Criseydes herte brynge.
> To this entent he koude nevere fyne;
> To fisshen hire, he leyde out hook and line. (V. 774–77)

The hunt seems embedded in the prehistory of the poem, enabling Cassandra to interpret Troilus's dream correctly by establishing Diomede's descent from Meleager, the mythological slayer of the Calydonian boar. Diomede's promises resemble Troilus's previous oath of service, and in this relationship as well, the lovers exchange (the same) jewelry. Language and action are essentially the same, if speedier, as when Troilus woos Criseyde—but for all the similarity, most readers find the two courtships very different. This results from a paradox of conventional language; when Troilus expresses himself with the time-honored words of *amour courtois*, we would gladly believe in the permanence he seeks to achieve by linking his love with tradition. Yet when Diomede uses the same words, precisely because they are conventional, he casts a shadow of mutability on the stability Troilus thought to guarantee. At this point in the poem, many readers pore back over the development of Criseyde's character, searching for clues of the emotional instability that would make her infidelity comprehensible. It is unlikely, however, that Chaucer intends full psychological realism here. Criseyde's betrayal was in the story as he found it; to this he adds a second betrayal, that of the conventional language of love. In giving Troilus and Diomede the same words to express their feelings, Chaucer confronts us with the impossibility of Troilus's idealist treatment of language. The words of love are conventions which mean only what we can agree that they mean; just as with proverbs, their significance is relative to context—speaker, listener, the worsening political circumstances in Troy—and their fixed form derives not so much from true semantic stability as from our desire for such an absolute relationship to reality: *ut nomina consequentia rerum sint.*

Troilus and Criseyde thus expresses a profoundly ambivalent attitude toward conventional love language. On one hand, religious parody exalts the love affair, embellishing it with the lovely poetic fiction of *amour courtois*: the use of convention in general, because of its history of repetition, mimes timelessness. Troilus seeks connection to the ideal and the timeless through convention, but his attempt imperils an inevitably imperfect human love, for the formative power of conventional language consists only in constituting his sights of what is possible. Mistaking the flexible reed of poetry for a sturdy oak, he expects the affair to take its nature from the words of love. But conventions derive their meaning from cumulative usage, and the meaning of love in this poem resides in the *relation* of convention to the new context supplied here. Criseyde recognizes the change her history works on tradition when she laments, "O, rolled shal I ben on many a tonge!" (V. 1061)—she becomes a new *topos* embodying not the correspondence between convention and context Troilus expected, but the difference. On this level, *Troilus and Criseyde* is about both the desire to fix an inherently mortal, transitory love permanently, and the impossibility of fulfilling that desire. When the poet proclaims as his purpose to help lovers to "pleyne," he refers to information not only about the steps of the "olde daunce," but also about the traps which await us if we begin to believe literally that love is the same thing as conventional love language.

It is now time to turn the tables and see what Chaucer's treatment of the love affair reveals about his poetic, for I think it a matter of reciprocal illumination. One of the most interesting recent articles on *Troilus and Criseyde* traces the parallels between Pandarus and the poet himself.[9] Just as Chaucer poses as an unsuccessful lover and servant to love's servants, so Pandarus, likewise unsuccessful, becomes such a servant by mediating between Troilus and Criseyde. In order to join potential lovers, Chaucer forges a link between his English audience and Lollius's old Latin history, and in general Pandarus's use of oral wisdom parallels the poet's use of written authority, "olde bokes." Chaucer constructs a poem to accomplish his historical and amatory mediations in which he follows the precepts of rhetorical theory, just as Pandarus, taking his cue from the same text—the *Poetria Nova*—constructs his own poem, the love affair. Given the analogous roles played by the two artists, it is not surprising that when Pandarus describes his part in furthering love, his words often have a double reference. They pertain not only to the immediate narrative context, but also to the poem as a whole. For example, leaping in to discover Troilus suffering in the throes of terminal lovesickness, Pandarus unleashes a barrage of proverbs, including: "I have myself ek seyn a blynd man goo / Ther as he fel that couthe loken wyde" (I. 628–29). This not only advertises Pandarus's skills as advisor to the lovesick, but also validates the poet's mediation. When Chaucer uses the same idea to rationalize his own inadequacies as a redactor ("A blynd man kan nat juggen wel in hewis," II. 21), he modifies it to include a pun on the colors of rhetoric, and so reinforces the analogies between Pandarus and poet, love affair and poem.

Why would Chaucer wish to incorporate into the text a poet-surrogate whose similarity comes at precisely the points where he ultimately fails, the furtherance of love and the attempt to fix experience in a stable context of authority? Through Pandarus, proverb-wielder and poet whose text is a love affair, Chaucer extends the instability clinging to the shifting reference of proverbs, and to the love affair itself, to his own artistic endeavor. Significantly, the poet participates fully in the conventional modes of expression whose equivocation he exploits. The loss of control Pandarus experiences in the latter portion of the poem is analogous to Chaucer's role as a translator who has no control over the text, who must tell the story of "how that Criseyde Troilus forsook, / Or at

9. E. T. Donaldson, "Chaucer's Three 'P's': Pandarus, Pardoner, and Poet," *Michigan Quarterly Review* 14 (1975): 282–301.

the leeste, how that she was unkynde" (IV. 15–16).[1] The poet describes his ambivalent relationship to his own poem most succinctly in his comment on Troilus's refusal to divulge the name of his beloved:

> For it is seyd, "man maketh ofte a yerde
> With which the maker is hymself ybeten
> In sondry manere . . ."
>
> (I. 740–42)

Chaucer is a maker, his poem the "yerde" (remember the flexible reed, or "yerde," of poetry) by which he is himself beaten. What so peculiarly disturbs us about Criseyde's second courtship is the betrayal of the conventional language with which Troilus had thought to secure permanence, and Chaucer's problem is the same. The instability which troubles him most deeply is not simply that of a mortal love affair, but that of his poetic language, his medium for drawing together the past tradition of "olde bokes," the present, and, he hopes, the future of that tradition. His solution is to go between the horns of the dilemma—dependence on his poetic language and simultaneous recognition of its mutability—by incorporating into the text a metalanguage in which the image of Troilus's and Criseyde's love refers to *Troilus and Criseyde* itself. Writing both sides of the dilemma into his text as a matter of thematic concern may not guarantee resolution, but Chaucer in a sense exorcises his devil by exposing it.

The mutual mutability of love and language conditions *Troilus and Criseyde*'s relationship to literary tradition. Chaucer's exhortation to his poem to "kis the steppes, where as thow seest pace / Virgile, Ovide, Omer, Lucan and Stace" (V. 1791–92) is analogous to the lovers' desire to fix their love permanently through conventional language. Throughout the poem (as indeed elsewhere in his writings), Chaucer seeks extratextual authentication, both in Lollius's old history and in the more recent literary tradition of Dante and Petrarch. Both elements inform the central passage on authentication, Book II's proem, which opens:

> Owt of this blake wawes for to saylle,
> O wynd, o wynd, the weder gynneth clere;
> For in this see the boot hath swych travaylle;
> Of my connyng, that unneth I it steere.
>
> (II. 1–4)

The conceit refers to the monumental effort required to write the poem (particularly for the inept poet Chaucer claims to be), but by postponing "of my connyng" to 1.4, the poet allows us to think at first that it refers to the love affair. Although he imitated these lines from Dante (*Purgatorio* i. 1–3), Chaucer would have found the *topos* in Petrarch as well, and in fact the *rime* give him a precedent for using conventional love language to talk about poetry. Typically, the Petrarchan poet/lover seeks union with Laura, who among other things is the laurel, a symbol for poetic immortality. By locating his poem in this particular tradition,

---

1. Again, Donaldson is best on the narrator's growing pain and helplessness in the last two books; see "The Ending of Troilus," in *Speaking of Chaucer* (London: Athlone Press, 1970), pp. 84–101.

Chaucer tells us why he needs its support: he too desires poetic immortality.

But he cannot rest easy with joining *Troilus and Criseyde* to a tradition which will help preserve it; seeking the poetic laurel does not guarantee that one will find it. In the rest of the proem, Chaucer discusses the problems he faces in saving ancient written tradition from time's oblivion—his own ignorance and changes in language and custom generally which might interfere with his mediation:

> Ye knowe ek that in form of speche is chaunge
> Withinne a thousand yeer, and wordes tho
> That hadden pris, now wonder nyce and straunge
> Us thinketh hem, and yet thei spake hem so,
> And spedde as wel in love as men now do . . .
>
> (II. 22–26)

Primarily, these lines ask his audience's indulgence for Lollius's old-fashionedness, but they also have a more proleptic significance. Chaucer's real concern is the same one implicit in his plea for the future of his own text, the fear that mutability in language will preclude Troilus and Criseyde's participation in the immortality of literary tradition.

If it weren't for the ambiguous figure of Lollius, we could consider this merely a modesty *topos*, the apology an inverted assertion of authenticity. Chaucer appeals to Clio, the muse of history, and even problems in transmission imply that transmission takes place. But the proem touches on a problem of deep concern: survival of a text is possible only by anchoring it in tradition, and Chaucer sees every word he writes qualifying that tradition, thus prefiguring the fate of his own text. Perhaps the failure to admit *Il Filostrato* as a source is "anxiety of influence," but I think a more distinct artistic purpose conditions the choice. While insisting on the need for authenticity, Chaucer quite deliberately pulls the rug out from under himself by basing his authentication on a fiction. To transmit old history is to assert the permanence of literary tradition through repetition. Of course, since Lollius never wrote a history, none could have survived for Chaucer to translate. If he believed that there once had been such a text, however, it would be the perfect example of the transience of language. His redaction would then constitute mediation between present and not only things past, but something passed entirely out of existence and mediating memory. The fiction of Lollius embodies the problematic authenticating endeavor more resonantly than admission of a newer, surviving source could have done. On this level, *Troilus and Criseyde* is about the poet's desire for permanence and stability in the medium he depends on, and the impossibility of fulfilling that desire because of the fundamental mutability of language.

I am dissatisfied with this essay because its dispassionate analysis cannot convey the sadness and poignancy of the situation it attempts to describe, that of a poet who has recognized the final and inescapable limitations of his language. I can try once more by extending the analogy between poem and love affair. Chaucer's attitude toward his poem is much the same as his attitude toward Criseyde: both affairs must eventually disappoint because of the "slydyng corage" of their participants.

Chaucer loves Criseyde, the "hevenyssh perfit creature" (I. 104), but he must finally and reluctantly admit that she is neither heavenly nor perfect, only extraordinarily lovely and lovable. Moreover, Chaucer's bittersweet relationship to poetry resembles the attitudes of both Troilus and Pandarus toward Criseyde. Pandarus, clearly a poet, plays on Criseyde as Chaucer does with the words he gives his stand-in, taking obvious joy in prodding her into conformity with his will. Yet at the end, no longer able to manipulate her, he can say, "I hate, ywys, Cryseyde" (V. 1732). Here Chaucer follows instead his second poet-figure, Troilus, who makes poetry through the mediation of Petrarch, whose words he speaks in his first lyric. As a Petrarchan lover, Troilus dons the mask of the poet who desires immortality of love and language. Just before the consummation, he prays to (among others) Apollo, the god of poetry, for aid:

> O Phebus, thynk whan Dane hireselven shette
> Under the bark, and laurer wax for drede,
> Yet for hire love, O help now at this nede!
>
> (III. 726–28)

The story of Apollo and Daphne constitutes a summation of the process of pursuit embedded in *Troilus and Criseyde*. Troilus's use of myth, like the use of proverbs and conventional language throughout the poem, stems from the desire to capture experience in the timeless repetition of traditional words. But by building this particular myth so integrally into his text, Chaucer shows the equivocation of formal, verbal stability. In the poem as a whole, he uses apparently stable conventions to talk about mutability, just as this myth disjoins its acquired fixity of form from its content—metamorphosis. The story does indeed immortalize Apollo's love, but in the form of a pursuit which can never succeed. Like Troilus's other attempts to fix Criseyde in the safe confines of tree-ness, it describes his desire rather than her essence; it is Troilus who later becomes "Ibounden in the blake bark of care." The myth also represents the desire for the poetic laurel which Petrarch embodied in Laura, and, I believe, Chaucer in Criseyde.[2] By analogies of this sort, Chaucer too becomes a crashing oak, failing always to fix the bending reed of his poetry. Troilus's helpless sorrow when he can no longer deny Criseyde's metamorphosis also represents Chaucer's final attitude toward his own faithless bride of poetry:

> . . . and I ne kan nor may,
> For al this world, withinne myn herte fynde
> To unloven yow a quarter of a day!
> In corsed tyme I born was, weilaway,
> That yow, that doon me al this wo endure,
> Yet love I best of any creature!
>
> (V. 1696–1701)

I am reminded of George Herbert's palinode, "The Forerunners," which describes his relationship to poetry as a marriage of equivocal worth. His

---

2. Schibanoff (note 8 above) states that, in contrast to her parents' names, Criseyde's name plays no role in determining her character, destiny, or symbolic value. This bit of Greek may not have been available to Chaucer, but it is an interesting coincidence, if nothing more, that Criseyde's name means "daughter of gold," linking her to one of the puns Petrarch makes on Laura: *l'oro*.

rejection notwithstanding, however, what speaks most strongly in that poem, as here, is Herbert's love of the words which fail him:

> Farewell sweet phrases, lovely metaphors,
> But will ye leave me thus?
>
> . . .
>
> Lovely enchanting language, sugar-cane,
> Hony of roses, whither wilt thou flie?[3]

Chaucer offers two escapes from this impasse at the end of *Troilus and Criseyde*. The first is silence, the route taken by his two surrogates. When Pandarus leaves the stage, his last words are "I kan namore seye" (V. 1743), and when Troilus's soul is translated out of "this litel spot of erthe" (V. 1815), he leaves behind not only love but also language. He says nothing, and his final destination is not recorded in words. The second solution Chaucer offers is to ground language in the only power capable of transcending all change and referential shifts, the Christian Word so markedly absent from the pagan world of the rest of the poem. Following the same impulse that motivates the Retraction at the end of the *Canterbury Tales*, Chaucer chooses this second course, ending the poem with a prayer to the Trinity. In both cases the poet dissociates himself from the equivocal language of mortals, because the fundamental nature of human love and human poetry is tied to this sublunary world. The flowers of rhetoric are as any other worldly flowers, of which Chaucer writes: "Al nys but a faire, / This world, that passeth soone as floures faire" (V. 1840–41). They cannot transcend their own limitations, and I think it is for this reason that the concluding prayer describes the Trinity as "uncircumscript." Its nature, resolving all change in an all-encompassing unity, is beyond the scope of this poet to write about, and as the poem ends, he too falls silent.

LEE PATTERSON

Troilus and Criseyde and the Subject of History†

> "He believed that nothing can be finally known that involves human motive and need. There is always another level, another secret, a way in which the heart breeds a deception so mysterious and complex it can only be taken for a deeper kind of truth."

In the late fourteenth as in the late twentieth century, Chaucer's *Troilus and Criseyde* attracts attention for reasons that go far beyond its famous tale of love betrayed, however engrossing at the level of psychological realism. In rewriting Boccaccio's romance, Chaucer was, to be sure, engaging the erotic literature of contemporary aristocratic society. But

---

3. George Herbert, "The Forerunners," ll. 12–13, 19–20, in *The Works of George Herbert*, ed. F. E. Hutchinson (Oxford at the Clarendon Press, 1941, reprint ed., 1970), p. 176.
† From *Chaucer and the Subject of History* (Madison: University of Wisconsin Press, 1991), pp. 84–99, 104–114, 137–155, 161–64. Reprinted by permission.

his poem went far beyond the *Filostrato* in exploring the idea of antiquity—not in its own right precisely (whatever that might mean) but rather for what it could tell him about his own place in historical time. For Chaucer, the story of Troilus and Criseyde was a definitive moment in the founding myth of Western history in the Middle Ages, the myth of Trojan origins. And as a poem of origins, the *Troilus* was by definition available to a meditation upon the nature of history per se.

The context of that meditation was, initially, the contest between Augustinianism, with its supervening transcendentalism, and the late-medieval counterimpulse to preserve and create a secular historiography. The linked genres by which this secular tradition could be carried were legendary history and romance, narrative forms that allowed for a more ambitious program than "literature" is sometimes thought capable of sustaining. But when Chaucer embarked on his own essay into the philosophy of history, he soon discovered that the project was fraught with internal contradictions. Nor was it only history-as-event whose unanticipated difficulties Chaucer staged in the poem; it was also history-as-story. For the *translatio verborum* by which the text of history was rewritten proved to be as errant as the line of descent posited by the translation of empire itself.

The second context of Chaucer's project, both enabling and disabling, was Christian spiritualism's opposite—the resistance to human praxis of the material conditions of medieval life. The sheer inertia of medieval society, its difficulty in imagining and fulfilling specific historical programs, encouraged the Middle Ages to conceptualize progress not as the directed advancement toward a future goal but as the recovery of a golden past. Change was experienced as loss, development understood as reformation.[1] It is in "the former age," as Chaucer calls it, when men's "hertes were al oon," that value is to be found; "cursed was the tyme" when men embarked upon the civilizing ventures that have brought them only "doublenesse, and tresoun, and envye, / Poyson, manslawhtre, and mordre in sondry wyse."[2] This yearning for an original, unitary state, uninfected by "doublenesse," is a profoundly and pervasively Chaucerian theme and nowhere more extensively than in the *Troilus*. It must have been given special urgency for Chaucer by the disasters of the 1380s. For this was a decade that saw alarming threats to the kingdom from both within (the Rising of 1381) and without (the anticipated French invasion of 1386, the victory of the Scots at Otterburn in 1388); that witnessed an unnerving increase in both the military incompetence of the ruling class (the Despenser crusade of 1383, Richard II's impressively prepared but miserably anticlimactic campaign against Scotland in 1385, Gloucester's dismal *chevauchée* of 1387) and its political fragmentation (the "loyal conspiracy" of the Lords Appellant and their Merciless Parliament of 1388). Even Chaucer's own financial and personal security came under threat.

It is remarkable (and often remarked) how little of the pressure of

1. Gerhart B. Ladner, *The Idea of Reform: Its Impact on Christian Thought and Action in the Age of the Fathers* (Cambridge: Harvard University Press, 1959).
2. *Riverside Chaucer*, 650–51. See James Dean, "Time Past and Time Present in Chaucer's Clerk's Tale and Gower's *Confessio Amantis*," *ELH* 44 (1977): 401–18, and "The World Grown Old and Genesis in Middle English Historical Writing," *Speculum* 57 (1982): 548–68.

historical events is directly recorded in the poem itself. While Gower placed the analogy between Troy and London at the center of his diatribe on the Rising of 1381, Chaucer provides only oblique glances at current events in his explicitly Trojan poem. Instead we have a progressively more inward focus on the subjectivity of the protagonists, a self-reflexive attention to the problematics of writing, and above all, a conceptualization of history not as a series of temporally contingent and humanly tractable events but instead as a total form of being, history as a trans-historical idea rather than as a material reality. *Troilus and Criseyde* is (or tries to be) a meditation on history that effaces the historical. And what replaces the historical, as we should know from similar strategies in our own time, is the meditating mind itself, a consciousness that rises above and incorporates the conflicting interests of the medieval historical imagination.

This is precisely the moment of modernism, the moment that absorbs the past into a fully present selfhood from which an equivalently self-present significance can issue. Reality is founded in, and controlled by, the self: the disappointments of history are redeemed by an act of understanding that empowers consciousness and projects it forward into the future.[3] But as I have already argued, Chaucer was not in fact able to rest with the modernist moment, to proclaim the dominion of the transcendent mind. On the contrary, *Troilus and Criseyde* everywhere proclaims the fragmentation of subjectivity, both that of its protagonists and of its author. In so doing, it admits that there is no immunity from historicity, that the attempt to find it in thought is as great or greater a betrayal as that of faithless love.

The Medieval Writing of History

It is a truism that the development of a secular, causal historiography is impeded in the Middle Ages by the radical devaluation of both historiography and the historical life entailed by the spiritual imperatives of Christianity. History is the realm of the mundane and the unstable, a welter of events whose meaning remains resolutely hidden to the human observer. We are living in the Sixth Age, in the time of the Fourth Empire; the world is growing old (*mundus senescens*), traversing a vacant and meaningless period of time about which nothing useful can be said.[4] History may be, as Augustine put it, God's poem, but only God can read it; and those who are living it should concern themselves not with the means by which He works His mysterious purposes but with the pressing needs of their own salvation.[5] History is significant only as the stage on

---

3. See above, Introduction, 3–7, 11–13, 20–21; David Kolb, *The Critique of Pure Modernity: Hegel, Heidegger, and After* (Chicago: University of Chicago Press, 1986); and Gordon Teskey, "Milton and Modernity," *Diacritics* 18 (Spring, 1988): 42–53.
4. As Amos Funkenstein points out, for an Augustinian historiography, "all that could be said about [the present] was that the world grows older" ("Periodization and Self-Understanding in the Middle Ages and Early Modern Times," *M&H* 5 [1974], 8); and see R. A. Markus, *Saeculum: History and Society in the Theology of St. Augustine* (Cambridge: Cambridge University Press, 1970): "There is no sacred history *of* the last age: there is only a gap for it *in* the sacred history" (23).
5. On history as God's poem, see Augustine, *PL* 33:527, *PL* 34:410, and *De civitate Dei*, 11, 18; 4, 17; Bonaventure, *Breviloquium*, in *Works*, trans. José de Vinck (Paterson: St. Anthony Guild Press, 1960), 2:11–12; on the dangers of an overcurious interest in the interpretation of history, see Augustine; *PL* 33:420 and *De doctrina christiana*, 2,44.

which to enact individual choices between the City of God and the City of Man; it is a *via peregrinationis*, a place of exile, a land of unlikeness.[6] Since the usefulness of post-Incarnation history resides solely in its ability to teach us to disdain history, its value is wholly personal. It is a locus not of accomplishment but purification, not of fulfillment but healthful loss. Whether conceived as a desert place of exile, a chaos of random events, or, as in Boethius's view, a repetitive cycle of meaningless acts of rise and fall, history is significant only in terms of its impact upon the inner spiritual lives of those caught in its web.[7]

Much of the history that was actually written in the Middle Ages reflects these assumptions. Monastic historians, who have provided so much of the material with which we now reconstruct the medieval past, were in fact deeply divided about the legitimacy of the very scholarly activity in which they were engaged. For Peter Damian, history amounted to nothing more than "ludicrously useless annals, frivolous telling of frivolous old wives' tales"; while Ernald, Abbot of Rievaulx, commissioned William of Newburgh to write his history of England because he did not want any of his own monks engaged in so dubious an activity.[8] Monks displayed an admirable concern with factual inclusiveness and, especially, chronological accuracy; but rarely is the monastic historian concerned with structural coherence or linear development.[9] For Henry of Huntingdon, writing in the early twelfth century, the succession of foreign dominations that God has imposed upon Britain—the Romans, Picts and Scots, Angles, Danes, and now Normans— are punishments for wickedness. They have no legitimacy in and of themselves but stand as part of a scenario whose meaning is to be read entirely in the spiritual terminology of human sinfulness and divine wrath.[1] R. W. Southern's comments on monastic annals can be extended to include more ambitious monastic historical projects as well: "They are a resolute, undeviating record of human disorder in the midst of cosmic order. . . . This ambiguity in history, which made it at once wholly irrational and [from a divine perspective] wholly rational, at once wholly coherent and wholly incoherent, was one of the most carefully cultivated experiences of the early Middle Ages."[2]

The sense of coherence, of history as divinely superintended, did of course find historiographical expression, although rarely in a form that

6. Augustine, *De civitate*, 1, preface; 18, 51.
7. According to F. P. Pickering, *Literature and Art in the Middle Ages* (Coral Gables: University of Miami Press, 1970), all medieval Christian literature "falls into one of the two categories, according to Augustine *or* according to Boethius" (179). But as far as the problem of the legitimization of the historical life is concerned, there is little difference between the two: for both Augustine and Boethius, history is exile.
8. For Peter Damian, see Marie-Dominique Chenu, *Nature, Man, and Society in the Twelfth Century*, trans. Jerome Taylor and Lester Little (Chicago: University of Chicago Press, 1968), 164 n. 4; for Ernald of Rievaulx, see Bernard Guenée, *Histoire et culture historique dans l'occident médiéval* (Paris: Aubier, 1980), 47–48. In his important review article in *History and Theory* 12 (1973), Robert Hanning discusses the "tensions between the historian's craft and the world-rejecting monastic profession" (423).
9. See Guenée, *Histoire*, 110–11.
1. For Henry of Huntingdon, see Nancy F. Partner, *Serious Entertainments: The Writing of History in Twelfth-Century England* (Chicago: University of Chicago Press, 1977), 11–48. As she says about the form of the monastic chronicle, "The essential point is simply the universality of episodic, nondevelopmental, serial organization" (202).
2. R. W. Southern, "Aspects of the European Tradition of Historical Writing: 1. The Classical Tradition from Einhard to Geoffrey of Monmouth," *TRHS*, 5th ser., 20 (1970) 180–81.

encouraged the development either of causal modes of historical explanation or explorations of the relation of the individual to the course of historical events. The genre of history writing that best expressed the medieval sense of providential order without violating its equally powerful sense of the worthlessness of the historical (i.e., secular) life was the ecclesiastical history. Perhaps the most familiar instance is Bede's *Ecclesiastical History of the English People*; its origins were in Eusebius's *Ecclesiastical History*, and its assumptions continued in force in Orderic Vitalis's twelfth-century history, also entitled *Ecclesiastical History*.[3] The purpose of these histories—enacted in a pure form only by Bede but providing the legitimizing assumptions for the others—is to show how God's chosen people come together in the Church in preparation for history's apocalyptic fulfillment. Secular events are of interest only insofar as they are relevant to the workings of this process, and they enter into the historical record only when appropriated by the totalizing force of the Church.[4] Yet despite its severity, this model historiography is compromised by the intrusion of secularity in two forms. One is the simple interest in historical events of all kinds, regardless of their ecclesiastical relevance, that is a growing characteristic of historical writing from the twelfth century on. The other is the development, also most marked in the twelfth century but derived from earlier models, of a full-fledged *Heilsgeschichte*, in which not just ecclesiastical but also secular foundations are endowed with a role in God's providential design.

This latter historiographical conception, which is often (and wrongly) taken to be not only the characterizing form of medieval historiography as a whole but a straightforward and unproblematical expression of medieval religious values, in fact runs counter to Augustinian principles. For Augustine denied not only the so-called Augustus-theology that would make of the Roman Empire an earthly *imperium* underwritten by God for special historical purposes but also the claim that *any* moment of secular history, no matter how momentous, can be understood in terms of a providential purpose.[5] As Theodor Mommsen has said, "To him history was the *operatio Dei* in time, it was 'a one-directional, teleological process, directed towards one goal—salvation,' *the salvation of individual men, not of any collective groups or organizations.*"[6] And R. A. Markus points out that "Augustine's excision of Roman history from sacred history has left not only Rome, but all historical achievement, problematic."[7]

But this Augustinian severity could withstand neither the late classical

3. See Arnaldo Momigliano, *Essays in Ancient and Modern Historiography* (Middletown: Wesleyan University Press, 1975), 107–26.
4. Walter Ullmann speaks of a " 'totalitarian' ecclesiastical history" underwritten by "the ecclesiologically conceived theme of totality—the Church embracing the totality of life" (*Medieval Foundations of Renaissance Humanism* [London: Elek, 1977], 64).
5. For the phrase "Augustus-Theologie," see Theodor Mommsen, "Aponius and Orosius on the Significance of the Epiphany," in *Medieval and Renaissance Studies*, ed. Eugene Rice (Ithaca: Cornell University Press, 1959), 319. There was, it is true, one very brief moment, around 399–400, when Augustine entertained the possibility of an *imperium Romanum* in which divine providence and secular dominion would come together so that God's purposes might be enacted historically through the agency of an earthly foundation; see Markus, *Saeculum*, 33–37.
6. Theodor Mommsen, "St. Augustine and the Christian Idea of Progress: The Background of *The City of God*," *Medieval and Renaissance Studies*, 293; my italics. The cited phrase in Mommsen's statement is from Karl Löwith, *Meaning in History*.
7. Markus, *Saeculum*, 63.

devotion to the idea of Rome nor the more general commitment to the belief that the historical life is per se significant. Augustine denied special value to either the rise or fall of Rome, but his own rigorous dismissals were being softened at the very moment they were being put in place: Orosius's *Seven Books of History Against the Pagans* was supposed to be an expression of Augustinian historical conceptions but proved in the event to foster attitudes diametrically opposed to an authentic Augustinianism. For while Orosius devalues the Roman empire by analogizing it to Babylon and by almost entirely suppressing the myth of Trojan origins in favor of the fratricidal violence of the founders Romulus and Remus, he simultaneously accords to Rome the special status of being the bearer of God's final earthly purpose and so invests a sense of development and progress in the *translatio imperii* from Troy to Babylon, to Persia, and then to the fourth of Daniel's four empires, Rome. It is this "Christian progressivism," as Mommsen calls it, that in the last analysis drives Orosian historiography and that served to legitimize the topos of translation for medieval historians.[8] Hence it was almost to be expected that in the secularizing twelfth century, with its interest in historicizing values that had previously been regarded as atemporal absolutes, a writer like Otto of Freising would subvert Augustine's insistence on the internal and private nature of the two cities. Asserting the primacy of an institutional unity denominated "Christendom," whose existence was marked by its political formation into the significantly named Holy Roman Empire, Otto declared that historical actuality should be endowed with providential legitimacy.[9] Otto's *Geschichtstheologie* was widely shared throughout the later Middle Ages, and not only by historians: it also underwrites, perhaps by way of Joachim of Flora's prophetic history, the political vision of Dante's *Commedia*.

Troilus and Criseyde is, of course, located within the *other* tradition, the body of foundational narratives inspired precisely by what Augustine rejected—Virgil's Roman mythography and what followed from it. Throughout the Middle Ages historians constructed Trojan genealogies for the later European *imperia*: in his authoritative *Historia destructionis Troiae*, Guido delle Colonne designates first Britain (Brutus), then France (Francus), Venice (Antenor), Sicily and Tuscany (Sicanus), Naples (Aeneas), and Calabria (Diomedes) as Trojan foundations; and other claimants included the Danes and the Normans (Antenor again). Turkey (Turcus), Fiesole (Dardanus), Belgium (Bavon), the Saxons, the German Emperors, and the Capetians.[1] Even at the very end of the

---

8. Mommsen, "St. Augustine," and "Orosius and Augustine," in *Medieval and Renaissance Studies*, 325–48. Robert W. Hanning, *The Vision of History in Early Britain* (New York: Columbia University Press, 1966), provides a valuable account of these issues (1–43).
9. Markus, *Saeculum*: "Augustine's conception of history as the careers of two [historically] interwoven [if] eschatologically opposed cities has here become the very thing which it was designed to undermine: the theological prop of a sacral society, of a Christian political establishment in which the divine purpose in history lay enshrined" (164). For discussions of the development of an imperial ideology, with suggestions as to its relation to the topos of *translatio*, see Walter Ullmann's "Reflections on the Medieval Empire," *TRHS*, 5th ser., 14 (1964): 89–108, and "Dante's 'Monarchia' as an Illustration of a Politico-Religious 'Renovatio,' " in *Traditio-Krisis-Renovatio aus theologischer Sicht: Festschrift Winfried Zeller*, ed. Berndt Jaspert and Rudolf Mohr (Marburg: Elwert, 1976), 101–13; and Geoffrey Barraclough, *The Mediaeval Empire: Idea and Reality*, Historical Association Pamphlets, G17 (London: Historical Association, 1950).
1. Nathaniel Edward Griffin, ed. (Cambridge: Mediaeval Academy of America, 1936), 11–12. The claim for the Britains was originally made in the ninth century by Nennius and for the Franks in

Middle Ages the famous historian Johannes Trithemius proved the Trojan origins of the German emperor Maximilian by inventing two nonexistent scholarly sources, and it cost Polydore Virgil much labor, and obloquy, to disprove the Trojan foundation of Britain.[2] For virtually all medieval historians, Troy represented an originary moment analogous to the biblical moment of Genesis. According to Isidore of Seville, Moses is the first sacred historian and Dares the first pagan, and in most universal chronicles it is with the Troy story that pagan history enters into the controlling context of scriptural history.[3] Jean Malkaraume, for instance, goes so far as to insert the thirty thousand lines of Benoît de Sainte-Maure's *Roman de Troie* into his versification of the Bible, appropriately introducing it after Moses's Pentateuch.[4] Other writers use less drastic strategies of incorporation: in the *Story of England*, a translation of Langtoft's *Chronicle*, Robert Mannyng of Brunne traces the genealogy of the Trojan kings back to Noah and describes Troy as the first city built after the flood;[5] and several Troy stories prefaced their account with the Judgment of Paris in order to assimilate Eve's apple to the golden apple of Discord.[6]

As we should expect, Trojan origins provided a powerfully legitimizing tool for medieval rulers. The location of historical authority in a single source naturally appealed to a medieval monarchy interested in promoting its own role as an exclusive source of political power, and the linearity of *translatio imperii* was convenient support for hereditary

the seventh or eighth by "Fredegar." For Denmark (and the Normans), see Benoît de Sainte-Maure, *Chroniques des Ducs de Normandie*, ed. Carin Fahlin (Uppsala: Almqvist and Wiksells, 1951), 1:19–20 (lines 645–60); for Turcus, see pseudo-Vincent of Beauvais, *Speculum Historiale*, 2, 66 (Douai: Bellerus, 1624), 68; for Fiesole, see the *Chronica de origine civitatis* (before 1231), discussed by Nicolai Rubinstein, "The Beginnings of Political Thought in Florence: A Study in Medieval Historiography," *JWCI* 5 (1942): 198–227. The Trojan origin of the Saxons was first promulgated by Widukind, for the Normans by Dudo of St. Quentin, for the German emperors by Ekkehard, and for the Capetians by Suger and the Monks of St. Denis: see Southern, "Aspects, I," 173–96. Lovato Lovati, a judge at Padua (1241–1309) who devoted much of his energy to the recovery of ancient texts, "also tried his hand at archaeology, and identified a skeleton which some workmen had turned up as the remains of the legendary founder of Padua, the Trojan Antenor, a gorgeous error" (L. D. Reynolds and N. G. Wilson, *Scribes and Scholars* [Oxford: Clarendon Press, 1968], 104). The *Chronicon Briocense*, a chronicle of Brittany begun in 1394, claims that the Breton language is the purest surviving form of Trojan; see Michael Jones, " 'Mon Pais et ma Nation': Breton Identity in the Fourteenth Century," in *War, Literature and Politics in the Late Middle Ages*, ed. C. T. Allmand (Liverpool: University of Liverpool Press, 1976), 145.

2. For Trithemius and the Emperor Maximilian, see Guenée, *Histoire*, 144; on Polydore Vergil, see F. J. Levy, *Tudor Historical Thought* (San Marino: Huntington Library, 1967), 63–68.

3. For Isidore, see *Etymologiae* 1, 42, 1: "Historiam autem primus apud nos Moyses de initio mundi conscripsit. Apud gentiles vero primus Dares Phrygius de Graecis et Trojanis historiam edidit" (*PL* 82:122–23). Isidore doubtless promotes Dares above Dictys because Dares was a Trojan. For the chronicles, see Karl Heinrich Krüger, *Die Universalenchroniken*, Typologie des sources du Moyen Age, fasc. 16 (Turnhout: Brepols, 1976). For a fourteenth-century English instance, see Ranulf Higden's *Polychronicon*, ed. Churchill Babington, Rolls Series (London: Longmans, 1885), 2:402–18.

4. J. R. Smeets, ed., *La Bible de Jehan Malkaraume*, 2 vols. (Assen: Gorcum, 1978). Benoît had already posited this chronology by asserting that Calchas's tent had previously belonged to the Pharaoh who was drowned in the Red Sea (Leopold Constans, ed., *Le Roman de Troie*, SATF, 6 vols. [Paris: Firmin Didot, 1904–12], lines 13819–21).

5. Robert Mannyng of Brunne, *The Story of England*, ed. F. J. Furnivall, Rolls Series (London: Longmans, 1887), 1:15–16. The same genealogy is given in one of the manuscripts of the so-called *Histoire ancienne jusqu'à César*; see Paul Meyer, "Les premières compilations françaises d'histoire ancienne," *Romania* 14 (1885), 68.

6. Two instances are the *Libro de Alexandre* and the *Ovide moralisé*; see E. Bagby Atwood, "The *Excidium Troiae* and Medieval Troy Literature," *MP* 35 (1937–38), 125. See in general, Margaret J. Ehrhart, *The Judgment of the Trojan Prince Paris in Medieval Literature* (Philadelphia: University of Pennsylvania Press, 1987).

dynasties and genealogical claims.[7] This was especially the case in England, where the stability of the monarchy and even the continuity of national identity (from Celts to Anglo-Saxons to Danes to Normans) was so much in question. While Geoffrey of Monmouth's political sympathies remain obscure, his narrative was quickly appropriated by the initially insecure and then imperialistic Henry II, who almost certainly sponsored Wace's translation; and it was again at Henry's court that Benoît wrote *Le Roman de Troie*, the central document of Trojan historiography for the Middle Ages and a crucial model for *Troilus and Criseyde*. Moreover, at the end of Henry's reign Joseph of Exeter composed his *Bellum Troianum*, a text that perhaps provided Chaucer with one of the most powerful and enigmatic moments of his own poem.[8] But the invocation of Trojan origins was not confined to England: in 1204 Pierre de Bracheux tried to justify the unjustifiable Latin conquest of Byzantium by claiming that since the Franks were descendants of the Trojans they were now reconquering territory the Greeks had wrongfully seized some two thousand years before.[9]

The power of Trojan precedents was still in force in late medieval England. Not only did Trojan historiography continue to interest royal and noble families—Edward II's Queen Isabelle owned a volume called *De bello troiano*, and Humphrey of Bohun, Earl of Hereford (d. 1322), named his youngest son Eneas—but it appears in some unexpected contexts.[1] One of the charges laid against Nicholas Brembre by his opponents in 1386 was that he wanted to change the name of London to *Parva Troia* and have himself styled duke of Troy—in effect, an accusation of harboring royalist ambitions.[2] On the other side, during Richard II's elaborate tournament at Smithfield in October 1390—for which Chaucer as clerk of the king's works supervised the building of the scaffolds—London was referred to as "la neufe troy."[3] Not surprisingly, the

---

7. For the centrality of lineage in medieval thought, see R. Howard Bloch, *Etymologies and Genealogies: A Literary Anthropology of the French Middle Ages* (Chicago: University of Chicago Press, 1983); Gabrielle M. Spiegel, "Genealogy: Form and Function in Medieval Historical Narrative," *History and Theory* 22 (1983): 43–53; and for a literary-philosophical insight, Patricia Drechsel Tobin, *Time and the Novel* (Princeton: Princeton University Press, 1978): "By an analogy of function, events in time come to be perceived as begetting other events within a line of causality similar to the line of generations, with the prior event earning a special prestige as it is seen to originate, control, and predict future events. When in some such manner ontological priority is conferred upon mere temporal anteriority, the historical consciousness is born, and time is understood as a linear manifestation of the genealogical destiny of events" (7–8).

8. On Henry II as a patron, see Walter F. Schirmer and Ulrich Broich, *Studien zum literarischen Patronat im England des 12. Jahrhunderts* (Cologne: Westdeutscher Verlag, 1962), 27–203; Diana B. Tyson, "Patronage of French Vernacular History Writers in the Twelfth and Thirteenth Centuries," *Romania* 100 (1979): 180–222, 584; and Reto R. Bezzola, *Les Origines et la formation de la littérature courtoise en Occident*, 500–1200, vol. 3, pt. 1 (Paris: Champion, 1963). I have provided a more detailed account of both the specific question of Henry's historiographical interests, Arthurian and Norman as well as Trojan, and of the ideological function of the *Gründungssagen* in general, in *Negotiating the Past: The Historical Understanding of Medieval Literature* (Madison: University of Wisconsin Press, 1987), 199–210.

9. Robert de Clari, *La conquête de Constantinople*, ed. Philippe Lauer (Paris: Champion, 1924), 102.

1. For Isabelle's book, see Juliet Vale, *Edward III and Chivalry: Chivalric Society and Its Context, 1270–1350* (Woodbridge: Boydell Press, 1982), 50; for Eneas de Bohun, see John Barnie, *War in Medieval English Society: Social Values and the Hundred Years War* (London: Weidenfeld and Nicolson, 1974), 101.

2. John P. McCall and George Rudisill, Jr., "The Parliament of 1386 and Chaucer's Trojan Parliament," *JEGP* 58 (1959), 284 n. 25.

3. The proclamation or Crie des Joustes for the tournament is printed in F. H. Cripps-Day, *The History of the Tournament in England* (London: Quaritch, 1918), xli–xlii; see Sheila Lindenbaum, "The Smithfield Tournament of 1390," *JMRS* 20 (1990): 1–20. See also Juliet R. V. Barker, *The Tournament in England, 1100–1400* (Woodbridge: Boydell, 1986), 100.

usurping Lancastrians appropriated Trojanness: Bolingbroke's son, the future Henry V, commissioned Lydgate's *Troy Book* as well as a personal manuscript of *Troilus and Criseyde*.[4] And on the other side of the channel, the aspiring dukes of Burgundy were avid collectors of Trojan materials. Philippe le Bon owned seventeen manuscripts dealing with Troy, two of which may even have been copies of the *Troilus*, and he also commissioned Raoul Lefèvre's *Recueil* and founded the Order of the Golden Fleece, which took as its exemplary chivalric event the voyage of the Argonaut that stood, in many Trojan histories, as the initiating event of the war.[5] So too, in Italy the library of the ambitious Visconti contained no less than four manuscripts of Guido delle Colonne's *Historia destructionis Troiae* and six other "Troy books."[6] Substantial and specific political value was thus invested in the idea of Trojan origins—a fact that gives the literary initiative undertaken by Chaucer, who remained loyal to his beleaguered monarch throughout the factional 1380s, an inevitably political dimension.

The invocation of Troy assumes that a legitimizing power is located within the processes of secular history itself, that earthly foundations can find authorization within the scope of their own historical existence, with no necessary recourse to a transcendental realm of value. That these powerful interests ran counter to medieval spiritualism was occasionally made explicit. In 1153 Hugh of Fouilloy attacked bishops who adorned the walls of their palaces with pictures of Trojans rather than giving their riches to the poor: his concern was with not only episcopal charity but the intrusion of secular historiography into the ecclesiastical world.[7] And in his *Scalacronica*, written in the 1350s and 1360s, Sir Thomas Gray began with a vision of the ladder of history resting upon two books, the Bible and "la gest de Troy." But once having established this familiar equivalence, Sir Thomas hastily revised it: according to the Sibyl who is his guide, "veiez cy sen et foly, le primer livre la bible, le secounde la gest de Troy."[8] Similarly, in the *Miroir de mariage*, Eustache Deschamps says that he will rest his argument

---

4. The Campsell manuscript, described by R. K. Root, *The Textual Tradition of Chaucer's Troilus*, Chaucer Society, 1st ser., 99 (London: Kegan Paul, Trench, Trübner, 1916), 5.

5. Alphonse Bayot, "La légende de Troie à la cour de Bourgogne," *Société d'Emulation de Bruges, Mélanges* 1 (Bruges: de Plancke, 1908); Muriel J. Hughes, "The Library of Philip the Bold and Margaret of Flanders, First Valois Duke and Duchess of Burgundy," *JMH* 4 (1978): 145–88; for the Burgundian ownership of a manuscript of the *Troilus*, see Eleanor Hammond, "A Burgundian Copy of Chaucer's *Troilus*," *MLN* 26 (1911): 32. See also André Bossuat, "Les origines troyennes: leur rôle dans la littérature historique au xvᵉ siècle," *Annales de Normandie* 45 (1963): 91–118.

6. A. Pratt, "Chaucer and the Visconti Libraries," *ELH* 6 (1939), 195. For the Trojan story in other aristocratic libraries in the later Middle Ages, see Pierre Champion, *La Librairie de Charles d'Orléans* (Paris: Champion, 1910), 40–41; S. Edmunds, "The Library of Savoy: Documents," *Scriptorium* 24 (1970): 318–27; 25 (1971): 253–84; 26 (1972): 269–93 (especially items number 106 and 148); and Margaret Kekewich, "Edward IV, William Caxton, and Literary Patronage in Yorkist England," *MLR* 66 (1971): 481–87.

7. Antoine Thomas, "Le *De claustro anime* et le *Roman de Troie*," *Romania* 42 (1913): 83–85. I am indebted to Prof. David Jacoby for this reference, who accepts the ascription of this work to Hugh of Fouilloy (Thomas, following Migne, ascribes it to Hugh of St. Victor).

8. Ed. Joseph Stevenson (Edinburgh: Maitland Club, 1836), 2. For this text, see Beryl Smalley, *English Friars and Antiquity in the Early Fourteenth Century* (Oxford: Basil Blackwell, 1960), 13–14; Derek Pearsall, *John Lydgate* (London: Routledge and Kegan Paul, 1970), 122; M. D. Legge, *Anglo-Norman Literature and Its Background* (Oxford: Clarendon Press, 1963), 283–87; and especially Antonia Gransden, *Historical Writing in England II: c. 1307 to the Early Sixteenth Century* (London: Routledge and Kegan Paul, 1982), 92–96.

En saincte Escripture esprouvée,
Non pas en histoire trouvée
D'Erculès ou des Troïens.[9]

More centrally, the founding text of English legendary history—Geof-frey of Monmouth's *Historia regum Britanniae* (c. 1136)—was by impli-cation and design antiecclesiastical. In about 1200 the monastic historian William of Newburgh unfavorably compared Geoffrey's work with its theologically orthodox predecessor, Bede's *Historia ecclesiastica gentis Anglorum.* The point for William was not simply that "our Bede, . . . of whose wisdom and integrity none can doubt," was truthful whereas Geoffrey told lies, but that Geoffrey's narrative substituted for ecclesiastical history (in which the crucial event was the conversion of the *gens Anglorum*) a purely secular history centered on the rise and fall of the *reges Britanniae* and both climaxed and encapsulated by the career of Arthur.[1] Hence, William pointed out, Geoffrey allowed Arthur's exploits to preempt the central event of Bede's *Historia*, the conversion-ary moment of the arrival of St. Augustine in England. In Geoffrey's account the conversion of the British passes virtually unnoticed, and Bede's Ethelberht, who "embraced the easy yoke of Christ at the preach-ing of Augustine," is displaced by the fraudulent hero Arthur. In sum, the history that Geoffrey traces is governed not by a Christian providence but by a *translatio imperii* whose shape was first sketched not in Euse-bius's *Historia ecclesiastica* (Bede's mastertext) but in Virgil's *Aeneid*; and the fatality that brings down the Arthurian empire locates causality at the level not of divine superintendance but human action.

The secular and causal historiography articulated by Geoffrey's *His-toria* began to flourish in the twelfth century and continued to develop in many forms.[2] To be sure, only in *quattrocento* Italy did there emerge a fully and confidently humanist historiography that sought to explain "the inner workings of historical phenomena and particularly of political institutions" by reference to "psychological elements."[3] But it was the legendary histories and the romances of the Middle Ages that served in the interim to protect this humanist interest against the effacement of historically specific secondary causes entailed by religious imperatives. With their focus upon the nature of the self and its relation to its society, and their freedom from the necessarily limiting plot ordained by Chris-tian history, these ubiquitous narratives provided the environment in which events could begin to be understood in human terms. At the cen-ter of the narrated action is a human agent who does not merely react to events but also creates them: in the world of romance, history is less given than made. And the linearity of romance narrative, as distinct from

9. Eustache Deschamps, *Le Miroir de mariage*, lines 9101–4, in Le Marquis de Queux de Saint-Hilaire, ed., *Oeuvres complètes d'Eustache Deschamps*, SATF, vol. 9 (Paris: Firmin Didot, 1890).
1. Joseph Stevenson, trans., *The Church Historians of England*, vol. 4, part 2 (Glasgow: Seeleys, 1856), 399, 401. William's *Historia rerum Anglicarum* is edited in the Rolls Series by Richard Howlett, *Chronicles of the Reigns of Stephen, Henry II, and Richard I*, vols. 1–2 (London: Long-mans, 1884–85). For this citation, see the Proemium, in which William characterizes Bede as "de cujus sapientia et sinceritate dubitare fas non est" (1:18).
2. The secularization of twelfth-century historiography is a commonly observed phenomenon; see, for example, Ullmann, *Medieval Foundations*, 61–67. On the "historicization" of culture generally in the twelfth century, see Chenu, *Nature, Man, and Society*, 162–201.
3. Donald J. Wilcox, *The Development of Florentine Humanist Historiography in the Fifteenth Century* (Cambridge: Harvard University Press, 1969), 45.

that of ecclesiastical history, implies a causality that is, however obscured by enigma or thwarted by chance, finally grounded in the human will. As we shall see, Trojan historiography provided a particularly focused opportunity for this kind of historiographical interest, and the efflorescence of Trojan writings, first in the twelfth and then in the fourteenth centuries, corresponds to the analogous flourishing of various forms of secular and causal historiography.[4]

There was, however, a philosophical problem inherent in this new secular history, a problem raised by precisely that principle of continuity expressed in the idea of *translatio imperii*. This was the problem of repetition. In the *City of God* Augustine cited the Psalmist's phrase, "the ungodly will walk in a circle," in order to attack pagan theorists of history who believe in the idea of temporal recurrence. The phrase is relevant, he says, "not because their life is going to come round again in the course of those revolutions which they believe in, but because the way of their error, the way of false doctrine, goes round in circles." These pagan philosophers are wandering in "a circuitous maze, finding neither entrance nor exit, for they do not know how the human race, and this moral condition of ours, first started, nor with what end it will be brought to a close."[5] Contrasting the unidirectional linearity of Christian history, firmly anchored by the biblical paradigm of an initiatory Genesis and a conclusive Revelation, with the Platonic circularities of eternal return, Augustine's faith in a God who transcends and encompasses history offered itself as an antidote to the pagan entrapment within the historical cycle itself. Yet he also articulated the condition of all men living in the Sixth Age, whose historical life bears a meaning that remains resolutely unavailable to them and for whom the translations of secular history articulate a meaningless pattern of ceaseless rise and fall. The only significant history is that lived within the church (i.e., ecclesiastical history) since it is Fortune's turning wheel that controls the dynastic world. And as Origen's history implied, each successive empire articulates the same pattern: as Troy, so Babylon, so Persia, so Rome—and so on until the empty recursions of history have been finally brought to a definitive end.

This specter haunts the romances and the legendary histories, for which heredity is both the basis of legitimacy and the cause of failure. Troy is the original city, the *Parva Troia* or Troynovaunt of London heir to its glory.[6] Yet as Gower hysterically insists in the first book of the *Vox*

4. The dominance of secular modes of understanding in later medieval historiography is shown by the virtual disappearance of the monastic chronicle, with its insistence upon the random nature of historical events relieved only by an occasional invocation of providential intervention, and its replacement by the aristocratic history, with its location of the motive force of history in the human will and its concern to provide causal explanations for events; see Bernard Guenée, "Histoires, annales, chroniques: essai sur les genres historiques au moyen âge," *Annales* 28 (1973), 1007.
5. Henry Bettenson, trans. (Harmondsworth: Penguin Books, 1972), 488–89. "*In circuitu impii ambulabunt* [Psalm 11:9]; non quia per circulos, quos opinantur, eorum vita est recursura, sed quia modo talis est erroris eorum via, id est falsa doctrina. Quid autem mirum est, si in his circuitibus errantes nec aditum nec exitum inveniunt? quia genus humanum atque ista nostra mortalitas nec quo initio coepta sit sciunt, nec quo fine claudatur" (Bernhard Dombart, ed. [Leipzig: Teubner, 1909], 12, 14–15). Momigliano shows that the idea that pagan historians posited a circular pattern for historical time is derived not from classical histories themselves but from polemical Christian misrepresentations (Momigliano, *Essays in Ancient and Modern Historiography*, 179–204).
6. See John Clark, "Trinovantum—The Evolution of a Legend," *JMH* 7 (1981): 135–51. A text written in the same place and at the same time as the *Troilus* (London in the second half of the

clamantis, just as Troy was brought down by internal dissension so will London collapse into the chaos of the Rising of 1381.[7] A purposive linearity cannot maintain itself, and the historical process gives way to reveal an underlying recursiveness, a circularity that calls into question all merely historical beginnings and endings. *Troilus and Criseyde* represents, I believe, Chaucer's investigation of this central dilemma of the medieval historical consciousness. And he makes his point by extending the line of descent backwards, by showing the specular resemblance that exists between the events of Trojan history and those that took place earlier, at Thebes. If this resemblance is deeply troubling, it followed that the later connections forged by medieval historians between Troy and their own societies must be ridden by the same disastrous determinism.

In choosing Thebes as his starting point, Chaucer was somewhat eccentric. That Theban history preceded Trojan was of course known to the Middle Ages, but Thebes never attained the same historiographical status.[8] For one thing, it lacked the Virgilian mythography that served to define Troy as the originary moment; and for another it was known to the Middle Ages primarily through a variety of literary sources that lacked the historical authority that Dares's and Dictys's "eyewitness" accounts could claim. Indeed, the Thebes story functioned in medieval historiography primarily as a prefiguration of Troy: it is significant, for instance, that the *Roman de Thèbes*, in both its original, versified forms and in its prose *remainiements*, always appears in the manuscripts only within the context of ancient history and almost always as linked specifically to Troy, while the Troy story often stands on its own or as the initiatory movement from Troy to Rome and so to the modern world.[9] But Chaucer seems to have intuited what it was about Theban history that might well have caused its strategic marginalization: he shows that

---

1380s) that also stresses the continuity between the contemporary city and its Trojan origins is *St. Erkenwald*. For a suggestive discussion, see Gordon Whately, "Heathens and Saints: *St. Erkenwald* in its Legendary Context," *Speculum* 61 (1986): 330–63.

7. The following passage from 1, 13 is not untypical: "The Trojan victory was lost in defeat, and Troy became a prey to the wild beast, just like a lamb to the wolf. The peasant attacked and the knight in the city did not resist; Troy was without a Hector, Argos without its Achilles. No boldness of a Hector or Troilus defeated anything then, but instead those who were defeated suffered the whole affair without courage. Priam did not shine then with his usual honor; instead, the master put up with whatever the servant did to him. Even Hecuba's chambers could scarcely remain undisturbed, without suffering agitating then; the faint hearts within them. Nor indeed could Ilion then defend from the madmen the man enclosed within its lofty towers" (Eric W. Stockton, trans., *The Major Latin Works of John Gower* [Seattle: University of Washington Press, 1962], 71–72).

8. For example, the early-thirteenth-century compilation called by scholars the *Histoire ancienne jusqu'à César* is divided into seven parts: Genesis; the founding of the kingdoms of Assyria, Egypt, and Greece; the early days of Assyria and Greece; Theban history; the stories of the Minotaur, Amazons, and Hercules; Trojan history; and the founding of Rome (Meyer, "Les premères compilations," 1–81).

9. On the manuscripts of the *Roman de Thèbes*, see Giovanna Angeli, *L'"Eneas" e i primi romanzi volgari* (Milan: Ricciardi, 1971), 60 n. 1; on the prose *remaniements*, see Brian Woledge, *Bibliographie des romans et nouvelles en prose française antérieurs à 1500* (Geneva: Droz, 1975), 120–21. Of the twenty-eight (more or less) complete manuscripts of the *Roman de Troie*, sixteen present the *Roman* alone, while only two precede it with the *Roman de Thèbes*; in five manuscripts it is followed by the *Roman d'Eneas*. The manuscripts are described by Constans, *Le Roman de Troie*, 6:1–105. See also the *Excidium Troiae*, which provides a version of the Troy story, then a prose *Aeneid*, and finally a history of Rome to Augustus (E. Bagby Atwood and Virgil K. Whitaker, eds. [Cambridge: Mediaeval Academy of America, 1944]). A similar text is the *Compendium historiae Troianae-Romanae*, H. Simonsfeld, ed., *Neues Archiv der Gesellschaft für ältere deutsche Geschichtskunde* 11 (1886): 241–51.

the Trojan origin, and all historical origins, are undone by a subtext that repudiates the very idea of originality.

* * *

[Omitted here is a section in which Patterson treats Chaucer's *House of Fame* and the medieval idea of metaphor, *translatio*. The *House of Fame* posits that "the labyrinth of historical writing is an unfounded and ceaseless process of mediation, a *translatio* of nothing but itself"—*Editor.*]

History versus Romance

There is, it must be acknowledged at the outset, something inherently paradoxical about either a historiographical or a historical reading of *Troilus and Criseyde*. For the action of the poem seems conspicuously, even aggressively, to resist the attention to either its Trojan or its contemporary context that would encourage us to regard history as its ultimate reference. The poet defines his project at the outset in entirely amorous terms: he addresses his bidding prayer to "ye loveres, that bathen in gladnesse" (1, 22), defines his subject as "swich peyne and wo as Loves folk endure" (1, 34), and calls himself "the sorwful instrument, / That helpeth loveres, *as I kan*, to pleyne" (1, 10–11). And he shortly issues a polemical statement explicitly disclaiming any historical interest:

> But how this town com to destruccion
> Ne falleth naught to purpos me to telle;
> For it were a long digression
> Fro my matere, and yow to long to dwelle.
> But the Troian gestes, as they felle,
> In Omer, or in Dares, or in Dite,
> *Whoso that kan* may rede hem as they write. (1, 141–47)[1]

This disclaimer is then matched at the end of the poem by an analogous stanza that justifies the poet's lack of interest in the martial deeds that comprise the public record:

> And if I hadde ytaken for to write
> The armes of this ilke worthi man,
> Than wolde ich of his batailles endite;
> But for that I to writen first bigan
> Of his love, I have seyd *as I kan*,—
> His worthi dedes, whoso list hem heere,
> Rede Dares, he kan telle hem alle ifeere. (5, 1765–71)

1. "Whoso that kan:" while this gently qualifying phrase seems in the first instance directed to those without Latin, since Homer was unavailable to virtually *every* medieval reader Chaucer begins by invoking one of the original accounts of the Trojan War only to remind us of its absence. The phrase, and the preceding "as I kan" of 1, 11, also echos the opening "if I kan" of the *House of Fame* ("I wol now synge, if I kan / The armes and also the man" [143–44]), a phrase that simultaneously marks the difference between the medieval minstrel and the classical poet and registers, in John Fyler's words, "the uncertain ability of art to be true to the facts," especially when—as in the case of the Dido-Aeneas episode—those facts are notoriously in dispute (Fyler, *Chaucer and Ovid*, 33; see A. C. Spearing, *Medieval to Renaissance in English Poetry* [Cambridge: Cambridge University Press, 1985], 22 n. 18). Moreover, the phrases prefigure the nervous "I have seyd as I kan" with which the poem concludes; see the next citation in the text.

Having initially defined his project in wholly amorous terms, the narrator feels justified in referring us elsewhere for historical details that are, for him, simply distractions from the matter at hand.

But before assuming that the narrator's dehistoricizing of the Troy story represents a straightforward Chaucerian initiative, we should take note of two other textual facts. One is that in subordinating the historical world of events to the inner world of erotic action the narrator's behavior imitates that of his protagonists, thus following a program that we know better than to regard as exemplary. When Troilus first falls in love, "Alle other dredes weren from him fledde, / Both of th'assege and his sava-cioun" (1, 463–64). This does not mean, however, that he abandons his martial duties. As soon as Pandarus leaves Troilus at the end of Book 1, Chaucer adds a passage to the *Filostrato* to tell us that

> Troilus lay tho no lenger down,
> But up anon upon his stede bay,
> And in the feld he pleyde tho leoun;
> Wo was that Grek that with hym meete a-day! (1, 1072–75)

And this martial prowess continues even during the height of the love affair:

> In alle nedes for the townes werre,
> He was, and ay, the first in armes dyght
> And certeynly, but if that bokes erre,
> Save Ector most ydred of any wight;
> And this encrees of hardynesse and myght
> Com hym of love, his ladies thank to wynne,
> That altered his spirit so withinne. (3, 1772–78)

"Bokes"—the "Troian gestes" of Homer, Dares, and Dictys are doubtless meant—testify to Troilus's bravery, and the narrator here explains its inner meaning. A matching phrase later locates in the *records* of heroism ("As men may in thise olde bokes rede" [5, 1753]) the fact that Troilus continues his martial ferocity after Criseyde's departure, though now motivated by rage and jealousy. Inspired first by love and then by hate, Troilus enacts throughout the narrative a heroism that is admirable (historically worthy of record) because it both testifies to the intensity of his amorous feelings and shows him fulfilling his role as an *alter Hector*—"and next his brother, holder up of Troye" (2, 644).

In effect, then, the narrator manages to provide for the "Troian gestes" a rich texture of private motivation and psychological depth without ignoring their significance as history. He thereby protects his story from the simplistic moralization that characterizes so much medieval histo-riography—and too much modern criticism.[2] The problem with moral-

2. In "The Trojan Scene in Chaucer's *Troilus*," *ELH* 29 (1962), John P. McCall ascribes the fall of the city to "the criminal lust of Troy" (263 n. 3), claiming that this interpretation is common in "the medieval encyclopedic tradition" (264 n. 4). This may well be so, but it is almost entirely absent from historiographical accounts, including those of Benoît de Sainte-Maure, Joseph of Exeter, Guido delle Colonne, and the various prose histories (e.g., *L'Histoire ancienne jusqu'à César*), the primary means by which classical history was transmitted to the medieval aristocratic world within which Chaucer wrote. Modern readings of the poem in these terms are offered by such diverse critics as D. W. Robertson, Jr., *A Preface to Chaucer* (Princeton: Princeton University Press, 1962), 472–502, and "The Probable Date and Purpose of Chaucer's *Troilus*," *M&H* 13 (1985): 143–71; Chauncey Wood, *The Elements of Chaucer's* Troilus (Durham: Duke University

izing Trojan history, whether Chaucer's or those of Benoît and Guido, is not that it is wrong, in the sense that it ignores another, more obviously correct understanding, but that categorical moral judgments reduce complex patterns of motivation to simple ideas of choice, or, more seriously, make all stories alike. For, while this narrative foregrounds private amorousness, it also resists the structure of blame. It not only refuses to draw any straightforward causal connections between Troilus's failed love and the fall of Troy, but seems to imply that there is no connection between these two events at all. As I shall argue, in this poem the private stands wholly apart from and seeks to efface the public, just as, at the level of genre, romance, a story focused on the fate of a single individual, seeks to preempt tragedy, a story about (in the definition of Isidore of Seville) *res publicas et regum historias*.[3] And at a still further level of complexity, the reader is so entangled in the inward world of eroticism and delicate feeling that, if he or she has learned anything from modern discussions of reading, the experience should be one not of moral superiority but rather complicity. For the characters, their narrator go-between, and the poem's audience all come to share the desire to suppress the historical consciousness.[4]

At certain points this inwardness is dramatized within the poem itself and thematized in particularly intricate ways. One telling instance is the scene at Deiphoebus's house, where Pandarus's manipulations have succeeded in momentarily creating a space within which the lovers can, in a necessarily constrained and tentative way, begin to express their love. Pandarus's busy weavings create a bustle of activity, both physical and interpretive, that allows for the brief appearance of a local enclave of pure privacy, and one which not even the reader is fully able to penetrate.[5] The same process is at work in an even more elaborately articu-

---

Press, 1984), especially 32–33 and 63–98; Winthrop Wetherbee, *Chaucer and the Poets*, for whom "an excessive preoccupation with love is the folly at the heart of the *Troilus*, . . . and the ultimate downfall of Troy is foreshadowed by the intensity of this preoccupation, the importance assumed by the 'siege of Criseyde' in the midst of the larger war" ([Ithaca: Cornell University Press, 1984], 118); and Eugene Vance, "Mervelous Signals: Poetics, Sign Theory, and Politics in Chaucer's *Troilus*," *NLH* 10 (1979): 293–337, who argues that "the heroic young prince is not only re-enacting Adam's loss of primal innocence, but Mars's erotic downfall in a coma of heroic inactivity as well" (324). But Chaucer takes pains to show us that Troilus is far from inactive.

3. In medieval literary discussions private and public concerns are generically distinguished in terms of comedy and tragedy, as in the authoritative definition by Isidore cited in the text: "Sed comici privatorum hominum praedicant acta, Tragici vero res publicas, et regum historias; item tragicorum argumenta ex rebus luctuosis sunt, comicorum ex rebus laetis" (*Etymologiae*, 8, 7, 6 [*PL* 82: 308]). Paul Strohm has shown that the term *romaunce* is most often used to designate a narrative about an individual rather than a society: "the majority of the works designated in this way recount the chivalric (martial and occasionally amatory) deeds of a single notable hero" ("The Origin and Meaning of Middle English *Romaunce*," *Genre* 10 [1977], 13); see also Strohm's important "*Storie, Spelle, Geste, Romaunce, Tragedie*: Generic Distinctions in the Middle English Troy Narratives," *Speculum* 46 (1971): 348–59. In terms of medieval genre theory, the *Troilus* wants to be a romantic comedy but is reluctantly constrained to the form of a historical tragedy; and when Chaucer at the conclusion designates his poem "litel myn tragedye" (5, 1786) he implicitly acknowledged the triumph of history.

4. A fifteenth-century example is described in Patterson, *Negotiating the Past*, 115–53; for twentieth-century instances, see E. Talbot Donaldson, ed., *Chaucer's Poetry*, 2d ed. (New York: Ronald Press, 1975), 1129–44, and his "Criseide and Her Narrator," *Speaking of Chaucer* (London: Athlone Press, 1970), 65–83; Evan Carton, "Complicity and Responsibility in Pandarus' Bed and Chaucer's Art," *PMLA* 94 (1979): 47–61; and Richard Waswo, "The Narrator of *Troilus and Criseyde*," *ELH* 50 (1983): 1–25.

5. The phrase "local enclave" is taken from Norbert Wiener, *The Human Use of Human Beings: Cybernetics and Society* (Garden City: Doubleday, 1954): "While the universe as a whole, if indeed there is a whole universe, tends to run down, there are local enclaves whose direction seems

lated form in the consummation scene, where we are simultaneously made complicit in the eroticism enacted before us and yet denied full access precisely by the ostentatious mediations of both Pandarus and the narrator, a series of multiform goings-between designed to persuade us that at their center is a moment of utterly unmediated confrontation. In part our conviction derives from the sense of progressive inwardness that the very topography of the setting communicates. Situated within a room that is itself surrounded by another room, itself surrounded by the house and its walls, by the city and *its* walls, then by the beseiging Greeks, and with the whole encased within a rainstorm, the lovers retreat first to a bed, then to a mental space that only they share, and finally to a wordless union that leads them (and perhaps us) to believe that they have passed beyond the world of history to a transcendent "Love, that of erthe and se hath governaunce" (3, 1744).

We are likewise made aware throughout the first three books of the poem that the historical is both unavoidably present and nonetheless placed at the service of the erotic action. Although the poem opens with Calkas's defection to the Greeks because of his understanding of the shape that events will assume, this dark premonition is quickly preempted by the theatrical scene of Criseyde pleading before Hector. And Calkas is reduced in these opening lines from "a lord of gret auctorite" (1, 65) and "a gret devyn" (1, 66) to a "traitour" who has committed a "false and wikked dede" (1, 87, 93)—a reduction in which the narrator himself participates with his trivializing pun, "whan this Calkas knew by calkulynge" (1, 71). As I have already suggested, by describing Calkas as a "lord of gret auctorite," Chaucer recalls the final line of the *House of Fame*—"A man of gret auctorite" (2158)—and invokes in this new context the questions of literary authority with which that earlier poem deals. These questions, moreover, become insistent a few lines later when Chaucer states, both gratuitously and disingenuously, that his sources do not tell him whether or not Criseyde had children; in fact, of course, Boccaccio explicitly describes her as childless (*Filostrato* 1, 15). In dispensing with Calkas's authority, therefore, the poet opens the way for other forms of deviation from authority, implying that the story as a whole can be told only if both the Trojan history that is its context (presided over by Calkas) and the literary history that provides its materials (here represented by Boccaccio) can be set aside.

Yet—and this is our second textual fact—if the events of the war seem to enter the narrative only as occasions for erotic action, the historical consequence that is excluded nonetheless reenters by the textual back door. Criseyde's first sight of Troilus is as he returns from battle, and her romantic admiration fastens on, but hardly effaces, the signs of his heroic achievement. Pandarus uses as a pretext to visit Criseyde the arrival of a Greek spy with news (2, 1111–13), and while he never tells her, or us, what the news might be, it remains a disturbing possibility. More tellingly, the gathering at Deiphoebus's palace is called to solve a problem whose triviality seems to efface the larger historical crisis it

---

opposed to that of the universe at large and in which there is a limited and temporary tendency for organization to increase. Life finds its home in some of these enclaves" (12).

displaces: Pandarus imagines some kind of legal action against Criseyde managed by "false Poliphete," an obscure figure whom Criseyde fears only because of "Antenor and Eneas, / That ben his frendes" (2, 1467, 1474–75)—although even then she regards the threat as insignificant: "No fors of that; lat hym han al yfeere" (2, 1477). Yet in fact this confected conspiracy is derived from a real conflict. Antenor and Aeneas will shortly join together in a plot against Troy itself, and there is evidence that Chaucer thought of Poliphete as a co-conspirator. For the name derives not from medieval versions of the Troy story but from Virgil's "Polyphoetes [or Polyboetes] sacred to Ceres" in *Aeneid* 6, one of the fallen Trojans whom Aeneas sees in the underworld.[6] There Polyphoetes is linked with the group Virgil calls "tris Antenoridas," Glaucus, Medon and Thersilochus, and Servius's gloss says that "multi supra dictos accipiunt quod fals[os] esse Homerus docet, qui eos commemorat."[7] However Chaucer may have understood this gloss, he seems to have believed that "false Poliphete" was an associate of Antenor, and that the conspiracy Pandarus imagines against Criseyde, and which she here dismisses as trivial, was later to be enacted in a darker, less fictive form. Similarly, just as a crucial moment in Trojan history is here prefigured in a trivialized form so does the "tretys and . . . lettre" with which Troilus distracts Helen and Deiphoebus involve a public matter of grave importance "If swych a man was worthi to ben ded, / Woot I nought who" (2, 1699–1700)—that serves as a pretext to occupy two of the leaders of Trojan society who have themselves, we suspect, an amorous agenda that will also figure in the final catastrophe.[8]

This dynamic of simultaneously invoking and suppressing the crucial issues of Trojan history also shapes the exchange between Troilus and Criseyde in the temple that initiates the erotic action in the first place. The event takes place on the feast of the Palladion, here represented as a moment of natural impulses, as

> the tyme
> Of Aperil, whan clothed is the mede
> With newe grene, of lusty Veer the pryme,
> And swote smellen floures white and rede. (1, 155–58)

Because the Greeks "hem of Troie shetten, / And hir cite biseged al aboute" (1, 148–49), the Trojans are denied access to the extramural world of nature where springtime celebrations traditionally take place; and yet they nonetheless continue to perform their "observaunces olde" (1, 160). To those familiar with Trojan history, however, the feast of the Palladion signifies more than springtime release. For at its center is the "relik" (1, 153) whose theft, according to Trojan historians, is one

6. "Cererique sacrum Polyphoeten [Polyboeten]" (6, 484); for an earlier version of this suggestion, see G. L. Hamilton, *The Indebtedness of Chaucer's* Troilus and Criseyde *to Guido delle Colonne's Historia Trojana* (New York: Columbia University Press, 1903), 97 n. 3. As I discovered after completing this chapter, the reference to Virgil's Polyphoetes is also proposed by John Fyler, "Auctoritee and Allusion in *Troilus and Criseyde*," *Res Publica Litterarum* 7 (1984): 73–92.

7. G. Thilo and H. Hagen, eds. (Leipzig: Teubner, 1884), 2:72–73.

8. These suspicions are discussed by McKay Sundwall, "Deiphoebus and Helen: A Tantalizing Hint," *MP* 73 (1975): 151–56, and by John V. Fleming, "Deiphoebus Betrayed: Virgilian Decorum, Chaucerian Feminism," *ChR* 21 (1986–87): 182–99. On Helen's thematic function in the poem, see Christopher C. Baswell and Paul Beekman Taylor, "The *Faire Queene Eleyne* in Chaucer's *Troilus*," *Speculum* 63 (1988): 293–311.

of the conditions of the fall of Troy.[9] The Trojans' turn away from the war into a sanctuary where they can celebrate the reappearance of a springtime from which they are excluded—a turn then reenacted by Troilus in his retreat into first his chamber and then the "mirour of his mynde" (I, 365)—is thus shadowed by a linear temporality that will finally overcome them. However brave or persistent, their attempts to evade the demands of the historical world are evidently bound to fail.[1]

If Books 1 through 3 show us lovers, and a society, determined to avoid their implication within a tragic history, Books 4 and 5 show instead that the local enclave of love can neither withstand nor transcend the pressures of history. "It shal be founde at preve" (4, 1659), says Troilus as Criseyde leaves Troy, and the proving of the affair is devastating in its results. For what is revealed is a fatal weakness not just in Criseyde but in the constitution of the affair as whole: whatever it is that makes her unwilling either to stay or to return has been an element of her character that has, from the beginning of the story, been both manipulated and overlooked by a devious Pandarus and an enamoured Troilus. Is the weakness of the private world of love then morally identical with (if not responsible for) the weakness that brings down Troy? Not only the narrative symmetry between the fate of the city and the fate of the lovers solicits such a question. For the exchange of Antenor for Criseyde fulfills another of the dark prophecies about Trojan history, that Troy would not fall as long as Troilus lived: in removing from Troilus his reason for living, the exchange removes as well a necessary condition for the survival of the city.[2] Are we then to think that Troilus, falling in love in such a way and with such a woman, rendered himself vulnerable to a loss that served to undermine the city to which he owed his largest allegiance?

9. In his commentary to *Aeneid* 2, 13, Servius says that the survival of Troy was dependent upon the preservation of three things: the Palladion, the tomb of Laomedon, and the life of Troilus; see E. K. Rand et al., eds., *Servianorum in Vergilii Carmina Commentariorum* (Lancaster: American Philosophical Society, 1946), 2:316–17. In the *Filostrato* Boccaccio refers to this relic as "il Palladio fatale" (1, 18); and in his gloss to *Aeneid* 2, 166, Servius has a long discussion of the theft of the Palladion by Ulysses and, significantly, Diomedes; see Rand et. al., 2:367–69.

1. Another echo of an excluded but visible Trojan history are the ominous suggestions of a connection among Criseyde, "Eleyne [and] Polixene" (1, 455), all of whom brought their lovers to disaster. Helen appears at Deiphoebus's house, and in circumstances that disturbingly prefigure her later liaison with (and betrayal of) her host; and Polyxena is then referred to explicitly by Troilus when, in Book 3, he offers to be a go-between for Pandarus with "my faire suster Polixene" (409). Perhaps it is also Polyxena who is the composer of the song Antigone sings in Book 2. The song is written, we are tantalizingly told, by "the goodlieste *mayde* / Of gret estat in al the town of Troye, / And let hire lif in moste honour and joye" (2, 881–82) and is addressed to an absent lover ("Now good thrift have he, whereso that he be!" [2, 847]). These are conditions that would seem to fit particularly aptly a Polyxena who was pining for Achilles.

2. Chaucer could have found this prophecy implicit in the ecphrasis in the temple of Juno in *Aeneid* 1, 474–78, where not only does the *infelix puer* Troilus stand for all the victims of the Trojan War, and of the Italian Wars to come, but his death fits into a larger pattern of prophecy that Aeneas reads but fails to understand. An example of a medieval history that promotes the military role of Troilus in order to link his death to the city's destruction is the *Chronique Martinienne*, a translation of the *Cronica* of Martin of Poland made in 1458 by Sébastien Mamerot (Pierre Champion, ed., *Cronique Martiniane* [Paris: Champion, 1907], xlvi). The connection between the eponymous Troilus and his city is exploited by a number of Trojan texts: for instance, Albert of Stade's *Troilus* establishes in its poem an analogy between the fact that Troilus was named after the city and that the poem is also called *Troilus* because it is named after the Trojan War, which is its subject: "Troilus est Troilus Troiano principe natus / Et liber est Troilus ob Troia bella vocatus" (Albertus Stadensis, *Troilus*, ed. T. Merzdorf [Leipzig: Teubner, 1875], 9: these lines may be an interpolation into Albert's original). According to the *Compendium historiae Troianae-Romanae*, Troy was named after Troilus: first it was called Neptunia, but "que post modo, a Troiulo eius nepote, Troia apellata fuit" (ed. Simonsfeld, 242).

The poem forces us to ask this question, but it declines to provide a clear answer. Chaucer's narrative persistently resists the equation of the erotic and the martial, even at the level of analogy or synecdoche—as Troilus, so Troy. Rather, the fate of the city is seen to be overdetermined by a multitude of causes, and Troilus's behavior, if anything, to be *less* culpable, more genuinely heroic, than Trojan society in general. We have already seen how even after the loss of Criseyde Troilus maintains his heroic defense of the city (5, 1751–57); more to the point, the events surrounding the exchange of Criseyde for Antenor are themselves embedded in a set of explanations that preclude Troilus's culpability. In describing the capture of Antenor at the beginning of Book 4, Chaucer returns to the "authentic" accounts of Benoît and Guido that show that Antenor was captured not *with* the other listed Trojans but *despite*— "maugre"—their presence.[3] His purpose is evidently to present this event as a military misadventure caused by an overly aggressive Trojan militarism: the Trojans themselves initiate the battle—"Ector, with ful many a bold baroun, / Caste on a day with Grekis for to fighte" (4, 33–34— and yet (in a passage original with Chaucer) "The folk of Troie hemselven so *mysledden* / That with the worse at nyght homward they fledden" (48–49). Yet another explanation for the fall of the city, and one that also posits a general Trojan culpability, is provided by Calkas immediately prior to the scene of exchange: he explains to the Greeks (in a passage also added by Chaucer) that because Laomedon failed to recompense Apollo and Neptune for building the walls of the city the gods will now bring down vengeance on the "folk of Troie" (4, 122). And yet a third explanation is then provided by the account of the Trojan parliament (another of Chaucer's additions), in which the expediency of the "folk" (4, 198, 202) overrides the moral force of Hector's blunt objection: "We usen here no wommen for to selle" (182). In sum, the event that Chaucer presents as decisive for the fall of Troy—the ironically designated "deliveraunce" (202) of Antenor—is *also* represented as a function of Trojan folly in a wide variety of forms.

Moreover, while we are certainly entitled to see Troilus's love for Criseyde as self-deluded, the poem is careful to exculpate its protagonist from simple selfishness. For just as Hector seeks by his intervention to protect Criseyde (as he had promised), so does Troilus by his silence. "With mannes herte he gan his sorwes drye" (154), and his thought is "*First*, how to save hir honour" (159). At the very moment Criseyde is being sold by his fellow citizens, Troilus is seen as preferring "resoun" to "love" by choosing silence over speech (162–68), an act that defines his devotion to Criseyde—his "trouthe"—as very different from the narrow self-interest that motivates the "peple" (183) of Troy. Far from being complicit in the process that is to bring about their downfall, the lovers are here represented as victims, set apart at the levels of both practice and morality from the world of military, religious, and political action that will serve to drive them apart.

In sum, Chaucer forces upon his historiographically informed reader an interpretive dilemma that allows no easy solution, perhaps even no

---

3. On the revision of 4, 50–54, see Stephen Barney's notes in the *Riverside Chaucer*, 1044–45.

solution at all. Ostentatiously setting aside the historical context, he then persistently if surreptitiously reinvokes it; and yet having done so, he not only fails to impart any clear sense of its relevance but offers explanations that insist upon its irrelevance. In allowing the collapse of the local enclave of love and the civic world in which it is nested to be occasioned by the same event, Chaucer establishes a connection at the level of event that is then denied at the level of causality. This denial is all the more unsettling because he implies that both events are motivated by a self-destructive blindness: "O nyce world, lo, thy discrecioun" (4, 206) he apostrophizes the Trojan parliament, echoing his earlier apostrophe to the love-struck Troilus—"O blynde world, O blynde entencioun!" (1, 211). But then by here setting Troilus's "reasonable" silence (further legitimized by Hector's high-minded defense) against the clamorous "noyse of peple" (183), the poet insists upon the moral difference between two similar acts of self-destruction.

The effect of this juxtaposition is to bring the reader to an interpretive impasse. We have been encouraged to see the complex erotic relationship that constitutes the subject matter of the poem as providing an interpretive purchase upon the large historical event in which it is embedded; but then at this moment of crisis we are denied the means to do so. Troilus's love fails, Troy fails: these symmetrical events come finally to provide a statement not about the meaning of history but instead about its profound meaninglessness. We can of course find reasons for each individual failure, but it is the lack of connection that is distressing, especially since the narrative seems to assert it so insistently. At best, we are allowed only a metaphoric relation: both Troilus and the Trojans behave foolishly. Not only is this conclusion banal, but it leads to the monkish conclusion that history is by definition simply a record of human folly. Denied a stance within the historical world itself, then, the only critical purchase we can gain upon the action is one that stands outside history altogether—a position that necessarily denies the significance that the poem, by its very definition as a Troy book, seeks to express. How far this impasse can be attributed to a structural weakness in medieval historiography (as distinct from looking beyond Chaucer's poem to its own historical environment) must be our next question; and the first route to its answer is an investigation of previous Trojan history writing, especially that of Benoît de Sainte-Maure in the *Roman de Troie*.

* * *

[Omitted here are two sections. In the first Patterson reviews the idea of history presented by accounts of Trojan history from Dares and Dictys to Guido delle Colonne, focussing on Benoît's *Roman de Troie*. He finds in them a historiographical impasse: the catastrophe of Troy is finally enigmatic, and not easily moralized. Boccaccio's response was in effect to remove the love story from its problematic historical setting.

The second omitted section treats the story of Thebes as embedded in *Troilus and Criseyde*, which forms an analogue to the story of Troy, but which likewise displays the moral meaninglessness and empty recursiveness of history—*Editor*.]

The Form of Subjectivity

The subjectivity represented in *Troilus and Criseyde* is as doubled, as duplicitous, as that of *Anelida and Arcite*. The love story the poem tells is about how two people strive, unsuccessfully, to become one; and their failure is a function of their own lack of oneness or integrity—a quality that must be understood in psychological as well as ethical terms. The condition to which both Troilus and Criseyde aspire in the poem is conceived as a love that overcomes difference—what the narrator calls, in reference to himself, "unliklynesse" (1, 16)—by establishing a unifying concord. As Pandarus, optimistically but finally inaccurately tells the lovers, "ye two ben al on" (4, 592).

"Love is he that alle thing may bynde" (1, 237), and as criticism has well shown, for Troilus this "holy bond" (3, 1261) not only unites him to Criseyde but "cercle[s] hertes alle" (3, 1767) in a universal, cosmic harmony.[4] Criseyde's aspirations are less philosophical, but criticism too rarely acknowledges that she also yearns for an unmediated mutuality, as the account of her inward conversion to love in Book 2 shows. First she listens to Antigone's song, which describes love as the reciprocal and unstinting exchange of hearts: the lady of the song loves a knight "In which myn herte growen is so faste, / And his in me, that it shal evere laste" (2, 872–73). Then she dreams a literal enactment of this exchange, with an eagle playing the role of Troilus. For Troilus Criseyde is firmly "iset" (3, 1488) in his heart, and for Criseyde Troilus is in turn "so depe in-with myn herte grave" (3, 1499) that he could (she says) never be turned out. "I am thyn, by God and by my trouthe" (3, 1512) she avers, and Troilus similarly tells Pandarus that "I thus am hires" (3, 1608)—a reciprocal self-surrender that allows for an apparently instinctive and equivalent mutuality: "ech of hem gan otheres lust obeye" (3, 1690). As the narrator says, "This is no litel thyng of for to seye" (3, 1688).

That Troilus and Criseyde posit as their goal unmediated mutuality and universal harmony both defines desire as privation and accounts for its inevitable unfulfillment. Both lovers are in search of a completeness that will minister to a sense of need that they differently but mutually express. For Troilus desire is experienced as the discomfort of absence: he burns with "the fyr of love" (1, 436), a metaphor invoked throughout the poem to articulate appetite as self-consumption. As he says at the outset, "at myn owen lust I brenne" (1, 407). For Criseyde the situation is more complicated, since the cultural constraints placed upon the representation of female sexuality allow it only a displaced expression. But in the one moment when her desire does emerge directly, it too adopts a metaphor of privation. Catching sight of Troilus returning from battle, she famously exclaims, "Who yaf me drynke?" (2, 651): the sight of Troilus is a love potion that quickens rather than slakes thirst. Love is an appetite that grows by feeding; lovers are driven by yearnings that cannot be relieved by each other.

This is an economy of desire that can easily be accommodated to

---

4. See, for example, Rowe, *O Love! O Charitee!*, passim. On the ambivalence of the imagery of binding in the poem, see Stephen Barney, "Troilus Bound," *Speculum* 47 (1972): 445–58.

traditional medieval paradigms. In Boethian terms the lovers are driven by an *amor conversus* that seeks to return to the *fons et origo* from which they originally derived but that has been misled into the false good of each other. In Christian terms the lovers are tormented by a *concupiscentia* that is the effect of the fall, an endless desire that they have, in the words of the *Parson's Tale*, "wrongfully disposed or ordeyned" so that they now "coveite, by coveitise of flessh, flesshly synne" (X, 336). But Chaucer is unusual in not allowing these absolutist positions either to foreclose his exploration of the dynamic of desire or to prescribe its terms. Much of the burden of the poem concerns the nature of the subjectivity that at once produces and is produced by the historical world; and while we are never allowed to forget its endemic insufficiencies, it is described with a particularity and intensity that frustrate appropriation by any essentializing interpretive scheme, whether medieval or modern.

Central to Chaucer's independence from absolutist schemes is his concept of *entente:* he transforms the Boethian concept of *intentio naturalis* into a historicized and therefore irreducibly complex notion of intention—part motive, part goal, part meaning. At the opening of the poem the audience is enjoined to "herk[en] with a good entencioun" (1, 52), and throughout the first three books we are encouraged to think that a similarly benevolent—and largely indeterminate—intention is shared by the characters as well. Pandarus assures Troilus at the outset that "myn entencioun / Nis nat to yow of reprehencioun" (1, 683–84) and tells Criseyde that "I speke of good entencioun" (2, 295), that "myn entent is cleene" (2, 580). He seeks to foreclose the very possibility of interpretation: his meaning is at once self-evident—"This al and som, and pleynly oure entente" (2, 363)—and benevolent: "What so I spak, I mente naught but wel" (2, 592). Criseyde is apparently persuaded. Troilus, she believes, "meneth in good wyse" (2, 721), Antigone's song was written "with . . . good entente" (2, 878), and she listens to the nightingale "in good entente" (2, 923). And like Pandarus, she wants to believe that her own intention is "pleyn": " 'For pleynly myn entente,' as seyde she, / Was for to love hym unwist, if she myghte" (2, 1293–94). When at Deiphoebus's house she asks Troilus "to telle [her] the fyn of his entente" (3, 125), Troilus outlines a program of courtly service that Criseyde accepts with the semicontractual and yet resolutely vague phrase, "as I wel mene, eke menen wel to me" (164).

Yet as the poem proceeds this vagueness is asked to bear an intolerable weight of implication. At the beginning of Book 3, for instance, Troilus and Pandarus struggle to articulate the nature of their relationship, with Pandarus finally sliding off the issue with a dismissive gesture: "Al sey I nought, thow wost wel what I meene" (256), he says, to which he later unhelpfully adds, "For wel I woot, thow menest wel, pardee" (337). In describing the consummation scene the narrator has continual recourse to bland, justificatory formulas. When Criseyde allows Troilus into the bedroom, we are told that, "Considered alle thynges as they stoode, / No wonder is, syn she did al for goode" (923–24); and then when she allows him into her bed, the formula reappears again, although now with an awkward qualification: "for every wyght, I gesse, / That loveth wel, meneth but gentilesse" (1147–48). Criseyde then explains to Troilus that "In alle thyng is myn entente cleene" (1166)—later she "Opned hire herte, and tolde hym hire entente" (1239)—while Troilus embraces her "as he that mente / Nothyng but wel" (1185–86) and then makes known his "clene entente" (1229). Finally, to complete this picture of well-meaning, "Pandarus with a ful good entente / Leyde hym to slepe" (1188–89).

What precisely is the content of this *entente?* The question becomes increasingly urgent as the narrative moves from its comic ascent in Books 1–3 to the tragic collapse of Books 4 and 5. When in Book 4 Pandarus is about to send Troilus to discuss their dilemma with Criseyde, he assures him that "by hire wordes ek, and by hire cheere / Thou shalt ful sone aperceyve and wel here / Al hire entente" (655–57); and as Criseyde works her persuasions on Troilus the narrator hopefully adds that "al this thyng was sayd of good entente" (1416), that she "spak right as she mente" (1418). Yet we can doubt whether even Criseyde knows what she means, anymore than she did in Book 2. Even as she prepares in Book 5 to accept Diomede's proposal, she plaintively assures herself that "in conclusioun, / I mene wel" (5, 1003–4), and when she writes her final, unworthy letter to Troilus she concludes with a painfully self-revealing apology for its brevity: "Ek gret effect men write in places lite; / Th'entente is al, and nat the lettres space" (5, 1629 30). When Troilus sees his brooch on Diomede's armor he thinks that this *entente* is now clear, for he assumes that Criseyde meant to make a public profession of her love—"for that ye mente / Al outrely to shewen youre entente" (5, 1693–94). The fact is apparently unarguable, but Criseyde (and the reader) may well feel that both more and less was meant.

We are continually tempted toward irony and even cynicism by the language of *entente*, which often seems simply a disguise for embarrassing motives. Yet such a reading is included within the poem in a form that makes it increasing difficult to accept, since to do so requires us to identify with the cynical Pandarus. Unable to understand that motives (including his own) may be complex and even conflicted, Pandarus focuses only on what the narrator calls "the fyn of his entente" (3, 553) and seeks to foreclose the process by which that conclusion is to be achieved as of no interest. As he himself says to Criseyde,

> Nece, alwey—lo!—to the laste,
> How so it be that som men hem delite
> With subtyl art hire tales to endite,
> Yet for al that, in hire entencioun,
> Hire tale is al for som conclusioun. (2, 255–59)

This conclusion is to bring Troilus and Criseyde to bed, after which "Pandarus hath fully his entente" (3, 1582). But is it adequate to say, with Pandarus, that the conclusion to which the lovers' *entente* is directed is the sexual act? And that in having it *they* have fully their *entente?* And are the elaborate means by which that *entente* is brought to fulfillment (the entire first half of a very long poem) simply a form of erotic deferral, an elaborately extended foreplay?

To grant Pandarus's view interpretive authority is to reduce *Troilus and Criseyde* to the *Filostrato*. For in that poem a lofty idealism—compounded largely of Boethian and Dantean materials—is undercut by a deeply misogynist cynicism about the nature of desire. This cynicism is, significantly, most explicitly voiced by Boccaccio's Pandaro:

> I believe indeed that every lady leads an amorous life
> in her wishes, and the only thing that restrains her is
> the fear of shame; and if for such yearning a full
> remedy can virtuously be given, he is foolish who does
> not despoil her, for in my opinion the distress vexes
> her little. My cousin is a widow, she desires, and
> should she deny it I would not believe her.[5]

When Criseida shortly does deny it, Pandaro repeats his opinion with exasperation (2, 112), and Criseida instantly drops the pretense: she smiles in assent (113), and in her subsequent interior monologue admits to herself and to us her desire for a consummation: "would that I were now in his sweet embrace, pressed face to face!" (117).[6] According to the logic of Boccaccio's poem, these carnal impulses find their inevitable moral extension in her later infidelity, motivated as it is by the "lies, deceptions and betrayals" (53, 18) that lurk within her. The *Filostrato* must, therefore, end with a misogynist outburst ("Giovane donna è mobile" [53, 30]) qualified only by the claim that there does exist, somewhere, a "perfetta donna" who is at once amorous and faithful. Nor are these ambivalences absent from the dramatic frame in which Boccaccio's poem is set. Written to persuade the poet's own "donna gentil" of the intensity of his passive suffering, the poem also demonstrates the poet's active power as moral arbiter and propagandist. The lady is disingenuously advised to apply to herself only those "praiseworthy things" written about Criseida and to regard the "other things" as there just for the sake of the story—a selective reading that is meant to be impossible. Should she not return to her adoring poet, runs the clear implication, "la donna gentil" is in danger of becoming known as another "Criseida villana" (8, 28) through the agency of the same poet, now grown vengeful. His poem is, he tells us at the beginning, the "forma alla mia intenzione" (Proemio), and it accurately embodies the complex mix of emotions that women elicit from the men who are simultaneously their victims and masters.

Chaucer's poem, as C. S. Lewis argued many years ago, consistently excludes the misogyny that provides one pole for Boccaccio's amorous dialectic.[7] Pandaro's account of female desire is both sharply truncated in the corresponding speech by Chaucer's Pandarus and generalized into a human quality, characteristic of both men and women:

---

5. Trans. Nathaniel Edward Griffin and Arthur Beckwith Myrick (New York. Biblo and Tannen, 1967 [1929]), 2, 27.

6. For Criseida's earlier expressions of desire, see Boccaccio's account of her meditation on Troiolo (2, 68–87).

7. In "What Chaucer Really Did to *Il Filostrato*," Lewis contrasted Boccaccio's "cynical Latin gallantries" with what he took to be Chaucer's commitment to the code of courtly love (75); but as Sanford Meech showed, what Chaucer was really doing was installing in the place of the *Filostrato's* misogyny reductions a fully articulated conception of the self in the process of being in love (*Design in Chaucer's "Troilus"* [Syracuse: Syracuse University Press, 1959]). For moralizing readings of the *Filostrato*, however, see Robert P. apRoberts, "Love in the *Filostrato*," *ChR* 7 (1972): 1–26; and Chauncey Wood, *Elements of Chaucer's* Troilus, 3–37.

Was nevere man or womman yet bigete
That was unapt to suffren loves hete,
Celestial, or elles love of kynde;
Forthy som grace I hope in hire to fynde.   (1, 977–80)

Similarly, Pandaro's second use of this Ovidian *topos* (2, 112) is wholly
revised by Chaucer to become a comment not on women's amorousness
but on their *daunger* (2, 1149–52), and Criseida's answering smile
becomes in Criseyde both less knowing and less specific to Pandarus's
comment. Finally, the explicit antifeminism of Boccaccio's ending (8, 3)
is wholly excluded in Chaucer's poem. But Chaucer does more than
protect Criseyde from antifeminist reductions. His revisions also allow
into his poem a more capacious representation of subjectivity—the
whole inner world so inadequately designated by the single word
entente—than the *Filostrato* can accommodate. Boccaccio's poem
remains within the generic confines of erotic literature, a typical if prom-
inent example of the Ovidian tradition of the Middle Ages. His charac-
ters are defined by the genre: lovers and only lovers, they draw their
motivations from the store of recognized erotic impulses and define their
lives solely in terms of their amorous fates. But Chaucer's poem expands
these generic boundaries in order to explore the nature of subjectivity
itself, and in doing so it shows how the notion of intention, as defined
by either philosophy (Boethius) or moral theology (the Parson), is in-
adequate to an account of human action.

To reduce the subjectivity of the *Troilus* to intentionality is to assume
that human beings exist as singular, self-identical, and self-present indi-
viduals, an assumption that the poem throughout calls into question.
Instead, we would do better to think of the subjectivity of the *Troilus* as a
site where not one but many intentions—in effect, many selves—are in a
ceaseless process of constitution. In one sense, the character who most
ostentatiously displays the multiplicity of selves that typifies this subjec-
tivity is the Janus-faced Pandarus. Mercurial in mood as in function, he
alternates easily between modes of behavior that we usually think of as
distinct: as he shuttles visitors in and out of Troilus's sickroom at Dei-
phoebus's house, for instance, he adopts and divests himself of a wide
variety of roles, and in his manipulation of the consummation scene he is
equally adept at assuming—and perhaps even experiencing—radically
disparate forms of behavior. He is, moreover, equally at home at Troilus's
"beddes syde" (3, 236, 1589; 5, 294) or at Criseyde's (3, 682, 1555–82),
and he displays throughout the narrative a sexual interest that is at once
genderless and double-gendered, without specific affect and therefore
capable of multiple cathexes. It is true that the very facility that makes it
possible for Pandarus to transfigure himself as he manipulates others
might render his subjectivity less rather than more problematic: in defin-
ing him as less than fully invested in any of his roles, the poem invites us
to understand him as an instance of a simple, in the sense of deliberate
and therefore wholly controlled, hypocrisy. But even this kind of simplic-
ity is delusive. The turmoil of selves that he displays comes finally to sur-
round a strange emptiness at the center—we never finally do understand
his own motivation, and neither, so far as we know, does he.

Just as Pandarus is more of a mystery than he may at first appear, so too are the lovers; and while we (and they) are tempted to stress their difference from him, the narrative insists that they are to an important degree equivalent. That Criseyde is changeable is the central fact about her: linked imagistically to the moon, to "slydynge fortune," and to the unstable world itself, she is an object of exchange whose subjectivity alters with her circumstances.[8] With Troilus she is a courtly lady anxiously aware that all worldly happiness is "fals felicitee" (3, 814), aggrieved and saddened by her lover's jealousy, and yet finally prepared to yield herself wholly to him: "And at o word, withouten repentaunce, / Welcome, my knyght, my pees, my suffisaunce!" (3, 1308–9). Yet immediately after this wholehearted yielding she engages in a notoriously ambiguous flirtation with Pandarus that causes even the narrator to turn away in embarrassment—"I passe al that which chargeth nought to seye" (3, 1576)—and she finally becomes the woman whose self-interest allows her to accept the matching selfishness of Diomede's brutal protection. It is all too easy to decide that the last of these Criseydes is the real one, but to do so requires us to impeach all the rest by assuming a self-consistency—a constancy of selfhood—that the poem itself shows to be an illusion.

For not even Troilus, endowed (as Criseyde herself recognizes) with "moral vertu, grounded upon trouthe" (4, 1672), is exempt from variableness. Two examples of his complexity—a complexity that he himself seeks to efface and that criticism has been equally reluctant to acknowledge—will suffice. After each of the dramatized meetings with his lady, Troilus engages in a conversation with Pandarus that reveals a sharply different self than had previously been in evidence. In the bedroom at Deiphoebus's house Troilus is a tongue-tied lover, unable to manage the elaborate game of role playing that Pandarus has fabricated: when Criseyde declines to be the courtly beloved but insists instead on acting the threatened victim pleading for protection, Troilus collapses into blushing silence (3, 78–84). Similarly, and even more drastically, at Pandarus's house the fiction of Horaste—and Criseyde's apparent belief in it—renders him not just silent but unconscious: unable to extricate himself from Pandarus's web, he faints.

But after each of these scenes he is a wholly different, and far less appealing, person. When Pandarus worries that he might be thought a bawd, Troilus provides not just the expected disclaimers but also an offer to be himself a bawd in return. Not only does this offer reinstate the sleaziness that he and Pandarus have been trying to deny, but it is delivered in a language far more blunt that any that Pandarus would use:

> I have my faire suster Polixene,
> Cassandre, Eleyne, or any of the frape
> Be she nevere so fair or wel yshape,
> Tel me which thow wilt of everychone,
> To han for thyn, and lat me thanne allone.   (3, 409–13)

Similarly, when after the lovers' night together Pandarus again comes to Troilus, not only does Troilus "telle hym of his glade nyght" (3, 1646)

8. For these comparisons, see Rowe, *O Love, O Charite!*, 57–91.

but he is "nevere ful to speke of this matere" (1661). "This tale ay was span-newe to bygynne, / Til that the night departed hem atwynne" (1665–66): for an entire day Troilus rehearses with his friend the night they have *together* (we unhappily remember) spent with Criseyde—men discoursing together about a woman they have, in some indefinable but nonetheless real way, already shared. Here it is Criseyde who is the mediating third term: at once present in memory and absent in fact, she is the means by which two men spend a day together—and a day apparently spent, moreover, in bed.[9]

We can, if we wish, draw a moral distinction between Criseyde's abandonment of Troilus and Troilus's talking about Criseyde with Pandarus, but we should not allow it to obscure the similarity between the two lovers. In fact, Chaucer continually insists that not one but both the lovers are simultaneously knowing and unknowing, at once conscious of the nature of their desire and the means of its fulfillment and yet profoundly, and necessarily, unaware. Criseyde must know, for example, that the meeting at Deiphoebus's house is not required by Poliphete's threat—which she herself has dismissed (2, 1477–78)—and both the secret pleasure she takes at the discussion of Troilus's illness and virtues ("For which with sobre cheere hire herte lough" [2, 1592]) and her lack of surprise at the absence of Helen and Deiphoebus in his bedroom certainly suggest that she knows the true purpose of the meeting. But does this mean that her continued playing of the role of threatened victim is simply hypocrisy, an empty gesture toward conventions of seemliness? Or does it not rather express hesitations and anxieties that are deeply a part of her character? Similarly, the night at Pandarus's house where the lovers will, as the narrator delicately says, "leiser have hire speches to fulfelle" (3, 510) is prepared for by innuendo and even outright suggestion (see, e.g., 3, 566–67); indeed, the very pretext that keeps Criseyde from going home—that it is raining—is itself empty, since it was raining not only before she came but when the invitation was first accepted (see 3, 562). Yet does that mean that Criseyde's shock on being awakened by Pandarus, and her protestations about receiving Troilus, are meaningless? If they are, why does Pandarus confect the story about Horaste in the first place? The fact is that this semiawareness is a necessary condition for the love affair. No doubt Criseyde is in Pandarus's house because she wants to make love with Troilus: as she finally says to him, "Ne hadde I er now, my swete herte deere, / Ben yolde, ywis, I were now nought here!" (3, 1210–11). But because her world proscribes the explicit representation of female sexual desire, she cannot admit this want either to others or to herself. Indeed, the obsessive secrecy that surrounds and perhaps even dooms the affair is best understood as a metaphoric displacement of this need for *self-concealment*: it is less "every pie and every lette-game" (3, 527) who threaten the affair than the guilt and shame with which sexuality, and specifically female sexuality, is invested.

9. When Pandarus first arrives he sits on the "beddes syde" (1589) to talk with Troilus, but Troilus leaps up and gets on his knees in thanksgiving. Then, however, "down in his bed he lay" (1615), and we never hear of him getting up again: just as the first conversation takes place with Pandarus on the "beddes syde" (3, 236) and Troilus lying down, so too does this one.

When Chaucer describes how Criseyde falls in love, he shows not only that desire is experienced by her as an external force that comes upon her, but that even when it has become a part of her—when it has become *her* desire—she is unable to represent it to herself as her own. Aroused first by Pandarus's words, her feelings are intensified by the sight of Troilus returning from battle to the point where she can understand them only as a form of almost chemical change: "Who yaf me drynke?"[1] Retreating into her closet, she then retreats yet further into her own mind: by debating the question of love she hopes to gain a conscious purchase upon it. This process is not resolved but merely sealed by a series of symbolic events (all of them Chaucer's invention) that serve to present love, and specifically passion, as an entity at once a part of and apart from the female subject who experiences it. First there is the over-hearing of the *Canticus Antigoni* (as several manuscripts call it). A song of love as mutuality, it alienates Criseyde's desire from itself by its double vicariousness: it is not even Antigone's own song much less Criseyde's (and hence its difference from the *Canticus Troili* of the previous book) but the song of the unnamed "goodlieste mayde / Of gret estat in al the town of Troye" (880–81). Then there is the "lay / Of love" (921–22) sung by the nightingale in the cedar tree, a wordless song that by its oblique allusion to Philomela images passion as a function only of the rapacious male and so simultaneously invokes and mutes the female fear of desire. And finally there is the dream of the bone-white eagle with his "longe clawes" (927), who in rending from her her heart and replacing it with his own fulfills the promise of mutuality offered in Antigone's song and so redeems the violence of the means: "she nought agroos, ne nothyng smerte" (930). Criseyde remains the passive recipient of actions performed not only upon her body but with her will—and yet at no point does either body or will find representation. By this point, Criseyde has, as she will later, passively say, "ben yold" (3, 1210), but her accession to that yielding—much less her desire for it—remains unspoken and unacknowledged. She knows and doesn't know that she desires: she has heard it and dreamed it, and the knowledge is at once part of and apart from her.

The unreflective, subterranean way in which love comes upon Criseyde is a function not of moral failure but of cultural necessity: all we need do to demonstrate this to ourselves is to try to imagine in what terms she might acknowledge her own sexuality. For then she immediately turns into a character like the Miller's Alison, or Alison of Bath—and she perforce exits from the world of this poem. The precondition of Criseyde's existence as Criseyde, in other words, is that she *not* know the burden of that name.

Troilus's Oedipean blindness is also prescribed by cultural imperatives. After his sight of Criseyde in the temple he composes the *Canticus Troili*, asserting his utter passivity before the transcendent force that has possessed him. So too does Chaucer assert his passivity in receiving the translation of this song from "myn auctour called Lollius" (1, 394). But

---

1. That Criseyde has been prepared by Pandarus's words is suggested by the description of "al hir meyne" rushing to welcome him with a cry of remarkably sexual suggestiveness: "cast up the yates wyde! / For thorwgh this strete he moot to paleys ride" (615–16).

just as the "tonges difference" (1, 395) that is the condition of all writing subverts the disingenuous claim of the poet, so do the circumstances of the lover's song call into question the singleness of his *entente:* it is one of the means by which Troilus will *"arten* hire to love" (1, 388), and its strategic value stands in awkward opposition to its transcendent claims.[2] Neither poet nor lover is in touch with an origin (Love, Lollius) that legitimizes their analogous projects. Indeed, as soon as the metaphor of Cupid shooting lovers with his arrows is invoked in the temple scene in Book 1 (206–10) it is immediately undone by the heavily sexualized eye play in which Troilus and Criseyde then engage. Troilus's "eye percede, and so depe it wente / Til on Criseyde it smot, and ther it stente" (1, 272–73); but when she responds with her "somdele deignous" glance, "He was tho glad his hornes in to shrinke" (300). Rather than proceeding from a transcendent source, desire is a function of human sexuality, and the metaphor of Cupid's arrows is revealed as a mystification of its physical source.

But if sexuality is the ground of Troilus's desire, it is in no sense its whole content. Indeed, if it were, the loss of Criseyde would be easily consoled. To "arten" Criseyde solely for the purposes of sexual gratification would be as much a betrayal of Troilus's *gentilesse* as it would be to "ravisshe" her out of Troy. Hence the necessity of Pandarus, whose function for Troilus is to enact those aspects of his *entente* to love that he cannot acknowledge. It is because Pandarus is available not only to handle the embarrassing details of the consummation but actually to undress Troilus and install him in Criseyde's bed that Troilus can afford to faint. The point is not, as D. W. Robertson has memorably said, that Troilus loves Criseyde for nothing more "than her pleasing 'figure' and surpassing competence in bed," but that his desire is initiated by and necessarily includes a sexuality that he wishes both to enact and, for reasons we are surely meant to admire, to disavow.[3]

Willful ignorance is thus the condition of the lovers' very existence. Endowed with a subjectivity that is irreducibly complex, and driven by a desire that at once includes sexuality and aspires to a satisfaction that sexual possession can never provide, their unification can only be accomplished by means of a go-between whose very presence necessarily betrays, and betrays it to, its own multiplicity. To acknowledge that Pandarus represents the mediated and therefore unsatisfactory gratification at which all desire arrives is not, however, to establish him as the cause of the failure. On the contrary, the tragedy of desire is that its efforts to recover that which has been lost serve to confirm how truly lost it is: the condition of desire is always to rebegin. This rebeginning is enacted by the lovers in Book 4, which repeats (as we have seen) the structure of the action of Books 1–3. An effort at closure, Book 4 not only, and necessarily, fails of its desire but then opens onto the saddest act of repetition of all, the parodic reenactments of the past that occupy Book 5. With Diomede Criseyde not only engages in a foreshortened and debased reenactment of her courtship with Troilus, but as the poem

---

2. The verb *arten* is derived, according to the *MED*, from *arctare* and means to compel, force, or induce; but it also absorbs ominous connotations from its homonym, art.
3. Robertson, *Preface to Chaucer*, 496.

leaves her she recognizes that her fate is to be "rolled . . . on many a tonge" (5, 1061) by historians who are the literary equivalent of Diomede with his "tonge large" (5, 804). This is both a Dantesque vision of the endless historiographical recording in which she is condemned to re-enact her original crime and, with Chaucer's invocation of the "tonge" with which both Diomede and historians like himself manipulate her, a disturbingly vivid reminder of the sexual abuse implicit in misogynist writing.

In describing Criseyde's betrayal, as with the other decisive moments of his poem, the narrator insists that the process by which actions unfold is so imperceptibly gradual and so compounded of motives and circum-stances that the search for a single or simple explanation—"the cause whi"—is inevitably thwarted. At the conclusion of Diomede's interview with Criseyde in her tent, "he roos and tok his leve."

> The brighte Venus folwede and ay taughte
> The wey ther brode Phebus down alighte;
> And Cynthea hire char-hors overraughte
> To whirle out of the Leoun, if she myghte;
> And Signifer his candels sheweth bright
> Whan that Criseyde unto hire bedde wente
> Inwith hire faders faire brighte tente,
>
> Retornyng in hire soule ay up and down
> The wordes of this sodeyn Diomede,
> His grete estat, and perel of the town,
> And that she was allone and hadde nede
> Of frendes help; and thus bygan to brede
> The cause whi, the sothe for to telle,
> That she took fully purpos for to dwelle.   (5, 1016–29)

The astronomical machinery represents not only the relentless passage of time—Criseyde had promised Troilus she would return "Er Phebus suster, Lucina the sheene, / The Leoun passe out of this Ariete" (4, 1591–92)—but also the workings of forces that operate in ways that are necessarily not fully available to self-reflection. Now as the moon leaves Leo so does Criseyde leave the lover who has just been described as "Yong, fressh, strong, and hardy as lyoun" (5, 830).[4] Venus is somehow in Diomede's train here, and she in turn dominates Phoebus Apollo: to say that love overcomes wisdom is a not inaccurate translation of the astronomical symbolism, but neither is it fully adequate as an account of Criseyde's decision. The Zodiac bears signs, but their meaning is not available to Criseyde, an ignorance that is both the condition of her very existence and a key constitutive of her decision—if "decision" is the right word. Lying in bed, Criseyde "returns" Diomede's words as the heavens turn, a scene that itself returns to the night some three years before when "lay she stille and thoughte" (2, 915) of Troilus's words, of Pan-darus's, and of Antigone's. Then she had heard the "lay / Of love" sung

---

4. And see also 1, 1074, where we are told that "in the field [Troilus] pleyde tho leoun." The symmetry between Troilus the lion and his rival Diomede the boar perhaps derives from the *Thebaid*, where Adrastus is given a prophecy that his two daughters will be married to a lion (Polynices) and a boar (Tydeus); see *Thebaid* 1, 395–400.

by the nightingale, had dreamed the dream of the eagle, and had awakened (we were prepared to believe) in love.[5]

In deciding to stay with Diomede and abandon Troilus, Criseyde not only continues her earlier behavior but reveals her life to be a continuous process that cannot be endowed with a precisely demarcated beginning and ending, in the sense of either a single motive or an intended goal. If it were true, as Pandarus had said, that "th'ende is every tales strengthe" (2, 260), now that we reach that conclusion we should be able retrospectively to evaluate the meaning of the events that have occurred: "But natheles men seyen that at the laste, / For any thyng, men shal the soothe se" (5, 1639–40). Criseyde's liaison with Diomede ought then to tell us what her liaison with Troilus meant: at the end of her career in the poem her actions will have made clear what she meant at the beginning, just as when Troilus and Criseyde ended up in bed we knew (apparently) that this had always been "the fyn of hir entente." But in fact, far from clarifying the enigma of her character and motivation, much less of human actions in general, Criseyde's behavior in Book 5 serves to compound the difficulty: her end does not gloss but replicates her beginning.[6]

It seems that the narrator himself finds this narrative inconclusion painful. So, at least, we might judge from his last-minute attempt to suppress it. In the midst of Diomede's second and successful assault on Criseyde, he suddenly introduces into the poem portraits of the three protagonists. Technically, the presence of these portraits is sanctioned by the historiographical tradition: Dares, Benoît, and Joseph of Exeter all include similar passages in their histories, and Chaucer's version may owe some details specifically to Joseph.[7] But the point about their late appearance in *this* version of the story is that they evade the very problem of interpretation on which Chaucer has hitherto insisted. By substituting for the detailed representation of subjectivity woodenly externalized *effictiones* ornamented with brief judgments—Diomede has the reputation of being "of tonge large" (804), Criseyde is, notoriously, "slydynge of corage" (825), Troilus is "trewe as stiel in ech condicioun" (831)—the narrator suddenly implies that the relation of character to action has

---

5. For an account of the symmetry between Criseyde falling in and out of love with Troilus, see Donald R. Howard, "Experience, Language, and Consciousness: *Troilus and Criseyde*, II, 596–931," in *Medieval Literature and Folklore Studies: Essays in Honor of Francis Lee Utley*, ed. Jerome Mandel and Bruce A. Rosenberg (New Brunswick: Rutgers University Press, 1970), 173–92.

6. As we would expect of a Troy poem, *Troilus and Criseyde* is saturated with the language of beginnings and endings: see, for example, 1, 377–78; 1, 973; 2, 671–72; 2, 790–91; 2, 1234–35; 2, 1565–66; 2, 1595–96; 3, 462; 4, 1282–84; 5, 764–65; 5, 1003–4; and 5, 1828–33.

7. Ever since R. K. Root's essay on "Chaucer's Dares," *MP* 15 (1917–18): 1–22, it has been assumed that Chaucer knew Joseph of Exeter's *Ilias Daretis Phrygii* and used it in these portraits. But the evidence is very slight. There is also no firm evidence that Chaucer knew either Dares or Dictys directly, but given their assimilation into Benoît and Guido it is unlikely that we would be able to recognize their direct presence in Chaucer's poem in any case. It is possible, however, that his reference to Geoffrey of Monmouth as a Trojan historian in the *House of Fame* (1470) shows that Chaucer was misled by one of the several manuscripts of Geoffrey's *Historia* that was prefaced with Dares's *Historia* into thinking that Geoffrey was the author of the entire Trojan-British compilation. He may have read Dares's *Historia*, in other words, thinking it was by Geoffrey, and assumed that Dares's work was something else again. *Pace* Root, it seems unlikely that he would have thought that Joseph of Exeter's tortuously stylized poem, with its several references to twelfth-century events, was Dares's eyewitness history. For a fourteenth-century version of this technique, see George B. Stow, ed., *Historia vitae et regni Ricardi Secundi* (Philadelphia: University of Pennsylvania Press, 1977), in which the author includes a portrait of Richard II just after his death but prior to the end of the book (161).

become self-evident. But the very narrative that these portraits mean to gloss belies such interpretive confidence.

The circularity traced by Criseyde in Book 5 is traced as well by Troilus, who pathetically (and, for many readers, irritatingly) repeats the lovesick behavior he originally performed in Book 1. When in Book 1 Troilus returned from the temple he made "a mirour of his mynde, / In which he saugh al holly [Criseyde's] figure" (1, 365–66), and in Book 5 he reactivates the imaginative faculty as a cushion against the intrusion of the historical world. "Refiguryng hire shap, hire wommanhede, / Withinne his herte" (5, 473–74) and revisiting the "places of the town / In which he whilom hadde al his plesaunce" (5, 562–63), including her darkened palace, he deliberately tries to recreate the past. And he recreates it in less self-aware ways as well. As soon as he was stricken with love in Book 1 Troilus adopted a series of mortal poses. He was "refus of every creature" and devoted to death; overwhelmed by "sorowe and thought," he "mot nedes deye," to "sterve, unknowe, of [his] destresse," and even Pandarus admitted that he endured "wo / As sharp as doth he Ticius in helle" (1, 570, 579, 573, 616, 785–86). In Book 5 both the suffering and the theatricalization of suffering return. Troilus cries out for death (e.g., 5, 206) and prescribes both his funeral arrangements and his final memorial (the ashes of his heart are to be conserved in a golden urn and bequeathed to Criseyde "for a remembraunce" [5, 315]).[8] "Of hymself ymagened he ofte / To ben defet" (5, 617–18), and he is soon "so defet" (5, 1219) that he has to walk with a stick. When asked the nature of his illness, Troilus is stoically (and gallantly) vague but then meaningfully adds that "he felte a grevous maladie / Aboute his herte, and fayn he wolde dye" (5, 1231–32); and he now confirms Pandarus's original account of his infernal sufferings by retreating to his bed where he "torneth / In furie, as doth he Ixion in helle" (5, 211–12). The torments of the unacknowledged lover in Book 1 become the anguish of the rejected lover in Book 5 and are in both cases an inextricable compound of deep feeling and play acting, the authentic and the theatrical. As does Criseyde, Troilus in his ending returns to his beginning, and nowhere with more poignance than in the scornful laughter from the spheres that echoes the scornful laughter in the temple when he first entered upon his circular course.

Telling the story of Troilus's "double sorwe," the narrative of *Troilus and Criseyde* is itself pervaded with doubleness. In revising Boccaccio, Chaucer consistently added replicating counterparts to what are in the *Filostrato* single incidents. Troilus is seen from Criseyde's window not once but twice; Criseyde gives Troilus a brooch and Chaucer has Troilus reciprocate; love letters are exchanged twice, an event that is then itself repeated in the less amiable exchange of Book 5; Troilus's self-revelation to Pandarus is represented twice, first by the narrator and then by Pandarus himself, who characteristically doubles the incident into two acts of revelation (first in the garden, then in Troilus's room); the added meeting at Deiphoebus's house prefigures the consummation scene; and Criseyde not only has two lovers but has the second woo her twice. So

8. Significantly, Troilus's imagination of his death derives from Arcita's similar imagination in the *Teseida*; see the note in the *Riverside Chaucer* to 5, 280.

too does the Theban story appear in Book 2 in two versions, in both its French and Latin forms, and it then reappears in Cassandra's discourse in Book 5. Nor is the habit of repetition confined to details. As the narrative proceeds it gradually reveals itself to be organized by a whole armature of repeating structures, the most obvious being the recapitulation of Books 1–3 in Book 4 and then, as we have just seen, the further matching of Book 1 and Book 5. And the poem as a whole opens with a Theban phrase ("double sorwe") derived from Dante's rewriting of Augustine in *Purgatorio* 22 and closes with a Christian prayer addressed to "Thow oon and two and thre, eterne on lyve, / That regnest ay in thre and two and oon" (5, 1863–64) that echoes Dante's account of the singing of the "holy circles" in *Paradiso* 14.

The doubleness of the narrative is a symmetrical counterpart to the equivocal subjectivity that is so much the poem's center of attention. A doubled self—in a sense that includes both moral duplicity and the endless psychological multiplicity that defines subjectivity itself—is at once encased within and enacted as a doubled history. Yet the meaning of this symmetry remains enigmatic. We can establish clear causal lines in neither direction: the poem will not allow us to say that the failed love of Troilus and Criseyde causes the fall of Troy nor that the fall of Troy causes the failure of the love affair. Lacking "the cause whi," all we can remark upon is the symmetry itself. The public world of history and the private world of the self stand as mirror images of each other, a specularity that itself reduplicates the doubleness of which they are constituted. And as an act of historiographical analysis the poem itself becomes what Petrarch called a *lavor doppio*, a doubling of the "original speech" or *sermo prisco* of the ancients by a modern respeaking. Past and present become hopelessly intermingled, and the original story disappears in the act of its recovery.

In the *Boece* Lady Philosophy describes man as a being helplessly caught in the middle of a process that he can neither evade nor understand. "Certes," she says, "ye men, that ben erthliche beestes, dremen alwey your bygynnynge, although it be with a thynne ymaginacioun; and by a maner thought, al be it nat clerly ne parfitely, ye loken from afer to thilke verray fyn of blisfulnesse" (3, 3, 1–6). It is this world of mediation, of replicated acts that foreclose the quest for either beginning or end, that Chaucer represents in *Troilus and Criseyde*. Boethianism offers to its believers the knowledge of a *fons et origo* that is not only itself unmediated but identical with the "oon ende of blisfulnesse" (3, 2, 8) to which man's *intentio naturalis* instinctively converts him. Yet for all their striving, not only does this consoling vision finally elude the poem's protagonists, but the terms of its relationship to the historical world requires that it should. Invoked throughout the poem by an elaborate set of allusions, Boethianism functions not as a mode of being available to them and willfully ignored but as a norm of judgment that stands outside and apart from a historical world it weighs in the philosophic balance and finds wanting.[9] When Troilus does finally escape from his own historicity

9. For these allusions, and various Boethian readings of the poem, see Theodore A. Stroud, "Boethius' Influence on Chaucer's *Troilus*," *MP* 49 (1951–52): 1–9; John P. McCall, "Five-Book Structure in Chaucer's *Troilus*," *MLQ* 23 (1962): 297–308; three important articles by Alan Gaylord, "Uncle

by an ascent through the spheres, the Boethian "ful avysement" (5, 1811) at which he arrives is a scornful dismissiveness that condemns all historical experience to "blynde lust" (5, 1834). Yet by drawing his account of Troilus's ascent from the *Teseida*, Chaucer manages to locate even this apparently definitive Boethian moment within a Theben context, and by correlating Troilus's final enlightenment with his youthful ignorance, Chaucer manages to suggest the ultimate impotence, even irrelevance, of Boethianism. Rather than a mode of understanding that is fully aware of the experiential world it presumes to judge, the poem implies, Boethianism is an ideal dream of order that is not only continually belied by experience but is itself motivated by recursive yearnings. Far from prescribing how history either should or could be, Boethianism yearns for a utopian world in which origin and end are simultaneously possessed—a world, that is, from which the embarrassment of history has been entirely banished. In the course of urging Troilus not to despair at the news of Criseyde's exchange, Pandarus offers him (in a stanza original with Chaucer) good Boethian advice about the dangers of trusting in a world governed by Fortune (4, 386–92). This advice is, however, not only impeached both by its source in the poem and by its accompanying proposal that Troilus should transfer his affections to another woman, but Troilus's reply itself offers the definitive statement about the limitations of Boethian transcendence: "O, where hastow ben hid so longe in muwe, / That kanst so wel and formerly arguwe?" (4, 496–97).

We remember that in his *Scalacronica* Sir Thomas Gray founded the ladder of history upon two books, the Bible and "la gest de Troy." Yet in Chaucer's retelling the Trojan source gives way to reveal beneath it yet another source, and one that compulsively insists that beginnings are always rebeginnings, that action is always repetition. Just as Lollius is revealed upon inquiry to be a mumbling together of sources, disparate and even contradictory;[1] and just as the lovers' *entente* is shown in enactment to be a tangled and finally unfathomable compound of idealism, self-regard, and appetite; so the Trojan origin becomes equally inextricable from its own, unacknowledged past. The poem defines historical experience in Theban terms as iterative and compelled, and like Troilus before Cassandra, habitually—and necessarily—blind to its own mean-

---

Pandarus as Lady Philosophy," *Papers of the Michigan Academy of Science, Arts, and Letters* 46 (1961): 571–95; "Chaucer's Tender Trap: The *Troilus* and the 'Yonge, Fresshe Folkes,' " *English Miscellany* 15 (1964): 25–45; and "Friendship in Chaucer's *Troilus*," *ChR* 3 (1968–69): 239–64; John M. Steadman, *Disembodied Laughter: Troilus and the Apotheosis Tradition* (Berkeley: University of California Press, 1972); McAlpine, *Genre* of Troilus and Criseyde; Rowe, *O Love O Charite!*; and Wood, *Elements of Chaucer's* Troilus.

1. As Kittredge pointed out in "Chaucer's Lollius," *Harvard Studies in Classical Philology* 28 (1917): 47–133, Chaucer almost certainly got the idea that Lollius was a Trojan historian from Horace's *Epistle* 1, 2, probably as (mis)cited by John of Salisbury in the *Policraticus*. But he could not have been ignorant of the fact that the ME verb *lollen* meant to mumble or to sing (which is one of the modern explanations offered for the term Lollard: see Malcolm D. Lambert, *Medieval Heresy: Popular Movements from Bogomil to Hus* [London: Edward Arnold, 1977], 302). A native word for indistinct singing then endowed with a classical suffix, "Lollius" is an economical representation of the situation of the vernacular poet who combines a wide variety of postclassical materials (the *Filostrato*, Petrarch, the *Roman de la Rose*, Guido delle Colonne, Benoît de Sainte-Maure, et al.) in an effort to recreate an unavailable classical origin. It was a commonplace of Trojan historiography to complain at the outset of each retelling of the story about the inadequacies and inaccuracies of previous tellings, and in particular to berate Homer for his Greek bias and his predilection for fabling; see, for example, the Prologus to Guido's *Historia* and Chaucer's own account of the rivalry among the Trojan historians in the *House of Fame* (1475–80).

ing. This message preempts not only local lessons about the meaning of Criseyde's betrayal and Troilus's disillusionment but large-scale historical hypotheses about the fall of Troy and the meaning of history itself.

If history has no meaning, or at least none available to human understanding, then Chaucer's essay in the philosophy of history must end as inconclusively as both Criseyde's career and Troilus's life. Criticism has often described what Lowes long ago called "the tumultuous hitherings and thitherings of mood and matter in the last dozen stanzas of the poem," descriptions that provide vivid evidence of the interpretive impasse to which the poem brings both its narrator and its readers.[2] The final stanza is a tacit admission of this abandonment of authorial control. It is a prayer directed to God, the divine *scriptor* who is "Uncircumscript and al maist circumscrive" (5, 1865), and it expresses both distance from this divine source and faith in its availability. The stanza itself speaks to the Creator largely through the mediation of others' language: it is Chaucer's version of Dante's version of a hymn by Bernard of Clairvaux; and as spoken by a man threatened by "visible and invisible foon" (5, 1866), it is an evening prayer that corresponds to the bidding prayer with which the poem opens. But this sense of distance, of a speaker mired in the historical world and alienated from the divine origin, is both enforced and countered by the prayer's content. On the one hand, it begins with a circularity that includes, and presumably transcends, the recursions of both Thebes and Boethius, addressing itself to "Thow oon and two and thre, eterne on lyve, / That regnest ay in thre and two and oon" (5, 1863–64). And on the other, it concludes with a reference first to the human member of the Trinity, who can mercifully make His creation worthy of Him—"for thi mercy, digne" (5, 1868)—and then to the fully human Mary, "mayde and moder thyn benigne" (5, 1869). In thus coming to rest on the Mother of God, who (as the Second Nun, citing the same Dantean source, says) "nobledest . . . oure nature" (VIII, 40), perhaps the poem means finally to acknowledge that the enigma of the historical world encompasses at least the possibility of a divine sanction. And yet the consolation here offered remains wholly private, a gesture of inclusion spoken out of faith rather than hope.

✳ ✳ ✳

[Omitted here is Patterson's treatment of the "dialectic between self and history" in terms of the troubled state of England in the early and middle 1380s, and the likelihood that Chaucer's own troubled career and financial insecurity were a result of large-scale conflicts between king and magnates. The conclusion follows—*Editor*.]

What then of a mere controller of customs who had the effrontery to set himself up as the purveyor of Trojan history? As European monarchs (including England's Henry II and the future Henry V) knew, the Trojan myth provided above all a typology of monarchical legitimacy: as empire descended from the Trojans, so too monarchy enjoyed a genealogical authority. The Richard of the 1380s, threatened with deposition and

---

2. *Geoffrey Chaucer and the Development of his Genius* (Boston: Houghton Mifflin, 1934), 153. An exemplary account is given by Donaldson, *Speaking of Chaucer*, 84–101.

denied his full authority, could not have been insensitive to these meanings. Moreover, throughout the 1380s, as into the 1390s, Richard made great efforts to fashion for himself a fully chivalric identity: he led his army into the field in the Scottish campaign of 1385—the first time an English monarch had done so since Edward III's last campaign of 1369, he sponsored and even participated in tournaments, and he adapted both the insignia and the habits of his illustrious father and grandfather to his own purposes. A fully chivalric poem recalling to his subjects their glorious Trojan past would certainly have been consistent with these strategies—especially for a king who, in his self-composed epitaph, compared himself to Homer, the author of all Trojan histories.[3]

Yet of course *Troilus and Criseyde* is not really that kind of poem. Despite the royalist attitudes that govern its account of the Trojan Parliament, despite the generally affirmative effect that any Trojan narrative has upon royal authority, *Troilus and Criseyde* cannot really be aligned with specific monarchical interests. On the contrary, its meditations on history are both too general and too profound to be contained by any narrowly partisan purpose. It is neither a militarist nor a pacificist poem: unambiguously celebrating martial achievement, it also measures the cost of war upon the amorousness that is the other crucial element of the chivalric life-style, and it shows the noble life at odds with itself, fulfilling its deepest romantic needs in a context that dooms them to extinction.[4] If we read the poem topically, we can see that its representation of a society under siege that undoes itself through parliamentary miscalculation has a general rather than specific and partisan relevance. The 1380s were a time of disputed sovereignty, conspiratorial factionalism, and disastrous militarism—all issues upon which *Troilus and Criseyde* reflects. The poem's continual concern with authority, as both literary source and metaphysical foundation, is a textual analogue to the troubled, and finally unresolved, constitutional debate over sovereignty. Similarly, the figure of Pandarus is a comic version of the malign conspiratorial manipulator who pervaded the poet's historical world, while the poem's privileging of *trouthe*, even when the object of loyalty is unworthy, reflects a time of broken commitments and dark betrayals.[5]

3. Richard said he was "lyke to Homer" (cited by George B. Stow, "Chronicles versus Records: The Character of Richard II," in *Documenting the Past: Essays in Medieval History Presented to George Peddy Cuttino*, ed. J. S. Hamilton and Patricia J. Bradley (Woodbridge: Boydell, 1989), 165.
4. It should be added that the poem's emphasis upon the intensity of personal feeling must have seemed relevant to Richard's own capacity for passionate engagements, first with Robert de Vere, the Earl of Oxford, then with Anne of Bohemia. For the evidence, see Stow, "Chronicles versus Records," 161 n. 33, 163.
5. In fact, in Book 4 Pandarus's conspiratorial instincts become less comic as he tries to persuade Troilus to violate the parliamentary decision, ratified by the king, to exchange Criseyde for Antenor. That Pandarus is here initiating a factional dispute is made clear when he pledges his loyalty to Troilus in terms that assume civil disorder.

> I wol myself ben with the at this dede,
> Theigh ich and al my kyn upon a stownde,
> Shulle in a strete as dogges liggen dede,
> Thorough-girt wth many a wid and blody wownde,
> In every cas I wol a frend be founde. (624–28)

An earlier version of this factionalism is implied in Pandarus's mobilization of the royal family (Hector, Helen, Deiphoebus, and Troilus) against Polyphete and his supporters, Aeneas and Antenor. To a governing class riven by internecine rivalry, these conspiracies must have seemed painfully relevant. Lines that also have a powerfully contemporary relevance in the context of the 1380s are Criseyde's suggestion in Book 4 that the war will soon be over because "men purposen

And Chaucer's meditations on history go even deeper than these general analogies, opening up disquieting profundities. For the poem's deepest message is not about the failure of any particular historical moment but about the failure of history, and of historical understanding, per se. Telling a story of complicity and victimization, it shows us a historical world that is simultaneously created by and yet set apart from the men and women who seek to live their lives within it. The final message is one of bafflement before a narrative—and a world—that defies understanding and forecloses consolation: we could hardly expect a poem that stands silent before the tragedy of secular history to offer anything more than an uncommitted reflection on its own historical moment. Deriving from and speaking to the unhappy world of the 1380s, the *Troilus* refuses to offer any clear message; and this lack of clarity itself expresses the dilemma the poem represents. All engagement in the world of history is dangerous and finally disappointing, and yet engagement cannot be avoided; the act of representation is itself an act of loyalty, but the results are both of uncertain authenticity and hardly worth the risk; survival is an imperative, but what of *trouthe?* And to what—or to whom—should one be true? These are the questions that Chaucer's experience in the 1380s must have forced upon him, and his poem asks them as both fictive form and historical act. But the very conditions that entail their asking foreclose the possibility of an answer: stranded before the enigma of his own and his nation's history, Chaucer's final response is to offer up a prayer for release.

LOUISE O. FRADENBURG

"Our owen wo to drynke": Loss, Gender and Chivalry in *Troilus and Criseyde*†

> "Therto we wrecched wommen nothing konne,
> Whan us is wo, but wepe and sitte and thinke;
> Oure wrecche is this, our owen wo to drynke."
> —CRISEYDE[1]

There are histories of suffering and of violence. The interdependence of such histories must seem obvious, yet their links can be, and have been, obscured often enough because of the political inarticulacy of those who suffer and because those who commit violence rarely remind us of what it is like to suffer, except insofar as they rewrite the suffering of others as their own capacity to suffer gloriously *"for"* lord, king, nation.[2] Such

pees on every syde" (1350; and see 1352–58). Both passages are either added to Boccaccio or revised in the direction of contemporary relevance.

† From *Troilus and Criseyde,* ed. R. A. Shoaf. MRTS Vol. 104 (1992): 86–106. Copyright © Arizona Board of Regents for Arizona State University. Reprinted by permission.

1. *T&C* 2.782–84.
2. See Elaine Scarry's chapters on "The Structure of Torture" and "The Structure of War" in *The Body in Pain: The Making and Unmaking of the World* (New York: Oxford Univ. Press, 1985).

a heroization of suffering *for*, in the history of the West, typically de-
valorizes actual suffering, and devalorizes those who attempt to avoid it
as well as those prohibited from inflicting it. For the heroic ideal, survival
is a non-noble goal; it is ignoble to complain of physical pain; those not
categorically permitted to wound others have no honor in themselves,
but only through relations of dependence on those who bear arms.

The heroization of suffering *for* has in fact been one of the chief means
of occluding the history of suffering and its relation to the history of
violence. The foregrounding and idealization of an *intentional* relation-
ship to violence has, for example, made it difficult to treat the effects of
disease, war, dispossession, rape, and psychic trauma as potentially
related "patterns of suffering" constructed, at least in part, by "theory,
action, and perception," and endured by "embodied" selves.[3] The hero-
ization of suffering has also played a central part in the development of
what Marcuse called "the ideology of death"—the inculcation of the
acceptance of death as the ground for all forms of domination, the incul-
cation of "compliance with the master over death."[4] In what ways has
consent to the "transvaluation" of death—to its transformation from that
which ends our lives into that which gives meaning to our lives—been
solicited? How have subjects been brought to serve as "arms of the
state"? Moreover, if the primary site of the construction of the subject's
consent to sacrificial violence is (however diversely formed) the "family,"
or "household," what relations might we imagine between familial prac-
tices of violence as well as of desire, on the one hand, and violence
practiced by community or nation?[5] Finally, if there are rhetorics that
speak and produce violence, how have "literature" and literary study
participated in the violence of glorification, the politicization of loss, the
domination of "the scene of writing" itself?[6]

These questions are important ones for readers of *Troilus and Criseyde*
because it is a poem in which both violence and its occlusion have in
some ways been very successful.[7] Its apparent preoccupation with "inti-
mate desires" and with psychic trauma, with private spaces and secret
conversations and innermost thoughts, has by and large, and not at all
surprisingly, been replicated in a critical tradition more concerned with
the vicissitudes of love than war. Given that the occasional appearances
made by psychoanalytic criticism within this tradition (as within studies
of mourning in general) have tended to confirm the irrelevance of com-

3. See David Michael Levin's argument for a "cultural epidemiology" in *Pathologies of the Modern
Self: Postmodern Studies on Narcissism, Schizophrenia, and Depression* (New York: New York Univ.
Press, 1987), 5, 7.
4. Herbert Marcuse's essay "The Ideology of Death," in *The Meaning of Death*, ed. Herman Feifel
(New York: McGraw-Hill, 1959), 64–76, analyzes the relations between the treatment of death
in Western philosophy and larger cultural strategies of domination.
5. Teresa de Lauretis argues that "violence is en-gendered in representation"; "violence between
intimates must be seen in the wider context of social power relations; and gender is absolutely
central to the family." See "The Violence of Rhetoric: Considerations on Representation and
Gender," in *The Violence of Representation: Literature and the History of Violence*, ed. Nancy
Armstrong and Leonard Tennenhouse (London: Routledge, 1989), 240–41.
6. For an analysis of the rhetoric of violence in Italian humanist texts, see Stephanie Jed, "The Scene
of Tyranny: Violence and the Humanistic Tradition," in *The Violence of Representation*, 29–44,
at 29, 41.
7. Three helpful discussions of these issues are Diamond, "Politics"; Sally Slocum, "Criseyde among
the Greeks," *NM* 87 (1986): 365–74; and David Aers's discussion of Criseyde in *Chaucer*. I differ
from Aers's account and from Diamond's chiefly in my stress on *TC's recuperation* of aristocratic
loss.

munal violence to desire and loss, what might readers of *Troilus and Criseyde* have to gain by exploring psychoanalytic discourses on loss?[8] How could attention to such discourses help us think more deeply about the patterning of violence and suffering in and around Chaucer's poem? And is it, further, possible that *Troilus and Criseyde* might in turn contribute importantly to our understanding of rhetorics of loss?

Here I can do little more than suggest a few ways of approaching these questions. When we consider psychoanalytic theories of mourning in terms of histories of suffering, such theories seem to emerge in a cultural "place" once occupied by the exaltation of the masculine chivalric subject's *capacity* to confront and endure infinite loss, and by the depreciation of the feminine chivalric subject's claims to reparation. Psychoanalytic theory seems to occupy this cultural location partly because some of its developments are implicated in the heroization of suffering, as is suggested by the derivation of the Oedipal paradigm from classical tragedy, the association of the Oedipal paradigm with mourning through the theory of identification, and the frequent recurrence in Freud and elsewhere of nostalgic, archaicizing allusions to bygone elites.[9] Julia Kristeva's work in *Black Sun* offers a way of bringing out some aspects of a psychoanalytic rhetoric of violence relevant to *Troilus and Criseyde*.

Kristeva writes:

> The child king becomes irredeemably sad before uttering his first words; this is because he has been irrevocably, desperately separated from the mother, a loss that causes him to try to find her again, along with other objects of love, first in the imagination, then in words.[1]

Black Sun is Kristeva's tragic *Poetics*, a lamentation for irredeemable grief, irrevocable separation, the exposed and abandoned male child, the disinherited heir, kinged finally through struggle; her collocation of the irredeemable with the "triumph" of sublimation—of creativity in the form of art—is in the mode of tragedy. In her chapter "Psychoanalysis—A Counterdepressant," we move from the irrevocable and desperate and apparently unwanted separation of the Oedipal child king from his mother to the revelation of "matricide" as "our vital necessity," and the "inversion of matricidal drive into a death-bearing maternal image," the "bloodthirsty Fury": "For man and for woman the loss of the mother is a biological and psychic necessity, the first step on the way to becoming autonomous." Though Kristeva sees loss as a necessity for woman as

---

8. For an analysis of the elegy, and of studies of grief, in this connection, see my essay "Voice Memorial: Loss and Reparation in Chaucer's Poetry," *Exemplaria* 2 (1990): 170–202, esp. 184–85.

9. The importance of the activity of identification in mourning, and in the construction of the psychoanalytic subject, was pointed to by Freud in passages like the following from "Mourning and Melancholia": "all the time the existence of the lost object is continued in the mind. Each single one of the memories and hopes which bound the libido to the object is brought up and hyper-cathected"; Freud's further association in that essay of the process of mourning with the formation of the superego helped to situate mourning and identification within the Oedipal trajectory. On the contribution made by "Mourning and Melancholia" to the theory of identification, see Jean Laplanche, *Life and Death in Psychoanalysis*, trans. Jeffrey Mehlman (Baltimore: Johns Hopkins Univ. Press, 1976), 79; see also Julia Kristeva, *Black Sun: Depression and Melancholy*, trans. Leon Roudiez (New York: Columbia Univ. Press, 1989), 11.

1. Kristeva, *Black Sun*, 6.

well as for man, however, there is no child queen in this chapter.[2] The "peculiar" difficulty of the feminine subject's travail in separating from the mother does not, unlike that of the masculine subject, produce *in and of itself* the triumph of creativity. As happens so often in the rhetoric of loss, "good" and "bad" mourning are gendered.[3] The grief of men leads in a relatively straightforward renunciatory path, an *ascesis*, away from the maternal object, through identification with the "father," to sublimation and "poetic form."[4] In contrast the grief of women remains inglorious, inarticulate, its object encrypted—"Our wrecche is this, oure owen wo to drynke," says Criseyde—"[u]nless," writes Kristeva (30),

> [*another*] massive introjection of the ideal succeeds . . . in satisfying narcissism with its negative side *and* the longing to be present in the arena where the world's power is at stake.

Moreover, when lack—valued by some psychoanalytic theory as enabling the construction of the subject—is given in some privileged way to the "father," the "mother" *is* lacked, but cannot generate the kind of "creative" lack that constructs a subject; thus while the mother may be granted a role in biological reproduction, she is granted no role in the process of the social birth of the subject.[5]

Kristeva's invocation of matricide thus brings out the potential for violence in the psychoanalytic rhetoric of mourning: the destruction of the "mother" by her daughters as well as by her sons. Whether daughter or son is involved, rescue—in the form of cultural participation—arrives in the form of the father, who exacts a price, demands the sacrifice of the mother in order for the process of "substitution" to begin. The consequences of such a narrative imperative for the feminine subject seem to be, in Kristeva's thought, the uncertainty of her participation in culture—her identity somehow doubly uncertain, problematic. The submission of the masculine subject is also demanded, if he is to inherit, if nothing else is to be taken from him: he is threatened with isolation if he continues to grieve unremittingly, and is bought off for his renunciation with promises of future wealth, life, power, art. There is a strict economy in such rhetorics of mourning—in their inculcation of the consent to death, their offers of compensatory cultural glories. Discourses of loss—some psychoanalytic theory among them—have coercive designs on, and coercively design, the course of the subject's desire, and they embed those designs in the formation of the subject's gender iden-

---

2. On sublimation, see Kristeva, 22. Kristeva contends (*Black Sun*, 27–30) that because woman, unlike man, must identify with the mother *as* woman, but also must separate from her, it is more difficult for the feminine subject to turn affect into symbol, "matricidal drive" into a "death-bearing maternal image": "Indeed, how can She be that bloodthirsty Fury, since I am She . . . She is I?" The result of the woman's travail is her "constant tendency to extol the problematic mourning for the lost object . . . not so fully lost, and it remains, throbbing, in the 'crypt' of feminine ease and maturity."
3. On the distribution of "good" and "bad" mourning according to gender, see Fradenburg, "Voice Memorial," 185.
4. The "father" has some complicated meanings in this connection which are explored by Kristeva at pages 23–24 in her discussion of "symbolic lineage."
5. Maurice Bloch's "Death, Women, and Power" in *Death and the Regeneration of Life*, ed. Maurice Bloch and Jonathan Parry (Cambridge: Cambridge Univ. Press, 1982), 211–30, shows how women—perhaps because of their association with biological birth, and certainly because of their cultural devaluation—can be made to stand, in funeral rituals, for division, death, and sorrow, whereas men will be associated with rebirth into, and of, the community.

tity. At the same time it is unquestionably true that such violence works to substantiate and further masculine privilege.

And yet is there something psychoanalytic theory can contribute to the understanding of mourning besides permitting us to decipher within some of its manifestations the presence of an accommodation of violence?[6] Juliana Schiesari's recent work stresses the potential productivity of mourning for female solidarity and community, a productivity achieved not through triumph or mastery over an irrevocably lost maternal object but through a continued relationality with the figure of the mother and hence with female communities.[7] Other work that has been done on the productive agency of the mother in the cultural as well as biological construction of the subject would include Sara Ruddick's argument that one aspect of the practice of mothering is precisely the conforming of a child to the "rules" of its culture.[8] There is also, in Melanie Klein's work, a powerful analysis of the infant's experience of maternity as anticipating any and all future dialectics of lack of fullness that might be thought fundamental in the construction of subject-positions; and in Laplanche's analysis of "maternal care" the mother, far from contributing only the figure of an object of nostalgia, becomes herself a bearer of

> intrusion into the universe of the child of certain meanings of the adult world. . . . The whole of the primal intersubjective relation—between mother and child—is saturated with these meanings. . . . In the final analysis the complete oedipal structure is *present from the beginning.*[9]

Psychoanalysis has offered languages with which to talk in detail about the historicity, the artifactuality, of the subject, and therefore about the role of loss in the subject's construction (not, again, as an experience to be "mastered" or "triumphed" over but as what Marcuse might call an external fact to be grieved). Psychoanalysis thus allows us to think about "fantasy" (which does not mean that something is "unreal" or has never happened, but means rather than whether or not it "actually" happened it inhabits one's psyche in a specifically elaborated way) in connection with the practice of violence. Once psychoanalysis has historicized for us the mourning subject, war can no longer so easily be posited as a privileged "reality" to which all other experiences must measure up if they are to be taken seriously, nor can attempts to articulate the experience of suffering so readily be undermined as doubtful, mere

6. Freud himself, as Lorraine Siggins puts it, repeatedly affirms "that a loved object is never really relinquished"—see "Mourning: A Critical Survey of the Literature," *IJP* 47 (1966): 14–25, at 17, where she cites Freud's "Letter to Binswanger," in *Letters of Sigmund Freud*, ed. E. L. Freud (New York: Basic Books, 1960). I have argued elsewhere ("Voice Memorial," 182–83) that such an understanding might provide a basis for the revaluation rather than the punishment of mourning, for the rethinking of problematic concepts like "substitution" for the lost object and "mastery of grief."

7. Schiesari, "Appropriating the Work of Women's Mourning: The Legacy of Renaissance Melancholia," *Working Paper* No. 2, Univ. of Wisconsin-Milwaukee Center for Twentieth-Century Studies (1990–91), 10.

8. See Sara Ruddick, "Maternal Thinking," in *Mothering: Essays in Feminist Theory*, ed. Joyce Treblicot (Totowa: Rowman and Allanheld, 1984), 213–30; and *Maternal Thinking: Toward a Politics of Peace* (Boston: Beacon Press, 1989).

9. Laplanche, *Life and Death in Psychoanalysis*, 44–45. Klein's work is easily available in *The Selected Melanie Klein*, ed. Juliet Mitchell (New York: The Free Press, 1986).

artfulness.[1] To this extent psychoanalytic theory has enabled the very critique of its own complicities with the rhetoric of violence which we have been at pains to examine, and in thus exposing the very strategies of isolation in which it sometimes participates, furthers a shareable political discourse about loss and desire.

If the interiorized and interiorizing tragedy of the subject becomes one of the chief modes whereby psychoanalytic discourse en-genders loss and heroizes masculine suffering, and if the historicizing of the mourning subject becomes the chief psychoanalytic countertext to sacrificial melancholy, what connections useful to a reading of *Troilus and Criseyde* can we make between these figurations of the subject and earlier rhetorics of loss? Tragedy, Aristotle insisted long ago, is about great men, and Kristeva wants to remind us also of "the relationship philosophers have maintained with melancholia . . . black bile (*melaina kole*) saps great men."[2] Is there a philosophical articulation of greatness in relation to melancholia during the later Middle Ages? What, during the later Middle Ages, did the work of, or occupied the cultural location, now taken by psychoanalysis? There were, for example, traditions on *tristitia* and despair that provided powerful narrative models for the production of "truth" through valorization of suffering both physical and psychic, creating for the soul an experience of interiority *through* suffering that may well have helped to make the place of the tragic subject of Kristevan psychoanalysis: "Without a bent for melancholia there is no psyche, only a transition to action or play."[3] The Middle Ages also saw the elaboration of extremely powerful models for the valorization of suffering: the Crusades, the chivalric orders, spectacular punishment, penitential theory and practice, the centering of communal and individual piety around the Passion, the melancholy of the courtly lover. The rhetoric and practices of loss characteristic of the warrior culture of the medieval aristocracy will be the particular concern of the following discussion of *Troilus and Criseyde*.

Troilus and Criseyde is a poem about loss, communal as well as private; the poem is centrally concerned with the construction of the aristocratic subject *for* loss, for the delectation and transvaluation of loss, and with the production of an aristocratic poetry whose future is figured as equally uncertain. *Troilus and Criseyde* examines the production of a heroic attitude which *prepares for* rather than obstructs the *ascesis* of military endeavor at the end of the poem (the futility of Troilus's search for Diomede), so that even the masculine chivalric subject's loss of the ability to assert his honor through violent confrontation with his double contributes to the honoring, as it were, of his infinite capacity to inhabit the space of loss. That the reward is a vision of the littleness of the earth,

1. In the Preface to *Images of Women in Peace and War: Cross-Cultural and Historical Perspectives*, ed. Sharon Macdonald, Pat Holden and Shirley Ardener (Madison: Univ. of Wisconsin Press, 1987), xvii, Pat Holden and Shirley Ardener note that the definition of "war" itself is always problematic and is itself an object of contestation. And yet "war" is repeatedly used rhetorically as a touchstone for reality; see my chapter on "Soft and Silken War" in *City, Marriage, Tournament: Arts of Rule in Late Medieval Scotland* (Madison: Univ. of Wisconsin Press, 1991). On doubt and pain, see Scarry, *The Body in Pain*, 4.
2. Kristeva, *Black Sun*, 6–7.
3. Susan Snyder, "The Left Hand of God: Despair in Medieval and Renaissance Tradition," *SR* 12 (1965): 18–59; Kristeva, *Black Sun*, 4.

of the absurdity of mourning, is, from the standpoint of aristocratic culture, merely a raising of the stakes, one which *enables* the communalization and spiritualization of Troilus's trajectory, making the most transcendent meanings of all—Christian ones—for "yonge, fresshe folkes, he or she" (5.1835), *out of* Troilus's loss: *Troilus and Criseyde,* I would argue, shows how the aristocracy of the later Middle Ages substantiated itself partly *through* its melancholic embroidering of embarrassment, rejection, humiliation, betrayal, defeat, valorizing them as a means of preventing their implications from posing radical questions about the heroization of suffering.[4]

Thus by the end of the poem, we might say, Troilus dies, but his honorable fate—honorable *through* psychic agony, through the very exhaustion of his chances, through his reduction to a desire completely incapable of achieving its aims and finally suffused with a sense of the vanity even of the attempt—acquires discursive power just at the moment when the text is flooded with metapoetic concerns. Criseyde, by contrast, dishonorably survives, and knows that she will be destroyed by books—"thise bokes wol me shende" (5.1060)—and that she is powerless to affect her reputation. Does this mutually exclusive distribution of life and good literary reputation mean that Chaucer writes completely from the point of view of the aristocratic delectation of loss, desirous perhaps of the power of such an effective strategy for his "litel . . . tragedye"? (5.1786) Does his text (also) activate counter-strategies that perform cultural work similar to those psychoanalytic insights that actually enable mourning *not* in the service of the transcendentalization of violence? Can we suggest what those strategies might have been for such a poet writing in the later Middle Ages? The lynchpin here is precisely the contrast between Criseyde and Troilus. Does *Troilus and Criseyde,* while displaying with extraordinary fullness the aristocratic power to recuperate loss for the practice of violence, ask us at the same time to deheroize suffering and to grant to "mere" survival, not a mirroring heroic privilege, but more simply the depth of our desire for it, and the ultimately political power of the possibility that survival, as ideology and as practice, might go unpunished? Does Criseyde become the bearer of a valued ability to mourn in a way that makes a future, permits survival, without celebrating renunciation and legitimating violence? Or does the suppression of Criseyde's grief by Pandarus in Book 4—"So lef this sorwe, or platly he wol deye. / And shapeth yow his sorwe for t'abregge, / And nought encresse, leeve nece swete!" (4.924–26)—mean that once again woman's mourning leads nowhere unless to a man's greatness, that Criseyde will become the bearer not of a valued wish to live on, but of "inconstancy"? And what might be the relation between the feminization of survival in *Troilus and Criseyde* and heroic constancy in *The Legend of Good Women,* on the one hand, and, on the other, of Chaucer's own need to survive the vagaries of a political career?

These are difficult questions to answer, partly because Criseyde's capacity for survival itself bears to some extent the marks of a fantasy, that fantasy being that only men die in war, that women are less subject

---

4. See "Sovereign Love" and "Soft and Silken War" in *City, Marriage, Tournament* for a fuller discussion of this issue.

to physical violence than men during either peace or war, that men risk their bodies to protect those of women ("youre body shal men save," says Hector to Criseyde [1.122]); women prove their honor, if they prove it at all, through the difficulty of their choices, through the heroic preservation of their chastity, not through the practice of arms—i.e., they prove their honor through tests of faith, trials of consent.[5]

Though we can have no hope of cataloguing with any fullness here the role of violence in late medieval women's lives, it is worth pausing to call a few facts and images to mind. We know that both noble and non-noble women were "unofficially" engaged in the practice of warfare when, as was often the case, husbands were absent or dead, and they had frequent occasion to defend themselves from rape, injury and death during times of peace as well as in times of war. In one local study, moreover, Kathryn Gravdal describes "life" as it appears in the records of the Abbey of Cerisy in Normandy during the time of the Hundred Years' War and the difficulties women faced in seeking reparation for violence inflicted on them:

> We find a picture of poverty, broken family structures, quotidian sexual violence, incest, demoralization, and social instability. The court is notably lax in sentencing, practically flaunting canon law. The names of the jurors in any given sitting frequently include those of men convicted of criminal behavior in the preceding sessions.[6]

In one of the rape cases tried by this court, the accused man was convicted and fined for rape, and the woman in question fined three times as much for allowing him to have carnal knowledge of her (Gravdal 213). And the *Registre Criminel de la Justice de Saint-Martin-des-Champs a Paris*

> clearly suggest[s] that women, who commit far fewer crimes, receive the death penalty three times more frequently than men;

their punishments were burial alive (in order to shield their modesty from hanging) for "lesser offenses," as when in 1342 Ameline La Soufletiere is buried alive for the theft of a man's purple cloak, and burning at the stake for "grave" offenses;[7] when Criseyde is introduced in Chaucer's poem, and the town, angered by her father's betrayal, wants to burn her—"al his kyn"—"fel and bones" (1.91), this is no fantasy of pagan barbarism. Shulamith Shahar writes in *The Fourth Estate* that women died "by the cruellest methods of execution known to the cruel society of the Middle Ages." As Gravdal remarks of medieval French law: "Slow

---

5. See Sharon Macdonald, "Drawing the Lines—Gender, Peace and War: An Introduction," 1–26, in *Images of Women in Peace and War*, esp. page 4 on the role played "in the creation of a well-ordered [martial] ideology, [of] dualities such as all women as potential mothers and all men as potential warriors." See also *Society at War: The Experience of England and France During the Hundred Years War*, ed. C. T. Allmand (Edinburgh: Oliver and Boyd, 1973), 26–27, for an example of an oath "to maintain the honour of womanhood, . . . and to do this with our bodies, if need be," on the part of a military order founded by the Duke of Bourbon.
6. Kathryn Gravdal, "The Poetics of Rape Law in Medieval France," in *Rape and Representation*, ed. Lynn A. Higgins and Brenda R. Silver (New York: Columbia Univ. Press, 1991), 211.
7. Gravdal 215–16; Shulamith Shahar, *The Fourth Estate: A History of Women in the Middle Ages*, trans. Chaua Galai (London: Methuen, 1983), 21.

to protect and quick to punish, this society gives every sign that it values female life less than male."[8]

Gravdal also remarks that widows (Criseyde's station in life) were the most frequent victims of rape because they were "unprotected" by father or husband (Gravdal 217). Her research suggests at the same time that relatives and guardians and friends and acquaintances could as easily be the source of violence as of protection. So, perhaps, does evidence from Chaucer's own life: of the witnesses present on Chaucer's behalf at Cecily Champain's well-known release of Chaucer from "*omnomodas assiones tam de raptu meo tam* [sic] *de aliqua alia re vel causa*—actions of whatever kind either concerning my rape or any other matter"—Donald Howard remarks of the witnesses who were present on Chaucer's behalf that they were "some very big guns indeed, which means he thought the matter grave"; if Cecily is to be identified as the stepdaughter of Alice Perrers, who had been the mistress of Edward III,

> it means that Chaucer raped or seduced the stepdaughter of an old friend who had done him many favors. . . . Or it means that his old friend's stepdaughter brought against him a vindictive accusation.[9]

The vulnerability of women to intimate violence is also registered in the late fifteenth-century theologian John of Ireland's commentary on the Annunciation in his *Meroure of Wyssdome*, in which he warns ladies to eschew "worldly plesance" in the form not only of the company of strange men, but also that of kinsmen and friends, because "gret perell js . . . to be allane with [th]ame jn secret placis and tyme."[1] And Georges Duby has argued of medieval France that incest was not a stigmatized aberration nor even an overlooked occasional vice, but rather a central practice and sign of seigneurial power.[2]

Troilus and Criseyde was written during the Hundred Years' War, during the period of decline in England's fortunes and glory. The poem's interiorization and spiritualization of loss and its apparent rejection of the meaningfulness of mortal combat with one's enemy (Troilus is not allowed a battle to the death with Diomede) refigure late fourteenth-century disappointment in the prowess of chivalry, in its powers of protection. Such disappointment would have been exacerbated by the demoralization of civilians during the Hundred Years' War. C. T. Allmand notes that

> one of the biggest changes in warfare which occurred at this period was the way in which, as the scale of war continued to expand, this expansion was made to embrace larger proportions of the populations of both England and France than ever before.[3]

---

8. Gravdal, 216. For a broad review of the treatment of rape in medieval law, see Shahar, *The Fourth Estate*, 16–17.
9. Donald R. Howard, *Chaucer: His Life, His Works, His World* (New York: E. P. Dutton, 1987), 317, 318.
1. *The Meroure of Wyssdome . . . by Johannes de Irlandia*, ed. Charles Macpherson, vol. 1 (Edinburgh: William Blackwood and Sons, for the Scottish Text Society, 1926), 137.
2. See his chapter on "Incest, Bigamy and Divorce among Kings and Nobles," in *Medieval Marriage: Two Models from Twelfth-Century France*, trans. Elborg Foster (Baltimore: Johns Hopkins Univ. Press, 1978). Critics who argue that Chaucer could not possibly even have dreamed of implying that Pandarus may have had incestuous desires for Criseyde should reconsider the family history of the period.
3. *Society at War*, ed. Allmand, 9.

The war made on the civilian population was most grievous in its effects in France, whose "unhappy fate" it was "to provide the battleground for much of the war," as Chaucer himself well knew, having participated in the 1359 campaign;[4] but England was raided frequently during the latter part of the fourteenth century, when England's fortunes turned for the worse, and there was great fear of invasion (Allmand 9, 11)—a fear of perforation which seems, in Chaucer's poem, to be displaced onto Criseyde in the form of her anxieties, her ambiguous loyalties, her uncertain nationality, the general fragility of her borders. For England as well as for France, "war was a form of human activity which had by now come to pervade all the ranks of those societies in or between which it was being fought" (Allmand 13). Though Allmand does not expound on them, the consequences for women must have been terrible; during the English siege of Limoges in 1370, Howard notes, Edward the Black Prince, "borne in on his litter, watched while the soldiers, on his orders, ran about killing the citizens—men, women, and children."[5]

Thus, when Pandarus arrives at Criseyde's house to tell her about Troilus's love for her, and she says "is than th'assege aweye? / I am of Grekes so fered that I deye" (2.123–24), we might reasonably conclude that her fears—here and at any other moment in the poem—are more than justified. But many of her critics have wanted to see Criseyde as unheroic, concerned "only" with survival; they have isolated her anxieties from the historical contexts that explain them (as indeed do some her interpreters within the poem itself), positing those anxieties as part of an essential character and thereby perpetuating fantasies of male rescue and feminine weakness. C. S. Lewis wrote that Chaucer

> so emphasized the ruling passion of his heroine, that we cannot mistake it. It is Fear—fear of loneliness, of old age, of death, of love, and of hostility; of everything, indeed, that can be feared. And from this Fear springs the only positive passion which can be permanent in such a nature; the pitiable longing, more childlike than womanly, for protection, for some strong and stable thing that will hide her away and take the burden from her shoulders.[6]

To treat fear as a characterological matter where Criseyde is concerned is of course to fail to analyze the extent to which the question of violence done to Criseyde, and its role in the construction of her desires, is constantly both raised and occluded in *Troilus and Criseyde*, a poem which represents only chivalrous knights as braving actual violence: Troilus goes off to fight the war and comes back with arrows hanging off him, an image treated as erotic as well as heroic: "Who yaf me drynke?" says Criseyde (2.651). But, again, inside Troy, inside those private Trojan spaces in which love is pursued, the potential for violence against Criseyde is brought before us even as it is made to disappear.

---

4. See Howard, *Chaucer*, 69–73.
5. Howard, *Chaucer*, 128.
6. C. S. Lewis, *The Allegory of Love: A Study in Medieval Tradition* (New York: Oxford Univ. Press, 1958), 185; cited in Kaminsky, *Critics*, 145–46; for bibliography on the question of Criseyde's fear, see Kaminsky, 200 nn58 and 59.

There are, to begin with, the threat of Criseyde's being burned to death for her father's treachery; her fear of the Greeks; the forcefulness of some of Pandarus's gestures towards her ("And in hire bosom the lettre down he thraste," 2.1155); the coerciveness of his rhetoric ("And therfore, er that age the devoure, / Go love," 2.395–96). When Book 2 opens, Pandarus, who has been feeling "his part of loves shotes keene" (2.58), is awakened to his "grete emprise" by the song of the swallow Procne; the allusion is rendered in such chillingly neutral tones that it is difficult to believe either that Chaucer expected his audience to draw the inference or that he did not: Procne

> so neigh hym made hire cheterynge,
> How Tereus gan forth hire suster take,
> That with the noyse of hire he gan awake.   2.68–70[7]

In a further tableau which itself seems to allude to the tableau of Pandarus's awakening, Criseyde listens to the song of Procne's raped and mutilated sister, Philomela, in the form of the "nyghtyngale"—here described by Chaucer as male, and as singing "*Peraunter* . . . a lay / Of love" (2.921–22; my emphasis)—just before she falls asleep and dreams (2.925–31) of the eagle who painlessly rips out her heart and leaves his behind—a simultaneous evocation and denial of violence, an image at once of overwhelming invasive power and of apparent reciprocity ("herte lefte for herte").[8] Book 2—the book in which Criseyde is brought to desire—is thus marked by a series of allusions to invasive violence and rape whose import is nonetheless rendered completely ambiguous. But this doubleness is at work everywhere in *Troilus and Criseyde*'s poetics of violence.

One of the most important moments that stage what Lynn A. Higgins and Brenda R. Silver refer to as the "elision of the scene of violence" characteristic of literature about rape is the consummation scene in Book 3.[9] Here the specter of rape is raised by Troilus himself—"Now yeldeth yow, for other bote is non!" (3.1208)—and is then made to vanish when Criseyde utters the words that might seem to confirm her consent, not only to her "capture" at this moment, but to the entire course of the affair:

> "Ne hadde I er now, my swete herte deere,
> Ben yold, ywis, I were now nought heere!"   3.1210–11

But just previous to this moment, the narrator has posed the following rhetorical question:

---

7. The story is told in Ovid's *Metamorphoses* 6 of how Tereus, married to Procne, raped her sister Philomela, subsequently imprisoning her and cutting out her tongue so that she could not accuse him of his crime. Philomela weaves a tapestry telling her story and sends it to her sister; they revenge themselves upon Tereus and are turned into a swallow (Procne) and a nightingale (Philomela). The story is also told in Chaucer's *Legend of Good Women*; he leaves out the sisters' revenge against Tereus. For a brilliant reading of this myth that is relevant to my concerns in this essay, see Patricia Joplin, "The Voice of the Shuttle is Ours," in *Rape and Representation*, 35–64.

8. Images of coupling, of "twoness," that suggest both reciprocity and dominance, consent and coercion, reappear elsewhere in the poem, indicating again the extent to which the abjection of the later fourteenth century's experience of the war is being both recalled and denied in *Troilus and Criseyde*; fear of violation is at once expressed and suppressed. See, e.g., the irony of Troilus's use of the expression "we tweyne" just when he informs Criseyde "Now be ye kaught" (3.1207), and the pastoral image of the "wodebynde" twisting about its tree (3.1230–31).

9. "Introduction: Rereading Rape," in *Rape and Representation*, 5.

> What myghte or may the sely larke seye,
> Whan that the sperhauk hath it in his foot?   3.1191–92

He adds that "Criseyde, which that felte hire thus itake, / . . . / Right as an aspes leef she gan to quake" (3.1198, 1200). A picture of maidenly modesty? Or are we indeed to question what the innocent, helpless and possibly foolish lark is supposed to say when the sparrowhawk has it in its foot? Possibly "Ne hadde I er now, my swete herte deere, / Ben yold, ywis, I were now nought heere"?[1]

But what of the fact that the exquisite pastoral images used to describe the lovers' pleasure in Book 3 (1226–32) are followed immediately by a simile that compares Criseyde's *language* to that of the nightingale?

> And as the newe abaysed nyghtyngale,
> That stynteth first whan she bygynneth to synge,
> Whan that she hereth any herde tale,
> Or in the hegges any wyght stirynge,
> And after siker doth hire vois out rynge,
> Right so Criseyde, whan hire drede stente,
> Opned hire herte, and tolde hym hire entente.   3.1233–39

Are we to hear behind Criseyde's (to us) inaudible voicing of her "entente" the mutilated mouth of Philomela? The poem at this moment recalls for us the occlusion of the voice of the survivor—Philomela, Procne, and Criseyde are all women who survive to tell their stories but whose voices are in various ways rendered inaudible or ambiguous. The possibility of Criseyde's rape can be spoken only through a kind of intertextual haunting. Is Book 3, then, like the garden in Book 4 of *Daphnis and Chloe*, what John Winkler has called "a microcosm of the pastoral world—protected, fertile, flowering, with a structure of recollected violence in the center"? Do Troilus and Criseyde discover here that "sexual violence is not merely an unhappy accident that might be avoided, but is a destiny written into the very premises of socially constructed reality?"[2] It seems likely that they do, though not in such a way as to become "aware" of their circumstances.

This moment of consummated love, of overheard but inaudible privacy, is itself both a preservation and a violation of inner space; the presence of such a silence at the structural core of *Troilus and Criseyde* bespeaks the extent of the poem's fixations on violence that cannot be articulated, and explains as well its fascination with the uncertainties of speech, its defensive garrulities (the Narrator and Pandarus, for example). The consummation scene is written to produce an ambiguity that *cannot be resolved* through interpretation; we cannot "decide" whether Criseyde has consented or not, whether she had been raped or not. We can only see that the possibility had been raised and then made undecidable; and this suggests that for a woman in Criseyde's position sexual violence may *be* what she has for love, may *be* the medium of her consent. It suggests also that such ambiguity is in part designed to protect

1. Aers (*Chaucer*, 127–28) recognizes that "male domination" makes the question of desire very problematic in this scene; but even he posits a "genuine love" that can be distinguished from "social practice and ideology."
2. John J. Winkler, "The Education of Chloe: Erotic Protocols and Prior Violence," in *Rape and Representation*, 15–34, at 25.

the delectation of invasive violence, and is talismanic for the masculine chivalric subject—who by means of such occlusion may retain the conviction both of his masculinity and of his honor.

We could of course argue that part of what Chaucer is trying to achieve in *Troilus and Criseyde*—this would perhaps be true of some of his sources as well—is an avoidance of rape, an attempt to avoid tragic repetition of the circumstances of Helen's abduction (elopement? rape?). Certainly Book 4 presents Troilus, Criseyde, and Pandarus attempting to imagine solutions to their predicament that have not already proved destructive, and may suggest that their failure to do so is "tragic"—not because they lack imagination, but because their culture provides no real alternatives (see, for example, 4.547–609). So that, though they avoid the "ravyshhyng" of women, Criseyde is apparently doomed to repeat her reliance on the ambiguities of male "protection," and Troilus to turn his rage and sorrow inward. But is Troilus heroized *because* he refuses rape? To what extent is the refusal of rape a recuperation of the warrior ideal in *Troilus and Criseyde*, part of Troilus's ennobling *ascesis*?

Or is the undecidability of Chaucer's text designed not just to occlude violence but to make us "see" its occlusion? For it may be that "seeing" the occlusion of violence (that is, seeing the trace of what has been made to dioappcar) was about as far as Chauccr was able to go by way of a deheroization of suffering. Further, it may be that the value placed at the end of the poem on vision rather than effective action marks the presence of an ideological *cul-de-sac* in which nonetheless a real struggle over the value of "survival" is taking place—one which would break out again with the *Legend of Good Women*, a poem also centrally concerned with the workings of gender in the heroization of suffering and the devalorization of survival, and one in which the Chaucerian narrator is himself somewhat accommodating and obedient. Chaucer's own career, after all, was not one in which heroism was easily affordable.[3]

This in itself raises another set of complex issues; for the poem's privileging of vision cannot be unrelated to the voyeurism (apparent voyeurism? does he watch, or does he deflect the voyeuristic gaze by reading, and what has the world gained by his so doing?) of Pandarus's behavior in Book 3—"And with that word he drow hym to the feere, / And took a light, and fond his contenaunce, / As for to looke upon an old romaunce" (3.978–80). The poem's privileging of vision might therefore also be related to the coy, prurient ambiguity of yet another moment of undecidability that follows on the morning after Troilus and Criseyde's first night together: the moment that *might* be read, but I would argue could never *definitively* be read, as Pandarus's incestuous dalliance with Criseyde:

> With that she gan hire face for to wrye
> With the shete, and wax for shame al reed;
> And Pandarus gan under for to prie,

3. See Paul Strohm, *Social Chaucer* (Cambridge: Harvard Univ. Press, 1989).

. . .
I passe al that which chargeth nought to seye.
What! God foryaf his deth, and she al so

3.1569–76

From the pastoralization of violence, to the avuncularity of incest? Chaucer's poem indeed treads the finest of lines between the perception of the occlusion of violence and the desire to participate in it. And yet I think it is a line that can be read: it may be, in Chaucer's poem, what there is in the place of an awareness willing to read the strength of the wish for survival, willing in particular to read the ways that, in cultures committed to the uses of death, the wish for survival constructs the subject to desire where there is no desire, and to deny desire where it might be. The simultaneous detachment and curiosity of Chaucer's narrators seems to tread this line; they look on, but change nothing, and so perhaps can be said neither to do violence nor to prevent it, neither to hurt nor to rescue; what they desire is never clear, though it is always clear that they desire something, that they are "in it" for something, even if it seems that they are "in it" only for "protection." The close intercalation in Book 3 of Pandarus as go-between and of the *Galeotto* of canto 5 of the *Inferno* is relevant here—does he merely look on or does he make desire happen where it would not? is he responsible for sexual violence, has he tried to cover up its traces? "kep the clos" (3.332); and yet Chaucer doesn't take himself off the hook by putting anyone in hell, and doesn't much glamorize his own search for "vision."[4] We should question, however, whether unheroic avuncularity—"erand" rather than "grete emprise" [2.72–73]—is preferable to heroization. While Chaucer's refusal to heroize Pandarus, or the narrator of *Troilus and Criseyde*, may inscribe a sense of the kinds of contributions a courtier must make to the glorification of his betters' losses—while Chaucer's apparent neutrality, his ambivalence, his devotion to "both sides," may be a problem rather than an intention—such ambiguities are perhaps there in the first place because, as the Prologue to *The Legend of Good Women* attests, he sees in ways that bring out conflict and danger, even if the screen of ambiguity breaks out afresh each time we seem ready to see the scene of violence done to as well as by desire. Criseyde's survival may be read as a countertext to the heroization of suffering, but only when it is read alongside of the narrator's preoccupation with the question of whether he can do anything to "rescue" her, and thus to that small degree asks a question about whether he has maintained "the honour of womanhood," has helped "widows, virgins and ladies."[5]

If the question of engendered consent to violence impels the narrative of *Troilus and Criseyde*, then one of the crucial things that does the work of psychoanalysis in this poem is precisely the poem's reconsideration of the motifs of courtly love, and the resulting fullness of attention given to the construction of subjects of desire; the ways in which the procedures involved enforce the experiential transformation of what Pierre Bourdieu calls "coerced relations" into "elective" and "reciprocal"

4. See Karla Taylor's fine chapter on "A Text and Its Afterlife" (*Chaucer Reads*, 50–77), which charts the intercalation I have just mentioned.
5. *Society at War*, ed. Allmand, 27.

ones;[6] and the difficulties posed thereby for the notion of consent. It is well known that Chaucer in effect brought out Criseyde's consent *as a problem*, whereas in Boccaccio she is more straightforwardly eager and in charge of the narrative that brings about the fulfillment of "her" desires, "double" only in an *intentional* difference between depth and surface; and Chaucer calls attention to this issue also when he counter-poises the incredible, if powerfully handled, conventionality of the way Troilus falls in love—the subtle streams of her eyes, and so on—with the songs and dreams and interventions of the gaze and the promptings and coercions of Pandarus that characterize the way Criseyde falls in love. Chaucer, moreover, pushes the point of the contrast upon us with the following:

> Now myghte som envious jangle thus:
> "This was a sodeyn love; how myght it be
> That she so lightly loved Troilus,
> Right for the firste syghte, ye, parde?"
> Now whoso seith so, mote he nevere ythe!
> For every thing, a gynnyng hath it nede
> Er al be wrought, withowten any drede.   2.666–72

Book 2 begins with the narrator's famous meditation on change; it is also in this book that Criseyde remarks, "That erst was nothing, into nought it torneth" (2.798), and it is no accident that once again Criseyde is made the bearer of an examination of the historicity, as opposed to the melancholy, of desire, given subsequent events. But nonetheless the departure taken here by Chaucer allows us to read an important con-struction of the feminine subject of chivalric culture.[7]

In Book 2, long before the completion of the trajectory that reveals Criseyde's story to be partly that of the feminine chivalric subject, a subject produced *for* consent—that is, for an enervation of will/desire refigured as the paradox of an obedient choice—Criseyde ponders the (for her, as feminine chivalric subject) defining irruption of an "other" desire into the disciplined camouflage of her survival as a traitor's daugh-ter in Troy—a situation in which that other desire that comes to claim her will do so as the desire of something that is *not* other, but is rather at home in Troy, surrounded by brothers and parents, she living in Troy, after all, chiefly on the *grace* of the masculine chivalric subject. Now, where Book 1 is concerned, while Hector's grace in intervening for Cri-seyde's life by definition can ask for nothing in return without departing from the economy of honor, Criseyde's meditations in Book 2 on whether or not to allow Troilus to take over and serve as a more intimate "protector" suggest that such grace will count for nothing in the absence of a deheroized feminine practice of calculation, quietude, survival. Thus the disappearance of the betraying, abandoning, imperfect human father, Calcas, clears the stage for the heroizing of the masculine chi-valric subject's paternal powers: Hector's "grand" gift of her life to her,

---

6. Pierre Bourdieu, *Outline of a Theory of Practice*, trans. Richard Nice (Cambridge: Cambridge Univ. Press, 1977), 171.
7. The "feminine chivalric subject" I describe below does not exhaust the possibilities for the subject-positions of aristocratic medieval women, but it was one of the most powerfully enforced and culturally validated of such positions.

grand because of its apparent positioning beyond any possible return that she could make to Troy's best warrior, grand also because of its willingness to risk, to stake itself on her innocence, to refuse to read a difference between her surface and her depths.

Criseyde is generously deracinated, defathered—"Lat your fadres treson gon / Forth with meschaunce, and ye yourself in joie / Dwelleth with us, whil yow good list, in Troie" (I.117–19)—so that she may be, as feminine subject, "rescued" for, taken by, called to, the ideality of chivalric culture, as object of its lavish and absurd expenditures of trust and effort. The scene of her entry into the ideality of chivalric culture, which is also the scene of her entry into Chaucer's poem, is one of two moments in *Troilus and Criseyde* that does not seem in any way to ironize the genre of chivalric romance—the other also being Hector's intervention, also a refusal of ignoble exchange, of the "charge" of that "natural" father whose own choice had, after all, been survival: "Syres, she nys no prisonere"; "I not on yow who that this charge leyde"; "We usen here no wommen for to selle" (4.179–82). Criseyde is thus prepared, through the fact of her paternity, as exclusively *for* the desire or at least purposes of the masculine chivalric subject, by honorably cutting her loose from her history, thus marking her with the "chance" of honor, the opportunity to provide "aventure" for the masculine chivalric subject, making her as adventitious as the damsels of uncertain identity encountered in the pages of Malory's own obsessive work on rescue and threat.

The fantasy—and the lethal message—is that the "life" of the feminine chivalric subject has no history of its own, is owed not even to the paternity (let alone the maternity) of blood or to the participation of that subject in social relationships, but rather is refounded upon the nature of the masculine chivalric subject's desire with respect to her, at least when they meet in those romance encounters and exchanges that structure the meaning and even the possibility of identity. Where the chivalric fantasy of rescue is concerned—and I am arguing that this is a founding fantasy for the construction of the gendered aristocratic subject in the later Middle Ages—the lineage, history, origin of the romance heroine acquires meaning only through the arrival of desire from the place of the masculine subject, in the sense that she will be his "aventure," she will seem to break in upon his life with the force of a risk, a chance, that founds his honor. And as in the *Knight's Tale* as well this founding moment remakes conquest and takes the form, for her, of an appeal to him, that is, of a request, a question, a wish—in Hector's speech the terms of Criseyde's residence in Troy will be "whil yow good list." The wish is, ultimately, for life, or to put it another way, for a life free of the threat of violence, but since the figure who grants this wish does so through his possession of a superior power of violence [violence being the medium that gives risk its honorable meanings—he may choose either to rape or to rescue, to slay tyrants (Theseus) or be one (Creon), to wage war against women (Theseus) or to save them from the effects of war (Theseus)]—the appeal is for a life figured as free of the threat of death, but only by gift of the other, and therefore as not free at all. Thus the power of death gives meaning to, makes possible, the life of the feminine chivalric subject; and her appeal inscribes her as desiring the intervention of the male subject, as consenting to the loss of the meaning of her history, even as his desire defines her. Moreover, since violence is the medium that gives risk its honorable meanings, the wish to live or to be free from violence, posited as proper to the feminine chivalric subject, places her *as subject* outside the very chivalric ideality that takes her in and on which she is brought to depend. The consensual desire of the feminine chivalric subject is thereby constructed, through loss and violence, for domination: for "compliance with the master over death," for the acceptance of death as the condition whereby life may be refigured as the gift of the ruler. Since she is not recognized as having any capacity in herself to give this kind of symbolic, culturally valorized gift of life, moreover, it is not such a far distance for the feminine chivalric subject to become the bearer of death for the masculine subject, hence wielder of violence from a very different kind of place.

Thus the feminine chivalric subject is constructed to enter the "symbolic order" of chivalric culture through the renunciation of all desire that does not take the form of an appeal for a life free of violence, hence through an erotization of borrowed power, of bonded freedom, of forgiven debt. When she gains entry into language, she will articulate an appeal for freedom to love, for the right of consent to love, as with the formel eagle in the *Parliament of Fowls*; but as the obvious limitations on the choices available to the formel eagle make clear, that very appeal will be predicated on the constitution of an authority whose power of protection and rescue, whose power to rape and kill, may be petitioned.

The profound role of loss and violence in the construction of the feminine chivalric subject, in particular of that subject's gendered relation to bodily suffering, is brought out by Criseyde in the lines that I have used as the epigraph to this essay:

> "Therto we wrecched wommen nothing konne,
> Whan us is wo, but wepe and sitte and thinke;
> Oure wrecche is this, our owen wo to drynke."   2.782–84

When, that is, the masculine rescuer turns out to be the seducer, traitor, rapist (as happens repeatedly in *The Legend of Good Women*), appeal fails and there is no further recourse to be had from chivalric ideality: that is, *feminine* "complaint," as opposed to appeal, must inevitably fall upon deaf ears as there is no feminine subject-position within chivalric ideality from which complaint can be spoken, from which losses can be articulated. Chaucer's poetry—*Anelida and Arcite, The Legend of Good Women, The Squire's Tale*, Alcyone in *The Book of the Duchess*—repeatedly stages, indeed comes to grief upon, the scene of the inefficacy of any feminine complaint addressed, as it were, to the "rescuer" about *himself*, in his guise of thief or rapist or abandoning lover of "novelrie" (in the case of Ceys it is a matter of his death, when he can no longer offer protection but only unheeded advice spoken by a simulacrum);[8] and these are possibly the circumstances of patronage as well, as the Prologue to *The Legend of Good Women* seems to attest. That, in Chaucer's poetry, this kind of attempt at communication is repeatedly made—

8. See Fradenburg, "Voice Memorial," 171–72.

and equally repeatedly not only broken off but apparently implicated in the breaking off of the narrative of which it is a part—clearly demonstrates that complaint is the impotent obverse of those founding moments of successful feminine appeal (and thereby of consent to the transvaluation of death) in the beginning of works like *The Knight's Tale* and *Troilus and Criseyde*. Narrative begins as it does in *Troilus and Criseyde* and in *The Knight's Tale* because each work situates the masculine interlocutor of the female subject as rescuer and not as tormentor; as a result the question that is asked, the appeal that is made, can produce a future, "new life," a media success as it were, in the form of narrative. But Criseyde's lines about women's woe hint at that narrative paradigm wherein the coincidence of rescuer and tormentor in the same person turns the feminine subject's affect—her "wo"—into body: she is language-less, somatized, and figured as the source of her own unpleasure: "our owen wo to drynke." Once again loss will turn the language and affect of woman's woe back into the body unless a renunciation of the lost object intervene—the heroism of which renunciation, for the feminine subject, will in turn be depreciated by all the factors we have just established as constituting her petitionary position in chivalric culture, to the point that renunciation of the lost object becomes a renunciation of the subject's right even to hope for reparation.

JILL MANN

From *Feminizing Chaucer*†

*   *   *

The question of literary authority is the central concern of the *House of Fame*, as critics have long agreed. In Book II, Chaucer comically protests a faith in bookish authority so extreme that it can entirely dispense with experiential proof: to the Eagle's offer to show him the stellar constellations so that he will be able to confirm what the books say from firsthand experience, Chaucer replies that he believes what he reads about them just as firmly as if he had seen it with his own eyes—and in any case, his eyesight wouldn't stand the glare (993–1017). The vision of the House of Fame in Book III shows the problems attendant on credulity of this sort: the medley of truths and falsehoods, of obliterating silences and unsubstantiated reputations, renders the recovery of historical truth effectively impossible. As in the *Livre de Leesce*, so here too Homer is accused of writing 'lyes / Feynynge in hys poetries', which are to be dismissed as 'fable' (1477–80). Chaucer's vision of the true source of poetic authority is to be found not in Book III, but at the very outset of his dream, in the presentation of Dido. It is located, not in a rigorous

† Excerpts reprinted from Jill Mann, *Feminizing Chaucer* (Cambridge: D. S. Brewer, 2002), by permission of the author and publisher. Revised from her *Geoffrey Chaucer* (London: Harvester Wheatsheaf, 1991). The selections are from Chapter I, "Women and Betrayal," pp. 13–25, and Chapter V, "The Feminized Hero," pp. 129–33.

historical accuracy, but in the liberating ability of the imagination to invest the two-dimensional outlines of a text with their own autonomous life and movement. If Chaucer's Dido visualizes herself shrinking to the two-dimensional figure of gossip and literary *exemplum*, then in imagining that moment of anguished anticipation Chaucer has reversed the process: he has in imagination gone behind the literary sources to recuperate the living individual from whom they take their origin. It is his own act of imaginative retrieval that Chaucer emphasizes at the very heart of Dido's lament, intervening to make the point that here he has left his literary sources behind:

> In suche wordes gan to pleyne
> Dydo of hir grete peyne.
> As me mette redely—
> Non other auctour alegge I. (311–14)

Ovid's importance to this passage is not that he creates a Dido more acceptable to Chaucer; on the contrary, it is that his response to Vergil is the model for Chaucer's similarly independent act of imaginative retrieval. Just as Ovid could isolate a female perspective from Vergil's story of male destiny, so Chaucer can reconstruct Dido afresh from the point where her story makes contact with common human experience as he knows it.

The significance of this early work of Chaucer's, therefore, is not simply that he takes the 'woman's side' in the Dido-and-Aeneas story; it is rather that he dramatizes the adoption of this standpoint as *an act of retrieval*: the woman's viewpoint is rediscovered in the story of male heroism. Chaucer's Dido represents an affirmation of faith that such a retrieval is a permanent possibility—that the writ of literary authority runs no further than the point at which it meets the reader's own corrective or confirmatory experience.

To come to *Troilus and Criseyde* from the *House of Fame* is to see with full clarity how surprising—indeed, how apparently inexplicable—is Chaucer's choice of subject here. After his fervent identification with the victims of male deceit, he chooses to tell the classic story of female betrayal. Like Dido, Criseyde anticipates her own afterlife in story and song, but in her case there is the added pain of knowing that her tale will fan the flames of antifeminism.

> 'Allas, of me, unto the worldes ende,
> Shal neyther ben ywriten nor ysonge
> No good word, for thise bokes wol me shende.
> O, rolled shal I ben on many a tonge!
> Thoroughout the world my belle shal be ronge!
> And wommen moost wol haten me of alle.
> Allas, that swich a cas me sholde falle!
>
> Thei wol seyn, in as muche as in me is,
> I have hem don dishonour, weylaway!
> Al be I nat the first that dide amys,
> What helpeth that to don my blame awey?' (V 1058–68)

Criseyde's lament has a source in Benoît, whose Briseida similarly envisages with dismay her own future disgrace in story and song ('De mei n'iert ja fait bon escrit / Ne chantee bone chançon': *Roman de Troie* 20238–9), but his imagination of her distress does not prevent him (as it does Chaucer) from drawing the usual antifeminist moral (13438–56, 13471–91); for him, Briseida's prophetic vision of the meaning that will be given to her story simply repeats and endorses the meaning that he himself assigns to it—that women are inconstant and emotionally shallow (cf. Mieszkowski, 1971, 81–7, 103–4). The greater prominence that Chaucer gives to his own role as narrator of Criseyde's story invests the passage with a quite different significance: it becomes an accusation of his own role in adding to the 'bokes' that chronicle her shame. The responsibility is all the greater since Criseyde's very existence is a literary fiction; the poets invent the female inconstancy that they purportedly record. And whereas the *House of Fame* represents Dido's story as having painful consequences for herself alone. Criseyde's story is here represented as impinging on the real lives of other women, present and future. Chaucer here vividly realizes one of the special burdens that women have to bear: the knowledge that they cannot escape the burden of meaning. Whether good or bad, their actions will always be interpreted by reference to a model of 'woman', and will share willy-nilly in the responsibility for the nature of that model. The possible repercussions of this story on the lives of women are brought to the foreground again in the Prologue to the *Legend of Good Women*, where the God of Love upbraids Chaucer for having written *Troilus* precisely on the ground that women will be the sufferers from it.

> 'And of Creseyde thou hast seyd as the lyste,
> That maketh men to wommen lasse triste,
> That ben as trewe as ever was any steel.' (F 332–4)

Given this sensitivity to its antifeminist effects, why *did* Chaucer decide to tell this story? Are his expressions of sympathy for betrayed women to be seen as mere conventional gallantries, replaced at will by an equally conventional readiness to see women as fickle deceivers? That this is not the case is suggested by the fact that on two of the three occasions when Chaucer depicts female betrayal, he deliberately—even, it might seem, perversely—reverses the exemplary direction of his story when he comes to summarize its import. At the end of *Troilus and Criseyde*, he not only apologizes for his story to the female members of his audience[1]—

> Bysechyng every lady bright of hewe,
> And every gentil womman, what she be,
> That al be that Criseyde was untrewe,
> That for that gilt she be nat wroth with me.
> Ye may hire gilt in other bokes se;

---

1. The audience addressed may be the implied rather than the actual audience, since Richard Green has shown that the number of women at court was probably small: "Women in Chaucer's Audience," *Chaucer Review* 18 (1983–4): 146–54. Such apologies to women for antifeminist material are frequent enough in medieval literature to be regarded as conventional (Jill Mann, *Apologies to Women* [Cambridge: Cambridge UP, 1991]); but Chaucer's use of the convention is different from that of other writers by his immediate addition of remarks critical of men.

And gladlier I wol write, yif yow leste.
Penelopeës trouthe and good Alceste. (V 1772–8)

—he also, astonishingly, represents it as a warning to beware of false-hood in *men*:

N'y sey nat this al oonly for thise men,
But moost for wommen that bitraised be
Thorugh false folk—God yeve hem sorwe, amen!—
That with hire grete wit and subtilte
Bytraise yow. And this commeveth me
To speke, and in effect yow alle I preye,
Beth war of men, and herkneth what I seye! (V 1779–85)

The same reversal of direction occurs in similar circumstances in the *Manciple's Tale*. Having reached the point where he has to relate the adultery of Phoebus's wife, Chaucer swerves aside into a long digression on the impossibility of eradicating natural characteristics, illustrating this point with the Boethian example of the bird who flies off to the wood the moment its cage door is left open. Similarly, he continues, a cat's appetite for mice will never disappear, no matter how well fed it is, and a she-wolf characteristically expresses her 'vileyns kynde' by choos-ing the 'lewedeste wolf that she may fynde' (160–86). This last example was a favourite with antifeminist writers,[2] and one awaits—given the nature of the story Chaucer is telling—the inevitable conclusion on female lustfulness. But the trait that Chaucer identifies as naturally implanted in human beings is not lust, but 'newfangelnesse', and it is not women whom he identifies as most tainted with it, but *men*.

Alle this ensamples speke I by thise men
That been untrewe, and nothyng by wommen.
For men han evere a likerous appetit
On lower thyng to parfourne hire delit
Than on hire wyves, be they never so faire,
Ne never so trewe, ne so debonaire.
Flessh is so newefangel, with meschaunce,
That we ne konne in nothyng han plesaunce
That sowneth into vertu any while. (187–95)

The 'we' is significant: not 'men', but 'we men'. With these at first baffling contradictions between story and moral, Chaucer delicately negotiates the problems of a male author telling a story of female betrayal. He acknowledges his own masculinity, rather than dissolving it in the imper-sonal authority of the invisible author, and deflects the moral of his story on to the sex of which he can speak with personal authority. There are no such contradictory frameworks to complicate his stories of male betrayal; his exclamations against male deceit endorse and amplify the natural implications of the narrative rather than running against its grain. Setting the story at odds with the comment on it in the cases of female betrayal is thus not an instance of the 'ambivalence' so often

2. See Reid, T. B. W., "The She-Wolf's Mate," *Medium Aevum* 24 (1955): 16–19; *Romance of the Rose* 7761–6 (trans. Frances Horgan [Oxford: Oxford UP, 1994]); Matheolus, *Lamentations* I.904–6 (ed. G. Van Hamel [Paris: Emile Bouillon, 1893–1905]).

invoked in Chaucer criticism as a convenient way of halting further analysis, but rather an overt recognition of the need for a male author to *situate himself* in relation to these tales, and thereby to redress the asymmetrical balance created by the alignment of the male author and the male victim in the story.

The *Manciple's Tale* has yet more light to shed on *Troilus and Criseyde*. For it shows us that the male author not only has a general responsibility for telling or not telling a story, he also has a specific responsibility for *how* he tells it. It is he who chooses the style that will determine whether we see sexual congress as romantic passion or as a bestial coupling. No sooner has Chaucer turned back to the story of Phoebus's wife than he digresses from it again, this time to comment on his own use of the word 'lemman' to denote her lover.

> Hir lemman? Certes, this is a knavyssh speche!
> Foryeveth it me, and that I yow biseche.
>   The wise Plato seith, as ye may rede,
> The word moot nede accorde with the dede.
> If men shal telle proprely a thyng,
> The word moot cosyn be to the werkyng.
> I am a boystous man, right thus seye I:
> Ther nys no difference, trewely,
> Bitwixe a wyf that is of heigh degree,
> If of hir body dishonest she bee,
> And a povre wenche, oother than this—
> If it so be they werke bothe amys—
> But that the gentile, in estaat above,
> She shal be cleped his lady, as in love;
> And for that oother is a povre womman,
> She shal be cleped his wenche or his lemman.
> And, God it woot, myn owene deere brother,
> Men leyn that oon as lowe as lith that oother. (205–22)

The story-teller determines attitudes to women by the style he chooses for his story; it is he who makes woman an Isolde or a whore. The power of rhetoric to re-create women in its own mould is depressingly illustrated in Phoebus's sentimental reconstruction of his wife after he has murdered her in jealous rage:

> 'O deere wyf! O gemme of lustiheed!
> That were to me so sad and eek so trewe,
> Now listow deed, with face pale of hewe,
> Ful giltelees, that dorste I swere, ywys!' (274–7)

Phoebus's wife is not only the victim of male violence, but also the victim of male rhetoric (Mann, 1991c, 222). We never penetrate behind this rhetoric to an intimate knowledge of her, her lover, or the nature of the relationship between them; we see only the various stereotyped models in terms of which she might be presented.

It is style that is crucial in Chaucer's telling of the story of Criseyde. It is his style, rather than his final protestations of good intentions, that prevents this story, against all probability, from being read as a classic example of feminine fickleness and deceit. So successfully did Chaucer fend off this apparently inevitable interpretation that scholars were long convinced that the hostile stereotyping of Criseyde came only *after* Chaucer, and was largely attributable to Henryson and Shakespeare. Gretchen Mieszkowski's exhaustive documentation of the Cressida story from its inception in Benoît de Sainte-Maure shows however that she was already a byword for female mutability (and worse) when Chaucer came to write. It is Chaucer who not only abandons Boccaccio's moral on the fickleness of women, but who also creates a Criseyde to whom this moral seems entirely inappropriate. Despite the fact that Chaucer makes clear from the outset that the story will tell how Criseyde 'forsook' Troilus 'er she deyde' (I 56), this inevitable ending fades from the reader's consciousness in the moment-by-moment excitements of the love-affair. When in Book III Criseyde exclaims, in response to Pandarus's trumped-up story of Troilus's jealousy, 'Horaste! Allas, and falsen Troilus?' (806), the idea of her being unfaithful to Troilus is as unthinkable to us as it is to her. The character of betrayer is one with which events invest her, not one we are persuaded is hers from the beginning, whether by virtue of her sex or by virtue of her individual character. The final moment when Criseyde visualizes her own entrapment within the bounds of this stereotyped character thus reveals to us the full extent of the living indeterminacy which Chaucer has recuperated from its unpromising outline. No less than Chaucer's Dido, Chaucer's Criseyde represents an act of imaginative retrieval. Yet the very success of this act of retrieval raises even more acutely the question of how the betrayal comes about. If it is *not* due to female fickleness, what is its cause?

In answering this question, we come near to the heart of Chaucer's continual concern with betrayal. For it is, in his eyes, the bitterest manifestation of the most fundamental characteristic of human nature: the capacity for change. On two occasions in the *Canterbury Tales*, Chaucer adapted the Boethian metre on the ineradicability of natural impulses, complete with its illustrative image of the bird in the cage (*Consolation of Philosophy*, III m.2). The passage from the *Manciple's Tale* which I have already discussed is one of these instances; the other is in the *Squire's Tale*, where it forms part of the lament of the female falcon, deserted by her lover, and thus accounting for his betrayal of her:

> 'I trowe he hadde thilke text in mynde,
> That "alle thyng, repeirynge to his kynde,
> Gladeth hymself;" thus seyn men, as I gesse.
> Men loven of propre kynde newefangelnesse,
> As briddes doon that men in cages fede.
> For though thou nyght and day take of hem hede,
> And strawe hir cage faire and softe as silk,
> And yeve hem sugre, hony, breed and milk,
> Yet right anon as that his dore is uppe
> He with his feet wol spurne adoun his cuppe,
> And to the wode he wole and wormes ete;
> So newefangel been they of hire mete,
> And loven novelries of propre kynde,
> No gentillesse of blood ne may hem bynde.' (607–20)

In both cases what Chaucer adds to his Boethian source is an identification of man's 'propre kynde' as 'newefangelnesse', the ineradicable movement towards change and 'novelries'. It is this same impulse towards 'a newe' that Dido had identified as the source of men's betrayal (*House of Fame* 302). Neither lust, nor greed, nor vanity, is necessary to account for betrayal: it is the simple and inevitable reflex of the changeability that is the very life of human beings.

Troilus and Criseyde is Chaucer's most extended and most profound exploration of human changeability, and it is worth investigating this in some detail in order to see how it can give rise to, and yet resist being reduced to, female betrayal. The long and complex narrative allows us to see change not only as the sudden reversal it appears to be in the condensed summaries of *exemplum* or lament, but also as a series of minute adjustments to the changing pressures of daily living. To this end, the first three books of the poem are even more important than the last two. For it is in the slow process of Criseyde's acceptance of Troilus that we learn to understand how, when the time comes, she will gradually abandon him for Diomede. Between the Criseyde who rejects Pandarus's first overtures with distress and indignation, and the Criseyde who in joyous ecstasy entwines her body round Troilus's as tightly as honeysuckle round a tree, there lies a linked sequence of shifts and adjustments so small that they pass almost unnoticed at the time; yet the change they effect is as major, when we stand back to take the long view of it, as the one effected in the betrayal. It is the comparability of the two processes that cleanses the betrayal of its antifeminist implications, and it is to the earlier process that we should look if we want to understand how Chaucer rescues the betrayal from an antifeminist meaning.

The pressure towards change in Criseyde comes from without—from Pandarus's revelation of Troilus's love in the first case, and from the exchange with Antenor and Diomede's wooing in the second—but these external stimuli would fail of their effect were it not for the internal mutability they find to work on—the capacity of the mind to adapt, to absorb the overturning of the status quo into its own processes until it becomes a new status quo, a point of new departure. Chaucer's first indication of this capacity for absorption comes in the carefully casual question Criseyde addresses to Pandarus when all the first agitations over his announcement of Troilus's love have died down, and the subject appears to have been dropped: 'Kan he wel speke of love?' (II 503). The threatening aspect of Pandarus's startling news is, we see, wearing off: fear is replaced by curiosity, rejection by a readiness to admit at least the hypothesis of a hypothesis. The knowledge of Troilus's love has become part of Criseyde's 'mental furniture'; tossed into the ceaseless play of her thoughts and emotions, it causes them to shift, to rearrange themselves around it, to regroup into new formations to take account of it (Mann, 1989, 223–6).

This process of rearrangement can be seen in all its subtlety of detail in Chaucer's account of Criseyde's private thoughts when Pandarus has left her and she sits down to reflect on the 'newe cas'. She has barely got beyond reassuring herself that no woman is obliged to love a man however passionately he is in love with her (II 603–9), when she is distracted by shouts outside hailing Troilus's return from the battlefield. Watching this young hero ride by, she sees him with new eyes in the light of Pandarus's revelation, and blushes with consciousness of the thought that this is the man whose life, according to Pandarus, depends on her mercy. The serene detachment of which she has just been assuring herself evaporates at its first test; the secret excitement that arises spontaneously with the thought that this brave and modest hero is dying with love for *her* creates an embarrassment that of itself constitutes an implicating relationship with Troilus, despite his obliviousness to her gaze or her blush. It is not—as Chaucer hastens to make plain—that 'she so sodeynly / Yaf hym hire love', but that the pressure of the moment creates a pull towards him: 'she gan enclyne / To like hym first' (II 673–5).

> And after that, his manhod and hys pyne
> Made love withinne hire [herte] for to myne,
> For which by proces and by good servyse
> He gat hire love, and in no sodeyn wyse. (II 676–9)

As Chaucer turns back to his account of Criseyde's thoughts, we can see this 'proces' getting itself under way, as her mind accommodates itself to the new fact of Troilus's love. In contrast to the deliberate calculations of Boccaccio's Criseida, who weighs pros against cons and allows Troiolo's handsome person to tip the balance (*Filostrato* II 69–78, 83), Criseyde's reflections proceed in a random, spontaneous, disorganized manner. Their zig-zagging movement is conveyed in the loose, additive nature of the phrases that introduce each new idea: 'Ek wel woot I . . . Ek sith I woot . . . And eke I knowe . . . Now sette a caas . . . I thenke ek . . . ' (II 708–36). The self-conscious organisation of thought at the opening, as Criseyde decorously addresses herself to questions of 'worthynesse' and 'honour', and attempts worldly wisdom ('better not to make an enemy of the king's son') dissolves into spontaneous wonder that this dazzling personage, who could claim the noblest lady in Troy as his love, has chosen *her*; equally spontaneous is the immediately succeeding thought that this is not, after all, so odd, since—as everyone says—she is the most beautiful woman in Troy. It would be a mistake to interpret this last reflection as revealing vanity in Criseyde: an outstandingly beautiful woman can hardly be unaware of her own beauty, although social decorum obliges her to conceal her knowledge, as Criseyde recognises ('Al wolde I that noon wiste of this thought': II 745). Criseyde's private awareness of her own beauty escapes being vanity precisely because the vigilant supervision of her more public self brings it under scrutiny and control. What is revealed by this most private of thoughts is the level of intimate reflection to which we have penetrated: we have moved from the level of thought that is prepared for public scrutiny—that would translate itself without difficulty into speech—to a level of instinctive reaction that could hardly be made public without changing its entire character. What it is not vanity to know, it is vanity to speak. This sense of *levels* of thought is the result of our perception of the constant movement between them; the self-conscious aspect of the mind (in our terms, the super-ego) constantly doubles back on what has been spontaneously thought, correcting and criticizing. As her awareness of her beauty is 'corrected' by the self-reminder that no one else must know of this awareness, the prudential consideration that Troilus is no boaster is immediately 'corrected' by the reflection that he will of course have nothing to boast of.

So it is that the possibility of loving Troilus, which first appears only as a hypothesis to be rejected ('although it is out of the question to grant him my love . . . '; 'and he won't have anything to boast of . . . ') finally appears as a positive without any *logical* preparation for the change. Having begun to contemplate her own beauty—to look at herself, that is, with Troilus's eyes—she is led quite naturally into fashioning a new image of herself: the picture of sober widowhood which has been the model for her behaviour hitherto (II 113–19) gives way to a new conception of herself as her 'owene womman', in comfortable circumstances, 'Right yong', and free from obligations to a husband (II 750–6). For such a person love seems not only permissible but desirable.

> 'What shal I doon? To what fyn lyve I thus?
> Shal I nat love, in cas if that me leste?
> What, pardieux! I am naught religious.' (II 757–9)

So she admits the possibility of loving Troilus as one that is, indeed, open for her to choose.

What is important in this long sequence of thought is not so much its representation of *what* Criseyde thinks as its representation of *how* she thinks (Howard, 1970). Her mind moves of its own accord, flitting from one aspect of the situation to another, animated by the sudden emotional impulses that thwart the attempt at a logical progression by starting off in an unrelated direction. It is not surprising, then, to find that one of these impulses causes her thoughts suddenly to reverse themselves completely, the corrective agent here being not the super-ego but simple fear: *since* she is free, should she jeopardize this freedom by subjecting herself to the anxieties, quarrels, jealousies and betrayals so frequent in love? The spontaneous nature of this reversal in mood is emphasized by the natural image Chaucer chooses to express it:

> But right as when the sonne shyneth brighte
> In March, that chaungeth ofte tyme his face,
> And that a cloude is put with wynd to flighte,
> Which oversprat the sonne as for a space,
> A cloudy thought gan thorugh hire soule pace,
> That overspradde hire brighte thoughtes alle,
> So that for feere almost she gan to falle. (II 764–70)

Sun and shade alternate within the human mind as inevitably as in a March day; the mind too 'chaungeth ofte tyme his face'. So this reversal in turn eventually reverses itself.

> And after that, hire thought gan for to clere,
> And seide, 'He which that nothing undertaketh,
> Nothyng n'acheveth, be hym looth or deere.'
> And with an other thought hire herte quaketh;

> Than slepeth hope, and after drede awaketh;
> Now hoot, now cold; but thus, bitwixen tweye,
> She rist hire up, and wente hire for to pleye. (II 806–12)

'Now hoot, now cold': here is change working at its most fundamental and ineradicable level. The bold outlines of observable change are formed out of the *pointilliste* minutiae of this ceaseless movement of thought and emotion, absorbing and responding to external stimuli. In the sequence that follows we see how a new set of external stimuli gradually transforms the continual to-ing and fro-ing into a single directional flow: Antigone sings her song in praise of love which answers Criseyde's fears of 'thraldom'; the nightingale sings under Criseyde's window as she falls asleep; she dreams of the eagle who tears her heart out without pain. The current of events is pulling her towards love, but it could not do so without the existing presence in her mind of the thoughts and emotions which it can endorse and bring into the foreground. The seething possibilities in Criseyde's mind are the seed-bed for new developments; chance determines which of these possibilities—the attraction to nobility, openness to adventure—will realize themselves in the immediate sequence of events, but the other possibilities—cautious timidity, prudent self-interest—do not disappear; they remain, to be called into play by the new set of external pressures created by Criseyde's isolation in the Greek camp and Diomede's insistent wooing.

It is the slow process by which Criseyde's thoughts and feelings adapt themselves to the fact of Troilus's love until it becomes part of her own being that teaches us to understand how they can equally adapt to his loss and set Diomede in his place. This time Chaucer does not show us her thoughts in detail, but his summary indicates with beautiful subtlety the way that this process mirrors that in Book II. After Diomede's first visit, Criseyde goes to bed in her father's tent.

> Retornyng in hire soule ay up and down
> The wordes of this sodeyn Diomede,
> His grete estat, and perel of the town,
> And that she was allone and hadde nede
> Of frendes help; and thus bygan to brede
> The cause whi, the sothe for to telle,
> That she took fully purpos for to dwelle. (V 1023–9)

The betrayal dissolves itself in the invisible flux of Criseyde's thoughts; the stanza concludes, not with a decision, but with the mere germination of the *cause* of a *purpose*—and a purpose that realizes itself not as action, but simply as the will's endorsement of a status quo, so that the moment of that endorsement is inaccessible to outward observation.

And yet, having shown us Criseyde's change of heart as a slow process of incremental adjustment, in the very next stanza Chaucer re-presents it with a brutal abruptness of style that becomes a characterisation of the deed itself:

> The morwen com, and gostly for to speke,
> This Diomede is come unto Criseyde;
> And shortly, lest that ye my tale breke,

> So wel he for hymselven spak and seyde
> That alle hire sikes soore adown he leyde;
> And finaly, the sothe for to seyne,
> He refte hire of the grete of al hire peyne. (V 1030–6)

The shift in narrative perspective effects a shift in emotional attitude. The first stanza takes a 'long view' of Criseyde's change of heart, seeing it as a gentle and quasi-inevitable process of reorientation; the second 'shortly' summarizes this process until its outlines appear in cruel clarity. Taken together, they answer the question of how betrayal comes about: the bewildering volte-faces castigated in the denunciations of 'newefangelnesse' spin themselves out into the subtle filaments of fluctuating mood and thought. We do not see Criseyde deciding to betray—we do not even see her betraying—we see her realizing, at the end of the almost invisible process, that she has betrayed (Mann, 1986, 82). Just as she never formally decides to yield to Troilus, but comes to realize that she has yielded ('Ne hadde I er now, my swete herte deere / Ben yolde, ywis, I were now nought heere!': III 1210–11), so her betrayal too is a matter of retrospective acknowledgement ('I have falsed oon the gentileste / That evere was': V 1056–7) rather than present decision. In neither case is there a single moment of choice, but rather a gradual and spontaneous movement through a series of finely discriminated stages leading from common civility to declared love, each stage providing not only the basis for the next but also its *raison d'être*: 'since *that* has been granted, surely it obliges you to *this*'.

Criseyde's yielding to Diomede thus ironically repeats and mirrors her yielding to Troilus. The reorientation of the self which is applauded and welcomed when it leads to her ecstatic union with Troilus is bitterly parodied in her supine capitulation to Diomede. In the formal portraits of Criseyde and her two lovers which Chaucer interpolates into the narrative action of Book V, as if to freeze their outlines before they finally recede from us into history, the two manifestations of her capacity for change appear as two versions of her character:

> Ne nevere mo ne lakked hire pite,
> Tendre-herted, slydynge of corage. (V 824–5)

'Slydynge' is the adjective used to characterize Fortune in Chaucer's translation of Boethius's *Consolation* (I m.5.34); applied to Criseyde's mind, it underlines with brilliant economy Chaucer's profound perception that Fortune exists not only in external vicissitudes—the exchange of Antenor for Criseyde—but also as an ineradicable part of the human mind, as the constant variability which forms itself into the larger evolutions of an individual story. But if Criseyde's 'slydynge corage' is the ugly face of human changeability, its benign face is 'pite', the quality in the beloved on which the lover pins his hopes, as innumerable medieval love-poems—among them Chaucer's *Complaint unto Pity*—make clear. Criseyde's 'pite' leads to Troilus's happiness, her 'slydynge corage' to his betrayal.

It is at this point that we are ready to see how this story of betrayal both is and is not, in Chaucer's mind, appropriately told of a woman rather than a man. It is *not*, in the sense that changeability, as Chaucer shows it to us, is not specifically female but is simply a human condition. If Troilus remains faithful, that is not only because of his own stability, but also because his social context remains unaltered. For him, Criseyde's departure creates an absence, a vacuum into which his whole being strains; for her, it creates a new set of presences, obliterating the structure of relationships in which Troilus held the central place. The external change, not her own fickleness, precipitates her betrayal. Yet there is at the same time a special appropriateness in mediating the tragic experience of mutability through a woman, since it is in women that the capacity for change, for adaptation and graceful responsiveness, has been traditionally most admired. So in the *Knight's Tale* it is Emily's 'wommanly pitee' to which Theseus appeals in order to transform the grief at Arcite's death into rejoicing over her marriage to Palamon (3083). It is this womanly responsiveness which Chaucer surely has in mind in his generally misunderstood comment on Emily's 'freendlich' reciprocation of Arcite's happy gaze after he has won her in the tournament:

> (For wommen, as to speken in comune,
> Thei folwen alle the favour of Fortune). (2681–2)

The ready changeability which gives women a special affinity with Fortune can manifest itself as treacherous instability or as a blessed (from the male lover's point of view) susceptibility to external pressure; in Criseyde we see it in both its forms. Its role as part of an ideal of womanhood is manifest in Criseyde's graceful adaptations of her tone and manner to her companions and her situation: relaxed, poised and witty in her verbal fencing with Pandarus, she is dignified, open and passionate with Troilus. This is how men would have their women be, instinctively adapting to the contours of their personalities and moods. But if this is what they want, they must accept that women can be equally chameleon-like with *other* men, until they are changed beyond recognition.[3] The real tragedy of *Troilus and Criseyde* is not simply that Troilus is separated from Criseyde, it is that she ceases to exist as the Criseyde he has known and loved: she has become, in Shakespeare's words, 'Diomed's Cressid'. Troilus's fidelity is enslavement to a ghost.

To say that Chaucer roots Criseyde's betrayal in the fundamentally human capacity for change is to say that there is no reason why we should not take his final protestations against an antifeminist interpretation of his story at face value. But it is not to say that Criseyde's betrayal thereby becomes excusable or acceptable or a 'realistic compromise'. If Chaucer professes 'routhe' for Criseyde and an inclination to 'excuse' her in order to deflect *our* inclination to blame the tragedy on female weakness, this does not prevent him from narrating her betrayal in terms that make it far uglier than it is in Boccaccio's story. For one thing, Boccaccio's Diomede is a far nicer person, who has genuinely fallen in love with Criseida, and who has all the attractiveness and nobility of Troiolo. Chaucer's Diomede, in contrast, is a calculating seducer who seems simply to want another female scalp for his collection—and

3. Cf. C. Saintonge, "In Defense of Criseyde," *Modern Language Quarterly* 15 (1954): 312–20. P. 313: "the same qualities that made [Criseyde] desirable brought about her fall from grace."

will even, it is suggested, boast about it afterwards ('som men seyn he was of tonge large': V 804). It is likewise Chaucer who displays in full the cheap dishonesty of Criseyde's letter to Troilus (V 1590–1631; cf. *Filostrato* VII 105; VIII 5), and who imports from Benoît (*Roman de Troie* 20275–8) the pathetic protestation of fidelity to her new lover with which she tries to cover over the implications of what she has done. Yet if we read the story aright, we understand how Chaucer can make these changes without incurring the charge of antifeminism. His aim is not to blacken women, but to show human change in its fully tragic dimensions, and for this Criseyde's loss is not enough: we need to see the deformation of her personality. But if antifeminism is not the aim of Chaucer's story, it may still be its unintended *effect*, as Chaucer himself acknowledges in the God of Love's accusations in the Prologue to the *Legend of Good Women*. It is to Chaucer's attempt to meet these accusations in the *Legend* that we must now turn.

*   *   *

> '. . . pitee renneth soone in gentil herte.'
> (*Knight's Tale* 1761)

It is nowadays a commonplace that the meaning of a term is not fixed in isolation, but only in relation to the cultural or linguistic structure of which it forms part. So the value assigned to 'woman' or 'womanhood' cannot be fully determined without reference to the values invested in the term 'man'. To make 'woman' into a moral positive is not enough, if she becomes thereby merely the 'silent bearer of ideology', as Mary Jacobus puts it (1979, 10)—if, that is, her morality acts only as a salving conscience for the men who are left free to practise the *realpolitik* required for effective action in the world. The question of how Chaucer conceives of men is thus the last and most crucial element in determining the status of women in his writing.

Male heroes are, as I have already noted, few and far between in Chaucer. In the *Canterbury Tales*, the moral high ground is occupied by Constance, Griselda, Cecilia, Prudence, and no man is accorded the central and dominating position in the narrative that they enjoy. It is only in *Troilus* that a single male consciousness becomes the central locus of poetic meaning; whatever the prominence given to Criseyde, the central subject of this poem is the loss of happiness, and it is to Troilus and not to Criseyde that this experience belongs. The question raised by this experience—the question of what meaning can be attached to human happiness in a mutable world—has urgency only if we believe that it was a *true* happiness, and also that its loss cannot simply be written down to failings or vices—female fickleness, male inertia— which could be avoided by those wishing for better fortune. Chaucer takes pains, therefore, to present Troilus as admirable throughout; he is 'this ilke noble knyght' to the last (V 1752). In his final emotional rejection of human love, Chaucer still speaks, not of Troilus's weakness or folly, but of his 'grete worthynesse' and his 'noblesse' (V 1829, 1831). It is to Troilus that we should look first, therefore, for evidence of Chaucer's conception of a masculine ideal.

It is in Troilus that we can first clearly perceive that the male hero in Chaucer is a *feminized* hero. I have shown * * * that Troilus is divested of the coerciveness characteristic of the 'active' male, and that his unreserved surrender to the force of love is for Chaucer not a sign of weakness but of a generous nobility. He is feminized not only in his reverence for woman but also in his vulnerability and sensitivity of feeling. 'Feminized' is not to be equated with 'effeminate'; Troilus's physical prowess and bravery are carefully established at numerous points in the poem, most notably in the visual image created by the description of his return from the battlefield, watched by the curious Criseyde:

> So lik a man of armes and a knyght
> He was to seen, fulfilled of heigh prowesse,
> For bothe he hadde a body and a myght
> To don that thing, as wel as hardynesse;
> And ek to seen hym in his gere hym dresse,
> So fressh, so yong, so weldy semed he,
> It was an heven upon hym for to see. (II 631–7)

Troilus is not lacking in the conventional attributes of 'manhod' (II 676)—courage, strength, dignified self-restraint. It is with 'manhod' that he controls his words and deeds so as not to betray his relationship with Criseyde to anyone (III 428), and 'with mannes herte' that he suppresses his emotions when the exchange of Criseyde for Antenor is being debated in the Trojan parliament (IV 154); similarly when leading her out from Troy, he 'gan his wo ful manly for to hide' (V 30). But the domination implied in this conception of manhood is a domination of self, not a domination of others. It stands in implicit but eloquent contrast to the notion of manhood assumed in Pandarus's impatient advice on how to prevent the loss of Criseyde:

> . . . 'Frend, syn thow hast swych distresse,
> And syn the list myn argumentz to blame,
> Why nylt thiselven helpen don redresse
> And with thy manhod letten al this grame?
> Go ravysshe here! Ne kanstow nat, for shame?
> And other lat here out of towne fare,
> Or hold here stille, and leve thi nyce fare.
>
> Artow in Troie, and hast non hardyment
> To take a womman which that loveth the
> And wolde hireselven ben of thy assent?
> Now is nat this a nyce vanitee?
> Ris up anon, and lat this wepyny be,
> And kith thow art a man; for in this houre
> I wol ben ded, or she shal bleven oure.' (IV 526–36)

Pandarus speaks for the conventional notion of 'manhod' as aggressive egoism; 'showing oneself a man' slides with ease into 'ravishing women'. His protest that 'It is no rape' (596), because Criseyde's willingness can be presumed[4]—indeed she would probably think Troilus foolish if he did

---

4. In terms of fourteenth-century law, Pandarus is mistaken; the term *raptus* covered cases where the woman consented to her own abduction—i.e., what we would now call elopement (Cannon, 2000).

not assert himself in this way (598–9)—reincarnates the male assumption of female willingness, and the need to exercise responsibility on her behalf, that we saw illustrated in *Pamphilus* and Peter of Blois's lyric. Like Galatea, she will 'a lite hire greve', but allow herself to be quickly appeased (603–4). The same conception of 'manliness' is evident when Pandarus repeats his advice a little later:

> 'Forthi tak herte, and thynk right as a knyght:
> Thorugh love is broken al day every lawe.
> Kith now somewhat thi corage and thi myght;
> Have mercy on thiself for any awe.
> Lat nat this wrecched wo thyn herte gnawe,
> But manly sette the world on six and sevene;
> And if thow deye a martyr, go to hevene!' (IV 617–23)[5]

'Manliness', for Pandarus, means acting vigorously in one's own interests and letting the rest of the world go hang. This is the 'mannishness' that is repudiated in the Sultaness and Donegild in the *Man of Law's Tale*; this scene in *Troilus* shows us that it is not only in women that this kind of manliness is to be rejected, but also in men. Chaucer carefully dissociates Troilus from Pandarus's ideas of manliness, locating true manhood instead in Troilus's rejection of 'ravysshyng of wommen' (IV 548),[6] and in his 'passive' suppression of self to the interests of others—the people of Troy and Criseyde herself (McAlpine, 1978, 159–62). When Chaucer speaks of Troilus's manhood he habitually pairs it with the 'feminized' characteristics—capacity for feeling or suffering, 'gentilesse'—that cleanse it of aggression: 'his manhod and his pyne', 'manly sorwe', 'gentil herte and manhod' (II 676, III 113, IV 1674).

It is not only in his refusal of coerciveness that Troilus is a 'feminized' hero. It is also in the fact that the story in which he is set casts him in a feminine role in that it assimilates him to the women of Ovid's *Heroides*—abandoned and betrayed by his lover, immobilized, frustrated of action and movement, finding relief only in memory, lamentation and fruitless letter-writing. Roland Barthes writes of the essentially feminine nature of this situation.

> Historically, the discourse of absence is carried on by the Woman:
> Woman is sedentary. Man hunts, journeys; Woman is faithful (she
> waits), man is fickle (he sails away, he cruises). It is Woman who
> gives shape to absence, elaborates its fiction, for she has time to do
> so; she weaves and she sings; the Spinning Songs express both
> immobility (by the hum of the Wheel) and absence (far away,
> rhythms of travel, sea surges, cavalcades). It follows that in any man
> who utters the other's absence *something feminine* is declared: this
> man who waits and who suffers from his waiting is miraculously
> feminized. A man is not feminized because he is inverted but
> because he is in love. (Myth and utopia: the origins have belonged,

---

5. The repeated emphasis on 'manhood' and 'being a man' is Chaucer's own development from the single word 'virilmente' in the corresponding speeches in *Filostrato* (IV.64–5, 71–5).
6. This too is Chaucer's addition (cf. *Filostrato* IV.67), as is the crucial condition, "so it were hire assent" (IV.554), attached to his consideration of the possibility of asking King Priam to grant him Criseyde in marriage.

the future will belong to the subjects *in whom there is something feminine.*)

(1979, 13–14; cf. Lipking, 1988, xix)

Whether or not this is 'historically' true, the influence of the *Heroides* fixed it as a mental model for the Middle Ages. So Troilus finds himself in the situation of Dido, Ariadne, Penelope, endlessly yearning into a void, imprisoned in inaction and emotional paralysis. The Ovidian lament, after centuries of history, is uttered by a male voice. It is Boccaccio, of course, who earns the credit for first transposing this essentially feminine genre into masculine form, but in the *Filostrato* its function is simply to add lyrical pathos to his appeal to his mistress: 'whenever you find Troiolo weeping and grieving over the departure of Criseida, you may understand and recognize my own words, tears, sighs, and torments', he writes to Maria d'Aquino in his Prologue. In Chaucer, it acquires extra significance by being linked with a distinct conception of masculinity which bears the stamp of female experience. If Constance and Griselda are characterized by suffering, so is Troilus; there is no division between active male and suffering female.

This is one final reason for Chaucer to tell a tale of female betrayal: that it enables him to break down the apparently inevitable division between the active male betrayer and the passive female sufferer. That he was conscious of the Ovidian nature of Book V of his poem can be deduced, I think, from a typically bland witticism which he added to Boccaccio's narrative in Book I: Pandarus, affirming his ability to help Troilus even though he himself is unsuccessful in love, quotes from a 'lettre' written by an 'herdesse', Oenone, to Troilus's brother Paris, to the effect that Phoebus, inventor of medicine, was able to cure all complaints except his own love (I 652–65). The 'lettre', as the quotation from it shows, is nothing other than Epistle V of the *Heroides*, here treated as if it were a historical document rather than a product of the imagination—as if, that is, it were a real-life letter that Paris showed to some of his friends and might well have shown to his brother Troilus. In his note on this passage, Barry Windeatt draws attention to its submerged link with Criseyde's vow of fidelity to Troilus in Book IV (when the River Simois flows backwards to its source, then alone will she be untrue: 1548–54), which echoes Paris's vow of fidelity to Oenone, quoted in the same *Heroides* epistle (V 29–30, with Xanthus in place of Simois), and is destined to the same fate as his. The pattern of Troilus's life merges with the pattern of Oenone's life; her 'lettre' ceases to be a mere source of apt simile and becomes instead the mirror that reflects his own experience.

Troilus is not the only Chaucerian hero to find himself in the *Heroides* posture, abandoned and grief-stricken. *The Complaint of Mars* likewise climaxes a narrative of female betrayal with an extended lament by the betrayed male lover. If the narrative in this case is a witty astrological allegory rather than a serious exploration of human love, the complaint itself has a lyrical intensity that makes it a genuine expression of feeling. Here it is not only a male who suffers, but also a god: as in the *Man of Law's Tale*, his power is reinscribed as impotence by the planetary role that separates his heavenly course from that of his beloved Venus. The male sufferer is also the focus of attention in the *Book of the Duchess*, although in this case it is bereavement rather than betrayal that has deprived him of his mistress. Here it is the predicament of the abandoned lover that introduces the spectre of betrayal, which presents itself, as it does in the *Franklin's Tale*, as a possible result of death. To Chaucer's jocular comment that the Black Knight's long rehearsal of his love is a case of 'shryfte withoute repentaunce', the Knight makes passionate reply:

> 'Repentaunce? Nay, fy!' quod he,
> 'Shulde y now repente me
> To love? Nay, certes, than were I wel
> Wers than was Achitofel,
> Or Anthenor, so have I joye,
> The traytor that betraysed Troye,
> Or the false Genelloun,
> He that purchased the tresoun
> Of Rowland and of Olyver.
> Nay, while I am alyve her,
> I nyl foryete hir never moo.' (1115–25)

Forgetting is betrayal, but forgetfulness of the absent is, as Barthes says, 'the condition of survival': 'if I did not forget, I should die' (1979, 14). 'Hit was gret wondre that Nature / Myght suffre any creature / To have such sorwe and be nat ded', as Chaucer says of the Black Knight (467–9). Nature resists the stasis imposed by absence, pressing towards the emotional movement that is the condition of life.

Like Troilus, the Black Knight is condemned to stasis by his 'trouthe', perennially arrested by fidelity to a past that is forever sundered from the living movement of the present. Like Troilus—and like Griselda, for whom likewise the only way out of stasis is betrayal, not only of the beloved but also of the self. Chaucer's heroes share the same experiences as his heroines; the only 'active' males in the early poems are the villains of the *Legend of Good Women*, who inflict suffering without feeling it.

*   *   *

Glossary

These very common words are not always glossed in the text. The letters *i* and *y*, *k* and *c* are interchangeable.

and   and, if
anon   immediately
atones   at once
ay   always
ayeyn   again, in turn
be(n)   are, be
bet   better
breste   burst
but, but if   unless
certes   certainly
couthe   could, knew, known
do   do, cause
drede   fear, doubt
eft   again, in turn
ek   also
em, eem   uncle
er   before, previously
falle(n)   fall, happen, befall
forthy   therefore
fro   from
gan   began, (aux.) did
han   have
hem   them
hewe   hue, complexion
hire   her, their
ich   I
ilke   same, very
kan   can, know, know how
kynde   nature
like(n)   please, like
list(e)   it pleases
lust   pleasure, desire
men   men, one
mot, moot   must
muchel   much
namely   especially
nas   *ne was*
nathelees   nevertheless
ne   not, nor
neigh   near, nearly
ner, neer   nearer, near

nolde   *ne wolde*
not   *ne wot*
nyce   foolish
nyl   *ne wil*
nys   *ne is*
nyste   *ne wiste*
o   one
parde   by God, indeed
pleyne(n)   complain, lament
quod   said
rede(n)   counsel, advise, read
sik, sike(n)   sigh, to sigh
sith   since
soth   true, truth
swych   such
syn   since
than   then, than
that   that, who, that which
thilke   that same
thinken   seem
tho   then, those
to   to, too
triste(n)   trust
tweyne   two
wax   grew
wende(n)   think, suppose
wight   person, creature
wise   manner, way
wist(e)   known, knew
wolde   wished, would
wood   insane
worship   honor
wot   knows
wroth   angry
wys   certainly, indeed
yë(n)   eye(s)
yif   if
yive(n), yeve   give
ynough   enough
ywis   certainly

Selected Bibliography

*indicates a work included or excerpted in this Norton Critical Edition.

BIBLIOGRAPHIES AND HANDBOOKS

Annual bibliographies of Chaucer studies appear in the journal *Studies in the Age of Chaucer*. The University of Texas at San Antonio maintains a compilation of these bibliographies on the internet at <uchaucer.usta.edu/cgi-bin/Pwebcon.cgl?DB=local&PAGE=First>. Annual reviews of more important studies appear in *The Year's Work in English Studies*.

Baird, Lorrayne Y. *A Bibliography of Chaucer, 1964–73*. Boston: Hall, 1977.

Baird-Lange, Lorrayne Y. *A Bibliography of Chaucer, 1974–1985*. Hamden, CT: Shoe String Press, 1988.

Boitani, Piero, and Jill Mann. *The Cambridge Chaucer Companion*. Cambridge: Cambridge UP, 1986.

Bowers, Bege K., and Mark Allen. *Annotated Chaucer Bibliography, 1986–1996*. South Bend, IN: U of Notre Dame P, 2002.

Brown, Peter, ed. *A Companion to Chaucer*. Oxford: Blackwell, 2000.

Kaminsky, Alice R. *Chaucer's 'Troilus and Criseyde' and the Critics*. Ohio UP, 1980.

Pugh, Tyson, and Angela Jane Weisl, eds. *Approaches to Teaching Chaucer's 'Troilus and Criseyde' and the Shorter Poems*. Forthcoming. New York: Modern Language Association, 2006.

Rowland, Beryl, ed. *Companion to Chaucer Studies*. Rev. ed. Oxford: Oxford UP, 1979.

Windeatt, Barry. *Oxford Guides to Chaucer: Troilus and Criseyde*. Oxford: Clarendon, 1992.

EDITIONS OF *TROILUS AND CRISEYDE*

Barney, Stephen A., ed. *Troilus and Criseyde*, with Explanatory and Textual Notes, in Benson, ed., *Riverside Chaucer*.

Baugh, Albert C., ed. *Chaucer's Major Poetry*. New York: Appleton Century Crofts, 1963. Uses Robinson's text.

Benson, Larry D., gen. ed. *The Riverside Chaucer*. Boston: Houghton Mifflin, 1987. Thorough revision of Robinson; the standard edition.

Donaldson, E. Talbot., ed. *Chaucer's Poetry: An Anthology for the Modern Reader*. New York: Ronald, 1975.

Fisher, John H. *The Complete Poetry and Prose of Geoffrey Chaucer*. New York: Holt, Rinehart and Winston, 1977.

Pollard, Arthur W., et al., ed. *The Works of Geoffrey Chaucer*. Globe Edition. London, Macmillan, 1898. W. S. McCormick edited *Troilus and Criseyde* for the Globe edition.

Robinson, F. N., ed. *The Works of Geoffrey Chaucer*. 2nd ed. Boston: Houghton Mifflin, 1957.

Root, Robert Kilburn, ed. *The Book of Troilus and Criseyde*. Princeton: Princeton UP, 1926. Excellent notes.

Skeat, Walter W. *The Complete Works of Geoffrey Chaucer*. 6 vols. Oxford: Clarendon, 1894.

Windeatt, B. A., ed. *Geoffrey Chaucer: Troilus & Criseyde*. London and New York: Longman, 1984. Prints the Italian text of the *Filostrato* (Pernicone 1937) in parallel and all substantive variants.

COLLECTIONS OF ESSAYS

Barney, Stephen A., ed. *Chaucer's 'Troilus': Essays in Criticism*. Hamden, CT: Archon, 1980.

Benson, C. David, ed. *Critical Essays on Chaucer's 'Troilus and Criseyde' and His Major Early Poems*. Toronto: U of Toronto P, 1991.

Salu, Mary, ed. *Essays on 'Troilus and Criseyde'*. Cambridge: D. S. Brewer, 1979.

Schoeck, Richard J., and Jerome Taylor, ed. *Chaucer Criticism, II: 'Troilus and Criseyde' and the Minor Poems*. South Bend, IN: U of Notre Dame P, 1961.

Shoaf, R. A., ed. *Chaucer's 'Troilus and Criseyde'—"Subgit to alle Poesye": Essays in Criticism*. Binghamton, NY: Medieval & Renaissance Texts & Studies, SUNY Binghamton, 1992.

REFERENCE WORKS

Benson, Larry D. *A Glossarial Concordance to the Riverside Chaucer*. 2 vols. Hamden, CT: Garland, 1993.

Burnley, J. David, *A Guide to Chaucer's Language*. Basingstoke: Macmillan, 1983.

Crow, Martin M., and Clair C. Olson, ed. *Chaucer Life Records*. Oxford: Clarendon, 1966.

Davis, Norman, et al. *A Chaucer Glossary*. Oxford: Clarendon, 1979.

Kökeritz, Helge. *A Guide to Chaucer's Pronunciation*. Rev. ed. Toronto: U of Toronto P, 1978.

LIFE AND TIMES

Boase, Roger. *The Origin and Meaning of Courtly Love: A Critical Study of European Scholarship*. Manchester: Manchester UP, 1977.

Brewer, Derek S. *Chaucer in His Time*. London: Longman, 1973.

Burnley, David. *Courtliness and Literature in Medieval England*. London: Longman, 1998.

Cannon, Christopher. "Chaucer and Rape: Uncertainties Certainties." *Studies in the Age of Chaucer* 22 (2000): 67–92.

Green, Richard Firth. *Poets and Princepleasers: Literature and the English Court in the Late Middle Ages*. Toronto: U of Toronto P, 1980.

Howard, Donald R. *Chaucer: His Life, His Works, His World*. New York: Dutton, 1987.

Keen, Maurice. *Chivalry*. New Haven: Yale UP, 1984.

Pearsall, Derek. *The Life of Geoffrey Chaucer: A Critical Biography*. Oxford: Blackwell, 1994.

Saul, Nigel. *Richard II*. New Haven: Yale UP, 1997.

Strohm, Paul. *Social Chaucer*. Cambridge: Harvard UP, 1989.

BOCCACCIO AND OTHER SOURCES

•apRoberts, Robert P., and Anna Bruni [Seldis] Benson, trans. *Giovanni Boccaccio: Il Filostrato*. New York and London: Garland, 1986. Reprints the Pernicone text of Boccaccio with a facing-page translation and valuable introduction.

Bianciotti, Gabriel, ed. *Le Roman de Troyle*. Rouen: University of Rouen Publications 75, 1994. An early French translation of the *Filostrato* by Beauvau.

Boitani, Piero, ed. *Chaucer and the Italian Trecento*. Cambridge: Cambridge UP, 1983.

———, ed. *The European Tragedy of Troilus*. Oxford: Clarendon, 1989.

Branca, Vittore. *Boccaccio: The Man and His Works*, trans. Richard Monges. New York: New York UP, 1976.

———, ed. *Tutte le opere di Giovanni Boccaccio*. Vol. II: *Filostrato* and *Teseida*. Milan: Mondadori, 1964. The *Filostrato* text is a slightly revised version of Pernicone 1937.

Fansler, Dean S. *Chaucer and the 'Roman de la Rose'*. New York, 1914. Repr. Gloucester, MA: Peter Smith, 1965.

Frazer, R. M., trans. *The Trojan War: The Chronicles of Dictys of Crete and Dares the Phrygian*. Bloomington: Indiana UP, 1966.

Ginsberg, Warren. *Chaucer's Italian Tradition*. Ann Arbor: U of Michigan P, 2002.

Griffin, Nathaniel E., and Arthur B. Myrick, ed. and trans. *The Filostrato of Giovanni Boccaccio: A Translation with Parallel Text*. Philadelphia: U of Pennsylvania P, 1929.

Gordon, R. K., ed. and trans. *The Story of Troilus as Told by Benoît de Sainte-Maure, Giovanni Boccaccio, Geoffrey Chaucer, Robert Henryson*. London: Dent, 1934. Repr. Toronto, Medieval Academy Reprints for Teaching, U of Toronto P, 1978.

Hanly, Michael. *Boccaccio, Beauvau, and Chaucer: 'Troilus and Criseyde'—Four Perspectives*. Norman, OK: Pilgrim Books, 1990.

Havely, N. R., ed. and trans. *Chaucer's Boccaccio: Sources of 'Troilus' and the Knight's and Franklin's Tales*. Cambridge: D. S. Brewer, 1980.

Meek, M. E., trans. [Guido delle Colonne] *Historia Destructionis Troiae*. Bloomington: Indiana UP, 1974.

Minnis, Alastair J. *Chaucer and Pagan Antiquity*. Cambridge: D. S. Brewer, 1982.

Nolan, Barbara. *Chaucer and the Tradition of the Roman Antique*. Cambridge: Cambridge UP, 1992.

Pernicone, Vincenzo, ed. *Il Filostrato e il Ninfale fiesolano*. Bari: Laterza, 1937.
Roberts, Gildas, trans. *Joseph of Exeter: The Iliad of Dares Phrygius*. Capetown: A. A. Balkema, 1970.
Schless, Howard H. *Chaucer and Dante: A Reevaluation*. Norman, OK: Pilgrim, 1984.
Wallace. David. *Giovanni Boccaccio*. Cambridge: Cambridge UP, 1991.
Wimsatt, James I. *Chaucer and His French Contemporaries: Natural Music in the Fourteenth Century*. Toronto: U of Toronto P, 1991.

HENRYSON

Benson, C. David. "Critic and Poet: What Lydgate and Henryson Did to Chaucer's *Troilus and Criseyde*," *Modern Language Quarterly* 53 (1992): 23–40.
Fox, Denton. "The Scottish Chaucerians." In *Chaucer and Chaucerians*, ed. D. S. Brewer. Tuscaloosa: University of Alabama, 1964. 164–200.
———, ed. *The Poems of Robert Henryson*. Oxford: Clarendon, 1981. The standard edition with excellent notes.
Gray, Douglas. *Robert Henryson*. Leiden: Brill, 1979.
———, ed. *The Testament of Cresseid*. In *The Oxford Book of Late Medieval Verse and Prose*. Oxford: Oxford UP, 1988. 288–304.
Kindrick, Robert L. *Robert Henryson*. Twayne Series 274. Boston: G. K. Hall, 1979.
•———, ed. *The Poems of Robert Henryson*. Kalamazoo: TEAMS, Western Michigan UP, 1997.
MacQueen, John. *Robert Henryson: A Study of the Major Narrative Poems*. Oxford: Clarendon, 1967.
Patterson, Lee. "Christian and Pagan in *The Testament of Cresseid*." *Philological Quarterly* 52 (1973): 696–714.

GENERAL CRITICAL STUDIES OF CHAUCER

Burrow, J. A. *Ricardian Poetry: Chaucer, Gower, Langland and the Gawain Poet*. London: Routledge & Kegan Paul, 1971.
Dinshaw, Carolyn. *Chaucer's Sexual Poetics*. Madison: U of Wisconsin P, 1989.
Donaldson, E. Talbot. *Speaking of Chaucer*. New York: W. W. Norton & Company, 1970.
Gaylord, Alan T., ed. *Essays on the Art of Chaucer's Verse*. New York and London: Routledge, 2001.
Kelly, Henry Ansgar. *Chaucerian Tragedy*. Cambridge: D. S. Brewer, 1997. Discusses Henryson and Boccaccio as well as Chaucer.
Hansen, Elaine Tuttle. *Chaucer and the Fictions of Gender*. Berkeley and Los Angeles: U of California P, 1992.
•Mann, Jill. *Feminizing Chaucer*. Cambridge: D. S. Brewer, 2002. Rev. from *Geoffrey Chaucer*. London: Harvester Wheatsheaf, 1991.
Muscatine, Charles. *Chaucer and the French Tradition*. Berkeley and Los Angeles: U of California P, 1957.
•Patterson, Lee. *Chaucer and the Subject of History*. Madison: U of Wisconsin P, 1991.
Payne, Robert O. *The Key of Remembrance: A Study of Chaucer's Poetics*. New Haven: Yale UP, 1963.
Taylor, Karla. *Chaucer Reads the Divine Comedy*. Stanford: Stanford UP, 1989.

STUDIES OF *TROILUS AND CRISEYDE*

Barney, Stephen A. *Studies in 'Troilus': Chaucer's Text, Meter, and Diction*. East Lansing, MI: Colleagues, 1993.
———. "Troilus Bound." *Speculum* 47 (1972): 445–58. Repr. in Shoaf 1992.
Benson, C. David. *Chaucer's 'Troilus and Criseyde'*. London: Unwin Hyman, 1991.
•Bloomfield, Morton W. "Distance and Predestination in *Troilus and Criseyde*." *PMLA* 72 (1957): 14–26. Repr. in Barney 1980.
Brenner, Gerry. "Narrative Structure in Chaucer's *Troilus and Criseyde*." *Annuale Mediaevale* 6 (1965): 5–18. Slightly rev. and repr. in Barney 1980.
Brody, Saul N. "Making a Play for Criseyde: The Staging of Pandarus's House in Chaucer's *Troilus and Criseyde*." *Speculum* 73 (1998): 115–40.
•Delany, Sheila. "Techniques of Alienation in *Troilus and Criseyde*." In *The Uses of Criticism*, ed. A. P. Foulkes. Bern: Peter Lang, 1976. 77–95. Repr. in Shoaf 1992.
•Donaldson, E. Talbot. "The Ending of *Troilus*." In *Early English and Norse Studies, Presented to Hugh Smith*, ed. Arthur Brown and Peter Foote. London: Methuen, 1963. 26–45. Rev. in Donaldson 1970: 84–101 and repr. in Barney 1980.

•Fradenburg, Louise O. " 'Our owen wo to drynke': Loss, Gender, and Chivalry in *Troilus and Criseyde.*" In Shoaf 1992: 88–106.

Fyler, John M. "The Fabrications of Pandarus." *Modern Language Quarterly* 41 (1980): 115–30. Repr. in Shoaf 1992.

Ganim, John M. "Tone and Time in Chaucer's *Troilus.*" *English Literary History* 43 (1976): 141–53.

•Green, Richard F. "Troilus and the Game of Love." *Chaucer Review* 13 (1979): 201–20.

Howard, Donald R. "Experience, Language, and Consciousness: *Troilus and Criseyde* II, 596–931." In *Medieval Literature and Folklore Studies . . . in Honor of Francis Lee Utley,* ed. Jerome Mandel and Bruce A. Rosenberg. New Brunswick: Rutgers UP, 1970. 173–92. Repr. in Barney 1980.

Kolve, V. A. "Looking at the Sun in Chaucer's *Troilus and Criseyde.*" In *Chaucer and the Challenges of Medievalism: Studies in Honor of H. A. Kelly,* ed. Donka Minkova and Theresa Tinkle. Frankfurt am Main and New York: Peter Lang, 2003. 31–71.

•Lewis, C. S. "What Chaucer Really Did to *Il Filostrato.*" *Essays and Studies* 17 (1932): 56–75. Repr. in Barney 1980.

McCall, John P. "The Trojan Scene in Chaucer's *Troilus.*" *English Literary History* 29 (1962): 263–75. Repr. in Barney 1980.

Meech, Sanford B. *Design in Chaucer's 'Troilus'.* Syracuse, NY: Syracuse UP, 1959.

Mieszkowski, Gretchen. "The Reputation of Criseyde 1150–1500." *Transactions of the Connecticut Academy of Arts and Sciences* 43 (1971): 71–153. New Haven: Archon, 1971.

Sams, Henry W. "The Dual Time-Scheme in Chaucer's *Troilus.*" *Modern Language Notes* 56 (1941): 94–100.

Spearing, A. C. "A Ricardian 'I': The Narrator of *Troilus and Criseyde.*" In A. J. Minnis, Charlotte C. Morse, and Thorlac Turville-Petre, eds., *Essays on Ricardian Literature: In Honour of J. A. Burrow.* Oxford: Clarendon, 1997. 1–22.

Steadman, John M. *Disembodied Laughter: 'Troilus' and the Apotheosis Tradition.* Berkeley: U of California P, 1972.

•Taylor, Davis. "The Terms of Love: A Study of Troilus's Style." *Speculum* 51 (1976): 69–90, rev. in Barney 1980.

•Taylor, Karla. "Proverbs and the Authentication of Convention in *Troilus and Criseyde.*" In Barney 1980. 277–96.

Wetherbee, Winthrop. *Chaucer and the Poets: An Essay on 'Troilus and Criseyde'.* Ithaca: Cornell UP, 1984.